JONATHAN DIMBLEBY
DESTINY IN THE DESERT

The Road to El Alamein –
The Battle That Turned The Tide

P
PROFILE BOOKS

This paperback edition published in 2013

First published in Great Britain in 2012 by
PROFILE BOOKS LTD
3A Exmouth House
Pine Street
Exmouth Market
London EC1R 0JH
www.profilebooks.com

1 3 5 7 9 10 8 6 4 2

Typeset in Aldus by MacGuru Ltd
info@macguru.org.uk

Printed and bound in Great Britain by
CPI Group (UK) Ltd, Croydon CR0 4YY

A CIP catalogue record for this book is available from the British Library.

ISBN: 978 1 84668 445 6
eISBN: 978 1 84765 467 0

For Kitty,
in memory of her grandfather,
Richard Dimbleby

CONTENTS

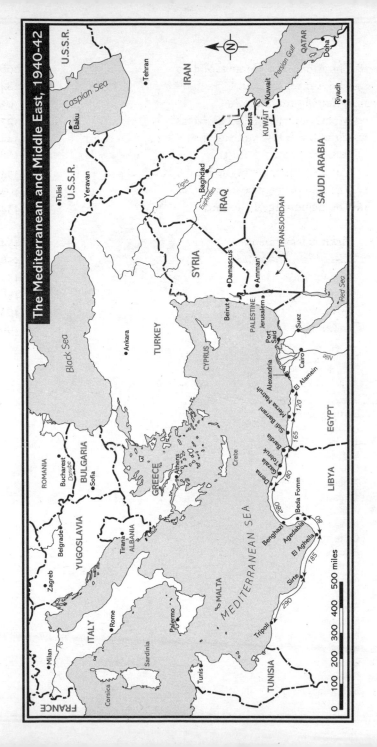

The Mediterranean and Middle East, 1940–42

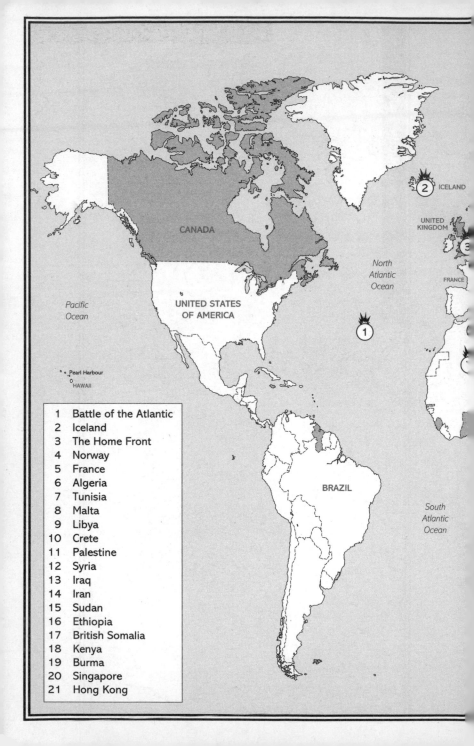

Pacific Ocean

CANADA

UNITED STATES
OF AMERICA

Pearl Harbour
HAWAII

North Atlantic Ocean

ICELAND ②

UNITED
KINGDOM

③

FRANCE

①

BRAZIL

South Atlantic Ocean

1	Battle of the Atlantic
2	Iceland
3	The Home Front
4	Norway
5	France
6	Algeria
7	Tunisia
8	Malta
9	Libya
10	Crete
11	Palestine
12	Syria
13	Iraq
14	Iran
15	Sudan
16	Ethiopia
17	British Somalia
18	Kenya
19	Burma
20	Singapore
21	Hong Kong

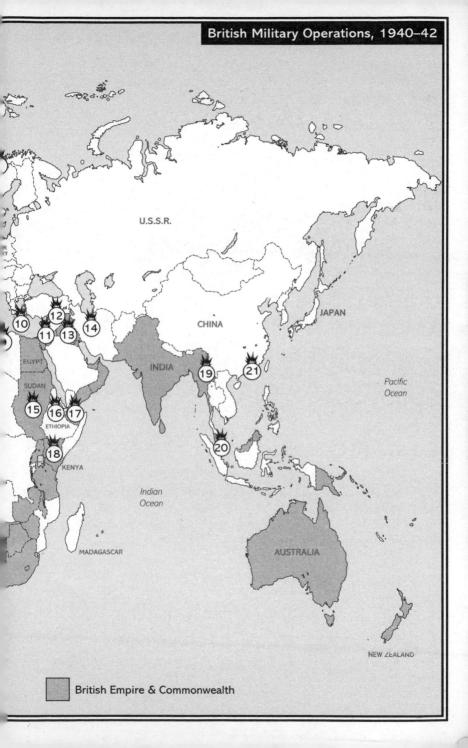

PREFACE:
A PIVOTAL STRUGGLE

The victory of the British Eighth Army at the Battle of El Alamein in November 1942 yielded one of Churchill's most famous aphorisms: 'This is not the end, it is not even the beginning of the end, but it is, perhaps, the end of the beginning.' For the British Prime Minister and for the nation it was a moment to savour after the long months of failure, defeat and humiliation which had followed the evacuation of the British Expeditionary Force from France at Dunkirk in June 1940.

El Alamein soon entered a hallowed pantheon of historic British victories among the likes of Blenheim and Trafalgar. In the mythology in which it was soon to be shrouded, the battle also acquired its own Marlborough or Nelson in the person of Lieutenant General Bernard Montgomery. Like his illustrious predecessors, 'Monty' was given his place in the accompanying roll call of great military leaders. Moreover, he was destined to become the only British general of the Second World War to have an entire chamber devoted to his exploits in that very real pantheon in London which houses the Imperial War Museum.

The myths of El Alamein endure. The battle, which was fought over twelve gruelling days and nights between two war-weary armies, was billed as though it were a prize fight between two military superstars: Monty versus the Desert Fox. This was perhaps inevitable. Field Marshal Erwin Rommel had already acquired the semi-mythical status which that admiring sobriquet bestowed on him by the British suggests. From the moment of his arrival in the North African desert in February 1941, Rommel had repeatedly out-dared, outmanoeuvred, and outsmarted Montgomery's predecessors on the battlefield. To Churchill's growing dismay, his Panzerarmee Afrika seemed destined to run rings round the Eighth Army indefinitely. At a moment of acute crisis, the appointment of Montgomery to command that weary British force in the Western Desert seemed like the Prime Minister's last throw of the military dice.

By the late summer of 1942, as the new British commander rehearsed for the Battle of El Alamein, the Eighth Army had been so reinforced with men and armaments that it enjoyed overwhelming superiority on the battlefield and in the air. This has led most military historians – on both sides – to conclude that while a British victory was hardly inevitable, defeat was virtually inconceivable. Nevertheless, after so many setbacks on so many fronts, Churchill, by then desperate for good news, was in a state of the highest anxiety. So, when the news reached him that Rommel's army had crumbled and was in full retreat, the Prime Minister's exhilaration was unbounded. He at once cabled his congratulations to the Middle East Command, declaring, 'it is evident that an event of the first magnitude has occurred which will play its part in the whole future course of the World War.' Later, in another of his grandiose aphorisms, he purred memorably, 'Before Alamein we never had a victory. After Alamein we never had a defeat.'

In fact there had been victories before El Alamein and there were to be defeats afterwards, which is doubtless why Churchill was careful to preface that exultant affirmation with five cautionary words 'It may almost be said ...' However that qualification has been widely ignored, further contributing to the enticing myths by which El Alamein has become encrusted. Not that this should diminish the significance of the victory which came at a critical moment for Churchill and for Britain's fortunes. After more than three bone-wearying years of war against Hitler, it finally demonstrated – for the first time – that the British could not only resist the Nazi threat to the home front but were able and willing to take the war to the enemy on a foreign field and emerge with a comprehensive victory. At Churchill's command, Britain's church bells, silent since the outbreak of war, were rung out across the nation in celebration and relief.

But there is far more to El Alamein than the fact that it salvaged Britain's morale and reputation. Although it came to be regarded as a defining moment in British history, it cannot usefully be seen in isolation from the drama of which it formed the climax. Eminent military historians have fought and re-fought every moment of a desert conflict which lasted for two years – the longest British campaign on land in the Second World War. They have untangled every move in the back-and-forth struggle across a terrain so implacably hostile that the challenge of human survival, let alone warfare, was as testing as anywhere on the planet. They have analysed the tactics adopted by both armies, rigorously detailing the strengths and weaknesses on each side. Yet, even seventy years after El Alamein, the battle itself and the tsunami of global events which led up to it are still a source of intense and acrimonious controversy.

There are those who have argued that, far from being 'an event of the first magnitude' as Churchill believed, El Alamein was a battle that need not have been fought, that it was militarily redundant, and therefore that those 13,500 men – from Britain, Australia, New Zealand, India, South Africa, Poland, and 'Free' France – who spilled their lifeblood in the sand for Montgomery's victory, died for little purpose. Some have gone further, arguing that the entire desert campaign between 1940 and 1942 was an unnecessary diversion which squandered precious resources that should have been preserved for a frontal assault against the German enemy in Europe. From these twin standpoints, such historians concede that El Alamein may have had a certain utility as propaganda – an heroic riposte to those who had come to believe that the British Army had no stomach for the war against Nazi Germany – but it was nonetheless a marginal achievement on a peripheral war front.

xvi DESTINY IN THE DESERT

This perspective sidesteps or ignores the critical fact that Churchill fought the Second World War as much to save the global reach of the British Empire as to destroy Nazism. It was for this reason above all others that the protagonists on both sides were sucked into the cauldron of the Middle East and North Africa, and it is only against this background that it is possible to make sense of what otherwise would have been indeed a peripheral struggle in the blood-soaked sand of a faraway and irrelevant desert.

Though this book places that military and human drama played out over the vast emptinesses in Egypt and Libya at the heart of the story, it also seeks to place the Desert War in a much wider context. From this standpoint the victory at El Alamein was a providential triumph on a war front that, so far from being peripheral, was pivotal to the struggle between the Allies and the Axis for control of a vital front in a Mediterranean theatre which, in large measure, shaped the course of the Second World War.

For Britain, the Mediterranean was 'the carotid artery of empire', crucial both to safeguarding the nation's vital assets in the Middle East and in sustaining the great outposts of Empire in India, Africa, and the Far East, to all of which Churchill, his government and parliament were unequivocally committed. Britain was still the world's greatest maritime power, holding sway over the lives of two-fifths of the planet's population spread over five continents. At that time almost all British citizens subscribed to a vision of the world in which the sun would never set on their great empire. To argue – as later generations with the benefit of hindsight would come to do – that the Empire was at best an anachronistic delusion and at worst an exploitative and rarely benign system of colonial oppression would have seemed unpatriotic if not treasonable to most of His Majesty's British subjects. Of course there were those who campaigned for an end to Britain's global hegemony, but they were few in number and lacking in impact. That the Second World War would hasten the demise of empire and accelerate the decline in the nation's global influence was, for most people, an unimaginable prospect. As Churchill himself proclaimed a few days after the victory of El Alamein, 'I have not become the King's First Minister in order to preside over the liquidation of the British Empire. For that task, if it were ever prescribed, someone else would have to be found.'

Moreover, short of obliterating Germany with bombs, the North African desert was the only theatre where Britain could battle effectively against Nazi Germany. Churchill's challenge was extreme. In the two and a half years leading up to El Alamein, when defeat seemed as likely as victory, Britain came under acute pressure on all fronts in a region which encompassed what is now generally known as the Arab World. The Middle East Command in Egypt was on constant alert against the threat of pro-Nazi insurrection or subversion in neighbouring Arab countries.

Even more threatening was the prospect of a full-scale Nazi blitzkrieg southwards, either from Russia via the Caucasus or through Turkey. From whichever route it might come – and it was under constant consideration by the German High Command – British strategists feared that any such thrust would be designed to link up with Rommel's Panzerarmee forcing its way across from the Libyan desert to Cairo and the Suez Canal. Had Hitler been gifted with strategic vision rather than a blinkered obsession with the destruction of the Soviet Union, it is more than probable that those threats would have been realised, in which case, the consequences would have been cataclysmic, not only for the Empire but for Britain itself.

Thus, from Churchill's perspective, victory or defeat in the struggle against Rommel came to represent respectively triumph or disaster in a crucial theatre of war where the very survival of the British Empire was at stake. As he told a press conference in Cairo two months before the Battle of El Alamein, 'We are determined to fight for Egypt and the Nile Valley as if it were the soil of England itself.' This unshakeable resolve placed what might otherwise have been a minor military campaign on a faraway battlefield at the heart of a prolonged political and diplomatic drama.

With the fall of France in June 1940, Churchill was fully aware that the industrial and military might of the United States would be essential for the defeat of Hitler and the preservation of the Empire. His genius, over the course of the six testing months which followed the bombing of Pearl Harbor by Japan in December 1941, was to seduce President Roosevelt into sharing his strategic perspective: firstly persuading him that the European front should have priority over the defeat of Japan in the Pacific and then – against the fierce advice of almost all the President's men – that a joint invasion of North Africa, which Churchill was to codename Operation *Torch*, should precede any direct military assault against the enemy on mainland Europe.

One of the reasons the Americans were initially so suspicious of Churchill's war strategy was a profound aversion to the very idea of an empire from which the people of what later became the United States had liberated themselves only a little over a century and a half earlier. But by the summer of 1942, Roosevelt – despite the profound scepticism of his senior military advisors – had come to share the Prime Minister's view that victory in North Africa was crucial to the triumph in the West. Once the President had made this decision, the two leaders' common purpose – in one of the many ironies of the Second World War – placed this military theatre in which the Eighth Army was fighting to sustain the British Empire at the very heart of the Allied war effort.

For Churchill, the arduous, frustrating and often acrimonious months of negotiation between London and Washington which led up to America's decision to join the fray in North Africa was intimately linked to the alarmingly uneven performance of the Eighth Army in the Western Desert. Following a string of setbacks and defeats in Europe and the Pacific, the failure of Britain's forces to make headway against Rommel had confirmed Roosevelt's most senior advisors in their aversion to deploying American troops against the Axis powers in North Africa rather than on the mainland of Europe.

As a supplicant, seeking to establish himself as an equal partner in a new special relationship, Churchill had to prevent the President's military advisors from poisoning the chalice from which he needed Roosevelt to drink. For this reason, he regarded it as imperative that Britain's potential should be demonstrated on the battlefield as well as in the conference chamber. As the Middle East and North Africa formed the only available battlefront on which to display any military prowess against the otherwise all-conquering Germans, the struggle for victory in the desert was of overriding importance.

This led the Prime Minister to dabble constantly in the details of military strategy on a battlefront about which he was perforce often ill informed or ignorant. The abrasive character of this interference dismayed, irritated and even infuriated his most senior military advisors, who found themselves unable to curb his restless urge to direct the struggle from afar. His successive commanders-in-chief at Middle East HQ, Cairo, were subjected to a bombardment of prime ministerial missives exhorting, harrying, bullying and occasionally threatening them towards ever greater and more urgent effort.

By the time Montgomery arrived in the desert in August 1942 (ostensibly to serve under General Harold Alexander, Churchill's third commander-in-chief in fifteen months) the Prime Minister's desire for victory against Rommel had become all-consuming. After more than six months of fraught negotiation, he had finally persuaded the Americans that their first military campaign against Hitler should take the form of Allied landings in North Africa rather than via a cross-Channel invasion of France to open a second front against Hitler in Europe. To restore the tattered credibility of the Eighth Army after the loss of Tobruk in June 1942, and to reassert his own stature as the Prime Minister of a war-winning nation after a long series of military setbacks, Churchill was desperate for a victory at El Alamein before the start of Operation *Torch*, which was scheduled for the autumn. Unlike his predecessors, Montgomery refused to be harried into precipitate action, but he did not disappoint: the Eighth Army's victory at El Alamein in November 1942 preceded the American landings in North Africa by four symbolic days.

From today's perspective it may seem astonishing that the aspirations or rights of the millions of people who inhabited that vast swathe of territory which stretched from Iran in the east to Morocco in the west were quite irrelevant to the contesting foreign powers who fought with such ferocity over their lands. Except in so far as they could be coaxed, co-opted, or coerced into acquiescence, the Arabs of the Middle East were of no account to the principal protagonists. As Montgomery's Chief of Staff, Major General Sir Francis de Guingand acknowledged, 'The civilian population suffered terribly and we had to destroy cities, communications, towns, harbours and the lot.'

The troubled and often violent history of the Arab World in the twentieth century is largely the story of subject peoples rising up against their colonial masters. This long – and still unresolved – convulsion was temporarily arrested by the Second World War and held in suspended animation. By wheeling and dealing with national leaders, imprisoning recalcitrants and suppressing nascent uprisings, the British – and to a lesser degree the Germans, Italians and Vichy French – merely checked the wheel of history in the Arab World; nor did they significantly affect its future alignment, direction or momentum. For this reason, though it is an important area of study for historians of the Arab World, the Arabs themselves play only a walk-on role in this, as in other, accounts of the battles that were fought over their homelands and too often over their dead bodies.

It is a truism that without the astonishing resolve and terrible suffering of the Russian people which culminated in the Nazi defeat at Stalingrad, the world today would have been very different. Set against the massive scale of that decisive struggle and the eventual destruction of Nazism by the Allies in Europe, the Desert War is sometimes relegated to the status of a minor drama in a provincial theatre. Leaving aside the fact that the enormous logistical effort required to sustain the Eighth Army in the desert could have been achieved only by a maritime power of Britain's unique reach, this is to indulge a form of historical and strategic myopia. When Churchill wrote later that the victory at El Alamein represented 'the turning of the hinge of fate' he was not so much indulging his penchant for hyperbole as pinpointing the symbolic moment which did indeed mark 'the beginning of the end'.

Of course, the hinge had not turned very far by the autumn of

1942. At that stage, Hitler's invading armies had yet to be expelled from the Soviet Union and the Japanese had yet to be broken in the Pacific. But the long campaign in the Western Desert which culminated at El Alamein had borne fruit. Rommel was on the run, the imminent arrival of the US invasion force made the defeat of the Axis powers in North Africa a foregone conclusion (though it took much longer than anticipated), the Middle East was secure, the Mediterranean would fall under Allied control, and the Germans would find themselves forced to confront an Allied invasion on their southern flank in Italy. The self-delusional lodestars by which both Hitler and Mussolini had been guided had started to fade towards oblivion.

The lion's share of the credit for this has to be given to Churchill. The strategic vision which fuelled his restless meddling in military detail far exceeded in clarity and conviction all his contemporaries. The physical and intellectual energy that kept him up half the night dictating ill-judged memoranda to desert generals was also the source of the inspirational authority with which he had convinced the American president that victory in the Mediterranean theatre should precede the liberation of Europe and the conquest of Japan. This agreement both shaped the subsequent course of the war and – to the intense irritation of Stalin – defined the respective roles of the Allies in the final victory over Nazism. It is inconceivable that Roosevelt would have acceded to Churchill's imperatives if the Prime Minister had not fought with such unquenchable fervour for two years to defend the British Empire on the desert battlefield.

This book tells the story of the events which led up to the victory at El Alamein. It is about the high drama played out between and within the war capitals of London, Washington, Berlin, Rome and Moscow. It is about politicians and generals, diplomats and civil servants, soldiers and civilians. It is about forceful characters and the tensions and rivalries between them. It is about stress, confusion and misunderstanding. It is about momentous decisions that bore directly on matters of life and death, victory and defeat. And it is no less about the resilience and resolve of those who fought in the desert and for whom, for month after month, even year after year, days of extreme danger were interspersed with weeks of supreme boredom. It is about all those, on whatever side and at whatever level, who played their part in a gruelling conflict in which mercifully the forces of light eventually triumphed over the forces of darkness.

August 2012

A NOTE TO THE PAPERBACK EDITION

After the publication of *Destiny in the Desert* a small number of correspondents wrote to me in the kindest terms but also pointing out errors of fact. I am most grateful to these assiduous readers and I hope they will be satisfied with my corrections.

I would also single out a memorable encounter with 'Jimmy' James, who introduced himself to me at a literature festival. In 1942, he was a nineteen-year old pilot, charged with flying the Bristol Bombay carrying Lieutenant-General 'Strafer' Gott. It was shot down on 7 August. Gott, who had just been appointed to command the Eighth Army, was trapped in the fuselage and died. I had written of this tragic incident that he had been 'incinerated' in the flames but, according to 'Jimmy' James, this was not the case. Rather, Gott died from wounds inflicted by the machine-gunners in the Messerschmitt squadron which, after downing the Bombay, returned for a second run after James had managed to crash-land in the desert. This rare, perhaps unique, 'return visit' suggested to him that the Germans had intelligence that an important figure was aboard the doomed plane. I promised the modest but courageous Mr James (a detailed account of his sang-froid in the midst of disaster may be found in *The Battle of Alamein* by John Bierman and Colin Smith) that I would 'incinerate' the word 'incinerate' from future editions of the book. I have done so.

Some readers, on the basis of their first-hand experience in the desert, have intimated that I have been too harsh on Gott's successor, Lieutenant-General Montgomery. They have argued that 'Monty' was an inspirational figure who (as Churchill judged similarly) re-invigorated the Eighth Army in the run-up to the final battle of El Alamein. In particular, Peter Willet described his first sighting of Montgomery on Ruweisat Ridge. 'I came to the edge of a deir, and caught sight of a staff car crossing in a cloud of dust, with a small figure wearing a beret sitting in the back; and in some magical, inexplicable way, my spirits were suddenly lifted and a feeling of optimism replaced the formerly pervasive feeling of resignation ...' Other readers, with similar first-hand experiences in the Eighth Army, have volunteered that, to the contrary, my comments about this most colourful and controversial of Second World War generals are well founded. I appreciate all the insights of which I am now the fortunate beneficiary.

March 2013

ONE

STARTING POINTS

'An hour marked by destiny is striking in the sky of our country; the hour of irrevocable decisions.'

Benito Mussolini

London

In his first speech as Prime Minister, on 13 May 1940, Winston Churchill told the House of Commons, 'I have nothing to offer but blood, toil, tears and sweat.' As he spoke, the British Expeditionary Force in France was in full retreat towards Dunkirk, its stubborn but forlorn rearguard action powerless to arrest the German advance. Only Hitler's bizarre and unexpected decision to call off the chase allowed the bulk of the BEF and the First French Army to reach the beaches at Dunkirk. The Führer's decision infuriated his army commanders and, especially his Chief of Staff, General Franz Halder, who noted bleakly, 'Now we must stand and watch countless thousands of the enemy get away to England right under our noses'.

On 26 May, with the panzer force only eighteen miles away from the port itself, the Royal Navy, supported by a flotilla of trawlers and other small craft, began a remarkable rescue operation. By 4 June – the day on which the Swastika was raised over Dunkirk – some 338,000 Allied troops had escaped across the Channel. The only consolation for the victors was the massive jumble of discarded tanks, guns, trucks and ammunition which littered the French landscape, a bleak testimony to a national humiliation that even the 'Dunkirk spirit' could not entirely obscure.

On the same day, acknowledging the 'colossal military disaster' of Dunkirk, Churchill roused the House of Commons with his second imperishable speech as Prime Minister, declaring, 'We shall fight on the beaches, we shall fight on the landing grounds, we shall fight in the fields and in the streets, we shall fight on the hills; we shall never surrender'. However, for obvious reasons of national security he forbore to tell his parliamentary colleagues that in the week leading up to the evacuation at Dunkirk the War Cabinet had met in secret for five days in succession to explore the grim options facing the government. The Foreign Secretary, Lord Halifax, had argued in favour of negotiating terms with Hitler (initially via Italy's dictator, Benito Mussolini, who had yet to declare war on Britain). Churchill begged to differ but – mindful of the fact that he could not yet rely on the unequivocal support of his colleagues against a powerful alliance of appeasers ranged against him in parliament and beyond – even he did not entirely rule out the prospect of cutting a deal with the Führer.

Among a host of senior figures – not to mention many ordinary citizens – who believed that defeat was now all but inevitable, the Director of Military Intelligence, Major General Francis Davidson, told a BBC correspondent privately in the midst of the Dunkirk fiasco, 'We're finished. We've lost the army and we shall never have the strength to build another.' Faced by such a groundswell of pessimism, Churchill had little choice but to tread with care. However, he eventually secured the support of key members of the War Cabinet (former Prime Minister Neville Chamberlain, Labour leader Clement Attlee and Attlee's deputy, Arthur Greenwood), which gave him the authority to speak with such unequivocal defiance in the House on 4 June.

In the midst of this perilous turmoil, Churchill summoned General Archibald Wavell, the Middle East commander-in-chief, from Cairo to London. The Prime Minister was on the warpath. Filled with romantic memories of the Boer War – 'where we owned nothing beyond the fires of our own camps and bivouacs, whereas the Boers rode where they please all over the country'

– his purpose was to galvanise Wavell to confront an Italian army which was mustering on the border with Egypt.

Wavell's responsibilities encompassed a huge triangular swathe of the Middle East and East Africa from Iran in the east to Abyssinia (Ethiopia) in the south and Egypt in the west. The troops under his command were spread widely and thinly across this vast region, protecting the British Empire from all-comers but especially a resurgent Italy, whose ruler harboured imperial dreams to rival the imperial realities of the United Kingdom.

Churchill's commitment to sustaining a British Empire which still ruled most of the waves and covered two-fifths of the globe was unequivocal. His presumption was widely shared in the nation and endorsed by the overwhelming majority of his senior colleagues in government, parliament, the armed forces, and Whitehall, for whom the very identity of the United Kingdom was umbilically linked to the scores of colonies, dependencies, protectorates, and dominions around the world which were either ruled or controlled by Britain. The exploitation of these possessions and the global reach they afforded was almost universally thought to be vital to the prosperity and prestige of the nation. To harbour a dissident opinion was generally thought to be eccentric if not subversive. Moreover, without access to the raw materials, resources and man-power of the Empire, it would not have been possible for Britain to challenge the expanding hegemony of the Third Reich.

For these reasons, the protection of the Middle East was in Churchill's unyielding judgement second only in importance – and a close second at that – to the survival of the United Kingdom itself. Egypt, though nominally independent, was geographically and strategically at the heart of the Empire, linking Britain via a network of arteries to its possessions around the world, the 'fount of British military power in the Middle East' with its capital, Cairo, 'an epicentre of the British imperial world.'

The C-in-C, Middle East left Cairo to arrive in London on 8 August 1940. Churchill was in abrasive mood, Wavell was on the defensive. The two men were very different in character and temperament: where the Prime Minister was emotional, volatile and loquacious, Wavell was cool, measured, and taciturn. The soldier was also gifted with a richly complex intellect that contrasted sharply with the impetuous certainties by which the politician was guided. To complicate their relationship further, Churchill was prone to distrust and despise generals and Wavell was, in the words of his biographer, 'suspicious of politicians and thought politics too serious a matter to be left in their hands'. Their attitudes to warfare were also deeply at odds. Churchill was a romantic who had a zest for battle and conquest. Wavell, on the other hand, judged all wars to be 'deplorably dull and inefficiently run'; nor could he see any reason why the human race, 'so inefficient in matters of peace, should suddenly become efficient in time of war'.

Not surprisingly, their first encounter was very far from being a meeting of minds. Though Churchill acknowledged that the Middle East Command 'comprised an extraordinary amalgam of military, political, diplomatic and administrative problems', he could not restrain himself from telling Wavell that the forces at his disposal were either deployed in the wrong places or – effectively – standing at ease a long way behind the front when they should have been eagerly preparing to repel the enemy on the Libyan border. If Wavell had been so minded, he could have pointed out that up until recently he had been forbidden to put his 36,000 troops in Egypt on a war footing for fear of provoking the 100,000-strong Italian army to launch a pre-emptive strike on Cairo: Wavell's conventional caution was grounded in military common sense.

Though Wavell's loyalty to his political masters was never in question, his disdain for the Prime Minister's conceptual grasp of military strategy was ill concealed – not so much by what he said but by his failure to say almost anything at all. From the general's perspective, Churchill was both overly inclined to meddle in matters of operational detail that he did not understand, and unwilling to grasp the scale and complexity of the challenges facing him on the many other fronts under his command. Only later did he allow himself the indulgence of the barbed reflection that 'Winston's tactical ideas had to some extent crystallised at the South African [Boer] war.'

It was an uncomfortable encounter which Churchill described

as 'a prolonged hard fight against the woolly theme of being safe everywhere', in the course of which, he boasted, 'I put my case in black and white.' Wavell did not yield easily, and on at least one occasion, by his own account, 'succeeded in convincing' Churchill that he was wrong, or rather, 'I convinced him that I wouldn't do it.' Eventually however, the general was wrestled into compliance and was issued accordingly with a lengthy and detailed 'General Directive' drawn up by the Imperial General Staff at the Prime Minister's behest and approved by the War Cabinet. Afterwards, Wavell reflected, 'I am pretty sure that he [Churchill] considered my replacement by someone who was more likely to share his ideas, but could not find any good reason to do so. Winston has always disliked me personally.' There is no evidence that the feeling was other than mutual: a disaffection which boded ill for what was to become a crucially important relationship.

In the two months following Italy's declaration of war on 10 June, small units of Wavell's Western Desert Force had engaged in a series of hit-and-run raids against Italian outposts on and behind the Libyan border, destroying tanks and taking prisoners in skirmishes that harassed the enemy but inflicting insignificant damage on either of the two Italian divisions mustering on the Libyan side of the frontier. But now much more was required. On 16 August Wavell was formally instructed 'to assemble and deploy the largest possible army upon and towards the western frontier' to confront 'a major invasion of Egypt from Libya ... All political and administrative considerations must be set in proper subordination to this.' Duly chastised, Wavell returned to Cairo to oversee the rapid redeployment of his troops from other parts of the Middle East Command to prepare for the coming clash in the Western Desert.

Rome

The British Prime Minister was not to know that, so far from being poised to invade Egypt, the Italian army in North Africa was profoundly reluctant to leave the comparative security of its Libyan colony. This lack of resolve infuriated the Italian dictator, Benito Mussolini, who was driven by a demonic urge to conquer the Middle East. On the same day that he declared war on Britain, Il Duce had appointed himself 'Supreme Commander of the Armed Forces in the Field'. That evening he stood resplendently on his balcony overlooking the Piazza Venezia in Rome while below him in the square a large crowd dutifully cheered him on as he issued his clarion call to war.

'Blackshirts of the Revolution and of the Legions, men and women of Italy and of the Empire,' he declared, 'An hour marked by destiny is striking in the sky of our country; the hour of irrevocable decisions. We are entering the lists against the plutocratic and reactionary democracies of the West, who have always hindered the advance and often plotted against the very existence of the Italian people … And we will conquer … People of Italy, to arms! Show your courage, your tenacity and your worth.' Aside from the fascist diehards in the Piazza, this faintly ludicrous call to arms found little favour with the Italian people. Instead of a mass display of support for their leader's bellicose meanderings, the writer Christopher Hibbert, who was present at the time, noted that 'an atmosphere of gloom hung over the dreadfully quiet city'.

Mussolini – who had already appointed himself 'Duce of Fascism and Founder of the Empire' – believed that Italy's natural right to be a great imperial power had been thwarted by Britain's control of the Mediterranean, which he regarded as an Italian lake, the 'fourth shore' of which was North Africa. In the middle of May, Churchill had written to Mussolini in the remote hope of keeping Italy out of the conflict. 'Is it too late', he had inquired, 'to stop a river of blood from flowing between the British and Italian peoples?'

Mussolini's resentful rejection of the Prime Minister's overture at least had the virtue of candour. In 1935, he protested, Britain had led the call for sanctions (in the form of an arms embargo) during the Abyssinian crisis, when Italy, as he put it, was merely 'engaged in securing for herself a small space in the African sun'. Nor was that all. 'May I remind you', he added 'of the real and actual state of servitude in which Italy finds herself in her own sea.' The belief that the Mediterranean was not only Italy's maritime backyard but a legitimate possession was no less sincere for being utterly bizarre.

His vision of the twentieth-century Roman Empire not only encompassed the Mediterranean but much of the Middle East and Africa as well. Libya – which had been an Italian colony since 1912 when it was ceded to Rome by the Ottoman Empire – was to be the springboard from which to drive the British from the entire region. The conquest of Egypt would be the first step towards the realisation of that dream. Il Duce was consumed by a vaulting ambition which far exceeded his reach. Vanity and bombast were his hallmarks. 'War alone brings up to their highest tension all human energies and puts the stamp of nobility upon the peoples who have the courage to meet it,' he had once declared in a flush of fascist passion.

But, though his grasp of military strategy was haphazard at best, he was not without cunning. Under the Pact of Steel, which he had co-signed with Hitler on 22 May 1939, each side agreed to come 'immediately' to the aid of the other if either were involved in 'hostilities', but Mussolini had refrained from declaring war against Britain until – following the debacle of Dunkirk – he judged that Hitler would soon reign supreme in all Europe. Convincing himself that hostilities would end within three months, he informed his Chief of General Staff, Pietro Badoglio, that he only needed 'a few thousand dead so that I can sit at the peace conference as a man who has fought' and lay claim to a fair share of the spoils. The most propitious means of achieving this objective was to engage the British on the battlefield in the Western Desert, and thus to establish himself as a serious military ally rather than the Führer's clowning cheerleader.

To this end, he demanded that Marshal Rodolfo Graziani, the commander-in-chief of the Italian forces in North Africa, be instructed to launch an early invasion of Egypt. But Graziani at once revealed a stubborn reluctance to mount any kind of aggressive action against the British. On 3 August Mussolini's Foreign Minister and son-in-law, Count Galeazzo Ciano, made a caustic note in his diary to the effect that, 'principally because of the heat', the much-decorated commander – whose penchant for bloody reprisals in Abyssinia had earned him the sobriquet 'The Butcher of Ethiopia' – was unwilling to mount any offensive until the following spring.

Summoned back to Rome to explain himself, Graziani told Ciano on 8 August that 'the attack on Egypt was a very serious undertaking' for which 'our present preparations are far from perfect'. The marshal was understating the case: the poorly trained and ill-equipped men under his command were almost entirely unfit to wage war. Though on paper they far exceeded in strength the modest forces available to Wavell, his warning that premature action against the British would 'inevitably develop into a rapid and total disaster' was prescient. When Graziani insisted that he 'would rather not attack at all, or, at any rate, not for two or three months' Mussolini was incensed. Believing that the Nazi invasion of Britain was 'very imminent', he despatched a telegram on 19 August instructing him to invade Egypt 'as soon as a German patrol lands in England'. But – confirming that a victor's place at the conference table was dearer to him than outright conquest – he added, 'there are to be no territorial objectives ... I am only asking you to attack the British forces facing you'.

Within days, however, as he contemplated the fruits that would fall into his lap were Graziani to march all the way to Cairo, his quixotic ambition once more ran away with him. Encouraged in this flight of fancy by no less an authority than the Chief of Staff of the Supreme Command of the German Armed Forces, Field Marshal Wilhelm Keitel, Mussolini informed Ciano on 27 August that 'Keitel also thinks that the taking of Cairo is more important than the taking of London'. Presumably because he was accustomed to his father-in-law's vacillating bombast, Ciano did not bother to contrast the self-contradictory objectives of which – within the space of a week – Mussolini had thus delivered himself.

In any event, Mussolini was now in a great hurry. At the very least, he needed a victory in the desert – and thereby those 'few thousand dead' – before Britain fell under German tutelage. A date was set for the invasion of Egypt: 6 September 1940.

Berlin

Following the British retreat from Dunkirk, detailed plans were laid in Berlin for the invasion of Britain. The launch of the invasion, codenamed Operation *Sealion*, was scheduled for 27 September.

Throughout the summer of 1940, the Luftwaffe subjected southern England to a daily bombardment with the purpose of destroying the RAF's ability to protect Britain's cities and thus to drive
Churchill to the bargaining table. By early September, the Battle of
Britain was reaching its crescendo. On the 13th, German bombers
not only hit Buckingham Palace but the West End, the House of
Lords, the Law Courts and eight Wren churches, an onslaught
which prompted the commander of the United Kingdom Home
Forces, General Brooke, to note in his diary, 'Spent morning in
the office studying increasing evidence of impending invasion ...
Everything looks like an invasion starting tomorrow from the
Thames to Plymouth! I wonder if we will be hard at by this time
tomorrow.' At a meeting of the War Cabinet, Churchill said that
he was sure this indicated the Germans 'meant business'.

But Hitler's mind was already elsewhere. On 31 July 1940,
at a meeting with his Army Chief of Staff, Franz Halder, Hitler
discussed the relationship between the Third Reich and its ostensible ally, the Soviet Union. 'Britain's hope lies in Russia and the
USA,' Halder recorded the Führer as saying. 'If Russia drops out
of the picture, America, too, is lost for Britain ... Decision: Russia's destruction must therefore be made part of this struggle ...
The sooner Russia is crushed the better. The attack will achieve
its purpose only if the Russian state can be shattered to its roots
with one blow.'

Eleven months earlier, on 23 August 1939, the German Foreign
Minister, Joachim von Ribbentrop, had sat solemnly alongside his
Soviet counterpart, Vyacheslav Molotov, in Moscow as they put
their signatures to a non-aggression pact between the two totalitarian states. As part of their treaty, they agreed that if one were
attacked the other would come to the rescue; in a secret protocol,
they also agreed that they would devour northern Europe and
divide the spoils between them. The cynicism was mutual: Hitler
had no intention of abiding by the Molotov/Ribbentrop Pact,
while Stalin could have had little doubt that the pact was simply a
means of postponing an inevitable clash between the two ideologi-
cally opposed giants of continental Europe.

Now, in the summer of 1940, Hitler told Halder, 'If we start in May, 1941, we will have five months to finish the job.' With this commission, the question for Halder and his colleagues in Oberkommando der Wehrmacht or OKW, the German High Command, was – on the face of it – quite simple: which should come first – the defeat of Britain or the destruction of the Soviet Union?

The answer was unequivocal. On 15 September, London was assailed by 100 bombers and 400 fighters but with 56 of those aircraft shot down, OKW concluded that such losses were unsustainable; as it turned out, therefore, the date on which the Battle of Britain is commemorated marked not only the zenith but also the nadir of Germany's efforts to destroy Britain's aerial defences. At the time, however, the Luftwaffe's onslaught formed an appropriately ominous backdrop for a Secret Session of Parliament on 17 September at which Churchill advised his fellow MPs that more than 1,700 self-propelled barges and 200 seagoing ships were 'already gathered at the many invasion ports in German occupation' and that these vessels were laden with all the munitions needed 'to beat us down and subjugate us utterly'. Warning that this flotilla could transport nearly half a million men across the Channel in one crossing, he insisted that Britain's forces would defeat this 'most tremendous onslaught', but felt bound to add that 'whatever happens, we will all go down fighting to the end'.

By a fateful quirk of history, Hitler chose that very day to call off the invasion of Britain. His decision was based on a shrewd calculation of the odds against success. The prospect of adverse weather conditions in the Channel combined with an appreciation by OKW that the combination of the Royal Navy, the British Army and the yet-to-be-eliminated RAF would offer stiff resistance formed a compelling argument against launching *Sealion* prematurely. Far better, he judged, to stay his hand in the expectation that in due course Britain would be obliged to acknowledge the New Order in Europe and seek an accommodation with the all-conquering Third Reich. This, he allowed himself to believe, would become inevitable once the Wehrmacht had destroyed the Soviet Union to become the master of all continental Europe. Most of Hitler's military advisors shared this perspective but some argued to the contrary – that the defeat of Britain should not only precede the invasion of Russia but that it could be accomplished by an alternative strategy. Instead of a cross-Channel invasion, they advocated that the panzer divisions should be despatched in the opposite direction to secure the Mediterranean and to seize the most vulnerable and valuable link in Britain's chain of imperial possessions: the Middle East. This, they claimed, would compel the British government to sue for peace.

In a meeting with Hitler on 6 September (and again on the 26th) the commander-in-chief of the German Navy, Grand Admiral Erich Raeder, 'thinking in global rather than continental terms', spelt out this alternative vision. Urging a major offensive to capture Suez and thence to advance through Palestine and Syria into Turkey, he advised that this démarche would not only cripple the British Empire but, by opening a route into the Soviet Union from the south, would make it 'doubtful whether an advance against Russia in the north will be necessary'.

Although the Führer was unconvinced by Raeder's proposal (which was also endorsed by Ribbentrop, who similarly favoured a 'Britain first' strategy), he was not entirely immune to its wider implications. Although he had shown little sign of being drawn to the romantic vision of those nineteenth-century German colonists who had long dreamt of recreating a Mittelafrika to complement Mitteleuropa, he did not entirely dismiss the thought that those African colonies which had been confiscated from Germany by the victors at the Treaty of Versailles might in due course be reclaimed. Though this momentary shift of focus from a continental to a global perspective was never to sharpen into a coherent military strategy, it became lodged in the back of his mind as part of his vivid if vague aspiration to dominate the world. For the next two years it was also to haunt Britain's military planners and its Prime Minister.

The sharp disagreements in OKW about whether the defeat of Britain or Russia should have the priority led to 'weeks of cajoling, bullying, and tantrums' before the Führer's staff fell into line behind his unshakeable conviction that the defeat of Russia would inevitably lead to the collapse of British resistance. However, all were able to agree about one thing: the panzer divisions which were not now needed for the invasion of the British mainland – at least until the spring of 1941 – could be redeployed to support the Italians in North Africa. Hitler did not share Mussolini's imperial delusions but he was persistently agitated by the threat posed to Germany's southern flank from the British presence in the Middle East and the Mediterranean. To forestall this, his quixotic ally Mussolini would be an essential partner.

Washington

Across the Atlantic the nascent drama in the Middle East barely registered on the political Richter scale. President Roosevelt was personally far from indifferent to the dark clouds which had gathered over Europe following Hitler's rise to power, but he was also a consummate politician and he had his mind on more pressing matters. Already campaigning to be returned for an unprecedented third term in office, he was only too aware that the majority of those voters who had twice returned him to the White House not only lacked a global perspective but were strongly averse to being dragged into foreign imbroglios of any kind. The opinion polls suggested that most of his fellow citizens favoured staying out of the European war even if this were to mean the defeat of Britain. This attitude was not only reflected in the press but was expressed with vehemence in Congress.

In an often overlooked passage at the very end of his 'We shall fight on the beaches' speech in June, Churchill had ended by claiming that if Britain 'were subjugated or starving' then the Empire would continue the struggle against Hitler until the United States 'with all its power and might, steps forth to the rescue'. This sentiment expressed the essence of a grand strategy from which Churchill would never waver: the war against Nazism would have to be waged on a global scale but victory would be secured only once the United States had been persuaded to form a grand alliance to protect the British Empire from the Axis threat. To this end, Churchill had to convince the White House that America was no less threatened by Nazism than the United Kingdom. But faced with an apparently implacable cohort of American isolationists,

Churchill confronted a political and diplomatic challenge which would surely have seemed insuperable to a lesser being.

The Prime Minister, who had only met Roosevelt once before, opted for a frontal assault. Cabling the President on 15 May 1940 in the first of thousands of wartime telegrams, he wasted little time on diplomatic niceties. Warning of the gravity of the threat, he wrote, 'I trust you realise that the voice and force of the United States may count for nothing if they are withheld too long. You may have a completely subjugated, Nazified Europe established with astonishing swiftness ... All I ask now is that you should proclaim non-belligerency, which would mean you would help us with everything short of actually engaging armed forces.' To help counter the very real prospect of invasion, he specifically requested 'the loan of forty or fifty of your older destroyers'. He got short shrift. It was 'not opportune' the President replied as approval for the loan would be required by Congress which, he inferred, would not be forthcoming.

Roosevelt himself was by no means unmoved by Britain's plight, but it was impossible for him to swat away the implacable forces of isolationism by which the White House was surrounded. His political supremacy in America rested upon his domestic triumphs. By leading America out of the depths of the Great Depression with a New Deal spending programme which had brought relief to tens of millions of unemployed and impoverished citizens, he had become a national hero. In 1936 he had secured the presidency for a second time with a landslide victory and, whatever his private inclinations may have been, he was a canny politician who knew instinctively how votes could be lost as fast as they could be won; he had no appetite for winning an argument but losing an election.

So powerful was the 'anti-war' sentiment in Congress that he had even recoiled from seeking approval for the resources needed to protect America's own borders, let alone those required to engage a faraway enemy on a foreign field. In 1935 he had approved the Neutrality Act, which expressly forbade the United States to ship arms to any combatant nation unless the weaponry were paid for in cash. Two years later his so-called 'Quarantine Speech', which proposed treating militarily aggressive states as a 'public health hazard' to be isolated, was fuzzily ambiguous. At least until 1938, when Roosevelt began to fear that Nazi subversion might contaminate the US's own 'backyard' in South America, the White House insisted that Hitler's regime was distasteful but a problem for Europe not the United States.

On the eve of the European war in September 1939, American commentators started to speculate that he might lead the nation into battle against Hitler. Roosevelt responded at once by summoning a press conference to insist there were no circumstances in which he would join a 'stop-Hitler' bloc. Furthermore, he promised that if Czechoslovakia were invaded, America would remain neutral.

As it was, the United States was in no condition to go to war. Earlier in the year, his newly appointed Chief of Staff, General George Marshall, was so dismayed by the gimcrack state of the nation's defences – which absorbed no more than a nugatory 1.7 per cent of GDP – that he had started a one-man campaign to lobby Congress. Warning that it was dangerous and irresponsible for a major power with an economy that was the largest and most robust in the world to maintain armed forces so pitifully inadequate as to be outranked by sixteen other nations, including Spain and Portugal, he demanded a crash programme of military investment. His efforts were in vain. However, refusing to accept that he had embarked on a 'mission impossible', he did not relent, telling the President in exceptionally blunt terms that if the necessary resources were not appropriated, 'I don't know what is going to happen to this country.'

Churchill was similarly resolute. Five days after his initial rebuff, he tried again. On 20 May – as the British Expeditionary Force was still beating the retreat to Dunkirk – he addressed Roosevelt in almost apocalyptic terms. While making it clear that his government would never 'consent to surrender', he warned that if the Nazis were to occupy Britain, others would assuredly come to the fore, willing 'to parley amid the ruins ... [and that] if this country were left by the United States to its fate no one would have the right to blame those responsible if they made the best terms they could for the surviving inhabitants. Excuse me, Mr President, putting this nightmare bluntly. Evidently I could not answer for my successors, who in utter despair and helplessness might well have to accommodate themselves to the German will'.

On 14 June, ten days after the evacuation from Dunkirk and as yet with no intimation of further US support, Churchill went even further. Reiterating that a 'pro-German government' in Britain 'might present to a shattered or starving nation an almost irresistible case for entire submission to the Nazi will', he spelt out the baleful implications of this surrender for the United States. The entire might of the British fleet, he warned, would almost certainly fall into Hitler's hands. Once joined with the Japanese, French and German navies, the Nazis would possess a totalitarian armada which would have a 'decisive' impact on the future of the United States. Piling on the pressure, he conjured up a fearsome image of a 'revolution in sea-power' that would very soon be able to dominate the world. 'If we go down you may have a United States of Europe under the Nazi command far more numerous, far stronger, far better armed than the New World. I know well, Mr President, that your eye will have already searched these depths, but I feel I have the right to place on record the vital manner in which American interests are at stake.'

This prime ministerial bombardment did not lack eloquence, clarity or passion but Roosevelt still failed to respond. Only after the fall of France, later in the month, was the President able to begin the delicate and tortuous task of weaning Congress away from its isolationist instincts. Evidence from France of the apparently irresistible march of Nazism across Europe finally alerted American public opinion to the threat Hitler might eventually pose to their interests. This altered mood by no means constituted a volte-face, but it led to a detectable shift on Capitol Hill, where a Bill was now approved increasing the military budget by $5 billion. To secure this concession, Roosevelt was obliged to make it clear that the new funds would be used solely to meet a direct attack on what he described as 'vital American zones'.

However, the slowly shifting mood of Congress also allowed the President to offer some comfort to Churchill. Within the formal constraints of the Neutrality Act, he brokered a deal to deliver the ancient destroyers for which Churchill had implored him. After a long bout of intense negotiation, the United States agreed to supply Britain with fifty of its obsolescent warships. In return, Britain was obliged to grant ninety-nine-year military leases on seven British colonies – Newfoundland, Bermuda, the Bahamas, Jamaica, St Lucia, Trinidad and British Guiana. It was a remarkably one-sided outcome. Estimating the scrap value of the destroyers – which he described as being 'on their last legs' – at between $4,000 and $5,000 apiece, Roosevelt reassured doubters that he had pulled off a spectacular deal, noting with satisfaction that, at a cost to the US Treasury of some $250,000, the price tag for the bases America thus acquired from Britain was 'extremely low'.

In other circumstances it would have been a humiliation, but Churchill chose to look on the bright side, concluding that it not only bound the Americans closer to Britain but – unconvincingly – that it marked the transformation of the United States 'from being neutral to being non-belligerent'. Not surprisingly, he failed to reveal the full character of the negotiations, preferring to tell the House of Commons that the military leases had been granted to the United States 'spontaneously' – without any haggling – to the mutual benefit of both governments and the British Empire. To put it mildly, this was to be economical with the truth: Roosevelt had insisted that the bases were a quid pro quo for the destroyers. Indeed, though the first geriatric vessels were delivered in September 1940, the lawyers took so long to finalise the agreement that it was not ready for signature until March the following year.

Although Washington had indeed taken one small step towards entering the war alongside the British Empire, Roosevelt faced a Republican challenger, Wendell Willkie, who, by the autumn of 1940, was closing the gap in the race for the White House. To secure a third term, Roosevelt's stance sounded almost as isolationist as his opponent's. Again and again he repeated that the only reason the government had reintroduced the draft, under which 16 million Americans faced possible conscription, was to protect the United States from a direct attack. On the eve of the poll, he even went so far as to make what – in retrospect – was an exceptionally rash promise: 'I have said this before, but I shall say it again and again and again,' he told a crowd in Boston, 'your boys are not going to be sent into any foreign wars.' In November, the notion that, within two years, the speaker of those words would be authorising the despatch of American soldiers to fight against Germany not in Europe but in North Africa would have seemed quite preposterous.

Moscow

Like Roosevelt, but for very different reasons, Joseph Stalin also hoped to avoid becoming embroiled in the conflict between Britain and Germany. The Soviet dictator had his mind on matters much closer to home, where his cynical rapprochement with the Führer was under growing strain. The final capitulation of Paris on 17 June 1940 had come as much as a shock to Stalin as to Roosevelt. The Soviet dictator had now lost any residual hope that – as in the First World War – Germany and France might fight each other to a standstill in the mud of Flanders. 'Couldn't they put up any resistance at all?' he complained when he heard the news of the French collapse.

Although he was unaware of Hitler's plans, Stalin was assuredly acquainted with those passages in *Mein Kampf* in which Hitler made it clear that Germany would in due course need to seize Russia to meet the Fatherland's growing demand for raw materials, to satisfy the Third Reich's appetite for greater *Lebensraum*, and to destroy the bacillus of Bolshevism. Concluding that his best hope of postponing a German démarche was to humour his German counterpart, Stalin not only increased the flow of food, petroleum, phosphate, and iron ore from the Soviet Union to Germany but even invited Berlin to use Russia as a corridor for the transhipment of vital raw materials from Romania, Iran, Afghanistan and the Far East.

At the same time, following their joint dismemberment of Poland in 1939, Stalin was still busily cleansing his half of that broken nation. As in the Baltic States of Estonia, Latvia and Lithuania, which had already been subjugated by the Red Army, those citizens who dared to challenge the Soviet diktat were liquidated. With summary executions and mass purges – the most notorious of which had been the massacres at Katyn in April and May 1940, when more than 21,000 Polish army officers, policemen, and members of the intelligentsia, were summarily executed on the express orders of the Politburo – the Soviet leader was as assiduous as the Führer in seeking to eliminate every vestige of opposition to his tyranny.

The Red Army's readiness to commit war crimes on Stalin's behalf was far more apparent than its military potential. In a 'Winter War' which began in late 1939, a small Finnish army had outfoxed and outfought the lumbering Russian invader on an Arctic battlefield. Only weight of numbers eventually forced the Finns to sue for peace. In March 1940, under the so-called 'Moscow Peace Treaty', the Soviet Union seized 11 per cent of its neighbour's territory and 30 per cent of its economic assets. But it was a hollow triumph which had accounted for the lives of many more Soviet than Finnish soldiers.

Nor did the dismal performance of the Red Army pass unnoticed in Berlin, where the General Staff concluded its analysis of the campaign with the scathing verdict that 'The Soviet "mass" is no match for an army and superior leadership.' This not only confirmed Hitler's prejudice 'that no Slav fighting force could stand up to the racially superior Germans' but, according to Alan Bullock, more than any other factor convinced him that he would be justified 'in gambling on defeating the Russians in a single campaign' the following year.

Stalin was no less aware that the Red Army – which, seized by the compulsion of paranoia, he had purged of its most experienced commanders – was poorly led as well as being ill equipped and ill trained. It was an urgent priority to turn this peasant army of 7 million soldiers into a fighting force capable of withstanding a Nazi invasion. Though he had used the breathing space provided by the non-aggression pact to create a security zone around the Soviet Union which, through occupation and annexation, extended from Finland in the north to the Black Sea in the south, the Russian leader was increasingly anxious about the fragility of the 'buffer' states which separated Russia from German-occupied eastern Europe. Similarly the Dardanelles, a narrow waterway linking the Black Sea to the Mediterranean and an important artery for Soviet shipping, was a source of growing concern to Moscow. Though the Dardanelles fell within Turkey's territorial limits, Stalin did not trust Hitler to keep his hands off a strategic choke point from where the Wehrmacht could easily strangle the Soviet economy. His prime task remained the postponement of the inevitable.

In the autumn of 1940, the idea that a campaign in a remote desert in North Africa – about which Stalin knew little and cared less – would thwart his own demands for an Allied second front in Europe against Hitler would have seemed as outlandish in the Kremlin as in the White House.

TWO

OPENING SALVOS

'The desert roused to fury, flaying us with a thousand whips
of sand that stung our faces and knees unbearably, choking
us and covering our bodies and luggage with a yellow screen.'
Richard Dimbleby

On 13 September 1940 the Italian Tenth Army finally trundled across the Libyan border into Egypt. A small 'covering force' of British troops fell back steadily before this stately progress, harrying the flanks of the 80,000 troops who were advancing across the desert in the general direction of Alexandria. Mussolini was 'radiant with joy' to hear the news, believing, as he told his Foreign Minister, Galeazzo Ciano, that 'The English [sic] are withdrawing with unforeseen rapidity.' His delight was premature.

Marshal Graziani had only crossed into Egypt because he feared the wrath of Italy's mercurial dictator if he procrastinated any longer. The original deadline set for the attack – 6 September – had come and gone without a single Italian soldier setting foot on Egyptian soil. The Italian commander-in-chief's reluctance to engage the British was supported by Marshal Badoglio, the most senior officer in Comando Supremo, the Italian High Command. Like Graziani, the Chief of the General Staff understood only too well that, although the 150,000 Italian troops massed on the Libyan side of the border enjoyed a five-to-one numerical advantage over the Empire and Commonwealth troops available to the British Middle East Command, Graziani's under-funded, ill-equipped and ill-trained troops were quite unprepared to do serious battle.

The memories of those conscripted into Mussolini's venture reinforce Graziani's realism.

'In September I was taken from the Tunisian frontier to Cyrenaica [eastern Libya]' a Private in the Tenth Army recalled. 'I was told we were to invade Egypt. Morale was not very high among the few people that I worked with and knew. I had a very jovial officer, but not a great leader; he was not very inspiring.' Lieutenant Paolo Colacicchi noted that his men 'were tired and wanted to go home; they were thinking of their fields left unattended. they had no aggressive feelings ... We realised that the British Army we were facing in Egypt, even though considerably smaller than ours, was better trained and better equipped, especially in transport, tanks, and armoured cars.'

Moreover, whereas the British force was mechanised, the great majority of Graziani's men had to slog it across the desert on foot. Combined with a shortage of water both to drink and with which to cook the men's basic diet, pasta, this meant that the Italians were wholly unprepared for any significant aggressive operation. But when Graziani sought a further month's delay, Mussolini vetoed the request, making it clear that he would be unceremoniously removed from his post unless the Tenth Army advanced into Egypt forthwith. Faced by this ultimatum, Graziani finally gave way. As Italy's Foreign Minister noted drily, 'Never has a military operation been undertaken so much against the will of the commanders.'

Had Mussolini not been so strategically inept, he could have played a trump card which he did not even realise he held. Though Hitler had been careful to conceal his intention to invade Russia, Mussolini should have realised that his principal utility to Hitler was as a guardian of the Third Reich's southern flank, which – had he not been so purblind – gave him great scope to press his Axis partner for military support not only in southern Europe but in North Africa as well. Indeed, on the day which had been supposed to mark the Italian démarche against Egypt – 6 September – Hitler confirmed this by offering to send 250 panzers from Europe to assist Graziani's desert campaign. But, puffed up with vainglory and suspecting that Hitler would use this apparent largesse as a

Trojan Horse in which to muscle his way into a dominant role in 'his' theatre, Mussolini rejected the Führer's gesture. His intention was to fight 'a parallel war' to assert in the Mediterranean his right to be regarded as equal with Hitler when the time came to divide up the spoils of victory at the conference table. This was to prove an expensive error of judgement.

As it was, the Italian advance into Egypt was more of 'a pantomime offensive' than a serious military operation. Motorcycle outriders 'protected' the front and rear of a long column of light tanks, support vehicles and truckloads of infantry, a formation which left the Tenth Army so vulnerable to attack that one contemptuous British officer likened its progress to 'a birthday party in the Long Valley at Aldershot'.

The British executed a tactical withdrawal, harrying Graziani's army along the way. Wavell, who was not prone to self-delusion, reported that the British withdrawal 'was effected with admirable skill [and] very serious losses were inflicted on the enemy' because Graziani 'made little attempt to use his immensely superior numbers or his mobility to outflank and overwhelm our small force'. The Western Desert Force was under the command of General Richard O'Connor, who had established a forward base at Mersah Matruh, a small port 120 miles east of the Libyan border and 200 miles west of Alexandria. It was here that the British commander, with two divisions totalling 31,000 men, prepared to arrest the Italian advance.

His ADC was Earl Haig, the son of the First World War field marshal. Haig was at once impressed with his new boss: 'Small in stature, dressed in shorts, he displayed a personality which was vigorous and intense, and deeply serious. Behind the friendly facade lay an expression of grim determination – of vigilance. He seemed like a horse which is eager and almost fretful. Without any small talk, he spoke with temperament [sic] often tinged with anxiety and frustration.'

If O'Connor harboured any anxieties about the size of the Italian force he was about to engage, they were short lived. After four days, by which time the Italians had covered no more than fifty miles, Graziani called a halt at Sidi Barrani, a small fishing village on the edge of the Mediterranean – which was as far as his unmechanised army could advance without running out of essential supplies. An Italian gunner, Sergeant Emilio Ponti, was one of the first to reach the harbour. 'A general came up, I was told he was General Bergonzoli, a famous Italian General. We called him General *"Barba Electrica"* – "Electric Whiskers". He said, "Lads, you have conquered Sidi Barrani, but we won't let you put your flag up."' Ponti protested, saying 'The Arabs and British have left. We didn't kill anybody. They just went. And this is our first town in Egypt, and we are entitled to it.' However Bergonzoli told them that it was to be handed over to Mussolini's 'Blackshirts', who had played no part in the proceedings but were to enjoy the fruits of their work. Not unnaturally this irked Ponti and his fellow foot soldiers.

That night the Royal Navy lobbed some shells into the port which hit a few of the fascist lorries. Some of them were killed. The gunners reflected, 'That could have been us. But as they get much more pay than us, it serves them right.' Ponti commented, 'You become really cruel when you are in the Army.' The hierarchies of status, pay and conditions within the Tenth Army could hardly have been better calculated to lower the morale of the Italian infantry. The officers were lavishly accommodated with comfortable beds, silk sheets, wardrobes for their uniforms, and a mess room in which to relax after dinner with fine Italian wines. Aside from water and pasta, the men were fed on bully beef and hard biscuits.

At Sidi Barrani, the Italians constructed a chain of fortified camps running south from the Mediterranean for fifty miles into the desert. It was soon clear that these garrison townships were to form a semi-permanent forward base from which Graziani had no intention of advancing any further. Wavell, who had feared an all-out onslaught on Egypt, was greatly reassured.

The lassitude of the Italians allowed O'Connor both to relax and to seize the initiative. His conversation, according to his ADC, was often 'about hunting and point-to-points' and he paid particular attention to the quality and preparation of dinner in the officers' mess: 'When he brought back some asparagus from Cairo, with strict instructions to see the long stalks were left on and served with butter sauce' he was less than pleased when 'his orders fell on deaf ears and the asparagus was served butterless and nearly stalkless in the middle of a large dish'. On the battlefield, however, he was very far from precious. He used small mobile columns, formed from the British 7th Armoured Division, in hit-and-run operations that, in Wavell's words, 'continually engaged and harassed the enemy'. The scene was set for a struggle which would pit men and weapons as much against the elements as each other in a theatre of conflict as inhospitable as anywhere on the planet.

The desert battlefield evoked powerful and contrary emotions even in the same individual. Men who were persecuted by intense heat in the day and bitter cold at night also had to endure ferocious sandstorms which penetrated every vehicle, every tent, and every human orifice. 'The desert roused to fury, flaying us with a thousand whips of sand that stung our faces and knees unbearably, choking us and covering our bodies and luggage with a yellow screen,' the BBC's correspondent, Richard Dimbleby, scribbled in his diary after his first experience of a *khamseen*.

'The sandstorm came at us like an express train at about 40 m.p.h, with increasing gusts of wind,' Bob Sykes, a tank crewman, wrote. 'All oxygen seemed to go out of the air, and the flies were maddening and swarming. The heat was terrific and I sweated so the sand caked onto me.' Sykes took shelter in his dugout but the sand found its way through every crack, making him fear that he would be buried alive. 'I fought my way out … the sand was whipping the skin off my face and hands. It was almost pitch black and I felt entirely alone. Then a light appeared and the sun began to look a dirty orange. The noise slowly abated and the wind died down. I had ridden out my first sandstorm.'

'Our worst enemy at that time was the desert sore,' a private in the Durham Light Infantry said later. 'If you cut yourself, septicaemia set in and it was difficult to treat … our MO invented a way of treating wounds with ground up M and B tablets and Vaseline and soldiers were told to keep the bandage on for as long as possible.'

The founding commander of the Long Range Desert Group (LRDF), Major Ralph Bagnold, wore Arab headgear partly as a means of disguise and partly because it offered some protection against the intense heat, since 'it flapped in the wind and kept one cool, and in a sandstorm you could wrap a piece of cloth round your face'. The LRDF was a piratical reconnaissance force of military adventurers with intimate knowledge of the remotest parts of the desert. Their task was to penetrate deep behind enemy lines, scouting for any sign of enemy movement. Bagnold evidently relished the extreme conditions. 'There were no flies in the deep desert, no animals, nothing for a fly to live on … No diseases in the desert either … It was so dry, you would sometimes come across a camel that had wandered off and died, perhaps fifty years before. The skin was dry and cracked, but you could look inside, see the organs intact, shrivelled up but otherwise complete.'

Except for those in thrall to the self-flagellatory predilections of T. E. Lawrence, the desert was alien and hostile, a surreal, hallucinatory space that seemed properly to belong not to the human species at all but to the hare, the gazelle, the scorpion, the snake and the squadrons of clinging, stinging flies that settled on food and in latrines, spreading diarrhoea and dysentery. But the terrible beauty of this environment also provoked awe. 'Here in the desert,' my father, the BBC correspondent, noted, 'where you live with the strict relentless rhythm of the sun and the moon and the stars, you come to a close understanding of your own unimportance … the feeling of humility never left me when I was living in the desert.'

In a series of colourful despatches, a correspondent for *Time* magazine likened fighting in the desert to 'playing chess with nothing but rooks and pawns. Whole areas of strategic gambit are impossible, and even admissible tactics are confounded and confused by nature. Water is as vital as ammunition; sand finer than talcum makes its way into eyes, carburettors and rifle breeches; heat averaging 120 degrees out of doors becomes incineration inside a tank or behind an airplane engine.'

Competing for apt metaphors, others likened the desert to a polo ground, although, from extremity to extremity it covered approximately the same area as India, and so far from being a level playing field was corrugated by gullies, large stones and outcrops of impassable rock. The British war correspondent Alan Moorehead, whose trilogy *The Desert War* would become the most celebrated contemporary account of the Middle East conflict, wrote,

> I began to see that desert warfare resembled war at sea. Men moved by compass. No position was static ... There were no trenches. There was no front line ... always the essential governing principle was that desert forces must be mobile: they were seeking not the conquest of territory or positions but combat with the enemy. We hunted men, not land, as a warship will hunt another warship, and care nothing for the sea on which the action is fought.

Unlike the sea, however, the topography of the desert is as unchanging as it is unyielding; a terrain with fixed points for which adversaries competed to establish a tactical advantage, by avoiding exposure to enemy fire or achieving protection from it. Very often the difference between success and failure, life and death, was possession of a small salient either as a forward niche from which to attack or a protective bunker in which to hide.

With Graziani sand-anchored at Sidi Barrani, Wavell was at his Cairo headquarters, planning the Italian's eviction. Richard Dimbleby was based in the Egyptian capital. 'Cairo is a babel,' he wrote, 'a yellow and white, dusty smelly city of shouting, screaming men and women, of screeching trams and crazy buses, of lunatic motor drivers and dreaming pedestrians, of starved and beaten cab-horses, mangy dogs, of rabies, venereal disease and dysentery. Anything can be bought in Cairo if you are prepared to pay the price, any price can be lowered if you are willing to argue.' Despite the dirt, the dust and the heat of a city 'pervaded by the familiar smell of the urban Middle East: the blend of exhaust fumes, overworked pack animals, cheap incense and manure', Cairo was an exotic watering hole, well away from the front line.

For the minority of expatriate politicians, diplomats, spies, soldiers, traders, travellers, and journalists who occupied the most salubrious parts of the metropolis, the crowded streets of the Old

City provided an alluring if sometimes unsavoury backdrop to their own congenial and leisurely lifestyles. They were then the masters, a transient colonial class who, with few exceptions, felt themselves to be socially, if not always economically, a cut above their Egyptian peers. They lived in airy apartments and were lavishly attended by servants who danced upon their every need. They frequented luxurious emporia which furnished all manner of personal or household supplies. At Groppi's, the famous coffee shop, they whiled away long hours in torpid gossip about the amatory exploits of this or that beau and belle.

New arrivals from the rigours of the desert or from war-stricken Britain – whose inhabitants had become accustomed to nightly bombing raids by the Luftwaffe – were shocked to discover the dissolute torpor which seemed to pollute the expatriate community. Nor were the British staff officers who liked to congregate at the Gezira Sporting Club or the Turf Club immune from such insouciance. One evening, a young British officer called Gordon Waterfield, newly arrived from London, entered the dining room of the Continental Hotel wearing shorts. He was swiftly informed that the hotel did not serve officers in such casual attire and told to leave. He protested but to no avail. Later he shared his irritation at such stiff-necked formality with a group of fellow officers at the Turf Club. So far from consoling him, however, they clearly deprecated his attitude, to the point where a lieutenant-colonel evidently 'sprang to his feet, and said hotly that captains had no right to an opinion on the matter'.

A more stimulating ambience was to be found at the Anglo-Egyptian Club, where those with a taste for the arts and literature gathered for congenial bookish evenings. Wavell, who was an aesthete and intellectual, was a frequent visitor, the imposing austerity of his presence enhanced by the fact that he had lost an eye in the Great War. The novelist and poet Lawrence Durrell, who arrived as a refugee from Greece with his wife and a small child in the spring of 1941, was admiring of the general's scholarly mien. 'Wavell had an extraordinary weakness for poets and poetry and was in fact at that moment doing an anthology and a treatise on generalship, which is one of the more amusing and sensitive books

I think ever written by a general.' he recalled. 'A side of him was withdrawn, not exactly morose but he had a wall eye, and wall eyed people give a feeling of dryness and moroseness ... [but] we liked him very much. He was a great addition to the circle and he used to come down very modestly ... he always had an anthology of verse under his arm.'

The Anglo-Egyptian Club offered Durrell – in his unlikely guise as a British military attaché – a measure of relief from the distressing sights, sounds and smells of a city that he and his wife came to loathe. The dust, the dirt, and the flies offended their senses, no less than the grinding poverty which also assailed them. 'Such a country ...' Durrell wrote splenetically to a friend, 'cripples, deformities, ophthalmia, goitre, amputations, lice, flies. In the street you see horses cut in half by careless drivers or obscene dead black men with flies hanging like a curtain over their wounds.'

A somewhat more sybaritic environment than the Anglo-Egyptian Club was provided by Shepheard's Hotel, which had long been the most sought after oasis for visitors from all over the Middle East, and since the outbreak of war had become the place to be seen in the maze of intrigue that made Cairo so deliciously notorious. Combining Moorish grandeur with Victorian cosiness, Shepheard's offered faded opulence and an air of intrigue which meant that no foreign correspondent strayed far from its Long Bar, where champagne flowed as freely as whisky and soda. It was the place above all others where a journalist could learn the truth about what was happening both at the front, more than two hundred miles away, and in the political furnace of the city itself. Editors back home might blanche at the expenses thus incurred, but the reporter could always insist that there was no other way of competing for a scoop in the Cairo hothouse – though, in the case of the BBC's correspondent, Shepheard's provided a rather more congenial environment than his own office, which was situated on the ground floor of a building which also housed a brothel.

Despite its reputation, the Long Bar failed to deliver any hint of the first big wartime story to emerge from Cairo. This was for the very good reason that Wavell had gone to some lengths to ensure that no leak should emanate from his own headquarters about the counter-attack he was planning to launch against the Italians. To guarantee surprise – essential in order to maximise the impact of his own numerically inferior forces and to avoid arousing suspicion in Cairo that might reach enemy spies – Wavell avoided putting his plans on paper. He discussed the details of the offensive with just a dozen or so senior commanders and staff officers. Their troops were told only that they were to participate in a training exercise.

Even Churchill was kept in the dark about the planned operation until his Secretary of State for War, Anthony Eden, returning from a visit to Cairo in October, gave him news of the impending assault in person – and even this disclosure was forced on Wavell. 'I realised Winston's sanguine temperament and desire to have at least one finger in any military pie,' he wrote later. 'I did not want to arouse premature hopes, I did not want Winston to make detailed plans for me ... But Eden was proposing to sap my strength in aircraft, A.A. guns, transport etc., in favour of Greece, thinking I had only a defensive policy in mind, to such an extent that I had to tell him what was in my mind to prevent my being skinned to an extent that would make an offensive impossible.'

During the preceding weeks, with the threat of an immediate Nazi invasion of Britain receding, the Prime Minister had become increasingly restless for action, demanding that the Chiefs of Staff find somewhere – anywhere – to confront the enemy. According to one of Whitehall's most senior staff officers, the Director of Military Operations, Major General John Kennedy, Churchill not only 'fretted at the delays which are inseparable from the preparation of modern fighting' but pressed the Chiefs 'to grapple with the enemy' and, in his thirst for action, kept coming up with proposals which, Kennedy drily observed, 'had no attraction for the Chiefs of Staff.'

When Eden returned to London with the news that such an offensive was already in preparation, the War Cabinet gave immediate approval to what Churchill described as Wavell's 'splendid enterprise', which, he insisted, 'should take first place in all our thoughts and have, amid so many other competing needs, first claim upon our strained resources'. Later the Prime Minister recalled 'purring like six cats at the prospect of engaging the enemy'. His appetite for action was insatiable. According to Kennedy, he discussed the impending offensive nearly every day and, in so doing, 'magnified the possible results out of all proportion' while refusing to recognise 'the hard realities of the problem of supply in the desert'.

However these realities could not be ignored. Since early summer the Mediterranean had been effectively closed to British merchant shipping via the Straits of Gibraltar because the Axis had command of the skies over so much of the seaway. As a result, all reinforcements for the Middle East could only be despatched safely via the Cape of Good Hope. The 'Cape route' involved a looping voyage down through the Atlantic, round the Cape and up through the Red Sea to Suez – a journey of some 13,000 miles which took up to three months to complete. Churchill found this hard to endure and, in June, pressed the Admiralty to risk the Mediterranean route, dangerous though it might be. When the Admiral of the Fleet, Sir Dudley Pound, warned of the perils this would entail, the Prime Minister reacted sharply. 'From time to time and for sufficient objects this risk will have to be faced,' he admonished, adding, 'Warships are meant to go under fire' – a gratuitous slur which the Admiralty refused to dignify with a response.

In August, the Prime Minister's frustration had boiled over once again. At the height of the threatened invasion of Britain, he ordered a brigade of fifty infantry tanks – 'nearly half our best available tanks' as he described them – to be despatched forthwith to reinforce Wavell's Western Desert Force against the threatened Italian invasion. When the Admiralty told him that this armour would be sent via the Cape rather than through the Mediterranean, Churchill erupted. 'I cannot accept this proposal to use the Cape route … which deprives us of invaluable resources during a most critical period … there can be no question of them or their personnel going by the Cape, thus making sure they are out of everything for two months.' Two days later he wrote icily to the First Lord of the Admiralty and the First Sea Lord reproaching them for the 'standard of danger-values now adopted in the Mediterranean' and informing them that he would take 'full responsibility' for any tanks that might be lost en route. However, Pound stood his ground, an exercise of rightful authority which prompted Churchill to growl later that he had been both 'grieved and vexed' by the admiral's intransigence. He even considered invoking the authority of the War Cabinet to overrule the First Lord but in the end resisted the temptation to take such an incendiary route. However, no sooner were the tanks on their way via the Cape to Egypt (where, as it happened, they arrived in time to strengthen O'Connor's counter-offensive), than Churchill – gambling that Hitler would not invade Britain in the near future – began once again to urge the Chiefs of Staff to supply Wavell with more resources: infantry units from Australia and New Zealand should be rapidly mobilised for the desert conflict as well as armoured units and aircraft from Britain itself.

The Prime Minister's restless quest for early action led him to complain repeatedly about the apparent inertia of the Middle East Command. To the intense frustration of his advisors in Whitehall, he found it impossible to appreciate that not every soldier in the Middle East could be deployed on the desert front line; other fronts needed protection as well. To make matters worse, he was also unable to appreciate why the 'ration' strength of a mechanised army in the twentieth century was bound to exceed by far the numbers of men on its 'fighting' strength; that without a vast support structure of staff officers, engineers, mechanics, drivers, quartermasters and orderlies, not to mention doctors, dentists and nurses, the men in tanks or in slit trenches at the front would be quite unable to wage war at all.

If Churchill heard what he was told, he rarely appeared to listen. Thus in late October, 'hungry for a turn to the offensive' he told Eden (who had not yet returned from Egypt) to investigate. 'I fear that the proportion of fighting compared with ration strength is worse in the Middle East than anywhere else. Please do not be content with the stock answers ... Not only the best, but the second and third best, must be made to play their part,' he cabled.

The Prime Minister's urge to interfere with such incontinent ferocity in operational details which should not have detained him was inspired by an unwavering conviction that victory in the Middle East was crucial to the survival of the Empire. Thus, on 28 November, soon after Eden's return from Cairo with the glad tidings of an imminent offensive in the Western Desert, he could not refrain from cabling Wavell to pile on the pressure once again: 'News from every quarter must have impressed on you the importance of *Compass* [the codename given to his planned offensive] in relation to the whole Middle East position, including Balkans and Turkey, to French attitude in North Africa, to Spanish attitude, now trembling on the brink, to Italy, in grievous straits, and generally to the whole war.' This was not mere grandiloquence: for Churchill, *Compass* offered a critical opportunity to demonstrate to those hard-pressed nations in southern Europe and the Balkans which had not yet succumbed to the Axis threat that Britain could be trusted to fight back on their behalf.

On the afternoon of Saturday, 7 December 1940, the British commander-in-chief attended a race meeting at the Gezira Club with his wife and two daughters and later that evening he hosted a dinner party at the Turf Club for a group of his senior colleagues. It was a calculated demonstration of military sangfroid. Back at his desk on Monday morning, he summoned the British war correspondents to his office at nine o'clock. Alan Moorehead described sitting with his colleagues in a semi-circle around Wavell as he told them, with a rare smile, 'Gentlemen, I have asked you to come here this morning to let you know that we have attacked in the Western Desert.' Operation *Compass* was underway. Clearly relieved to discover that none of the correspondents had heard even a whisper of the impending attack, he added a cautionary note which would assuredly have vexed his intemperate Prime Minister. 'This is not an offensive and I do not think you ought to describe it as an offensive as yet. You might call it an important raid.'

Ever mindful of Churchill's pressure, Wavell had cabled London the previous day to advise General Sir John Dill, the Chief of the Imperial General Staff, against extravagant expectations. 'Feel undue the hopes being placed on this operation which was designed as raid only,' he wrote. 'Please do not encourage

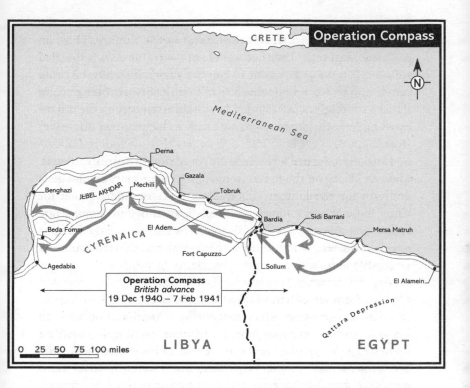

CRETE   **Operation Compass**

Mediterranean Sea

Derna

Gazala

Benghazi   JEBEL AKHDAR   Mechili   Tobruk

Beda Fomm   El Adem   Bardia   Sidi Barrani   Mersa Matruh

CYRENAICA   Fort Capuzzo

Agedabia   Sollum   El Alamein

Operation Compass
British advance
19 Dec 1940 – 7 Feb 1941

Qattara Depression

0   25   50   75   100 miles

LIBYA   EGYPT

optimism.' When the CIGS forwarded this missive to Churchill, he reacted testily. 'If with the situation as it is, General Wavell is only playing small, and is not hurling on his whole available force with furious energy, he will have failed to rise to the height of circumstances.'

Later Wavell explained the cautious tone of his cable to Dill. 'I always meant to go as far as possible and exploit any success to the full, but I was a little apprehensive that Winston might urge me to do too much, as limitations of supply and transport never made any great appeal to him.' Without the mutual suspicion and disdain by which their relationship was marred, a great many wearisome and damaging misunderstandings might have been avoided – to the benefit of both men and to the conduct of the war in the Middle East and the Mediterranean during an intensely testing period.

A few days later, scrambling to catch up with the advancing British armour, the BBC's correspondent came across the 'gutted tanks and armoured cars blistering in the sun, petrol and diesel lorries with burst tyres and broken backs, exploded ammunition trucks standing like black skeletons in pools of their own debris. The Italians themselves lay tangled in the mess with the desert fleas crawling over them and the savage flies tormenting their swollen faces.'

Initially Graziani's Tenth Army fought with stubborn resolve against O'Connor's men. But, confirming that a small mechanised army supported by infantry tanks can wreak havoc against a much larger force of foot soldiers, their resistance was short lived. With agility and aplomb, the British mobile units soon found a way round to the rear of the Italians at Sidi Barrani and trapped thousands of them in their front-line garrisons. With no means of transport, Graziani's men had little choice but to die or surrender. Most of them were swift to take the latter option.

'The Italians were utterly lamentable,' Artillery Captain Bob Hingston noted. 'We were pretty green but they were appalling soldiers. The first thing I saw was four of their guns perched right out in the open, not dug in. Why they'd put them there when there was quite a bit of cover around I cannot imagine. They started firing and so I managed to range on to them and gave them a good plastering; that was the end of them.' A brother officer Captain Philip Tower recalled, 'It was a complete walkover. I saw thousands of Italian prisoners, delighted that the war was over.' One of those prisoners, Private Mario Cassandra, described his own surrender. 'The first time I saw an Englishman I was lying in a hole … I heard a lot of noise, people shouting and people running, and as we were going we saw all these Italians sitting down and realised they were prisoners, and joined them.'

To widespread astonishment, and somewhat to his own surprise, O'Connor's 'raid' had swiftly turned into a rout. The Western Desert Force with 31,000 troops – the Indian, Australian and New Zealand battalions which formed the 6th Infantry Division, the British 7th Armoured Division and the 7th Battalion, Royal Tank Regiment – had forced an army that was five times larger to scramble out of their front-line fortress at Sidi Barrani and stumble back in chaotic cohorts to the Libyan border.

The detritus of battle littered the desert. Not only dead soldiers sprawled grotesquely on the ground under blankets of flies or starving pack-mules, braying wildly for water, but, as Dimbleby's colleague Alan Moorehead wrote, an officers' mess with 'beds laid out with clean sheets, chests of drawers filled with linen and an abundance of fine clothing of every kind'. The British correspondents wondered in disbelief at the richly embroidered uniforms, bedecked with medals of honour and gold lace, the polished jackboots, the tasselled belts and peacock hats, all neatly arranged as though their tenants were preparing to participate in a parade-ground march past, rather than fleeing for their lives. That evening, the war correspondents sat amid this booty, helping themselves to jars of bottled cherries, tins of ham, anchovies, and bread 'that had been baked somehow here in the desert'. There was a splendid array of excellent Italian wines and casks of brandy and other liqueurs – all crated and carted from Italy across the Mediterranean to Tripoli or Benghazi 'across a thousand miles of sea and desert by ship and car and mule team'.

A signaller in the Royal Horse Artillery, Ted Whitaker, described how his unit came across 'piles of Italian kit ... There was a large store of tinned food and condensed milk. My mother had always stopped me from eating condensed milk with a spoon, and [here] there was no one to stop me. We found a gramophone and a pile of opera records. So for some time we sat and ate tinned food with Nestlé's condensed milk and listened to opera. I found a nice silk black shirt.' They discovered a cache of pistols and revolvers forgotten in the rush to retreat. A collection of pullovers and black woolly hats with pom-poms was irresistible. Flushed with the triumph, Whitaker and his friends donned the Blackshirts' clothes but were told smartly to 'take that bloody stuff off and look like soldiers'.

The desert breeze stirred waste paper and the pages of lost letters that were meant for the eyes of loved ones only. In a letter which would never reach its destination, an infantryman wrote, 'God watch and keep our beloved Federico and Maria and may the blessed Virgin preserve them from all harm until the short time, my dearest, passes when I shall press thee into my arms again. I cry. I weep for thee here in the desert and lament our cruel separation.'

Others, though, expressed greater defiance, notably that minority who were committed to Mussolini and the fascist cause. One officer, in a letter which he must have written about the hit-and-run skirmishes that had preceded O'Connor's counter-offensive, complained:

> But for the cowardice of the English who flee from even our lightest shelling and smallest patrols, we would have committed the wildest folly in coming to this appalling desert. The flies plague us in millions from the first hour in the morning. The sand always seems to be in our mouths, in our hair and in our clothes, and it is impossible to get cool. Only troops of the highest morale and courage would endure privations like these ... We shall soon be at Alexandria. We shall soon now be exchanging this hellish desert for the gardens of the Nile.

By the time Moorehead picked up this letter, its author was either dead, captured, or hurriedly retreating back to the Libyan fortresses of Bardia or Tobruk, well on the other side of the border.

Ten miles to the west of Sidi Barrani, the war correspondents came upon a sight 'that seemed at first too unreal, too wildly improbable to be believed'. The 7th Armoured Division under General Creagh had captured many thousands of prisoners who, as Moorehead watched, 'plodded four abreast in the sand on either side of the metal strip ... [a] stupendous crocodile of marching figures stretched away to either horizon ... they were tired and dispirited beyond caring. I found no triumph in the scene – just the tragedy of hunger, wounds and defeat.'

The victory was not without cost. A gunner from the Royal Horse Artillery, Sergeant Ray Ellis, was out in the open when he heard 'a screaming sound' and hurled himself to the ground. 'There was this devastating flashing, crashing and blast – it went quiet. Then there was another scream and a soldier came out into the street. He was holding his guts in and all his stomach had been torn open and his entrails were trickling through his fingers. He was screaming. He sank to his knees, his screaming changed to a gurgle and he just dropped, almost at my feet. He was the first man I saw die.' An Italian bomber had hit its target.

A British Cruiser tank was hit by an Italian shell and burst into flames. Its driver was killed instantly but his foot remained on the accelerator and the vehicle continued to trundle forward as its radio transmitted to their listening colleagues the terrible sounds emanating from those trapped inside the doomed vehicle. The commander, who had had his hand blown off, yelled, 'the tank's on fire' and then, one of them recounted, 'all we heard were the most terrible screams of agony; they were being burned alive while their tomb of fire went on towards the enemy'.

Total British casualties numbered 500, of whom 133 were killed and 387 wounded but O'Connor's men had captured large quantities of equipment – including 237 artillery pieces and 73 tanks – in addition to more than 38,000 prisoners. In the crude audit of warfare, it was a singular triumph. As an officer in the Coldstream Guards counted the prisoners, he reported witheringly, 'We have about five acres of officers and 200 acres of other ranks'.

When Churchill received the news that Sidi Barrani had fallen and that the Italians were scurrying back into Libya, he was relieved and exultant. On 16 December he sent a jubilant telegram to Wavell. 'The Army of the Nile' he wrote, using the romantic designation that he had personally accorded the Western Desert Force, 'has rendered glorious service to the Empire and to our cause, and we are already reaping the rewards in every quarter … Your first objective now must be to maul the Italian Army and rip them off the African shore to the utmost possible extent.'

Churchill's delight was boundless. At last – and for the first time since the start of hostilities – he could boast that the British Army had engaged the enemy and had emerged triumphant. He was swift to cable Roosevelt and the Prime Minister of Australia, Robert Menzies, writing to the latter, 'I am sure you will be heartened by the fine victory the Imperial Armies have gained in

Libya ... We are planning to gather a very large army representing the whole Empire and ample sea-power in the Middle East, which will face a German lurch that way.' The Prime Minister's euphoria was premature. He was not to know when this 'lurch' might occur, what form it might take, or how devastating it would prove to be.

THREE

MUSSOLINI'S MISTAKE

'You have done great deeds and won much glory. We are fighting for freedom and truth and kindliness against oppression and lies and cruelty, and we shall not fail.'
Archibald Wavell

In Rome, news of the British seizure of Sidi Barrani hit the Foreign Ministry like 'a thunderbolt'. But though Ciano realised that the Tenth Army had 'had a licking', Mussolini appeared quite impervious to the gravity of the situation. By now, according to the timetable he had projected three months earlier, he should have been celebrating victory with Hitler as an equal partner with his German ally. That vision had turned to dust in the desert, crumbling so fast that even so delusional a leader as Mussolini should have found it impossible to swat away the bitter truth that his Tenth Army had been comprehensively humiliated. On 10 December Ciano noted, 'Things are going really badly in Libya. Four divisions can be considered destroyed, and Graziani, who reports on the spirit and decision of the enemy, says nothing about what he can do to parry the blow.' Despite this, his father-in-law became 'more and more calm', maintaining vapidly that 'the many painful days through which we are living must be considered inevitable in the changing fortunes of every war'. His insouciance did not yield to reality until a 'catastrophic' telegram arrived from Graziani warning that he might well have to withdraw his forces all the way back to Tripoli, a prospect that, according to Ciano, left him 'very much shaken'.

In his canny fashion, however, Il Duce was swift to appreciate the likely impact on public opinion. For the most part, the Italian people had been reluctant combatants who felt they had been press-ganged into a war which promised no discernible benefits. When Ciano urged that steps should be taken to improve morale, Mussolini listened carefully. 'We must speak to the hearts of the Italians,' the Foreign Minister advised. 'We must make them understand that what is at stake is not Fascism – it is our country, our eternal country, the country of us all, which is above all men and times and factions.' There was little evidence to suggest that such vacuities would have any impact on an increasingly sceptical population that continued to have difficulty in recognising why its eternal identity was at stake in the sands of the North African desert.

The Italian winter matched Mussolini's bleak mood. On Christmas Eve 1940 he stood at a window in his palace, watching the falling snow, and then turned to his son-in-law. 'This snow and cold are very good,' he avowed. 'In this way our good-for-nothing men and this mediocre race will be improved. One of the principal reasons I have desired the reforestation of the Apennines has been to make Italy colder and more snowy.' The dictator's bizarre meditations on the contemptible nature of his subjects provided him with a ready excuse for holding them responsible for the manifold ills of the nation rather than his own lamentable performance as their leader. He would return to the same theme again and again, on one occasion deploying two clumsily mixed metaphors to complain, 'It is the material I lack. Even Michelangelo had need of marble to make statues. If he had only had clay he would have been nothing more than a potter. A people who for sixteen centuries have been an anvil cannot become a hammer within a few years.' Though his 'soft and unworthy people' were not yet disposed to turn against him, his humiliation by the British was the culmination of a disastrous few weeks in which he had also been humiliated on another Mediterranean front.

Two months earlier, on 28 October, half a million Italian troops had crossed the border from Albania into Greece. The invasion had been prescribed by Il Duce in a sudden fit of pique. It followed an Alpine meeting with Hitler at the beginning of the month. On the face of it, it had been a remarkably congenial and collusive encounter as the two men sat in the Führer's well-upholstered railway carriage at the Brenner Pass on 4 October discussing their shared objectives. The German leader had been in an exceptionally ebullient mood.

A week earlier, on 27 September, the Japanese ambassador had joined Hitler and Ciano to sign the Tripartite Pact which ostensibly committed the three dictatorships to provide mutual military support if one or other of them were to be attacked. The Pact also mooted a 'New Order' in Europe and Greater East Asia. The Führer must indeed have felt that he now bestrode the world like a Colossus. At their meeting on 4 October he informed Mussolini that the British were in 'a hopeless situation militarily' and 'titanic efforts' were being made by the Third Reich to prepare for the 'final battle' which would bring about the defeat of the British Empire. Careful though he was to avoid mentioning Operation *Barbarossa*, he did let slip that the Soviet Union was too weak to pose any military threat to the global ambitions of the new tripartite alliance. His only concern seemed to be the United States. Explaining that it would be 'prudent to prepare for a confrontation', he informed his ally that he was minded to establish a German bridgehead in North Africa to face any challenge from across the Atlantic.

The apparent openness with which Hitler spoke – not only railing against Bolshevism but indicating as well that he intended to accord more importance to the Mediterranean theatre – put Mussolini in an unusually good humour. He returned to Rome elated and invigorated, convinced that theirs was a true partnership of equals, the suspicion and envy which habitually curdled his feelings about the Führer banished from his mind. The euphoria did not last.

Within days he discovered that – without informing, let alone consulting him – Hitler had despatched the Wehrmacht into Romania, an acquiescent staging post from which the German army could penetrate deeply into any part of the Balkans. When the Italian leader heard about this démarche, he lost his temper.

'Hitler keeps confronting me with a fait accompli,' he shouted. 'This time I shall pay him back in his own coin; he will learn from the newspapers that I have occupied Greece. The equilibrium will be restored.' On witnessing this outburst, Ciano, who was himself an advocate of the folly which was about to unfold, commented with the complacency of an ingénue, 'I believe the military operation will be useful and easy.'

Mussolini's generals knew better. Protesting that an operation of such magnitude would require at least twenty divisions and take months to organise, Badoglio, the Supreme Chief of the Italian General Staff, even threatened to resign if the invasion went ahead, a threat which merely provoked Mussolini to fly into a violent rage. When Hitler heard about the plan, he did his best to dissuade his junior partner from a venture which he knew would inflame passions throughout the Balkans, thereby undermining the diplomatic offensive he had already unleashed to corral the region into the Axis camp by political thuggery rather than brute force.

Mussolini was undeterred. When the Italian army duly crossed the border, it found itself up against a Greek force inferior in numbers but not in patriotism and willing to fight for the soul of the nation with a ferocity which the Italians had failed to foresee. Within three weeks the invaders had not only been halted but, in a humiliating reverse, had been driven firmly back into Albania. Mussolini's precipitous and whimsical act of imperial aggression had turned into a military debacle.

Hitler was furious, but was careful to frame his written rebuke in measured language, warning his partner that the complex situation in the Balkans had been made even more difficult; moreover his precipitate action would inevitably have (unspecified) repercussions for the Axis campaign in Egypt. When he read the Führer's letter, Mussolini was left in no doubt that he had provoked great displeasure. 'This time he really has slapped my fingers,' he commented.

When the Führer met the Italian Foreign Minister at the Berghof (Hitler's headquarters in the Bavarian Alps) on 18 November, he was far more severe. 'He is pessimistic and considers the situation much compromised by what has happened in the Balkans,' Ciano noted. 'His criticism is open, definite and final. I try to talk to him, but he does not allow me to proceed.'

Yet within days Hitler had relented. At their next meeting, in Vienna on 20 November, Ciano saw that the Führer had 'two big tears in his eyes' as he declared that he would never forget Mussolini's support during the Anschluss (Germany's annexation of Austria in March 1938). Indeed, he had just sent his Italian ally a further message to reassure him that 'I am at his side with all my strength'.

For Il Duce, this conciliatory note was a two-edged sword. Though he distrusted the Führer's motives and found his manner irksome – he had every reason still to regard him as 'a gramophone with seven records' – he could no longer deceive himself that he was an equal partner fighting in parallel with Germany against a common enemy, albeit on a different front. He was trapped in a relationship, a marriage of necessity, in which protestations of goodwill concealed a mismatch of power and, ultimately, bad faith.

That Hitler chose to humour and console his partner did not alter that brutal truth. General Ubaldo Soddu, Mussolini's Undersecretary for War, who had been put in command of the defeated Italian troops in Albania, was soon obliged to report that the military situation there was so dire that the only way of escape was 'through political intervention'. Mussolini was moved to despair and soon sacked Soddu. But he could not ignore the truth. 'This is grotesque, but it is a fact,' he told Ciano on 4 December. 'We shall have to ask for a truce through Hitler.' With an uncharacteristic display of emotion Ciano noted, 'I would rather put a bullet through my head than telephone Ribbentrop [the German Foreign Minister].'

At the time, Italy's ambassador to Berlin, Dino Alfieri, was back in Rome convalescing from an illness. On a visit to Mussolini's office at the Palazzo Venezia, he found his leader 'plunged in the depths of depression. I had never before seen him look so dispirited. His face was pale and drawn, his expression sad and preoccupied ... He paced slowly round his big desk, taking short steps ... passing his right hand nervously across his chin and face, turning now to Ciano, now to me, as though seeking approval or support for his theories and justification for his hopes.'

But there was no reprieve. The twin disasters on either side of the Mediterranean had exposed as hubris on stilts Mussolini's dream of bestriding his 'Lake' no less colossally than Hitler bestrode great swathes of Europe; through his clumsy self-delusions he had incontrovertibly revealed his ineptitude and his dependency on the goodwill of his German patron. It was his good fortune that, for his part, Hitler retained a loyalty and even an affection for his fellow dictator. More to the point, however, was his persistent anxiety about the threat from the British to his southern flank, which drove him to the ineluctable conclusion that he needed Mussolini as much as Mussolini needed him. For this reason, the Führer was about to throw a lifeline to his wayward ally which was to change the whole course of the conflict in the Middle East.

After taking Sidi Barrani in mid-December, General O'Connor was poised to exploit his initiative and anxious to hound the Italian Tenth Army further back into Libya. However, without warning, his advance was brought to a juddering halt when he was ordered by Wavell to release the 4th Indian Division for immediate redeployment against the Italians in East Africa. The Indians were to form the northern arm of a pincer movement designed to drive the Italians out of Eritrea and Ethiopia (which Mussolini had colonised in 1936) and thereby to destroy the Italian Empire in East Africa and, in the process, to secure beyond doubt the safety of Britain's crucial supply lines to the Middle East via the Red Sea and the Suez Canal.

The strategic significance of Wavell's decision was not lost on O'Connor, but he was nonetheless dismayed. It was not only a 'complete and very unpleasant surprise', he complained later, but 'it put paid to the question of immediate exploitation. I don't doubt the desirability, if not the necessity, of those troops being brought to East Africa. But it all arose from the fact that they didn't expect a big success in the desert and when it came they weren't prepared to alter the plan ... The net result was that we lost surprise altogether.'

Wavell's decision had indeed given Graziani a brief respite. He used this breathing space to reinforce the Tenth Army's defences at Bardia, a Libyan port eighteen miles to the west of the Egyptian border. Though the town was fortified along a seventeen-mile perimeter with machine-gun and anti-aircraft-gun emplacements, while the port itself was girdled by an anti-tank trench and barbed wire, Bardia was nonetheless vulnerable. But Mussolini's orders were unambiguous: 'I have given you a difficult task but one suited to your courage and your experience as an old and intrepid soldier,' he instructed General Bergonzoli. '[It is] the task of defending the fortress at Bardia to the last. I am certain that "Electric Whiskers" and his brave soldiers will stand at whatever cost'. Bergonzoli reacted with corresponding braggadocio. 'I am aware of the honour and I have today repeated to my troops your message … In Bardia we are and here we stay.'

The Australian 6th Infantry Division, which had disembarked at Alexandria in December to replace the Eritrea-bound Indian 4th Division, was not only unblooded by battle but ill-equipped and untrained in desert warfare. They were not only short of weapons like machine guns but so lacking in supplies that they were only permitted to fire one practice round of anti-tank ammunition before they were sent into action. The leather jerkins needed to ward off the wind and the cold at night were provided only on the eve of the battle for Bardia. Similarly, the wire-cutters and gloves vital for breaching the town's defences arrived only at the very last moment.

At the end of December, just before the start of the ground attack on Bardia, the port was pounded by the Royal Navy's heaviest guns while, over two nights, the RAF dropped 50,000 pounds of bombs on the Italian positions around the town. The final assault began on 3 January 1941. It had already become the knee-jerk custom for the British – and the Germans – to mock the Italian soldiers for a lack of fighting spirit, a readiness to lay down their arms at the slightest pretext and to run for cover rather than stand their ground for a cause in which they had little faith. But there were numerous examples of unflinching obedience under fire.

'In you go!' a company commander of the 6th Australian

Infantry Division yelled as three of his platoons moved towards the town's perimeter, suffering heavy losses as they went. 'All hell was let loose' one of his lieutenants, Jack Tramp, recorded as the Italians staged a counter-attack. 'They came at us in droves and for about two hours we were kept busy as they advanced within two hundred yards of us. But finally we beat them off.' By nightfall the three platoons could muster only thirty survivors. Between them, they carried the dead – their own and the Italian – to the bottom of a wadi, 'where we covered them with loose stones'.

Assigned to provide artillery support to the advancing Australian infantry, Gunner L. E. Tutt described fighting his way through the perimeter wire at Bardia. 'We came across a battery of Italians. It became the fashion to decry the Italians as soldiers; this may have been true of their infantry but not of their artillery. In this instance they had died at their guns. Their bodies were scattered close to their firing positions and they must have remained in action until our infantry tanks and the Australians had overrun their gun sites.'

But once this line had been breached, it became pointless to heed Mussolini's orders. An Australian infantryman, Corporal Rawson, described what happened when his battalion became entangled with 'Eyetie [prisoners] trying to get through to our lines ... There was moderate small arms fire ... an artillery post but it didn't give us much trouble ... The only other resistance our company met was from a machine-gun nest behind a built-up earthworks. We took cover and decided what to do. Our section leader gave an order to charge, but before we got very far a row of white flags went up as if by signal. The gunner in the centre had apparently been shot in the head and when he was killed the others surrendered.'

For all their inexperience the Australians were clinically efficient and quite fearless. 'We admired the Australians very much. They were tall men, bronzed and casual,' said Stephen Hawkins, serving in a unit of the Royal Horse Artillery, which provided covering fire for the 6th Australian Division as it advanced towards the town in the early hours of 5 January. 'At dawn', Hawkins recalled, 'the Aussies went in. They went in groups of about six, with their long bayonets.' There was no return fire; Bardia had fallen. Bombadier Dawson watched as 'thousands upon thousands' of Italian prisoners came out to surrender. 'They looked pathetic, calling "Aqua, Aqua". We couldn't spare any water to give them. In the afternoon we drove through an area we had been shelling, and there were lots of Italian bodies lying there. I laughed, more hysteria than anything.' Without water to drink or trucks to escape in, the Italians once again had no choice but to surrender or perish.

That evening, a small group of war correspondents followed the Australians into the town. 'On either side of us in the gloom' the BBC's correspondent Richard Dimbleby reported, 'were gathering crowds of enemy officers and men – with their guns ... they did nothing; they just stood and watched us drive through ... they were gathering voluntarily to surrender to the first British troops they saw ... several of them actually ran up to me with their hands up, crying "surrender".'

As he walked through the throng of prisoners, a young soldier seized him by the arm, begging him to find an ambulance for a wounded comrade who was lying on the ground in a greatcoat soaked with blood from a gaping stomach wound. Dimbleby turned for assistance to an Australian guard, who was unimpressed: 'Put a bloody wop in an ambulance? What about our boys?' Two British ambulances passed, already overflowing with casualties. The third stopped and the wounded Italian was lifted inside, provoking much grumbling from within the crowded vehicle. 'But', Dimbleby noted, 'two of them made a pillow for the youngster as he lay at their feet and someone else threw a coat over him. The doors were shut again and the ambulance moved off into the darkness.' His friend, who had escaped the onslaught with a broken ankle, watched his friend depart. Dimbleby helped him to the side of the road. 'Then he burst into tears and cried more bitterly than I had ever seen a man cry before.'

With 1,000 dead, 3,000 wounded and 36,000 captured, only 5,000 of an original force of 45,000 men under Bergonzoli's command escaped to fight again. At a cost of 456 casualties, the Australians also took 130 tanks and hundreds of field guns, machine guns and rifles along with 700 other vehicles. It had taken two days to expose Mussolini's injunction to 'stand whatever the cost' as another example of the preposterous rhetoric which in due course would make him an object of ridicule in his own country as well as the rest of the world.

From Bardia, O'Connor's men advanced rapidly towards the port of Tobruk, meeting hardly any resistance. As a tank gunner in Graziani's Tenth Army, Sergeant Ponti was one of the few to have a mechanised means of transport to reach Tobruk before the Australians. On the way, he clattered past piteous groups of exhausted fellow countrymen – 'cannon-fodder' as he described them – who had no choice but tramp through the heat of the day.

The Tobruk perimeter, an arc around the town of some fifty kilometres in length, was strongly fortified with tank traps, barbed wire and underground concrete bunkers which should have provided a confident army with more than adequate protection against even the heaviest bombardment. But Italian morale had been broken. On 21 January the British artillery fired their opening salvoes. Sergeant Ponti was almost immediately deserted by his commanding officer. 'The firing was terrific. I stayed inside the tank. I wasn't going to be killed ... We had no enthusiasm. We didn't believe we were doing the right thing. To get killed for some madman seemed stupid ... There was pandemonium, no one knew what they were doing. The officers were all hidden ... We got in a ditch ... My mate got hit. But I was all right. I took my pistol out and threw it away.' When there was a lull in the fighting, Ponti crawled and then ran into the nearest medical centre to find that 'it was packed with officers, not with the sick. A short while later an Australian walked in, bayonet at the ready. In Italian he said, "Hands up". I pulled out my white handkerchief and went out first.'

A British doctor, who was among the first to enter the town, passed 'the litter of a rout' – half-open suitcases, weapons, helmets, a tatter of torn uniforms – and climbed a small rise and looked down towards the sea. At first glance – when seen at a distance – Tobruk was a dazzling sight with its flat-roofed, white houses clinging to the flank of a low slope overlooking a brilliantly blue bay. Dr Stephanides was struck by 'the immense amount of Italian shipping sunk in the harbour; masts stuck up everywhere out of the water like pins in a pin cushion'.

The doctor also witnessed an unlikely camaraderie between soldiers who so very recently had been trying to kill one another. The town, he noted, was silent 'except for occasional shots fired as a feu de joie by over-exuberant Australians. We encountered a few of these, together with Italians, waving bottles of wine, singing and exchanging hats.' The Australians had captured 25,000 Italian prisoners, along with a substantial collection of guns, tanks, and trucks at a cost of 49 dead and 306 wounded.

With the news that Tobruk was taken, Wavell allowed himself an uncharacteristic burst of enthusiasm, reaching for an extended hunting metaphor, of the kind much favoured by his peers in the cavalry. 'Hunt is still going,' he reported, 'but first racing burst over, hounds brought to their noses, huntsmen must cast and second horses badly wanted. It may be necessary to dig this fox.' The prosaic gist of this signal – which was designed to be incomprehensible to any Italian eavesdropper – was 'We have paused to take stock, we are moving cautiously forward, seeking out the enemy, and we are urgently in need of reinforcements.'

But O'Connor was not in a mood to pause. With characteristic panache he ordered that the Italians should be given no respite. Bergonzoli was soon on the move again, leading the Italian retreat a further 280 miles to Benghazi, a major port midway between the British headquarters at Alexandria and the Italian headquarters in Tripoli. Rather than simply following the Italians along the coast road, O'Connor despatched two units in a straight line to speed across uncharted desert to Beda Fomm, a coastal town between Benghazi and Tripoli. Their task was to block Bergonzoli's line of retreat to the Libyan capital, thus leaving any remaining Italians in Cyrenaica trapped and isolated. It was a daring ruse but it worked.

On 5 February the retreating Tenth Army was duly brought to a sudden halt at Beda Fomm. 'The enemy's position was desperate, with a confused mass of vehicles almost twenty miles in length pinned to the roads between our Armoured Brigades in the South and the Northern detachment in the Soluch area,' Wavell reported. But the Italians did not give up without a struggle. Though some surrendered, others attempted to break out. Their efforts were repulsed, but only after some of the most intense fighting of the campaign. Witnessing the way in which the British armour picked off the fatally exposed Italian tanks, the Australian war correspondent Chester Wilmot was also impressed by the resistance they offered. 'It was a really hard job, and we fought them all afternoon. By dark there couldn't have been more than thirty left.'

On 7 February, after a final bid by thirty tanks to escape the British noose, General Bergonzoli finally gave up. His main force was now trapped in the Benghazi salient, where they surrendered to a unit of the 6th Australian Division. Benghazi itself was occupied on the same day and within two days the Australians had reached the port of El Agheila, some 470 miles west of Tobruk. Emulating his CO's penchant for hunting metaphors, O'Connor signalled Wavell, 'Fox killed in the open'.

Not all O'Connor's men appreciated the significance of their achievement. Bombardier Dawson's regiment was not in Benghazi for 'the kill' but some miles behind the front. A brigadier came up to his unit and said to the sergeant in command, 'I thought you'd like to know, we've taken Beda Fomm, and Bergonzoli's in the bag.' 'Thank you, sir,' the sergeant replied. 'I'll tell the men that, sir, they will be delighted.' 'Jolly good show,' the brigadier said, and drove off. After he had gone, the sergeant said, 'Who the fuck's Bergonzoli?'

Although a combination of enemy firepower and mechanical breakdown had left the 7th Armoured Division with no more than 145 tanks, O'Connor was undaunted. Despite being 700 miles from his forward base at Mersah Matruh, he was confident that he retained enough firepower to advance a further 400 miles to Tripoli and thus complete the destruction of the Italian military presence in North Africa. In one month, his men had destroyed the bulk of the Tenth Army, capturing 130,000 men, 845 guns, and 380 tanks at a cost of 550 dead or missing and 1,373 wounded.

On 14 February, Wavell issued a Special Order of the Day: 'You have done great deeds and won much glory. We are fighting for freedom and truth and kindliness against oppression and lies and cruelty, and we shall not fail.' Operation *Compass* had been an unequivocal triumph. It was to be the last for a very long time.

FOUR

A CHANGE OF PLAN

*'We felt deflated and sad … We felt there must be pretty
weighty factors which robbed us of a prize which to us sitting
in Cairo glittered so brightly and appeared so desirable.'*
'Freddy' de Guingand

With the Italian Tenth Army at O'Connor's mercy, Churchill now made a fateful decision. On 24 February 1941, two days after the fall of Beda Fomm, he ordered that four of the British divisions which had helped secure Benghazi and which O'Connor hoped to lead into Tripoli should be withdrawn from the Libyan front and despatched to Greece instead. When O'Connor heard this news he was appalled. Already frustrated by Wavell's decision two months earlier to transfer the 4th Indian Division to Eritrea, which had delayed his westward progress towards Benghazi, he could barely contain his disappointment that the prize of Tripoli was now to be snatched from him when it was almost in his grasp. 'I ought to have pressed straight on, on the afternoon of Beda Fomm' he reflected later. 'It would not have been a matter of disobeying orders: at the time I had no orders. I blame myself.' But he paused, and by the time the formal order came through from GHQ Cairo, he had no choice but to obey. Any hope of completing the destruction of the Italian military presence in North Africa had been postponed indefinitely.

Wavell's staff were equally horrified when they discovered what was afoot. Lt Colonel 'Freddy' de Guingand, a senior staff officer at GHQ Cairo, was in a planning meeting when a 'Most Urgent' signal arrived from London.

We read it together and our faces fell ... This meant that [our] high hopes could be relegated to the waste paper basket ... The message changed the framework of our strategy. Greece was now to become our top priority. Forces must be collected to enable us to take Greece ... All this to us was a bitter blow, and we felt deflated and sad. We did not at that moment know anything of the high policy behind the decision, but we felt there must be pretty weighty factors which robbed us of a prize which to us sitting in Cairo glittered so brightly and appeared so desirable.

Churchill had not taken the decision lightly. As Britain's only remaining ally in Europe not to have been overrun by the Wehrmacht, Greece's strategic location in the southern Mediterranean provided a potentially important buffer against a possible German assault on the Middle East. As Churchill himself put the case for the diversion of forces from the desert, 'This grave step was required not only to help Greece in her peril and torment, but to form against the impending German attack on a Balkan front comprising Yugoslavia, Greece, and Turkey.' Straddling Europe and the Middle East, Turkey's location was equally important to Britain and Germany; its neutrality, if not its allegiance, was a strategic imperative for both Churchill and Hitler. Nonetheless the Prime Minister's critical decision was not in fact reached with the degree of confidence that his use of the term 'required' might suggest.

Churchill had begun to press the case for sending military aid to Greece in the autumn of 1940, soon after the foiled Italian invasion. On 2 November he telegraphed Eden who was with Wavell at GHQ Cairo, where – unbeknown to Churchill – the final preparations were underway for Operation *Compass*. 'Greek situation must be held to dominate all others now,' he wrote imperiously. 'We are well aware of our slender resources. Aid to Greece must be attentively studied lest whole Turkish position is lost through proof that England never tries to keep her guarantees.' This concern to protect Britain's international credibility also had a wider dimension: his urge to impress on the Americans that Britain was both a force to reckon with and to be relied upon. Fired by this combination of strategic vision and national prestige, the Prime Minister was impatient. GHQ in Cairo was aghast. 'We cannot from Middle East forces send sufficient air or land reinforcements to have any decisive influence upon course of fighting in Greece,' Eden cabled. 'To send such forces from here, or to divert reinforcements now on their way or approved, would imperil our whole position in the Middle East'.

Churchill did not relent. Day after day, he kept up the pressure both on his commanders in the Middle East and on the Chiefs of Staff in London, a prime ministerial bombardment which was only suspended when Eden returned from Cairo with the news that Wavell was soon to go on the offensive in the desert against the Italian Tenth Army.

But by January 1941, with Operation *Compass* exceeding all expectations, Churchill began to press the case for Greece once again. British intelligence had discerned that a Wehrmacht invasion was in the offing, though its precise timing was a matter of conjecture. Armed with this information, the Prime Minister sent a note to General 'Pug' Ismay, his trusted assistant and go-between with the Chiefs of Staff. 'It is quite clear to me that supporting Greece must have priority after the Western flank of Egypt has been made secure,' he wrote. Three days later, Wavell – who was at this point overseeing O'Connor's advance towards Tobruk and Benghazi – was told in unequivocal terms that Greece was henceforth to take precedence over all other operations in his command.

The general did not attempt to conceal his dismay. In a cable to London, he argued that the German concentration in Romania was merely 'a move in the war of nerves' designed both to prop up the Italians and to induce the Chiefs of Staff to arrest the advance in Libya and 'disperse our forces in the Middle East ... We trust the COS will reconsider whether the enemy's move is not bluff'.

In Whitehall, the Director of Military Operations, Major General John Kennedy, strongly sympathised with Wavell's reluctance to divert forces from the desert to Greece. He made an appointment to see Dill, the CIGS and his immediate superior. Insisting that his team judged that 'at least twenty divisions, plus a considerable airforce' would be needed simply to hold Salonika, let alone to confront a full-scale Wehrmacht invasion, he argued tartly that the Germans 'could overrun Greece with the utmost ease if they wanted to do so', and concluded that 'we stood more to gain by winning the African coast for ourselves than by denying Greece to the Germans.' Kennedy did not prevail. The Chiefs of Staff sided with Churchill, whose response to Wavell was brusquely dismissive.

'Our information contradicts the idea that German concentration in Roumania is merely a "move in the war of nerves" or "a bluff to cause dispersion of forces",' he told Wavell in a cable on 10 January. On the contrary, there was 'a mass of detail' confirming that the build-up was the prelude to an early and 'deadly' onslaught against Greece which would 'eclipse victories you have gained in Libya'. Instructing his Middle East commander-in-chief to 'conform your plans to larger interest at stake', he peremptorily closed off further discussion with the words, 'We expect and require prompt and active compliance with our decisions, for which we bear full responsibility.' As a loyal soldier, Wavell had little choice but to obey or resign.

With Air Chief Marshal Sir Arthur Longmore, his RAF counterpart in the Middle East, at his side, Wavell was soon in Athens to offer military assistance to the Greek dictator, Ioannis Metaxas. At this point, with the Greek army comfortably holding the Italians at bay in Albania, General Metaxas feared that Britain's offer would merely goad Germany into the invasion which he still hoped to avoid. He firmly declined Wavell's proposal. But on 29 January – providentially from Churchill's perspective – Metaxas died suddenly from a severe infection of the larynx which led to a fatal toxaemia. His successor, the weak and pliable Alexandros Koryzis, was eager to reopen talks with the British.

Convinced by now that the Germans intended to invade sooner rather than later, and fearful that Hitler's objective was to use Greece as a stepping stone for an attack on the Middle East, Churchill sent the fateful cable to Wavell requiring that four divisions be made ready for redeployment to Greece. It was at this point that Wavell ordered a halt to O'Connor's advance.

At the same time, belatedly heeding his Director of Military Operations, Dill decided to throw his weight behind GHQ Cairo. On 11 February he told a meeting of the War Cabinet that Wavell's troops in the Middle East 'had their hands full' and that none could be spared for Greece. At this – as Dill related the moment to Kennedy – Churchill 'lost his temper with me. I could see the blood coming up his great neck and his eyes began to flash. He said: "What you need out there is a Court Martial and a firing squad. Wavell has 300,000 men, etc., etc.," I should have said, Whom do you want to shoot exactly? but I did not think of it till afterwards.'

By this point, according to Kennedy's memoirs, both he and Dill agreed that Churchill 'was now trying to force an unsound policy down Wavell's throat, and down the throats of the Greeks and Turks'. They were convinced that by sending troops across to the other – European – side of the Mediterranean, they would be playing into Hitler's hands and that 'if they were sent, they were certain to be annihilated or driven out again'. What was more, the dispersion of British forces in this way would leave 'the vital centres of Egypt and Palestine unduly exposed to attack'. But Dill was unable to force the issue with Churchill because two of his fellow chiefs – Air Chief Marshal Portal and the First Sea Lord, Admiral Pound – supported the Prime Minister.

A few days later, on 16 February, Kennedy was a guest at a weekend house party at Ditchley Park, a retreat near Oxford used by Churchill when a full moon made it too risky for him to stay at Chequers. At 10.30 a.m. he was summoned to Churchill's bedroom, where he was to give a review of the military situation on all fronts. He found the Prime Minister sitting up in bed wearing a dressing gown patterned with dragons. Several telephones were at his side. Papers and files littered the bed. Churchill offered him a cigar and then listened intently as the Director of Military Operations, referring only to some scribbled notes on a postcard, delivered an overview of the military challenges facing Britain. Kennedy did not refrain from expressing his severe doubts about the Greek enterprise, fully expecting this to provoke a similar show of anger to that which Dill had aroused at the earlier meeting of the War

Cabinet. Instead, according to Kennedy, the Prime Minister did not demur.

Whether or not he had been disconcerted by Kennedy's analysis, Churchill now displayed a rare moment of indecision. On 21 February he signalled Eden, who had been shuttling between Cairo and Athens accompanied by Wavell, 'Do not consider yourselves obligated to a Greek enterprise if in your hearts you feel it will only be another Norwegian fiasco [a reference to the evacuation of the British military contingent from Narvik in June 1940]. If no good plan can be made please say so. But of course you know how valuable success would be.'

But by now the diplomatic and military momentum had become virtually unstoppable. For reasons that remain unclear – though it is sometimes suggested that Roosevelt's 'Special Representative' William Donovan, who had just completed a tour of the region might have influenced them – both Dill and Wavell, who had hitherto been deeply sceptical, had executed a startling U-turn and expressed themselves in favour of the Greek operation. Eden, who had been promoted to Foreign Secretary following the departure of Halifax to become ambassador to the United States, now stamped his own authority on events. Praying in aid his two converts, Eden's breezy cable to Churchill betrayed no doubts. 'We are agreed,' he signalled, 'we should do everything in our power to bring the fullest measure of help to Greeks at earliest possible moment. If the help we can offer is accepted by the Greeks we believe there is a fair chance of halting a German advance and preventing Greece from being overrun.' This improbable assessment flew in the face of military reason, but it was enough to rally a wavering Prime Minister. On 24 February, Churchill signalled Eden, 'Full steam ahead'.

No sooner had this instruction been despatched than it was the turn of the Chiefs of Staff to get cold feet. In a portentous note which ended with the phrase, 'The hazards of the enterprise have considerably increased', they advised Churchill of their trepidation at the proposed venture. This last-minute frisson of alarm prompted Churchill once again to offer Eden an eleventh-hour chance to change his mind. But with 57,000 troops on their way from Alexandria to Piraeus, the Foreign Secretary was not to be dissuaded. Conceding that the British might indeed be ignominiously ejected by the Wehrmacht, he argued that 'to have fought and suffered in Greece would be less damaging to us than to have left Greece to her fate'. Churchill strongly shared this view, claiming that if his government were to dishonour Britain's pre-war undertaking to 'guarantee' Greece's borders, the credibility of all other British commitments in the region would be in doubt, if not in tatters. To abandon the Greeks to their 'torment' would almost certainly reverberate widely: morale at home, already damaged by a string of setbacks and defeats, would be further eroded. No less worryingly, American isolationists would have yet more ammunition with which to denigrate Britain as an unreliable ally, or even a broken nation, with whose leader Roosevelt should sup only if using a very long spoon.

In a letter to the President written on 10 March (which he did not reproduce in his own history of the Second World War), Churchill sought to explain why – notwithstanding the temptation 'to push on from Benghazi to Tripoli' – he had decided to send 'the greater part of the Army of the Nile' to Greece. Claiming that there was 'a good fighting chance' of success, he went on to add – with wanton speculation – that it was 'quite possible that the whole situation in the Balkans might [thereby] be transformed ... in our favour'. By this time, the 6th Australian Division, the New Zealand 2nd Division and the British 1st Armoured Brigade had already landed on Greek soil to reap an imminent military whirlwind.

FIVE

ROMMEL TO THE RESCUE

*'We wanted an adventure, and nobody thought about getting
killed. We were all in high spirits.'*

Fritz Zimmermann, Afrikakorps gunner

On the same day that Churchill despatched his fateful 'Full
steam ahead' message to Wavell, a small unit of German
tanks came across a British patrol in the desert near Benghazi
and destroyed two scout cars and a truck, capturing three British
soldiers and their commanding officer in the process. A thousand
miles away in Cairo, with his attention focussed on the Greek
crisis, Wavell declared himself to be unperturbed by the skirmish. As Basil Liddell Hart, the 'godfather' of tank warfare, was
to observe, 'on normal reasoning' the Middle East commander-in-
chief was justified in reaching this conclusion but 'such reckoning
did not allow for a Rommel'.

General Erwin Rommel had arrived in Tunis twelve days
earlier as the virtually unknown commander of the newly formed
Afrikakorps. Although they included 120 panzers (the German
tanks renowned for speed, reliability, and firepower), the forces
at Rommel's disposal hardly posed a significant threat to the
'Army of the Nile' – even allowing for the withdrawal of four
divisions for the Greek venture. Nor could GHQ Cairo imagine
that the Afrikakorps would be in a fit state to take the offensive
for several weeks at least. Later Wavell acknowledged his 'great
error' in judging 'that the enemy could not put in any effective

counter-stroke before May at the earliest'. As one of his senior staff officers, Brigadier Harding conceded, 'I didn't know enough about Rommel at the time, I ought to have known more ... we underestimated Rommel's drive and energy.'

Rommel was Hitler's favourite general. Highly decorated for his exploits in the First World War, he had risen to take command of Hitler's personal protection squad, the Führerbegleitbataillon, where his loyalty and efficiency made a powerful impression on his patron and – auspiciously – on Joseph Goebbels, the Nazi propaganda minister. His reputation as a bold and imaginative leader on the battlefield had already been established by his dazzling performance during the blitzkrieg which precipitated the British retreat from Dunkirk and the fall of France. Though he was disliked and distrusted by most of his superior officers, who resented his intimacy with the Führer and viewed him as a vainglorious upstart, Hitler himself told Mussolini that Rommel was the most outstanding tank general in the German army.

On 6 February, with the Italians broken at Beda Fomm, Hitler summoned his favourite to a meeting to announce that he intended to go to the rescue of the Italian Tenth Army in North Africa and that he, Rommel, was to take command of the Afrikakorps. The Führer's decision to divert Wehrmacht units to North Africa was taken without enthusiasm. Although he had flirted with the idea the previous autumn, he had made it abundantly clear in a New Year message to Mussolini that he had no intention of becoming embroiled in the Western Desert at this stage. In a strategic tour d'horizon, he boasted that 'the war in the West is itself won', but, following O'Connor's triumph, he warned that he was unwilling as yet to provide the forces required to mount 'any counter-attack on a large scale' against the British in North Africa, an operation which, he advised, 'would take a minimum of three to five months' to prepare.

Hitler had continued to toy with the prospect of 'a detour through the Mediterranean and Africa on the way to world empire', but it was very far from being a priority. Although a number of his senior commanders, notably Grand Admiral Erich Raeder, continued to argue that the Mediterranean and North Africa should be a strategic priority, Hitler's blinkered attention was focussed elsewhere. By comparison with Operation *Barbarossa*, the Mediterranean theatre was peripheral to his overriding purpose. Obsessed with the destruction of Bolshevism, he was unable to see that the Axis could 'deliver a devastating blow to the only country against which he was still at war' by confronting the British in the Middle East before the invasion of Russia. When – but only when – *Barbarossa* had been accomplished, would he order the Wehrmacht to advance through the Caucasus to topple the British from the epicentre of their Empire.

But Italy's humiliation in the desert had forced his hand. On 18 January, with the Italian Tenth Army on the retreat and the British poised to seize Tobruk, the two dictators met at the Berghof. Though Mussolini's twin humiliations in Greece and Libya were implicitly at the core of their conversations, Hitler, as usual, was once again careful not to patronise his ally. 'There are no hidden condolences in the air – condolences that Mussolini feared,' Ciano noted with relief. Instead the Führer was careful to maintain the pretence that they were still equal partners in a joint crusade. The reality, however, was obvious to both of them. Mussolini urgently needed military assistance in the desert and because he was always anxious about the security of his southern flank in Europe, Hitler, who, only a week earlier had issued a directive (22), insisting that Tripolitana (western Libya) 'must be held', had little choice but to provide it.

The Führer's affable manner towards him and his boundless optimism about the progress of the war reassured and invigorated Mussolini. Presumably mindful of his own recent meeting with Hitler, when he had been treated to a severe dressing down following the Balkan fiasco, Ciano was surprised and relieved that the meeting between the two leaders had been so 'spontaneously cordial' while Mussolini, according to his son-in-law, returned to Rome 'elated as he always is after a meeting with Hitler'.

The mood in OKW was very different. When Major General Baron von Funk (whom Hitler had charged with overseeing the despatch of the Wehrmacht units that he had already committed to North Africa) returned from Libya and Rome, he delivered a damning report on the incompetence and feebleness of the Italian military leadership, advising that the position could only be recovered by the despatch of a further panzer division to the desert. According to Major General Engel, Hitler's adjutant, the Führer seemed 'shattered' by Funk's assessment.

It was only now that Hitler began seriously to analyse the full import of an Italian rout. In a key meeting on 3 February he told his most senior commanders that if the Italians were defeated in North Africa, 'Britain could hold a pistol at Italy's head. The British forces in the Mediterranean would not be tied down. The British would have free use of a dozen divisions ... We must make every effort to prevent this ... We must render effective assistance in North Africa'. It was a pivotal judgement with far reaching consequences.

There was a further disturbing prospect. If the Italians were defeated in North Africa, O'Connor might not only seize Tripoli but very probably advance further west to threaten Tunisia and even Morocco. Faced by this threat, Hitler feared that the Vichy commanders in those two French colonies might opportunistically switch their allegiance from the Axis to the British. In this case, any chance that the Axis might have of securing a stronghold on the western approaches to the Mediterranean or the Atlantic littoral from which, in due course, to confront the United States would be greatly diminished.

It was at this point – when he saw no other option – that Hitler began to grapple seriously with the complexities of embarking on a military campaign in North Africa. Ordered to examine the force levels required to mount a successful operation to prevent the Italians from being driven from their colonial capital and military headquarters in Tripoli, the Führer's senior advisors were soon sharply at odds with one another. A minority, led by Admiral Raeder, supported Funk's plea for more troops and armour to be sent to Libya. But the majority was adamantly opposed to such a commitment to what they regarded as a secondary front; any such venture, they argued, would compromise the prospects for *Barbarossa*.

The fierce argument in OKW over North Africa closely mirrored the anxious debate within the British High Command which had preceded the decision to divert troops from the Middle East to Greece. It is not hard to detect the historic irony that, at this point in the war, each side fundamentally misinterpreted the principal objective of the other: Churchill's priority was to safeguard the Middle East, Hitler's obsession was the invasion of Russia. While the Prime Minister feared a German démarche through the Caucasus, the Führer was sensitive only to the threat that the British might knock Italy out of the war.

Rommel's Afrikakorps was to consist of two panzer divisions (totalling some 300 tanks), an infantry regiment, and an artillery battalion. They were to fight as a unified force under his command rather than being dispersed among the Italian units. But Hitler's urge to preserve the illusion that North Africa was still Mussolini's battlefront added a further complication which led almost immediately to a dog's breakfast of confusion in the chain of command. It was made clear to Rommel that, on the one hand, his title 'Commander of the German troops in Libya' meant that he would be answerable to OKW and OKH (the Oberkommando des Heeres or Army High Command) while, on the other, he would be required to take his battle orders from General Italo Gariboldi (who had replaced Graziani after the latter's ignominious retreat from Egypt) and, through him, to Italy's Supreme Commander, Il Duce. Rommel soon became adept at playing off these rivalrous authorities against one another, secure in the knowledge that he could appeal over their heads at will to the ultimate authority, the Führer.

Rommel landed in Tripoli on 12 February 1941, brazenly resolved to fight his own campaign in his own way. It was immediately clear to him that the Italians were deeply demoralised by their humiliation at the hands of the British. It was no less obvious that the Italians were immediately suspicious of the assertive forty-year-old general who had been foisted on them by Berlin to avert further disasters in the desert. When Rommel outlined his plan of campaign, which he had conceived before his arrival, Gariboldi was unimpressed and said so. Rommel not only ignored his superior officer's advice but proceeded to reconnoitre his chosen battleground in the desert.

Unaware that O'Connor had been instructed to advance no further than El Agheila – his forces severely depleted by the redeployment of four divisions to Greece – Rommel had selected a salient around Sirte, a small port in an otherwise empty quarter of sand dunes and salt marshes midway between Tripoli and Benghazi, as his front-line defence of the Libyan capital against the expected British onslaught.

On 13 March he attempted to fly from Tripoli to Sirte. Soon after take-off his plane flew into a sandstorm, at which point, he wrote later,

> the pilot, ignoring my abuse and attempts to get him to fly on, turned back, compelling me to continue the journey by car … Now we realised what little idea we had had of the tremendous force of such a storm. Immense clouds of reddish dust obscured all visibility and forced the car's speed down to a crawl … Sand streamed down the windscreen like water. We gasped in breath painfully through handkerchiefs held over our faces and sweat poured off our bodies in the unbearable heat. So this was the Ghibli [sandstorm]. Silently I breathed my apologies to the pilot.

That evening, protected by the sandstorm which also made it impossible for the RAF to frustrate its arrival, the first contingent of the Afrikakorps started to disembark at Tripoli – the advance guard of a 25,000 force equipped with 8,500 vehicles, together with 26,000 tons of supplies, which were to arrive in Libya within the next two months. They were at once despatched to the Sirte front, some 200 miles east of the capital. According to one member of that advance party, Fritz Zimmermann, a gunner with the Afrikakorps, he and his fellow conscripts were elated at the prospect of battle. 'We wanted an adventure, and nobody thought about getting killed. We were all in high spirits … we made our way to the front through the night. We had to travel without lights, and it was very dangerous ... Soon it was daylight and the sun shone in a clear blue sky. The scenery was bleak – all sand and desert.'

Rommel had devised an ingenious plan to deceive the British into believing that he had many more panzers than had yet arrived. Captain Hans-Otto, one of his adjutants, was at the port when Rommel ordered an engineer to build him 150 dummy tanks. 'The engineer looked stupefied and Rommel asked, "Don't you have timber here in the harbour, and canvas covers for vehicles?" "Yes, sir." "So you can give me 150 tanks," replied Rommel.' A few days later, scores of converted Volkswagen 'panzers' formed part of a parade through the city to create the impression that he had a huge military force at his disposal.

Rommel was in a hurry. On 19 March he flew back to Hitler's headquarters where the army's commander-in-chief, Field Marshal Walther von Brauchitsch, told him that he could not expect any reinforcements in the near future as, for the time being, the Führer had 'no intention of striking a decisive blow in Africa'. However, Brauchitsch was careful to avoid explaining the reason for this: that Operation *Barbarossa* was now in the final stages of preparation and was to be launched in almost exactly three months' time. To mollify Rommel, he advised that, as soon as the 15th Panzer Division had disembarked (scheduled for the end of May), he would very probably be permitted to start an offensive designed to recapture Benghazi.

Rommel was undeterred. On 24 March, using their great mobility to strike suddenly and swiftly, the panzers captured the British forward position at El Agheila and, with XIII Corps (as the Western Desert Force had been renamed in January) on the retreat, advanced to take Agedabia, which put them within striking distance of Benghazi, less than a hundred miles away. The legendary German tanks inspired awe and trepidation among the retreating British troops. 'We saw tanks coming over ... wireless aerials with pennants atop, like a field full of lancers,' recalled Gunner L. E. Tutt of the Essex yeomanry. 'Men of the Tower Hamlets went forward to face them in Bren carriers and were virtually destroyed in a matter of minutes; their bravery was unquestioned but they should never have been asked to face such odds ... Once we pulled out of our positions the rot seemed to set in ... There seemed to be no overall direction. Too many units were on the move at the same time, a mistake which contributed to a growing panic.'

In his report of the retreat Wavell wrote, 'Our intention was that the armoured force should maintain a position from which they would be on the flank of the enemy advance by the main road to Benghazi.' Instead the British defences crumbled in disarray. 'It is painful to attempt to describe the muddle in which the column withdrew. Armoured cars, trucks and tanks were mixed up without regard to their units; jumbled, jolting forward at a speed which indicated that the panic of the higher command had communicated itself to the troops,' one retreating infantryman, Roy Farran, recorded.

To make matters worse, O'Connor had been forced to return to Cairo with a stomach ailment. His replacement was Philip Neame, a fellow general who had won a VC in the First World War and a Gold Medal for rifle shooting at the 1924 Olympics. But, as a staff officer based in Cairo, he had no experience of the desert. He was an ill-chosen and inadequate substitute for O'Connor, who was the only British general capable of rivalling Rommel's guile on the battlefield. On 16 March Wavell flew up from Cairo to see his new appointee. It was a discouraging encounter. 'I found Neame pessimistic and asking for all sorts of reinforcements which I hadn't got,' Wavell wrote later. 'And his tactical dispositions were just crazy ... I came back anxious and depressed from this visit, but there was nothing much I could do about it. The movement to Greece was in full swing and I had nothing left in the bag. But I had forebodings and my confidence in Neame was shaken.'

On Wavell's instructions, Neame abandoned Benghazi. On 3 April, advised by an Italian priest who had come out of the town to meet them that the enemy had departed, a German reconnaissance battalion nudged cautiously into the outskirts of the city to discover that the British had indeed left. In the absence of any coherent plan to counter Rommel's sudden assault, the retreat soon became a rout. 'Suddenly the road was full of vehicles going westwards, with infantry riding on them,' Bombadier Dawson recalled. 'In no time at all we were racing down the road … It was a farce.' Roy Farran described the 'spirals of black smoke which marked the retreat of a defeated army. If a truck broke down, even for a small thing like a puncture, the drivers were afraid to lose the main column by halting to repair it. Instead they put a match to the petrol tank and leapt on a passing vehicle.' One of his colleagues, Ray Ellis, detected 'signs of panic … It seemed that everyone in the Army of the Nile was doing their best to put the greatest distance between themselves and the enemy – everybody was rushing headlong back to Egypt.'

Their commanding officers were at a loss. 'I was surprised at the speed at which Rommel advanced from Tripoli in a full-scale offensive, driving us back; and at their opportunist tactics, their excellent recce, the performance of the battle groups,' Brigadier Harding recalled. Rommel had gambled on the gullibility of the British, maintaining the illusion that he had indeed embarked on a full-scale offensive when in reality, as he boasted happily, he was in no position to undertake any such a venture. His bluff had worked.

Although the Afrikakorps had been the key to Rommel's triumph, the Italians also played their part – though, partly because of his contempt for their commanders, Rommel rarely gave them the credit they deserved. But the fighting spirit of those Italian divisions which were most loyal to the fascist cause was not in doubt. The letters sent home by Lieutenant Pietro Ostellino, a tank officer in the Ariete Division, to his new wife, reveal a steely commitment. On the eve of Rommel's offensive he wrote that 'things here are going well and our re-occupation of Cyrenaica, the land which has been in enemy hands, is a matter of days or even hours away. We rush to the front line for the honour of the Patria. You must be proud and offer your suffering to the cause for which your husband is fighting enthusiasm and passion.' And a little over a week later, on the 14th, he described 'chasing away the English', promising that all would go well, 'because ours is a holy cause and God is with us'. Even allowing for military censorship, it is unreasonable to suppose that such sentiments were composed merely for the benefit of his senior officers.

With Benghazi back under Axis control, Rommel returned to Tripoli, where he was 'berated violently' by Gariboldi for defying orders. Instructed to 'discontinue all action and undertake no further moves without his express authority', Rommel responded by stating his views 'plainly and without equivocation'. When Gariboldi insisted that he should make no further moves without instructions from Rome, 'the conversation became somewhat heated ... I was not going to stand for it, and said I intended to go on doing what I felt I had to do in whatever situation might arise. This brought the conversation to a climax. At that very moment, a signal arrived – deus ex machina – from the German High Command, giving me complete freedom of action, and settling the argument exactly as I wanted it.' That evening, 3 April, he wrote exultantly to his wife:

> Dearest Lu,
> We've been attacking since the 31st with dazzling success. There'll be consternation amongst our masters in Tripoli and Rome, perhaps also in Berlin too. I took the risk against all orders and instructions because the opportunity seemed favourable. No doubt it will all be pronounced good later and they'll say they'd have done exactly the same in my place ... The British are falling over each other to get away. Our casualties are small. Our booty can't yet be estimated. You will understand that I can't sleep for happiness.

With the British in full retreat from Cyrenaica, Rommel received a telegram from the Führer, congratulating him on his unexpected success and encouraging him to further feats in the desert. But the Führer's mind was already elsewhere.

SIX

DANGEROUS DIVERSIONS

*'Do you play poker? Here is the hand that is going to win
the war: a Royal flush – Great Britain, the Sea, the Air, the
Middle East, American aid.'*

Winston Churchill at a dinner party

The drama in the Balkans – on which so much hinged for all the warring parties in the region – had started to unfold at extraordinary speed. The apparent threat posed by Britain to his southern flank on the European side of the Mediterranean agitated Hitler far more than the passing thought that Rommel could inflict a devastating blow against the enemy on the African side. What if the British were to succeed in forging a common front with the Greeks and the Yugoslavs? How would Turkey react? Would the Balkan states join the enemy camp? The questions nagged and the Führer had a simple answer to them: if diplomatic brutality failed, the threat would have to be eliminated by military force. It took him very little time to settle on the latter option.

On 25 March Paul of Yugoslavia, the prince regent, was finally pressurised into joining the Tripartite Pact which the three Axis powers had signed six months earlier. This news prompted a serious riot in Belgrade between the Serbian and Croatian communities. Two days later, on 27 March, Prince Paul was overthrown in a British-supported bloodless coup by the heir to the throne, his seventeen-year-old cousin Prince Peter II. Rendered 'incandescent with rage' by this impertinence, Hitler ordered the Wehrmacht to cross into Yugoslavia and crush the uprising. As Andrew Roberts has written, 'The brutality can be gauged by the fact that 17,000 Yugoslavs were killed by the Luftwaffe on a single day, almost as many certified deaths as the RAF were to cause in Dresden in February 1945.' On 6 April 500,000 German troops marched on Belgrade. After a valiant resistance which lasted eleven days, at a cost of 100,000 Yugoslav casualties, the capital surrendered.

At the same time, ten Wehrmacht divisions – 680,000 men with more than 1,000 tanks supported by 700 aircraft – blitzed their way from Bulgaria into Greece. Operation *Marita*, as the invasion was codenamed, had a simple purpose: to complete the task which – to his intense anger – Mussolini had blindly initiated and hopelessly fumbled. But whereas the Greek army had seen off the Italian invaders, it soon started to disintegrate under the ferocity of the German onslaught. By 20 April (which coincided with Hitler's fifty-second birthday), 75,000 Greek soldiers had been killed or wounded. On the 23rd, the government in Athens surrendered. By the 27th, the Swastika was flying over the Acropolis.

By this time, Wavell had already ordered the Allied commander in Greece, Henry Maitland Wilson, to evacuate all British troops. As wiser military heads in London had predicted, they had been swept aside by the German blitzkrieg, outnumbered, outgunned, and – not for lack of courage – outfought as well. The retreat was perilous. The Luftwaffe had virtually destroyed the port at Piraeus, forcing the escaping units to make for the beaches to scramble aboard a waiting flotilla of Royal Navy ships, fishing smacks, and even Sunderland flying boats. Alan Moorehead, who had witnessed 'horrible carnage' at the front, observed the evacuation. 'On the beaches, the British set about destroying the last of their equipment, putting bullets into car tyres, ramming shells the wrong way down gun barrels and firing the charges, smashing engines with crowbars, draining oil sumps and leaving the motors running, plunging vehicles over cliffs, shooting horses, firing dumps of munitions, oil and food.' As the troops marched to the ships they came under concentrated enemy fire. The order went out: 'Don't take shelter, or if you do you will be left behind. Carry your wounded and leave your dead.'

A bleak communiqué issued from Cairo on 1 May did not attempt to conceal the scale of the disaster. 'The enemy, by the employment of greatly superior numbers, had obtained complete command of the air ... Consequently re-embarkation had to take place from open beaches against continuous enemy pressure on land and heavy and repeated attacks from the air ... Rear-guards which cover this withdrawal may have to sacrifice themselves to secure the re-embarkation of others.' Remarkably, some 43,000 men managed to escape, though 15,000 soldiers – a quarter of the original cohort – were either killed, wounded or captured along with the tanks and heavy weapons which had not already been destroyed in battle or on the beaches.

The evacuation fully earned its grim portrayal as a 'second Dunkirk'. Militarily the venture had been a fiasco, a disaster that had been foreseen and repeatedly foretold. As Wavell noted ruefully in his later despatch, 'the expedition to Greece was ill-starred ... something in the nature of a gamble, the dice were loaded against it from the first'.

However, the gamble was a classic example of the Clausewitzian dictum that 'war is a mere continuation of politics by other means'. Still wholly unaware that the Führer's obsessive and over-riding priority was the invasion of Russia, Churchill's strategic objective had been – as Hitler had suspected – to form a defensive bloc with the triumvirate of Greece, Yugoslavia and Turkey. But his immediate intention had not been (as Hitler feared) to assault the Führer's southern flank but to establish a bulwark against any German move on the Middle East. It had been a forlorn objective, based on faulty intelligence, a misreading of the political dynamic in all three countries, and a failure by British diplomats to stitch together even the most threadbare canopy under which the three target nations would all be willing to shelter.

Nevertheless, after the debacle, even as the remnants of the British task force scrambled to escape, he was rewarded, on 1 May, with a remarkably generous message from the President. 'You have done not only heroic but very useful work in Greece.' And three days later, on 4 May, he cabled again to express 'the admiration which the American people hold towards your generals, admirals, airmen and sailors who fought in Greece and are now fighting in the Mediterranean and Africa'. Of greater material utility, he also promised that 'supplies in so far as they are available here are to be rushed to the Middle East. Thirty ships are now being mobilised to go within the next three weeks to the Middle East ... I know of your determination to win on that front and we shall do everything that we possibly can to help you.' Churchill's decision to explain the raison d'être for the Greek enterprise in advance to his American sponsor had paid off handsomely. That this support was to be provided through the mechanism of the new Lend-Lease Bill, which – on paper at least – imposed strict terms of trade on the British government, did not distract from Churchill's satisfaction at this reassuring outcome.

The Prime Minister's transatlantic antennae were highly tuned to the political mood music in Washington. Almost three months earlier, during the same weekend at Ditchley Park at which his Director of Military Operations, Kennedy, had expressed his grave reservations about the Greek venture, Churchill had opined that the Americans were 'moving into the war by sentiment', though he added delphically, 'I could make out a very strong case why it would pay America to keep out'. At dinner that evening he held up his hand with the fingers spread out and asked his guests rhetorically, 'Do you play poker? Here is the hand that is going to win the war: a Royal flush – Great Britain, the Sea, the Air, the Middle East, American aid.' He could not have known it beforehand, but he could now comfort himself that he had pulled one chestnut at least from the Greek inferno.

This commitment may have owed something to the 'sentiment' that nestled in the Presidential breast, but it assuredly owed rather more to a hard-headed calculation of America's own strategic interests in a worsening conflict. Roosevelt realised that the growing Axis threat in the Atlantic from the rapidly expanding U-boat flotillas posed a grave challenge to America's national security. Distasteful though the prospect remained to most American citizens, the United States was being drawn ineluctably closer to war. Roosevelt grew increasingly frustrated. In a blunt letter to an isolationist, he wrote, 'Slowly and in spite of anything we

Americans do or do not do, it looks as if you and some other good people are going to have to answer the old question of whether you want to keep your country unshackled by taking even more definite steps to do so – even firing shots – or, on the other hand, submitting to be shackled for the sake of not losing one American life.' And in a brusque letter to another isolationist in Congress, James O'Connor, he demanded, 'When will you Irishmen ever get over hating England? Remember that if England goes down, Ireland goes down too. Ireland has a better chance for complete independence if democracy survives in the world than if Hitlerism supersedes it ... do stop thinking in terms of ancient hatreds and think of the future.' Later in May, he took the political risk of warning the American people that 'unless the advance of Hitlerism is checked now, the Western Hemisphere will be within range of the Nazi weapons of destruction.'

In his correspondence with the President, Churchill repeatedly laced his pleas for military assistance with eloquent attempts to cast the struggle against the Nazis in terms which presented the Mediterranean theatre as pivotal to victory and the loss of the Middle East as a catastrophe for the United States. But despite Churchill's persistence and his own 'sentiment', the President refused to be harried into a formal declaration of belligerence against Germany. Although American opinion was starting to shift in favour of military intervention, he had no doubt that the electorate would resist being hustled into what was still widely regarded as 'Britain's War'.

In the meantime Rommel had not been idle. Hardly pausing at Benghazi, he pressed on across the desert towards Tobruk and the Egyptian border. The blistering speed of his advance left General Neame frozen both tactically and psychologically in the headlights of the advancing panzers. Unable to seize the initiative, he was also incapable of masterminding the retreat while his adversary never paused or relented but was always near the front, goading his commanders into more aggressive and rapid action.

On 8 April, in one of his almost daily letters to his wife, Rommel wrote, 'We've been attacking for days now in the endless desert and have lost all idea of space or time … things are going very well. Our main force [the 15th Panzer Division] is on its way up after a 220-mile march over the sand and rock of the desert. I flew back from the front yesterday to look for them and found them in the desert. You can hardly imagine how pleased I was … I'm very well. You need never worry'.

He omitted to report that in the space of two days he had narrowly missed death when his plane came under enemy fire. To get a bird's eye view of the confusion on the battlefield, he frequently took to the air in his Storch, a reconnaissance aircraft that could fly at very low speed and land almost anywhere. On 7 April he flew low over the desert, trying to distinguish his own forces from those of the enemy. Looking down, he noted 'long black columns of vehicles' which he took for one of his own armoured brigades. 'Several men laid out a landing cross between the vehicles. At the last moment I suddenly spotted the flat helmets of the British troops. We immediately banked and made off, followed by machine-gun fire from the British troops. We were lucky to get away practically unscathed, with only one hit in the tail.' The next day he was almost a victim of 'friendly fire'. Flying no more than 150 feet above the desert, he approached an Italian battalion. The Italians had evidently never seen a Storch before and, when he was little more than fifty yards away, they opened fire from all directions. 'It was a miracle that we were not shot down,' he wrote later, 'and it did not speak well for Italian marksmanship'.

In the chaos of the British retreat, the two armies often became entangled as they got lost in the dust and the dark. One of Rommel's intelligence officers, Captain Behrendt, described an occasion on the road to Derna (about halfway between Benghazi and Tobruk) when he and the army commander encountered a British soldier with his broken-down motorbike. The despatch rider asked if they were heading for the 3rd (British) Armoured Brigade. Behrendt confirmed that this was indeed their destination. 'He got into my car, and after a while he said "strange car". "Yes, you are right, this is a German car, and we are Germans," I replied. All he said was "Oh". I admired him for his coolness.'

As the rout accelerated, Wavell – who was still masterminding the deployment to Greece but had also only just arrived back from the Eritrean front, flew hurriedly to Neame's headquarters at Derna. 'I soon realised that Neame had lost control and was making no effort to regain it by the only possible means, going forward personally ... no one seemed to have much idea where our own troops or the enemy were.' After the meeting, Wavell discussed the crisis with Harding, who was serving as Neame's Chief of Staff. By his own account, Harding 'begged' Wavell to send O'Connor back to the desert to take over from Neame. O'Connor, who respected Neame, was reluctant to step into his colleague's shoes at such short notice and when very little could be done to alter the immediate course of events. Instead, therefore, Wavell agreed that O'Connor should 'hold Neame's hand' – which Harding judged to be 'a mistake'. As it was, their collaboration would be short lived.

Although the British did their best to dodge marauding panzer units, it was a perilous flight from Benghazi across Cyrenaica towards the Egyptian border. 'The going was rough with scrub and some wadis' recalled Captain William Bolton of the Royal Horse Artillery (RHA). 'It wasn't possible to spread out and we moved head to tail; thank God there was no air interference.' Navigating their way across towards the coast, they were dismayed to receive orders diverting them to a desert outpost called Mechili. As dusk fell, they stopped for 'a brew up'. After a while, 'a huge staff car came up and the chap inside asked where we were going. When we told him, he said "You had better hurry because Mechili is under attack ..." In that car were Generals Neame and O'Connor. Not long afterwards they went into the bag. We were the last to see them before that happened.'

Later that night, 7 April, the two British generals lost their way. In the early hours of the following day their conspicuous Cadillac was intercepted by a detachment of German motorcyclists reconnoitring the German advance. Captain Behrendt was present at the scene and noted nonchalantly, 'We reached Derna, picking up on our way British soldiers and generals, amongst them the famous General O'Connor who had defeated the Italians at Sidi

Barrani, and General Neame and other officers and men.' Neame and O'Connor were taken into captivity and confined to an Italian POW camp. 'It was a great shock and I never thought it would happen to me; very conceited perhaps but it was miles beyond our own front,' O'Connor wrote later.

It was a loss that Wavell could ill afford. 'This tragic accident,' the historian Correlli Barnett wrote, 'robbed the British of the greatest of all their desert generals.' With an officer class lacking experience, talent, or the proven qualities of leadership so urgently required, no one of similar calibre was readily available to replace the one general with the flair, imagination, and bravado to match Rommel.

By now the panzers were only a little over 200 miles from the Egyptian border and – which was of even greater import – they were threatening to surround Tobruk. In a vainglorious moment of exultation, Rommel signalled OKW that the strategically important port would soon be in German hands. The seizure of Tobruk would not only remove the British from a military stronghold from which they could threaten any further Axis advance towards Egypt but it would play a part – albeit a modest part – in easing Rommel's growing logistical predicament. The Afrikakorps had now advanced more than 700 miles from Tripoli but was still dependent on the Libyan capital for the stockpiles of fuel, weaponry, ammunition, equipment, food and all the other stores essential to sustain a fighting force of more than 15,000 troops in the desert. The further and faster Rommel advanced from Tripoli, the more fragile and tenuous the lengthening supply line became and, like a taut elastic band, it was now stretched close to its limits. The task of maintaining a flow of supplies across so long a distance over such difficult terrain would have been challenging at any time; in war, with the threat of counter-attacks on the ground and bombardment from the air and sea, it was so daunting that only the boldest commander would hazard the extreme risks entailed in sustaining a major offensive so far from the relative security of his main base. Rommel was disposed to take such risks but the capture of Tobruk would immeasurably enhance his prospects of advancing into Egypt to seize Alexandria, Cairo, and the Nile Delta.

Well aware of all this possibility – but by no means beholden to the totemic status which Tobruk was soon to acquire – Wavell decided that it was 'essential' to prevent Rommel's purpose. To this end, troops were rushed from Alexandria by sea and by road. As soon as they arrived they were ordered to 'dig in' on the shallow escarpment which formed the town's defensive perimeter. Driver Bill Hutton, with the RHA, tried to do as he had been instructed. 'I got a pick and shovel and it was just like rock. I hit the ground and sparks flew up from my pick. I thought "to hell with it", made up my bed and went to sleep. I woke up next morning and some cocky chap came along and said, "We're the last in, Rommel's out there with his panzers." "Who's Rommel, and what's a panzer?" I asked.'

On 10 April, Wavell's decision to hold Tobruk was endorsed by the Prime Minister who had been greatly agitated by the precipitous retreat from Benghazi. Unable to resist giving his commander-in-chief the benefit of his advice, Churchill not only wrote to inform Wavell that Rommel would have great difficulty in taking Tobruk, but advised, with an intensity that was not warranted by any clear military imperative, that 'it seems to be a place to be held to the death without thought of retirement'.

The next day Wavell flew up to Tobruk to see for himself. He was met by Brigadier Harding, who, in the forced absence of O'Connor and Neame, was doing his best to buttress the town's defences. Wavell asked if it would be possible to keep Rommel at bay. Harding replied, 'I think we can hold it provided the navy can keep us supplied and Rommel doesn't wheel a mass of heavy tanks and attack us.' According to Harding, Wavell then said 'Hold it' and immediately afterwards took a piece of foolscap paper and wrote out a directive to that effect. The C-in-C then returned to Cairo.

But he must have had second thoughts because when he got back to his headquarters in the capital, he cabled London to warn that it would be very difficult to hold Tobruk against a determined enemy onslaught. Much put out by this apparent U-turn, Churchill drafted a curt riposte insisting that it was 'unthinkable that the fortress of Tobruk should be abandoned without offering the most prolonged resistance'. Happily, as this message was about to be sent, Churchill received word that, despite his reservations, Wavell had just reaffirmed his decision to hold Tobruk. The prime ministerial reproof was swiftly recovered from the out tray and consigned to the archives.

But this suppressed contretemps foreshadowed a far more serious outbreak of hostilities between London and Cairo. For Wavell – whose overriding priority was the protection of Egypt – Tobruk was of little strategic importance. So long as the Royal Navy and the RAF could interdict the maritime supply route to the port, it mattered little whether or not the town itself was in British hands. For Churchill, however, the town had a symbolic importance that far exceeded its military significance: in his mind, Tobruk epitomised Britain's resilience and resolve. So when Wavell was unwise enough to refer to the Tobruk salient in technically correct but somewhat casual terms, he was sternly rebuked by the Prime Minister. 'We feel it vital that Tobruk should be regarded as a sally-port and not, please, as an "excrescence".'

With Washington always on his mind, Churchill sent an upbeat telegram to Roosevelt on 13 April, reiterating his commitment to Tobruk as 'an invaluable bridgehead'. A few weeks later, in conversation with Averell Harriman, who had been sent to London by Roosevelt as his special representative, Churchill went much further. Tobruk, he avowed, was crucial to the protection of Egypt and the Suez Canal – and therefore to the entire Middle East. Were the Middle East to be lost, he explained, Spain, Vichy France and Turkey would embrace the Axis powers and a 'robot new order' would be created in 'a world in which Hitler dominated all Europe, Asia, and Africa'. This, he warned, would give 'the United States and ourselves, no option but an unwilling peace'. To invest Tobruk with such pivotal significance was to transform a modest port of limited utility into a political symbol of global moment – an emblematic albatross which would weigh heavily indeed in the months ahead.

By 11 April, with a characteristic contempt for caution, Rommel had accelerated his offensive to such effect that he had driven the British back to the Egyptian frontier at Sollum (from where O'Connor had started his onslaught against the Italians four months earlier) with one panzer division and encircled Tobruk with another. Although his progress had been hampered by lack of fuel and supplies, by sickness and disease, by breakdowns and repairs, by units which went astray and got lost in the desert, he had nonetheless advanced 400 miles in little over a fortnight. To maintain the momentum, he even flew over the Axis columns dropping notes to his hard-pressed troops which read, 'If you don't get a move on, I'll land – Rommel'. He had broken every rule of conventional warfare: he had imperilled his supply lines, he had defied his superiors, who were aghast at the rashness of his blitz-krieg, and – with the tacit support of Goebbels, who was mesmer-ised by his buccaneering spirit – he had even dared to circumvent a clear instruction from the Führer himself, issued on 2 April, that 'there should be no full-scale offensive'. And against the odds, he had triumphed. So far, it had been a spectacular coup.

Now, however, he succumbed to hubris. Allowing himself to believe that the British would abandon Tobruk, he expected to seize the town without meeting significant resistance. Without taking the elementary precaution of reconnoitring the surround-ing terrain or the defences which the British had hurriedly erected around the town, he was unaware that the 30,000 British and Aus-tralian troops entrenched within its perimeter – some of whom, in what Wavell described as 'race against time', had just arrived from Alexandria by sea – had no intention of surrendering Churchill's 'sally-port'.

When the Afrikakorps, led by the 5th Light Division, tried to force an entry into the town from the south, it met far stiffer resistance than Rommel had imagined and was forced to retreat. Undeterred, he sent his troops into battle again the next day when, once again, the British – in the form of the 9th Australian Division which had only recently arrived from the United Kingdom – held them at bay. Their commanding officer, General Leslie Mors-head, who was nicknamed 'Ming the Merciless' on account of the demands he made of his men, instructed, 'There'll be no Dunkirk here. If we should have to get out, we shall fight our way out. There is to be no surrender and no retreat.'

Instead of facing what should have been a self-evident truth that his reckless progress had left him with too few men to capture the fortress and not enough supplies to nourish their needs, Rommel still behaved as though the capture of Tobruk were imminent. Accordingly he repeatedly sent his tanks and infantry 'over the wire' with scant regard for either their lives or the chances of taking the town (which his superiors at OKW had correctly judged to be a 'mission impossible').

They swiftly ran up against the Royal Horse Artillery and soldiers such as Lance Sergeant Harold Harper. 'The tanks came over the ridge probably about six hundred yards away, which rather shook us as we were used to firing at eight [hundred], nine [hundred] or a thousand yards,' he recalled. 'They didn't attack in strength. The firing was almost incessant. It was rather like a cup tie – when you knocked out a tank, everybody cheered. I think we managed to knock out three or four before they retired.'

There was hand-to-hand fighting as well. An NCO with the 9th Australian Division watched a bayonet charge 'which demoralised the enemy, and those who escaped were driven back through the wire … We kept on firing through the night … we had been told to stick there and we did.'

Joachim Schorm, a lieutenant in the 5th Panzer Regiment (which formed a core part of the 5th Light Division), described the mayhem which Rommel's foolhardiness had inflicted on his troops:

> Some of our tanks are already on fire. The crews call for doctors, who dismount to help in this witches' cauldron. Enemy anti-tank units fall on us with their machine-guns firing into our midst … Our own anti-tank guns and 88s are almost deserted, the crews lying silent beside them … now comes the gap and the ditch … the vehicle almost gets stuck but manages to extricate itself with great difficulty. With their last reserves of energy, the crew gets out of range and returns to camp.

Rommel had driven his troops to the limits of endurance but, in thrall to his obsession with the conquest of Egypt, he refused to admit failure. In the early hours of 14 April he launched another foolhardy attempt to breach the perimeter wire. In a ferocious battle, his tanks and infantry were repelled yet again, losing sixteen out of thirty-eight tanks to the concentrated fire of the Royal Horse Artillery's 25-pounders in the process. Wavell reported that the Australians had captured 250 Germans, many of them apparently weeping with despair. 'Their morale is definitely low,' he added. Churchill commented, 'Perhaps it was because their morale and expectations had been so high that they wept.'

In letters to his wife during April, Rommel sustained his self-delusion that Tobruk was about to fall. However, on the 22nd, an intriguing note of reality crept into a letter which one of his adjutants, Major Schraepler, wrote to Frau Rommel about the 'worrying' days that her husband had to endure in this period. 'We have too few German forces and can do nothing with the Italians. They either do not come forward at all, or if they do, run at the first shot. If an Englishman [sic] so much as comes in sight, their hands go up. You will understand, Madam, how difficult this makes the command for your husband.'

On 1 May, Rommel finally came to terms with reality and called off the assault. By this time, most of his troops were at the point of exhaustion and many of his senior officers could no longer refrain from voicing their dismay at his style of leadership. Among the latter, Major General Kirkheim had already complained formally to General Halder, head of the Army General Staff. 'For days Rommel has given none of us a clear report,' he wrote. 'I feel, however, that the thing has gone from bad to worse. It appears from reports of officers coming from the front, as well as from personal letters, that Rommel is [in] no way up to his command duties. All day long he races about between his widely scattered forces, ordering raids and dissipating his troops.'

Rommel's progress had not only been thwarted at Tobruk. A tenacious stand by the British on the border at Sollum had forced him to call a halt on the Egyptian frontier as well. Although the main British line of defence was now well back from the border at

Mersah Matruh, Rommel was now dangerously, if not critically, over-extended. Recognising this, OKW instructed him to suspend his campaign; nor was he to renew either the offensive against Egypt or the assault on Tobruk until ordered to do so. Halder – who loathed Rommel – despatched General Friedrich Paulus (a senior staff officer who was later to lead the German assault on Stalingrad) to bring the errant desert commander to heel. 'Perhaps he is the only one who can exercise his personal influence on this officer, who has gone mad,' Halder noted. Paulus was one of Rommel's few old friends among the staff officers at OKW but, on his return to Berlin, even he reported that Rommel had seriously misjudged the situation in North Africa. More especially he had failed to take adequate account of the acute supply problems by which he had now ensnared himself. His inability to seize the port of Tobruk, the acquisition of which, with its capacity to offload up to 20,000 tons a month, would to some extent have alleviated this predicament, meant that the logistical challenge he now faced was quite extraordinarily daunting.

The Afrikakorps required 30,000 tons of supplies a month, the Italians – military and civilian combined – needed a further 100,000 tons. But the port at Tripoli could only handle 45,000 tons a month and Benghazi, which had a theoretical capacity of 35,000 tons, was under frequent bombardment from the RAF. To make matters worse, the Royal Navy held sway in the Mediterranean, posing a constant threat to the supply convoys on the hazardous crossing between Italy and North Africa. The supplies offloaded at Tripoli were transported by a fleet of 3,600 trucks shuttling back and forth between the Libyan capital and the front, a round trip of more than 2,000 miles across bone-crunching terrain in scorching heat. Moreover, these vehicles, which consumed seventy-five litres of fuel a day each – a total of almost 6,000 tons a month – were a further drain on scarce resources. As a result, Rommel's forces were chronically short of the means required to maintain his army's capacity to wage war, which left him little choice but to bide his time. However, he had already achieved one important objective. By forcing the issue against the British in the desert, he also forced it upon the attention of OKW and Hitler; in the process he had – almost accidentally – demonstrated that, so far from being a strategic backwater, the Mediterranean was potentially a pivotal theatre in the Second World War.

SEVEN

TROUBLE AT HOME AND AWAY

'I am sure that you, better than anyone else, must realise how difficult it is for a soldier to advise against a bold offensive plan ... One lays oneself open to charges of defeatism, of inertia, or even of "cold feet" ... It takes a lot of moral courage not to be afraid of being thought afraid.'
Sir John Dill to Winston Churchill

April 1941 had been a cruel month for the British. With Rommel on the warpath in the desert and the Wehrmacht slicing through Greece, morale in the higher echelons of the Imperial General Staff had fallen sharply. It was clear to his colleagues that the CIGS, General Dill, was 'worn and anxious', so 'tired mentally' on one occasion 'that he could not concentrate on the papers for cabinet'. Many of his staff officers were under similar stress. Overstretched and overworked, they were under a constant barrage of what, according to the Director of Military Operations John Kennedy, they regarded as 'unsound and impractical propositions' emanating from a hyperactive and intemperate Prime Minister.

In these testing days, it did not take much to incur Churchill's wrath, especially if your name was Archibald Wavell. On 24 April, while Rommel was still pressing the assault on Tobruk, the C-in-C, Middle East sent the Chiefs of Staff a note to warn that most of the troops under his command were not 'battle-worthy, being either unsuitable or insufficiently equipped ... We are fighting, as we have done since the beginning of this war, with improvisations, and insufficiencies.'

Included with this memorandum was a copy of an 'intensely

secret' document, spelling out his 'Worst Possible Case' strategy. The theoretical assumption in this paper was that Rommel was unstoppable and that Egypt would fall to the enemy. In this eventuality Wavell intended to evacuate his troops to Sudan, or overland to Palestine or by sea to other destinations. It would not necessarily mean the end of the war but it would be a grave setback indeed; nonetheless, Kennedy regarded the document as 'merely soldierly precautions ... there was no question of a secret Achilles' heel of pessimism'.

Three days later, on 27 April, Kennedy was invited to stay the night at Chequers. At dinner, the Prime Minister asked him for his assessment of the situation in Egypt. Kennedy argued that it was vital to cut the German means of communications both across the Mediterranean and through the desert from Tripoli. Otherwise, he warned, the Germans could assault Egypt from both the East and West, in which case it would be impossible to hold the line. To insure against that risk, five armoured divisions would be required – reinforcements that unfortunately were unavailable. This unpalatable analysis provoked Churchill's immediate wrath. 'Churchill flushed at this, and lost his temper,' Kennedy recalled. 'His eyes flashed and he shouted, "Wavell has 400,000 men. If they lose Egypt, blood will flow. I will have shooting parties to shoot the generals."'

By now Kennedy was well aware that among the Prime Minister's idiosyncrasies was a tendency to relieve his feelings of exasperation with such outbursts. But when Churchill went on to accuse Kennedy of 'defeatism' by even contemplating the loss of Egypt, the latter had difficulty controlling his own anger. Unlike so many of his senior colleagues, who were prone to retreat under prime ministerial fire, the Director of Military Operations chose instead to refer the Prime Minister to Wavell's 'Worst Case' strategy which he presumed – wrongly – had been placed before him. 'This comes as a flash of lightning to me. I have never heard such ideas,' Churchill exclaimed in even greater rage. 'War is a contest of wills. It is pure defeatism to speak as you have done.'

The next day, Churchill sent a dyspeptic directive to his Chiefs of Staff. 'The loss of Egypt and the Middle East would be a disaster

of the first magnitude to Great Britain, second only to successful invasion and final conquest ... It is to be impressed upon all
ranks, especially the highest, that the life and honour of Great
Britain depends upon the successful defence of Egypt.' For once,
this grandiloquent volley of prime ministerial fire did not intimi-
date the Chiefs, who responded by defending Wavell for preparing
a 'Worst Possible Case' and advising that it was now essential to
devise ways of blocking the Suez Canal to thwart Rommel's east-
ward progress were this theoretical prospect to be realised.

Tension between Churchill and his commanders both in Whitehall and in the Middle East was inevitable but their disputes were
never fiercer than during this anxious period. It is notable, though,
that – in contrast with modern British political conflicts – none
of the antagonisms that rose to the surface appear to have been
animated by personal enmity or trivial rivalry. All those involved
were facing great dilemmas with grave implications, the scale of
which were matters of properly disputed conjecture. Thus, when
the Chiefs of Staff came under renewed pressure from Churchill
to send further reinforcements to the Middle East, Dill was goaded
to respond forcefully on their behalf, warning on 6 May that it
would be premature to discount the threat of a German invasion
of Britain; that German successes in the Balkans and Libya had
demonstrated 'the paramountcy' of the Wehrmacht's 'armoured
forces supported by a powerful Air Force'; and that to provide the
requisite number of armoured divisions and tank brigades to 'give
security' to the United Kingdom, it would be necessary to suspend
the flow of additional tanks and armaments to the Middle East.

Dill went on to challenge Churchill on the nub of the issue:

> The loss of Egypt would be a calamity which I do not regard as
> likely, and one which we would not accept without a most des-
> perate fight; but it would not end the war. A successful invasion
> alone spells our final defeat. It is the United Kingdom therefore
> and not Egypt which is vital, and the defence of the United
> Kingdom must take first place. Egypt is not even second in
> order of priority, for it has been an accepted principle in our
> strategy that in the last resort the security of Singapore comes

before that of Egypt. Yet the defences of Singapore are still considerably below standard.

Churchill's reaction was scathing and incredulous. 'I gather you would be prepared to face the loss of Egypt and the Nile Valley, together with the surrender or ruin of the Army of half a million we have concentrated there, rather than lose Singapore. I do not take that view,' he replied on 13 May. Instead, offering a great hostage to fortune, he went much further – asserting that the defence of Singapore would need only a very small fraction of the troops required to protect the Nile Valley; that were Japan to enter the war, it would not be to besiege Singapore at the outset; and – in a reminder of how much strategic and diplomatic capital he had invested in wooing Roosevelt – that in these circumstances the United States 'would in all probability come to our side'.

For once, the usually emollient CIGS held his ground. 'I am sure that you, better than anyone else, must realise how difficult it is for a soldier to advise against a bold offensive plan,' he wrote in a pained rebuke, 'One lays oneself open to charges of defeatism, of inertia, or even of "cold feet". Human nature being what it is, there is a natural tendency to acquiesce in a defensive plan of doubtful merit rather than to face such charges. It takes a lot of moral courage not to be afraid of being thought afraid.'

The Prime Minister refrained from replying to this plea for better understanding; nor did he include it in his voluminous memoirs, contenting himself instead by preening that he had 'no difficulty in convincing my political colleagues ... My views therefore prevailed and the flow of reinforcements to the Middle East continued unabated'. Of course, Churchill was arrogant and imperious but, as so often, his refusal to accept military logic and instead to gamble against the odds put his genius to the test – and on this occasion it was not found wanting. Even Kennedy, the most outspoken of Churchill's military advisors, was swift to concede later that, despite 'the effects of his constant bludgeon-strokes on our daily work', he and his colleagues 'never ceased to be aware of his stature or to feel other than deeply privileged to serve him. He towered over us all like a Colossus.'

Towards the end of May, reports from all fronts made dire reading: Crete was under assault from an airborne German invasion, Syria was at the point of collapsing into Hitler's embrace, an uprising in Iraq had not yet been crushed, Greece was lost and Rommel hovered menacingly on the Egyptian border. As yet unaware that the Wehrmacht was about to invade the Soviet Union, Churchill's military advisors feared that the pincer movement they had long feared might very soon throttle the Middle East.

Burdened by the gravity of these threats, the Prime Minister chose to place the blame on Wavell. Though his axe would not fall for another month, he decided that the Middle East C-in-C should be sacked. Deploying a graceless metaphor, made even less attractive by the fact that it was not written in the heat of the moment but with the benefit of hindsight, he later wrote, 'It might be said we had ridden the willing horse to a standstill.'

Unaware of Churchill's decision, the 'willing horse' was devoting all his attention to the alarming situation which now promised to engulf his command. 'I was threatened with having to undertake operations simultaneously in no fewer than five theatres with my resources in men and material very seriously depleted by the losses in Greece ... To deal with these many responsibilities my resources were completely inadequate,' he wrote with grim frustration. His predicament was in no way ameliorated by the unrelenting torrent of advice, exhortation and instruction Churchill inflicted on him, second-guessing his strategic and operational judgement. Flailing around for a way of escape, the Prime Minister demanded action on all fronts, often using language so fierce that it would surely have driven a lesser man than Wavell to despair.

If the Greek debacle had sapped Wavell's morale, Crete gave him no respite. The defence of the island was led by Major General Bernard Freyberg, the British-born commander of the New Zealand Expeditionary Force. Nicknamed 'the Salamander' by Churchill for his legendary eagerness to face enemy fire, he had already earned a VC and three DSOs in the First World War for his courage in combat, notably at Gallipoli. No one doubted his resolve but the forces available to him were pitiful: a total of 30,000 men, 15,000 of whom were a motley collection of battle-weary evacuees from Greece who had left their equipment behind on the beaches. He had virtually no artillery and only a score of elderly RAF fighters with which to protect this strategically significant outpost. Despite this, his men put up far greater resistance to the airborne armada – Operation *Merkur* – that Hitler unleashed against Crete on 20 May than OKW had predicted. Nonetheless, at the end of a week during which more than 700 aircraft, including 430 bombers, had dropped some 25,000 soldiers on the island, the New Zealanders were at bay.

The Royal Navy, under the command of Admiral Andrew Cunningham, swept back and forth between Crete and the mainland, intercepting, sinking or scattering several flotillas of fishing boats laden with German troops. But Cunningham's ships came under heavy bombardment from the Luftwaffe, which, in the space of two days (22 and 23 May) managed to sink two cruisers and three destroyers as well as seriously damaging the battleship *Warspite*. Such heavy losses led Cunningham to conclude that he could not afford to risk any further vessels in the defence of Crete without jeopardising his ability to protect other vital areas in the Eastern Mediterranean. On the 26th, Freyberg signalled Wavell in Cairo that it was impossible for his men any longer to endure the concentrated bombing that the Luftwaffe had inflicted on them over the previous week. He added gallantly: 'I feel that I should tell you that from an administrative point of view the difficulties of extricating this force in full are insuperable ... The troops we have, with the exception of the Welsh Regiment and the Commandos, are past any offensive action. If you decide, in view of the whole Middle East position, that hours will help we will carry on.'

When this news was passed on to Churchill, he cabled solicitously, 'Your glorious defence commands admiration in every land. We know the enemy is hard pressed. All aid in our power is being sent.' This do-or-die missive was false in two respects. The enemy had endured serious casualties but was by no means 'hard pressed'; nor was further aid on its way. Indeed, though Churchill simultaneously instructed Wavell, 'Victory in Crete essential at this turning-point in the war. Keep hurling in all aid you can,' the Middle East commander-in-chief knew that all was already lost and that he had little choice but to ignore the Prime Minister's command. On the 28th, he ordered Freyberg to evacuate Crete forthwith, an operation that was so fraught with danger that it had soon to be called off: too many ships had been crippled or sunk by the Luftwaffe and too many sailors and soldiers had been massacred by a sustained bombardment which left the decks of British destroyers and cruisers awash with blood. In all, 5,000 soldiers and sailors had been killed, wounded or were missing in action, while 12,000 men were stranded on the beaches, to be taken into German custody.

For their part, the Germans had been badly bruised, losing 5,670 paratroopers and with more than 350 planes put out of action. That this elite force should have suffered such heavy losses came as a shock to Berlin and the Nazi leadership reacted with characteristic brutality. In retaliation for their alleged collaboration with the enemy, the Luftwaffe's commander-in-chief, Hermann Goering, authorised the mass execution of Cretan villagers. Hitler himself was so affected by the losses that he came to regard all airborne operations as a hostage to fortune which should not be risked again.

Nonetheless, in strategic terms, the German victory posed an additional threat to the British. Should they choose to make full use of Crete's facilities, the Luftwaffe was now in an even more powerful position to challenge the British in the Eastern Mediterranean and the Middle East. Pumped up by their success, senior officers in the Luftwaffe started to canvas ambitious plans for seizing control of the entire theatre. Colonel Günther Korten, a staff officer attached to 4 Air Fleet, proposed 'an island-hopping operation' from Greece to Crete, Rhodes and Cyprus, then on to Alexandria, Beirut, Haifa and Jaffa. Arguing that this would not only give Germany command over the Eastern Mediterranean, but open the way for the German army 'to advance in North Africa and strike at the heart of the British Empire in India', he convinced Goering, who, with Hitler's endorsement, gave the go-ahead for the island-hopping project. On 18 April, OKW formally approved this change in strategy: Greece was to become the launch pad for an aerial bombardment of Alexandria and Suez.

A lesser man than Wavell would have been drowned by the cascade of military crises which befell him between April and May 1941. On the eve of the German invasion of Greece and with his own forces reeling before Rommel in the Desert, he was confronted by yet another challenge which posed an immediate and fundamental threat to Britain's capacity even to prosecute the war in the Middle East or the Mediterranean.

On 1 April, an Iraqi general, Rashid Ali, led a military coup d'état against the pro-British regime in Baghdad. Iraq had been a British colony until 1930, when it formally became an 'independent' kingdom (though ruled by a branch of the Hashemite royal family which had been placed on the throne by the British); its location made it an important conduit between Egypt and the jewel in Britain's imperial crown, India.

Of even greater significance and more immediate moment, the British forces protecting the Mediterranean and the Middle East depended entirely on oil from Iran and the Iraqi oil fields at Mosul and Kirkuk. Without this lifeline, the Empire's army, navy and air force would have been paralysed. Accordingly the terms imposed by Britain on Iraq at the time of independence required Baghdad to permit British troops to transit Iraq and, in the event of war, 'to give all aid, including the use of railways, rivers, ports and airfields' to the British government. In addition, Baghdad undertook to protect the pipelines carrying the oil from the British refineries in Iraq to Haifa and the Mediterranean.

Reflecting a growing resentment at these constraints on Iraq's right to self-determination, Rashid Ali's uprising dramatically put at jeopardy Britain's entire strategy in the region. Within days the nationalist leader suspended the flow of oil from Mosul and Kirkuk. On 18 April (by which time Rommel had laid siege to Tobruk and the Swastika had been raised over Athens) an Indian brigade – the vanguard of the 10th Division en route from Delhi – landed at Basra. In response, Rashid Ali assembled an Iraqi force of 9,000 men and besieged Britain's military base at Habbaniya which housed 9,000 civilians and was protected by a total of 2,000 imperial troops.

Habbaniya's principal role had been to train newly recruited RAF pilots, who honed their skills over the desert in a collection of elderly biplanes. Hoping to avert a military clash, Wavell intended to negotiate a face-saving compromise with Rashid Ali to avoid diverting troops from other hard-pressed fronts to secure Iraq. On 4 May, however, with skirmishes around Habbaniya threatening to topple into all-out combat, he was overruled by Churchill, who cabled, 'The security of Egypt remains paramount. But is essential to do all in our power to save Habbaniya and to control the pipeline to the Mediterranean.' Next day, Wavell protested in the bluntest terms he had yet used. 'Your message' he wrote, 'takes little account of realities. You must face facts … I feel it my duty to warn you in the gravest possible terms that I consider the prolongation of fighting in Iraq will seriously endanger the defence of Palestine and Egypt. The political repercussions will be incalculable … I therefore urge again most strongly that a settlement should be negotiated as early as possible.' His clear emphasis was on the word 'negotiated'.

Churchill was contemptuous of what he interpreted as his commander-in-chief's pusillanimity; 'Wavell gives me the impression of being tired out' he noted scornfully. Aware, through cable intercepts, that the Iraqi regime had been pressing the Axis powers for military assistance, the Prime Minister formally instructed Wavell to engage Rashid Ali's forces before the Germans could come to his assistance. The commander-in-chief backed off. Within a week a force of 5,800 men, spearheaded by the Transjordan Frontier Force, was on its way at speed across the 500 miles of desert which separated Palestine from the British base in central Iraq.

As it turned out, the siege of Habbaniya was over even before their arrival on Iraqi soil. Raiding parties from within the base, supplementing a sustained assault by a squadron of Wellington bombers and fighter aircraft newly arrived from Egypt, managed to break the siege. The Iraqi air force was virtually destroyed and Rashid Ali's troops fell back towards Baghdad. Wavell sought to use this advantage as a basis for a renewed attempt to find a negotiated settlement with the Iraqi leader but the Prime Minister was in no mood to compromise: Rashid Ali was to be driven from power by force.

The Iraqis did not surrender without a struggle. Fighting a grim rearguard action, they retreated to the city of Fallujah, from where they were dislodged only after a fierce battle with the reinforcements which had by now arrived from Palestine. Just in time to be too little too late, the Luftwaffe finally despatched a small number of warplanes to Mosul.

Rashid Ali's coup had taken Berlin as well as London by surprise. Immersed in preparations for *Barbarossa* and orchestrating the final stages of Hitler's Balkan campaign, OKW had yet to develop a diplomatic policy let alone a military strategy for Iraq. This was made glaringly apparent on 23 May, when Hitler belatedly issued Directive No. 30, a document resonant with vague aspiration rather than practical plans. 'The Arab Freedom Movement is our natural ally against England [sic] in the Middle East' he declared. Rashid Ali's 'rebellion', he predicted, would extend across the Iraqi frontiers, interrupt British lines of communication, and tie down both English troops and English shipping space at the expense of other theatres of war. 'For these reasons,' he continued, 'I have decided to push the development of operations in the Middle East by going to the support of Iraq.' However, he continued, 'Whether and how it may be possible, in conjunction with an offensive against the Suez Canal, finally to wreck the British position between the Mediterranean and the Persian Gulf, is a question that will be answered only after *Barbarossa*.'

This imprecise disquisition was of precious little utility to the new Iraqi dictator. The British were already poised to take Baghdad and, by the end of May in the absence of any military support from Germany, the capital duly surrendered. Dismayed by the failure of the Germans to rally to his support, Rashid Ali fled to Teheran accompanied by a gaggle of German and Italian ministers. On 31 May the Emir was reinstated and Iraq once again fell firmly under British control.

Both because he had failed to develop a strategy by which to realise the ambitions he harboured for the Middle East and because he was wholly absorbed in the final stages of the planning for Operation *Barbarossa*, Hitler had missed a real chance to disrupt fatally Britain's oil supplies in the Middle East and therefore to render his enemy impotent not only in that theatre but – with the United States as the United Kingdom's only other source of oil – in many other parts of the world as well.

In London, the Chiefs of Staff rewarded Wavell's success against Rashid Ali by transferring Iraq – which had hitherto 'belonged' to the Indian Command – to the Middle East Command, a decision which prompted Wavell to cable Dill, 'What a baby you have given me on my 58th birthday'. Dill replied, 'Yes, what a baby, but I hope you soon kill the little brute.'

In overriding his commander-in-chief's reluctance to use force in Iraq the Prime Minister had been ruthless, but his judgement had been proved correct. Reflecting on the success of an operation which had both secured the oil arteries on which the Middle East Command depended and strangled a nascent uprising which could have threatened to usurp Britain's regional hegemony, Churchill noted with satisfaction, 'Hitler certainly cast away the opportunity of taking a great prize for little cost in the Middle East.'

Wavell's summary of the episode was ruefully defensive. 'Rashid Ali and his adherents seemed to have lost heart at the weakness of the support accorded to them by the Germans ... had the Germans sent sufficient forces to enable the Iraqi rebels to score a success, the whole country might well have risen against us'. As it was, the collapse of Rashid Ali's coup (which was to have lasting repercussions in Iraq and the Middle East in the decades following the end of the Second World War) did not mark a turning point in the Arab World; it was also an impressive demonstration that the British Empire had no intention of surrendering its imperial hegemony in the region.

On reflection, Wavell later paid gracious tribute to Churchill's resolve. 'I told Winston that I was doubtful whether the force ordered across to Habbaniya was strong enough to effect its purpose ... He ordered me to send it, a bold and correct decision, which I always felt I really ought to have taken myself.' Churchill was less generous. By May, his lack of faith in his commander-in-chief, which bordered on personal animosity, had reached the point of no return. On the 6th, after a meeting with Churchill, the CIGS told Kennedy, 'The Prime Minister wants to sack Wavell and put General Claude Auchinleck into the Middle East.' Auchinleck, the commander-in-chief of the Indian Army, had been far more supportive of military action against Rashid Ali and had provided reinforcements to protect Basra, an alacrity which prompted Churchill's observation that Wavell appeared tired out. Later, he added that Auchinleck 'gave us the feeling of a fresh mind and a hitherto untaxed personal energy'.

As if Wavell did not face more than enough challenges with the unfolding crisis in the Western Desert, the concurrent campaigns in East Africa and Eritrea, the debacles in Greece and Crete, and the coup in Iraq, he now had to face another threat which was no less taxing of his energy, his resources, and his strategic intelligence. At precisely the moment Rashid Ali's forces opened their assault against the British in Iraq, the Vichy authorities in Syria agreed to give Axis warplanes landing rights. By the end of May, a hundred German and twenty Italian warplanes had duly landed in the French colony to serve belligerent notice on the British.

The threat was obvious: if the Germans were to acquire control of Syria, then Egypt and the Canal Zone, the British oil refineries at Abadan and the communication links between Iraq and Palestine would all be at risk of bombardment by the Luftwaffe.

Once again Wavell came under intense pressure from the Prime Minister. Brushing aside complaints that the Middle East Command lacked a large enough force to intervene effectively, Churchill demanded action. Once again, Wavell at first demurred. On 21 May he signalled London that he was preparing to mount a joint British and Free French operation to take Syria by force – if the situation were to prove 'favourable' – but, unaware of his imminent dismissal, he added with rare finality, 'you must trust my judgement or relieve me of my Command'.

Churchill replied with brutal condescension in a telegram approved by a characteristically compliant War Cabinet. 'Our view is that if the Germans can get Syria and Iraq with a few aircraft, tourists and local revolts, we must not shrink from running equal small-scale risks, nor from facing the possible political aggravation of political danger from failure. We of course take full responsibility for this decision and should you find yourself unwilling to give effect to it, arrangement will be made to meet any wish you may express to be relieved of your Command'.

The Prime Minister was now in a hurry to rid himself of a commander he not only regarded as excessively cautious and pessimistic but found personally uncongenial as well. Had he been dealing with a lesser figure, his peremptory cable would most certainly have achieved that outcome. But Wavell was both a loyal servant of the Crown and a deeply committed commander-in-chief who was unlikely to fall on his sword out of pique. Nonetheless, Dill was evidently fearful that this time the Prime Minister might have pushed his friend and colleague too far. That evening he sent a letter to Wavell urging him to stay in his post:

> What a time you are having. How I wish I could be of more help to you. I do not know whether or not you will pack up on receiving the telegram from the Defence Committee – or rather the PM ... From your own personal point of view you will be sorely tempted to hand in your portfolio – you could hardly go on a better wicket – but from a national point of view it would I feel be a disaster. And yet I feel that the P.M. has only two alternatives – to trust or to replace. But even if he does not trust it would, I feel, be disastrous for you to go *at this moment* when you are handling so many difficult, if not critical situations.

It is not clear when this letter reached Wavell, but it was almost certainly not in time to influence the commander-in-chief's decision. Although he must have been exceedingly unhappy at Churchill's offensive tone, he refrained from escalating their 'misunderstanding' – Churchill's term – any further. Instead he confined himself to reiterating that the invasion force he had eventually been able to muster was 'much smaller' than he considered necessary for the task required of it. He was also disturbed at having to rely on the Free French as allies, not only because he – rightly – distrusted their overly optimistic analysis of the political situation in Damascus but also because he judged – correctly – 'that it would be likely to stiffen the resistance of the [Vichy] French in Syria.' Churchill was not disposed to be moved either by such niceties or by Wavell's acquiescence. At a dinner on 25 May he told the assembled party that, if he could be placed in Wavell's shoes, he would 'gladly lay down his present office – yes, and even renounce cigars and alcohol!'

The Syrian invasion, codenamed Operation *Exporter*, was launched on 7 June and was accompanied by a blitz of propaganda leaflets dropped from the air. This had no effect on the Vichy forces, who resisted with so much ferocity that, as he had feared, Wavell was obliged to summon troops from Iraq and Egypt to avoid a humiliating rebuff. But the fratricidal bitterness that he had foreseen was not invariably evident. The BBC's correspondent witnessed a poignantly farcical skirmish when a group of Free French fighters found themselves confronting a battalion from the Foreign Legion to which they had both previously belonged. As the adversaries prepared for battle, they recognised each other and, instead of opening fire, pointed their guns at the sky. Faced with this mutual refusal to obey orders, the opposing commanders met and agreed to withdraw their men from a confrontation that neither was willing to face.

Nonetheless, the Vichy troops did not yield easily or without bloodshed. By the time Syria finally succumbed, the casualties numbered 6,500 on the Vichy side and 4,600 on the British side (of whom 1,300 were Free French fighters) – a remarkably heavy price for what Churchill had described as an operation carrying 'small-scale risks'. But the Prime Minister had his victory and it counted.

Combined with the defeat of Rashid Ali in Iraq, the neutralisation of Syria reinforced Britain's authority in the Middle East, allowed Churchill to boast that the Axis attempts to use those territories as a springboard to advance on either Egypt or Iran had been foiled. Nevertheless, Wavell did not concede the strategic ground on which he had stood when he expressed his reluctance to enter the Syrian fray. His official account of Operation *Exporter* ended with the defiant comment, 'We must again be considered fortunate in achieving our objective with forces which were really insufficient for their task.'

As in the case of Iraq, the success of the Syrian operation was achieved only because the Prime Minister had forced Wavell either to obey or to resign. The relationship between them was beyond repair. By 12 July, the date Damascus finally came under British control, Wavell was no longer in command.

A FIGHTBACK FAILS

*'One thing seemed quite certain to us, that if the battles were
to be fought from London, a mess would be made of them.'*
Major General John Kennedy

In Cairo and in London, the Western Desert remained the most important battlefront and greatest headache. At his headquarters in Cairo Wavell surveyed his demesne with gloom. On 15 May, as he prepared to invade Syria, he also launched an attack on Rommel's front line which was – appropriately – codenamed Operation *Brevity*. Believing that 'the enemy strength in armoured fighting vehicles in the forward area was small and that he was in difficulty with his supplies', he decided to launch an attack in the expectation of retaking Sollum and Capuzzo on the Egyptian side of the Libyan border, which he regarded as 'a good jumping off place for an attack on a large scale'. But Rommel's battlefield intelligence alerted him to Wavell's plans. He at once despatched an additional panzer squadron to reinforce the units already dug in on the top of the escarpment which marked the border. The British were forced to withdraw. As they did so, Rommel advanced rapidly to wrest control of the high ground at Halfaya Pass, a stronghold some four miles to the south of Sollum, which gave him even greater control over the surrounding terrain. Wavell's abortive offensive had done nothing for his own morale or for Churchill's confidence in his hard-pressed commander-in-chief.

But the failure of Operation *Brevity* served only to whet the prime ministerial appetite for action. On 27 May, as Rommel's troops dug themselves in above Halfaya Pass, he sent a note to the Chiefs of Staff blithely insisting – in the face of the evidence – that 'the opportunity for a decisive military success' had presented itself in the Western Desert. The purpose, he avowed, should be nothing less than 'the destruction' of Rommel's army 'in a decisive battle fought with our whole strength. It should be possible in the next fortnight to inflict a crushing defeat upon the Germans in Cyrenaica'. With his usual reluctance to look beyond a crude 'headline' figure, he reminded the Chiefs that Wavell had upwards of 400 heavy tanks at his disposal against 130 heavy tanks on the other side; and, with a breathtaking disregard for the military realities of the Middle East, he demanded that Wavell should 'strike with the utmost strength in the Western desert against an enemy already in great difficulties for supplies and ammunition. Here is the only chance of producing a major military success, and nothing should stand in its way.'

The Chiefs were aghast. As they surveyed the pressures on Wavell's forces, stretched to the very limit by overlapping and competing operations across the entire Middle Eastern theatre, they recoiled from Churchill's bombastic simplicities. 'One thing seemed quite certain to us,' Kennedy noted, 'that if the battles were to be fought from London, a mess would be made of them.' But Churchill was not to be thwarted. On 28 May, overriding the protests of an unusually assertive CIGS, he cabled Wavell to emphasise yet again the need for victory in the desert. 'Everything must now be centred upon destroying the German forces in the Western Desert,' he declared. 'Now ... is the time to fight a decisive battle in Libya and go on day after day facing all necessary losses until you have beaten the life out of General Rommel's Army.'

This roused Dill to protest with uncharacteristic vehemence. 'My dear Prime Minister,' he wrote, 'I have of course despatched your telegram of today to Wavell. At the same time I feel I should let you know that there is much in it that I do not like.' But Churchill was undeterred even when Dill crossed Whitehall to 10 Downing Street to press the point; his telegram would stand.

Interpreting the Prime Minister's ill-judged missive as an instruction to press ahead with *Battleaxe* (as the proposed 'large scale' counter-attack against Rommel was to be codenamed), Wavell signalled the Chiefs of Staff to express his reluctance to engage with Rommel prematurely.

'I think it right to inform you that the measure of success which will attend this operation is in my opinion doubtful,' he wrote with laconic understatement. His pessimism was born of what he described as some 'disquieting features' which were bound to make progress difficult: his armoured cars were too lightly armoured to resist enemy aircraft and, having no guns, were 'powerless' against the German eight-wheeled armoured cars; his infantry tanks were too slow for desert warfare and were easily destroyed by the superior anti-tank guns of the enemy; and his cruiser tanks enjoyed no advantage over Rommel's medium tanks. For these reasons among others, Wavell concluded, 'We shall not be able to accept battle with perfect confidence in spite of numerical inferiority, as we could against the Italians.' These were not the forebodings of a defeatist but constraints on military action which it would have been folly for Wavell – or the Chiefs of Staff – to ignore but which Churchill, driven by the political imperative for a victory, refused to contemplate.

As soon as he saw Wavell's gloomy telegram, Churchill rang Dill to complain that it was 'the message of a tired and beaten man'. Dill responded spiritedly. 'You must not forget, Prime Minister, that we started this war without an army. Although we are getting on, it is not an army yet, except in name, and it is not too easy to build it up and to fight at the same time.' Churchill reacted by suggesting that reinforcements should be sent to the Middle East. Dill demurred, saying, 'we cannot risk sending any more units from here'. When Churchill put the phone down, Dill and Kennedy discussed Wavell's predicament, the latter repeating 'we were not beaten yet in the Middle East' and insisting, 'we should not lose the war in an effort save Egypt'.

Still unaware that Hitler was now only three weeks away from launching what would prove to be his catastrophic invasion of

Russia, the Chiefs of Staff in London believed that the war was poised on a knife edge and that the British Empire was in deepening peril. Still fearful of a blitzkrieg by the Wehrmacht towards the Middle East via Turkey and Syria in combination with a massive air assault on the British positions in the desert, and especially on Tobruk, they were as dubious about a premature offensive against Rommel as Wavell. But the pressure on the Middle East commander-in-chief did not abate. Nor did Churchill's urge to get rid of him. On 30 May, Dill emerged from a meeting of the War Cabinet to tell Kennedy that the 'question of Wavell was becoming very urgent' because 'the Cabinet had lost faith in him'.

But the Prime Minister stayed his hand. On 4 June he sent Wavell a long telegram which, with its promise of greater administrative support and the prospect of further reinforcements over the next four months, seemed to offer the weary general a measure of comfort. But the Prime Minister was unable to restrain his growing exasperation: 'You have at the present moment 530,000 soldiers on your ration strength, some 500 field guns, 350 A.A. guns, 450 heavy tanks, and 350 anti-tank guns. In the months of January to May upwards of 7,000 mechanical vehicles have reached you ... yet you are evidently hard put to find a brigade, or even a battalion, and in continual telegrams you complain of your shortage of transport, which you declare limits all your operations.'

Churchill's frustration was compounded by the fact that a few weeks earlier he had put the full authority of his office on the line in Wavell's cause. In April, the Middle East C-in-C had sent a series of messages to London both to warn that the Afrikakorps was about to be greatly strengthened by the imminent arrival in Tripoli of the 15th Panzer Division, and to remind the Chiefs of Staff of the great disparity in the number and quality of the British tanks available to him on the Egyptian front by comparison with Rommel's panzers. These 'alarming messages', as Churchill assessed them, had led him to take a drastic decision. Overriding the objections of his CIGS and the reluctance of the Admiralty, he had ordered a naval convoy, laden with 295 new and reconditioned tanks, to make the perilous journey to the Middle

East via the Straits of Gibraltar and through the Mediterranean rather than taking the time-consuming Cape route.

In a memo to the Chiefs of Staff, he spelled out the reason for this decision in apocalyptic terms. 'The fate of the war in the Middle East, the loss of the Suez Canal, the frustration or confusion of the enormous forces we have built up in Egypt, the closing of all American co-operation through the Red Sea – all may turn on a few hundred armoured vehicles.' Acknowledging that the 'risk of losing the vehicles, or part of them, must be accepted' he asserted that the operation would be worthwhile 'even if half got through'.

This was a strategic gamble that, unlike his meddling in battlefield tactics, marked his greatness as a wartime leader. Not pausing to consider the political opprobrium that he would endure should the venture fail, he relished the drama and the challenge he had inflicted on his military subordinates. 'Secrecy' he avowed with barely concealed excitement, would be 'of the highest importance, and no-one outside the highest circles need know of the intention to turn off at Gibraltar. Everyone onboard the convoys must think they are going round the Cape.'

His ruse worked. Only one vessel laden with 57 tanks was lost on the way to Alexandria where the remaining 238 'Tiger Cubs', as the tanks were nicknamed, were safely disembarked. With a forgivable absence of modesty, Churchill could not refrain from preening himself on 'the brilliant success of Tiger' and 'the risks I had successfully run in sending out the Tiger Cubs ... through the deadly Mediterranean at so much hazard and with so much luck'. However, his exuberance did not last long.

As Wavell recorded wearily in his final despatch, the process of unloading the tanks took longer than expected, while one ship had to be diverted to Port Said because the cranes at Alexandria were not strong enough to lift the heaviest armour. Moreover, it was a prosaic fact of mechanical reality – which Churchill was not disposed to appreciate – that the newly arrived vehicles had to be painstakingly readied for the rigours of the Western Desert. Many of them needed a thorough overhaul and all of them had to be fitted with sand filters and painted with appropriate camouflage.

As a result the Tiger Cubs were not ready for action until the first week in June.

This delay allowed Rommel to deploy the full might of the 15th Panzer Division to the front line comfortably before Wavell was ready to launch Operation *Battleaxe*. But none of this weighed with Churchill. After the political and military risks he had taken to reinforce the 'Army of the Nile', Churchill found it especially galling that Wavell remained so pessimistic about the prospect of early success.

It was in this inauspicious atmosphere that Operation *Battleaxe* finally trundled into action against the enemy on 15 June. Wavell's Western Desert Force numbered 25,000 men. Incorporating the 4th Indian Division and the 7th Armoured Division – now reinforced by Churchill's Tiger Cubs – *Battleaxe* was under the field command of General Noel Beresford-Peirse. Advancing in three columns, their immediate purpose was to retake Sollum, Capuzzo and Halfaya.

The Durham Light Infantry formed part of the Capuzzo contingent. Lance Corporal Joseph Lamb attended a church service on the eve of the attack but was unimpressed by his battalion padre, who took it upon himself to tell the congregation, 'a lot of you won't be coming back'. Lamb said to himself, 'I thought, you should bloody well be going yourself.'

They set off in a dust storm led by Major Peter 'Crackers' May, who described their first encounter with the enemy: 'I can only assume they didn't put their sights down because all the bullets were going over our heads until we got close. Then they started hitting. These were Italian gunners ... a gunner with whom I crossed bayonets parried my point. Having done bayonet fighting, which was useful, I forced him down, and turned to one of my soldiers and said "Fix this bloody wop." He plunged his bayonet in and said, "Got him, Sir."'

'We got the order to get out and form up and fix bayonets,' recalled Lance Sergeant Wilson. 'I felt "I'm going to get it or come out of it alive." I just kissed my bayonet ... We shouted and screamed as we charged ... I was aware of men going down

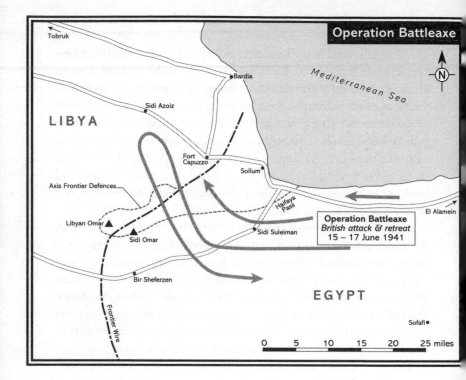

around me ... Young Woodall was ahead of me wrestling with an Italian. I bayoneted him and because I had one up the spout I shot him.'

But, as with *Brevity*, Rommel was forewarned by his field intelligence – the intercept of radio communications between British units – which also gave him precise information about Beresford-Peirse's every manoeuvre. Thus the Desert Fox was able to arrest the British advance with a speed and accuracy which flummoxed the British commanders.

Lamb watched in dismay as six 'Matilda' infantry tanks trundled forward. 'I waved at the tanks, hoping they would pepper the enemy front. No way they went straight in on into the 88s [German anti-tank guns with devastating fire-power] and they were all wiped out. Then about an hour after, I looks and all of a sudden there were about six Jerry tanks coming for us, and I shouted, "Right lads, every man for himself. Live to fight another day or else you've had it. Follow me." And we dashed away ... We ran like hell.'

The fighting barely lasted three days. On the 17th, the infantry was ordered to withdraw. Lamb described the moment 'when the reaction set in' the day after he and the rest of his battalion found themselves back at their 'starting-line' with fellow survivors of A Company. 'One of the lads starting crying. I started laughing like hell. We lost half our battalion, and we lost half the company. Out of about ninety men only 46 got out.' Although they had managed to take Capuzzo, they had failed to capture Halfaya and Sollum, where the British attackers had been decimated by the power, range, and accuracy of the German anti-tank guns.

The following day Wavell cabled London. 'I am sorry to have to report that "Battleaxe" has failed.' For the C-in-C, Middle East, it was the end of a dispiriting episode in a bleak chapter of setbacks, and for once, he was unable to contain his feelings. 'This was the only time I saw Archie Wavell in tears', one of his senior staff officers, Brigadier John Harding wrote subsequently. By contrast, Rommel, who had initially expected a 'hard fight', wrote jubilantly to his wife, 'The three-day battle has ended in complete victory. I'm going round the troops today to thank them.'

Churchill was alone at Chartwell, his country retreat in Kent, when he heard the news. Having invested so much of his personal credibility in *Battleaxe*, he was more than usually downcast by the outcome. By his own account, he 'wandered about the valley disconsolately for some hours', reflecting on yet another defeat on a battlefield in which a British force had been comprehensively outfoxed and outfought. Although they had managed to escape before the Afrikakorps cut off their line of retreat, the British had suffered severe losses: 381 men dead or missing and 588 wounded. Rommel had endured heavier human casualties but he had lost only twelve tanks. The British had lost almost eight times as many, ninety-one tanks, two-thirds of the total which had gone into action three days earlier. Wavell's gloomy prognosis about the likelihood of success had proved distressingly well founded.

'The operation which went by the codename *"Battleaxe"*

was a sorry affair,' de Guingand, commented later, noting wryly, 'The name was symbolic, for it achieved just about as much as that ancient weapon would have done if used in a modern battle.' Pinpointing the reason for the failure to achieve a 'laudable aim', de Guingand noted that 'the tools with which to carry it out were terribly weak'. The only benefit derived from *Battleaxe*, he concluded, 'was the fact that we were now left in no doubt as to how far behind we were in both tank and anti-tank gun design'.

Battleaxe was Wavell's personal nemesis in the Middle East. On 21 June he received a cable from Churchill informing him that, 'after the long strain you have borne, a new eye and a new hand are required in this most seriously menaced theatre'. The commander-in-chief was in the middle of shaving when he heard the news. He showed no emotion but said simply, 'The Prime Minister's quite right. This job needs a new eye and a new hand.' Accepting his dismissal with dignity, he wrote privately to his friend Dill to say that he was 'sorry he had not done better'.

Though they had endorsed Churchill's decision to sack his commander-in-chief, the Chiefs of Staff were as disquieted by the pressures which the Prime Minister had put on him as by the general's readiness to yield to his political master even when he was convinced that the demands made on him were excessive or ill-judged. But when – after his departure – the Prime Minister launched an attack on Wavell's integrity, even Dill was roused to indignation. On 11 July Churchill sent an unofficial note to the Cabinet in which, according to Kennedy, he implied that Wavell had acted deceitfully by disguising from London the fact that he had been 'resigned to disaster' in the desert. This roused Dill to write to the Prime Minister to express his dismay. 'I feel I must let you know how shocked I am that you should make such an attack on General Wavell,' he protested. Churchill was unabashed. Brushing aside the CIGS's rebuke with haughty disdain, he admonished, 'I must retain the right to address my Cabinet colleagues as I think fit upon such information as is before me at any time.'

Dill had made his point and knew when to retreat. 'I sincerely hope that you do not think that I for one moment wished to question your obvious right to address your cabinet colleagues as you think fit,' he replied, adding diplomatically, 'I am sure, for your part, you will not take it amiss if I seek to defend commanders who I think have been criticised without a full hearing.' By this time the subject of their contretemps was already en route for Delhi where, with characteristic grace, he had accepted a demotion to become C-in-C, India.

Wavell's departure from Egypt was a sad occasion for those who had seen him in action at first hand. He was widely admired by his colleagues in the army and by those outsiders who had cause to meet him on a regular basis. Alan Moorehead, who had been 'deeply sorry' to hear the news, likened him to Tolstoy's General Kutuzov in *War and Peace*. 'His fine head, his lined and leathery face, even his blind eye, give you the feeling of strength and sagacity and patience, though there is little in what he says normally to suggest any of these qualities. He listens intently. One feels one can tell him anything.' When the war correspondents were summoned to GHQ to bid their farewells, the *Daily Mail*'s Alexander Clifford noted that, though 'his dark face was lined, he was precise, as steady and as cheerful as I can remember'. Moorehead 'saw suddenly how sincere he was, how hard he had tried – tried, fought, organised, argued and held on. There went out of Cairo and the Middle East that afternoon one of the great men of the war.' This view was shared by the general who had twice – in *Brevity* and *Battleaxe* – worsted him on the battle-field in the desert. According his son, Manfred, Rommel regarded Wavell as 'a military genius'.

The writer and explorer Freya Stark, who had befriended Wavell, was on the tarmac for his departure from Cairo. 'He looked tired and sad, and kind, and the huge empty aerodrome, the sandy edges of the hills, the pale colour-wash – ochre and blue – of the early day, seemed all to lie in attendant as a frame to a picture, round the group of uniforms and the weather-beaten faces, and the solitary figure … the image was not inspired by any thought of lost causes, but by an atmosphere of loyalty and devotion which hung about the scene.'

Wavell's admirers came to regard Churchill's decision to rid himself of his loyal commander-in-chief as unjust and unwarranted.

Citing his victories in East Africa, where he had taken 200,000 Italian prisoners, his success in *Compass*, where another 200,000 were captured, and noting that between February and June 1941 he had conducted no fewer than six major campaigns, 'never less than three at a time', the historian Correlli Barnett judged, 'No other British soldier of the day had the strategic grasp, the sagacity, the cool nerves and the immense powers of leadership to do all these things and steer a course free of total disaster.' Acknowledging that his career 'had been latterly clouded by defeat', Barnett concluded that Wavell's dismissal, 'in fact if not in intention, made him a scapegoat for Churchill's own mistakes'.

However, writing without such benefit of hindsight but enjoying a unique perspective from within Whitehall, John Kennedy took a harsher view. In every engagement for which Wavell had been responsible, with the exception of Operation *Compass* and the East African campaign, the Director of Military Operations judged that the Middle East C-in-C had been guilty of 'grave errors of judgement and strategy', most of which he attributed to his willingness to bow to Churchill's ill-judged pressure.

Kennedy's verdict formed part of a deeply pessimistic review he had written for the Chiefs of Staff in which he analysed the predicament facing Britain.

> Whether we can hold on in the Middle East depends on one thing and one thing alone – whether the Germans concentrate seriously against us there. If they do, they will be able to develop their attacks in considerable strength from the west through Libya, from the north through Turkey, and possibly from the north-east through the Caucasus and Persia. We cannot produce sufficient strength in the Middle East in the near future to secure our position in face of serious attack from even one of these fronts ... If we hold on in the Middle East over an appreciable period it will therefore be only because the Germans are fully occupied elsewhere.

There could have been no better exposition of the harsh

reality confronting the Chiefs, albeit one that was anathema to Churchill, for whom Britain's imperial presence in the Middle East was only marginally less important than the survival of the United Kingdom. The departure of Wavell was intended to bring fresh energy and a bolder strategy to the Middle East Command; but if Kennedy's analysis was well founded, it mattered not who became C-in-C, Middle East. He – and Britain – would be at the mercy of the Führer's whim.

On the same day that Churchill dismissed Wavell, Kennedy and Dill met to discuss the failure of *Battleaxe*. Dill commented bleakly, 'I suppose you realise we shall lose the Middle East.' Kennedy replied, 'Well that depends on the Boche. If he concentrates on the Middle East, I agree we cannot put in sufficient resources to hold it. But he may not concentrate on it and he may get into trouble elsewhere.'

A few hours later in Berlin, at 4 a.m. on Sunday, 22 June, the German Foreign Minister, Joachim von Ribbentrop, delivered a formal declaration of war to Vladimir Dekananozov, the Russian ambassador. Apologising to Dekananozov, the egregious Nazi diplomat even claimed that he had sought personally to stop the war. As it was, Operation *Barbarossa*, the largest, most brutal, most fateful military campaign in history, was underway.

During the night, Jock Colville, Churchill's private secretary, was told by telephone that the invasion had started, but, under instructions to wake the Prime Minister only if Britain were invaded, he did not disturb him until 8 a.m. Churchill spent much of that day preparing a broadcast to the nation, hastily scheduled for the evening. It was another memorable performance. 'The Nazi regime is indistinguishable from the worst features of Communism,' he rumbled. 'It is devoid of theme and principles except appetite and racial domination. It excels all forms of human wickedness in the efficiency of its cruelty and ferocious aggression.' But, restraining his aversion to the Bolsheviks, he conjured a potent image of the Russian people at bay. Where he had once seen the repressive might of the Soviet state, he now saw Russian soldiers 'standing on the threshold of their native land, guarding the fields which their fathers have tilled from time immemorial' and seeking to protect 'the ten thousand villages of Russia where the means of existence is wrung so hardly from the soil, but where there are still primordial joys, where maidens laugh and children play.' Faced with 'the hideous onslaught' of the Nazi war machine, 'with its clanking, heel-clicking, dandified Prussian officers' and 'the dull, drilled, docile, brutish masses of the Hun soldiery plodding on like a swarm of crawling locusts, the past with its crimes, its follies, and its tragedies, flashes away'. Britain, he pronounced, had only 'one aim and one single, irrevocable purpose. We are resolved to destroy Hitler and every vestige of the Nazi regime.' He then declared 'we shall give whatever help we can to Russia and the Russian people.' The warmth of these words was matched by their vagueness, a deliberate if not wholly unconstructive ambiguity.

Churchill's haunting images of Russia's plight disguised a profound and – within the British elite though not among the wider population – widely shared aversion towards the Soviet regime. Most of the Prime Minister's colleagues at Westminster, in Whitehall, and in the armed forces not only loathed their Russian counterparts with unwavering intensity but would have been delighted to see the totalitarian protagonists fight one another to a standstill in the mud of the Russian steppe, twin Leviathans locked in a hellish embrace. But they did not for a moment believe that such a happy outcome was even a remote possibility.

It was almost universally presumed that the Soviet Union would be overrun by the panzers within a matter of weeks. In June 1941 the suggestion that the Russian people would sustain the struggle for four years and – at a cost of at least 25 million military and civilian lives – emerge victorious would have been almost universally ridiculed. It was inconceivable that the Red Army, vast in number but ill equipped, ill provisioned, ill trained and incompetently led by demoralised generals, could prevail against an Axis strike force, numbering 4,300,000 troops, 4,200 tanks and 4,400 aircraft.

Such pessimism lay at the heart of the instructions that Kennedy gave to Major General Noel Mason-MacFarlane, the reluctant leader of a hastily cobbled-together military mission to

Moscow, four days after the invasion. 'We don't think this is any-thing more than an off-chance. But we can't afford to miss even a poor chance like this. Your job will be to do what you can to help keep the Russian War going, and so exhaust the Boche. Even if we only manage to keep it going in Siberia, as we did with the White Russians, that will be something.' Quite how the unfortu-nate major general was supposed to help to 'keep the war going' was never made clear to him and the British mission was soon consigned to the margins of military diplomacy in Moscow.

As far as Whitehall was concerned, the anguish of the Russian people was of no great moment: the crucial role of the Red Army was less to save Russia than to impede the German advance through the vast wasteland of the Russian interior. This, in turn, would provide Britain with urgently needed breathing space in which to strengthen the nation's depleted defences on the home front and to reinforce the frontiers of the Empire overseas against the eventual and inevitable German onslaught.

This cynicism was not shared with a British public who, not unnaturally, presumed that Churchill's eloquent promises of support for Russia had been sincerely made, and for whom they became an effective rallying cry for the 'second front' that was soon to cause him much political trouble.

Mussolini had learned of the invasion only a few hours before Churchill, and then only because Ciano had him woken in the early hours of 22 June. Il Duce was not amused. 'Not even I disturb my servants at night but the Germans make me jump out of bed at any hour without the least consideration,' he railed. But he was nonetheless anxious indeed to offer Hitler practical support. Unhappily for Il Duce, the Führer was almost equally reluctant to accept it.

'The thing that is nearest to Il Duce's heart is the participa-tion of one of our contingents,' Ciano noted, but, after reading a long message from the Führer, he added, 'from what Hitler writes it is clear that he would gladly do without it.' Nonetheless, Mus-solini was insistent, asserting – ludicrously – that his divisions were 'superior to the German, both in men and equipment'. Under this embarrassing pressure and mindful of his southern flank and Mussolini's thin skin, Hitler, relented. On 24 June Ciano was able to note with relief, 'Our first contingents will leave in three days. Il Duce is very much excited at the idea of this participation of ours in the conflict, and telephones me to say that tomorrow he will review the troops.' In so far as his commitment of troops to the Russian Front constituted a strategic decision, it was motivated by the hope that the war would either end with a compromise which would protect the new balance of power in Europe or that it would last for a long time and thus give Italy a chance to secure by force of arms what he described as 'our lost prestige'. After listening to this interminable disquisition, Ciano sighed into his diary, 'Oh, his eternal illusions.'

Britain now needed America more than ever and, accordingly, Churchill wooed Roosevelt with even greater persistence. Week after week he deluged the President with letters and cables to report progress and to explain setbacks, in terms which elaborately cajoled and flattered the object of his political ardour. As the historian Max Hastings has put it, 'Few lovers expended as much ink and thought upon wartime correspondence as did the Prime Minister on his long letters to Roosevelt.' Even at the direst moments, when he was irritated, frustrated, or impatient with the White House – and even more so by Congress – he adopted an uncharacteristically patient tone, subtly adapting his assertive personality to seduce an audience that was still averse to becoming embroiled in any foreign war. But it was not until the early summer of 1941 that his ardour really began to bear fruit, giving him cause to hope that his blandishments were worth the expenditure of time, effort and eloquence that he had devoted to the purpose.

Roosevelt's landslide victory in November 1940 had not only made him the first President in history to win a third term in office but it had also given him even greater prestige and the authority to display his true colours as an internationalist who had no doubt that the rapid advance of Nazi Germany posed a grave threat to the United States which would have to be confronted. But, mindful of the isolationist sentiment which still infected American opinion, he had moved far more cautiously towards that end than the British Prime Minister had hoped. On the eve of Roosevelt's victory, Churchill had told his Private Secretary that he 'quite understood the exasperation which so many British people feel with the American attitude of criticism combined with ineffective assistance; but we must be patient and we must conceal our irritation'.

Throughout this period he had managed an exquisitely balanced *pas de deux* with the President, pressing his cause with a suitor's ardour but without quite losing his dignity in the process. Thus on the morrow of the President's election, he wrote to congratulate him in adulatory terms, confessing, 'I feel you will not mind my saying that I prayed for your success and I am truly thankful for it', but concluded almost proprietorially, 'that in expressing the comfort I feel that the people of the United States have once again cast these great burdens upon you I must avow my sure faith that the lights by which we steer will bring us all safely to anchor'.

The British ambassador to Washington, Lord Halifax, who had been removed from his post as Foreign Secretary to make way for Eden at the turn of the year, did not share that sense of comfort. Stiff, aloof and formal, he could not abide the easygoing, casual style which he discovered to be the Washington way of doing business. Clearly wishing himself to have been sent anywhere than to the American capital, he was heard to observe wearily that trying to pin down the Americans was 'like a disorderly day's rabbit-shooting'. In his aristocratic disdain for the vulgarity of the American elite with whom he came in contact, he was not alone. In the upper echelons of British society, the Americans were widely regarded as arrogant upstarts who were only too happy to see British soldiers die to save their – American – bacon. 'They are a quaint lot – they are told that if we lose the war they will be next on Hitler's list ... and yet they seem quite content to leave the actual fighting to us; they will do anything but fight,' a Conservative MP jibed contemptuously.

This animosity was returned in full measure by many in Washington who were not only viscerally hostile to the British

Empire but, in the words of the historian Michael Howard, then a student at Oxford, 'had some reason to regard the British as a lot of toffee-nosed bastards who oppressed half the world and had a sinister talent for getting other people to do their fighting for them'.

This degree of mutual mistrust and disdain required from Churchill a great deal more patience than he was accustomed to exercise or found it easy to command. That he achieved such self-restraint was to play no small part in delivering Britain from defeat. Without the unique relationship that he gradually established with the President, it is hard to imagine how the Americans would have been prevailed upon not only to form a military alliance with Britain but to give priority to Europe over the Far East and to open their account with Nazism not in continental Europe but in a North African desert. It was a bravura performance by a supremely adroit politician in the face of seemingly overwhelming odds.

By the beginning of 1941 Britain's financial predicament was so severe that it would dwarf all such subsequent crises. Following the 'destroyers for bases' deal, the government had to pay for all American supplies in cash. By November 1940 it had paid out $4,500 million leaving only $2,000 million in the Treasury coffers. As Churchill later recorded with enviable sangfroid, 'It was plain that we could no longer go on in this way.' In fact, Britain was teetering on the edge of insolvency. 'Even if we divested ourselves of all our gold and foreign assets,' Churchill recorded, 'we could not pay for half we had ordered, and the extension of the war made it necessary for us to have ten times as much.' The government's ability to prosecute the war had thus come to depend on the repayment terms which the United States was prepared to accept for the armour and weaponry without which Britain would assuredly have had to sue for peace.

But Washington was deeply sceptical about London's confession of approaching bankruptcy. At the height of the Battle of Britain, the US administration had questioned 'whether Churchill's government had honestly revealed its remaining assets' and insisted on the presentation of audited accounts to prove its probity. In November 1940, Roosevelt dismissed the British Treasury's protestations, telling his Cabinet, 'England still has sufficient credits and property in this country to finance additional war supplies.' On 1 December, when Henry Morgenthau, the Treasury Secretary reported that the British had claimed that they did not have the $2,000 million to pay for arms they had bought in October, the President replied briskly, 'they aren't bust'.

Churchill was so alarmed by this dismissive attitude, that, on 8 December, he sent the President what he regarded as 'one of the most important' letters he ever wrote. He did not beat about the bush. 'The more rapid and abundant the flow of munitions and ships which you are able to send us, the sooner will our dollar credits be exhausted,' he wrote. 'The moment approaches when we shall no longer be able to pay cash for shipping and other supplies … I believe you will agree that it would be wrong in principle and mutually disadvantageous in effect if at the height of this struggle Great Britain were to be divested of all saleable assets, so that after the victory was won with our blood, civilisation saved, and all the time gained for the United States to be armed against all eventualities, we should stand stripped to the bone.'

The letter was delivered to the President in the Caribbean, where he was on a yachting holiday. According to those who were with him, Churchill's appeal finally made an impression on Roosevelt. On 17 December, after his return to the White House, he told the Washington press corps that it was in America's self-interest to do 'everything possible to help the British Empire to defend itself'. That he did not shrink from seeking to commit the United States to the support of the Empire as well as the kingdom was a mark both of his remarkable authority and his understanding of the deep currents of American opinion that flowed beneath the agitated political surface.

Adept politician that he was, he alighted upon the folksiest of metaphors to sell this vision to the American people. 'Suppose my neighbour's house catches fire and I have a length of garden hose four or five hundred yards away and connect it up to his hydrant, I may help him put out the fire. Now what do I do? I don't say to him before that operation, "Neighbour, my garden hose cost me fifteen dollars; you have to pay me fifteen dollars for it." No! What is the transaction that goes on? I don't want fifteen dollars – I want – I want my garden hose back after the fire is over."'

A fortnight later, on 29 December, in one of his regular 'fire-side chats', the President warmed to this theme, saying, 'There is danger ahead ... But we all know that we cannot escape danger by crawling into bed and pulling the covers over our heads ... If Britain should go down, all of us in all the Americas would be living at the point of a gun, a gun loaded with explosive bullets, economic as well as military. We must produce arms and ships with every energy and resource we can command ... We must be the great arsenal of Democracy.' But mindful of the fact that the polls showed that 40 per cent of the electorate still believed that it was more important to keep out of war rather than aid England, he was careful to add, 'You can, therefore, nail any talk about sending our armies to Europe as a deliberate untruth. Our national policy is not directed towards war. Its sole purpose is to keep war away from our country and our people.'

The 'great arsenal of Democracy' still expected a very big buck for its bang. Clearly unmoved by Churchill's plea that Britain should not be 'stripped to the bone', the US Treasury exacted terms of trade for American military hardware which ruth-lessly exploited Britain's dire financial predicament. British assets held in the United States had to be sold off at far less than their book value – and often at knock-down prices. On the day after Roosevelt's heart-warming fireside chat, Churchill found himself obliged to write to the President imploring him not to despatch an American warship to Cape Town to claim Britain's last reserves of gold bullion. 'This will disturb public opinion here and throughout the Dominions and encourage the enemy ... If you feel this is the only way, directions will be given for the available Cape Town gold to be loaded on the ship. But we should avoid it if we can.' Church-ill's plea was ignored and the gold reserves were duly removed from South Africa against the settlement of Britain's debts.

Only when the American Treasury was finally persuaded that Britain's gold reserves were indeed exhausted did it permit the flow of direct aid from the United States across the Atlantic effectively free of charge. The mechanism for this was Lend-Lease, a scheme dreamt up by Roosevelt and sold by him to the American nation with great political adroitness. Steered through a suspicious Congress and into law on 11 March 1941 as 'An Act to Further Promote the Defense of the United States', Lend-Lease was to provide Britain and later Russia with an inexhaustible flow of armaments and other supplies over the next four years on terms which were both exceptionally easy and impossible to fulfil. 'The thing to do', Roosevelt had explained to Henry Morgenthau, the Treasury Secretary, is to 'say to England, we will give you the guns and the ships that you need, provided that when the war is over you will return to us in kind the guns and ships that we have loaned to you.' Lend-Lease was a vital step forward which signalled to the Axis and the rest of the world in unequivocal terms that the United States was no longer a neutral state except in name. However, Lend-Lease gave Washington far greater leverage over British strategy than before, which meant that Churchill had to navigate his Middle Eastern strategy with great dexterity through the uncharted diplomatic waters which now beckoned if he was to avoid it being holed below the waterline by its opponents on the other side of the Atlantic.

Secret talks between the British and American military planners earlier in the year had produced an outline strategy for the defeat of Germany but the White House was still a long way from making the military commitment without which, as the Prime Minister knew only too well, victory would not be possible. Churchill kept up the pressure on Washington, both directly by harrying the White House, and indirectly by reaching out to the American people whenever he was given the opportunity. Thus in a radio broadcast from London on 16 June 1941, at a low point in Britain's military fortunes, his rhetoric soared into the stratosphere. 'A wonderful story is unfolding before our eyes,' he promised his listeners across America. 'How it will end we are not allowed to know. But on both sides of the Atlantic we all feel – I repeat, all – that we are part of it, that our future and that of many generations is at stake.' And then, in an astute reference to the threat posed by Nazism, he added, 'The grand freedoms of which the President of the United States has spoken so movingly are spurned and chained. The whole stature of man, his genius, his initiative, and his nobility, is ground down under systems of mechanical barbarism and of organised and scheduled terror.' The message was plain: if you want to retain your freedoms, you had better be ready to fight for them.

Notwithstanding the impact which his grandiloquence may have had on the imagination of his listeners, it still cut little ice with hard-nosed legislators on Capitol Hill, or with the financial and military advisors who surrounded the White House. America was not yet ready or willing to take up arms for what still seemed to be a faraway cause.

NINE

A NEW BROOM IN THE DESERT

*'We have sought no shooting war with Hitler. We do not seek
it now ... But when you see a rattlesnake poised to strike, you
do not wait until he has struck you before you crush him.'*

Franklin D. Roosevelt

Wavell's successor as C-in-C, Middle East was General Sir
Claude Auchinleck, who arrived in Cairo on 30 June 1941
from India, where he had enjoyed a similar titular status but in
a far less demanding theatre of operations. 'The Auk', as he was
nicknamed, had not been regarded as a high-flyer. At Wellington School he had failed to distinguish himself academically; his
achievement in winning the Derby Gift – for industry and good
conduct – presciently identified those qualities with which he
was most readily associated. Although his imposing appearance,
spartan tastes, modesty and integrity commanded respect, he was
widely thought by his peers to lack the experience, perspective
or dash required of a commander-in-chief in such a complex and
demanding theatre as the Middle East. In the First World War he
had served with distinction in the Indian Army and remained in
this imperial outpost in the inter-war years. Socially he was an
outsider, a 'loner' who was unfamiliar with the upper-class camaraderie of the officers' mess in the mother country – a culture
which had been effortlessly transferred to Cairo. It was tempting
to underestimate the Auk, and especially his resolution, which,
tinged with obstinacy, suggested great strength of character.

These qualities were to bring him both high esteem and

deep turmoil; if Wavell had difficulties with the Prime Minister, Auchinleck was to have double trouble. In the measured words of his biographer, '[H]e was a soldier, not a diplomat, and his insistence on making decisions for military, rather than political reasons, would soon begin to alienate Churchill's sympathies.' Conflict between the two was inevitable and not long in coming.

Soon after his arrival in Cairo, Auchinleck received a remarkable letter from the CIGS, Sir John Dill. Outlining the chapter of crises by which Wavell had been ensnared, Dill homed in on the pressures that the new C-in-C was likely to face:

> The fact is that the Commander in the field will always be subject to great and often undue pressure from his Government. Wellington suffered from it: Haig suffered from it: Wavell suffered from it. Nothing will stop it ...
>
> You may be quite sure that I will back your military opinion in your local problems, but here the pressure often comes from very broad political considerations; these are sometimes so powerful as to make it necessary to take risks which, from the purely military point of view, may seem inadvisable. The main point is that *you* should make it quite clear what risks are involved if a course of action is forced upon you which, from the military point of view, is undesirable. You may even find it necessary, in the extreme case, to dissociate yourself from the consequences.
>
> The time will come when we can strike out with effect ... But in the meantime we have a grim fight to fight and we cannot afford hazardous adventures. So do not be afraid to state boldly the facts as you see them.

The new commander-in-chief was very soon put to the test. With the British government in financial hock to the United States, Churchill could not easily pursue a military course of which the White House disapproved. There was intense competition for the planes, tanks, and ships which started to roll off the production lines at a rate that only the world's most dynamic economy could achieve. The US Chief of Staff General George Marshall wanted the arms and equipment for the rapidly growing US military. And he did not refrain from reminding the White House that every weapon that was despatched across the Atlantic to Britain or around the Cape to the Middle East was a weapon that was not available to his own generals and admirals. Churchill was thus under great pressure to demonstrate that armaments supplied to Britain under the terms of Lend-Lease were put to good use.

This was especially the case in relation to the Middle East and North Africa. Despite what Roosevelt had said in December about coming to the aid of the 'British Empire', Washington was profoundly sceptical about the scale of Britain's commitments in this distant theatre. Roosevelt's most senior advisors found it virtually impossible to conceive that Europe had to be liberated via North Africa and supposed, rather, that for all his rhetoric about freedom and democracy, Churchill was essentially an old imperialist bent on safeguarding Britain's global hegemony. Since there was some truth in this perception, Churchill was hungry for success in the Western Desert, both to counter the growing sense across the Atlantic that Britain was a 'loser' and to demonstrate that Hitler could be challenged outside the continent of Europe and thereby thwart his global ambitions.

Less than a month before Auchinleck's arrival in Egypt, in a stern cable to his predecessor, Churchill made a point of highlighting the need to deploy rapidly and effectively the weaponry the US was delivering to the Middle East: 'President Roosevelt is now sending, in addition to the thirty ships under the American flag, another forty-four vessels, which carry among other things, 200 additional light tanks from the United States Army Production and many other important items … It would be disastrous if large accumulations of American supplies arrived without efficient measures for their reception and without large-scale planning for the future.'

Auchinleck, who took up his post formally on 5 July (after a five-day briefing from Wavell), found himself almost immediately subjected to very similar pressures. On 4 July Churchill had cabled Roosevelt depicting 'the greatly increased vigour and drive in our effort in the Middle East' that would follow from Auchinleck's appointment, which would ensure 'that the fullest use is made of the formidable resources steadily accumulating there from the United Kingdom, the overseas Empire, and the United States'. His upbeat prognosis was very far from Dill's analysis of the challenge facing the Middle East Command or from Auchinleck's own assessment once he had had a chance to survey his demesne for himself.

In London, the Axis threat to the Middle East assumed ever larger proportions. In July, the widespread assumption that Hitler would complete his destruction of the Soviet Union by the end of August was underpinned by a detailed analysis of the predicament facing Britain in the Middle East presented to the War Cabinet by the Joint Intelligence Sub-Committee (JIC). All the available evidence made it reasonable to conclude that, with Russia at his mercy, Hitler would turn on the Middle East. The Wehrmacht would be ordered to cross into Turkey and then Syria before throttling the carotid artery of the British Empire by seizing Egypt and the Suez Canal. At the time this threat not only seemed alarmingly real but – serendipitously – the analysis on which it was based also happened to be remarkably well founded.

A draft of Hitler's Order Number 32, dated 11 June 1941, called for the destruction of the British position in the Mediterranean and western Asia 'by converging attacks from Libya through Egypt, from Bulgaria through Turkey, and possibly from Transcaucasia through Iran'. In a memorandum at the beginning of July, only a week after the invasion of Russia, General Paulus (who had visited Rommel outside Tobruk at the end of April) produced plans for an assault on the Middle East spearheaded by three panzer divisions. In his role as Deputy Chief of the German General Staff, he proposed that – with Ankara's acquiescence – the Wehrmacht should transit Turkey, crossing into Syria and Palestine, before reaching the Suez Canal that November. This operation would be timed to coincide with a renewed offensive by Rommel planned for the same month. Nor was this the end of Paulus's ambition. With the Middle East securely under Axis control, he explained, two panzer corps 'would secure the land bridge to India, from the Nile to the Tigris' and thus destroy the British Empire.

A detailed examination of the German military archives by the historian Martin Kitchen has unearthed compelling evidence that Paulus's scheme was far more than one general's whim and that, at this stage of the war, Hitler's hubristic vision knew few bounds. Rommel was not informed of these proposals but Brauchitsch, the commander-in-chief of the army, was deputed to produce a detailed memorandum for OKW on the options facing the Third Reich after the conquest of Russia. Brauchitsch not only endorsed the Paulus plan but went further, proposing a parallel attack on the Persian Gulf via the Caucasus. Judging that Ankara would refuse to allow the panzer divisions to criss-cross its sovereign territory, he argued that Turkey would very probably have to be subdued by force. To ensure the success of the attack on the Persian Gulf, it would also be necessary to seize Gibraltar and Malta. To guarantee the success of this grand scheme, it would be essential for Rommel to capture Tobruk (which had now been under siege for two months). By this means the Axis would acquire a stranglehold over the entire Mediterranean.

With the benefit of hindsight such vaulting ambitions may seem fanciful, but at the time they were consistent with London's own appreciation of the likely extent of Hitler's ambition. Had *Barbarossa* been as successful as both OKW and Whitehall then presumed, it is more than probable that a version of the Paulus/ Brauchitsch plan would have been essayed. From a contemporary British perspective it would have seemed treasonably irresponsible to have presumed otherwise. For this reason alone, it is bizarre that the conflict in the Middle East and North Africa is sometimes dismissed as a 'sideshow' merely because Hitler failed to make it a priority to rival *Barbarossa*.

The Middle East Command was the most extensive in the British Army. From its epicentre in Cairo, Auchinleck's empire covered North Africa, East Africa, the Mediterranean and the Arab World as well as the Middle East itself. Mindful both of his responsibility to protect his northern and eastern fronts and of the need to face down Rommel in the Western Desert, Auchinleck swiftly concluded that he lacked the manpower and weaponry to challenge Rommel in the desert while simultaneously protecting his other flanks. This immediately put him at odds with Churchill, who still found it impossible to appreciate that a high proportion of the million British imperial troops scattered across the territories under the Middle East Command were 'artificers, engineers, labourers, dockers, administrators, and lines-of-communications workers required for sustaining modern war in a primitive and remote land' and, for this reason, not available for front-line duties.

On 4 July Auchinleck sent Churchill a telegram to advise that to launch a campaign against Rommel before Syria had been properly secured (the Vichy French had yet to surrender) would 'invite failure on both fronts'. The Prime Minister was thoroughly irritated and again pressed his new C-in-C to go on the offensive. Auchinleck – doubtless mindful of Dill's advice – resisted. Each mustered competing arguments in which the caution of the soldier stood in ever sharper contrast to the impatience of the politician. It was very soon clear, as Churchill commented later, that 'there were serious divergences of views and values between us'.

Auchinleck had other reasons to resist the Prime Minister. In his very first formal 'Appreciation' for the Chiefs of Staff in the middle of July, he explained that, after the 'bewildering rapidity' of Wavell's campaigns, the army he had inherited required 'a comprehensive programme of reorganisation, improvisation, re-equipment and training' before it could undertake any major military operation. Churchill was having none of it. Generals 'naturally prefer certainty to hazard', he responded tartly, pressing again for a 'hard and decisive battle in the Western Desert before the situation changes to our detriment, and to run those major risks without which victory has never been gained'. But in Auchinleck, the Prime Minister had met his match. The former's biographer may have exaggerated when he wrote that Churchill was the only man who could have inspired the nation towards victory, but that 'most people near him realised that he was so ruthless as to appear at times almost venomous', but it was notoriously difficult to face down the Prime Minister. Nonetheless, Auchinleck refused to be bullied, insisting that 'to launch an offensive with the inadequate means at our disposal is not, in my opinion, a justifiable operation of war'.

On 21 July, belatedly replying to Dill's letter about the likely pressures from London, he wrote, 'What I would like to repeat is that it is not sound to take an unreasonable risk. I am quite willing to take a reasonable risk as you know but to attack with patently inadequate means is to take an unreasonable risk ... I am afraid I shall be quite firm on this point.'

With nothing to be gained from a further exchange of combative telegrams, the Prime Minister summoned Auchinleck to London. In meetings with the Chiefs of Staff and at the War Cabinet, Auchinleck made a compelling case for delay, powerful enough at any rate to persuade them that he should not be harried into a premature offensive against Rommel. Churchill invited his obstinate general to Chequers for the weekend, where his C-in-C's 'unquestioned abilities, his powers of exposition, his high, dignified, and commanding personality' made such an impression that the Prime Minister reluctantly conceded that the offensive against Rommel – to be codenamed *Crusader* – should not begin until 1 November 1941, fully three months later than he had originally demanded. Auchinleck had won his first bout with the Prime Minister, though the latter did not revise his opinion that the delay upon which the C-in-C had insisted was 'a mistake and a misfortune' which he was not disposed to forget.

The intensity of Churchill's correspondence with Auchinleck was not a mere spasm of frustration. Though Auchinleck would have been unaware of it, the Prime Minister was simultaneously confronting an unexpected and potentially damaging challenge from Washington that threatened to undermine his Middle East strategy altogether. America's initial scepticism about Britain's imperial pretensions in the Middle East was now compounded by a growing belief in Washington not only that the campaign in the Western Desert was doomed but also that it put at risk the United Kingdom's capacity to defend itself from a German invasion across the Channel.

This unpalatable message was entrusted to Harry Hopkins, who had first arrived in London as the President's emissary six months earlier, on 10 January 1941. Hopkins was tall, thin, and clearly frail, with a demeanour which added lustre to his natural charm and diplomatic acumen. He was very much more than an intermediary. His close friendship with Roosevelt gave him more influence than any official with the possible exception of the President's Chief of Staff, Marshall.

Before he arrived in London Hopkins had sought advice from the French diplomat Jean Monnet (the future architect of the European Common Market), who had played a significant part in persuading Roosevelt that America should become the 'great arsenal of Democracy' by putting the nation's industrial capacity on a war footing. Monnet advised him that 'Churchill *is* the War Cabinet, and no-one else matters.' Hopkins riposted, 'I suppose Churchill is convinced that he's the greatest man in the world.' For his part, Churchill was advised that Hopkins was a visitor of the very greatest importance. His trusted friend and Minister of Information designate, Brendan Bracken, was despatched to Poole airport to greet the President's emissary, who looked sick and seemed 'too tired even to unfasten his safety belt'. Bracken escorted him by special train to London, where he met Churchill the following morning.

Churchill, who did not know what to expect, was profoundly affected when, by his own account, Hopkins began their relationship by reporting that his President had sent him to London 'to tell you that at all costs and by all means he will carry you through, no matter what happens to him – there is nothing he will not do so for long as he has the human power'. Not surprisingly the Prime Minister at once recognised that 'here was an envoy from the President of supreme importance to our life'.

For the duration of Hopkins's first visit, Churchill was solicitous in the extreme. In the process he began to build a genuine personal friendship which allowed his American interlocutor to become one of the very few individuals who could both prick the Prime Minister's pomposities and bluntly contradict him without causing offence. On one occasion, the American envoy told

Kennedy, he had interrupted one of Churchill's frequent harangues by saying, 'Now Mr Prime Minister I don't want a speech – I want something I can take back to convince the President you are right.'

By July, however, on his second visit, Hopkins was the bearer of distressing news: Roosevelt's chief military advisors, he warned, had come to believe that British policy in the Middle East was 'mistaken' and the position there 'quite hopeless'; and therefore that to send further reinforcements to that theatre would be like 'throwing snowballs into hell'. For this reason, Hopkins advised the British Chiefs of Staff that the Americans would be unwilling to provide a large quantity of armaments 'if we mean to allot them to the Middle East, especially in view of the fact that the British Isles and other vital areas ... are still inadequately defended'. To ram the point home, Hopkins added bluntly that, if the British persisted, the Americans 'would prefer to keep the equipment for themselves rather than let it go to the United Kingdom'.

Even more disconcertingly, in a conversation with Churchill, Hopkins not only reiterated this position but opened their exchanges by advising that, in any case, 'the new situation created by Hitler's invasion of Russia' would have an impact on the volume of Lend-Lease supplies available to Britain. In response to this, Kennedy wrote an aide memoire for the Chiefs of Staff on 23 July restating the British case for remaining in the Middle East – to protect India, the Persian Gulf, the Red Sea, and the Mediterranean – and arguing that to this end the Americans should be prevailed upon to supply 'large numbers of tanks and aircraft for the Middle East, before the end of the year'.

The next day, at a further meeting with Churchill and the Chiefs of Staff, Hopkins was accompanied by a small galaxy of US military personnel as well as Averell Harriman, another of the President's confidants, who had just returned from a fact-finding visit to Cairo. According to Churchill, Hopkins made it clear that 'the men in the United States who held the principal places and took decisions on defence matters' believed that 'the Middle East was an indefensible position for the British Empire', but – which was an important glimmer of light for Churchill – Roosevelt himself felt more inclined to support the war in the Middle East, on the grounds that 'the enemy must be fought wherever he was found'. The meeting ended inconclusively, though Churchill allowed himself to be left with the impression that 'our American friends' had been 'convinced by our statements.' As he would soon discover, this was very far from the case.

There was, though, one material crumb of comfort for the Prime Minister. A few days later, Hopkins invited Churchill to join Roosevelt for a tête-à-tête in the United States. The Prime Minister accepted with alacrity; he would go a-wooing with great pleasure and even greater purpose. Roosevelt was apparently almost as pleased as Churchill at the prospect of their first face-to-face meeting (aside from a chance encounter more than twenty years earlier). Codenamed *Riviera*, the talks were to be conducted in conditions of the utmost secrecy in two warships in Placentia Bay, off the coast of Newfoundland. Roosevelt, who revelled in cloak-and-dagger dramas as much as Churchill, did not even tell his ailing eighty-six-year-old mother about his plans. Writing to her on 2 August, he pretended that he was off for a short break in the presidential yacht, to 'cruise away from all newspapermen and photographers and I hope to be gone ten days'. He did indeed board the *Potomac* that evening at the New England naval base, but the following day, once he was in Long Island Sound, he was spirited off the vessel – which continued to fly the presidential flag in his absence – and taken aboard the USS *Augusta*. Accompanied by a flotilla of US naval vessels, the *Augusta* steamed at speed to his rendezvous with Churchill. 'Even at my ripe old age I feel a thrill in making a getaway', he noted in expectation of what he termed the 'Big Day' ahead.

Churchill had already left from Scapa Flow in HMS *The Prince of Wales*, a battleship very much larger than the *Augusta*. As they zigzagged across the Atlantic to avoid marauding U-boats, he read C. S. Forester's *Captain Hornblower, RN*, 'brooded on the future battle in the Desert', and, with his entourage, rehearsed for his forthcoming meeting with the President. After a five-day crossing, he joined Roosevelt in the *Augusta*, where the two 'prima donnas' (as Hopkins had once referred to them) evidently impressed one another greatly. Little of immediate utility was accomplished in their talks, but from today's perspective, it had a memorable outcome. On 12 August the two men put their signatures to a joint declaration of high principles, which the President named the Atlantic Charter.

The Charter's purpose was not to define a blueprint for a joint military strategy but to assert a simple set of political, social and economic principles with which to confront the hideous values and purposes of the Third Reich. Historically important because its text would later be embodied in the founding Charter of the United Nations, the document's immediate significance for Churchill was that it incorporated as a prime objective 'the final destruction of the Nazi tyranny'. America, ostensibly a neutral power, had formally and publicly linked arms with one of the protagonists in a global war.

The Prime Minister's satisfaction was not matched by the reaction in the United States, where the high-minded purposes of freedom and democracy enshrined in the Charter found little favour with an electorate that was still averse to direct military engagement abroad. America was not yet ready to become a belligerent in deed as well as word: at a press conference after the Placentia summit the President felt obliged to insist the US was no closer to entering the war than it had been before.

From Britain's perspective the most practical outcome of the Placentia Bay talks was Roosevelt's undertaking to step up America's unofficial role as a participant in what would soon be known as the Battle of the Atlantic. Since the start of the year, the rate at which German U-boats were hunting down and sinking British merchant vessels in the Atlantic had reached alarming levels. In the three months leading up to May 1941, German submarines had sunk 142 of them, a rate of destruction which came dangerously close to matching the capacity of British or American yards to replace the lost tonnage. The Atlantic convoys were a lifeline for the people of Britain and without them, the government's ability to prosecute the war against Hitler – not least in the Middle East – would have been fatally imperilled. Yet the balance of power in the Atlantic had tipped alarmingly in Germany's favour.

Urged on by Churchill, Roosevelt decided to retaliate by

extending America's 'security zone' in the Atlantic to protect all the waters of the Western Hemisphere. American warships (some of which were withdrawn from the Pacific for this purpose) and aircraft were instructed to patrol these waters and to alert the British to the whereabouts of any marauding U-boats that might threaten the Atlantic convoys. Despite the mood in Congress, Roosevelt used a speech, broadcast on 27 May, to proclaim a 'national emergency'. Declaring, 'The Battle of the Atlantic now extends from the icy waters of the North Pole to the frozen continent of the Antarctic,' he warned, 'It would be suicide to wait until they [the enemy] are in our front yard.'

By September Roosevelt had ratcheted up American policy to match his Presidential rhetoric by declaring that US naval escort vessels accompanying the merchant convoys across the Atlantic were free to attack any U-boat within a radius of up to 300 miles. In a calculated move on 4 September, a US destroyer provoked a U-boat in the North Atlantic into releasing a torpedo at its tormentor. Two days later Roosevelt used this act of 'piracy' on the high seas to announce a 'shoot on sight' policy. In by far the most bellicose speech he had yet essayed, he said, 'It is time for all Americans, Americans of all the Americas, to stop being deluded by the romantic notion that the Americas can go on living happily and peacefully in a Nazi-dominated world ... We have sought no shooting war with Hitler. We do not seek it now ... But when you see a rattlesnake poised to strike, you do not wait until he has struck you before you crush him.' America was yet another step closer to war.

TEN

AUCHINLECK STANDS FIRM

'The Desert Army may add a page to history which will rank with Blenheim and Waterloo. The eyes of all nations are upon you. All our hearts are with you.'
Winston Churchill

In the Western Desert, Rommel waited in frustration and discomfort. 'One lies in bed tossing and turning and dripping with sweat,' he wrote to his wife on 3 July. 'The news of victories in Russia is very good to hear. It's all quiet here so far. But I'm not being taken in. Our stubborn friends on the other side will be back sooner or later.' On that other side, the imperial 'Army of the Nile' – the British, the Australians, the New Zealanders, the Indians, the South Africans, and a smattering of Free French and Poles – similarly sweltered in the heat.

For every man of every rank on both sides it was a test of endurance and character that most human beings are never called upon to undertake. Life for the ordinary soldier at the front during the long summer of 1941 was a daily grind that barely changed for week after week. Food – or its absence – preoccupied every soldier. The British lived off tins of spam and bully beef, the Germans made do with sardines. The lack of fresh vegetables and fruit exacerbated stomach upsets and caused dysentery – 'gyppy tummy' as it was called by the British soldiers – while flies, drawn to the waste, appeared in swarms to settle on food and plates, on lips and cups, on sores and cuts.

For a few, but only a few, the challenge was exhilarating. David

Lloyd Owen, a captain in the Long Range Desert Force, clearly relished the challenge of patrolling the remotest parts of the desert for up to six weeks at a time.

> Water was unobtainable anywhere, except in the main oases and in the odd well which we knew of; but most of them had been poisoned by the Germans, or by ourselves, or were rancid with camel dung ... We never relied on maps – they were useless. We used a piece of paper, worked out longitude and latitude within a mile or two, and fixed it exactly at night by star sights using a theodolite. There was intense boredom sometimes, and intense anxiety at others ... We had some narrow escapes, but the enemy was usually pretty easy to avoid; we were so well trained and alert. You could see the dust of moving vehicles miles away ... What we were more frightened of were enemy aircraft. We hated them ... If spotted by aircraft we would disperse to the four winds as fast as we possibly could and then go flat out in any direction to make it as hard as you could for the aircraft to hit us ... with luck, you might get away with only one vehicle destroyed.

For most men however, the sheer boredom of waiting and watching was interrupted only by repetitious war-games for a future battle, the precise purpose of which was at best unclear and at worst incomprehensible.

It was no better in Cairo. 'There is an enervating quality about the heat which lies upon the city from March until November every year,' Alan Moorehead wrote. With his customary astuteness, Moorehead detected an air of unreality that permeated the mood of the British community in the capital. 'There was through this quiet time,' he wrote, 'something definitely and deeply wrong with the mental attitude of the British forces in the Middle East ... Everywhere you went the men were "in good heart" – or so their officers told you. Probably this was true but it was largely the good heart of ignorance ... Everyone looked forward to the winter campaign with enthusiasm and dangerously brimming hope ... Unlike Wavell's first campaign, there

was no secret about this offensive whatsoever. The only question
was – When?'

Auchinleck had not allowed Churchill to bully him into a premature offensive but he had not been idle. When Moorehead drove
along the coast road from Alexandria towards the front line, he was
reassured to find himself caught in a traffic jam. There were tanks,
trucks, transporters, heavy artillery, anti-aircraft guns, and water
wagons – all lumbering towards the front. He saw squadrons of
new aircraft, vast petrol dumps and an arsenal of weaponry. To his
obvious relish, he could not even recognise the once-primitive war
correspondents' camp at Bagush. 'It was like coming into a hotel.
An officer met us, took our names, allotted us to tents – *tents* we
never had tents before – and our bed-rolls were carried off for us.
They said dinner would be ready in an hour, and if we did not want
a swim we could go into the bar.' And, he added, drily, 'The only
thing lacking was war. It was dead quiet at the front.'

Auchinleck was not at all complacent about the scale of the
build-up. 'We were working to very close margins as regards
equipment and training,' he wrote later. Countering Churchill, who in Auchinleck's view, 'thought that troops could come
straight out of a ship and be put into battle in a week', he made it
clear that 'it would take at least two months before those troops
were fit to go into battle'. His preparations were not assisted by
the Prime Minister, who, in his role as Minister of Defence, could
not resist deluging him with tactical advice laced with frequent
doses of strategic admonition. Auchinleck stonewalled, respond-
ing to the Prime Minister's spirited prose in a stiff and formal
tone which Churchill found abhorrent. At one point, the Prime
Minister's Chief of Staff, General Ismay, tried to broker a better
relationship between the two, urging Auchinleck to write Churchill a 'long personal chatty letter occasionally … I know normally
you would recoil in your modesty from doing so. But he isn't
a normal person (Thank God), and these aren't normal times.'
Auchinleck did his inadequate best to follow Ismay's well-meant
but ill-judged advice but the Prime Minister simply peppered him
with more of the same.

Partly because every soldier and all supplies from Britain – with the sole exception of the aforementioned Tiger Cubs – had to be sent via the 13,000-mile Cape route while those arriving from India, Australia and New Zealand also faced long sea journeys, and partly because of an acute shortage of shipping, it soon became clear to Auchinleck that many of the 100,000 troops under his command were unlikely to be battle ready before the date he had agreed with Churchill for the start of the offensive, 1 November. In the middle of October, therefore, he informed London that Operation *Crusader* should be delayed by a fortnight. Churchill was irked. On 18 October, in a cable to the Middle East C-in-C, he fumed 'It is impossible to explain to Parliament and the nation how it is our Middle East armies have had to stand for 4½ months without engaging the enemy while all the time Russia is being battered to pieces.'

In suggesting that Russia's predicament was threatening to provoke a political storm in Britain, Churchill did not greatly exaggerate. The public had been moved by the plight of the Russian people following the invasion and Stalin had been no less swift to detect an exploitable opportunity. On 18 July, in his first direct communication with Churchill, the Soviet leader had proposed that the British should open a second front in Northern France, which, he advised, 'could not only divert Hitler's forces from the East, but at the same time make it impossible for Hitler to invade Great Britain'. With a temerity that clearly irked Churchill, he went on to add that such a move 'would be popular with the British Army, as well as with the whole population of Southern England'. The Prime Minister's reply, two days later, was robust. 'I beg you to realise [the] limitations imposed on us by our resources and geographical position,' he wrote. 'The Chiefs of Staff do not see any way of doing anything on a scale likely to be of the slightest use to you.' But that was very far from being the end of the matter. By September, the Soviet leader was again agitating for a second front. Led by the Minister of Aircraft Production, Lord Beaverbrook, pressure was also mounting in the Cabinet and even at his own hearthside, where his wife, Clemmie 'felt very deeply that our inability to give Russia any military help disturbed and distressed the nation increasingly'. He had to tell her firmly that a second front was 'out of the question', encouraging her instead to lead a joint appeal by the British Red Cross and St John Ambulance for 'Aid to Russia' which he clearly hoped would siphon off the nascent public demand for an early second front.

Against that background, Churchill now admonished Auchinleck, 'I have hitherto managed to prevent public discussion, but at any time it may break out.' His implicit threat – though he never intended to act on it – was clear: if Auchinleck failed to take the offensive in short order, the Middle East would be starved of the material means required to conduct any offensive at all in order to feed a frenzy in favour of Russia.

Churchill's political frustration was as easy to understand as Auchinleck's military caution. The Prime Minister had already invested a great deal of military and political capital in Operation *Crusader*. In numerical terms, as a result of a constant flow of reinforcements over the previous months, Auchinleck's Eighth Army, as the Western Desert Force had been redesignated, now rivalled Rommel's Panzergruppe Afrika, as the German and Italian forces under his command had been renamed in August. To achieve this crude equivalence, Churchill had overcome the resistance of his own military advisors, fearful of denuding the home front, as well as the profound scepticism of the Americans on whose financial largesse Britain was so dependent.

With this always in his mind, Churchill bombarded the White House with detailed missives on every aspect of the war. 'Weekly and often almost daily I gave him the fullest tale of all I knew about our British thought and intention … There is no doubt that these interchanges commanded his closest attention and excited his lively interest and sympathy. His replies were naturally more reserved.' In fact, with other domestic and international issues pressing constantly upon him, the President sometimes failed to reply at all. This did not deter the Prime Minister. On 20 October, in an exceptionally long letter to Roosevelt, he put his strategic judgement on the line about the significance of the Middle East to the defeat of Hitler. Stressing the importance of the forthcoming offensive, he enthused that 'a victory in Cyrenaica of the British over the Germans will alter the whole shape of the war in the Mediterranean.' The impact of this would, he averred, stiffen Spain's resolve to remain neutral, weaken an already demoralised Italy, and, perhaps, most of all, 'Turkey may be consolidated in her resistance to Hitler ... As long as Turkey is not violated or seduced, this great oblong pad of poorly developed territory is an impassable protection for the eastern front of our Nile Army.' Roosevelt did not reply.

Churchill was so hungry for swift military action somewhere – anywhere – that he began to flail around in search of other possibilities to compensate for the postponement of *Crusader*. One of several speculative ideas which did the theoretical rounds in Kennedy's Directorate was the possibility that *Crusader* might be linked to an invasion of Sicily. Churchill seized on this option and, overruling all objections from his Chiefs of Staff, codenamed it *Whipcord*.

On 25 October, in a long telegram to the army, navy, and RAF commanders-in-chief in the Middle East, he urged a 'now or never' invasion of this small island at the toe of Italy. Pointing out that the Red Army had been so weakened by the German blitzkrieg – the panzers were now less than fifty miles from Moscow – that Hitler would soon be free to divert fully two-thirds of his invading armies to other fronts, he also proposed that *Whipcord* should coincide with a faster and deeper advance into Libya than Auchinleck had envisaged; this extended operation was to be codenamed *Acrobat*. Both *Whipcord* and *Acrobat* would hinge on the success of *Crusader*, and together they would lead on to the eventual seizure of Tripoli, which was to be codenamed *Gymnast*. 'Nothing gives us greater safety or baffles the enemy more than the sudden simultaneous upspringing of a great variety of targets,' he advised Cairo.

Whether or not Churchill's plethora of proposals would have 'baffled' Berlin, it certainly flummoxed the commanders-in-chief of the three services in the Middle East. Nor were they disposed to be blackmailed into adopting a strategy which they regarded as hare-brained. Ignoring Churchill's explicit threat to divert forces from their theatre to the Russian Front unless they complied, they informed London, in terms which barely disguised their disdain, that they did not regard *Whipcord* as 'either practicable or necessary'.

Faced with this unequivocal resistance from Cairo, Churchill for once backed down. *Whipcord* was abandoned and *Acrobat* was postponed. The Prime Minister's Director of Military Operations, Kennedy, who regarded these exhilarating forays into military strategy with wry exasperation, noted, 'Whenever an idea, however wild, was thrown up, he ordered detailed examinations, or plans, or both, to be made at high speed. Our stables were so full of these unlikely starters that we were hard put to it to give the favourites the attention they deserved. To cope with the situation adequately, it would have been worthwhile to have had two staffs: one to deal with the Prime Minister, the other with the war.'

In the absence of any other practicable alternative, the focus now returned exclusively to *Crusader*. On 15 November Churchill sent a grandiloquent message to Cairo for distribution to all soldiers serving in the Middle East:

> I have in command from the King to express to all ranks of the Army and Royal Air Force in the Western Desert, and to the Mediterranean Fleet, His Majesty's confidence that they will do their duty with exemplary devotion in the supremely important battle which lies before them. For the first time British and Empire troops will meet the Germans with an ample equipment in modern weapons of all kinds. The battle itself will affect the whole course of the war. Now is the time to strike the hardest blow yet struck for final victory, home and freedom. The Desert Army may add a page to history which will rank with Blenheim and Waterloo. The eyes of all nations are upon you. All our hearts are with you. May God uphold the right.

Auchinleck did not share Churchill's optimism. He knew only too well that the two armies were evenly matched on paper but not in practice. 'We were working to very close margins as regards equipment and training,' he was to write, 'the standard of training of many of the troops engaged left much to be desired. This was due to no fault of their own, but solely to lack of time and shortage of equipment.' He might have added that there was also an imbalance of leadership. The Eighth Army had a new commander, General Alan Cunningham, who was untested in the peculiar challenges of desert warfare whereas the guile and daring of the Desert Fox was not only well attested but haunted the prospective battlefield. In an extraordinary message to all commanders and chiefs of staff, Auchinleck had sought to counter the 'real danger that our friend Rommel is becoming a kind of magician or bogeyman to our troops, who are talking far too much about him. He is by no means a superman, although he is undoubtedly very energetic and able ... I wish you to dispel by all possible means that Rommel represents something more than an ordinary German general.' In future, he instructed, they should not always 'keep harping on about Rommel' but refer instead to 'the Germans' or 'the Axis powers' or 'the enemy'. This was easier said than done. In a personal letter to Ismay, Auchinleck obliquely if indirectly touched on Rommel's 'superman' qualities himself. 'I am not nervous about *Crusader*, but I wonder if you and those who sit at the council table with you realise what a peculiar battle it is going to be, and how everything hangs on the tactical issue of one day's fighting, and on one man's tactical ability on that one day. It is something quite different to battles as we knew them. All these months of labour and thought can be set at nought in one afternoon; rather a terrifying thought?'

Underlying Auchinleck's admission that Rommel seemed to be a 'magician' was a crucial – and remarkably paradoxical – contrast between the two armies facing each other on the desert battlefield. British propaganda liked to portray the German soldier as a goose-stepping automaton, rigidly and unthinkingly obedient to the Führer. The truth was otherwise. The Wehrmacht's military doctrine was known as *Aufstragstatik*, a 'command-and-control' system which emphasised individual initiative. Developed by the Prussian army in the nineteenth century and updated for the twentieth, the doctrine emphasised speed, flexibility and energy focussed at a decisive point against the enemy. The objective was 'not just to master a rapidly changing situation but actually to make the situation change as fast as possible so as to paralyse the enemy'. Thus the blitzkrieg, and thus the blistering and bewildering manoeuvres orchestrated by the Desert Fox. Furthermore, all German officers were given a mission (*Auftrag*) to fulfil, and an understanding of what their superiors intended. They were not told what they should do and how to do it but, rather, what to achieve and why it had to be achieved. Each officer and every NCO was also trained to a level two above their own in the chain of command. They were required to 'think' two levels up; but, to avoid constraining the initiative of their subordinates, they were only assigned tasks one level down.

In striking contrast, British military doctrine abhorred individual initiative. Instead of thriving on uncertainty, British commanders preferred to operate according to a master plan 'which specified what everyone was to do and how they were to do it'. Whereas German soldiers were expected to ignore their orders if the situation so dictated, British training emphasised unquestioning obedience. Except at the highest level, individual initiative was generally regarded as deplorable in principle and was frequently punishable in practice in a command structure that was inefficient, cautious, and inflexible. As a result, despite the inferior training of the poorly equipped Italian units under his command, Rommel's Panzergruppe Afrika was far better prepared and equipped for desert warfare than Auchinleck's Eighth Army.

During the summer lull Rommel had produced a grand scheme for a blitzkrieg across the desert which would annihilate the Eighth Army and so lead to the conquest of Egypt. Combined with a similar offensive by the Wehrmacht advancing via Turkey through Syria and Palestine (as, unknown to him, but as we have seen, General Paulus had already proposed within OKW), this pincer movement would bring the entire Middle East under Axis control. Inspired by this vision, he urged OKW to provide the means to such an ambitious undertaking. Berlin would have to sanction a massive naval and airborne attack in the Mediterranean designed to destroy the British fleet based in Alexandria, to annihilate the RAF, to protect Axis convoys bringing reinforcements to Tripoli and Benghazi, and to enforce a blockade of the Suez Canal. If these and other measures were approved, he advised OKW, the British Empire would in due course be paralysed. Unhappily for Rommel and mercifully for the eventual outcome of the Second World War, his strategic perspective clashed with Hitler's own imperative. To provide the Desert Fox with what he needed to prosecute the desert campaign effectively at this point would have compromised *Barbarossa*, and that was not a matter for negotiation. Only after the defeat of Russia, which OKW still thought to be a mere matter of weeks away, would the Führer be in a position to provide the firepower necessary to spring the trap on the British in the Middle East.

Rommel's frustration at the restraints imposed on him from above closely mirrored that of Churchill at the delays imposed on him from below. Just as the Prime Minister had fretted about Auchinleck's caution, so Rommel chafed at the restraints decreed by his own high command – both men arguing that the longer they waited, the stronger their adversary would become. Nevertheless, just as Auchinleck had good reason to resist Churchill, so the high commands in both Germany and Italy had strong grounds for restraining Rommel.

German liaison officers in Rome had become increasingly alarmed by the rate at which the Royal Navy and the RAF were consigning Italian cargo ships, laden with supplies and troops for North Africa, to the bottom of the Mediterranean. In the six months between January and August 1941, fifty-nine Italian and German vessels, totalling more than 250,000 tons had been sunk or damaged; a further thirty-two ships were destroyed in the seaway between Tripoli and Benghazi.

Even Rommel had begun to worry that, without a more consistent and greater tonnage of supplies and reinforcements reaching Libya, his Panzergruppe Afrika, would find it very difficult to make progress in the Western Desert. Although Hitler had been prevailed upon to divert six U-boats from the Atlantic, they made little impact and in the middle of September, the Italian navy suspended all efforts to replenish Rommel's desert army across the Mediterranean. It was seven weeks before a further attempt was made, when two 10,000-ton battle cruisers and ten destroyers left Italy to escort a convoy of merchant ships to North Africa. It was a catastrophe. 'An engagement occurred, the results of which are inexplicable,' Ciano recorded bleakly. 'All, I mean *all* our ships were sunk … The British returned to their ports having slaughtered us.' Describing the Italian naval commanders responsible for this fiasco as 'tragic clowns' Ciano also quoted Mussolini as judging that night, 9 November, as being the 'most humiliating day' for Italy since the start of the war.

On the same day, Rommel cabled Berlin to complain that he was not only short of troops and artillery but that, in October alone, a mere 8,000 tons of a promised 60,000 tons of supplies had reached Benghazi. It was obvious that unless this logistical haemorrhage could be staunched, it would be foolhardy to advance even as far as Tobruk, let alone to attempt any grander feat of arms. But, despite resolute attempts by the Italian air force to bomb the heavily fortified island of Malta into submission, the British continued to operate from that strategic stronghold as well as Alexandria with relative impunity.

At this point, Hitler, revealing once more his capricious attitude towards Rommel's theatre of operations, suddenly determined that – notwithstanding *Barbarossa* – the Mediterranean should be seen as 'a decisive area for the continuation of the war'. Observing the rapid reinforcement of Britain's Mediterranean fortress, he began to fear that the British intended to use the island as a launch-pad for an invasion of Sicily (ironically the very idea that Churchill was canvassing to such little avail at much the same moment). Were this to happen, he foresaw the collapse of Mussolini's regime, which was 'already tottering, because of food shortages and bombing raids from Malta'. In this case, his southern flank would be so seriously threatened as to have potentially catastrophic consequences not only in that theatre but for *Barbarossa* as well.

For this reason, and because he had already been alerted to his favourite general's predicament in the desert, Hitler ordered the transfer of a further eighteen U-boats from the Atlantic to protect the Axis convoys to Tripoli. This was too much for the commander-in-chief of the U-boat fleet, Grand Admiral Karl Doenitz, who protested, 'I cannot accept responsibility for an increase of the number of U-boats in the Mediterranean. It would weaken our efforts in the main theatre of operations, without a proportionate increase of our chances of success in the Mediterranean.' In this, Doenitz was both right and wrong. As Churchill noted subsequently, the German decision did indeed give 'further relief' in the Atlantic, where, in any case, the tonnage lost to the U-boats had started to fall sharply from its peak earlier in the year. But, as the Prime Minister also noted, the arrival of an additional twelve U-boats in the Mediterranean – six were sunk en route in the Straits of Gibraltar – sharply altered the naval balance of power in that theatre.

On 12 November the veteran aircraft carrier *Ark Royal*, on its way from Malta to Gibraltar, was struck by a torpedo from a German U-boat and sank only twenty-five miles from the British garrison at the mouth of the Mediterranean. As Churchill recalled, 'This was the beginning of a series of grievous losses to our Fleet in the Mediterranean and a weakness there which we had never known before.' Certainly, Rommel's prospects now began to take a turn for the better. He continued to plan for the seizure of Tobruk, which he had scheduled for 23 November, unaware – despite warnings from Oberkommando des Heeres in Berlin which he chose to ignore – that the full might of Operation *Crusader* was about to be unleashed on his unsuspecting front line.

On the night of 17 November a severe storm lashed at the desert. 'It rained in squalls of bitter sleet that night,' Moorehead wrote. 'Like artillery, the lightning came rushing from the Mediterranean and, as we lay awake and watching in the open, the water seeped through the bedding, blankets, groundsheets – everything. Men crouched against the sides of tanks and guns in the futile struggle to stay dry. The infantry sat numbly in their trucks with their greatcoat collars turned up over their ears ... It was a cold, miserable and disheartening start for the battle.' The next morning as the storm cleared the British armour rumbled forward towards the German front line. *Crusader* was underway.

Cunningham had under his command XIII Corps (led by General Reade Godwin-Austen) and the newly arrived XXX Corps (led by General Willoughby Norrie). Between them they had upwards of 700 tanks and 118,000 soldiers who came variously from Britain, the Empire (Australia, India, Canada, New Zealand, South Africa, Rhodesia …) and elsewhere (including Greece and Free France). The forces at Rommel's disposal included the Afrikakorps (made up of the 15th and 21st Panzer – formerly the 5th Light – Divisions, commanded by Lieutenant General Ludwig Cruewell), the 90th Light Division, and six Italian Divisions; in all 120,000 men and 400 tanks.

Though the Axis army was outnumbered in weaponry, the firepower at Rommel's disposal was formidable. Crucially, both his tanks and his anti-tank guns – especially the 88mm – were notably superior to their British equivalents. Although the British had the edge in the air, with some 700 RAF fighters and bombers against a combined force of 500 German and Italian warplanes, this was not to make any significant difference to the swirl of battle that was about to engulf the competing armies.

General Alan Cunningham, the younger brother of Admiral Andrew Cunningham (C-in-C of the British Mediterranean Fleet), had performed effectively against the Italians in the East African campaign earlier in the year. But that operation had been on a much smaller scale, against a much weaker enemy and on a far less complex battlefront. Churchill and the Chiefs of Staff had tried hard to persuade Auchinleck to appoint General 'Jumbo' Wilson (who had led the ill-fated campaign in Greece but was a far more experienced soldier) to command the Eighth Army, but the Auk had insisted that Cunningham was the better – and fresher – man for the task. The next few days, confronting a German commander who had acquired near-mythical status, was to put his leadership to a severe test.

The battle plan for *Crusader*, devised by Cunningham and approved by Auchinleck, was for XIII Corps to advance up to the Libyan border to surround the German frontier positions and cut off Rommel's line of retreat. Meanwhile XXX Corps, which

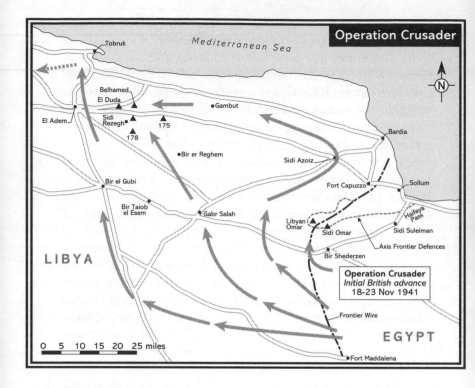

contained the bulk of the British armour, was to sweep widely into
the desert to 'seek out and destroy' the enemy panzers and then
head for Tobruk, where the besieged garrison had held Rommel
at bay for more than six months. The combination of a 'left hook'
and a 'right punch' was supposed to leave Rommel's panzers
reeling, allowing the British defenders in Tobruk to 'break-out'
and link up with the 7th Armoured Division under the command
of General William Gott. With his own lines of communication
severed, Rommel would have little choice but to order the panzers
to retreat to Benghazi. The plan was well enough laid in theory,
but the British commanders failed to agree how it would work in
practice. As a result it began to fall apart almost from the start.

Cunningham had expected the Desert Fox to react with alacrity by sending his panzers to confront the British. But Rommel
was more than seventy miles from the front, absorbed in the final

preparations for a renewed assault on Tobruk, and the British offensive took him totally by surprise. He had just returned from Berlin and Rome, where he had engaged in a series of furious arguments with his superior officers who had tried to prevent him seeking to capture Tobruk. At one point while he was in the Italian capital, he was so incensed that he telephoned OKW in Berlin. 'I hear you wish me to give up the attack on Tobruk,' he shouted at the German Chief of Operations Staff, Alfred Jodl. 'I am completely disgusted.' General Jodl, who had merely been reflecting the view that Hitler had himself expressed at a meeting with Rommel a few days earlier, gave way.

With Rommel buried in his maps at Tobruk, the panzers at the front failed to engage the British tanks. Somewhat at a loss, Norrie and Gott pressed Cunningham to allow them to spread out across the desert in search of their elusive quarry. Bowing to their experience, Cunningham gave them the go-ahead. It was a tactical error which had immediate repercussions. Had he not yielded to their impatience, the concentration of British tanks would have been far greater when called upon to confront the 21st Panzer Division's belated counter-offensive. As it was, General Friedrich von Mellenthin, one of Rommel's trusted staff officers, was able to note subsequently, 'Mercifully for us [Cunningham] had decided to split up his armour, and during the day the various formations of the 7th Armoured Division went off in different directions.' At this point, the 'fog of war' – literally as well as metaphorically – started to spread its pall across the vastness of a bleak battlefield.

Alerted to the British moves, Rommel abandoned his planned assault on Tobruk and moved swiftly to prevent Godwin-Austen's armour from linking up with the garrison. Hoping to drive a wedge between the two British formations, he ordered the 21st and 15th Panzers to attack the 7th Armoured Division – the 'Desert Rats' – at Sidi Rezegh, some ten miles to the south-east of Tobruk. On 21 November there began a major tank battle, the fiercest and largest yet of the campaign in the Western Desert. 'It was a wild, confusing, exhausting affair, fought on both sides by unslept, unfed, red-eyed men' in which the British commanders swiftly revealed that they lacked the dexterity of their German counterparts who were

– as yet – far better at 'orchestrating tanks, artillery, infantry and air-power into co-ordinated fighting units'. In contrast, the British preferred the derring-do of a suicidal nineteenth-century cavalry charge. This was not merely in romantic imitation of their horse-mounted forebears but forced upon them by the greater firepower at Rommel's disposal; it was the only way of getting in range of the enemy tanks and artillery.

Cunningham's tanks – British Crusaders and American M3 Stuarts (the 'Honeys', as they were known) – were outgunned and out-armoured. As a result their crews were only too aware that they could be knocked out by the panzers before they could themselves get within effective firing range. Aside from a pre-cipitate retreat, they concluded they had no choice but to 'charge' until they were close enough for their 2-pounders to penetrate the German armour. This was a rational, if desperate, tactic.

Alan Moorehead described how Brigadier A. H. Gatehouse, a British commander in the 7th Armoured Division

> sat on his tank watching the battle, estimating the strength of the enemy, the position of the sun, the slope of the ground. Then he lifted up his radio mouthpiece and gave his order. At his command the Honeys did something that tanks don't do in the desert any more. They charged. It was novel, reckless, unexpected, impetuous and terrific. They charged straight into the curtain of dust and fire that hid the German tanks and guns. They charged at speeds of nearly forty miles an hour and some of them came right out the other side of the German lines. Then they turned and charged straight back again. They passed the German Mark IVs and Mark IIIs at a few hundred yards, near enough to see the white German crosses, near enough to fire at point-blank range and see their shell hit and explode.

One of Gatehouse's colleagues, Brigadier Jock Campbell, who commanded the 7th Brigade (and later earned a Victoria Cross for his exploits), was one of the most colourful and buccaneer-ing members of that elite group of cavalry officers. According to Moorehead, Campbell was like a man berserk. He led his tanks into action riding in an open unarmoured staff car, and he stood there, hanging onto its windscreen, a huge well-built man [and] he shouted, 'Here they come. Let them have it.' When his car began to fall behind, he leaped onto the side of a tank as it went forward and directed the battle from there. He turned aside through the enemy barrage to his own twenty-five pounder gun and urged the men on to faster loading and quicker firing. He shouted to his gunners, 'How are you doing?' and was answered, 'Doing our best, sir.' He shouted back grinning, 'Not good enough.'

One of the 7th Armoured's crewmen, Bob Sykes, recalled,

I cannot describe the confusion of this all-out tank battle; we were here, there and everywhere ... I do not know who was keeping the score but we were losing a great deal of equipment and men ... we were weaving in and out of the battle zone, right in the thick of it. We had developed a tactic of going at the back of the German tank where it was only lightly armoured, and piling into it with some pretty disastrous effects to the engine. The noise, the heat and the dust were unbearable.

James Fraser, the driver of a Valentine tank, described what happened when it was hit by an armour-piercing shell which 'went through the back of the tank, right into the engine and stopped it ... We couldn't bale out then as there was all hell going round us. The lesser of the two evils was to remain in the tank. When night fell, the battle subsided and we found ourselves in the middle of the aerodrome, surrounded by burning tanks.'

At sunrise, his commanding officer climbed onto the top of the turret with his binoculars to see what was happening. 'An anti-tank rifle fired and chipped half his knee away. He was badly wounded. We put a tourniquet on it. By virtue of my seniority as a lance-corporal I had to take charge. I thought the only thing we could do was to try and make contact with our own lines ... In getting away we came under a hell of a lot of small arms fire, but we were dead lucky.'

Despite the rapidly changing shape of the battle, Cunningham stuck rigidly to his original – left-hook, right punch – battle plan and ordered the 'break-out' from Tobruk. This merely added to the gruesome melee by which the armies on both sides were soon engulfed. As Michael Carver, a young officer in the 7th Armoured Brigade (later to become Chief of Defence Staff), noted, 'This was a momentous decision, taken in conditions quite different to those originally envisaged and much less favourable.' But, in the confusion of battle, no one could yet tell where the balance lay or which side would prevail.

However, based on optimistic reports from the Eighth Army's forward headquarters, Auchinleck felt confident enough to cable the Chiefs of Staff in London on the same day – using yet another foxhunting metaphor – 'With luck earth stopped and the hounds in full cry.' But Rommel, who had taken personal charge of the battle, was equally confident, ordering all the German and Italian mobile forces to concentrate on 'the destruction of the enemy's main fighting force by a concentric attack of all German-Italian mobile forces' at Sidi Rezegh. It was at this point, Auchinleck wrote subsequently, that 'our difficulties began'.

Both sides displayed heroic qualities of resolve in the shambles that ensued as they fought with heavy weapons at close quarters and with death all about them. One of Rommel's ADCs, recently promoted to command a rifle company, followed a panzer regiment into the attack.

> We headed straight for the enemy tanks … Tank shells were whizzing through the air. The defenders were firing from every muzzle of their 25-pounders. We raced on at a suicidal pace … In front I saw nothing but belching guns. Then there was a violent jolt, a screeching and a hiss, and my car stopped dead. I saw a trench immediately ahead, leaped from the car, and plunged towards the slit. My driver leaped out even as I did. But before he could dive on his face, he suddenly stiffened up erect, spun on his axis, and then dropped limp … I wriggled down to the comfort of Mother Earth.

As this grim snapshot demonstrates, German battlefield tactics were not invariably superior to those of the British.

On the British side, a battalion of the 2nd Rifle Brigade, operating in support of Campbell's 7th Armoured Brigade, found itself under attack on the sloping edge of the airfield at Sidi Rezegh. A squadron of sixteen German tanks, supported by infantry, came over a ridge above them and advanced on their battalion headquarters. In the fire-fight that followed, as described by the Rifle Brigade's historian, 'the enemy gave everything they had'. Mortars, field guns, and machine guns pounded the British positions which were 'outranged and unarmoured'. With only three weapons capable of inflicting any damage on the German tanks – two 2-pounders and a Bofors gun – their crews remained 'completely composed, completely undaunted' as they were 'picked off one by one' by their assailants. The Bofors and one of the 2-pounders were quickly destroyed while 'all the crew of the remaining gun were either killed or wounded'. Two surviving gunners went forward to drag the dead bodies of the gun carriage away and started firing in their stead. The official history records that 'a little dog was running round from trench to trench trying hard to find its master and being distressingly friendly to each person in turn – distressing because its movements attracted a hail of machine-gun fire'. Within moments the gun carriage and two ammunition boxes were in flames. 'Ward Gunn, who had kept on firing throughout, was hit in the forehead and killed instantly. Pinney pushed his body out of the way and went on firing until further hits on the gun made it unusable.' The next day, Pinney was hit by a stray shell and was also killed.

A tank gunner in the 10th Royal Hussars, Victor Woodcliffe, was fired on by a detachment of Mark IV panzers, which had heavier guns with a far greater range than any British tank. He was knocked unconscious when one of the German tanks scored a direct hit. 'When I came to the tank was on fire, with flames whizzing round the turret. The heat was tremendous. I was gulping for air. My trousers were alight. I managed with difficulty to climb up and out through the top and threw myself to the ground, rolling over and over to extinguish the flames. The skin was hanging off my right leg. Bullets and shells were still flying round.' Though he suffered severe burns over much of his face and body, Woodcliffe miraculously survived.

In his despatch, Auchinleck described the 'pitched battle' on the aerodrome, as 'the clouds of dust and smoke raised by tanks and bursting shells made accurate shooting impossible and at times it was difficult to tell friend from foe'. But as darkness fell on the evening of 22 November, the outcome was no longer in doubt. 'At the conclusion of the battle which raged until after dark,' Auchinleck reported, 'our armoured brigades were finally driven off the aerodrome.'

Under cover of darkness, a panzer unit pounced on the headquarters of the 4th Armoured Brigade. Von Mellenthin later noted with glee how 'the tanks shone their headlights and the commanders jumped out with automatic pistols. The British were completely surprised and incapable of taking action. A few tanks tried to escape and were at once set on fire – the glare of flames made the battlefield as bright as day.' Acknowledging the enemy's 'spectacular' success, Auchinleck reflected that 'the 4th Armoured Brigade's 100 tanks' – which were now out of action – 'represented two-thirds of our remaining armoured strength'.

The next day, 23 November, the panzers closed in on the British defenders. As Sidi Rezegh was transformed into a desert charnel house, General Fritz Bayerlein, the Afrikakorps Chief of Staff, described the bloody climax of the battle. 'Guns of all kinds and sizes laid a curtain of fire in front of the attacking tanks and there seemed almost no hope of making any progress in the face of this fire-spewing barrier. Tank after tank split open in the hail of shells. Our entire artillery had to be thrown in to silence the enemy guns one by one.'

In the late afternoon the panzers went forward again while Bayerlein watched on as 'tank duels of tremendous intensity developed deep in the battlefield. In fluctuating fighting, tank against tank, tank against gun or anti-tank nest, sometimes in frontal, sometimes in flanking assault, using every trick of mobile warfare and tank tactics, the enemy was finally forced back … his only escape from complete destruction … a break out from the ring surrounding him.'

In the swirl of dust, of thrust and counter-thrust, of wheeling and whirling, of burning tanks and broken guns, no one on either side – from commanding officer to lowly private – could know who was winning and who was losing. Not until midnight, Bayerlein wrote, 'was it possible to gauge the results of the battle, to organize the formations, to assess losses and gains, and to appreciate the general situation'. Despite numerous examples of individual gallantry, the British had again been comprehensively outgunned and outmanoeuvred in a battle in which they had fought stubbornly but with little tactical coherence.

The dead had to be picked up from the battlefield and buried. It was a gruesome task that Sergeant Harold Atkins leading a platoon of the Queen's Royal Regiment could never forget. 'The sights were horrible. Some of those bodies had been lying out there for several days: no heads, limbs hanging off, green corpses, half a body ... You would come across a chap who had been killed and it was impossible to pick him up in one piece, legs and arms hanging by a shred. One had to use a shovel, and just chop off the limb, lay the main corpse in a blanket, put in the head or arm, or leg, and roll up the blanket and take it to the cemetery.'

Convinced that his victory at the Battle of Sidi Rezegh – or the Battle of Totensontag as it was known to the Germans (for whom that Sunday was a memorial day to those who had died in the First World War) – had settled matters on that front, Rommel returned to his field headquarters in what those about him described as a state of 'excited exultation' to plan his next moves. Later that evening, clearly calmer, he wrote to his wife, 'The battle seems to have passed its crisis. I'm very well, in good humour and full of confidence.'

By contrast, General Cunningham was at his wits' end. Hardly able to absorb the implications of what had happened – the loss of at least 350 fast cruiser tanks out of a complement of 400 and the 'annihilation' of the 5th South African Infantry Brigade – he sent an 'urgent request' to Auchinleck, asking his commander-in-chief to fly up to join him at Eighth Army headquarters. Recalling later – in language as measured as his demeanour – that the 'shifting in the balance of strength between the opposing armoured forces [had] produced a most critical situation', Auchinleck did not delay.

It was soon clear that the shattering impact of the last few days had driven the Eighth Army commander close to the edge. According to Auchinleck, his protégé was not only 'under great strain' but, even more grievously, he had 'lost his nerve ... I ... found him in a very shaky condition.' Surveying the wreckage of the high hopes invested in him by Churchill's valedictory message before the launch of *Crusader*, Cunningham argued that the Eighth Army should be ordered to retreat to protect Egypt from further onslaught. But Auchinleck – 'with the intuition that is the mark of a great general', drew the opposite conclusion. As he told Correlli Barnett, 'I thought Rommel was probably in as bad a shape as we were ... and I ordered the offensive to continue. I certainly gambled and Cunningham may very well have been proved to be right and I wrong.'

The following day he cabled Churchill. 'I am convinced that he [the enemy] is fully stretched and desperate, and that we must go on pressing him relentlessly. We may immobilise temporarily at least practically all our tanks in the process, but that does not matter if we destroy all his ... I have accordingly ordered General Cunningham to attack with all available resources.' Churchill was delighted, replying, 'Am immensely heartened by your magnificent spirit and will-power.' It certainly was a gamble on Auchinleck's part but, with both sides playing for the highest stakes, it was matched by an extraordinary move by the Desert Fox.

ELEVEN

THE TABLES ARE TURNED

'I came to understand something of the meaning of panic in this long nervous drive. It was the unknown we were running away from, the unknown in ourselves and in the enemy.'

Alan Moorehead

On the morning of 24 November 1941 Rommel took a gamble that defied military logic but caught the Eighth Army completely off guard. In what became known as his 'dash for the wire' he led his entire force in a headlong charge towards the Egyptian border, carving a route which took him directly through the British lines. Alan Moorehead watched 'the contagion of bewilderment and fear and ignorance' provoked by Rommel's own gamble as hundreds of British trucks, armoured cars and tanks 'came flying pell-mell across the desert' retreating from the Panzerarmee. Officers and men, who a moment before had been basking in the early morning sun, rushed to put on uniforms, pack kitbags, beds, and boxes of food, before leaping on any passing vehicle to join the retreat. In the confusion, which was exacerbated by clouds of swirling dust that blotted out the sun, men from one unit found themselves travelling in vehicles belonging to another. No one gave any orders, no one knew what was happening, why they were retreating or from what they were fleeing. Moorehead did not exempt himself from the general mood, 'I came to understand something of the meaning of panic in this long nervous drive. It was the unknown we were running away from, the unknown in ourselves and in the enemy.'

Within hours, Rommel was close to the border, penetrating as far east as Sollum, Halfaya and Bardia – names which, for both sides, were no longer denoted only on a map but hideously familiar battlegrounds to be won and lost and won and lost again. It was now clear that the Eighth Army had, in Auchinleck's phrase, 'grossly over-estimated' Rommel's tank losses at Sidi Rezegh and that, far from being on the point of collapse, the panzers were more than a match for the British armour. To make matters worse from the British perspective, the Germans, who now occupied the important airstrip at Sidi Rezegh, had been free to rescue and repair many more tanks from the ruins of that battlefield than the British had anticipated.

Though the battered Eighth Army was unable to arrest Rommel's advance to the border, there was some resistance, notably from XIII Corps, which, according to Auchinleck 'prevented the enemy from doing much serious damage' to the retreating British Army. Nonetheless as the two armies competed to reach the border first, they became hopelessly entwined: German vehicles joined British convoys; British soldiers used weapons captured from Italians or Germans and vice versa; men from both sides were captured, escaped, captured again, and escaped again; and, on one occasion, in an incident which would have been farcical were it not critical, 'A British truck driven by a German and full of British prisoners ran up to an Italian lorry. Out jumped a platoon of New Zealanders and rescued our men.'

Despite its apparent inspiration, Rommel's 'rush to the wire' soon revealed itself to have been as foolhardy as it was bold. His forces lacked the firepower, the communications, the supplies, let alone the coherent military trajectory to enable the operation to succeed. In the late afternoon of the 24th, as though casting about for ideas or fuelled by bravado, Rommel drove across the Egyptian border to the Halfaya Pass, where he took personal control of the 21st Panzer Division as it dug in on high ground overlooking this critical choke-point. On his way back to the border, his vehicle developed engine trouble and broke down in the sand. Unable to make contact with any nearby brigades, let alone with his own headquarters where he had left a relatively junior officer in command, he had no choice but to sit and shiver in the cold, waiting for a passing panzer to pick him up – or for the enemy to capture him.

It was his good fortune that the commander of the Afrika-korps, Lieutenant General Cruewell, who was usually as steady as Rommel was headstrong, happened to have taken the same track in a captured British command vehicle. Doubtless relieved to see his colleague, Rommel hitched a lift. Thus for some hours the two most senior officers in the Panzergruppe Afrika were lost in no-man's land and unable to find their way back through the wire into the relative security of Libya. When darkness fell they settled down for the night in a patch of desert which was patrolled sporadically by the British. In the morning they were disturbed by the noise of despatch riders, trucks and tanks. It was a British convoy on the move. But unaware that their vehicle – a Mammoth – had been captured by the Germans, let alone that it concealed the enemy's two most important generals, the British convoy rumbled by without a second glance.

Rommel's impetuous urge to be everywhere at once both impressed his troops and helped to secure his reputation as the Desert Fox, but it meant that too often he had no control over the direction of the battle, a weakness that a sharper, cleverer, and stronger adversary would have been swift to exploit. On this occasion, clearly emboldened by his exploit, he spent the rest of that day, securely camouflaged by the Mammoth, driving back and forth through the British lines visiting his own front-line units. However, he had both overreached himself and, in the process, given the advantage to Auchinleck, whose own gamble in overruling Cunningham now gave the Eighth Army cause for renewed optimism.

While Rommel was flitting back and forth across the desert, the Middle East C-in-C was at Eighth Army headquarters. An American war correspondent, Eve Curie, was with him. Noting that the British general was 'a strong sun-burned man with light-brown hair and blue eyes', Curie was impressed by his demeanour. As the conversation between Auchinleck and Air Vice Marshal Arthur Coningham (commanding the RAF Western Desert force) in the latter's caravan turned from one issue to another, Auchinleck sat 'in almost complete silence' until someone raised the danger posed by Rommel's thrust towards the Egyptian border. At this point he intervened calmly to say, 'He is making a desperate effort, but he will not get very far. That column of tanks simply cannot get supplies. I am sure of this.'

Cunningham was far less sanguine. Fearing that Eighth Army headquarters was in imminent danger of being overrun by the advancing panzers, he urged his commander-in-chief to return to Cairo. As Auchinleck was propelled towards his aircraft, he handed Cunningham a message for the troops. It was written with a clarity, simplicity and resolution that was not often attributed to him. 'His [the enemy's] position is desperate, and he is trying by lashing out in all directions to distract us from our object, which is to destroy him utterly. We will NOT be distracted and he WILL be destroyed. You have got your teeth into him. Hang on and bite deeper and deeper and hang on until he is finished. Give him NO rest ... There is only one order: ATTACK AND PURSUE. ALL OUT EVERYONE.'

Strategically, Auchinleck was sure that he had the upper hand over Rommel. But to be confident of success, he came to the reluctant conclusion that Cunningham had to be relieved of his command, a 'drastic decision' which Auchinleck took with deep personal regret. On 26 November his Chief of the General Staff, General Sir Arthur Smith, duly flew up to Eighth Army headquarters with a formal letter of dismissal. 'I have formed the opinion that you are now thinking in terms of defence rather than offence,' Auchinleck wrote, 'and I have lost confidence in your ability to press to the bitter end the offensive which I have ordered to continue.' This brutally frank notice of dismissal was leavened by a private note in which he wrote gently, 'It is no use, I am afraid, my telling you how I hate to have had to do this thing ... it is most painful to me because I like and respect you a very great deal, and I never thought I should have to act in this way towards you.'

Cunningham's replacement, Major General Neil Ritchie, who had flown up with Smith, took command at once. Ritchie did not inspire great confidence and it was unclear to everyone why Auchinleck should have chosen him. A staff officer of limited

battlefield experience, he was also modest enough about his abilities to have protested that he was unsuited for the great responsibility Auchinleck had unexpectedly thrust upon him. Decent
though he was, he was evidently not among the brightest of his
peers; his immediate superior, Smith, was to describe him bluntly
as 'straightforward and absolutely honest. If one could criticise
him he was a little slow.' However, his genial nature found favour
among his fellow officers (if not among the rank and file, who
lampooned him by chanting 'Ritchie – his arse is getting itchy!').
In Correlli Barnett's two-edged comment, he was 'handsome and
authoritative; good humoured in a slightly heavy manner. There
was a bovine strength about him.' At least, however, in the wake of
Cunningham's virtual collapse, Ritchie appeared to have the solid
and dependable qualities of character that would be required if the
demoralised and battered Eighth Army was to renew the offensive
with the vigour and resolution demanded by Auchinleck.

Auchinleck was not overly confident in his choice. As he
wrote later, 'Ritchie was perforce pitch-forked into a command at
a desperate moment, knowing little of his subordinate commanders or troops and told to retrieve an apparently lost battle.' In fact,
until his appointment, Ritchie had been several rungs lower in the
military hierarchy than the two corps commanders over whom he
now presided. Auchinleck decided that he had little choice but to
'hold [Ritchie's] hand' and 'make myself very readily available for
consultation at short notice'. In fact he soon took overall control of
what had – on both sides – become a wholly chaotic operation in
which the two armies had found themselves locked into a macabre
embrace both at the Egyptian border and at Sidi Rezegh. Nonetheless, as he peered through what he described, using the Clausewitzian cliché, as the 'fog of war', Auchinleck remained certain that
Rommel would be obliged to withdraw very soon and thereby
present the British with the victory that Churchill so urgently
sought. And he was right.

In Rommel's 'dash for the wire', the 21st Panzer Division had
passed within sight of two of the Eighth Army's largest supply
dumps which contained vast quantities of food, fuel, water, and
other equipment. But the Axis army pressed on regardless, not

pausing to commandeer the booty which was theirs for the taking. Had these supplies been captured, the British troops on the Sidi Rezegh battlefront would have been forced to retire, Rommel's assault on Egypt would have been far more likely to succeed and, at the very least, Rommel's noose around Tobruk could have tightened still further. As it was – as Auchinleck had deduced – the Germans were in deepening trouble, rapidly running out of the fuel and supplies needed to maintain their momentum. Although there had initially been some alarm, even panic, among the British defending the rear echelons at the scale and speed of Rommel's thrust, a good many officers came rapidly to the same view as their commander-in-chief. 'We just assumed that the German commander had made one hell of a blunder and in due course would get it in the neck,' wrote Robert Crisp, a South African Lieutenant serving in the Royal Tank Regiment.

By this time, Rommel's senior colleagues also came to realise that his rash decision to siphon off two panzer divisions from Sidi Rezegh for his Egyptian escapade had begun to look reckless rather than audacious. With the RAF inflicting severe damage on his advancing divisions, von Mellenthin wrote, 'the Afrikakorps was subjected to uninterrupted air attacks, which inflicted serious casualties, the more so as the Sollum front was beyond reach of our fighter cover. In short … we suffered heavy losses for little result.' For the first time, the Desert Fox had made a terrible tactical error which the British were swift to exploit.

The Tobruk garrison had been under siege for over seven months. For the first four of these, it had been held by the 9th Australian Division. Their spirit and their patience were indomitable. Between April and July they endured long days of discomfort and boredom occasionally interspersed by moments of intense danger. 'Night was the most active time. We patrolled the enemy areas every night. We didn't call it no-man's land; General Morshead, commanding the division and the Tobruk garrison, said it was our land,' recalled Captain Vernon Northwood, a company commander who, like his men, lived on daily rations of bully beef and biscuits. 'The water situation was pretty grim … You had a water bottle a day for drinking. I used to shave in a tobacco tin; after cleaning my teeth I would spit the water back into the tin and shave in it ... we shaved every day to avoid sores.' The shortage of water – almost all of which, like the rest of the garrison's supplies, had to be ferried by sea from Alexandria – was but one of the tribulations the Australians had to endure. 'Dust, flies, lack of water and boredom is what I remember about Tobruk,' Private Peter Salmon noted. 'I read my New Testament about ten times.'

'We had no pleasures ... Never did I see anyone breaking up under the strain, but there were quite a lot of them "desert happy" or part crazy,' the M3 Stuart crewman Bob Sykes wrote. 'Life here was more than tough: the heat by day, the cold by night and the continuous air raids and shelling made one feel it was going on for ever, and that we were actually living in an earthly hell.'

In an echo of the First World War, the besieged formed a strangely comradely relationship with the besiegers as though, despite knowing they would kill and be killed, they had a common bond through sharing the same ghastly rituals of war; mutual hatred was notable by its absence. Sergeant Bolzano, serving in the Afrikakorps, described an occasion when his unit was laying mines around the perimeter. In the darkness, he heard a voice say, 'What are you doing here?' One of his men replied 'We are laying mines.' The British soldier answered, 'That's exactly what we are doing.' According to Bolzano, 'Both sides went on laying mines, not shooting at each other; and left at the end.'

One of the Australians defending Tobruk, Company Sergeant Major Alan Potter, was on patrol when a lone Italian soldier rose up from the ground to lob a grenade at him. He and the junior officer he was accompanying were both hit in the head by shrapnel. Pulling a grenade from his pocket and yelling, Potter ran round a low wall towards the enemy soldier to find the Italian, who had a rifle across his chest to protect himself. 'I took the rifle from him, and thinking that there was a bayonet on it, I tried to stick him with it, but there wasn't a bayonet and all I did was prod him and take him prisoner ... I was losing blood, enough to drench me. Only a few minutes before I had been trying to kill him, and I asked him if he had any children in sign language, and he told me he had four and described their heights. I thought again; how crazy.'

After four months bearing the brunt of the siege, the Australians had acquired a powerful reputation for bloody-minded fearlessness. 'They were quite different to British troops. They were much more dedicated soldiers ...' commented Brian Wyldbore-Smith, a British staff officer based in Tobruk – who could not resist adding with the prejudice of his rank and class, 'They were a pretty rough lot ... Many of them were ex-jailbirds and convicts.' Whether there was any truth in this smear, the Australians were renowned for an egalitarian disregard of hierarchy, a trait which was widely admired by the British rank and file, though not by their superiors. Wyldbore-Smith, for example, observed with anxious disapproval, 'They hadn't got much use for their officers. They clipped their officers over the head every now and then.'

When, out of the blue, the Australian Prime Minister decided to do much the same – metaphorically speaking – to his British counterpart it caused consternation at the Eighth Army headquarters. In September, apparently resentful of the way in which the flower of the nation's manhood was being exploited in Tobruk and lacking confidence in the overall direction of the war, Arthur Fadden (who had just succeeded the far more amenable Robert Menzies as Prime Minister) suddenly demanded that every Australian soldier in Tobruk be withdrawn forthwith.

After a bitter exchange of correspondence between the two leaders, Churchill was forced to yield, as a result of which, Auchinleck, much against his will, was obliged to start the evacuation of the 'dedicated soldiers' of the 9th Australian Division from Tobruk. A few weeks later, Fadden was succeeded as Prime Minister by John Curtin, who proved to be even less amenable. To Auchinleck's fury, this meant he had had to ferry the Australians out of Tobruk and replace them with British units within a month of the planned start of *Crusader* and the intended break-out from Tobruk. Moreover, the operation took place under hazardous conditions as the sea lanes to Tobruk were under constant attack from Axis bombers. To add to Auchinleck's woes, the newly formed 70th Division – cobbled together from units formerly stationed in Palestine, Cyprus, and Crete – found itself thrust into the fray with barely enough time to find its way round the vast defensive complex which surrounded Tobruk before going into action.

The order to break out – the codeword was 'pop' – came on 20 November. By this time – with Rommel still virtually out of touch with the rest of his command at the Sollum front – the British had reoccupied the Sidi Rezegh salient and managed to rescue and repair many of the tanks they had been forced to abandon in the earlier battle. With their support, but after heavy fighting, the New Zealand Division, under Freyberg, reoccupied the aerodrome and from there advanced towards Tobruk. Between the 21st and the 27th, the New Zealanders and the 70th Division fought their way towards each other under day and night bombardment.

'It was a journey with a difference,' according to a Royal Artillery sergeant attached to the New Zealand Division, because

> all around us were burning vehicles whilst overhead streams of brightly coloured tracers passed in all directions ... every now and then a tank would blow up with a show of fireworks that would have done justice to any Guy Fawkes night: though such an explosion usually meant that a crew would be killed and roasted, I think the thought in everyone's minds was relief that it was someone else and not themselves. Selfish and callous though that might seem, the desire to survive was always uppermost in our minds ... [we could see] a vast number of bodies of troops of both sides.

The 70th Division's break-out from Tobruk was led by the 2nd Battalion, Black Watch, which marched towards the approaching New Zealanders in three lines led by a Scottish piper. They were supported by the Royal Horse Artillery, whose gunners laid down a 'creeping barrage' of fire some twenty or thirty yards in front of them as they marched towards and then through the besieging Axis forces.

Both British divisions took heavy casualties, but on 27 November they managed to make contact with each other just outside the town. The break-out had been accomplished. Soon afterwards, the commander of XIII Corps, Godwin-Austen, sent a signal to GHQ Cairo, saying: 'Tobruk is relieved but not half as much as I am.'

Rommel's situation was now critical. Lieutenant Colonel Siegfried Westphal, who had been left in command at the Panzerarmee's headquarters, was so alarmed that he countermanded his superior officer and ordered the panzer divisions at the front to return immediately to the Tobruk salient. Rommel, who had been out of contact with his own headquarters, had no choice but to accept Westphal's decision. He raced back to Tobruk, pausing on the way to raid the headquarters of the 2nd New Zealand Brigade, where he took 800 prisoners. But he was too late to rescue his own forces from the predicament into which he had placed them.

For once the British armour had the upper hand and the panzers were forced to retreat from the Sidi Rezegh salient, a battleground that had fallen silent, a testament to the desolation of war. 'Several aircraft had nose-dived into the ground and stood up-ended grotesquely,' Moorehead wrote. 'Every few hundred yards there were graves – the dead man's belt or perhaps his helmet flung down on top of the fresh earth and over it a cross made of bits of packing case: "Cpl. John Brown. Died in Action." Then the date. This scrawled in pencil.'

German and British graves were intertwined in the sand

as though the men had gone down together, still locked in fighting. Sometimes the dead were laid alongside the blackened hulks of their burnt-out tanks. The tanks themselves still smouldered and smelt evilly. Their interior fittings had been dragged out like the entrails of some wounded animal, for you would see the mess boxes, the toothbrushes and blankets of the crews scattered around together with their little packets of biscuits, their water bottles, photographs of their families, hand grenades, webbing, tommy guns, mirrors, brushes and all the mundane ordinary things that fill a soldier's kitbag and are a part of his life ... Over everything hung the same bleak winter's sky.

At the end of November, to aggravate his travails, Rommel received devastating news from Berlin and Rome. On account of Italian shipping losses in the Mediterranean, he was told, the tank reinforcements which he had expected to arrive within days would not in fact reach Tripoli for several weeks. This was the final straw. On 6 December he wrote home to his 'Dearest Lu', to inform her, 'I've had to break off the action outside Tobruk … I'm hoping we'll escape enemy encirclement and holding [sic] on to Cyrenaica. I'm keeping well. You can imagine what I'm going through and what anxieties I have.' On the following day, 7 December, the panzers began a full-scale retreat. The siege of Tobruk, which had lasted 240 days, was over. For the first time – though not for the last – the Desert Fox had been too clever by half.

Withdrawing in an orderly fashion and giving the British little chance to exploit their advantage, the Germans fell back to what was to become known as 'the Gazala Line', some forty-five miles along the coast to the west of Tobruk. It was soon apparent, however, that even here Rommel would not be able to hold the Eighth Army at bay. After what the German described as 'a very stormy argument' with 'Excellency Bastico' – as he chose drily to refer to General Ettoro Bastico, Graziani's successor, who wanted him to stand firm at Gazala – he was given permission to retreat again. On 20 December he wrote again to his wife, 'We're pulling out. There was simply nothing else for it. I hope we manage to get back to the line we've chosen. Christmas is going to be completely messed up … My commanding officers are ill – all those who aren't dead or wounded.'

As he followed the path of the Axis retreat, Alan Moorehead came across the pity of war in all its pathetic detail. At Gazala he saw a small group of Italian infantrymen, left behind in the rout and without any transport in which to escape, attempting to surrender to a passing platoon of British soldiers. At first the British ignored them. Only when the Italians pressed their case by throwing down their weapons, did the laconic squaddies point their dejected captives in the general direction of a nearby British camp where, safely in captivity, they might find water, food, and shelter.

At the port of Derna, which the Italians had evacuated the evening before, a group of Libyans who had 'gone through the township looting and destroying, and paying off old scores by firing the shops and warehouses' had also set light to a wing of the local hospital. Inside a number of sick and wounded British soldiers, who had almost given up hope of rescue, were lying in their dirty sheets or on the floor among puddles of water, which they had used to extinguish the fire. 'In utter weakness and despair', they had 'slumped down into deep sleep or a coma that served as sleep.' Further on, in what had been a lush valley, cultivated from moorland by Italian settlers into a land that once flowed with milk and honey, he noticed the rank crops, the broken fences, the flapping doors of abandoned homesteads, and a few lingering settlers who stood numbly staring at the surrounding dereliction. Moorehead reminded himself, 'Four armies – Graziani's, Wavell's, Rommel's and Auchinleck's – had crossed the valley in advance and retreat. They left a curse upon the place.'

As Rommel retreated before them, Auchinleck's army pressed on across the open desert towards Benghazi, following much the same route taken by O'Connor the previous year. 'It was an exhilarating journey for it seemed at long last that we had the enemy on the run,' Sergeant Gray recalled, even though it was 'impossible country', a barren land, strewn with boulders and rocky outcrops interspersed with flat sand-lakes where a few stunted bushes and clumps of coarse grass struggled to survive. Aside from the risk of breaking an axle on the rock – 'the thought of being left in the middle of nowhere certainly sharpened the minds and visions of all of us' – the most common problem was getting bogged in dry quick-sands or rain-storm bogs. 'Much sweat and much bad language followed when this happened.'

By Christmas, the Eighth Army had driven Rommel all the way back to El Agheila, the small township 180 miles south-west of Benghazi, and close to the 'starting line' at which he had begun his lightning advance across the desert ten months earlier. But by January 1942, the Eighth Army's own lines of communication and supply were stretched as close to breaking point in the west as Rommel's had been only three weeks earlier in the east, as the ineluctable laws of logistics imposed their rules of engagement with no less severity. Auchinleck had little choice but to instruct Ritchie to call a halt between Agedabia and El Agheila, a line in the sand which effectively became the new front between the opposing armies. Operation *Crusader* was over. With two-thirds of the Axis army effectively destroyed, Auchinleck could justly claim to have achieved a great victory.

In the course of *Crusader*, the Germans and Italians, who had begun the campaign with over 100,000 men, suffered 38,000 casualties – more than 8,000 dead or wounded and 30,000 captured or missing, along with the loss of 340 tanks and upwards of 300 aircraft. The Eighth Army's losses totalled more than 17,500, including 2,900 dead, 7,300 wounded and 7,500 missing, plus 278 tanks and 300 aircraft. In the raw statistics of suffering, these figures bear comparison in terms of human endeavour with the Battle of El Alamein itself but, because *Crusader* did not settle the matter finally, it is a battle all but forgotten in the annals of the Second World War except by those who endured it. In the absence of any other explanation, it may be for this reason that those who triumphed in the Eighth Army's first engagement were not entitled to wear the number '8' on their Africa Star – a bureaucratic cruelty which few of them were to forget.

As it was, those who fought their way to victory in the winter of 1941–2 – many of whom would go on to earn their '8' at El Alamein – were far less jubilant than might have been expected. According to one of the shrewdest observers in the campaign, the 7th Armoured Division's Michael Carver, 'a bitter taste remained' after the battle was over. Those who fought in the tanks 'cursed' those who had provided them with inferior armaments and inferior armour that constantly broke down; those who fought on foot, similarly armed with inferior weapons, spoke bitterly about the failure of the tanks to protect them; and the armoured commanders, 'hurrying from one spot to another to protect infantry from the threat of enemy tanks, which did not always materialise, blamed the infantry for wearing out their tanks and crews by such a misuse of the decisive arm in desert warfare'. Not for the first or last time, this front-line insight into the realities of war stood in stark contrast to the rhetoric of 'a common struggle' by which it was so often clouded.

Yet the Eighth Army's first battle in the desert had ended in victory. Not another Blenheim or Waterloo, as Churchill's inflated rhetoric had imagined, but clear evidence that Rommel was not a supernatural force but as mortal as any other member of the human race. Moreover, Auchinleck's 'gamble' had reaped dividends that Churchill was quick to turn to British advantage in the diplomatic and political arena. The Prime Minister was so buoyed by Auchinleck's triumph that, for a while, he even allowed himself to hope that the Eighth Army would press on with all haste towards Tripoli and thence to Tunis; Operation *Acrobat* – the conquest of all North Africa – which had been put on hold a few months earlier – was suddenly in prospect once again. After the avalanche of defeats which had marked 1941, the Eighth Army's success was a reprieve that caused him a rare moment of satisfaction. 'Here then,' he recorded sonorously, 'we reached a moment of relief, and indeed rejoicing, about the Desert war.'

And there were moments of celebration even as the battle continued. Richard Dimbleby was with the troops in Benghazi, which the British had retaken on Christmas Eve. As they prepared to welcome the New Year, he sat down at a battered piano and, on the stroke of midnight, played the opening chords of 'Auld Lang Syne'. As if on cue, there was an air-raid warning and a few moments later the bombs began to fall. 'I banged the old piano unmercifully trying to drown the din outside,' Dimbleby wrote. 'A stick of bombs fell with resounding crashes that shook the whole building. The louder the raid, the louder we sang. Our guns were sending their shells moaning over the roof, and a bomb whistled down and swayed the whole building as it burst … in the darkness we bellowed our song in defiance of the Germans above.'

TWELVE

ROOSEVELT JOINS THE FRAY

'Trust me to the bitter end.'
Franklin D. Roosevelt to Winston Churchill

By January 1942, Auchinleck's victory was almost forgotten, overtaken by the most momentous news of the war since the invasion of Russia the previous June. On 7 December, the very day that Tobruk was finally liberated, 353 Japanese aircraft launched an attack against the US Pacific Fleet anchored at Pearl Harbor in Hawaii. On that Sunday evening, Churchill was staying at Chequers with the American ambassador, John Winant, and Roosevelt's unofficial ambassador, Averell Harriman. They were alone at dinner when they heard the news on the wireless but the three men had been too absorbed in their own conversation to be certain of the facts. It was Churchill's butler who came into the dining room to confirm what had happened. Within minutes Churchill was on the phone to the White House. 'Mr President, what's this about Japan?' 'It's quite true' Roosevelt replied. 'They have attacked us at Pearl Harbor. We are all in the same boat now.'

The Prime Minister could scarcely disguise his delight. That night, drafting his memoirs, he wrote, 'Being saturated and satiated with emotion and sensation, I went to bed and slept the sleep of the saved and thankful.' Later, he added, 'No Americans will think it wrong of me if I proclaim that to have the United States at our side was to me the greatest joy … at this very moment I knew the United States was in the war, up to the neck and in to the death.'

The following day, Britain and Japan declared war on each other. Churchill told the House of Commons, 'In the past we have had a light which flickered, in the present we have a light which flames, and in the future, there will be a light which shines over all the land and sea.' At a meeting with the Chiefs of Staff, the next day, he allowed his exuberance of the moment to run away with his better judgement: when someone counselled a respectful caution in his new relationship with America, he riposted, 'Oh! that is the way we talked to her while he were wooing her; now that she is in the harem, we talk to her quite differently.'

A little later on the same day – once the President had secured the consent of the nation's legislators – America also declared war on Japan. Addressing both Houses in language reminiscent of his ally in London, Roosevelt declared, 'The forces endeavouring to enslave the entire world now are moving towards this hemisphere. Delay invites danger. Rapid and united efforts by all peoples of the world who are determined to remain free will ensure world victory for the forces of justice and righteousness over the forces of savagery and barbarism.' The national mood had been transformed by Pearl Harbor. Aroused into fury against Japan, most Americans were now more than ready to abandon the isolationism which had keep them out of the war for more than two years. On Capitol Hill, there was only one dissenting vote, a fiercely independent Congresswoman called Jeannette Rankin. A suffragette and a Republican, she had been the first woman to be elected to the House of Representatives and had joined forty-eight others in voting against war with Germany in 1916. In 1940 she had been re-elected on an openly pacifist ticket and now, convinced that the United States had provoked the Japanese attack on Pearl Harbor, she stood her ground despite the opprobrium that was heaped upon her. (Consistency was her hallmark: in 1968, at the age of eighty-seven, she led a Women's March on Washington to protest against the Vietnam War.)

On 11 December, Hitler and Mussolini – though not 'required' to do so under the terms of the pact between the three powers – declared war on the United States. Solemnising this grandiose act of folly, Hitler used the Reichstag to announce that, after victory has been achieved, 'Germany, Italy and Japan will continue in greatest co-operation with a view to establishing a new and just order.'

Over the last few months, Mussolini's incoherent world view had become increasingly unstable. Clearly overwhelmed by the swirl of events over which he had no control and little understanding, he had become incapable of developing, let alone defining, a grand strategy. One day, fulminating against the near total loss of his empire in East Africa, he told his Foreign Minister, 'I have sworn hatred against the British for all time, bequeathing this hatred to all Italians.' The next day, irked by some minor slight that offended his amour propre, he railed against the Führer and all things German. On one occasion, presumably with posterity in mind, he ordered Ciano to record his words precisely. 'I foresee an unavoidable conflict arising between Italy and Germany,' he dictated. 'I now seriously ask whether an English victory would not be more desirable for our future than a German victory.' Now, however, he stood on the balcony of the Piazza Venezia to pledge to the Italian people that the 'powers of the pact of steel' would emerge victorious. In their different and competing ways, both dictators had by now been borne aloft into a fantasy world where defeat was inconceivable and where the combined might of the British Empire, the Soviet Union, and the United States would in due course be vanquished.

On 9 December, pre-empting the formal declaration of war by the Axis powers, Churchill wrote to the President inviting himself to the White House to 'review the whole war plan in the light of reality and new facts'. With the mighty United States finally committed to military action, the British Prime Minister was impatient to discuss the future horizons of their joint enterprise. America had a capacity to produce soldiers and armaments at a rate which no other participant could match: the great question for him was where and when this potential might be deployed. For

Churchill it was a pressing issue that brooked no delay. Roosevelt, however, was in rather less of a hurry.

At first the President temporised, cabling back to warn the Prime Minister against the dangers entailed in crossing an Atlantic Ocean infested with U-boats. His eloquent solicitude, however, concealed a crude political calculation. Roosevelt had quite enough to contend with in Washington without the additional challenge of having to make house room for 'the overpowering personality of Britain's prime minister and the torrent of rhetoric with which he would assuredly favour the American people'.

Whether or not he suspected this, Churchill took the President at face value, cabling back to declare that 'it would be disastrous to wait for another month before we settled common action in face of new situation'. Thus challenged, Roosevelt relented, and on the 12th Churchill duly embarked from the Clyde aboard the *Duke of York*, accompanied by a protective phalanx of other warships. As they ploughed through stormy seas and incessant gales towards the United States (doubling the duration of the scheduled five-day voyage), Churchill and his entourage used their enforced confinement to plan for his second encounter with the President and his military advisors.

As they pitched and yawed towards their landfall at Hampton Roads on the Virginian seaboard, wretched news flowed in from the Pacific. HMS *Repulse* and HMS *Prince of Wales* had both been destroyed by a Japanese air attack, with a grievous loss of life – a heavy blow for a Prime Minister who had invested so much faith in the potential of these two battleships to defend Britain's territories in that theatre. According to General Alan Brooke, who had just succeeded Dill at the the CIGS, this grave news meant that 'from Africa eastwards to America, through the Indian Ocean and Pacific we have lost command of the sea'. To add to their conquests in French Indo-China and, in the course of a hideously cruel campaign, much of mainland China as well, the combined might of the Imperial Japanese Army and Navy was laying waste to Malaya and threatening Burma. The fall of Borneo was imminent, likewise Hong Kong. Singapore – a 'fortress' with which, Churchill had rashly declared, nothing compared in importance – was the next obvious target for a military machine which seemed virtually unstoppable: India or Australia or both might soon be in their sights.

Despite these multiple threats in the Pacific, Churchill never wavered from his Anglocentric belief that the survival of the British Empire required victory against Germany to have priority over the defeat of Japan. But with the Japanese simultaneously following up Pearl Harbor with an onslaught against the Philippines, Guam, and Midway, the Americans were almost certain to have a very different perspective. The critical test for Churchill – the greatest political challenge for him since the start of the war – was whether he could convince the Americans, in his words, 'that the defeat of Japan would not spell the defeat of Hitler, but that the defeat of Hitler made the finishing off of Japan merely a matter of time and trouble'.

To this end, mercifully untroubled by seasickness, he dictated four long papers which, taken together, have been widely judged to comprise 'an immense feat of intellectual effort and foresight' that formed 'one of the great state papers of the war'. 'WW1', as this four-part document was entitled, was a strategic tour d'horizon that shaped a grand strategy for the new Anglo-American Alliance. In the very first of these papers, he cut to the chase. Foreseeing – with unwarranted optimism – 'the total destruction of the enemy force in Libya before the end of the year', he argued for a joint Anglo-American campaign to occupy French-held North and West Africa. With Britain already in control of all the territory between Tunis and Egypt, this operation would 'secure free passage to the Levant and the Suez Canal' and should form the 'main offensive effort' of the Allies during 1942. The clarity of his vision was not in doubt: victory in the Middle East, North Africa and the Mediterranean should be the first major step along the way to the final destruction of the Nazi threat to the world.

This arresting proposal was unlikely to find favour in Washington. Although, in secret meetings at official level in the early months of 1941, both sides had agreed that, in the event of America entering the war, the Allies would make the defeat of Germany their priority, the participants had calculated without the impact of Pearl Harbor. Now the hunger for vengeance against the perpetrators of that outrage was bound to affect American attitudes even at the highest levels of government. In or out of the 'harem', Washington was not to be taken for granted. 'We were conscious of a serious danger,' Churchill recalled, 'that the United States might pursue the war against Japan in the Pacific and leave us to fight Germany and Italy in Europe, Africa, and the Middle East.' The challenge facing Churchill at Arcadia – as the series of meetings between the two leaders was codenamed – was immense. It would be hard enough to confirm a 'Germany First' strategy, let alone to persuade Roosevelt and his senior advisors that – so far from engaging the enemy directly on the soil of Europe – the destruction of Nazism should begin with an Allied invasion of North Africa, the whereabouts of which for many American voters remained an inconsequential mystery.

When Churchill and his party landed at Hampton Roads, they were flown straight to Washington, where the Prime Minister was heartened to see that the President himself was at the airport to greet them. Roosevelt's welcome was fulsome: Churchill was to stay at the White House for the duration of Arcadia as his personal guest. Even for so seasoned a statesman this was an entrancing prospect and the experience – over the following three weeks – fully lived up to its promise. The two leaders saw each other for several hours each day and always ate lunch in each other's company. In the evening Roosevelt prepared cocktails before dinner and, 'as a mark of respect', Churchill wheeled his host from the room – improbable as it may seem – likening himself to 'Sir Walter Raleigh spreading his cloak before Queen Elizabeth'. As both men did much of their work in bed – from necessity in the President's case, from eccentricity in Churchill's – they went to and from each other's sleeping quarters almost at will.

The Christmas celebrations proved especially delightful. There was a candlelit tree in the White House garden and, on Christmas Eve, both men spoke from the balcony overlooking the lawn. Churchill wooed his audience with characteristic eloquence: 'Here, in the midst of war, raging and roaring over all the lands and seas, creeping nearer to our hearths and homes, here amid all the tumult, we have tonight the peace of spirit in each cottage home and in every generous heart.' At church on Christmas Day he 'found peace in the simple service and enjoyed singing the well-known hymns, and one, "O little town of Bethlehem" I had never heard before"'.

Neither leader allowed himself to be distracted for long from the grave business before them. At their first meeting, on the evening of his arrival on 22 December, Churchill at once raised his proposal for a joint military operation in French North Africa (Morocco, Algeria, and Tunisia) to complement Britain's campaign in Egypt and Libya. The Prime Minister had first broached the subject the previous May, so this did not come as a complete surprise to Roosevelt. At that time, the President had resisted Churchill's request for a variety of supportive actions to counter the German threat to British interests in the Middle East. He had even suggested – in so many words – that it would not greatly matter if Britain were forced 'to withdraw further in the Eastern Mediterranean' and that it would not constitute a 'great debacle or surrender'. The war, he avowed, would be won in 'the Indian Ocean and the Atlantic Ocean'.

Churchill had been offended by the inference that the Middle East was of secondary importance and his reply was swift and blunt: to lose the Middle East would have 'grave' consequences, increasing 'the hazards of the Atlantic and Pacific and could hardly fail to prolong the war with all the suffering and military dangers that this would entail'. Urging Roosevelt to appreciate that Spain, Vichy France, Turkey and Japan would all be influenced by the outcome of the Middle East struggle, he had pressed for an early declaration of United States belligerency before 'vast balances' started to tilt 'heavily to our disadvantage'.

Clearly aware that he had trod heavily on a prime ministerial corn, Roosevelt responded in soothing tones, reassuring Churchill that he had not intended to minimise the gravity of the position in the Middle East. His previous message had merely been to indicate that a withdrawal from the Middle East would not of itself 'mean the defeat of our mutual interests' because the outcome would ultimately be determined in the Atlantic, insisting that 'unless Hitler can win there he cannot win anywhere in the world in the end'.

This was not Churchill's view. From Britain's perspective, safe passage across the Atlantic for the convoys bringing vital supplies to the United Kingdom and other war fronts – especially the Middle East – was essential, but only as a precondition for final victory. So far as Churchill was concerned, defeat in the Middle East and the Mediterranean would be a calamitous setback for the 'mutual interests' referred to by the President.

By December, Churchill felt himself to be on stronger ground. Not only had the Battle of the Atlantic tilted back in favour of the Allies, but in the course of their long conversations Roosevelt's attitude towards the Mediterranean had shifted as well. To Churchill's relief, the President began to warm to the British approach, agreeing – in principle – that North Africa should be the focus of the first Anglo-American military operation of the war. But – and it was a mountain of a 'but' – it was assumed by both men that this was contingent on Auchinleck's ability to deliver the success in Libya which Churchill had advised the White House would soon be accomplished.

In agreeing, even conditionally, that the first American troops to fire a shot in the Second World War would engage with the enemy apparently so far from the source of the immediate threat to America's vital interests, Roosevelt had acted on his own initiative without consulting his advisors beforehand. As soon as he broached the plan with them, he inevitably came up against a well-constructed wall of resistance which ranged from scepticism to outright opposition.

Initially, his Chief of Staff, George Marshall did not openly oppose the 'Germany First' strategy in principle. Moreover, as he recorded after the first formal session, he recognised that the President 'considered it very important to morale, to give the country a feeling that they are in the war, to give the Germans the reverse effect, to have American troops in active fighting across the Atlantic'. Nor, apparently, was he viscerally averse to an Allied landing in North Africa as a first step towards global victory against the Nazis.

At the President's request, he swiftly drew up plans for an early joint invasion of North Africa which – pirating the codename originally chosen by Churchill for the Eighth Army's advance into

Tunisia – would be called *Gymnast*. But Marshall's plan contained a crucial proviso: the Americans would need assurances that the Vichy French in Morocco, Tunisia and Algeria, would not resist an Allied landing on their territory. Since the avowed purpose of *Gymnast* was to inflict a damaging blow on an enemy with whom the Vichy French were presently collaborating closely, such a guarantee was virtually impossible to deliver.

If Marshall was cautious, some of his colleagues were utterly opposed to what they regarded as a foolhardy venture of no strategic value to the United States. According to General Joseph Stilwell, who was aptly nicknamed 'Vinegar Joe', Marshall had initially 'brushed aside' their warnings that Hitler's U-boats might scupper the North African landings by sinking the troop carriers on their way across the Atlantic. But under pressure from Stilwell and others he began to waver and, by 3 January, 'Vinegar Joe' was relieved to note that Marshall appeared to have done a volte-face. Evidently persuaded by them that Hitler would respond to *Gymnast* by instructing the Wehrmacht to march through neutral Spain (whether or not General Franco had given his consent) to throttle the Straits of Gibraltar, he joined his senior colleagues in judging the risk to the American convoys en route to the Mediterranean was too high to contemplate. *Gymnast* – from the military perspective – was, Marshall now agreed, a non-starter.

Stilwell, who referred habitually to 'the Limeys' and sarcastically to 'jolly old England', was animated by a bitter Anglophobia, but even Marshall, who harboured little, if any, such prejudice, conceded later that he too tended to regard Britain with suspicion. Though his colleagues were, for the most part, not given to conspiracy theories, they suspected that Britain's imperial pretensions weighed rather more with the Prime Minister than victory over Rommel per se, and that he had an ulterior motive in his insistent quest for *Gymnast*. 'The Limeys want us in, committed. They don't care what becomes of us afterward,' Stilwell sneered, 'because they will have shifted the load from their shoulders to ours.' For this reason, the President's military advisors grew increasingly dismayed by the influence that Churchill seemed to exert on 'Our Boy', as Stilwell referred to Roosevelt. 'The Limey's have his [Roosevelt's] ear, while we have the hind tit,' was his inelegant but accurate way of summarising their mood.

Stilwell's visceral hostility towards Britain reflected an attitude that was commonplace among the wider public; almost all Americans demanded a rapid response to Pearl Harbor but very many of them were less than enamoured of their European ally. At a private dinner one evening Roosevelt trespassed upon this delicate territory with impressive candour. Using a fellow guest as a foil, he said, 'You know, my friend over there' – gesturing towards Churchill – 'doesn't understand how our people feel about Britain and her role in the life of other peoples ... It's in the American tradition, this distrust, this dislike and even hatred of Britain – the Revolution you know and 1812; and India and the Boer War, and all that. There are many kinds of Americans of course, but as a people, as a country, we're opposed to imperialism – we can't stomach it.'

If Churchill was at all put out by such disclosures, he did not allow them to deflect him from his purpose. On Boxing Day he had been escorted by a posse of police outriders from the White House to Capitol Hill, passing what he described as 'great crowds' and 'cheering masses', before addressing both Houses of Congress. The reception for his speech did much to establish his standing in America. Despite the fact that most legislators deplored the British Empire and judged the Prime Minister's rhetoric on the subject as antediluvian, his carefully constructed vision of their shared destiny confounded their prejudice. When he avowed 'my hope and faith, sure and inviolate, that in the days to come the British and American peoples will for their own safety and for the good of all walk together side by side in majesty, in justice, and in peace', they were moved to reward him with a far from dutiful standing ovation. However, this display of transatlantic amity made little impact on Roosevelt's military advisors, whose suspicions about Churchill's imperial appetite continued to fester.

The symbolic centrepiece of the Arcadia Conference was a solemn 'Declaration by the United Nations' pledging an abiding commitment by its twenty-six signatories, including Russia and China, to the principles of life, liberty, religious freedom (to which the Soviets gave only grudging assent), justice and human rights. Codifying the Atlantic Charter, which the two leaders had signed at Placentia Bay five months earlier, the Declaration also had to be carefully negotiated between Britain and America, to ensure that it was so worded as to avoid exposing their deep underlying differences about empire, free trade (a shared principle which was nonetheless compromised by the 'Empire Preferences' with which Britain protected its imperial hegemony), and the rights of all people to self-determination.

More pressingly, the Declaration, which was signed on 1 January 1942, pledged the signatories to co-operate fully in their common struggle 'against savage and brutal forces seeking to subjugate the world'. Shorn of this high-flown rhetoric, the challenge for the Allies was, however, to agree where and when this united struggle should begin. Despite their tentative agreement to grapple with Hitler in North Africa, their efforts to transform this overarching objective into an agreed strategy for military action in the desert was to prove the most testing diplomatic challenge that either the Prime Minister or the President had yet faced. The Middle East would prove the litmus test of their good faith and mutual regard.

On 9 January Marshall sent Roosevelt a memorandum that 'breathed freezing cold over *Gymnast*'. Laying out a variety of logistical and tactical problems which reinforced his personal change of heart, Marshall warned that the risk of French resistance made *Gymnast* 'a very dangerous operation' which would have 'a very detrimental effect on the morale of the American people'. Roosevelt's political antennae were immediately receptive. Despite the understanding he had reached with Churchill, he now declared that America could 'take no chances on the possibility of our first major expedition being a failure ... if the risk looks great, we must think twice before we go ahead'.

Nonetheless Churchill remained optimistic. Despite the slow and sticky progress of the talks, he comforted himself with the thought that the President still agreed with him about the importance of North Africa. In an oblique reference to this presentiment, he commented sinuously, 'our thoughts flowed in the same direction, although it was not yet necessary for either of us to discuss the particular method'. His hopes were further fuelled by the President's decision during Arcadia to approve the despatch of four US Army divisions to Northern Ireland. This deployment was ostensibly to shore up Britain's defences and to form the vanguard of a future cross-Channel Allied invasion of France. But Churchill had another plan. For every American division to cross the Atlantic in the direction of the United Kingdom, he determined that an equivalent force could be despatched from Britain to the Middle East and North Africa – 'the first step towards an Allied descent on Morocco, Algeria or Tunis, on which my heart was set'. Brazenly conceding that 'few, if any, saw it in this light', he felt sure – without offering an explanation of how he came to this conclusion – that the President was 'quite conscious' that this was his intention. Churchill thus prepared to leave Washington confident that, notwithstanding the obstacles which might be put in his path by the American Chiefs, Roosevelt was still receptive to the grand strategy which he had enshrined in the strategic papers he had written on his way across the Atlantic.

As the Prime Minister prepared to take his leave of the White House, there was untimely news from Libya. So far from facing imminent destruction by the Eighth Army as he had predicted, Rommel's panzers were securely dug in on a defensive front line south of Benghazi and the British advance, at the end of its long logistical leash, had stalled. Whether or not Roosevelt was as committed to *Gymnast* as Churchill liked to suppose was no longer of immediate moment; it was obvious that he was now in no position to deliver his side of the bargain which he had struck with the American President at the start of their talks.

In a long memorandum which he drafted before his departure and shared with his hosts, he conceded that the 'stubborn resistance of the enemy' in Libya would 'retard or even prevent' the promised British victory in Libya; the capture of Tripoli was no longer the foregone conclusion that it had seemed to be three weeks earlier. Without *Acrobat*, there could be no *Gymnast*, which meant that any prospect of an Allied landing in North Africa would have to be put on hold until the battered Eighth Army was once again strong enough to launch an offensive finally to drive Rommel out of Libya. At the very least it would take four months to provide the reinforcements necessary to achieve this.

Despite this setback, Churchill departed Washington in good heart. As he left the White House on 14 January he was cheered by the fact that Roosevelt's parting words to him were, 'Trust me to the bitter end.'

Hitler's mood should have been rather less buoyant than he allowed it to appear. The projected annihilation of the Soviet Union had stalled. Instead of taking Moscow on schedule, the panzers had been repulsed virtually at the gates of the city by a Red Army clearly willing to sacrifice all to save the Motherland. Both sides had fought with a terrible ferocity, enduring a level of slaughter which bore comparison with any battle in history. But with temperatures falling to minus 40 degrees, the Russian winter was now claiming more Axis lives from frostbite and disease than were being lost in combat. The Führer's consolation was that, despite a massive counter-attack by the Red Army on all fronts, the Wehrmacht's three army groups had yet to surrender any captured territory of significance; the siege of Leningrad was slowly throttling the life out of the city; and in Berlin, OKW still felt confident enough to plan on the assumption that the Soviet Union would be broken within six months. Apparently untroubled by the fact that the awesome power of the United States was now poised to be directly and decisively deployed against him alongside Britain, Hitler approached 1942 with unbounded hubris, his vision for the One Thousand Year Reich intact.

Inspired by this fantastical prospect, he once again turned his attention to the Middle East. On 3 January he informed the Japanese ambassador that, as soon as the weather improved, he would march into the Caucasus and thence into Iran and Iraq. This, he explained patiently, would inspire the Arabs to rise up against the British. He also dusted off Order Number 32, which, six months earlier, had so enthused leading figures in OKW with its prospect of a twin-pronged attack on the Middle East. Convincing himself that the 'English' were in dire straits, stretched to the limit by the competing demands of North Africa, Russia, and India, he predicted that Churchill would soon be forced to pull troops out of North Africa. At this point, he avowed, Rommel would be provided with 'everything that he needed' finally to bring the British to the negotiating table.

In the course of his 1942 New Year's message to Mussolini, Hitler gave an extended résumé of the Wehrmacht's progress in Russia. The Italian Foreign Minister was unimpressed; Hitler's commentary, he noted was 'mostly excuses and not explanations' for the slow rate of progress. Nonetheless, with 200,000 Italian troops serving on the Russian Front, Il Duce was apparently 'cheered' by the Führer's appraisal.

Incoherently resentful of the German leader for failing to promise the restoration of his empire in North Africa, Mussolini was nonetheless astute enough to suppose that Hitler must have glossed over his setbacks in Russia by falsifying the evidence in the optimistic communiqués he issued from the headquarters which he had established in Poland at the 'Wolf's Lair', the huge military and administrative complex deep in the forest some thirty miles from the Soviet border from where he presided over *Barbarossa*. Hitler, Mussolini sneered, 'has used big figures to impress people like that jackass Roosevelt'. Warming to this theme, he added 'they are both big jackasses and belong to kindred races'. From Il Duce's demented perspective, America was not only run by a 'jackass' but peopled by 'Niggers' and 'Jews'; in Germany, meanwhile, the other 'jackass' had failed to use his power even to abolish the festival of Christmas, which 'reminds one only of the birth of a Jew who gave to the world debilitating and devitalising theories, and who especially contrived to trick Italy through the disintegrating power of the Popes'.

Such ravings were not infrequent. Reacting to a powerful speech by the American President earlier in the year, Mussolini had ranted that 'never in the course of history' had a nation been guided by 'a paralytic'; and that there had been 'bald kings, fat kings, handsome and even stupid kings but never kings who in order to go to the bathroom and the dinner table, had to be supported by other men'.

In their unhinged ways, Hitler and Mussolini inhabited a parallel universe of unreason which appeared to protect them from discerning with any clarity the devastating impact of the fact that the 'paralytic' in the White House had now committed the latent might of the United States armed forces to their total destruction. However, they were about to be confirmed in their self-delusions by the unexpected and astonishing performance of Hitler's favourite general in North Africa.

THIRTEEN

THE DESERT FOX GOES HUNTING

'Have you not got a single general in the army who can win battles, have none of them any ideas, must we continually lose battles in this way?'

Winston Churchill

On 17 January 1942, in an exuberant letter to his wife, Rommel wrote, 'The situation is developing to our advantage and I'm full of plans I daren't say anything about round here. They'd think me crazy.' The day before he had told Cruewell, his Afrikakorps commander, that they were to launch a counter-offensive against the British four days later, on the evening of 21 January. Because he was rightly convinced that his superiors would have forbidden it, the Desert Fox concealed his plans both from General Ugo Cavallero, the Axis commander-in-chief in North Africa, and from OKW. The preparations for the renewed offensive were made in complete secrecy under cover of dark. At Middle East Command in Cairo, relying on faulty and over-optimistic intelligence reports, Auchinleck drew the conclusion that 'the enemy seemed too weak to stage a counter-offensive'. For the second time Rommel was about to catch the British unawares.

In December the Royal Navy had sunk two ships loaded with tanks destined for Benghazi and Tripoli. Assuming that further shipments could not arrive until the end of January, Cairo flatly rejected reports from Eighth Army reconnaissance patrols that the enemy had nonetheless been reinforced by a significant number of replacement tanks. According to General Frank Messervy, temporarily in command of the 1st Armoured Division, this 'infuriated the forward troops who had actually seen them'. In reality, two Axis convoys, escorted by Italian battleships, had made it through the Mediterranean with fuel, ammunition and four panzer companies, thus, in von Mellenthin's words, 'greatly increasing the hitting power of the Afrikakorps'.

For the first time in many months, the Axis had wrested control of the sea lanes between Italy and the North African coast from the RAF and the Royal Navy. Malta was under sustained bombardment by Luftwaffe squadrons which had been released from the Russian Front for the purpose; and Alexandria, the headquarters of Britain's Mediterranean Fleet, had just been subjected to a daring assault by Italian commandos. On 18 December a posse of one-man operated 'human' torpedoes entered the harbour undetected and attached time-bombs to the hulls of the Royal Navy's two remaining battleships in the Mediterranean, the *Queen Elizabeth* and *Valiant*, scuppering both ships and putting them out of action for many months.

In a separate incident in the early hours of the following day, a British naval squadron – 'K' Force – hit a minefield. Several ships were severely damaged and one cruiser, HMS Neptune, sank; altogether this disaster cost the lives of 834 officers and men. As a result, except for 'the island's defiant guns and empty harbour, nothing remained in the two thousand miles between Gibraltar and Alexandria of Britain's mastery of the Mediterranean but three cruisers and a handful of destroyers and submarines'.

Within a matter of days, the positions in North Africa had been reversed: the Eighth Army, far from its main base, was fully extended and under-supplied while the Panzerarmee, close to its main base, was under-extended and fully supplied. With reinforcements arriving at a rate which even Rommel had not anticipated, the consequences for the British were immediate and disastrous.

Despite this, in response to an anxious cable from the Prime Minister (who was still in Washington), Auchinleck offered him a reassuring assessment. The enemy was 'hard-pressed more than we dared to think' and Rommel's divisions were 'divisions only in name ... much disorganised, short of senior officers, short of material, and due to our continuous pressure are tired and certainly not as strong as their total strength, 35,000, might be thought to indicate', he wrote on 12 January. Unhappily, Auchinleck had been misled by raw data, gleaned from deciphering 'Enigma' signals emanating from Berlin, in which Rommel, as usual, had exaggerated his weakness in order to wring reinforcements from OKW. British intelligence in Cairo made the mistake of accepting the Desert Fox's protestations at face value. Auchinleck had misread the runes in the sand.

Two weeks later, Sergeant Gray, on survey duties for his artillery regiment, was sitting on high ground by a beacon near the El Agheila front line. The sky was clear and visibility was good. 'I was at relative peace with the world as I "swept" the hills with my binoculars,' he recalled. 'I detected signs of activity. Closer examination showed a cluster of tanks approaching.' At first Gray assumed it was a British unit returning from patrol, 'then I began to have suspicions for it was a mighty big patrol ... I noticed a flash from the gun on one of the leading tanks ... and realised "our tanks" were "their" tanks.' He and two colleagues hurried back to their forward headquarters to find most of the staff there already 'packed and ready for the road ... Rommel and his merry men had overrun all forward positions and we had been given up for lost'.

The Desert Fox had launched his counter-attack with a speed and daring which left the British reeling and Auchinleck humiliatingly wrong-footed. Rommel's imagination had not ceased to inspire him with visions of an advance on Egypt to Suez and Palestine and beyond; nor would he pause until he had reached Iraq and Iran, where he would seize oil wells before advancing on Russia from the south. Given the resources at his disposal, this was an improbable meander, but his lightning attack on the morning of 21 January was nonetheless devastating.

The panzers, most of which were newly arrived from Italy, faced a greater threat from the topography and ground conditions – heavy sand dunes and deep swamps – than from the Eighth Army, whose forward positions soon crumbled. A German gunnery officer, Heinz-Werner Schmidt, described how he and his colleagues 'leapfrogged from one vantage point to another, while our panzers, stationary and hull down if possible, provided protective fire. Then we would establish ourselves to give them protective fire while they swept on again.' This fluid integration of armour and artillery contrasted sharply with the stratagems favoured by British commanders, who found it almost impossible to integrate their firepower with similar flexibility. As a result, Schmidt noted, 'despite the liveliness of his fire, the enemy's tanks were not able to hold up our advance'.

The following day Rommel, wrote exultantly to his wife, 'I wonder what you have to say about the counter attack we started at 8.30 yesterday? Our opponents are getting out as though they'd been stung. Prospects are good for the next few days.' Rommel's advance was so rapid that his panzers soon overran a number of abandoned storage depots bulging with restorative provisions. 'We obtained further things from Tommy's supply dump and slowly made ourselves become Tommies – our vehicles, petrol, rations and clothing were all English,' Wolfgang Everth wrote, reporting that he had 'breakfasted off two tins of milk, a tin of pineapple, biscuits and Ceylon tea.' But, in a reminder that the British were not entirely impotent, he added, 'Unfortunately, the reality of war soon returned again. The English made a low-level air attack [and] four men were killed and several wounded.'

Auchinleck remained stoical at the unexpected turn of the tide. He reported the bad news to London in a calm and measured way, although he acknowledged the setback was likely to 'upset' the British public. It certainly upset Churchill, whose plans for *Gymnast* had been put on hold but now seemed to be in tatters. An early Allied landing in North Africa rested upon Roosevelt's confidence in the Eighth Army's ability to conquer Libya, seize Tripoli and press forward into Tunisia driving Rommel's Panzer-armee Afrika into the clutches of the Allied divisions advancing from the west. In 'selling' this grand strategy to the President and his sceptical advisors three weeks earlier, Churchill had expended much political capital. Now the news from North Africa made all talk of *Acrobat* and *Gymnast* seem fanciful. Rommel had not only arrested the British advance in Libya but had reversed it. Worse was to follow.

On 24 January, three days after the start of Rommel's counter-offensive, Churchill was astonished to discover Ritchie, the Eighth Army commander, was poised to order the evacuation of Benghazi and Derna, which had been captured only a few weeks earlier. He could barely restrain his anger. 'I am much disturbed,' he cabled Auchinleck. 'I had certainly never been led to suppose that such a situation could arise ... Has our fresh armour been unable to compete with the resuscitated German tanks? It seems to me this is a serious crisis, and one to me quite unexpected.' Churchill evidently failed to appreciate the topography in Cyrenaica: with the loss of El Agheila, it was pointless to hold Benghazi and Derna, because a mobile force could advance directly across the desert from El Agheila, well to the south (as both O'Connor and Rommel had already done) and cut off the British line of retreat from both outposts. Unaware of this, the Prime Minister interpreted Ritchie's decision as further evidence that his strategy for victory in North Africa was falling apart. However, his cable to Auchinleck, which concluded bitterly, 'The kind of retirement now envisaged by subordinate officers implies the failure of *Crusader* and the ruin of *Acrobat*', was nonetheless disturbingly prescient.

As Rommel accelerated along the coast road towards the Egyptian border, the British commanders at the front were reduced to a state of utter bewilderment. In the hope of finding out what had gone wrong and how to put it right, Auchinleck flew up from Cairo to join the hapless Ritchie at Eighth Army headquarters. Like Cunningham before him, Ritchie was at a loss. So was Churchill, who, on the 28th, wrote again to Auchinleck, demanding an explanation for the 'defeat of our armour by inferior enemy numbers. This cuts very deep'. Auchinleck failed to respond directly to this severe rebuke.

Had he been disposed to aggravate Churchill's distress, the Middle East C-in-C might have pointed out that, over the last several weeks, a significant proportion of his most experienced troops had been redeployed to the Far East (the 7th Armoured Brigade, two Australian Infantry divisions, four squadrons of the Desert Airforce) and to India (the 70th Division) while two divisions promised to him by London had also been re-routed from Britain to defend outposts of the Empire in the Pacific. Auchinleck had thus been forced to revise his plans for the protection of the thousand-mile front under his command from the threats posed by the Wehrmacht from the north to Persia and Iraq as well as from the east.

This 'churn' of manpower from one front to another had created a vicious cycle of self-inflicted setbacks, a pattern of deployment and redeployment by which desert veterans were despatched to hold the line on other fronts to be replaced by inexperienced newcomers who struggled to cope with the harsh vagaries of desert combat. By the time these troops were battle-hardened, they were likewise either relieved or sent elsewhere. By contrast, Rommel's men – especially the Afrikakorps – were not only experienced but highly trained and, from the British perspective, alarmingly battle-hardened.

Auchinleck could have chosen this moment to explain that, following the redeployments to the Far East, he lacked both the men and the materiel required to sustain the desert campaign. Instead – for the time being – he confined himself to remarking that the enemy's tactics in the desert had been 'skilful and bold' and that he and Ritchie were seeking 'every possible means to turn the tables' on Rommel. In words which did nothing to restore Churchill's spirits, he insisted that the Eighth Army was not going to be routed and that there was 'no disorganisation or confusion, nor any loss of morale as far as I can see'.

This was not by any means how it seemed to the German generals on the spot. General von Mellenthin was astonished by the failure of the British to take a stand and at the speed with which their defences had collapsed. Noting that on 25 January 'it soon became apparent that the British tank units had no battle experience and they were completely demoralized by the onslaught', he went on to describe how 'the British columns fled madly over the desert in one of the most extraordinary routs of the war'. In one case the 15th Panzer Division managed to cover fifty miles in under four hours to take the airfield at Msus, where they found numerous supply columns and twelve aircraft readying for

take-off. Their 'booty of the day', von Mellenthin noted with satisfaction, was '96 tanks, 38 guns, and 190 trucks'.

On 31 January, Auchinleck offered a fuller explanation for the
Eighth Army's reverses, citing a combination of inferior armaments and a lack of leadership at the front. To round off this dispiriting verdict, he informed the Prime Minister that he had been
driven to conclude that, in such circumstances, the Eighth Army
could only confront Rommel with 'any reasonable hope of decisive success' when it enjoyed 'a two to one advantage' in men and
weaponry over the enemy. Although this was a sound military
judgement, Churchill found it impossible to accept such excuses;
nor was he to forgive Auchinleck for presiding over such a lamentable performance.

In one of the many ironies of the desert campaign, Churchill's
dismay at the failure of the Eighth Army to take the battle to the
enemy was matched by the fury of Italy's Comando Supremo at
Rommel for doing precisely that. Two days after the Desert Fox
launched his counter-attack, General Cavallero, accompanied by
Field Marshal Albert Kesselring, the German commander-in-chief
of the Mediterranean theatre, descended on Rommel's headquarters to instruct their insubordinate general to call off the chase.
'Make it no more than a sortie and then come straight back,' Cavallero ordered. Rommel retorted that he intended to 'keep at the
enemy' for so long as he had the troops and the supplies to do so.
Cavallero insisted that a 'shortage of fuel combined with acute
logistical problems made it imperative for Rommel to wait until
he had built up sufficient reserves'. Rommel, with an insolence
born of the confident belief that he had the support of Hitler, told
his commanding officer that 'nobody but the Führer could change
[his] decision'.

By 29 January, the Panzerarmee (minus part of the Italian
Corps, which had been forbidden to advance by a still seething
Cavallero) had overrun Benghazi. By the end of the month almost
all Cyrenaica had fallen. The Eighth Army had been driven back
over 400 miles across the desert until Ritchie called a halt thirty
miles to the west of Tobruk. Here they dug in along the 'Gazala

Line', which stretched southwards from the coast for forty miles to the military strongpoint of Bir Hacheim, to await Rommel's next move. But even the Desert Fox, his supply lines once again stretched to the limit, was forced to pause.

Making the best of a terrible job, the troops who had been so ignominiously swept aside by his advance, referred drily to their retreat as the 'Second Benghazi Handicap' (the 'First' being Wavell's similar humiliation ten months earlier). In a gleeful letter to his wife on 4 February Rommel reported that the Panzerarmee's advance 'went like greased lightning'. He had barely exaggerated.

In London Churchill was in a foul temper. Combined with a lengthening list of defeats in the Pacific, the Eighth Army's retreat to the Gazala Line was a bitter pill for him – and his fellow ministers – to swallow. According to Brooke, who had now been in this post at the CIGS for two months, meetings of the War Cabinet were often fractious occasions at which ministers were prone to turn their fire on the military. Brooke, who was far less equable than his predecessor, was exasperated by the Prime Minister's bombastic behaviour. 'He came out continually with remarks, such as: "Have you not got a single general in the army who can win battles, have none of them any ideas, must we continually lose battles in this way?"' he noted in his daily diary after one prime ministerial tirade. Judging such outbursts wrong in principle, he also thought them counterproductive in practice, especially when they encouraged other ministers to join him in making 'offensive remarks at the expense of the army'.

In Brooke, Churchill faced a sharper intellect and a less emollient senior advisor than Dill had been. Dill's moral courage and integrity were widely admired by his colleagues but he was physically and emotionally drained by long hours and the relentless demands of a Prime Minister who had become increasingly irritated by his measured diffidence in the face of disaster. According to his loyal lieutenant, Kennedy, many of Dill's colleagues had long taken to murmuring against him, saying that 'his brain was anyhow not agile enough for his job, that he had no drive, and that he was always half asleep at meetings of the Defence Committee and of the Chiefs of Staff'. On 18 November 1941 – the same day that Auchinleck finally launched Operation *Crusader* – Dill's genial reign came to a sudden end. He asked Kennedy to see him. 'The world is upside down for me. I am to go,' he said. 'The Prime Minister told me last night.' By this time, even Kennedy had reached the conclusion that his boss was 'much too tired to give of his best, and that it was right he should go before he became completely worn out'.

According to his successor, Dill often found Churchill's methods 'repulsive', but he accepted his dismissal with charac-teristic grace and without recrimination. Happily, his experience and expertise were not wasted. Although Churchill had intended to despatch him to oblivion by appointing him Governor of Bombay, he found himself obliged to take Dill with him to the Arcadia negotiations in Washington as Brooke was still coming to grips with his new role. This was a providential move. The former CIGS quickly established such cordial relations with the American team that Churchill wisely forgot about Bombay and instead made him his personal representative in Washington as head of the British Joint Staff Mission. Dill soon became 'the de facto British Ambassador for all matters military' and, following the formation of the Combined Chiefs of Staff (the coalescence of the British and American Chiefs of Staff agreed at Arcadia), he rapidly became 'a key figure in the higher direction of the war'. In a highly charged atmosphere where the new alliance was constantly assailed by mutual suspicion and rivalry, his dogged decency and transparent honesty soon caught the attention of Marshall, Roosevelt's most influential military advisor. The two men forged a bond of lasting friendship which was to be of incalculable benefit in the months ahead, particularly during the intense and tortuous negotiations over future strategy in the Middle East and North Africa which were soon to preoccupy both London and Washington once again.

Brooke was abrasive, impatient, and volatile. Despite an austere and remote demeanour, he was by no means reticent in argument. In the diary he kept throughout the war he did not shrink from the free expression of powerful emotions and waspish judgements, none of which appeared to have been recollected in tranquillity. In his previous role, commanding the United Kingdom Home Forces, Brooke's dealings with Churchill and his War Cabinet had left him less than starry eyed. Nor was he by any means overwhelmed by his new responsibilities as Chief of the Imperial Defence Staff.

Four days after taking up his new appointment in the middle of December, Brooke attended a Cabinet meeting at Number 10 Downing Street. Anthony Eden, the Foreign Secretary, was about to fly to Moscow for what was expected to be an uncomfortable meeting with Stalin about the second front. In Brooke's disparaging version of the occasion, Eden behaved 'like a peevish child grumbling because he was being sent off to see Uncle Stalin without suitable gifts while Granny Churchill was comforting him and explaining to him all the pretty speeches he might make instead'. Of course, Brooke noted, Stalin had to be appeased with more than warm words or empty gestures of fellow-feeling, but to provide him with more than a token number of tanks and aircraft would mean exposing the home front or denuding the Middle East Command. Nevertheless he recorded with characteristic asperity, for much of the Cabinet meeting, 'the conduct of the war seemed to have been pushed into the background, self-interests seemed to predominate'.

After dinner, Churchill had a further meeting with the three Chiefs of Staff. The conversation went round in circles and became heated. Finally, Churchill erupted. In 'the most awful outburst of temper, we were told that we did nothing but obstruct his intentions, we had no ideas of our own, and whenever he produced ideas we produced nothing but objections, etc. etc.! ... Finally he looked at his papers for some 5 minutes, then slammed them together, closed the meeting and walked out of the room! It was pathetic and entirely unnecessary ... It is all the result of overworking himself and keeping too late hours. Such a pity. God knows where we would be without him, but God knows where we shall go with him.'

Churchill was under intense pressure and growing strain. The defeats and setbacks abroad were followed by a crescendo of disapprobation at home. His Arcadia meetings with Roosevelt had been fruitful but the outcome could not be shared with the British public except in very broad terms. Otherwise the news was bad on all fronts and with every prospect that it would soon get worse. On his return from Washington he took the opportunity to provide a 'querulous' House of Commons with a prime ministerial tour d'horizon. To smoke out his critics, he decided to challenge them with a Confidence Vote.

The outcome was a foregone conclusion but the ruse at least gave him a very public opportunity to defend his conduct of the nation's affairs and to expose the irresolution of his adversaries. The debate began on 27 January. Claiming, disingenuously, that 'it had been privately intimated to me that I should be very reckless if I asked for a vote of confidence', he acknowledged that 'wrapped up' in the bad news from the Far East there would be 'many tales of blunders and shortcomings, both in foresight and action'. Urging that none of his colleagues should be 'mealy-mouthed' in debate or 'chicken hearted in voting' he proceeded to lay out his case in such terms as to intimate that the truly reckless act in this time of great crisis would be to vote against the government: 'It is because things have gone badly and worse is to come that I demand a Vote of Confidence,' he declared in an artful and persuasive performance that reassured his supporters and disarmed his adversaries.

Although he made no reference to the detailed discussions he had held with the President about *Acrobat* and *Gymnast*, he managed to make it abundantly clear that the Middle East occupied a pivotal status in both their reckonings. He returned frequently to the challenges facing Auchinleck's command and the multiple threats posed in the very recent past by 'the Panzer spearheads of the German Army' which menaced Turkey, Persia, Iraq, Syria and Palestine and thence the Suez Canal, Egypt and the Nile Valley. And while 'this menace defined itself with hideous and increasing reality …' in the east, Rommel was poised to advance into Egypt from the west. Only the personal intervention of Auchinleck, in ordering 'the ruthless pressure of the attack to be maintained without regard to risks and consequences', had prevented the Axis army from overrunning Egypt.

Although it was common knowledge that the British had evacuated Benghazi, he refrained from describing the Eighth Army's calamitous retreat to the Gazala Line. Nor, for obvious reasons, did he mention his thwarted hopes for *Acrobat* and *Gymnast*. Instead he spoke of the 'many ebbs and flows' in an 'heroic, epic struggle' which had 'proved not only that our men can die for King and country – everyone knew that – but that they can kill'. Then, as though to explain away future setbacks – and perhaps with a degree of envious chagrin – he paid Rommel an extraordinary tribute, describing him as 'a very daring and skilful opponent' and 'may I say across the havoc of war, a great general'.

His peroration held the House in thrall. 'Although I feel the broadening swell of victory and liberation bearing us and all the tortured peoples onwards safely towards the final goal, I must confess to feeling the weight of the war upon me even more than in the tremendous summer days of 1940 ... It is because I see the light gleaming behind the clouds and broadening on our path that I make so bold now as to demand a declaration of confidence from the House of Commons.' There followed three days of debate, at the end of which – to no one's surprise – the result of the vote was 464 to 1 in his favour.

Any comfort this result may have given Churchill or those about him was short lived. With Hong Kong overrun by the Japanese and Singapore at the point of collapse, the new CIGS wrote morbidly, 'I have during the last 10 days had an unpleasant feeling that the British Empire was decaying and that we were on a slippery decline ... I certainly never expected that we should fall to pieces as fast as we are and to see Hong Kong and Singapore go in less than three months plus failure in the Western desert is far from reassuring!' Two days later, with worsening reports from Burma as well as Singapore and the news that three of the most powerful German warships in the German Navy – the battleships *Scharnhorst* and *Gneisenau* and the battle cruiser *Prinz Eugen* – had escaped the blockade of Brest and slipped through the English Channel virtually unscathed, Brooke noted bleakly, 'These are black days.'

Singapore fell on 15 February with some 80,000 British, Australian, and Indian troops either killed, wounded or captured, adding to the 50,000 casualties already endured in the Malayan campaign. The sudden collapse of the colonial fortress – the largest base in the region – came as a shock to the British public though as little surprise to Churchill or his advisors, who had regarded this outcome as 'almost certain' since the middle of December. Nonetheless, the Prime Minister was devastated, ranking the loss of this 'impregnable fortress' as 'the greatest disaster in our history'.

The grim succession of setbacks unleashed a torrent of pent-up frustration in the national press. In a variety of newspapers and magazines, commentators and columnists conveyed the same message by asking the same question: was Churchill any longer competent to run the war or should someone else take the helm? Oppressed by the savagery of the criticism, Churchill's mood often blackened. When Roosevelt wrote to commiserate with him 'in these trying weeks' and to let him know 'that I think of you often', Churchill's reply gave a rare glimpse into his inner turmoil. 'I do not like these days of personal stress,' he wrote, 'and I have found it difficult to keep my eye on the ball.' Confiding in his close friend, Violet Bonham Carter, he said 'I feel very biteful [sic] and spiteful when people attack me,' bemoaning, 'I can't get victories. It's the victories that are so hard to get.'

Churchill's brooding anger at the lack of appreciation shown to him from those whom he regarded – often with good reason – as lesser mortals sometimes tipped towards self-pity. Following the loss of Singapore, he was driven to explain one humiliating setback after another at a Secret Session of Parliament on 23 April. In the course of an extended defence of his conduct as Prime Minister, he could not restrain his indignation. 'I am anxious', he glowered, 'that Members should realise that our affairs are not conducted entirely by simpletons and dunderheads as the comic papers try to depict … Any featherhead can have confidence in times of victory, but the test is to have faith when things are going wrong.'

For Churchill, a victory – somewhere, anywhere – had become a political imperative, both to buttress his own credibility at home and to impress upon America that Britain was not a busted flush but a force to be reckoned with. However, with the Germans still on the offensive in Russia and the Japanese running amok in the Pacific, the only part of the world in which he could conceivably hope for a clean victory in the foreseeable future was in the Western Desert – and even that now seemed a distant prospect.

This was not the moment for the kind of derring-do for which the Prime Minister yearned. Following the damage inflicted on the Eighth Army in its precipitate retreat to the Gazala Line, Auchinleck decided that radical action was required if his forces were to be melded into fighting units capable of confronting Rommel without further humiliation. To achieve this he needed time, and certainly more time than Churchill was prepared to allow him. Another stand-off between the general and the politician was inevitable.

After Pearl Harbor, Auchinleck had been required to surrender some of his most experienced units to add weight to the skeletal British presence in the Far East. In addition, he had to cope with the unexpected withdrawal from his command of two battle-hardened Australian divisions. This irksome decision followed an acrimonious exchange of telegrams between the prime ministers of each country, in which arrogant imperialism in London was matched by aggressive insecurity in Canberra.

The row surfaced in late December when the Australian PM, John Curtin, complained to Roosevelt about the 'utterly inadequate' British reinforcements sent by Churchill to counter the Japanese in the Far East. On Boxing Day – while Churchill was preoccupied with his address to the US Congress – Curtin gave vent to his widely shared resentment against the old colonial master in a signed article for the Melbourne *Herald*. 'We refuse to accept the dictum that the Pacific struggle must be treated as a subordinate segment of the general conflict,' he began, before putting the boot in with brutal precision. 'Without any inhibitions of any kind,' he avowed, 'I make it quite clear that Australia looks to America, free of any pangs as to our traditional links with the United Kingdom.'

Churchill was furious but elected to react with pained concern. 'Night and day', he wrote on 3 January, 'I am labouring here to make the best arrangements possible in your interests and for your safety.' The truth was otherwise. With the exception of

South Africa, represented in the person of his friend and ally Field Marshal Jan Smuts, Churchill rarely deigned to take cognisance of the disparate views held by the representatives of the Commonwealth, dominions and colonies. Though they provided the bulk of the British Imperial Army's infantrymen in the Middle East, he rarely bothered to consult them on any matter of substance. Nor was Curtin mollified: his reputation, as much as Australia's national interest, was at stake. He wanted his Australian boys out of the Middle East and back home to defend their own soil against the very real threat of an attack from Japan.

When a stray secret telegram alerted Curtin to the fact that the Chiefs of Staff in London were contemplating the evacuation of Singapore, he wrote to Churchill, on 23 January, to reprove him for even considering an option which, he said, would be regarded as 'an inexcusable betrayal' in Australia. Three weeks later, following the fall of Singapore, relations between the two leaders deteriorated even further: Curtin's truculence matching Churchill's high-handedness.

With Burma reeling from a severe Japanese onslaught, Churchill cabled the Australian Prime Minister to inform him that the 1st Australian Division, which was then on its way home from Egypt, was required for the defence of Rangoon. 'We are all entirely in favour of all Australian troops returning home to defend their native soil,' he wrote with ill-disguised sarcasm. 'But a vital war emergency cannot be ignored, and troops *en route* to other destinations must be ready to turn aside and take part in the battle.' The tone was distinctly *de haut en bas* and the implication – that the Australians were anxious to scuttle home rather than fulfil their imperial duty – was unfortunate. Not content with that, he threatened that if Curtin refused to allow his troops to be thrown into the fray against the Japanese, it would have 'a very grave effect upon the President and the Washington circle, on whom you are largely dependent'. He concluded brusquely by demanding 'an answer immediately'.

Assuming that Curtin would give way, Churchill sent orders that the convoy bearing the 1st Australian Division to Australia should be diverted to Rangoon. But Curtin did not yield. On 22

February, he insisted that it would be 'quite impossible to reverse a decision which we made with the outmost care'. Taken aback by this revolt, Churchill cabled the Australian Prime Minister to express his dismay but, having no choice but to comply with the stated wishes of a sovereign ally, he ordered the Australian convoy to return to its original course. Just over a fortnight later, Rangoon fell – though whether Curtin's stance affected the outcome is open to doubt; it is probable that the Australian contingent would have joined the melancholy throng who had to endure the cruelties imposed on Allied prisoners of war by their Japanese captors.

More significantly, the incident illuminated the undercurrent of tension within the imperial family as each nation struggled to assert its own identity and interest in the febrile atmosphere of a global crisis: Auchinleck needed the Australians in the desert, Churchill required them in Burma, Curtin demanded their presence in Australia.

FOURTEEN

TROUBLE AT THE TOP

'YOU MUST COME HOME ... *nothing matters so much as the*
removal of the wall of misunderstanding which has grown
up between you two.'
'Pug' Ismay to Auchinleck on his relationship with Churchill

In these black days, Churchill sometimes seemed so downcast that his intimates wondered for how long he would be able to withstand the pressure. His critics at Westminster and in the press continued to assail him for the catalogue of disasters over which he had presided. At private gatherings, to an extent that would have been inconceivable a year earlier, the London Establishment – politicians, editors, business leaders, diplomats, civil servants, and military commanders – discussed his performance with brutal disdain. On 5 March, Kennedy recorded a dinner conversation at which the prevailing view was that 'Winston was finished'. In a letter to Roosevelt, Averell Harriman reported that the confidence of the British people had been 'shattered to the core' and that a 'number of astute people, both friends and opponents, feel it is only a question of a few months before his government falls'. However, Harriman himself did not join this chorus, judging that the Prime Minister would soon bounce back 'with renewed strength'.

The Chiefs of Staff were not immune from the growing pressures of a worsening war. According to Kennedy, even the clinically cool CIGS seemed to be wilting under the strain: 'he was showing signs of wear and tear; he was inclined to be irritable; he did not laugh so much as during his first weeks in office'. More than any of his colleagues, Brooke had to bear the brunt of Churchill's gloomy tirades. 'I just sit silent,' he confided to Kennedy, 'and put up an umbrella.'

Auchinleck could not have chosen a worse moment at which to send the Chiefs of Staff a detailed account of his predicament in the Middle East. His formal 'Appreciation' landed in Whitehall with an unwelcome thud at precisely the moment that both Churchill and the Chiefs of Staff were casting about for a way out of the 'valley of humiliation', as the Prime Minister's wife, Clemmie, described the fevered atmosphere in London. Churchill had cabled Auchinleck on 26 February inquiring about his 'intentions' and advising him that Rommel 'may gain reinforcements as fast or even faster than you'. Reminding him that 'the supply of Malta is causing us increased anxiety, and anyone can see the magnitude of our disasters in the Far East', the Prime Minister's unstated message was clear: I want action against Rommel in the desert and I want it now.

But, so far from rekindling Churchill's spirits with a vision of the future triumphs in the desert for which he craved, Auchinleck's analysis was bleakly pessimistic. The Eighth Army, depleted by the redeployments to the Pacific and Australia was short of men, equipment and armaments, for which reasons he insisted that he would be unable to mount an offensive against Rommel until May at the very earliest, but more probably not before June.

Nothing could have been better calculated to incur Churchill's wrath. On 2 March he drafted a reply to Auchinleck in which, according to Brooke, 'he poured abuse on him for not attacking sooner and for sending us an appreciation in which he did not propose to attack until June!!' Three days after assuming his role as CIGS – at a point when *Crusader* still held out the promise of victory over Rommel in Libya – Brooke had noted, 'I am positive that our policy for the conduct of the war should be to direct both military and political efforts towards the early conquest of North Africa. From there we shall be able to re-open the Mediterranean and stage offensive operations against Italy.' But he did not approve of the means by which Churchill set about achieving that strategic goal, objecting strongly to the way in which his impatient and irascible political master interfered in operational decisions beyond his competence. Although he shared the Prime Minister's frustration at the prospect of further delay, he did not at all appreciate 'another example of Winston's interference with a commander in the field ... he is trying to force him to attack at an earlier date than is thought advisable, and what is more, tries to obtain his ends by an offensive wire'.

Churchill's draft, which contained such choice observations as 'armies were not intended to stand about doing nothing' and 'soldiers were meant to fight', was plucked from the prime ministerial out-tray and redrafted in less aggressive language. But, even when Brooke had toned it down, the message was stern enough. 'Viewing the war situation as a whole we cannot afford to stand idle at a time when the Russians are straining every nerve to give the enemy no rest, and when it is important to increase by every possible means the drain on the German armed forces ... Please reconsider the matter urgently and telegraph your views.'

Auchinleck was so distressed by the tone and content of Churchill's amended telegram that he despatched a fierce private note to Brooke, reproving him for endorsing a prime ministerial instruction which failed 'so signally either to appreciate facts as presented from here or to realise that we are fully aware of the situation as regards Malta in particular or the Middle East in general. We are trying here to face realities and to present to you the situation as it appears to us, not as you would wish it to be.'

Brooke was not disposed to offer Auchinleck much comfort. Although the Chiefs of Staff disapproved of Churchill's bullying interference, they had some sympathy with his impatience: the Middle East commander-in-chief's outlook had become overly 'defensive' and – despite the fact that his forces had been depleted by the withdrawals to the Far East – they judged that 'the longer he waited before he attacked Rommel, the poorer would be his chances of holding his position'. Moreover, there was urgent need to regain the Libyan airfields captured by Rommel during the 'Second Benghazi Handicap'; otherwise the RAF's Desert Air

Force would be unable to protect the convoys carrying supplies to the besieged island of Malta, which was now at grave risk of being starved into submission by an Axis air and sea blockade.

This Mediterranean fortress was of surpassing importance to the British Empire and had been so at least since the Napoleonic Wars. Moreover, as Churchill's confidant Lord Ismay wrote, Malta was 'almost one of our kith and kin. To lose her would be almost as painful as to lose a part of England herself.' It was also militarily unthinkable. To control Malta was to control a crucial seaway between Italy and North Africa. A staging post for bombers en route from London to Egypt, it was even more important as the only base from which the RAF and the Royal Navy could harass and interdict the supply lines from Naples, Taranto and Bari to Tripoli, Benghazi and Tobruk that were the sole means of provisioning Rommel's Panzerarmee. To lose Malta or to allow it to be starved into enforced neutrality would be to hand a massive strategic advantage to the Axis powers, giving them an immeasurably stronger position from which both to inflict great damage on British ships in the Eastern Mediterranean and to succour their forces in North Africa. 'This tiny island', as Ismay put it, was thus 'a vital feature in the defence of our Middle East position'.

It was against this background that Brooke sent Auchinleck a brisk response to the effect that 'his feelings would have been much more hurt if he had got the telegram the Prime Minister had intended for him'. This was hardly the most promising atmosphere in which to reach an agreement on the best way forward and – as might have been expected – it had quite the opposite effect. Auchinleck, assuredly mindful of Dill's original warning to him about resisting 'undue pressure from London', made it very clear once more that he would not yield to any pressure for a premature strike against Rommel, insisting that such a venture would be more likely to imperil Egypt than to secure victory.

Churchill was incandescent. 'Found the PM in an explosive mood today,' his doctor noted, quoting him as saying, 'The bloody man does not seem to care about the fate of Malta.' On 8 March, Churchill cabled Auchinleck demanding that he return to London 'at your earliest convenience' to discuss the conflict between them in person rather than by correspondence. To the Prime Minister's fury and the consternation of the Chiefs of Staff, Auchinleck bluntly refused to leave the Middle East. Despite a cable from Brooke urging him to change his mind, Auchinleck once again demurred, suggesting instead that the CIGS himself, accompanied by Air Chief Marshal Charles Portal, should fly out to Cairo. When the Prime Minister learned about this he was, according to Brooke, 'infuriated ... [and] once again suggested relieving [Auchinleck] of his command'. In a pained rebuke to Auchinleck, despatched on 15 March, Churchill expressed his 'extreme regret' at the Middle East C-in-C's refusal to meet him in London. 'I have done everything in my power to give you continuous support at heavy cost to the whole war,' he wrote despairingly. 'It would give me the greatest pain to feel that mutual understanding had ceased.'

That, of course, is precisely what had occurred, but short of sacking Auchinleck – which would have caused a degree of political embarrassment that he could ill afford – there was little the Prime Minister could do to bring his recalcitrant general to order. Drawing the obvious conclusion, Churchill noted later, 'It seemed to me that he conceived himself stronger in resisting from his own headquarters the requests which he knew would be made to him.'

Thwarted by Auchinleck's obstinacy, Churchill added a petulant coda to their correspondence, threatening to withdraw 'at least fifteen air squadrons from Libya to sustain the Russian wing in the Caucasus' unless Auchinleck agreed to advance the proposed date of his offensive. Churchill had no intention of carrying out this threat and, when Brooke saw the cable, he advised against escalating their dispute in this way. Churchill retorted, 'It will be a whip to him.' It wasn't. The relationship between the British Prime Minister and his commander-in-chief was rapidly approaching the point of no return.

Their stand-off was not solely a confrontation of obstinate egos. The pressures on both men were enormous. At issue were overlapping but competing political and military challenges of the greatest consequence which neither man was able or willing to view through the prism of the other. Against a darkening background of repeated disasters on land and at sea, Churchill's political imperative – a victory as soon as possible – was reinforced by a global strategic perspective which, perforce, Auchinleck lacked. But the Middle East commander-in-chief had a far clearer appreciation of the operational and logistical complexities by which he was constrained and knew that to launch an attack before his forces were very much better prepared to meet a Panzerarmee which had consistently shown its superiority in battle would be thoroughly irresponsible. The simple fact was that, from the start of the war, Britain had been trying to do too much with too little on too many fronts. The tension between Churchill and Auchinleck was essentially a reflection of this unhappy predicament.

In the lull which now ensued, Auchinleck continued the task he had set himself immediately after the 'Second Benghazi Handicap' – to put right some of the fundamental failings which had led to that rout. Some of these were technical, some organisational, some structural and some psychological. All were extremely serious and, in his judgement, had to be remedied before he could embark on yet another offensive. On 30 January, in a memorandum to his Chief of Staff, General Arthur Smith, Auchinleck had highlighted one of his principal concerns: the failure of the Eighth Army's armour to deliver the knockout punch of which on paper it should have been easily capable. It was an extraordinarily blunt assessment. 'We have got to face the fact,' he noted, 'that, unless we can achieve superiority on the battlefield by better co-operation between the army commanders and more original leadership of our armoured forces than is apparently being exercised at present, we may have to forgo any idea of mounting a strategic offensive because our armoured forces are tactically incapable of meeting the enemy in the open, even when superior to him in numbers.'

Notably, this apocalyptic indictment did not simply lay the blame on the comparative qualities of the British versus the German or Italian tanks, though these were of no small significance. In sheer firepower, the 2-pounders on the British tanks were like popguns in comparison to the 5cm guns mounted on the panzer Mark IIIs and IVs; the British tanks were also less mechanically reliable than their German equivalents and, after a three-month journey by sea via the Cape, most of them required time-consuming repairs and preparation for desert conditions before they could be put into service.

This imbalance of technical advantage had started to eat away at the spirit of the Eighth Army to the point where Auchinleck began to detect 'the growth of an inferiority complex among our armoured forces, owing to their failure to compete with enemy tanks which they consider (and rightly so) superior to their own in certain respects. This is very dangerous and will be most difficult to eradicate once it takes root, as I am afraid it is now doing.' Even the 'two to one' superiority in tanks which he advised Churchill would be required to face Rommel in the desert with any degree of confidence would not of itself be enough to secure victory. Auchinleck put his finger on the nub of the problem: without a radical overhaul, the Eighth Army would be persistently outmanoeuvred by Rommel and his panzers.

The origins of this inferiority lay deep in the history of the British Army and, as Auchinleck surely knew, it would take more than a few weeks to eradicate them. For the most part, the British armour was commanded by officers who still lived psychologically on the saddle of a horse, not in the stinking, clanking, broiling interior of a tank. Not for nothing did they instinctively use the language of the hunting field, the cricket pitch, the polo ground, or the race track when radioing one another from unit to unit in the hope of bewildering the German intelligence officers trying to decipher their messages. 'Gone to ground'; 'a chap has retired to the pavilion'; 'I've cast a shoe'; 'My horse and jockey have copped it' – all these phrases, and many more, belonged to a social class that regarded itself naturally as a cut above the rest. Cavalry officers looked back with nostalgia to the days when a charge was a charge, even though it might end up, so to speak, in 'the valley of death'. They did not lack for dash or bravery or patriotism, but they found it exceptionally difficult to display the kind of 'original leadership' required by modern tank warfare. Jealously protective of their own regimental histories and traditions, they still found co-operation with other tank regiments, let alone with artillery brigades and infantry battalions, a novel, baffling, and invidious concept. The resentments incubated by this snobbery nurtured a competitive disdain among the various fighting units of the Eighth Army, and especially between the cavalry and the infantry, 'the poor bloody foot soldiers' from Britain, the dominions, and the colonies. Rommel's panzer divisions succeeded by integrating tanks, artillery, and infantry into a single, flexible unit able to attack at speed with concentrated firepower on any flank. By contrast the Eighth Army was lumbering and inflexible, apparently doomed to be perpetually outsmarted and outfought.

There was a further problem, to which Auchinleck had referred fleetingly in his note to Smith: the low morale of the British Army by comparison with the Germans, the Russians, and the Japanese. After the collapse of Singapore, General Wavell in his new role as C-in-C, India identified as an underlying cause of that humiliation the loss of 'our hardness and fighting spirit ... Until we have again soldiers capable of marching twenty or thirty miles a day for a number of days running, and missing their full rations every second or third day, and whose first idea is to push forward and to get to grips with the enemy on any and every occasion and whatever the difficulties and odds, we shall not recover our morale or reputation.'

In London, the Director of Military Operations was not surprised. Kennedy had already discerned two reasons for the repeated failures on the battlefield. The first he attributed to the fact that the government had not begun to build up the British Army until after war had broken out and, as a result, it was as yet ill organised, under-trained and poorly equipped. The second reason was more startling and, from the perspective of the twenty-first century, quaintly primitive. The British, he avowed 'were undoubtedly softer as a nation than any of our enemies, except the Italians'. This, he mused, could be accounted for by the fact that 'modern civilisation on the democratic model does not produce a hardy race, and our civilisation in Great Britain was a little further removed from the stage of barbarity than were the civilisations of Germany, Russia, and Japan'. He was not alone in these sentiments. Brooke harboured similar doubts, though from a slightly different perspective. 'The more I see of democracy,' he confided in one diary entry after a particularly truculent meeting of the War Cabinet, 'the more I doubt our wisdom of attaching such importance to it.'

As Britain was supposed to be fighting in the name of democracy against tyranny, the CIGS's late night musing may seem perverse. On reflection, he explained that he had been 'embittered' by the criticisms directed at the military by the politicians. Conceding that Churchill was 'a wonderful national leader', he nonetheless observed, with mordant satisfaction, that his first act as Prime Minister had been virtually to convert that democracy into a dictatorship in which both parliament and cabinet 'were only minor inconveniences to be humoured occasionally'. This was a jejune analysis of the British political process but it contained a kernel of truth, the more disconcerting because Brooke so clearly relished Churchill's quasi-dictatorial power.

His concern about what he and Kennedy regarded as a crisis of leadership, morale and discipline in the army prompted Brooke to contact the senior officers under his command and alert them to the 'drastic measures' which were required to raise the standard of leadership throughout the army. 'We must be more ruthless in the elimination of those who seem unlikely to prove themselves determined and inspiring leaders in the field,' he insisted; it was also essential 'to raise morale and tighten discipline ... our men must be physically hard and fit ... they must possess a high sense of comradeship and discipline ... they must be taught to love the spice of danger'.

This was easier said than done – especially in the Middle East. This was not because the 120,000 men of the multinational Eighth Army believed themselves to be 'lions led by donkeys' – though some of them did – but because they found it difficult to appreciate why the war against Hitler had to be fought in the sand and rock of a distant desert. Crackling through the ether to them in the torpid atmosphere of a sweltering mess tent, Churchill's sonorous generalities from afar made little impact, while their own officers – themselves often unclear about the overall strategy of the war – were singularly inept at communicating its significance to a conscript army which expected explanations as well as orders.

Despite these failings, the Eighth Army's adversaries had acquired a deepening respect for the British troops. 'The British soldier fought very well in the desert, even though he might not have attained the *elan* of the German attack,' the Afrikakorps' Chief of Staff, Bayerlein, wrote of their gallantry during *Crusader*. 'Their officers fought with tremendous courage and self-sacrifice. Rommel too often expressed his admiration for his adversaries, and once said, on seeing a number of them as prisoners, that he would be happy to lead such men into battle.'

However, the German commanders were scathing about the tactics adopted by the British on the battlefield. Reviewing *Crusader*, Bayerlein wrote, 'Contrary to the principle that one can never be strong enough at the centre of gravity and must concentrate everything at this point, every attack was made by part only of the Eighth Army, and even the main offensive force, already too weak for its purpose, was thrown into battle dispersed.' As a result, 'the British formations were either badly battered or destroyed one after the other and disappeared from the theatre while the battle was still in progress.' These tactical errors were aggravated by their 'unwieldy and rigidly methodical technique of command, their over-systematic issuing of orders down to the last detail, leaving little latitude to the junior commander, and their poor adaptability to the changing course of the battle'. In short, closely echoing Auchinleck's own diagnosis, Bayerlein's assessment was that the British Eighth Army was no match for the Panzerarmee even when, on paper, they were evenly balanced.

Bayerlein would have been intrigued to read the British CIGS's bleak diary entry for 31 March.

> The last day of the first quarter of 1942, fateful year in which we have already lost a large proportion of the British Empire, and are on the way to lose a great deal more of it! During the last fortnight I have had for the first time since the war started a growing conviction that we are going to lose this war unless we control it very differently and fight it with more determination ... Half our Corps and Divisional Commanders are

totally unfit for their appointments, and yet if I were to sack them I could find no better! They lack character, imagination, drive and the power of leadership ... There are times when I wish to God I had not been placed at the helm of a ship that seems to be heading inevitably for the rocks.

Such sentiments were of little use to Auchinleck, who had no choice but to work with the clay at his disposal. At its most basic, his inheritance – 'the cumulative and accelerating effects of twenty years of military decadence' – was a force that was not yet 'fit for purpose' to do battle against an enemy as disciplined, organised and motivated as Rommel's Panzerarmee. Before confronting Rommel again, his overriding task was to ensure that the Eighth Army was reorganised and retrained to the point where he could be confident that it was capable of achieving victory. Until then he was not going to be rushed into a premature offensive. He would rather be deprived of his command than engage in such an act of self-defeating folly.

To help him implement these reforms, Auchinleck summoned from Palestine one of the most controversial staff officers in the British Army, Colonel Eric Dorman-Smith. No one doubted that 'Chink', as he was generally known, possessed one of the most brilliant and original minds in the army. He was fond of a quotation from A. A. Milne which he had pinned to his office wall, 'The third-rate mind is only happy when it is thinking with the majority. A second-rate mind is only happy when it is thinking with the minority. A first-rate mind is only happy when it is thinking.' He was as fastidious in dress (to the point of dandyism) as he was in thought. He was also impatient, arrogant, and uncompromising – characteristics that he did not deign to conceal from his colleagues, who, in consequence, generally found him insufferable. That he was also judged to have the wandering eye of a practised philanderer led envious rivals to regard him as something of a cad as well. Even among those who admired his intellect, he was thought to be dangerously rash in judgement and unsound in temperament, a maverick who was not to be trusted. Though he affected indifference to the hostility of those he despised, he was wounded to the point of embitterment by watching lesser beings climb more rapidly up the rungs of promotion. But in Auchinleck he had found a patron who not only revered his wayward genius but was deeply fond of him as well.

On 10 February Auchinleck cabled Ritchie at Eighth Army headquarters. 'I have given Dorman-Smith the job of inquiring into our present system,' he wrote. 'I feel we are still too rigid and hidebound and that we must modernise ourselves in this respect. He is excellent at this sort of thing ... It must be made clear that he is NOT snooping.' Dorman-Smith joined Ritchie on 15 February (the same day as the fall of Singapore) and stayed for just under two weeks. Dorman-Smith disdained the Eighth Army commander, whom he regarded as 'patronising, limited, and assured' and – which was even worse – had been appointed as Deputy Chief of the General Staff in the Middle East over his own head. According to his biographer, Dorman-Smith judged Ritchie to be an utterly 'repellent' individual, who 'hadn't been given a brain capable of having any needs except those foisted on by tradition and custom'.

Whether he was 'snooping' or not, Dorman-Smith returned to Cairo convinced that Auchinleck should sack the Eighth Army commander. This advice was not simply vengeful or malicious: Dorman-Smith's judgement that Ritchie was unsuited and ill equipped for the challenges facing the Eighth Army was widely shared. But, with some vehemence, Auchinleck demurred. It was out of the question to get rid of Ritchie so soon after sacking his predecessor, Cunningham; moreover, were he to do so, London would very probably send out General Bernard Montgomery, for whom Dorman-Smith also had a low regard, to replace him. This was a fateful decision: Ritchie's inadequacies, like those of Cunningham before him, were soon to be cruelly exposed, confirming for Auchinleck's admirers as well as his detractors that, whatever his other qualities, picking winners was not one of them.

Churchill chose this moment to divert Sir Stafford Cripps, the Lord Privy Seal, to Cairo from a crucial mission to India (see p.230). In the Egyptian capital he was to meet up with Lieutenant General

Sir Archibald Nye, Vice Chief of the Imperial General Staff, who had been despatched there at the same time from London. Their task was to investigate Auchinleck's refusal to go on the offensive. They were an odd, even perverse, choice: Cripps had no relevant military background while Nye, who had won a Military Cross for 'conspicuous gallantry' in the First World War, had served only as a staff officer at the War Office since 1940. If Churchill hoped that their delvings would act as a goad to prod Auchinleck onto the offensive, he was to be sorely disappointed.

On 21 March, after a long round of detailed conversations with Auchinleck and others, Cripps cabled Churchill: 'I am very satisfied with the atmosphere in Cairo after our talks ... I have no doubt of Auchinleck's offensive spirit but I think his Scottish caution and desire not to be misled by optimism cause him to over-stress in statement the difficulties and uncertainties of situation. I am convinced of his determination to face these, and am sure that it will help him very much if he can now be made to feel that all misunderstandings are at an end and there is no more questioning of his desire to take the offensive.' With a sensitivity for which he was not renowned, he added, 'It would, I am sure, help if you could send Auchinleck a short friendly telegram expressing your satisfaction that he will have all possible help from you to hit the target at the appointed time.'

Churchill was no more disposed to adopt that suggestion than he was to sign a peace treaty with Hitler. He also felt aggrieved by the failure of Cripps and Nye to hold the obstinate C-in-C to account. Presuming that the Lord Privy Seal had been of his mind, he had hoped 'by his personal force' that Cripps would bring about a solution on the spot. As it was, the Prime Minister grumbled, 'I was very ill-content with this.' He vented his ire in a sarcastic note to Nye: 'I do not wonder everything was so pleasant, considering you seem to have accepted everything they said.'

This was not the end of the matter. Auchinleck – to a much greater degree than Wavell had endured – now faced a united front against him in London. Though Brooke frequently deplored the tone of the Prime Minister's missives, he – and the Chiefs of Staff – shared his irritation at Auchinleck's refusal to advance the date for the renewed offensive against Rommel. Brooke's own respect for Auchinleck had been shaken three months earlier, when his overly optimistic reports and forecasts from the desert had been swiftly contradicted by the facts on the ground. In a waspish aside, reported by Kennedy, the CIGS had commented, 'If we had judged Rommel's condition by Auchinleck's reports and nothing else, we would regard him now as a prize-fighter in the last stages of exhaustion, lying back, practically unconscious, in his corner of the ring, with his seconds fanning him. It is quite funny, in a way, to see him rise up and deliver such a crack on Auchinleck's jaw.'

A few days after Churchill's sour response to the Cripps–Nye mission, General 'Pug' Ismay, the genial link man between the Prime Minister and the Chiefs of Staff, wrote to Auchinleck on 2 April in a last-ditch attempt to persuade him to come to London. In the most emollient terms, he sought to portray the breakdown in communications between the Prime Minister and his commander-in-chief as 'purely a temporary phase of a relationship which is marked by mutual esteem and, I might almost say, affection'. Virtually imploring Auchinleck to unbend, he offered a compelling insight into Churchill's complex personality, 'He is a mass of contradictions. He is either on the crest of a wave, or in the trough; either highly laudatory or bitterly condemnatory; either in an angelic temper, or a hell of a rage; when he isn't fast asleep he is a volcano.'

Ismay's innocent description of the Prime Minister's 'Black Dog' – as he himself referred to the recurrent bouts of depression by which he was afflicted – was intended to reconcile Auchinleck to Churchill's volatile character. But the Auk was unmoved. Although Ismay ended his letter by writing 'YOU MUST COME HOME [his capitals] … nothing matters so much as the removal of the wall of misunderstanding which has grown up between you two,' Auchinleck remained stubbornly in Cairo.

FIFTEEN

DEADLOCK

'A very dangerous man while being a very charming one!'
Alan Brooke on George Marshall

At the Gazala front, the Eighth Army waited in the wasteland, rehearsing for battle and reinforcing its defences. The Gazala Line was not an unbroken chain of defensive works like the Maginot Line but a series of 'boxes' – like castles in the sand, or 'cowpats', as cynical officers described them – linked by a chain of minefields. One infantryman 'digging-in' at one of these boxes described how his men first dug pits in which to conceal the Bren guns, then a narrow slit trench for a pair of riflemen, and finally 'bivvy holes' in which they lived and slept. 'These holes, usually six feet square, went as deep as the digger's patience; probably four feet: and the bivouac sheets were stretched flat over the top and camouflaged with nets and sand,' Lieutenant Billany reported. 'Each section position was a warren of underground dens and holes for stores. Everything went below the surface.' The boxes were protected by a perimeter fence made of flattened barbed wire – 'mattress' wire, as it was called – on which were hung booby traps and beyond which night patrols navigated their way about the minefields.

The men lived off a ration of bully beef and hard tack, supplemented by an occasional tin of pineapple chunks. 'To prevent scurvy,' Captain Harry Snell recalled, 'every day officers went round, put an ascorbic acid tablet on each man's tongue, and watched him swallow it.' Each man had a two-gallon tin for washing. 'You took Italian gas-mask filters and put them on top of the tin. After cleaning your teeth you spat the water into the filter, and it went through to the tin. Eventually you built about half a can of water. You washed your face, poured it back through the filter, washed your socks, and filtered again.' A ditty did the rounds succinctly contrasting the exigencies of life at the front with the sybaritic alternative enjoyed by staff officers in Cairo: 'Every time they pull the chain, three day's ration goes down the drain.'

The only relief from long days of boredom was a weekly truck ride across the desert to bathe in a balmy Mediterranean or a rare moment of excitement. 'We would go out and lie up until you saw a nice convoy, and shell it … shoot up as many of the lorries as we could, turn and race back, leaving some of the enemy trucks blazing.' As Peter Lewis, a lieutenant in the Durham Light Infantry recalled, 'It did not always go smoothly. On one occasion we unintentionally raided a column which had an ambulance with it.' By mistake they fired on the ambulance and drilled a hole through the engine. There followed an improbable moment of *Dad's Army* farce. 'There was a lot of shouting and screaming, and while we were busy apologising to the Italians, a couple of German Armoured Cars appeared on the horizon. We said we were jolly sorry, and tore off as fast as we could back behind the little escarpment we had come from.'

On the other side of the Gazala Line, the Panzerarmee similarly waited and rehearsed and, from Rommel's impatient perspective, dithered. After his success in forcing the Eighth Army back to Gazala, he intended to press his advantage before Auchinleck had time to regroup and re-equip his forces. But to his surprise and frustration he found himself thwarted by his two principal patrons in Rome and Berlin.

Knowing that the head of Comando Supremo, General Cavallero, lacked the stomach for an invasion of Egypt, Rommel suspected he would block his request for the five Italian infantry divisions which were then at ease in their safe havens at Mersa el

Brega, Agedabia, and Benghazi to be sent to his front at Gazala. But, knowing that Mussolini held him in high esteem, he felt confident that Il Duce would overrule Cavallero and that he would be granted the men and the supplies needed to sustain his offensive. Mussolini's contempt for his 'desktop general' Cavallero was unbounded, a disdain which was shared, with rare vehemence, by Ciano, who described Italy's most senior military officer as 'a complete clown ... who would even go so far as to bow to the public lavatories if this would be helpful to him'.

But Mussolini, weakened by his errors of strategic judgement, no longer enjoyed quite the dominion over Comando Supremo that he had exercised at the start of the desert campaign. And Cavallero, who was not in awe of the Desert Fox, had allies in Germany. His aversion to Rommel's planned assault was given swift and strong backing by OKW, whose own 'desktop' generals were still smarting from Rommel's persistent insubordination. This informal alliance between the most senior military commanders in Germany and Italy made it much harder for the two dictators to act in concert on Rommel's behalf.

Rommel decided to fly back to Europe to press his case. In Rome, he was rebuffed in person by Mussolini, who refused to give him full authority over the Italian as well as the German divisions under his battlefield command and thus made it impossible for him to order more Italian divisions to the front. In Germany he was baulked again. Although he knew that the acrimonious rivalries in OKW would tell against him, he was confident that he could appeal over their heads to the Führer. Instead, Hitler refused to promise more support in the form of either shipping or supplies; indeed, he went further, instructing Rommel that 'under no circumstances whatsoever' was he to launch an offensive aimed at the Suez Canal until 1943. Thus the stand-off in the desert between a German commander forbidden to race for the finishing line and a British commander refusing to leave the starting gate continued throughout the spring of 1942.

During this lull, the Americans startled Whitehall by launching a diplomatic offensive against their unsuspecting counterparts across the Atlantic. Their purpose was cloaked in the kind of mystery Roosevelt relished. On 2 April the President cabled Churchill to tell him that his closest confidant, Harry Hopkins, and his trusted Chief of Staff, George Marshall would be on their way to London within a few days. 'As I have completed [our] survey of the immediate and long-range problems of the military situations facing the United Nations (his preferred terms for the Anglo-American alliance), I have come to certain conclusions which are so vital that I want you to know the whole picture and to ask your approval,' he wrote. The following day, in a further note, he added, 'What Harry and Geo. Marshall will tell you all about has my heart and *mind* in it.' As the British were soon to discover, the purpose of the American mission – shorn of its diplomatic niceties – was to convince them that it was imperative to launch an early invasion of France to siphon off enough panzer divisions from the Eastern Front to ease the intense pressure on the Soviet Union.

There was no doubting the seriousness of Roosevelt's intent. On 6 April, in a personal letter to Queen Wilhelmina of the Netherlands, who was staying in London at the time, he wrote,

> I think we realize that the principal danger of the next six months is German success against Russia – for if Russia is driven to her knees this Summer Germany will be able to release very large forces against the Near East and the Middle East and seek to join hands with Japan.
>
> In other words we are forced to come to the conclusion that our major strategy must be the defeat of Germany in her Russian effort, for the very simple fact is that if this can be accomplished the probability is that Germany cannot survive another year.

This was a U-turn by the Americans, the polar opposite of the strategy which Churchill thought had been agreed at the Arcadia meetings three months earlier. However, he could not say so directly without jeopardising a relationship with the United States and with Roosevelt personally on which Britain's war effort was almost wholly dependent. To achieve his own goals in North

Africa and the Middle East, he would have to negotiate with great delicacy and patience against very powerful odds.

Aside from their own commitment to Roosevelt's plan, the American diplomats knew that the vision of a second front in France chimed with popular sentiment on both sides of the Atlantic. Only a few days earlier, on Sunday 29 March, a crowd of 40,000 had gathered in Trafalgar Square to campaign under the slogan, 'Second Front Now'. When the Russian ambassador to the Court of St James, Ivan Maisky, took to the streets of London he was cheered by crowds who asked for his autograph.

Three weeks later, in America – reflecting a widely held view – the newspaper magnate Lord Beaverbrook – one of whose famous columnists, John Gordon, had spoken from the platform at the rally in Trafalgar Square – addressed an audience of fellow publishers in New York. 'Communism under Stalin has won the applause and admiration of all the western nations,' he told them; and, as if to reinforce his well-earned reputation for shallow impetuosity, he urged the gathering, 'Strike out to help Russia! Strike out violently! Strike even recklessly!' A little over a month earlier the 'Beaver', as he was known, had resigned from the government of which he had been a notably unreliable, deceitful and scheming member. However, he remained unaccountably close to the Prime Minister, who had sent him to Washington on an ill-defined mission to further good relations with the President. Churchill's wife, Clemmie, could not abide Beaverbrook and had done her best to persuade her husband to exclude him from his inner circle. 'My darling,' she had written in February, just before the newspaper baron's resignation, 'Try ridding yourself of this microbe which some people fear is in your blood – Exorcise this bottle Imp and see if the air is not clearer and purer.' However, Beaverbrook's rant on behalf of Soviet communism merely prompted Churchill to offer him the stewardship of every British mission in Washington, an offer which Beaverbrook refused.

By this time the wily 'Imp' had infiltrated his way into Roosevelt's confidence as effectively as he had already suborned Churchill. The day after alerting the Prime Minister to the imminent arrival of Hopkins and Marshall, Roosevelt wrote to

1. Commander of the Eighth Army and victor at El Alamein, Lieutenant-General Bernard Montgomery, was fanatically driven, obsessively focussed, clinically organised and pathologically egotistical.

2. Hitler's favourite commander, General Erwin Rommel – the Desert Fox – seemed to be everywhere at once, urging his men on, devising new tactics, and all the time on the move.

3. General Cavallero, head of the Italian Comando Supremo. According to the Italian Foreign Minister, Count Ciano, he was 'a complete clown'.

4. Marshall Graziani – the 'butcher' of Ethiopia – only invaded Egypt in September 1940 because he feared the wrath of Italy's mercurial dictator if he procrastinated any longer.

5. Chief of the Imperial General Staff (1940–41) General John Dill: he went on to play a crucial diplomatic role in Washington.

6. With no experience of desert warfare, let alone of Rommel, Lieutenant-General Andrew Cunningham was soon at his wit's end.

7. General Claude Auchinleck was a soldier, not a diplomat; his insistence on making decisions for military, rather than political, reasons, soon alienated Churchill's sympathies.

8. General Wavell's loyalty to his political masters was never in question, but his disdain for the Prime Minister's conceptual grasp of military strategy was ill-concealed.

9. Hitler and Mussolini met in the Fuhrer's railway carriage at the Brenner Pass on 4 October 1940 where he informed Il Duce that the British were in 'a hopeless position militarily' and that the 'final battle' would destroy the British Empire. Mussolini returned to Rome 'elated and invigorated'.

10. British commanders preferred the derring-do of a suicidal nineteenth-century cavalry charge. This was not merely in romantic imitation of their horse-mounted forebears but forced upon them by the greater firepower at Rommel's disposal.

11. Officers and men were caught in the open, dive-bombed by German Stukas.

12. The 'ill-starred' British expedition to Greece cost 15,000 casualties and depleted Wavell's forces in the Middle East at a critical moment in the desert campaign. But this military debacle was hailed by Roosevelt as a 'heroic' effort to arrest Hitler's invasion of Britain's last ally on the European mainland.

13. Churchill's Imperial 'Army of the Nile' was a multi-national force incorporating infantry divisions from Australia, New Zealand, South Africa and India. By comparison with Rommel's Afrika Korps, it was ill-trained, ill-equipped and poorly armed.

14. The Australians earned a reputation for 'bloody-minded fearlessness' during the 240-day siege of Tobruk.

15. In July, 1942, the Eighth Army led by General Auchinleck foiled the Panzerarmee's repeated attempts to break through towards Cairo during the First Battle of El Alamein. It was not, however, in Churchill's mind to reward Auchinleck for this achievement.

16. A hot August at the British Embassy in Cairo. Churchill sits beside two
former Commanders-in-Chief, Middle East – Auchinleck, whom he had
just sacked, and Wavell who had been fired fifteen months earlier. Both had
failed to deliver the decisive victory on the battlefield for which he yearned
importunately. On the left (back row), General Alan Brooke, was Churchill's
choice to replace Auchinleck but he turned it down, claiming privately that
he had to remain as CIGS to 'exercise some control' over an impetuous
Prime Minister. To his left Admiral Harwood, Commander-in-Chief of the
Mediterranean Fleet and Richard Casey, who, as resident 'Minister of State' in
Cairo was an uneasy go-between Churchill and Montgomery who was at the
front preparing to do battle against Rommel.

Beaverbrook – the arch-advocate of the 'Second Front Now' campaign – indicating that his two emissaries had been anxious to take Beaverbrook with them. However, 'I had to make a personal decision,' Roosevelt wrote, 'and I put my foot down for the very good reason that I want you here. As you know, there is no one else I can talk to when we get word in the course of the next few days ... Thank the Lord the matter seems to be moving swiftly towards what I trust will be a momentous and successful conclusion.' The President was to be disappointed.

Although the Chiefs of Staff had some idea of what to expect from Hopkins and Marshall, they could not have imagined just how gruelling the transatlantic negotiations on which they were about to embark would become. Before leaving for London, Hopkins had sent a memorandum to Roosevelt (on 14 March), arguing, 'I doubt if any single thing is as important as getting some sort of front against Germany. This has got to be worked out very carefully between you and Marshall in the first instance, and you and Churchill in the second. I don't think there is any time to be lost, because if we are going to do it plans need to be made at once.' A week later, Marshall joined in, elaborating the reasons for making this a priority over all other options. Northern France, he argued, was the one place in the world 'in which a powerful offensive can be prepared and executed by the United Powers in the near future'. America's primary objective, he argued, should be the opening of a second front on mainland Europe as soon as possible and certainly before the vagaries of the weather in the Channel made the venture too perilous. This made September 1942 the latest realistic date for the invasion – a prospect which was anathema to Churchill and his military advisors. The stage was set for a very uncomfortable encounter indeed.

Churchill had already suffered a rebuff to his plans for *Gymnast* – the proposed Anglo-American landings in North Africa – which, following Auchinleck's setback in the desert, the Americans formally decided on 3 March should be postponed indefinitely. The ostensible reasons they gave for this decision were the competing demands on United States shipping and 'the extreme hazards' to which US troop movements were exposed in the Atlantic. However, this was window-dressing to disguise the fact that the US Chiefs feared failure in a venture for which they in any case had little appetite. The threat to Churchill's vision was now ominous: not only were the Allied landings in North Africa to be postponed but, if Washington were to get its way, they would be replaced by an Allied landing in France. Churchill's self-appointed – but monumental – task was to reverse that order of priorities by changing Roosevelt's mind.

Marshall and Hopkins arrived at Hendon airport on 8 April armed with a memorandum which had not only been agreed by the Joint Chiefs but approved by Roosevelt. Its message was blunt and unambiguous: 'Western Europe is favoured as the theatre in which to stage the first major offensive by the United States and Great Britain. Only there could their combined land and air resources be fully developed and the maximum support given to Russia ... The decision to launch this offensive must be made *at once.*' The American proposal envisaged a full-scale Allied invasion of Europe to be mounted in 1943, codenamed *Roundup* and involving forty-eight divisions and 5,800 aircraft. This massive operation was to be preceded in 1942 by *Sledgehammer*, a cross-Channel landing, probably on the Cherbourg peninsula on a much smaller scale. Its purpose would be to open an Allied bridgehead designed to draw off and tie down several panzer divisions that would otherwise be engaged on the Russian Front – and thereby prepare the way for *Roundup* the following year.

The British Chiefs supported *Roundup* in principle, though they doubted whether it would be possible to mount such a vast undertaking before 1944. But they regarded *Sledgehammer* with abhorrence. They were sure that a precipitate attack of this kind on that front would not only be very likely to end in another Dunkirk but very probably the loss of the Middle East and thereby the demise of the British Empire. To reinforce the case against *Sledgehammer*, Brooke asked Kennedy to prepare a map of Europe which would demonstrate 'the stupidity' of opening a second front by means of an early landing near Cherbourg. The map vividly contrasted the thousand-mile-long Russian Front with the twenty-mile-long front that would be opened by *Sledgehammer*. The comparison was designed to make a landing at Cherbourg appear 'so ridiculous ... as to make us the laughing stock of the world'. However, given the President's endorsement of the proposal, they had to avoid a head-on confrontation. Instead, led by Churchill, their negotiating tactics were so sinuously ambiguous as barely to fall short of outright duplicity.

The Prime Minister set about his task with treacherous charm. Despite the late hours that the American party was required to keep and the cigar-waving soliloquies they were obliged to endure, Marshall was rapidly seduced by the Prime Minister's display of magnanimity. 'What he did not realise', one of Marshall's devoted biographers noted, 'was that Churchill, while professing agreement, was filled with an inner determination to do everything he could to block what he considered the American's impetuousness and lack of military know-how.'

Brooke was not greatly impressed by Marshall. His diary records that after their first meeting, he came away thinking that the American Chief of Staff was 'a pleasant and easy man to get on with, rather over-filled with his own importance. But I should not put him down as a great man.' Later he added, 'The more I see of him the more I like him,' but could not forbear to conclude, 'A big man and very great gentleman, who inspired trust, but did not impress me by the ability of his brain.'

As each side eyed the other, brains were evidently under the microscope. Hopkins reported that 'Brooke made an unfavourable impression on Marshall, who thinks that although he may be a good fighting man, he hasn't got Dill's brains'. Another member of the American party said later, 'In our opinion, that is at the working level, Brookie wasn't the smartest of the British ... We didn't think he was really that smart.' The obvious conclusion to draw from their mutual disregard is that each Chief of Staff underestimated the other; it was not an auspicious start to what was to be a very intense working relationship. Yet each had much in common with the other. They were both cool, aloof, assured, somewhat unbending in manner and, in the words of Churchill's personal physician, Lord Moran, 'selfless men with a fine

contempt for the pressures of the mob'. Brooke certainly recognised his opposite number to be a figure of substance. Though he
did not have it in him to write with comparable warmth, there is
every reason to suppose that Ismay's assessment of Marshall – it
was 'impossible to imagine his doing anything petty or mean, or
shrinking from any duty, however distasteful' – resonated with
him. As much to the point, Brooke knew that, one way or another,
they would both have to work 'extremely closely together'.

Happily, Brooke was not required to work as intimately with
Marshall's senior advisor, General Albert C. Wedemeyer, who
not only represented the poisonous wing of the Anglophobic
party, but regarded Albion as being congenitally perfidious. But
Wedemeyer was no fool. On 9 April, after what he described as
an 'initial joust' between the two sides about the cross-Channel
invasion, he noted that his British counterparts were 'adept in the
use of phrases or words which were capable of more than one
interpretation … When matters of state are involved, our British
opposite numbers had elastic scruples … what I witnessed was the
British power of finesse in its finest hour, a power that has been
developed over centuries of successful intrigue, cajolery and tacit
compulsions.' Marshall was more sanguine and far less ready to
detect duplicity. After three days of talks he felt able to telephone
Washington to say that Churchill had 'virtually accepted *in toto*
the proposals I submitted to him … I regard this as acquiescence
in principle'. Had the matter been the subject of legal scrutiny, the
key term for lawyers would have been 'virtually'.

Marshall could have been forgiven for taking the British
Prime Minister at his word. The following day, Churchill himself
cabled Roosevelt to tell him that he was 'in full agreement in
principle' with the President's plans, and that if, 'as our experts
believe, we can carry this whole plan through successfully it will
be one of the grand events in all the history of war'. Two days
later, at what he described as a 'momentous' Defence Committee
meeting in 10 Downing Street, Brooke recorded that the British
formally accepted the plan for offensive action against Europe 'in
1942 perhaps and in 1943 for certain'. It is impossible to resist the
conclusion that, at least in respect of 1942, and probably 1943, the

British stance – notably the sinuous conditionality of their commitment – exemplified to perfection the constructive ambiguity which so incensed Wedemeyer. Brooke noted patronisingly, 'They had not begun to realise all the implications of this plan and all the difficulties that lie [sic] ahead of us'; and later he added dismissively, 'With the situation prevailing at that time it was not possible to take Marshall's "castles in the air" too seriously.'

By the end of the following day, after an 'eye-opener' of a conversation with Marshall, Brooke was even less impressed with his opposite number, describing Marshall's grasp of strategy as being so poor as to make him 'a very dangerous man while being a very charming one!' When Brooke pressed him to elaborate his ideas for *Sledgehammer*, it emerged that the American plan did not go beyond the landing itself. 'Whether we are going to play *baccharat* or *chemin de fer* at Le Touquet, or possibly bathe at Paris Plage is not stipulated! I asked him this afternoon – do we go east, south, or west after landing? He had not begun to think of it.' However, by confining this supercilious ridicule to his diary and agreeing in principle *Sledgehammer*, Brooke turned bad faith to British advantage by opening up the opportunity to discuss other priorities which he and Churchill thought should be the real focus of their attention.

Churchill had not for a moment lost sight of his own counter-proposal: the resuscitation of *Gymnast* and thereby the elimination of the German presence from North Africa and the salvation of the Middle East and the British Empire. This was strongly opposed by Marshall and the US Secretary for War, Henry Stimson, who had likened it to 'stopping up rat holes'. But Churchill could take some comfort from the fact that, despite his aversion to *Gymnast*, Marshall was not entirely unmindful of the significance of the Middle East to the Allied war effort.

A month earlier, on 12 March, Dill, who had forged a close friendship with Marshall, had telegraphed from Washington asking for the authority to tell the Americans, 'Unless the Middle East is reinforced strongly and fast, we shall be defeated there, and our combined efforts will not enable us to win the war for years.' This overtly placed the Middle East at the very heart of Allied strategy against both Japan and Germany. For Churchill this was axiomatic: the Middle East was no less crucial to the survival of the British Empire than it had been at the start of the war. For rather different reasons – he was vehemently anti-imperialist – Marshall had also come to share the British view that the Middle East was pivotal. Knowing that Britain's capacity to wage war in the region was dependent on the Persian and Iraqi oil fields, he also foresaw the 'disastrous consequences' of a pincer movement by the Germans advancing south from the Caucasus to link up with the Japanese advancing northwards towards the Persian Gulf and the Red Sea. His response to Dill's request for rapid reinforcement for the Middle East had been that the US Army would help 'in every practical way'.

At what he described as a 'momentous' meeting on 14 April, Churchill was careful to avoid any specific mention of *Gymnast*, though, in the words of Lord Ismay, who, at the Prime Minister's instruction took notes throughout, Churchill said, 'it was essential to carry on the defence of India and the Middle East. We could not possibly face the loss of an army of 600,000 [in the Middle East Command] and the whole man-power of India.' For this reason, and because Australia would need British protection, 'we could not entirely lay aside everything in furtherance of the main objective proposed by General Marshall'. Brooke reinforced the Prime Minister's caveat by stressing the strategic significance of retaining the Middle East to prevent Germany and Japan joining forces in this pivotal region. Hopkins reiterated that there was no doubt in Washington as to the importance of the Middle East.

The Anglo-American negotiations concluded with what appeared to be total agreement. On 17 April Churchill wrote to Roosevelt in extravagant terms to describe how their two nations were 'resolved to march forward into Europe together in a noble brotherhood of arms on a great crusade for the liberation of the tormented peoples'. The President replied the following day. 'I am delighted with the agreement which was reached between you and your military advisors and Marshall and Hopkins. They have reported to me on the unanimity of opinion relative to the proposal which they carried with them ... I believe this move will be very disheartening to Hitler, and may well be the wedge by which his downfall will be accomplished.' In reality, however, the transatlantic conflict of priorities was as sharp as ever.

Neither Churchill nor the British Chiefs of Staff had any intention of pursuing *Sledgehammer*. With the American Chiefs on their way back to Washington, Brooke noted, 'The plans are fraught with the gravest dangers. Public opinion is shouting for the formation of a new Western Front [i.e. to the west of the Eastern Front on which the Russians were fighting] to assist the Russians. But they have no conception of the difficulties and dangers entailed! The prospects of success are small and dependent on a mass of unknowns, while the chances of success or of disaster are great and dependent on a mass of well established military facts.'

Although Brooke had concealed his true feelings about *Sledgehammer* from the Americans, Marshall had read the runes astutely enough to realise that the 'meeting of minds' which Hopkins reported to the President did not amount to very much. In a letter home, he wrote that agreement had been reached only in principle. Most of the participants held 'reservations about this or that'; and, he added presciently, 'great firmness' would be required to avoid 'further dispersions'.

'Dispersion' was precisely what the British now had in mind – at least in the sense that both Brooke and Churchill were committed to the view that the invasion of Europe should follow rather than precede success in the Indian Ocean, the Atlantic, the Mediterranean and, especially, the Western Desert and North Africa, where, they believed, the defeat of Rommel should be followed by an assault on Hitler's southern flank in Europe. In his own account of these negotiations, Churchill was disarmingly mellifluous but less than candid when he described how he had used his 'influence and diplomacy in order to secure agreed and harmonious action with our cherished ally, without whose aid nothing but ruin faced the world'. In reality, by forbearing to share with the Americans his conviction that *Sledgehammer* was 'more difficult, less attractive, less immediately helpful or ultimately fruitful' than the alternative of an Allied landing in North Africa in the same year, he had, at the very least, dissembled by omission.

Was this duplicity or diplomacy? It mattered not at all, either then or later, to a Prime Minister who was resolved by either means to get his way. In his otherwise discreet memoirs, Ismay made it clear that he felt Churchill was wrong to have dissimulated on such a grand scale. 'No doubts were expressed; no discordant notes were struck,' he wrote. 'It is easy to be wise after the event but perhaps it would have obviated future misunderstandings if the British had expressed their views more frankly.'

SIXTEEN

STRETCHED TO BREAKING POINT

*'Germans shut their eyes in order not to see. But this does
not stop the more intelligent and more honest from thinking
about what America can do, and they feel shivers running
down their spines.'*

Count Galeazzo Ciano

Hitler spent much of the spring on his Eastern front at the Wolfsschanze (Wolf's Lair) in Eastern Poland, masterminding the plans for the next stage of his Russian campaign. According to Goebbels, who visited him there in March, 1942, the Führer seemed weighed down by the pressures of office. 'He has already become quite grey and merely talking about the cares of the winter makes him seem to have aged very much.' But his myopic certainties had not yet been contaminated by reality. Although the Wehrmacht had been horribly mauled by Stalin's counter-offensive, the Red Army's thrust had petered out and the panzers were about to launch a twin-pronged southern offensive with the objective of both capturing Stalingrad and seizing the oil fields of the Caucasus. The Führer still believed that the Third Reich would emerge triumphant from the carnage in the Soviet Union and that – as he saw it – Russia would become a vassal state, rather as India had been possessed by Britain. There were certain dissimilarities, not least that in seeking to achieve his objective, he had initiated, among many other hideous crimes, a pogrom which would lead to the liquidation of 2 million Russian Jews. As Heinrich Himmler, head of the SS and the principal agent of this cleansing operation, enthused, 'Just imagine what a sublime idea!

It's the greatest piece of colonisation the world will have ever seen, linked to a noble and essential task.'

Despite his deluded preoccupation with the destruction of Bolshevism, Hitler was not entirely immune to proposals for action elsewhere. Though he was not so absurdly hubristic as his Foreign Minister, Ribbentrop, who told a visiting Italian minister that the war in Europe was all but over and 'can be considered to be already won', he had managed to convince himself that the entry of Japan into the war had signed Britain's death warrant. On the face of it, in the wake of the fall of Singapore, the Japanese rampage through the Far East and the damage being inflicted by German U-boats on Allied shipping in the Atlantic, there were superficial grounds for this expectation. Buoyed by this presumption, he once again turned his capricious mind to the Middle East.

Although he was still unwilling to deplete his forces in Russia by siphoning them off to another theatre, he did not reject out of hand a renewed attempt by Admiral Raeder, the C-in-C of the German Navy, to persuade him that an offensive against the British in the Mediterranean could deliver a fatal blow to the Allies. Arguing that the Suez Canal and Basra were the 'western pillars of British domination in India', Raeder's view was that, were they to be destroyed, 'the strategic consequences would be devastating for the British Empire'.

The Führer's immediate response was non-committal. Although his one-eyed focus on Russia made it impossible for him to see that an Axis victory in Egypt and the Persian Gulf, might not merely 'devastate' the British Empire but, in the words of the military historian Sir Michael Howard, 'make it impossible [for Britain] to carry on the war at all', he allowed Raeder to elaborate his ideas. Thus encouraged, SKL (the Seekriegsleitung, German Naval Command) renewed the argument in favour of that very pincer movement in the Middle East about which the Chiefs of Staff in London were so apprehensive. Raeder's scheme was based on the assumption that the Japanese navy would soon dominate the Indian Ocean and close off the entrance to the Persian Gulf, at which point Rommel's Panzerarmee would advance on Suez to link up with Wehrmacht units advancing through the Caucasus to

Iran and Iraq. A precondition for throttling the British Empire by these means, however, would be the 'capture or total neutralisation' of Malta – an operation in which a naval blockade followed by a seaborne invasion would play a decisive part.

The naval commander's proposition put him at odds with others in OKW. Though Chief of Staff Halder accepted the case for a move against Suez, he argued that the attack should only come from the north via the Caucasus and not by Rommel from Libya. Either way, he insisted that any assault on Egypt should be given a green light only after the conquest of Russia. But Raeder persisted and, supported by the commander-in-chief of the Mediterranean theatre, Field Marshal Kesselring, he kept up the pressure on the Führer.

Both Raeder and Kesselring recognised that Malta was as important to the Axis campaign in the Mediterranean as it was to the British; that to control Malta was effectively to control the vital sea routes and airways between Italy and North Africa. From the start of Rommel's campaign, the Royal Navy and the RAF, both based at Malta, had persistently – and sometimes almost fatally – disrupted the regular flow of supplies to Tripoli without which the Axis campaign would have been doomed.

In a half-hearted attempt to bomb Malta into submission, the Italian air force had subjected the island to a fitful bombing campaign since the autumn of 1940. When the Luftwaffe joined the fray in January 1941, this aerial assault started to inflict far more damage than the display of flamboyant aerobatics to which the Maltese had previously been treated. The terror bombing of the island soon rivalled anything to which Britain had been subjected during the Blitz.

By the spring of 1942, the Maltese had been forced to give up all semblance of normal life. Though their island was now studded with anti-aircraft guns and crowded with more than 150 RAF bombers and fighters, operating from three hastily prepared airfields, they were given no respite. Kesselring, who, in December, had been tasked with the 'suppression of Malta', was given a boost when Hitler ordered the despatch of every available plane that could be spared from the Eastern Front to 'neutralise' the island fortress.

During the day, wave upon wave of German bombers assaulted the island; by night the Italians picked up the baton in a non-stop relay of aerial attrition that was as unsparing of the civilian population, which had started to live a troglodyte existence, as it was of the British defences. The agony of Malta has been vividly described by Douglas Porch: 'People fled to the countryside or spent the night standing in a fetid, urine-soaked, abandoned railway tunnel on the outskirts of Valletta that did duty for a public shelter, listening to an oratorio of screeching rats crazed by the bombing.'

Simultaneously, a naval blockade led to a drastic reduction in the number of British convoys reaching Valletta, the Maltese capital and main harbour; between January and April 1942 not one ship arrived. The population was very soon on starvation rations. 'Civilians queued for hours for a ladle of unappetising watery stew composed of dirty, poorly cooked vegetables flavoured with goat or horse meat ... Pasta ran out in April ... Electricity was scarce, and no kerosene was left for cooking, light or heat.'

On 15 April, in honour of their courage and to raise morale, George VI bestowed the George Cross on the entire population of Malta. But the graffiti writers were not overly impressed; the phrase *Hobz, mux George Cross* – Bread, Not George Cross – became the islanders' *crie de coeur*. So desperate was the situation that on 20 April Malta's governor, General William Dobbie, cabled London in despair to report that 'it is obvious that the very worst may happen if we cannot replenish our vital needs, especially flour and ammunition, and that very soon ... it is a question of survival'.

Between 20 March and 28 April the Axis dropped more than 6,500 bombs on the island, killing at least 1,000 people, wounding 4,500 more and destroying 15,500 buildings. Every surviving Royal Navy vessel was forced to flee the wreckage of the harbour at Valletta for the security of Alexandria, while the RAF had been reduced to a handful of serviceable planes. Their pilots were suicidally brave. One Rhodesian pilot recalled a day 'when only five of us were airborne and we encountered over 200 enemy aircraft – 40 109s [Messerschmitt Me109 fighters] escorting bombers – but the Spitfires shot down four bombers off Grand Harbour. Time after time as my wheels touched the ground I had to go up again to avoid being shot to pieces on the ground.' By late April Kesselring had, as instructed, managed virtually to neutralise Malta's capacity to threaten the Axis convoys in the Eastern Mediterranean.

It was against this alarming backdrop that Churchill found himself on the receiving end of a most unwelcome analysis of Britain's predicament from his Middle East commander-in-chief. On 27 April, in another gloomy assessment of the challenges facing his command, Auchinleck reported that the Axis powers were gaining control of the Eastern Mediterranean and there was little or nothing to be done about it; that his own forces were too weak to establish air superiority in the Western Desert; and that (in his biographer's summary), 'too much should not be expected' from his forthcoming offensive in Libya because he would probably lack the 'required tank superiority' and 'at the height of the battle' much of the air force 'might have to be withdrawn' to operate on the Northern Front (Iraq, Syria, and Turkey).

Auchinleck advised Churchill:

> If the immediate political and strategic results of an even partially successful offensive in Libya were likely to affect decisively the course of the war in this, or any other theatre I would not hesitate to advocate it. Even if fully successful, however, such an offensive could not materially affect the chances of a successful defence of our Northern Front, nor could it arrest the Japanese progress towards India and the Persian Gulf. It could have little material effect on the coming campaign in Russia. On the other hand failure on our part in Libya is likely to have an immediate and most far-reaching effect not only on the Middle East but on the whole world situation.

His reluctance to take the offensive against Rommel could not have been more clearly stated or well argued. However, his case imploded when he went on to make the astonishing proposal that he should send troops – 'every resource that can be spared' – from his own Command to India or Ceylon, 'to check the Japanese advance before it is too late'. He repeated this even more sharply in a letter to Brooke a few days later. Whether or not he was actuated by his own deep ties with India, he wrote on 3 May, 'The matter most in my mind at the moment is the threat to India ... I am seriously perturbed and cannot help wondering whether the dependence of the Middle East on India, strategically and materially, is fully realised at home.' With more than 200,000 Indian troops in the Middle East – roughly a fifth of what Churchill always referred to as his 'ration strength' – Auchinleck added that, although this was 'very nice for us [it was] hardly in keeping with her [India's] own very urgent need for all the trained soldiers she can muster'.

Stressing the degree to which the Middle East was dependent on India for munitions (90,000 tons had been delivered in March alone) as well as manpower, he concluded, 'I feel very strongly that the time has come when we must decide what is vital to our continued existence and what is not ... If I had to choose now between losing India and giving up the Middle East I would not hesitate. I believe that we can still hold India without the Middle East but that we cannot for long hold the Middle East without India.' His conclusion: the offensive in Libya, which had been brought forward to 15 May, should be postponed indefinitely.

Unwittingly, Auchinleck hit a raw nerve with his plea for India. Churchill's attitude towards Britain's Indian Empire was untouched by the emerging ideologies of the twentieth century, especially in relation to self-determination and democracy. A child of Victorian England, his imperial outlook had long since crystallised into a firm belief that white men – especially English white men – were inherently superior to the African and Asian natives over whom they ruled. This conviction was most unambiguously expressed in *The River War*, published in 1899, when he wrote admiringly of how, in Jeremy Paxman's phrase, 'Kitchener's machine guns made short work of poorly armed Sudanese', explaining that Britain's imperial mission was 'To give peace to warring tribes, to administer justice when all was violence, to strike the chains from the slave, to draw the richness from the soil, to plant the earliest seeds of commerce and learning, to increase in whole peoples their capacities for pleasure and diminish their chances of pain.'

Shorn of its seductive romanticism and applied to India, this attitude had fossilised into a disdain not only for the Indian demand for self-government but for a people whom he appeared to regard as children incapable of directing their own affairs. His aversion to Indian home rule was so extreme that his Secretary of State, Leo Amery, was driven to wonder whether, 'on the subject of India, he is really quite sane'.

In India itself, the nationalist movement, with Mohandas [Mahatma] Gandhi at its head, had long agitated for independence. In 1935 the British had been driven to promise self-government within the Empire but, on the outbreak of war in 1939, the Viceroy of India, Lord Linlithgow, press-ganged the country into supporting the British Crown. In an effort to restrain the growing frustration of the National Congress, Linlithgow also promised that the issue of self-rule would be reopened once the war was over. However, Gandhi's rapidly growing army of followers wanted India to stand apart from the conflict as a neutral state – a conviction that was reinforced by the rapid advance of the Japanese towards the Indian Ocean. Choosing to regard this stance as defeatist, the Prime Minister drew comfort from the fact that by 1942 an Indian Army of one million men had '*volunteered*' (Churchill's italics) to fight for the Empire; nor did he take kindly to being reminded by his own officials, however obliquely, that these brave soldiers were also 'mercenaries [who] fought for their pay and to support their families, also in the hope of rewards, of gratuities, pensions, and possibly grants of land'.

With the tensions in India bubbling ever more virulently, the American President decided it was time to proffer some advice on how to handle the demand for self-determination, a cause which was close to his heart. Churchill bridled at once. Attributing the White House's sudden interest less to high principle than to the fact that the Japanese were moving relentlessly towards the frontiers of Britain's most treasured possession, Churchill regarded it as unwarranted interference in the Empire's internal affairs. Moreover, he thought – with some justice – that Washington did not appreciate the complex rivalries and nascent hatreds between the Hindu and Muslim communities (which, five years later, after a communal bloodbath which cost at least half a million lives, would lead to the formal partition of India and the creation of Pakistan).

Roosevelt had raised his concerns about India at the Arcadia Conference in Washington. In the course of a lengthy lecture on British imperialism, Churchill had rebuffed him with such severity that the two leaders never spoke about the subject again. But India was too important for the President to ignore and the President was too important for Churchill to ignore. In the months that followed, the latter consented to keep the former apprised of the deteriorating political situation in the subcontinent.

By the spring of 1942, the President could ignore the issue no longer. In a 'Purely Personal' letter to Churchill on 10 March, he wrote, 'I have given much thought to the problem of India ... I have tried to approach the problem from the point of view of history and with a hope that the injection of a new thought to be used in India might be of assistance to you.'

Proposing the establishment of 'a temporary government' in India as the first step in the establishment of a permanent administration that would pave the way for full independence, Roosevelt reminded Churchill that such a move would be 'strictly in line with the world changes of the past half-century and with the democratic process of all who are fighting Nazism'. Though he was careful to concede that, 'strictly speaking', it was none of his business, he made it clear that his suggestion was 'part and parcel of the successful fight that you and I are making'.

Roosevelt's intervention, with its anti-imperialist tone, infuriated the Prime Minister but, mindful of both the President's growing concern and the rising tension in India itself, he decided to send Sir Stafford Cripps to Delhi to seek a way through a political impasse which now threatened to impede Britain's war strategy. In essence, the Lord Privy Seal was charged to promise 'full independence to India if demanded by a Constituent Assembly *after* [author's italics] the war'. However, as Churchill had fully expected, his emissary (whose arrival in the Indian capital had been delayed by his diplomatic diversion to Cairo) failed to find the common ground needed to progress.

When Roosevelt heard about Cripps's mission impossible, he dispensed with diplomatic nicety, protesting in a cable to Churchill on 11 April:

> I feel that I must place this issue before you very frankly …
> The feeling [in the United States] is almost universally held that the deadlock has been caused by the unwillingness of the British government to concede to the Indians the right of self-government … American public opinion cannot understand why, if the British Government is willing to permit the component parts of India to secede from the British Empire after the war, it is not willing to permit them to enjoy what is tantamount to self-government during the war.

Urging that Cripps should remain in Delhi in a further effort to secure a compromise that would bind India into the Allied war effort, he concluded that if – but only if – Churchill made this extra effort, the American people might be satisfied that a 'real offer and a fair offer' had been made by the British Government.

Once more, Churchill was enraged. Reflecting on the episode after the war, he wrote (with a contempt that no other disagreement between them was to provoke), 'I was thankful that events had already made such an act of madness impossible [Cripps had already left India to return to Cairo]. The President's mind was back in the American War of Independence, and he thought of the Indian problem in terms of the thirteen colonies fighting George III at the end of the eighteenth century. I, on the other hand, was responsible for preserving the peace and safety of the Indian continent, sheltering nearly a fifth of the population of our globe.' It was the authentic voice of the unreconstructed imperialist. But in Britain, he was far from being alone. Precious few voices were raised against him in the media or in the street while his Cabinet, including its Labour members, was staunch in support. Had it been otherwise, Churchill claimed, he 'would not have hesitated to lay down my personal burden, which at times seemed more than a man could bear'.

Churchill's response to Roosevelt's interference was measured but implacable, softened only by the emotional appeal with which he concluded his letter. 'Anything like a serious difference between you and me would break my heart and would surely deeply injure both our countries at the height of this terrible struggle.' For the time being, his warmth and eloquence ended the matter.

Within days Roosevelt, now clearly exerting his authority as the senior partner in the Anglo-American Alliance, was once again on the diplomatic offensive against Churchill. This time, yet again, the issue was Russia. Despite its valiant efforts, the Red Army had yet to beat back the Wehrmacht divisions which still threatened to turn an invasion into an occupation. While the people of Leningrad heroically refused to yield, the German noose around the city was slowly throttling the life from its starving citizenry. And, though neither threat had yet materialised, the prospect of a renewed offensive against Moscow or a thrust southwards towards the Caucasus put the Soviet regime under extreme pressure. To prevent a Nazi conquest, Stalin depended heavily on weapons and equipment from the United States and Britain. But in the spring of 1942, the damage inflicted by the Luftwaffe and the Kriegsmarine (German Navy) on the Arctic convoys from Britain and the United States had dramatically reduced the flow of supplies to the Russian Front. Armaments from the United States piled up in Iceland waiting for naval escorts to run the German gauntlet across the Barents Sea. But Britain lacked the necessary tonnage without diverting ships from other vital duties.

On 27 April Roosevelt cabled Churchill to say that he was 'deeply disturbed' by the prospective shortfall of deliveries of critical supplies to the Arctic ports of Archangel and Murmansk.

Once again – and so soon after the Indian imbroglio – Churchill found himself at odds with the President. In this case, however, he was on stronger ground. 'With very great respect,' he wrote, 'what you suggest is beyond our power to fulfil.' Warning of the 'disastrous consequences' that would follow any transfer of naval escorts from the Atlantic to the Arctic, he wrote 'I beg you not to press us beyond our judgement in this operation ... I can assure

you, Mr President, that we are absolutely extended.' Roosevelt
backed off.

Churchill's own imperative was to maintain the flow of supplies from the United States to Britain and especially to the Middle
East. The demand for a second front, for which public opinion in
the United States and Britain agitated with growing fervour, added
even more urgency to the campaign in the Western Desert. To
sustain Britain's status as an almost equal member of the newly
formed triumvirate alongside America and Russia, Churchill
had to demonstrate that the Eighth Army's desert campaign was
a crucial element in the overall strategy to defeat the Axis. For
immediate political as well as strategic reasons he also needed to
show that the resources being poured into the Middle East from
the United States – which might otherwise have been sent to the
Soviet Union – would bring early success against the Axis threat
in this theatre.

Against this extraordinarily fraught background, Auchinleck
could hardly have chosen a worse moment to propose both that the
Indian divisions under his command should be transferred from
the Middle East to their own home front and that the desert offensive should be postponed yet again. Summoning his considerable
reserves of sarcasm, Churchill's reaction was withering. 'While
we are grateful to you for your offer to denude the Middle East
further for the sake of the Indian danger,' he wrote on 5 May, 'we
feel that the greatest help you could give to the whole war at this
juncture would be to engage and defeat the enemy on your western
front. All our directions upon this subject remain unaltered in their
purpose and validity.' In private he now spoke openly of sacking
Auchinleck and of replacing him with General Alexander, who had
presided as commander-in-chief over the British Army's retreat
from Burma, though without significant damage to his reputation.

Two days later, somewhat chastened, Auchinleck reiterated
his case for postponing the offensive against Rommel but ceded
ground by agreeing that it could start on 15 June. He underlined
his case against any earlier attack with yet another detailed statement of the comparative strengths of the Eighth Army and the

236 DESTINY IN THE DESERT

Panzerarmee, especially in tanks, which gave the impression that Rommel enjoyed an insuperable advantage.

Later that day, the Cabinet met to discuss Auchinleck's message. Though Brooke was irked by Auchinleck's caution, and especially by his failure to appreciate the growing danger to the survival of Malta unless he moved swiftly against Rommel, he argued that it would be wrong to instruct the commander-in-chief to attack in the face of his considered advice from the front. The Cabinet accepted this guidance but Churchill could not disguise his impatience with Auchinleck, reminding him, in yet another cable, that the loss of Malta 'would be a disaster of the first magnitude to the British Empire, and probably fatal in the long run to the defence of the Nile Valley'. Urging him 'to attack the enemy and fight a major battle, if possible during May, and the sooner the better', he put his full authority on the line, advising, 'We are prepared to take full responsibility for these general directions.'

In perhaps his most serious – and, for him personally, disastrous – error of strategic and political judgement, Auchinleck cabled back to assert that the loss of Malta would not greatly affect Britain's position in the Middle East. 'This', Kennedy wrote later, 'was an incredible misconception. Apart from any question of prestige, the military value of Malta was great, not only as a check on traffic from Italy to North Africa, but as a staging point for aircraft in transit to the Middle East and India.' Moreover, some 30,000 soldiers and airmen were based on Malta and the thought of sacrificing them to the enemy was unacceptable. Auchinleck's insouciance about the possible loss of Malta was his undoing. Not only had he made a poor case but, according to Kennedy, 'The manner in which he had conducted the long discussions had lost him the confidence of both the Cabinet and the Chiefs of Staff.'

The War Cabinet now faced a grave dilemma. It would be a serious breach of protocol to override the commander-in-chief's judgement or to sack him merely because of his reluctance on military grounds to take the offensive against Rommel. Yet London was convinced that unless he could be goaded into action, Malta might fall. On 10 May, after a further meeting of the Cabinet, Churchill accepted Brooke's view that Auchinleck should be given a stay of execution. But, in what the Prime Minister described as 'a most unusual procedure' Auchinleck was given very clear orders which Churchill noted later he had either to 'obey or be relieved' of his command.

Churchill's message was unequivocal:

> We are determined that Malta shall not be allowed to fall without a battle being fought by your whole army for its retention. The starving out of this fortress would involve the surrender of over 30,000 men, Army and Air Force, together with several hundred guns. Its possession would give the enemy a clear and sure bridge to Africa, with all the consequences flowing from that. Its loss would sever the air route upon which both you and India must depend for a substantial part of your aircraft reinforcements. Besides this it would compromise any offensive against Italy, and future plans such as *Acrobat* and *Gymnast*. Compared with the certainty of these disasters, we consider the risks you have set out to the safety of Egypt are definitely less, and we accept them.

The 'very latest date for engaging the enemy which we could approve' was one that would distract the enemy's attention from a convoy of merchant ships laden with relief supplies which was scheduled to arrive at Malta on or around 15 June. Churchill's unstated but unambiguous threat could not have been lost on Auchinleck: if he wasn't prepared to do battle then Churchill would find someone who was.

The C-in-C, Middle East did not react for a full week. On 17 May Churchill cabled again, 'It is necessary for me to have some account of your general intentions in the light of our recent telegrams.' Two days later, Churchill finally got the answer he wanted. 'My intention is to carry out the instructions of your message of 10th May,' Auchinleck wrote with dignified *froideur*. With icy precision, he went on to seek clarification that the required offensive was not merely intended 'to provide a distraction to help the Malta convoy, but that the primary object of an offensive in Libya is still to be the destruction of the enemy forces and the occupation of Cyrenaica as a step towards the eventual expulsion of the enemy from Libya. If I am wrong in this assumption, then I should be so informed at once, as plans for a major offensive differ entirely from those designed merely to produce a distraction.' His disdain, concealed behind a mask of obedience, was crystal clear.

Churchill replied the following day, confirming that Auchinleck's presumption was correct and, in a belated attempt to warm the chill between them, adding, 'We have full confidence in you and your glorious army, and whatever happens we will sustain you by every means in our power.' Slightly mollified but clearly distancing himself from the decision that had been imposed on him, Auchinleck replied in the manner of a senior retainer, 'I am now absolutely clear as to my task and will do my utmost to accomplish it to your satisfaction … Am most grateful for your most generous expression in the army I command and in myself and for the assurance of your support, the measure of which has been proved to us so often and so amply in the past.' The die was cast: the offensive would begin as agreed in the middle of June.

This was to reckon without Rommel, who was chafing for action. For the first time since his arrival in North Africa, his military arsenal was overflowing with supplies. In February and March, as a result of the Axis bombardment and blockade of Malta, only 9 per cent of the supplies sent to North Africa from Italy had been lost en route; in April almost every ship reached Tripoli unscathed. As a result, the Panzerarmee was positively 'bloated' with fuel and armaments. Kesselring and Rommel were agreed in principle that the Axis offensive should start before the heat of summer but that Malta – already bruised but not broken – should be further pounded into submission.

The chief obstacle to this German *coup de main* was Cavallero, whose aversion to any offensive military action had been an albatross round Rommel's neck from the start. The head of Comando Supremo made it clear to Kesselring that he would oppose any attack on Malta unless success could be guaranteed by the use of overwhelming force. This, he knew, would not readily be forthcoming.

Thus baulked, Kesselring flew to Rome, where he managed to secure Mussolini's personal approval for an all-out attack on the British fortress. This, they agreed, should start at the end of May. From Rome, Kesselring flew to the Wolfsschanze, where, on 18 April, he 'treated Hitler to a heavily embroidered picture of the situation in the Mediterranean, and gave a glowing account of the Italians' preparations for a surprise attack on Malta'. Thus wilfully misinformed – the Italians had hardly begun to plan the assault, let alone to commit the resources required – Hitler finally cast aside his doubts and gave the formal go-ahead both for the invasion of Malta – to be codenamed *Herkules* – and for Rommel's offensive in the desert (which he had so recently forbidden).

This appeared to be the start of the great offensive for which Rommel had so long campaigned. On the face of it, Hitler had at last set in train a course of events which – in Rommel's mind – would lead to the beginning of the end of the British Empire in the Middle East and beyond. At this point in 1942, the Middle East was indeed at Hitler's mercy: the Eighth Army could have been annihilated, Egypt could have fallen, and the 'carotid artery' of the British Empire could have been severed, with incalculable consequences not only for a vast theatre of war stretching from Persia to Morocco, but for Britain's capacity to combat Nazism anywhere. But this was to calculate without the Führer's obsession with the Soviet Union which meant that, in reality, he willed only the ends, not the means. In so doing he assuredly made a strategic error to rival the invasion of Russia.

Perhaps to the relief of a timorous Comando Supremo, the Führer made it clear that, while he approved the seizure of Malta, he was not yet able to spare more than a token force of aircraft and parachute battalions for the operation. The Italians responded by sending OKW a military shopping list of such proportions that – as they must have foreseen – it was bound to be rejected. *Herkules* had been agreed in principle but would be impossible to mount in practice. No one, save Kesselring, who had a far sharper appreciation of the strategic importance of Malta than either Rommel or any other of his senior colleagues, was unduly dismayed by a delay which would prove to be fatal.

At the end of April 1942, Mussolini made one of his obligatory trips to the Berghof for yet another meeting with the Führer. Ciano's description of their arrival betrayed a weariness with these summits, which the Foreign Minister clearly believed had outlived their utility. 'The usual scene: Hitler, Ribbentrop, the usual people, the usual ceremony ... There is much cordiality, which puts me on my guard. The courtesy of the Germans is always in inverse ratio to their good fortune. Hitler looks tired.' Echoing Goebbels, he added, 'I see for the first time that he has many gray hairs.'

Ciano was haunted by the air of unreality which pervaded the talks. At one point, Ribbentrop, whom he loathed, informed him that after the Wehrmacht had advanced south and seized the Russian oil wells in the Caucasus, the 'British Conservatives, and even Churchill himself, who, after all, is a sensible man, will bow in order to save what remains of their mauled empire'. Ciano was no more convinced by that forecast than he was by the German Foreign minister's assertion – which was 'repeated by everyone, big and little, in the conference rooms and antechambers' – that America was 'a big bluff'. Ciano clearly thought that OKW was in denial. 'In my opinion,' he noted, 'the thought of what the Americans can and will do disturbs them all, and the Germans shut their eyes in order not to see. But this does not stop the more intelligent and more honest from thinking about what America can do, and they feel shivers running down their spines.'

The little of substance that was formally agreed in the space between the Führer's relentless monologues – 'Hitler talks, talks, talks, talks, talks,' noted Ciano irreverently – constituted an approval in principle for *Herkules* (but postponed until July at the earliest) and an immediate go-ahead for Rommel's next offensive.

On 12 May, Rommel wrote to his wife, 'Nothing much to report. Heat and lots of dust ... There's a certain nervousness on our front. The British are expecting us and we them. One day the two forces will measure their strength.' By now London was indeed expecting Rommel to launch an attack; the Ultra code-breakers at Bletchley Park had decrypted enough Enigma signals to judge that the Panzerarmee would be on the move by the end of the month.

But, unbeknown to Churchill, who laid great store by intelligence data from all sources and was an unusually assiduous interpreter of the evidence it provided, Rommel knew virtually as much about Auchinleck's plans as the Prime Minister. Some of this information came from decoding 'chatter' directly from Eighth Army units at the front. But much of this secret intelligence – which had already proved to be of quite extraordinary importance to Rommel – came from secret Allied messages sent from Cairo and intercepted in Rome before being passed on selectively to Berlin and thence to Rommel's North African headquarters. Since January, these intercepts had given the Desert Fox detailed reports of the strength and disposition of the British forces opposing him in the Western Desert. The source was known to him as 'Gute Quelle' (good source) and to Washington as Colonel Bonner Fellers, the US military attaché in Egypt.

From the opening of hostilities in the desert, Fellers had been given full access to the Eighth Army at the highest level, which meant that he was privy to the most secret data on its 'strengths, positions, losses, reinforcements, supply situation, plans, morale etc.'. But no one at Middle East Command was aware that, in addition to reporting back to Washington through the usual diplomatic channels, Fellers had been charged by his superiors in Washington to run a covert operation – effectively spying on the British – at the same time. Still less did they – or Fellers – have any inkling that within eight hours of his 'Most Secret' coded messages leaving Cairo for Washington they were 'under the gimlet eyes' of Mussolini, Hitler and Rommel.

Fellers was not only an astute analyst but socially adept; he swiftly became a trusted confidant of anyone who mattered in the Middle East Command. On the day that Wavell launched his first offensive in the late autumn of 1940, he was invited by the British commander-in-chief to join him: 'General Wavell told me they were going to do manoeuvres, so I went up as an observer, and God dammit,' he said later, 'it was the real thing.' But the more he saw and heard, the more critical and often contemptuous he became of the British efforts in the desert. On New Year's Day 1942, he had lunch with Hermione Ranfurly, a British aristocrat who worked for the Special Operations Service, which had four commando units in the Middle East. Countess Ranfurly doubled as a British spy. 'The trouble is your top brass is overconfident, which they've no right to be,' Fellers told her in his characteristically forthright way, continuing, 'your gear is still inferior to the enemy's, and you are less well led. Too many senior officers are sitting on their arses at GHQ.' The detailed analysis on which these censorious comments were based was of incalculable benefit to the Panzer-armee. One of Rommel's staff officers later commented that Gute Quelle's intelligence was 'stupefying in its openness' and 'contributed decisively to our victories in North Africa.'

Fellers sent his nightly messages to Washington using the standard 'Black Code' which the Americans believed to be impenetrable. And so it might have been, had not the Italian Servizio Informazione Militare (SIM) managed to plant two agents inside the US Embassy in Rome. One evening in September 1941, one of these agents, Loris Gherardi, opened the ambassador's safe, discovered the Black Code and handed it over to two colleagues waiting in a car outside. They took it to SIM headquarters, where it was immaculately copied. Later Gherardi took it back with him to the Embassy and discreetly replaced it.

According to Berlin's Chiffrierabteilung des OKW (the military cipher branch responsible for coding and decoding secret information), the knowledge unwittingly shared with them by Fellers from January 1942 provided 'all we needed to know, immediately, about virtually every enemy action'. This information had not only helped to nullify the impact of Operation *Crusader* but, as Rommel had detailed reports on the Eighth Army's operational plans, tactics, losses, and morale at his fingertips, had made an inestimable contribution to the dramatic success of his counteroffensive in late January when he had pushed Ritchie's forces back to the Gazala Line, where now, five months later – armed with the latest intelligence from 'Gute Quelle' – they awaited the next onslaught.

SEVENTEEN

THE WORST OF TIMES

*'These battles are hell. That's the fourth amputation today
and the fourteenth operation. I've been at it since eight
o'clock this morning and there's a queue like Bank Holiday
at the cinema.'*

Battlefield surgeon to Richard Dimbleby

On 27 May 1942, Lieutenant D. F. Parry overheard an exchange between a British 'forward' officer at the southernmost tip of the Gazala Line and a colleague embedded at XXX Corps headquarters at El Adem. Had it not been reported verbatim, the conversation might be presumed to have formed part of a Monty Python sketch forty years later.

OFFICER: There is a cloud of dust to the south; it has the
appearance of a military formation.
REPLY FROM XXX CORPS: There are no, repeat no, troops to your
south …
OFFICER: The cloud of dust is growing larger. It is undoubtedly
a military formation.
REPLY (*slightly irritable*): We repeat, there are no, repeat no,
troops to your south.
OFFICER: Through the haze I can now identify tanks, difficult
to identify but possibly German Mark IVs.
REPLY (*irritably*): We repeat, there are no troops, repeat no
troops, to your south.
OFFICER: I am counting Mark IVs – one, two, three, four, five,
six, seven – there is no doubt, repeat no doubt, that this is a

large German force. Mark IVs number over thirty, and there are also Mark IIIs and a large number of motorized infantry. This could be, I repeat, this could be the Afrikakorps moving at a speed of approximately 30 miles per hour towards El Adem.

REPLY *(with air of resignation)*: There are no forces in your area.

OFFICER: I have been spotted by the enemy and am under fire. I repeat, it is a large enemy formation and probably the Afrikakorps moving fast northwards.

REPLY *(very bored)*: There are no enemy forces in your area.

OFFICER: It is undoubtedly the Afrikakorps moving at speed towards El Adem. I am under …

In the background it was possible to hear the sound of exploding shells … Then there was silence. Rommel's blitzkrieg – Operation *Venezia* – had been unleashed.

'It will be hard, but I have full confidence my army will win it,' he had written to his wife the previous evening, 'After all, they know what battle means. There is no need to tell you how I will go into it. I intend to demand of myself the same as I expect from each of my officers and men.' Under cover of darkness he then took his place with the Afrikakorps, in a column, which along with the 90th Light Division and the XX Italian Corps, numbered 10,000 vehicles. 'I was tense and keyed-up, impatiently waiting the coming day. What would the enemy do? What had he already done? These questions pounded my brain.'

Six days earlier, Auchinleck, who was in Cairo, had sent a long letter to Ritchie at Eighth Army headquarters. Clearly concerned about Ritchie's well-attested limitations but anxious not to undermine his confidence, he wrote, 'Do not think I am trying to dictate to you in any way, but this coming struggle is going to be so vital that I feel you must have the benefit of our combined consideration here.' He identified two possible lines of attack that Rommel might open up. The first would be 'to envelop our southern flank, seizing or masking Bir Hacheim en route, and then driving on Tobruk'; the second would be 'a heavy attack on a narrow front …

with the object of driving straight to Tobruk'. This, he warned, might be accompanied 'by a feint against Bir Hacheim ... with the aim of drawing off the main body of your armour to the south and so leaving the way open for the main thrust'. While he was careful to remind Ritchie that he should be prepared to face either option, he judged that 'the second course is the one he [Rommel] will adopt, and is certainly the most dangerous to us'.

Unfortunately, Auchinleck had got it wrong. Rommel's plan of attack was precisely the opposite of what the British commander-in-chief supposed. His feint was to the north, not the south.

Five hours before Rommel's force headed for Bir Hacheim, his second-in-command, Cruewell, launched a frontal attack to the north. But this was not 'the main thrust' towards the Gazala Line which Auchinleck had anticipated. His entire strength consisted of two small armoured units accompanied by camouflaged trucks, each mounted with whirring aero-engines that kicked up great clouds of dust which wafted across the desert to provide a convincing impression that a major onslaught was underway. Meanwhile Rommel's 'right hook' advanced without impediment. Guided by dim lights concealed in used fuel cans planted in the sand, Rommel's column swept south along a meticulously prepared route until, a little before dawn, they reached a location some twelve miles to the south-east of Bir Hacheim, the southernmost fortress along the Gazala Line.

To begin with, Rommel's ruse went as planned. As soon as dawn broke, 'this great force' as Rommel described it, set off northwards in the direction of their ultimate objective, Tobruk, and very soon, 'in a swirling cloud of dust and sand, thrust into the British rear'. By 10 a.m. the 90th Light Division – to the initial disbelief of the hapless radio officer at XXX Corps headquarters – had reached El Adem, a mere twenty miles south of the Tobruk perimeter. The British 7th Armoured Division, almost alone in protecting the southern flank, was overrun. In the midst of what he was to describe as 'an awful muck of a battle', their commanding officer, General Frank Messervy (who had replaced the kilted Jock Campbell, killed in a motor accident two months earlier), was taken prisoner; but, after pulling off his insignia, he persuaded his captors that he was a humble batman and managed to escape soon afterwards to rejoin the division the following day.

In the confusion of these early hours, the British were at a loss. The commander of a Royal Horse Artillery battery, Major Jerry Birkin, scouting for evidence of the advancing panzers, sighted a dust cloud. At that moment a shell landed beside his armoured car. The next round scored a direct hit. 'I didn't realise it had hit us,' his driver, Bobby Feakins, recalled, 'and I turned round and there were two radio operators without heads – absolutely nothing from the shoulders. I had blood and muck all over me. Major Birkin slumped into my arms and he was actually dead at that point, hit right in the tummy. I was wounded in the legs. In the inter-battery wireless, I said, "We've been hit. We've been hit!"'

Under shellfire, the Major's brother, Captain Ivor Birkin, who belonged to the same regiment, arrived to witness the carnage: his brother's corpse, and, in the words of Sergeant Harper, his driver, 'those two lads, their hands still holding their mouthpieces, although their heads were lying on the floor', while Feakins, the only survivor, was 'gabbling out the message'. They managed to haul themselves onto the top of a passing tank but Feakins, who had lost the feeling in his legs, soon fell off into the sand.

After a while another tank came by heading vaguely in the direction of the enemy. 'The Commander said, "What the hell are you doing here?" "Having an afternoon cup of tea, you silly bugger." He replied, "Well I'm sorry old chap, I'm going into action now, but on my way back I'll pick you up." And he went away. An hour and a half, two hours, watching shells drop round me ... Fear because you didn't know what was going to happen. But he did come back, and I felt that heaven had opened up.'

Despite his blitzkrieg, Rommel was unable to maintain the momentum. As his panzers advanced northwards through the mine-laden military maze of the Gazala Line, they came under fire from British artillery dug in to the north, the east and the west. Even more seriously, they found themselves matched for the first time in the desert by the US-built M3 Grant tanks, recently arrived from America and in use on the North African battlefield for the first time. Despite their usually reliable intelligence, the Germans had also seriously underestimated the number of British tanks ranged against them; rather than the 85 they had thought, they faced 284, of which 167 were the fearsome Grants. Despite a heavy toll exacted by the German artillery, the 1st Armoured Division, which had been humiliated by Rommel's onslaught four months earlier, fought with heroic resolve and, in the words of General von Mellenthin, 'in some cases forced their way up to the very muzzles of the guns and wiped out the crews'.

In the afternoon the Axis columns came under such heavy and sustained fire that many of them broke in confusion, and, in Rommel's words, 'fled away to the southwest, out of the British artillery fire'.

By the evening, his advance had been forced to a standstill, and, as he noted ruefully, 'The advent of the new American tank had torn holes in our ranks. Our entire force now stood in heavy and destructive combat with a superior enemy.' Although the Panzerarmee had wrought havoc with the 7th Armoured Division and the 3rd Indian Motor Brigade, Rommel had lost more than a third of his entire armour; his transport columns were on the run from British motorised infantry units, the Light 90th Division had become separated from the Afrikakorps and Rommel himself had become separated from both. It was a grim reckoning at the end of a day which had started out so well for the Desert Fox.

The British, on the other hand, were mightily relieved not only to have survived the onslaught but to have seen off their attackers. The Gazala Line had held and the enemy advance had been arrested. According to Auchinleck's Director of Military Intelligence, Freddy de Guingand, 'Eighth Army were feeling quite pleased with themselves and everyone was quietly confident. We knew that the enemy's tank losses had been considerable, that his advance had been held up and that the coastal attack had been defeated. The enemy's main column stretched for miles ... Here the Desert Air Force found great opportunities and reports of hundreds of burning vehicles came pouring in. Our great belt of minefields had not been penetrated. So far so good.'

Over the next four days there was fierce, scattered and confused fighting along and behind the Gazala Line as Rommel, who had made contact again with the Afrikakorps and the 90th Light Division, once more marshalled his troops with his customary flamboyance and energy. During these decisive battles at the end of May, with the Afrikakorps coming under severe pressure, he came close to death twice on the same day. Soon after dawn on 28 May, as he scanned the horizon, detecting an enemy column on the move, his command post came under fire. 'Shells flew all round us and the windscreen of our command omnibus flew into fragments. Fortunately we were able to get away in our vehicles out of range of the British fire,' he wrote afterwards.

In the early afternoon, with the Afrikakorps virtually surrounded and under intense bombardment, Rommel – defying convention yet again and demonstrating an elan that few, if any, other army commanders would have dared to essay – set off with his Chief of Staff, General Gause, to find a way through to the beleaguered German armour. The alarming news that the 15th Panzer Division had run out of ammunition made it critically important to open up a supply line to the imperilled laager in which it was now at bay. Identifying a navigable route around the British positions, the two men set off back to Rommel's headquarters. On the way, as Rommel laconically described the encounters, they had 'a brush' first with a British and then with an Italian column. Unhappily the latter 'took us for hostile and opened up a wild fire, which we escaped by a quick withdrawal'. The next morning at daybreak, he led the supply column through to the beleaguered panzer division without being observed.

During these days, Rommel seemed to be everywhere at once, urging his men on, devising new tactics, and all the time on the move. There could not have been a greater contrast between his leadership and that of the Eighth Army's commander-in-chief, who preferred to oversee the battle from well behind the lines. This was not for want of courage on Ritchie's behalf but because he adhered to a stolid military convention which – like his immediate predecessor – he did not question. Cautious and plodding, he was psychologically and intellectually unable to react with the incisiveness required on a battlefield, the character of which altered as rapidly and dramatically as a constantly shaken kaleidoscope. Thus, rather than seizing the initiative at a point when his adversaries feared he would achieve 'a crushing victory', Ritchie dithered. In this vacuum, Rommel's commanders were able to regroup, repair armour and artillery, and take up defensive positions from which they were able to ward off the uncoordinated and sporadic attacks launched against them.

The balance and disposition of the two armies meant that Rommel should have been on his knees before the superior might ranged against him; instead the flexibility, ferocity and discipline of his troops served yet again as a reminder of how he had earned his nickname: he was quicker, more imaginative, and more skilled in the deployment of his armour. Even in retreat, the Axis troops – Italian as well as German – displayed a sangfroid and expertise that forced Auchinleck to concede, 'Although his lightning attack had failed, the enemy nevertheless gained a solid advantage.'

Describing one of the many confusing battles along the front, Auchinleck wrote with barely suppressed frustration of the way in which an entire Italian division (the Trieste) managed to escape through a British minefield (at Trigh Capuzzo) despite coming under heavy fire from Ritchie's tanks. 'Our armour strove to interpose itself between the enemy and the paths through the minefield,' he wrote, 'but he covered his retirement in characteristic fashion with a powerful anti-tank screen which our armour could neither penetrate nor outflank ... The whole of our armour was thus powerless to close on the gaps.'

It was even worse than that. In the many weeks during which they constructed the chain of boxes along the Gazala front, the Eighth Army commanders had failed to ensure that the minefields strung between them were adequately covered from each box by artillery fire to pick off any enemy tank seeking to navigate the maze of buried explosives. The result of Ritchie's oversight, as Auchinleck later confessed, was that after four days of sustained fighting, the panzers 'had succeeded in breaching our front and creating a dangerous salient in our main position'.

Nonetheless, the Germans were in a precarious situation. By

31 May, Bayerlein judged the panzer division under his command to be 'in a really desperate position, our backs against the mine-field, no food, no water, no petrol, very little ammunition … We were being attacked all the time from the air. In another twenty-four hours we should have had to surrender'. Accompanied by the commander of the Afrikakorps, General Walther Nehring, he therefore 'begged Rommel to break off the battle'. According to Bayerlein, however, 'he wouldn't hear of it'.

Instead Rommel ordered his panzers to launch an offensive against Got el Ualeb, one of the Gazala Line boxes, which was defended by 150th Brigade. Once again Ritchie was wrong-footed. As though numbed by Rommel's ruthless daring, instead of rushing troops and tanks in a co-ordinated move against the exhausted Germans and to support 150th Brigade, he failed to take any action at all. Thus the British brigade, which was at the point of exhaustion, was left to its own increasingly desperate devices.

'Yoicks. Tally ho, tally ho,' yelled a colonel leading a suicidal tank charge against a battery of 88mm anti-tank guns. One of the junior officers under his command, a Royal Horse Artillery observer, Captain William Pringle, was aghast and tried to stop him. 'When I eventually got him on the wireless, he told me he knew where he was going, and that it was my job to do what I was told. We went straight at them. The first gun was on him in seconds and BWHUUFF – he'd gone and the whole lot came to a screaming halt, there was total chaos everywhere.' Pringle ordered his driver to retreat. But the gears were stuck and the tank was trapped and disabled. Eventually, between them, they managed to engage reverse gear. 'We reversed seven miles. I told the driver, "Don't you stop, I'll murder you if you stop."'

Elsewhere in the chaos, Major Robert Daniell managed to make contact with his commanding officer. 'Bob, you are to stand and fight in the position where you are now, you are not to move,' he was instructed. 'Do you understand me? You are not to move at all.' Daniell told him that if he obeyed, he would lose every single man in his regiment. The brigadier replied, 'You are a Horse Artillery officer, you have been properly brought up and you know that in battle you will obey orders or take the consequence.'

Everywhere the British turned they seemed to come up against a well-concealed and perfectly positioned panzer tank or 88mm gun. Sergeant Ray Ellis, who, as we have seen, had narrowly avoided death at Sidi Barrani eighteen months earlier, was almost killed when a shell landed on his gunnery position, killing the rest of his unit. With no sense of bravado, he described how as one man fell, another came forward to take his place. One of them, who was not even a gunner, was caught by a burst of machine gun fire. 'He was terrified. I crouched down trying to console him, "You're all right lad, you're all right. Don't worry, you're not badly wounded, we'll soon have you away ..." Trying to ease his fear, I noticed sand settling on his eyes. He died in my arms.'

Soon Ellis was left alone. Every gun was out of action. He walked across to a British armoured vehicle. Inside he found two dead bodies, one of whom had been a good friend. 'I looked down on his lifeless face and burst into tears, seeing an old pal from the day I joined the regiment.' A few moments later a German tank rolled up and a sergeant beckoned him to jump aboard. 'We looked at one another, we'd been fighting each other all day. We both shrugged our shoulders and looked up to heaven – what a bloody silly thing it was. It was a matter of two enemies who had no enmity.'

By late afternoon, 150th Brigade had run out of ammunition and the panzers were about to overrun their positions.

With Ritchie in remote control away from the front, not only out of touch but ill informed by his own subordinate commanders, Rommel himself led the panzer infantry platoon which made the final break through the perimeter to seize the Got el Ualeb Box, where they took 3,000 prisoners and 124 guns.

The gallant remnants of 150th Brigade did their best to escape. According to Major Dobson,

it really became *sauve qui peut*. I went off with four or five others in a scout car. We hoped we might manage to drive through the minefield. We got a long way before there was the usual explosion and the wheel was blown off. We just sat there hoping we hadn't been seen, but we had and we were shelled

– it was very unpleasant. That night we set off to walk back towards (we hoped) our lines, but after a long night's walking we ran into a German LOC unit who, praise them, were very good to us.

The capture of Got el Ualeb not only marked a critical moment but came as a huge relief to the Axis forces. 'If we had not taken it on 1 June,' Bayerlein recalled, 'you [the British] would have captured the whole of the Afrikakorps ... we were surrounded and almost out of petrol. As it was, it was a miracle that we managed to get our supplies through the minefield in time.' But once they had found a route, they opened a relatively safe corridor through which the Axis commanders were able to resupply their front line. 'Our mines', de Guingand observed bleakly, 'were thus turned to the enemy's advantage, for they gave him much-needed protection.'

Richard Dimbleby visited a casualty clearing station a little to the rear of the mayhem but in the path of the advancing panzers. The noise of the battle shook the heavy canvas sides of the hospital tents and once or twice a heavier explosion rattled the medical instruments in the operating theatre. Inside, he saw three men robed in white bent intently over a polished steel table. Directly above them a powerful bulb shone against the shiny insides of some petrol tins which had been sliced open to form a wide reflector to direct the light onto the table. On the ground he saw a severed leg in a long enamel dish. Someone had thrown a cloth over the leg, 'leaving the toes sticking up, blue and grubby'. As the patient was wheeled away, two bombers roared overhead. The orderlies, clearing away the bloody instruments and dressings, took no notice. The surgeon, washing his hands at a bowl of steaming water, similarly ignored the intrusion. His face was tired and strained. 'These battles are hell,' he told the BBC correspondent. 'That's the fourth amputation today and the fourteenth operation. I've been at it since eight o'clock this morning and there's a queue like Bank Holiday at the cinema.' Outside, Dimbleby counted thirty soldiers waiting patiently for their turn on the operating table. All over the battlefield – on both sides – the grisly human detritus of war endured in pain and with patience.

A while later he came across a tank unit manned by members of the 3rd County of London Yeomanry. 'Most of them had been in action for twenty-four hours non-stop. They were covered with sand and dust and splashes of oil ... I spoke to three men from one tank as they sat against its tracks in a tiny pool of shade. The driver was a Bible seller in peacetime; his comrades were a bank clerk from Westminster and a hotel manager on the Great North Road.' They were remarkably phlegmatic, comparing the recently arrived American Grants with their own vehicle, which the Bible seller patted 'as affectionately as if it were a horse'. They asked Dimbleby what was happening on the rest of the battlefield; how were things? 'They could be better,' the reporter replied. 'You know I'm getting bloody fed up with this desert,' the Bible seller said, 'It's the same old tale every time. Push them back, and they come up to knock us down. It isn't getting us anywhere.'

With Ritchie paralysed by indecision, the soldiers under his command were left to protect a line of boxes which by now had lost all useful purpose. A signaller in the Royal Artillery, Robert Lee, recalled one incident:

> Coming at us, we had artillery shells, airburst rapid fire, machine gun-fire. German armour and German vehicles got right up on us. They were in full view ... Vehicles and Valentines [British infantry tanks] burning all around us, palls of that acrid smoke, the smell of human flesh roasting, burning. The first taste of hell. But not the last.
>
> All our positions were overrun like a farmer ploughing his fields. Their infantry and their quick-firing guns on portees were advancing on us ... We'd no alternative, apart from committing suicide. We laid down our weapons. We spread out. We walked towards individual soldiers with our hands raised and open. The young German I came to said 'Nicht boom-boom', and I said 'Nein'.

Rommel's troops swirled back and forth across the Gazala Line at a pace and with an ingenuity that left the Eighth Army floundering. His goal was still Tobruk, but he faced a familiar problem:

the reinforcement of supply lines which now extended forward to the new positions the panzers had taken up amid the minefields along the Gazala Line, a battleground which both sides referred to as the Cauldron. To this end Rommel had to establish a secure route around the southernmost edge of the Gazala Line. On 2 June, the panzerarmee commander duly despatched the German 90th Light and the Italian Trieste Divisions to Bir Hacheim, which was defended by the Free French under General Koenig, who had so far managed to stave off a succession of panzer attacks.

At Eighth Army headquarters, Ritchie and his senior commanders discussed how best to counter Rommel's latest moves. In a note to Auchinleck, he wrote, 'I am distressed over the loss of 150th Brigade after so gallant a fight but still consider the situation favourable to us and getting better daily.' Ritchie had no evidence to support this extravagant assessment and – given the dull-witted irresolution he now displayed – provided no grounds for supposing that he had any idea of how to seize back the initiative. One of his senior commanders, General William Ramsden, remembered hearing one of his colleagues emerging from one of many interminable staff conferences, to say 'I *think* Ritchie is going to do this or that.'

Auchinleck was filled with misgivings. 'It seemed to me', he wrote later, 'that, if the enemy were to continue to occupy a deep wedge in the centre of our minefield, the whole Gazala Line and Bir Hacheim in particular would become untenable.' With unconfirmed reports that large numbers of panzer tanks were advancing into the Cauldron, he concluded lugubriously – and in sharp contrast to Ritchie – 'We appeared to be rapidly losing the initiative we had gained by bringing his first attack to a standstill.' Unless Ritchie could regain the initiative, Tobruk would soon be in grave danger while the Eighth Army would have to contemplate a further retreat to the Egyptian border and beyond.

It was not until 5 June that Ritchie belatedly made his next move. In the early hours of the morning, units of the Eighth Army, under cover of an intensive artillery bombardment, launched a direct attack on Rommel's forces in the heart of the Cauldron. Had this counter-offensive been launched two days earlier, it might well have prospered, but Ritchie's days of indecision had given Rommel vital time to reinforce his key positions on a salient where the Axis was dug in on the high ground.

At first the British seemed poised to make a breakthrough as two Indian brigades supported by the 22nd Armoured Brigade drove the Italian Ariete Division off its stronghold on Aslagh Ridge. But when the British tanks advanced deeper into the Cauldron to take Sidi Muftah Ridge, they came under devastating tank and artillery fire and were forced to wheel off to the north, leaving the 9th and 10th Indian Divisions trapped in the middle of the minefield.

Everything now went wrong. With tight-lipped precision, Auchinleck described the dismal failure of another attempt to enter the Cauldron via an assault on Sidra Ridge, where 21st Panzer was dug in. 'The 32nd Army Tank Brigade', he wrote, 'was attacked on its right flank by enemy tanks, and having run onto an uncharted enemy minefield and so lost fifty tanks out of its original seventy, could give the infantry no support when they in their turn were attacked by tanks.' Von Mellenthin described the same attack from the German standpoint. Noting that it might have been 'gravely embarrassing' had it been made under cover of darkness, he wrote incredulously, 'the heavy British tanks lumbered forward in daylight, providing perfect targets for our anti-tank guns and ending up on a minefield where they were simply shot to pieces. From the tactical point of view this was one of the most ridiculous attacks of the campaign.'

Captain Rea Leakey was on one of the tanks spearheading this 'ridiculous' attack:

In the first second we must have received at least four direct hits from armour-piercing shells. The engine was knocked out, a track was broken and one shell hit the barrel of the 75-mm gun and broke it. Then quite a heavy high-explosive shell dropped on the mantlet of my 37-mm gun and pushed it back against the recoil springs ... I suffered nothing more than a 'singing in the ears'. But a splinter hit the subaltern in the head and he fell to the floor of the turret dead ... Almost every tank in the battle met with the same treatment.

With the Eighth Army reeling, Rommel stepped up the pace and variety of his assault and the panzers were soon running amok through the British positions. With tactical headquarters overrun, wireless sets destroyed, communications severed, tents and trucks set on fire, it was clear to Colonel Desmond Young (later to become Rommel's biographer), who was serving with the Indian Army, that the enemy 'had, indeed recovered the initiative which General Ritchie had wrested from him and had no intention of giving it up. 5 June was the turning point of the battle, though the chance of winning it outright went three days earlier.'

By 6 June, the Axis divisions which Rommel had despatched to Bir Hacheim four days earlier had surrounded the fortress. Now Rommel pressed home his advantage with ground and air attacks against the Free French who showed rare tenacity despite mounting losses. Ritchie was well aware of the importance of Bir Hacheim; that – in Auchinleck's words – its loss would require him to 'form a new and extended front facing southwards behind which we might be hemmed in and deprived of our power of manoeuvre. The threat to our rear would be increased.' Accordingly, he despatched tank and infantry units to confront the 90th Light and Trieste Divisions. Rommel countered by sending further reinforcements to the same location.

On 8 June, with cover from dive-bombing Stukas and artillery fire, an Axis unit penetrated a corner of the garrison. But, despite the continued aerial bombardment, the Free French refused to yield, resisting with such valour that von Mellenthin was moved to record that 'in the whole course of the desert war we never encountered a more heroic or well-sustained defence'. From London, General de Gaulle broadcast: 'General Koenig, know and tell your troops that the whole of France is looking at you and you are her pride.' Koenig responded 'We are surrounded. Our thoughts are always with you. Long live Free France.'

But by 10 June it was clear that heroism alone could not prevail. Ritchie gave the orders for the survivors to break out. Under heavy aerial and artillery bombardment but partially protected by the 7th Armoured Division, 2,400 of the original 3,700 defenders of Bir Hacheim fought their way out using bayonets.

An officer who observed them as they reached the British front line, noted that 'some of these tough, bearded Frenchmen were almost in tears when they described their anger and frustration ... They would have preferred to stay and die.' De Gaulle was greatly affected. In a flush of high-flown rhetoric, he proclaimed, 'When a ray of glory touched the bloodstained brows of her soldiers at Bir Hacheim, the world recognised France.' After the war, as President of France, he ordered a Métro station near the Eiffel Tower to be renamed 'Bir Hacheim' in honour of its defenders.

Rommel was now free to press his advantage. Cutting a swathe through the British defences, the panzers forced their way north until they reached the 'Knightsbridge Box'. With the battleground all but obliterated by a severe sandstorm, the Axis tanks and artillery supported by waves of Stukas assaulted the target area from all sides. German and Italian infantry advanced en masse into minefields which surrounded the box but were forced back by the Guards Brigade, which fought so valiantly as to earn a plaudit from Rommel for its 'tremendous courage and tenacity'. Casualties from both sides littered the ground, their bodies eerily illuminated by burning vehicles which gave an orange tint to the sandstorm which swirled about them.

Alan Moorehead likened the scene to another Battle of Waterloo:

> The English Guards with their strange and slightly automaton code of behaviour were peculiarly suited to this sort of action. It was something they understood. A position was given you to fortify and then you got the order to hold it to the last round and the last man ... So these odd gawky officers with their prickly moustachios, their little military affectations, their high pitched voices and their little jokes from the world of Mayfair and Ascot kept bringing their men up to the enemy, and the men, because they were picked soldiers of the regular army and native Englishmen and Scots, did exactly as they were told.

So resolute was their resistance that Rommel was forced to

call off the assault. Auchinleck signalled, 'Well done, 8th Army. Stick to it. Hang on to him. Never leave him. Do not let him get away. Give him no rest. Good luck to you all.'

But his congratulations were premature because his exhortations were ignored. 'I don't understand, why aren't we following up?' Colonel Young asked, his rhetorical question an expression of the bitter and widespread frustration at the failure of the Eighth Army's senior commanders to seize the initiative. 'We could have occupied the battlefield yesterday and grabbed all those Jerry tanks lying about. The Germans themselves are milling about all over the place. Why don't we push in and mop them up? … We will have to move quick or you can bet your life they will return to form a line. I can't understand it. I am only afraid that it is already too late.' His pessimism was well grounded. Rommel's heavy armour, concentrated in force, was perpetually on the move, feinting here and thrusting there while Ritchie's commanders floundered.

There were moments of memorable but long-forgotten heroism. One British division, seeking to escape from encirclement and surrender, hurled itself headlong at the enemy line under cover of darkness. The armour went first, followed by truckloads of infantry. In a moment of desperate fighting,

Germans and Italians alike shrieked for mercy from their slit trenches. Guns, tanks, defences, all were pulverised in the furious assault. A Valentine tank rode straight over an Italian mess tent in which enemy staff officers were having a late supper. Our men saw Germans on their knees, praying to be allowed to surrender. Some of the enemy who kept their heads manned every available gun and fired point-blank at the British transport columns plunging and bucketing through. In the glare of burning vehicles, the major commanding the Valentines saw a German climbing up the side of his tank with a bayonet raised to stab. The major was a boxer; a beautiful right hook sent the enemy sprawling under the tracks of the following tank.

But such moments of romantic valour made no difference to the imminent outcome.

As the Axis forces regrouped around the 'Knightsbridge Box', Rommel himself led the 15th Panzer Division in a simultaneous thrust towards El Adem, where one of their British victims – captured not killed – turned out to be Colonel Young (who soon came face to face with Rommel – a fortuitous meeting which led the British officer to write his influential and admiring biography of the German General after the war). Yet again, Rommel came close to death. On the evening of the 12th, he noted laconically, 'we were bombed by some of our own Stukas. They were being chased by British fighters and, lame ducks that they were, were forced to drop their bombs on their own troops for the sake of some extra speed. However the three of us – Bayerlein, the driver and I – escaped once again without a scratch.'

By 13 June, the Eighth Army was at the point of collapse. No longer able to hold out against the renewed assault, the exhausted Guards Brigade finally evacuated 'Knightsbridge'. With a sandstorm raging of such intensity that visibility was no more than a few yards, Rommel advanced towards Tobruk virtually unimpeded, recording that the 'slaughter of British tanks went on ... murderous fire struck from several sides into the tightly packed British formations, whose strength gradually diminished'.

The rout that was now in the offing did not spring from a lack of courage on the part of the British, Indian, Australian and Free French troops caught in this inferno but from the numbed and dilatory leadership of their commanding officers. Though Ritchie dithered, he was not alone to blame. His subordinates – Generals Norrie, Messervy and Lumsden – were not only out of touch with the calamitous turn of events on the battlefield but very often with each other as well. With their armour, artillery and infantry scattered and isolated, their commanders knew neither what was happening nor the extent of their losses. On that grim day, the 13th, when the mutual carnage of men and machines reached hideous proportions, the Eighth Army's official log was reduced to recording that there had 'evidently' been 'losses on both sides in these engagements'.

If Ritchie was in denial, Auchinleck, who returned on the same day to Cairo from a flying visit to the front, was at a loss, still unaware of how desperate the situation had become. But by the next day, with only seventy tanks left, Ritchie finally realised the scale of his defeat. He at once ordered the bulk of his forces to retreat to the Egyptian frontier in what became known – self-mockingly but despairingly – as 'the Gazala Gallop'.

Confusion soon became chaos as the British units trapped at the front fought their way out of the minefields and often straight through the Axis lines. 'I was lucky,' Captain Snell of the Durham Light Infantry recalled. 'My truck was hit by an anti-tank shell and blown to pieces but I and my driver got out. We went right through the dugouts with bayonets, tommy guns and grenades and cleared them out ... Our armoured cars shot all the machine-gunners. Our battalions went through. The Italians on each flank tried to stop them, but there was no concentrated effort on their part.' Snell led his company south into the desert, passing Bir Hacheim, and reached the wire between Egypt and Libya but 'we were shot up all the way, and by the time I arrived I had three armoured cars, myself and two other blokes. The rest of the company were wiped out.'

Earl Haig, who had just joined the 22nd Armoured Brigade, watched as 'like horses in a race ... the German units and ours were running neck and neck' for an isthmus in the desert, the last defensive position in Egypt from which it would be possible to arrest Rommel's headlong rush towards the Nile Delta and the Suez Canal. The retreat, noted Haig, 'was a very messy business and most unfortunate. Very sad ... rather I suppose like Dunkirk, we must have lost most of our supplies, our petrol dumps, our ammunition and so on.'

Rommel was cock-a-hoop. Rejoicing in the 'courage of the German and [a rare compliment] Italian soldiers' he rode with the panzers on the 14th, 'as British vehicles streamed east in their thousands' towards Egypt. Watching this retreat he noted the 'black dejection' on the faces of the retreating British troops. In a letter to his wife on the next day he wrote, 'The battle has been won and the enemy is breaking up. We're now mopping up encircled remnants of their army. I needn't tell you how delighted I am. We've made a pretty clean sweep this time.' He might have added, 'Next Stop: Tobruk.' One of the most fateful episodes of the Second World War was about to begin.

In London, Churchill did not realise how swift the collapse had been. With the 'Gazala Gallop' already in progress, he telegraphed Auchinleck, 'Your decision to fight it out to the end is most cordially endorsed. We shall sustain you whatever the result. Retreat would be fatal. This is a business not only of armour but of will-power. God bless you all.' Auchinleck, who had himself only just become aware that the Eighth Army was in full retreat – now alerted the Prime Minister to the galling truth that, save for two divisions which would remain to guard the approaches to Tobruk – the Eighth Army was on the way back to the 'old frontier'. Churchill cabled back in dismay, 'Do not understand what you mean by withdrawing to "old frontier".' More pointedly, he asked, 'To what position does Ritchie want to withdraw the Gazala troops? Presume there is no question in any case of giving up Tobruk. As long as Tobruk is held no serious advance into Egypt is possible.' The following day, Auchinleck replied, 'Although I do not intend that Eighth Army should be besieged in Tobruk, I have no intention whatever of giving up Tobruk.'

Auchinleck had good grounds for believing that this would be the end of the matter. Six months earlier, in January, the three commanders-in-chief in the Middle East, Admiral Cunningham, Air Marshal Tedder and Auchinleck himself, had come to 'the firm and unanimous decision that Tobruk should not again be held' were it to be invested by Rommel. On 19 January, Auchinleck made this unequivocally clear. 'It is not my intention to try to hold permanently Tobruk or any other locality west of the [Egyptian] frontier,' he wrote in Instruction No. 110, which was subsequently endorsed by the Middle East Defence Committee on 4 February. Two days later, the Head of Military Operations, Kennedy, sent a copy of this instruction to Brooke, with a note supporting Auchinleck's decision. On 11 February Auchinleck elaborated his position in Instruction No. 111, to Ritchie: 'If, for any reason, we should be forced at some future date to withdraw from our present forward positions [on the Gazala Line], every effort will still be made to prevent Tobruk being lost to the enemy, but it is not my intention to continue to hold it once the enemy is in a position to invest it effectively. Should this appear inevitable, the place will be evacuated, and the maximum amount of destruction carried out in it, so as to make it useless to the enemy as a supply base.' This instruction was still in force when the Gazala battle began in May. Unless Brooke had failed to read these instructions, or omitted to inform Churchill about them, the Prime Minister was dissembling when he wrote subsequently, 'At home we had no inkling that the evacuation of Tobruk had ever entered into the plans or thoughts of the commanders.'

As it was, the realisation that Auchinleck intended to evacuate Tobruk rather than subject its defenders to another siege appalled Churchill. His response to what he regarded as Auchinleck's 'equivocal' commitment to Tobruk was brusque. 'War Cabinet interpret your telegram to mean that, if the need arises, General Ritchie would leave as many troops in Tobruk as are necessary to hold the place for certain.' Churchill's anxious insistence that Tobruk should be held whatever the cost exposed a fundamental faultline that lay between London and Cairo: while the commander-in-chief regarded his overriding responsibility to be the defence of the Middle East and, as part of that, the defence of Egypt, the Prime Minister above all else wanted a victory over Rommel in the desert. For Auchinleck the port had utility as a supply depot for any further British advance deeper into Libya, but it was not critical to the defence of Egypt. For the Prime Minister Tobruk was symbolic of British resolve, a totem to the defeat of the Axis in North Africa and thereby to Britain's prestige in the world. To this extent Churchill's views mirrored those of Rommel – and Hitler – both of whom invested Tobruk with similar significance.

To the surprise and dismay of the Director of Military Operations in London, Auchinleck wilted under the pressure. On 16 June he cabled the Prime Minister to confirm 'War Cabinet interpretation is correct. General Ritchie is putting into Tobruk what he considers an adequate force to hold it even if it should become temporarily isolated by the enemy ... Very definite orders to this effect have been issued to General Ritchie, and I trust he will be able to give effect to them.'

Not surprisingly, Churchill took this to mean that the matter had been settled beyond all doubt and replied at once, that the Cabinet 'was glad to know that you intended to hold Tobruk at all costs'. Much relieved – but choosing to gloss over the implicit ambivalence of the word 'temporarily' – he set off in high spirits for his second prime ministerial visit to Washington where, as he put it, 'business of the highest importance to the general strategy of the war had to be transacted'.

As Churchill's flying boat droned steadily across the Atlantic, the Eighth Army continued in headlong flight to the Egyptian border. Tobruk was isolated and at the mercy of the panzers. 'To every man of us', Rommel wrote, 'Tobruk was a symbol of British resistance and we were now going to finish with it for good.'

By the evening of 18 June, Tobruk was cut off entirely and the surviving remnants of the Eighth Army beyond the perimeter wire joined the flight to the border, blowing bridges and laying mines as they went in a bleak effort to impede the progress of the pursuing panzers. Seen from a distance, the earthworks around the port seemed impressive – 'like the crenellated battlements of a mediaeval castle' – but on closer examination turned out to be no more than 'square piles of loose rocks' behind which the defenders 'lay pressed to the ground', horribly exposed to artillery fire and aerial bombardment.

Alan Moorehead, who arrived in Tobruk a few days before Rommel launched his attack, noted the lack of perimeter walls, anti-tank trenches and pill boxes. 'Indeed,' he wrote, 'as you went across this flat neutral coloured ground, you saw very little difference from the ordinary desert.' And there was good reason for this. Following Auchinleck's Instruction No. 111 of six months earlier, the once impenetrable barricades that had given Tobruk its talismanic reputation around the world, had been allowed to fall into disrepair. They were now half-ruined and largely neglected.

However, inside the town itself, the correspondent reported

an abundance of fresh water, millions of gallons of petrol in square cans, an arsenal of weaponry and ammunition, hospitals complete with medical supplies. He came across a great store of provisions – 'tinned tomatoes, peas and potatoes, tinned American beef, South African biscuits … sacks of tea and sugar, big tins of cheese, jam, and fish', enough comfortably to feed up to 30,000 men for three months. Nonetheless the place was dispiriting in the extreme. Tobruk was a decaying wreck of a town, which had been 'bombed into insensibility'. Aside from the light relief of the graffiti on one broken monument which read 'The Red Lion. Free Beer tomorrow', the 'depressing, degrading, levelling influence of war had made this place accursed'.

The troops defending Tobruk had been under enormous strain even before Rommel launched his final assault. Almost half their number – comprising two South African infantry brigades – had yet to be tested in battle while their commander, Major General Hendrik Klopper, who had been appointed only three days earlier, was similarly unblooded. On his arrival in Tobruk, Klopper had written to a South African colleague at GHQ to inform him, 'Things are going very well here, as spirits are very high, and I do not think morale could be better under present circumstances. There is a general feeling of optimism.' If so, it was alarmingly misplaced.

Following the collapse of the Gazala front, the South African recruits, very far from their own homeland, were obliged to watch as hundreds of lorries, overflowing with their exhausted brothers-in-arms, rumbled through Tobruk on their way back to the Egyptian border. Nor was the defenders' morale raised by the arrival of reinforcements – the 201st Guards Brigade and the 11th Indian Brigade – both of whose members had fought valiantly at 'Knightsbridge' and El Adem but were now drained of energy, famished with hunger and bruised by defeat. Within Tobruk's perimeter, a global symbol of British resistance, pessimism was the order of the day.

The Axis onslaught was brilliantly conceived and ruthlessly executed. Ritchie had presumed the panzers would strike at the perimeter from the direction of the Gazala Line and had instructed

Klopper to position his forces accordingly. But Rommel – in characteristic fashion – had opted for surprise. Instead of a head-on attack from the north-west he circled round to the south-east, where the panzers were least expected and which was therefore thinly defended. He had also persuaded Kesselring to despatch every available bomber to Tobruk, from as far away as Crete and Greece as well as the Axis airfields in North Africa.

The attack began early in the morning of 20 June. At dawn, the first wave of dive-bombers descended on the south-eastern perimeter, their air-activated sirens wailing with fearsome warning. Rommel and von Mellenthin stood on an escarpment overlooking the Tobruk perimeter. 'Kesselring had been good to his word and sent hundreds of bombers in dense formations; they dived on the perimeter in one of the most spectacular attacks I have ever seen,' von Mellenthin wrote. The bombardment – the first of 588 missions that day – had the desired effect. It was 'terrifying', a sergeant in the 6th South African Infantry Brigade reported. To make matters worse, he recalled, 'we didn't know what was happening as there were no orders from our officers. Confusion reigned, with fear and panic.' The German and Italian artillery had already laid down a ferocious barrage of fire on these ill-defended positions. This soon opened up a breach in the perimeter through which the first panzers bore down on the traumatised defenders who rose from their gun emplacements with their hands held aloft in surrender. The 'weak resistance' shown by the Indian and South African defenders under the crushing weight of the onslaught took the Axis commanders by surprise but allowed them to breach the outer defences with ease.

The Italian Trento Division was to the fore as the Axis forces swarmed into the town. A junior infantryman, Vittorio Vallicella, was in a patrol which took the surrender of 'hundreds' of black soldiers (very probably South African labourers, uniformed but unarmed), who 'at the sight of our small group, leap to their feet raising their hands in a sign of surrender … With surprise but also respect we look at these poor black soldiers who are at the service of rich England and who have come from afar to fight in a war which possibly they don't even know for whom or for what.'

As his patrol advanced further into the town, he was astonished to discover the 'luxury' in which their enemy had basked: there were showers, every officer had a mosquito net over his bed and, envy of envies, an abundance of food. Very soon, though, the food depots which they overran were taken over by the Germans. 'Even here our allies want to lord it over us,' Vallicella noted drily.

Shaken by both the direction and the ferocity of the Axis onslaught, Klopper all but gave up any attempt to arrest the enemy's advance. Though the panzers met some resistance as they trundled into the town, Klopper had barely started to regroup his troops before Rommel had himself crossed the perimeter and was on his way down to the port. In the late afternoon the harbour came under fire and Tobruk's fate was sealed. 'By nightfall it was obvious that Tobruk was in its death throes and Rommel was able to send off a triumphant signal to Berlin,' von Mellenthin noted, adding judgementally, 'Our losses during the day had been very small and out of all proportion to those of the enemy.' That evening, a number of British defenders managed to 'liberate' a case of gin from the officers' mess and 'got as drunk as lords, consuming a dozen bottles and singing patriotic songs such as "There'll always be an England ..."'. But across town, as Gunner W. A. Lewis recalled, it was possible to hear a counterblasting snatch of 'Deutschland uber Alles'.

In the early hours of the following morning, Klopper signalled Auchinleck to report, 'Situation shambles.' A while later he raised a white flag in surrender. Auchinleck's official report stated bleakly 'An order was circulated to all units in the garrison that a capitulation had taken place and that all vehicles, equipment and arms were to be destroyed.' Among the tens of thousands of fellow soldiers who surrendered in Tobruk, Lewis and his fellow revellers were rearrested in the tunnel where they had taken refuge during the night. 'Bodies lay everywhere,' he wrote later. 'At what was once the town square we found thousands of other prisoners ... My God, the humiliation of it all.'

By this time, Rommel was already at the port. 'Practically every building of the dismal place was either flat or little more than a heap of rubble,' he noted. As he drove out of town onto the

Via Balbia, he passed long columns of prisoners and burning vehicles on either side of the road; all about him he saw only 'chaos and destruction'. The Axis troops were elated. Reflecting the high hopes – and the relief – of the Trento Division, Vallicella noted, 'We have only one thought: Alexandria, Cairo, the Nile, Pyramids, palm trees, and women.'

Four miles to the west of Tobruk, Rommel reached Klopper's headquarters, where he took the formal surrender. Later that day he wrote exultantly to his wife, 'Tobruk! It was a wonderful battle.' In all, 35,000 imperial troops – South Africans, Indians, and British – were captured. In the annals of capitulation during the Second World War, this meant that Tobruk ranked second only to Singapore (where the Japanese took 85,000 prisoners). The defeat was as absolute as it was inevitable.

In his Order of the Day on 21 June, Rommel praised the 'Soldiers of the Panzerarmee Afrika' for their 'incomparable courage and tenacity' and promised them 'the complete destruction of the enemy' in the days ahead; later he wrote that for every one of 'my Africans', the victory at Tobruk 'was the high point of the African war'. Hitler was euphoric. The capture of Tobruk, he said, was 'destiny's gift to the German nation … an absolutely incredible success.' The next day a wireless message arrived from the Führer's headquarters to inform Rommel that, at the age of forty-nine, he was to be elevated to the rank of Field Marshal.

EIGHTEEN

THE AMERICANS COME GOOD

'What can we do to help?'
Franklin D. Roosevelt to Winston Churchill

Hitler's triumph was Churchill's humiliation. The day after his arrival in Washington on 18 June 1942, the Prime Minister left Brooke and the rest of his entourage in the capital and flew up to Roosevelt's private residence, Hyde Park, on the edge of the Hudson river. There, in the informal surroundings of the President's family home, the two leaders conferred in private on what was indeed 'business of the highest importance'. There were two main items on their agenda: the top-secret project to build and deploy the atomic bomb – codenamed 'Tube Alloys' – on which they found themselves in complete accord; and, more challengingly, the deepening transatlantic division over the grand strategy to be adopted in the year ahead.

Whatever he had – misleadingly – intimated in his discussions in London three months earlier, Churchill was in no doubt about his overriding objective: *Gymnast* (the Allied invasion of North Africa) had to precede *Sledgehammer* (the Allied attack on Cherbourg), which in turn was to precede *Roundup* (the full-scale invasion of France). For Roosevelt, the choice was more finely balanced. Earlier in the year, Marshall had tried to steer him away from *Gymnast*, but it still retained its residual appeal for the President. Although he had made it clear that his initial endorsement for the

North African operation was conditional on the near-certainty of success, he also had to consider 'the risks of *not* getting American ground troops into direct combat against the Wehrmacht before the [American] mid-term elections in early November'. Roosevelt's political imperative was to show the American people in advance of polling day that 'Our Boys' were directly engaged on the battlefield against the Nazi threat. He feared otherwise that the Republicans might triumph in the elections and, under pressure from the isolationist lobby, use their majority in Congress to repudiate Roosevelt's 'Germany First' strategy in favour of a campaign exclusively against Japan in the Pacific – an alternative which enjoyed strong support among the American electorate.

The details of their private talks at Hyde Park have yet to be revealed, but Churchill must have made the case for *Gymnast* with his characteristic eloquence and persistence. Roosevelt, who chose to regard himself as 'an amateur' strategist – and, in this respect, inferior to the 'former Naval person', as the Prime Minister dubbed himself in their secret correspondence – might be presumed to have been duly impressed.

The President may not have been a military strategist but he was an accomplished politician. The Prime Minister, who was similarly endowed, wrote a formal memorandum to Roosevelt on 20 June, to emphasise that *Gymnast* was the only available option capable of meeting the President's political requirements, not least because a 'substantial landing' in France before the November elections was out of the question. 'No responsible British military authority', he wrote, 'has so far been able to make a plan for September 1942 which had any chance of success unless the Germans became utterly demoralised, of which there is no likelihood. Have the American Staffs a plan?' In effect, Churchill was telling the President that it was *Gymnast* or nothing.

Simultaneously, Roosevelt received a letter from his Secretary for War, Henry Stimson, which expressed precisely the opposite view. In a ten-point document, Stimson argued that the best way to defeat Hitler was an early second front in Europe rather than an invasion of North Africa. Claiming, somewhat unconvincingly, that it was 'imperative' to despatch forces to Britain 'at top speed' to confront the threat of a likely Nazi invasion, he insisted that this could not be done if American ships were 'tied up with an expedition to *Gymnast*'. His message – which directly contradicted Churchill – was equally unambiguous: at least for the foreseeable future, *Gymnast* should be abandoned.

To complicate matters for Roosevelt, Stimson's opinion reflected the views of every one of the President's most senior military advisors, none of whom had abandoned their initial aversion to *Gymnast*, and one or two of whom expressed themselves with great vehemence. The amiable 'Pug' Ismay, Churchill's principal link to the British Chiefs of Staff, was present at a key meeting of the Combined Chiefs of Staff on 20 June in Washington, where he noted that Admiral King, the Chief of US Naval Operations, was 'blunt and stand-offish, almost to the point of rudeness'. He added that he was intolerant and suspicious of all things British. But it was Marshall's opposition rather than King's Anglophobia which was to weigh more heavily with the President. As the Army Chief of Staff, Marshall had already reiterated to Roosevelt – while Churchill was en route to Washington – that, on tactical and logistical grounds alone, he believed the case against *Gymnast* to be overwhelming. The landings in North Africa, he insisted, could be contemplated only if the preparations (codenamed *Bolero*) for the *Sledgehammer* landings in France were 'abandoned, or at best, indefinitely postponed'.

Brooke, who was in Washington for the first time as Chief of the Imperial General Staff, had not hitherto been required to declare his own position. He was, of course, party to Churchill's predilection for *Gymnast* but, at his first formal meeting with Marshall, he merely suggested that if it proved impossible to establish a Western Front in France during 1942, they should plan for *Gymnast* in one form or another; to this end, he argued, the US forces being readied for *Bolero* should be diverted to the North African operation. This equivocal contribution to the debate was scarcely the full-hearted endorsement of Churchill's vision that the Prime Minister might have wished from his most senior military advisor, and it sat uneasily with his earlier disdain for *Sledgehammer* but at least it kept *Gymnast* on the table.

However, after long hours of negotiation with Marshall and his colleagues, Brooke appears to have been persuaded to shift his ground towards the American position. When the Combined Chiefs met on the 20th, both sides agreed that the time was not ripe to proceed with *Gymnast* and that, instead, they should press ahead with *Bolero* in preparation for an attack on the Normandy coast around Cherbourg with all speed and energy. Had Churchill been apprised of Brooke's change of heart, he would most certainly have sought to veto the proposal. But the Prime Minister was still at Hyde Park, where, not surprisingly, both Marshall and Brooke were distinctly uneasy, in the latter's words, about 'the plans that the PM and the President had been brewing up' there. And so they should have been.

When the two leaders arrived back in Washington the next day, Churchill discovered what the Chiefs of Staff had been 'brewing up' in their turn. After a frosty meeting with the Prime Minister, Brooke noted, in his *Yes, Minister* fashion, that Churchill had been 'a bit peevish, but not too bad and after an hour's talk had him quiet again'.

It is impossible to know what would have happened to *Gymnast* – who would have won the argument between the generals on the one hand and the politicians on the other – and therefore to the future course of the Second World War, if fate had not at that point intervened to immediate and dramatic effect. On the afternoon of the 21st, while Brooke and Churchill were standing together by Roosevelt's desk in the White House, a secretary walked in and handed the President a slip of pink paper. Roosevelt passed it to Churchill without a word. It read, 'Tobruk has surrendered, with twenty-five thousand men taken prisoner.'

The news was devastating. Nor could it have come at a worse moment. For Churchill, Tobruk was a beacon and icon, a litmus test of triumph or disaster in the Middle East, vital to victory in the desert and to the protection of Britain's strategic interests in the Mediterranean and beyond. He had even vouchsafed that if Tobruk were to fall to the Germans, Hitler's 'robot world order' would eventually emerge victorious from the struggle. Moreover, his investment of so much political capital in a small sea port of uncertain military value was tied intimately to the strategic vision from which he never wavered: that *Gymnast* (the Allied landings in North Africa) and *Acrobat* (the Eighth Army's expulsion of Rommel from Libya) were twin-pronged operations that would together squeeze the life out of the enemy in North Africa and thence provide a springboard for the invasion of what he was later to describe – in a phrase that should have come to haunt him – as the 'soft underbelly' of the Axis in Italy. For the Eighth Army to lose Tobruk at this crucial moment had not only undermined his own credibility but, so it seemed at that moment, gravely imperilled his negotiating stance as he sought to persuade Roosevelt to adopt his global strategy for the defeat of Hitler.

For all these reasons, the fall of Tobruk shook Churchill to the core and, by his own account, he did not attempt to conceal his dismay from the President. 'It was a bitter moment. Defeat is one thing; disgrace is another,' he wrote later. What clearly grieved him most was that 'a garrison of twenty-five thousand [actually thirty-five thousand] seasoned soldiers had lain down their arms to perhaps one-half of their number … If this was typical of the morale of the Desert Army, no measure could be put to the disasters which impended in North-East Africa.'

There was silence in the room as Churchill contemplated his humiliation. Ismay, who had only met Roosevelt a few moments earlier, watched Churchill's reaction as he read the news. 'This was a hideous and totally unexpected shock,' he wrote, 'and for the first time I saw the Prime Minister wince.' A sensitive observer of human behaviour, Ismay had already noted the way in which the two leaders 'used to stroll in and out of each other's rooms in the White House, as two subalterns occupying adjacent quarters might have done. Both of them had the spirit of eternal youth.' That mutual regard was about to be put to the test.

After a long pause, the President spoke. Brooke was unable to recall precisely what Roosevelt said but he was 'vividly' impressed by his 'tact and real heartfelt sympathy'. As Churchill recalled the moment, there were 'no reproaches; not an unkind word was spoken. The President said simply, "What can we do to help?"' Confirming that indeed was what he had said, Ismay wrote, 'It was at moments like this that one realised what a priceless asset the Allies possessed in the intimate friendship and mutual understanding between Roosevelt and Churchill.'

In his memoirs, Churchill wrote that in response to Roosevelt's question, he at once replied, 'Give us as many Sherman tanks as you can spare, and ship them to the Middle East as quickly as possible.' Marshall, who by this time had been summoned to join them, responded by pointing out that the first few hundred Shermans had only recently come off the production line and that they had just been allotted to the US Army. But, according to Churchill, he went on to say that it was 'a terrible thing to take the weapons out of a soldier's hands … [but] if the British need is so great they must have them'.

Either Churchill's memory was at fault here or he deliberately condensed several days of tough negotiation into a single exchange. In fact Marshall's proposal was not merely to send tanks but the entire 1st Armored Division – men and tanks – to fight alongside the Eighth Army. On the face of it, this was an astonishing suggestion to emerge from someone who, until that moment, had been strenuously opposed to the early deployment of American troops anywhere except in Europe. However, Marshall was swift to realise that the calamity at Tobruk – in his words – 'threatened a complete collapse in the Middle East, the loss of the Suez Canal and the vital oil supply in the vicinity of Abadan. It was a very black hour.' After dinner that evening, as they digested the shock of Tobruk, Roosevelt, Churchill, Dill, Marshall, King, Hopkins, and Admiral Little (head of the British Admiralty delegation in Washington) discussed Marshall's suggestion at greater length. They continued to talk until 1 a.m., by which point, Brooke noted cryptically in his diary, Churchill had accepted the American offer, which 'may lead to USA front in ME at expense of the European front'.

The attractions of this for Churchill and Roosevelt were obvious. Both men, for distinct but overlapping reasons, wanted American troops in action on the battlefield. But quite why Marshall, who had been so averse to engaging with the enemy in North Africa, should have proposed this option remains unclear. What is in no doubt, however, is that the fall of Tobruk had dramatically redrawn the contours of the negotiations and – paradoxically – greatly to Churchill's advantage.

On the next morning, the protagonists not only discussed the deployment of the US 1st Armored Division to the Middle East but also agreed that plans for *Gymnast* (which the Combined Chiefs had postponed indefinitely only two days earlier) should be 'completed in all details as soon as possible'. This was a remarkable about-turn by the American Chiefs and a signal victory for Churchill and Roosevelt. Between the lines – and with the help of some ambiguous if not duplicitous phrasing – it also began to emerge that the Americans had conceded that there would be no invasion of France in 1942.

On the following day, the 23rd, the two leaders and their teams met in the Oval Office to discuss the Middle East in general and, in particular the logistical challenges posed by the deployment of an entire armoured division to the Western Desert. It was at this point, three days after the fall of Tobruk, that – for the first time – Marshall proposed sending Sherman tanks to the Middle East but without the 1st Armored Division's 15,000 troops. This 'new proposal', as Brooke referred to it, was for 300 Shermans and 100 105mm self-propelled guns to be transported by US vessels to the Middle East as soon as possible. This suggestion was far more to Brooke's liking as he had become uneasy at the implications of inserting an American-led tank division into the very heart of the Eighth Army. At lunch with Marshall and Dill, he enthused about the new proposal but warned that he might have 'great difficulty to get the PM to accept it as he would wish to conform to the President's desire to produce fighting troops instead of equipment'. As it happened, once Brooke had made it clear to him that 'the military aspect of this problem and its advantages outweighed the political considerations', Churchill readily agreed to accept the Shermans and the guns rather than the fully manned armoured division.

The negotiations which led up to this decision took place against a psychologically devastating backdrop to which none of the participants was ever to refer in public. It concerned one of the most sensitive and embarrassing aspects of the transatlantic relationship. As noted earlier, for at least eighteen months the US military attaché in Cairo, Colonel Bonner Fellers, had not only been privy to almost every piece of significant information about the Eighth Army but had routinely been transmitting his intelligence to Washington. This might not have mattered unduly had not the secret US code used by Fellers to encrypt his often contemptuous reports at some point been cracked by the Axis intelligence services. As a result, Berlin and Rome had almost instant access to his detailed commentaries and Auchinleck's battle plans. This appalling and embarrassing discovery came to light – as a result of some smart detective work at Bletchley Park – at precisely the moment when the Allies in Washington were digesting the full import of the fall of Tobruk.

For at least six months, Fellers's constant flow of detailed military secrets to Washington had not only filled the in-trays of Rome and Berlin but given Rommel invaluable information about the condition and disposition of the Eighth Army, knowledge which more than compensated for what the British had been able to glean from decoding Enigma messages. This massive breach of what had been presumed by the Americans to be an unbreakably secure system of secret communications had not only helped Rommel to inflict constant reverses on the Eighth Army but, in the process, contributed to the grievous military losses inflicted on Auchinleck's forces by the Panzerarmee.

The corrosive impact of Fellers's excoriating analyses of the Eighth Army's multiple frailties had almost certainly made a significant impact on Washington's policy makers. It would have been remarkable if his sustained critique had not reinforced the American Chiefs in their continuing aversion to a joint military operation with the British anywhere in North Africa. On 20 June, for example, the day before the fall of Tobruk, Fellers had sent a particularly harsh overview of the Eighth Army's performance. 'With numerically superior forces, with tanks, planes, artillery, means of transport, and reserves of every kind, the British Army has twice failed to defeat the Axis forces in Libya,' he wrote. 'Under the present command and with the measures taken in a hit and miss fashion ... The Eighth Army has failed to maintain the morale of its troops; its tactical conceptions were always wrong; it neglected completely co-operation between the various arms; its reaction to the lightning changes of the battlefield were always slow.'

This report, like its many predecessors, landed on the desk of America's most senior intelligence officer, Colonel William Donovan, the founding head of the Office of Strategic Services. Donovan was not only liked and respected by Roosevelt but was accustomed to sharing Fellers's insights with both Marshall and the President. At such a critical juncture, it would be astonishing if he had not forwarded on their military attaché's latest jeremiad to either or both of them. Indeed, there is circumstantial evidence to suggest that he did just that.

Late at night on the 21st – immediately after the British had accepted Marshall's initial offer of the 1st Armored Division – the President asked his Chief of Staff to stay behind in the Oval Office. Taking Marshall totally by surprise, he apparently suggested that they should send 'a large American force' to take control of the Middle East all the way from Teheran to Alexandria, including the entire Mediterranean seaboard and the Levant. Marshall was aghast but, 'not trusting himself to hold his tongue if the conversation continued much further', made it clear to the President that he was unwilling to discuss the matter at such a late hour and left the room. But that was not the end of the matter.

The President's proposal was tantamount to an outright rejection of Marshall's own clear view that *Bolero* – the build-up of US forces in Britain prior to a full-scale Allied invasion of France, now planned for 1943 – should precede all other American initiatives. In the course of delivering his late-night bombshell, the President evidently paid tribute to Fellers's secret critique of the British performance in the desert. Although he was openly Anglophobic, Fellers did not believe that the British should be left alone to endure the military consequences of what he regarded as their colonial delusions. On the contrary, he was convinced that – to protect American interests – a British defeat in the Middle East was to be avoided. To this end, he had consistently pressed for direct American intervention in the region to prop up Auchinleck's command. In his 20 June report, he specifically argued that Lend-Lease – the provision of US weaponry on the never-never – would not by itself save the British from defeat at the hands of Rommel. More, much more, was needed.

Marshall felt obliged to counter Fellers with a memorandum entitled 'American Forces in the Middle East'. Decrying Roosevelt's suggestion that US forces should commandeer the entire Middle East, he wrote, 'Fellers is a very valuable observer but his responsibilities are not those of a strategist and his views are in opposition to mine and those of the entire Operations Division.' To deploy US troops in the Middle East on the scale suggested, would 'deny the probability of assembling American forces of decisive power in any theater in this war'. And he went on, 'You are familiar with my view that the decisive theater is Western Europe. That is the only place where the concerted effort of our own and the British forces can be brought to bear on the Germans. A large venture in the Middle East would make a decisive American contribution to the campaign in Western Europe out of the question. Therefore I am opposed to such a project.' Marshall could hardly have expressed himself more bluntly; nor could the gulf between his perspective on the one hand, and that of both Roosevelt and Churchill on the other, have been more starkly exposed.

It was at this moment that, serendipitously, the code-breakers at Bletchley Park discovered that Fellers's coded messages from Cairo had been decrypted by Axis intelligence. It is impossible to establish the precise impact of this embarrassing discovery on the outcome of the Anglo-American talks – which had already been substantially recast by the fall of Tobruk – but, according to the American historian C. J. Jenner, who has sifted the available evidence, 'Whitehall handled Washington's disgrace, which was decisive in appalling loss of British blood and treasure, with adroit magnanimity.' From Jenner's account it appears that Churchill cleverly turned America's mortification to British advantage. Instead of reproaching Roosevelt for the Fellers debacle, he allowed the disgrace merely to hang in the air as he strove to secure the President's endorsement of his own strategic priorities.

Whether or not remorse for the role that Fellers had

inadvertently played in the loss of Tobruk did in fact play a significant part in American calculations, Churchill came away from Washington with every reason to be satisfied with what had been achieved. *Sledgehammer* had been postponed at least until 1943, *Gymnast* was still in the frame for 1942, and the Eighth Army was about to be massively reinforced with 300 of the latest and best tanks in the world. He could congratulate himself that, while Roosevelt saw very nearly eye to eye with him over future strategy in the region, the President's advisors, some of them seething at the way in which – as they saw it – 'Our Boy' had been manipulated by Churchill – had clearly been worsted. Paradoxically, so far from the humiliation at Tobruk weakening Churchill's hand, it had evidently had the opposite effect.

The talks in Washington were protected by a shroud of secrecy and, for this reason, the fact that Churchill had managed to pull so many strategic chestnuts from the fire was not apparent either in Britain or in the desert. The only story in London was the fall of Tobruk, which the press reported as though it were a national disgrace as well as a military disaster. The London correspondent for *Time* magazine, wrote, 'The Briton-in-the-street was as mad as a blitzed Briton.' Later, Churchill's Director of Military Operations recalled, 'We all felt immensely frustrated and disappointed and, indeed, rather ashamed that the Army was not doing better.' Kennedy even avoided going to his usual club in Pall Mall, hiding away instead at lunch or dinner at 'another unfrequented little club of which I was an honorary member'.

Beyond Whitehall, there was similar shame and resentment. 'I squirmed beneath the bedclothes and ground my teeth with rage', one woman noted in her private diary, when she heard the news from Tobruk; another wrote bitterly, 'We heard yesterday that we have lost Tobruk; the same old story – rotten leadership'; and another asked despairingly, 'Where can soldiers go where they have a reasonable chance? Tobruk has gone – what of Egypt, Suez and India? Nearly three years of war: WHY don't we get going – what stops us?'

The loss of national morale was reflected in a Censure Motion tabled on 25 June by a dissident Conservative backbencher which stated that the House of Commons 'has no confidence in the central direction of the war'. To prepare for the debate, Churchill asked Sir Stafford Cripps, the Lord Privy Seal, to produce a paper forewarning him of the challenges likely to come from the floor of the House. 'There is no doubt,' Cripps reported back, 'that there is a very grave disturbance of opinion both in the House of Commons and in the country.' To explain this he cited an alleged failure of leadership in the Middle East, distrust of an 'out of date' Supreme Command, the inferior quality of British weaponry but, above all else, what he described as 'over-optimistic News Reports from Cairo' which had 'undoubtedly done much to emphasise the shock of the loss of Tobruk'.

The BBC's Richard Dimbleby inadvertently found himself at the epicentre of this damaging accusation. As Middle East GHQ's favourite and most trusted correspondent, he was also – because the BBC had a global reach – its most important broadcaster. A little before the fall of Tobruk, Cairo had cabled the War Office urging that 'Dimbleby's facts be considered authoritative and that the tone for Libya news in all bulletins be taken from him in preference to all newspaper or agency reports'. Following the fall of Tobruk and the Cripps memorandum, the director-general of the Ministry of Information demanded to see all Dimbleby's reports from the desert. These were duly sent to him with an accompanying note from a senior BBC official, A. P. Ryan, who had been seconded to the BBC to become the Ministry's man at the Corporation. Ryan wrote, 'There is no doubt that Dimbleby says what Auchinleck wants said. There is equally no doubt that this reveals a grave misunderstanding by Auchinleck about public opinion in this country and all over the world outside the Middle East.'

Wholly unaware of the deepening strategic conflict between Churchill and Auchinleck, Dimbleby himself complained that GHQ Cairo had put him under pressure to 'emphasise our general defensive measures'. A little before Rommel's assault on the Gazala Line, he duly reported in his regular 'War Review', 'Fundamentally our task in the Middle East has been, and still is, defence.' Dimbleby chafed frequently under the censorship imposed on him by the Eighth Army. In the middle of June, after a number of his despatches had mysteriously failed to reach London, he noted in his diary, 'It is really disgraceful to cover up failures and I really believe that's what Cairo is doing.' Insisting that these reports had been 'suppressed' by GHQ Cairo 'in the hope that they would discover some grain of comfort to release the sad tidings', he noted astutely, 'The Cairo mind had still not caught up with the attitude of the public at home, who wanted only the facts, and as many of them as could be released without helping enemy intelligence.' It was thus hardly surprising that, after the shocking surrender at Tobruk, Cripps would identify 'over-optimistic' coverage of the Eighth Army's travails as a principal source of Britain's low morale on the home front.

Cripps was aware neither of the censorship imposed by Auchinleck's officials in Cairo nor of the degree to which this exacerbated the challenges of covering a battle which was confusing, fast-moving and scattered across a vast and often inaccessible front. To make matters worse, a forty-eight-hour time lag between the BBC's 'over-optimistic' reports reaching London and their rebroadcasting on the Forces Network to the troops in the desert placed Dimbleby in an unenviable predicament. On 6 June, for example, with the British in a worsening crisis around the 'Knightsbridge Box', he had listened with chagrin to his 'glowing news of our attack' two days earlier, which, he noted ruefully, 'was justified at the time it was sent off'. Such time lags – inevitable though they were – severely damaged the BBC's reputation in the desert as an embattled and weary Eighth Army listened to what seemed to be a travesty of the facts as they knew them to be and against which they had pitted themselves to such little effect.

Early in July, one of Dimbleby's allies at GHQ Cairo cabled the War Office in London in fury to report, 'The BBC should know that its name stinks in all British circles, civil and military throughout the Middle East.' Rightly or wrongly, another judged that the rank and file in the Eighth Army had 'come to loathe [Dimbleby] personally'. The fallout from the conflict between Churchill and Auchinleck and the consequential opprobrium heaped on the BBC correspondent was clearly unsustainable. Dimbleby was recalled to London without a word of explanation or gratitude for his work over the preceding two years. His predicament was a footnote to the history of those days but it does illuminate the extreme tensions that now prevailed in London and Cairo.

The Censure Motion was debated over two days, 1 and 2 July. Billed as a major challenge to the Prime Minister's authority, the scattergun attack which ensued lacked the drama which would have attended any possible risk that the motion might be carried. Only Aneurin Bevan, a formidable parliamentary performer whom Churchill loathed, added bite to the proceedings by charging, 'The Prime Minister wins Debate after Debate and loses battle after battle.' His wit and asperity was markedly absent from the lesser fry who followed him, but the debate did at least provide a flavour of the frustration and animosity which lurked below the surface of the wartime coalition. The Father of the House, Earl Winterton, concentrated his fire on Churchill personally, claiming clumsily and crassly that 'whenever we have disasters we get the same answer, that whatever happens you must not blame the Prime Minister; we are getting very close to the intellectual and moral position of the German people – "The Führer is always right."' The former Secretary of State for War, Leslie Hore-Belisha (who had been sacked by Chamberlain in 1940), reflected more precisely the pervasive anxiety in Parliament, Whitehall and the nation. 'We may lose Egypt or we may not lose Egypt – I pray God we may not,' he intoned, 'but when the Prime Minister, who said we hold Singapore, that we would hold Crete, that we have smashed the German Army in Libya … when I read that he said we are going to hold Egypt, my anxieties became greater … How can one place reliance in judgements that have so repeatedly turned out to be misguided?'

After a few thrusts of this nature, Churchill's critics lost their way. Early in the debate, they were made to look ridiculous as one of Churchill's supporters, an Independent Labour MP, Campbell Stephen, found an opportunity to intervene. With stiletto precision he pointed out that whereas Sir John Wardlaw-Milne had moved the Censure Motion 'on the ground that the Prime Minister had interfered unduly in the direction of the war', one of his principal seconders, Admiral Sir Roger Keyes, appeared to believe that 'the

Prime Minister has not sufficiently interfered in the direction of the war'. This crushing intervention, as Churchill noted gleefully, meant that 'the debate was ruptured from the start'.

Confident in the knowledge that he would survive by a comfortable margin, Churchill did not refrain from assailing his adversaries with all the authority and disdain at his command. Reminding the House of the 'military misfortunes' which had befallen the Eighth Army, he did not attempt to put a favourable gloss on the scale of the disaster. 'We are at this moment in the presence of a recession of our hopes and prospects in the Middle East and in the Mediterranean unequalled since the fall of France,' he rumbled; and then, as though daring his critics in the Chamber and beyond, he added sarcastically, 'If there are any would-be profiteers of disaster who feel able to paint the picture in darker colours they are certainly at liberty to do so.'

In reflecting on the 'bitter pang' of Tobruk he pitched cleverly for the sympathy of the House in his own adversity: 'Some people assume too readily that because a Government keeps cool and has steady nerves under reverses, its members do not feel the public misfortunes as keenly as do independent critics. On the contrary, I doubt whether anyone feels greater sorrow or pain than those who are responsible for the general conduct of our affairs.' Only a consummate politician would have dared to essay such a two-edged confession of frailty; and only an unassailable leader could have gone on to dismiss 'Lobby gossip, echoes from the smoking-room, and talk in Fleet Street [that] are worked up into serious articles seeming to represent that the whole basis of British political life is shaken, or is tottering,' before asserting that 'only my unshakeable confidence in the ties which bind me to the mass of the British people upheld me through those days of trial'.

His coup de grâce was to make it plain that if, as the motion implied, he should be barred from combining his authority as both Minister of Defence and Prime Minister, he would resign both positions. This, as even his critics realised, would have left Britain rudderless in the storm. Demanding a massive vote of confidence, the Prime Minister's peroration was defiant. 'If those who have assailed us are reduced to contemptible proportions and their Vote of Censure on the National Government is converted to a vote of censure upon its authors, make no mistake, a cheer will go up from every friend of Britain and every faithful servant of our cause, and the knell of disappointment will ring in the ears of the tyrants we are striving to overthrow.' He sat down to prolonged cheers and a white cloud of Order Papers. His performance prompted *Time* magazine to inform its American readers, 'He had not yet lost the power to charm Parliament, which still loved him for his gallantry under political fire.'

His success was not however entirely unclouded. While the 'No Confidence' Motion was defeated by 475 votes to 25 – proof, were it needed, that there was no other leader remotely capable of seizing the helm – 100 MPs refrained from entering either lobby, serving notice on the Prime Minister that for a significant section of the Commons, he was now on probation. Moreover, whether Churchill was capable of steering Britain through the maelstrom remained a matter of pessimistic conjecture not only in the Commons but beyond the confines of Westminster, and not only in Britain but around the world – and more especially in the Middle East.

NINETEEN

THE AUK'S LAST STAND

'Get out your frocks, we're on our way!'
German broadcast to the women of Alexandria

While Churchill commanded the House of Commons, the city of Cairo was gripped by panic. After seizing Tobruk, Rommel had advanced rapidly eastwards. By 23 June he had crossed the Egyptian border and – taking risks that, had he failed, would have marked him as one of the most irresponsible generals in the history of warfare – stormed towards Mersah Matruh, where Ritchie had unwisely opted to make a stand.

The following day Auchinleck cabled Churchill. 'I deeply regret that you should have received this severe blow at so critical a time as a result of the heavy defeat suffered by the forces under my command.' With an exceptional degree of grace and humility, he added, 'I thank you personally and most sincerely for all your help and support during the past year, and deeply regret the failures and set-backs of the past month, for which I accept full responsibility.' The only words missing from this *mea culpa* were 'and I therefore tender my resignation as C-in-C, Middle East'. For the time being, a chastened Auchinleck had decided to stay his hand.

Given the acute pressures to which he was subjected, Churchill's reply was surprisingly forgiving, though not entirely unbarbed. 'Whatever views I may have had about how the battle was fought or whether it should have been fought a good deal earlier, you have my entire confidence, and I share your responsibilities to the full.' Churchill too had decided to stay his hand. He may have judged that to dispense with Auchinleck at this juncture would be interpreted as an unseemly attempt to pass the buck or to divert attention from his own political troubles; in any case, it was militarily the worst possible moment to change the command, let alone to find an immediate successor from the limited pool of talent available to him.

Instead, writing from Washington on 25 June, Churchill urged Auchinleck yet again to make full use of what he insisted on describing as the Middle East Command's 'ration strength' – which stood at some 700,000 men. Assuming that Rommel would be unable to mount an assault on Mersah Matruh 'for three or four weeks', he demanded that 'every fit male should be made to fight and die for victory … You are in the same kind of situation as we should be if England were invaded, and the same drastic spirit should reign.'

But so far from waiting for 'three or four weeks', Rommel had barely waited twenty-four hours before advancing deep into Egypt in another lightning thrust which his most loyal lieutenants regarded as foolhardy and his superiors in Berlin and Rome did their best to prevent. On the day that Tobruk fell, Kesselring had flown to Libya, where he tried to stop Rommel in his tracks. In the course of a ferocious argument, Rommel said he intended to march on the Nile Delta forthwith. This provoked Kesselring to warn that he could not spare the Luftwaffe bombers needed to support Rommel's advance as they were needed for the long-delayed Operation *Herkules* against Malta. To transfer them from Malta would relieve the pressure on the beleaguered British fortress which would in turn once again jeopardise the Panzerarmee's vital supply lines across the Mediterranean. According to von Mellenthin, 'Kesselring maintained that the only sound course of action was to stick to the original plan [which had been agreed between Hitler and Mussolini two months earlier] and postpone an invasion of Egypt until Malta had fallen.'

Rommel would have none of it but argued vehemently that the

parlous state of the Eighth Army gave him a unique opportunity to make an immediate thrust for the Suez Canal. When Kesselring retorted that he would withdraw the Luftwaffe to Sicily, Rommel trumped his fellow field marshal by advising Kesselring that he had already sent his personal liaison officer to Hitler to plead his case. The following day, the 22nd, the Führer duly endorsed his favourite's plan despite what von Mellenthin described as 'the reasoned and powerful objections' of the most influential members of both OKW and Comando Supremo, signalling Mussolini, 'it is only once in a lifetime that the Goddess of Victory smiles'. It was a fateful decision: by agreeing that the capture of Cairo should precede the destruction of Malta, Hitler had made a strategic error of such magnitude as to seal Rommel's fate at El Alamein and, eventually, that of the Axis armies in North Africa.

This was by no means yet clear to anyone on either side. Only the lumbering and shambolic failure of the Eighth Army commanders to co-ordinate a response to Rommel's advance spared his depleted panzers and his exhausted troops. As von Mellenthin reflected, 'We got off very lightly, when one considers that concerted attacks by the greatly superior British forces could have terminated the existence of Panzerarmee Afrika.'

Instead, Mersah Matruh was soon in Rommel's hands along with 6,000 prisoners, most of whom surrendered without putting up significant resistance or suffering more than a handful of casualties. Despite some fierce infantry skirmishes and hand-to-hand fighting the tactical ineptitude of Auchinleck's commanders had allowed the panzers – though reduced to a few dozen in number – to run rings round a beleaguered and disorientated Eighth Army. Sergeant Nell, an NCO serving in the Green Howards, described what happened when his platoon was cut off and surrounded. He faced a simple choice: to order his soldiers to fight to the last man or to surrender. Nell chose the less glorious option but not before one of his men had pleaded with him to fight on:

> I pointed out to him that we should all be killed without advancing our war effort in the least ... He cried, actually sobbed, and pleaded with me to fight it out. But fighting was out of the

question, so I very carefully crawled out of the trench, stood up, and trying to look much braver than I felt, walked over to the Germans. It was only a short distance but it seemed an awful long way to me. One of them saw me. He shouted, 'Come on, Tommy! Come on, Tommy!' I shouted, 'All right lads, come out!' They came out with their hands up ... I felt a little ashamed.

By this time Auchinleck had taken the crucial decision to dismiss the hapless Ritchie and – as he had been urged by Churchill a month earlier – to take command of the Eighth Army himself. Judging swiftly that it would be impossible to hold Mersah Matruh, he cancelled Ritchie's instructions and, on 26 June, ordered the bulk of the Eighth Army to continue the retreat until they reached El Alamein, the last defensive position from which it would be possible to arrest Rommel's headlong progress towards the Nile Delta and the Suez Canal. 'Morale in good units of the Eighth Army was as good as it ever was,' General Harding recalled but 'the morale of the army as a whole was shattered because they were in a state of confusion and defeated.'

On the face of it Egypt was in danger of imminent collapse. Certainly, Rommel's confidence was unbounded. On the 29th, as the Panzerarmee took up positions facing the British line, he had a jovial conversation with one of his commanders at the front. 'Well, Briel,' he said, 'you will advance with your men to Alexandria and stop when you come to the suburbs. The Tommies have gone ... When I arrive tomorrow we'll drive into Cairo together for a coffee.' On the next day, a German radio station broadcast a message to the women of Alexandria on 1 July: 'Get out your frocks, we're on our way!'

No one was disposed to dismiss this braggadocio as empty posturing. Sir Henry Harwood, who had succeeded Admiral Cunningham, was so alarmed by the threat that he ordered the British fleet to evacuate Alexandria and to disperse to Haifa, Beirut and Port Said. Alexandria itself was placed under military curfew and the streets were eerily deserted of soldiers and trucks. In his somewhat accidental role as a British press attaché, Lawrence Durrell wandered the streets of the city, noting down the names of those shops which had put up signs welcoming the Germans and – with somewhat limited effect as most military personnel had departed – used his authority to declare them out of bounds to British troops.

Civilians loaded their cars or took to the trains and headed south into the Nile Delta. In Cairo, a hundred miles from Alexandria, the sky was soon filled with plumes of smoke not from an enemy bombardment but because staff at the British Embassy and GHQ had started to incinerate huge heaps of secret documents lest they fall into the hands of the advancing Panzerarmee. The day soon became notorious as Ash Wednesday. 'All day', Alan Moorehead wrote, 'groups of privates shovelled piles of maps, lists of figures, reports, estimates, codes and messages into four blazing bonfires ... I went into one office and the floor was covered in ashes and the smell of burning rags hung over the whole building.' A young captain in the Special Operations Executive, Julian Amery (later to become a leading Conservative MP), observed that the bulk of the papers 'were burnt in the open ... But then the wind got up and a mass of secret documents were blown away little more than scorched, rising like so many phoenixes from their ashes and pursued all over the city by irate and frenzied officers.' The scene would have more properly belonged in a Gilbert and Sullivan opera had there not been a genuine fear that Cairo would fall and soon afterwards that the panzers would be at Suez and into the Nile Delta. Auchinleck's Chief of Staff, Lieutenant General Thomas Corbett, imposed a night-time curfew on British troops and instructed all officers to carry revolvers at all times. The photographer Cecil Beaton noted sardonically that Cairo was 'in the most dreadful state of unrest, the streets jammed with traffic ... Flap is the word of the moment. Everyone puts a stopper on their panic by calling it a Flap.' His Majesty's Ambassador, Sir Miles Lampson, was one of the few to display the sangfroid on which the British liked to pride themselves. Although a special train had been laid on for him to leave, he remained at his post and ordered the white railings around the Embassy to be repainted.

By the time Churchill rose to his feet in the House of Commons to combat the Censure Motion against him, the 'Flap' had lasted for five days. British officials and their families were making preparations to evacuate the city and some had already left. The trains for Palestine were packed and tickets were at a premium. Others left by sea and road for destinations further afield. Margaret Coonan, the young daughter of a British Army officer, recalled that her family was given twenty-four hours to leave for South Africa. 'I remember we were told we couldn't take anything with us ... I was crying to bring a toy, and I was allowed one toy ... Jane [Margaret's sister] was allowed to take one of her toys too. We were given brown paper bags with chocolates and hard-boiled eggs, and put into lorries for the [4,000-mile] journey.'

The Egyptians were so used to having their sovereignty trampled on by imperial outsiders that they watched this kerfuffle with generally benign detachment. Most had no great animosity towards the Germans, whose propaganda in favour of Arab nationalism resonated with those who chafed under the nominal independence granted to them by the British. Others, though, had grown used to the presence of the old imperial power, and felt distinctly queasy about the prospect of living under occupation by either German Nazis or Italian fascists. Reflecting the prevailing ambivalence, Nahas Pasha, the Egyptian Prime Minister, who had been put in office at the behest of the British, apparently kept his counsel but hedged his bets by drafting a letter to Rommel 'assuring him that the sympathies of the Wafd were really with the Axis, but circumstances had forced them to co-operate with the British'.

Over the preceding months the Germans had made spasmodic efforts to prepare the Egyptian people for their liberation from the 'English' colonists. In a series of violently anti-Semitic pamphlets, the Nazi propaganda machine informed them that 'all people are God's people, except for the corrupt and parasitic Jews'. Explaining that the Third Reich had already taken steps to remove the Jewish 'professors, lawyers, artists, doctors, as well as industrialists and businessmen (who) are like maggots in the national flesh', Konstantin von Neurath, the liaison officer between Berlin and the Afrikakorps, proclaimed, 'We have the warmest possible sympathy for your struggle against the English and the Jews.'

Though this campaign made little impact on the Cairo populace, a number of Arab nationalists in the Egyptian army were willing to collaborate with the Nazis as members of the secret Free Officers Movement. One of these, a young signals officer called Anwar Sadat, arranged for two German spies in Cairo to establish radio contact with Berlin. In July both men (one of whom was a dissolute habitué of Cairo's fleshpots) were discovered and arrested by the British. They escaped the death penalty because the same sentence would have to have been imposed on Sadat as well, and to execute an Egyptian military officer was felt to be 'altogether too provocative in the tense atmosphere of July 1942'. Instead the future President of Egypt was stripped of his rank and sent to jail (from where he emerged to participate in the Egyptian Revolution of 1952 and, in 1979, to sign a Peace Treaty with Israel).

In 1942, such intimations of revolt did not yet menace the status quo. The British High Command felt confident enough about internal security to leave the Egyptian army in control of key installations; nor was it felt necessary to put British troops on alert to quell any possible uprising. Somewhat complacently, the British ambassador felt able to write that 'once the enemy appeared at the doors of Egypt there was a general realisation of the unpleasantness of a German occupation and a reversion of feeling in favour of us'. Nonetheless, in preparing for the worst, the Board of the Bank of Egypt ordered £6 million worth of new notes to be printed. On one side these are said to have showed Il Duce against a backdrop of the Pyramids; on the other, the Fascist Party slogan, *Summa Audacia et Virtus* ('daring and courage to the highest degree').

Mussolini was so confident that the Axis forces would very soon reach the Nile that, on 29 June, he flew to North Africa in preparation for what he imagined would be his magnificent entry into Cairo astride a white charger, which had been flown into Libya for the purpose. The plane bearing his own personage and a large retinue of followers was reported also to be carrying drums of black polish for his soldiers to buff their boots in preparation for the victory parade. Inauspiciously, however, the aircraft crashed on landing. Although the dictator escaped without injury, his barber and his chef were killed. Undeterred, he established his headquarters in the relatively congenial Mediterranean port of Derna, some 460 miles from the Axis front line at El Alamein where he liked to parade in front of the 'cages' where British POWs were held in captivity. Letting it be known that he expected Rommel to dance attendance upon him, he waited there – in vain – for the Panzerarmee commander to obey the summons.

This displeased Il Duce, who was already irked by the fact that the triumphs of the Axis forces on the Gazala Line, at Tobruk and reaching so far into Egypt had been so widely attributed to the 'genius' of Rommel rather than to the valour of the Italian troops. According to Ciano's diary for 26 June, Rommel's promotion to field marshal had caused Il Duce, 'much pain' because it had been done 'to accentuate the German character of the battle'. Nonetheless, borne aloft by the apparently irresistible momentum of Rommel's advance, he had visions of establishing an Italian commissariat in Alexandria 'before fifteen days are over'. But, before a week was out, Mussolini's confidence began to seem misplaced. 'There is a vague concern on account of the lull before El Alamein,' Ciano noted. 'It is feared that after the impact of the initial attack is spent, Rommel cannot advance further, and whoever stops in the desert is truly lost.' It was a prescient insight, though not yet appreciated either by Mussolini or by Cavallero, the Italian Chief of Staff, whom Mussolini had promoted from general to marshal to restore his nominal authority over Rommel. According to Ciano (who shared the widespread scorn for the character and judgement of the newly promoted marshal) Cavallero remained '100 per cent optimistic … he is certain that the superiority of the Axis forces will bring us immediately to Alexandria and in a short time to Cairo and the Canal'.

There was no such expectation among the men fighting for Mussolini's imperial cause. Although some units, notably the Ariete Armoured Division, were loyal fascists, most Italian conscripts had no political allegiance, saw no purpose in the Desert War, and wished only to be at home with their families. Among these men, optimism that the fall of Tobruk signalled the beginning of the end of the war in North Africa soon began to evaporate. The Trento Division was a case in point. On 2 July, Vittorio Vallicella, who two weeks earlier had looked forward excitedly to reaching palm trees and the women of the Nile Delta, noted miserably, 'We are stuck in this desolate plain of El Alamein, tired, hungry, and with little water, filthy and full of lice. We know that our Great Leader is … miles from the front because we have not been able to open the gates of Alexandria for him.'

In selecting El Alamein for the Eighth Army's last stand, Auchinleck had chosen well. Its only distinguishing feature was the station, just over a mile from the sea, on the single-track railway which ran from Sollum at the Egyptian border to Alexandria, sixty miles to the east. To the south of the station, forty miles away, lay the Qattara Depression, an empty quarter more than a hundred metres below sea level, pockmarked with quicksands and salt flats that made it virtually impassable except by camel. Rommel's only route to Alexandria, Cairo and the Nile lay through the forty-mile stretch of desert which separated El Alamein from the escarpment at the northern edge of the Qattara Depression. The terrain consisted principally of soft sand or broken rocks, which meant that even tracked vehicles could not move at speed. An otherwise featureless horizon was broken by three low ridges – Miteiriya, Ruweisat, and Alam el Halfa – which ran parallel with the Mediterranean, providing modest vantage points for the defending army.

Auchinleck established his battle headquarters on Ruweisat Ridge while the Eighth Army was deployed in and around a line of 'boxes' some – but not all – of which were protected by minefields and slit trenches. It was the bleakest of amphitheatres for what was to become one of the most famous battles in British history. In the mythology of twentieth-century warfare, El Alamein glitters gloriously; in mundane reality it lacked all glamour but was as godforsaken a battleground as anywhere on the planet. More to the purpose, the terrain and the topography favoured the defender more than the attacker – a fact which Rommel appreciated no less clearly than Auchinleck.

The series of fierce engagements which later became known

collectively as the First Battle of El Alamein began on Cairo's 'Ash Wednesday', 1 July, as Churchill prepared to face the censure of his peers in the House of Commons. Rommel tried his favoured technique: a diversionary attack by the 90th Light Division on the fortifications surrounding El Alamein itself, followed a few hours later by an attempt by the Afrikakorps to bypass El Alamein to the south. In both instances after fierce skirmishes in which an Indian brigade was overrun but eighteen of the Afrikakorps' fifty-five tanks were destroyed, Rommel's assault was repulsed. Later in the day, the 90th Light Division came under such heavy artillery bombardment that some German units even panicked. Later, Rommel described how, during this battle, he and his Chief of Staff came under 'furious artillery fire ... [as] ... British shells came screaming in from three directions, north, east and south; anti-aircraft tracer streaked through our force ... shell after shell crashed into the area we were holding ... our attack came to a standstill ... for two hours [General] Bayerlein and I had to lie out in the open.'

To make matters worse for Rommel, Auchinleck had far greater control over the movement of his own forces than Ritchie had ever achieved and he had already started to deploy them with far greater skill – displaying, in Rommel's phrase, 'an enterprise and audacity' which he could not forbear to admire. For the first time since the first phase of *Crusader* the Desert Fox had been outmanoeuvred on the battlefield. It was not only an unfamiliar experience but it evidently deflated him. 'The struggle for the last position is hard,' he wrote to his wife, Lu, on 3 July; and on the next day, 'Unfortunately, things are not going as I should like them. Resistance is too great and our strength exhausted. However, I still hope to find a way to achieve our goal. I'm rather tired and fagged out.'

After five weeks of fighting, with barely a pause, Rommel's Panzerarmee was as drained as he was. With Auchinleck using mobile forces to counter-attack as well as defend the line, it soon dawned on Rommel's troops that the vision he had held out to them of smiling girls offering salaams and more at their journey's end was slowly fading from their grasp, a mirage in the sand. One Italian soldier, drained of energy and hope, noted in his diary, 'We come out of our holes at night to take the air, otherwise we are buried all day, and with a slit trench as deep and narrow as mine it's no fun. There are two of us in mine and when we want to turn around it's agony, as we are as tightly packed in as anchovies in a tin.'

As the Eighth Army beat back one desperate assault after another, the attackers' morale plunged further. On 17 July a significant proportion of the Trento Division gave up the struggle and surrendered en masse. The rest were ordered to retreat. Private Vallicella found his way to a German field hospital. He had been taking supplies to the Trieste Division when his convoy was targeted by RAF bombers. He and his companions threw themselves under their truck just before it was hit. He survived physically unhurt but psychologically traumatised. When the doctors asked him what had happened, he broke down and needed two tranquillising injections before he drifted into a deep sleep. 'For 16 months we have led this life,' he noted. 'Maybe at this point we can only hope that a bomb takes us out and finishes our suffering.'

Nor was it only the Italians. The official War Diary of the 90th Division recorded that, to a man, it 'longed to have had a swim in the sea, and to sleep its fill' after the heavy fighting of the preceding days; and it bemoaned the fact that the Panzerarmee 'did not seem able to take this last fortress of the English in front of the Nile Delta'. By now Rommel knew it was not to be.

Outnumbered in men and tanks, critically low on fuel and ammunition, the Panzerarmee Afrika had very little hope of regaining the initiative. Rommel railed against Comando Supremo, which, 'with an almost unbelievable lack of appreciation of the situation', had inexcusably failed to deliver the fuel and weapons needed to sustain the advance into Egypt. He was especially outraged by the refusal of the Italian supply vessels on 'the Africa run' to take the risks required to make victory possible. To avoid the risk of being sunk by the RAF or the Royal Navy, they headed for the relative safety of Benghazi and Tripoli rather than docking at Tobruk or Mersah Matruh. As a result all replacements, spare parts, fuel, food and medical supplies had to be trucked for between 750 and 1,400 miles to the El Alamein front, which meant that the Panzerarmee was critically short of the means to prosecute the war. However, the blame properly rested as much with Rommel as with Comando Supremo or OKW. He had been told in no uncertain terms that to rush headlong into Egypt without ensuring that his army had the resources to sustain the advance was recklessly incautious but, in his arrogant certainty that the Nile Delta was ripe for the picking, he dismissed these warnings out of hand. However, though he never took his share of the blame, he was right to point out that in the conditions which he had helped to create, it was only 'the men's amazing spirit and will to victory that kept them going at all'.

And keep going they did. In what Rommel described as 'a series of violent and bloody battles' the fighting continued for three inconclusive weeks of attack and counter-attack. Unable to force the issue and woefully short of front-line manpower, Auchinleck was driven to improvise by breaking down the Eighth Army's divisions into ad hoc battle groups which were given names like Robcol, Squeakcol and Ackcol. These mongrel units – comprising an infantry battalion, an artillery regiment, a gun battery, anti-aircraft and anti-tank detachments – did not find universal favour among his commanders.

General Morshead, the forceful and outspoken commanding officer of the 9th Australian Division, whose men had given him the nickname 'Ming the Merciless', was not at all enamoured of Auchinleck's proposed reorganisation. He had earned his reputation in 1941 during the siege of Tobruk, when his 9th Division held Rommel at bay for six months between April and September. His preferred means of defence was attack; it is reported that at the height of the siege, he was shown an Eighth Army propaganda article headlined 'Tobruk Can Take It' which led him to retort, 'We're not here to take it, we're here to give it.'

Now he was equally forthright when Auchinleck asked him to break up his 9th Australian Division into battle groups and to send one brigade forward at once. By Morshead's own account, their conversation went as follows:

Auchinleck: 'I want the brigade right.'

Morshead: 'You can't have that brigade.'

Auchinleck: 'Why?'

Morshead: 'Because they are going to fight as a formation with the rest of the division.'

Auchinleck: 'Not if I give you orders?'

Morshead: 'Give me the orders and you'll see.'

In the course of this challenge, Morshead threatened to use the authority vested in him as the commander of a Commonwealth division to consult the Australian government (with which Churchill had an exceptionally prickly relationship) before complying with Auchinleck's instruction. Mindful, if resentful, of these diplomatic niceties, the commander-in-chief chose to relent.

This was not an isolated incident; there were other debilitating conflicts involving the Eighth Army's senior commanders about strategy and tactics, structure and organisation – clear evidence that for all his resolve and inventiveness, Auchinleck's multinational force not only lacked cohesion and clarity of purpose but was often dysfunctional as well. Auchinleck's inability to coordinate his defences or concentrate his forces for an effective counter-attack meant that the Eighth Army was unable to seize the initiative.

Nonetheless, the First Battle of El Alamein was marked by great fortitude. Morshead's Australians had a well-deserved reputation for pugnacity and forthrightness. Private Bill Loffman, an infantryman, required to liaise with an armoured brigade, was unimpressed by the Valentine tanks on which they rode into battle but admiring of their crews.

> These fellows were bloody heroes. They were going to take on the 88s and bigger tanks. Their tanks were still painted green [not camouflaged for the Desert]. British armour was crap taken into action by heroes. Our platoon commander was killed and the platoon sergeant had both legs blown off, and asked to be shot.

17. In August 1942, Churchill flew to Cairo where he appointed General Alexander (left) to replace Auchinleck as C-in-C, Middle East and summoned General Montgomery (right) from London to command the Eighth Army. Reflecting on the latter's abrasive character, he wrote to his wife Clemmie, 'If he is disagreeable to those about him, he is also disagreeable to the enemy.'

18. After Tobruk, Hitler promoted Rommel to Field Marshal. The ceremony took place in the Reich Chancellery, where obsequious courtiers noted that Rommel committed a faux pas by failing to remove his gloves before shaking hands with the Fuhrer.

19. In December 1941, immediately after the Japanese attack on Pearl Harbor, Churchill invited himself to the White House where he stayed for almost three weeks. He sought to persuade President Roosevelt that the Americans should fight the Germans and Italians in North Africa before defeating the Japanese in the Pacific.

20. Churchill's first meeting with Stalin in August 1942, whom he described as 'a profound Russian statesman'. But the mood in the Kremlin was 'bleak and sombre' as he explained that the 'true' second front would be in North Africa rather than in Europe.

21. Lieutenant-General Richard O'Connor after capturing the Libyan port of Derna during Operation *Compass*. The only battlefield commander to rival Rommel for panache, guile and daring, he was later captured when his staff car ran into a German patrol. He was incarcerated in an Italian POW camp from which he eventually escaped in 1943.

22. General Alan Brooke was an abrasive character with a tongue as sharp as his intellect. He handled Churchill's tirades with insouciance. 'I just sit silent and put up an umbrella,' he said.

23. General George Marshall, Roosevelt's Army Chief of Staff, and the President's most trusted military advisor. Described by Brooke as 'a very dangerous man'.

24. By the time Rommel reached the port, he noted, 'Practically every building of the dismal place was either flat or little more than a heap of rubble.' In a letter to his wife, he wrote, 'Tobruk! It was a wonderful battle.'

25. A British soldier is taken prisoner at Tobruk, one of 35,000 men who surrendered. Churchill said, 'defeat is one thing; disgrace is another'. Roosevelt said simply, 'what can we do to help?'

26. In May 1941, Hitler established his eastern headquarters in Poland at 'Wolf's Lair', a vast complex of underground bunkers hidden in the forest close to the Russian border, from where he masterminded Operation *Barbarossa*.

27. The fall of Tobruk, June 1942. As Rommel drove through the town in triumph, he passed long columns of prisoners and burning vehicles on either side of the road; all about him he saw chaos and destruction.

28. New Zealand casualties at Sidi Rezegh. Following a vicious tank battle in November 1941, at the start of Operation *Crusader*, one soldier wrote, 'Some of those bodies had been lying out there for several days: no heads, limbs hanging off, green corpses ...'

29. A communion service in the Desert: Montgomery's Chief of Staff recalled that the Eighth Army Commander had demanded that 'everyone – everyone – must be imbued with the burning desire to kill Germans. Even the padres – one per weekday and two on Sundays.'

30. On 3 November 1942, as the Axis troops surrendered in their thousands, Alexander cabled Churchill, 'After twelve days of heavy and violent fighting the Eighth Army has inflicted a severe defeat on the German and Italian forces under Rommel's command. The enemy's front has broken.'

31. Rommel was 'stunned' when, on 3 November, 1942, Hitler ordered him to 'stand fast' at El Alamein. 'This order demanded the impossible' he wrote, '… for the first time during the African campaign I did not know what to do.'

32. Three days after the Eighth Army's victory at El Alamein, American troops landed in North Africa to confront the Axis forces in Tunisia. Operation *Torch*, which shaped the future course of the Second World War, was a diplomatic triumph for Churchill.

Another private in the same Battalion, Peter Salmon described marching towards the enemy guns.

> The Germans concentrated their fire but the chaps kept going. The only people who stopped were people who picked up a rifle, stuck it in the ground by the bayonet, and put a helmet on top to mark where chaps were wounded, and walked on. Everybody is frightened, but you keep going to do the job.

The numerous engagements along the El Alamein front made quite extraordinary demands on the minds and bodies of the participants. In a scene reminiscent of the First World War, Vernon Northwood, a company commander serving in the 9th Australian Division, detected two truckloads of men setting up an 88mm gun in the moonlight only forty yards from his own trenches.

> I turned my company to face them, and said we must go in with the bayonet. We could see men taking up positions to defend the gun; we had to act quickly … I was shouting like a madman. You have to get yourself into a state of frenzy … I heard this noise behind me, all my men shouting and screaming … I only got a few paces, I took a bullet through the top of my steel helmet, above my forehead and scraped the top of my scalp, then one through the top of my arm. I thought I would lose it. It was like being kicked by a horse. Then wham, one through my neck, a fresh wound. I was thrown down and dropped my rifle and bayonet.

Northwood survived. His men reached the enemy gun emplacement and the Germans fled.

A fortuitous consequence of the attack at Tel el Eisa was that an Australian battalion, the 2/24th, captured one of the most vital units under Rommel's command, the cluster of radio antennae and trucks which comprised an invaluable listening station in the desert, known as the Long Range Reconnaissance Company 621 and operated by Captain Alfred Seebohm. By eavesdropping on the Eighth Army's radio traffic, Seebohm was able to transmit detailed battlefield intelligence directly to Rommel. So poor was British wireless security and so sharp was Seebohm's team that Lieutenant Hertz, the Captain's second in command, had been able to joke, 'We don't have to bother much about ciphers, all we really need are linguists, the sort who were waiters at the Dorchester before this war started.'

The loss of this service was devastating. On the morning of the 10th Rommel had asked for Seebohm's latest reports only to be told that 'Kompanie 621' was no longer in contact. 'Where is the company positioned?' Rommel asked. His liaison officer showed him on the map. 'Then it is *futsch* – lost!' Rommel expostulated in fury. Although the Eighth Army commanders had been 'dumbfounded' by the extent to which Seebohm had been tracking their every move, they were now swift to stop the flow of leaks. As a result Rommel was – for the first time – 'blind'. Combined with the fact that his 'Gute Quelle', Colonel Fellers, had been silenced by Bletchley Park's discovery, the loss of Seebohm's battlefield intelligence made it impossible for him to devise his own tactics in the light of what was happening on the other side of the line. His magical 'intuition' had deserted him, and with it, his ability persistently to outfox his adversary. He could still seize the initiative but he had lost an invaluable asset; the 'finger tip feel' which made him appear indomitable would never return.

Amid the heroism, there was a fatal combination of confusion and poor co-ordination. Spurred on by their commanding officer's rallying cry 'Let's make this a Balaclava, boys', the 23rd Armoured Brigade charged through a gap in a minefield to be confronted by deadly anti-tank fire followed by a panzer counter-attack. Casualties were severe. Tom Witherby, a gunner in the 46th Royal Tank Regiment, 'saw great clouds of black smoke. Then the wreckage of the attack coming back. The tank wounded, half-naked. Mortar bombs falling ... there must have been a kind of madness at the Army Command, a feeling that this was a once and for all chance to drive the enemy back and that all risks must be taken in the hope of success.'

In the early hours of 22 July, Earl Haig found himself 'trapped in a saucer' pinned inside his tank under fire from a panzer unit on a ridge above him. 'Shells were now landing all round us. I saw a New Zealander dreadfully wounded below the waist crawl pitifully towards my tank ... Our two pounder gun had no chance ... after about half an hour the enemy scored a direct hit on our tank. Smoke and flames came from the engine and my crew of three and I baled out, thankful to be alive and not wounded.' Haig leaped into a slit trench as the panzers advanced and surrounded the brigade. 'We rose from our trenches with arms raised in surrender,' he noted, observing that several of the German soldiers who took their surrender would have been happy to exchange places rather than remain on the battlefield. 'For you the war is over,' he quoted them as saying before they left wearily to return to the front line.

Towards the end of the month it became increasingly apparent that, while Rommel had lost any chance of breaking through the El Alamein line, the Eighth Army was incapable of destroying the Panzerarmee. Again and again – with some justification – Auchinleck blamed this frustrating impasse on one 'fundamental cause ... the lack of enough well-trained troops to keep up the impetus of the attack'. His resolve was not in doubt. 'I was firm in my intention to go on hitting the enemy whenever and wherever I could with the aim of destroying him where he stood.' But, helped by the fact that the trickle of supplies to his front line was once again starting to look more like a flow, Rommel's panzers did not fall back. As a result, according to von Mellenthin, a 'great opportunity for the British' soon passed. It was, he wrote, 'still possible for Auchinleck to defeat us but every day increased his difficulties'.

Rommel was less sanguine. His letters home, as the First Battle of El Alamein approached a sputtering denouement, reveal a pervasive and uncharacteristic sense of foreboding. On 12 July he wrote that, though a 'very serious situation' was being overcome, the air was 'still electric with crisis'. On the 13th, he referred to 'another decisive day in this hard struggle'. On the 14th, his 'expectations for yesterday's attack' had been 'bitterly disappointed. It achieved no success whatever.' On the 17th, things were 'going downright badly ... It's enough to make one weep.'

By the 18th, after a 'particularly hard and critical day', he noted that 'it can't go on like this for long, otherwise the front will crack. Militarily this is the most difficult period I've ever been through.' But Auchinleck's failure to make a decisive breakthrough somewhat restored Rommel's spirits. By the 26th, he felt able to write, 'The worst of our troubles are disappearing.' His intuition was well founded.

On the previous day, Auchinleck had urged his weary troops to make one more great effort to dislodge the enemy. 'You have done well,' he told them in a Special Order of the Day. 'You have turned a retreat into a firm stand and stopped the enemy on the threshold of Egypt. You have done more. You have wrenched the initiative from him by sheer guts and hard fighting and put HIM on the defensive in these last three weeks. You have borne much but I ask for more. We must not slacken. If we can stick it we will break him. STICK TO IT.'

But there was no breakthrough and, five days later, on 30 July Auchinleck reluctantly decided to call a halt. After a month of battle, both sides were exhausted, in need of respite, refreshment and reconstruction before once again locking horns. British casualties in July totalled more than 13,000 (of whom over half had served in the New Zealand and Indian infantry divisions). In addition, following the Gazala battle, the loss of Tobruk, the retreat to El Alamein, and the fighting along the Gazala Line, the Panzerarmee had taken 60,000 British, South African, Indian, New Zealand, Australian and French prisoners and destroyed more than 2,000 tanks and armoured vehicles.

Nevertheless, as Rommel noted later, 'the price to Auchinleck had not been excessive, for the one thing that mattered to him was to halt our advance, and that, unfortunately, he had done'. Critically, he went on, 'our attack came to a halt and our strength failed' in the July battles. Even more compellingly, he noted: 'Our chance of overrunning the remainder of the Eighth Army and occupying eastern Egypt at one stroke was irretrievably gone.' This reflection, made later in relative tranquillity, offers potent evidence that Churchill could as well have attributed his memorable phrase 'The End of the Beginning' to the First Battle of El Alamein as to the far more famous struggle which was to take place three months later in far more auspicious circumstances. However, it was not in Churchill's mind to reward Auchinleck for this achievement: the Prime Minister had neither forgotten nor forgiven.

TWENTY

ENTER MONTGOMERY

*'If he is disagreeable to those about him he is also
disagreeable to the enemy.'*
Winston Churchill on Montgomery

In London, Churchill's advisors had just put the finishing touches
to a secret document – 'Worst Possible Case' – which explored
the grim options were the Germans to occupy the Nile Delta. With
Auchinleck's failure to secure an outright victory over Rommel,
the central question facing the War Cabinet – addressed to London
from all three commanders-in-chief in the Middle East – was
which was more important: the Nile Delta or the Persian Gulf?
In this 'worst case', – with Rommel at the gates of Cairo – they
judged that it would not be possible to secure both fronts. The
military stalemate at El Alamein gave a longstanding question
greater urgency than ever.

Three months earlier, for the benefit of the Chiefs of Staff,
Churchill's Director of Military Operations had outlined the predicament facing the British government. From the purely military
perspective, Kennedy wrote, 'the retention of Iraq and Persia is
perhaps more important to us than the retention of Egypt itself.
This is so because the holding of these two countries is necessary for the protection of the oil at the head of the Persian Gulf.
Without this oil we should be unable to carry on the war in the
Indian Ocean.' However, if Cyrenaica (Eastern Libya) were to be
lost, it would prove difficult to hold Malta, and without Malta, it

would be exceptionally difficult to reinforce the Middle East and the Far East by air. Moreover, without 'destroying' Rommel, it would be equally difficult to free up enough men and weaponry to meet the growing threat from the north, via either Turkey or the Caucasus. According to Kennedy, everything now depended on the Russians, 'If the Russians are not defeated, there is a good prospect of holding the Middle East. If they are defeated, there is a poor prospect of doing so.'

In the intervening months, little had changed – except that the Russians had been unable to prevent the Germans from taking more territory: the Wehrmacht had seized the Black Sea port of Sebastopol; they had pushed the Red Army across the River Don and they were advancing rapidly towards Stalingrad; they had driven deep into the Caucasus, with every likelihood that – by one route or another – they would press on southwards towards Britain's oil lifeline in the Persian Gulf. Indeed, by July, evidently buoyed by his successes in the Caucasus, Field Marshal Ewald von Kleist, the commander of 1 Panzerarmee (Panzergruppe von Kleist), was already developing plans for the invasion of Persia and Iraq. This prospect was under such detailed consideration that the Deputy Head of Operations at OKW, General Walter Warlimont, was sent to Libya to impress on Rommel the vital importance of holding the line at El Alamein; in due course, he told Rommel, he and Kleist would be instructed to launch a co-ordinated pincer movement to throttle the British in the Middle East. However, like Rommel, Warlimont knew that the Panzerarmee's hold on the El Alamein line was exceedingly tenuous. He was also in no doubt that the final assault on the Middle East could not possibly start until the Red Army had been defeated at Stalingrad. When Ribbentrop informed the Japanese ambassador that the Kleist–Rommel pincer movement was still high on Hitler's agenda, and that the Wehrmacht was 'much closer to achieving this goal than the German leadership, even at its most optimistic, had ever imagined', he was not only echoing his Führer's capricious optimism but indulging a military fantasy in which even Rommel had started to lose faith.

However, this was by no means yet apparent in Cairo, and the threat from the north continued to agitate Auchinleck. In his unique position as both commander of the Eighth Army and C-in-C, Middle East (a combination of responsibilities that neither his predecessor nor his successor had to bear), he felt bound to raise his concerns with the Prime Minister. Churchill gave him short shrift, replying brusquely, on 12 July, that 'the only way in which a sufficient army can be gathered in the northern theatre is by your defeating or destroying Rommel and driving him at least to a safe distance ... It must be recognised, however, that if you do not succeed in defeating and destroying Rommel, then there is no possibility whatsoever of making a sufficient transference to the north, and we shall continue to be entirely dependent on the Russian front holding.'

Although Churchill judged that the Wehrmacht would not attack Persia before October, the dilemmas posed by this possibility were by no means theoretical; moreover, as Niall Barr has pointed out, 'they were of fundamental importance in shaping Auchinleck's conduct of the fighting at Alamein during July 1942'. In his reply to Churchill, Auchinleck conceded, 'I quite understand the situation ... My aim is to destroy him as far east as possible ... unless we can destroy the German forces here and so be enabled to transfer troops to Persia we stand to lose Iraq and the oil should the Russian front break.'

But the strategic challenges facing both Auchinleck and Churchill did not go away as easily as either of them would have wished. On 17 July, Kennedy was summoned to a meeting at Number 10, where the Prime Minister sat in the Cabinet Room 'with his back to a big fire, wearing his romper suit, and smoking a fat cigar' as they pored over a sketch map of the El Alamein battlefield. They were joined by Eden as they discussed the prospects of victory. Apparently concluding that the British had so far been saved by the Italians, Churchill said lugubriously, 'If Rommel's army were all Germans, they would beat us,' and, reflectively, 'much hangs on this battle'.

Afterwards, Kennedy and Brooke worked out a theoretical timetable for a possible German advance into Persia and explored various plans for defending the Gulf oil supplies, 'even if Auchinleck had to evacuate the Delta'. Later Kennedy noted that this focus served to show 'how narrow we considered the margin to be between defeat and victory in the Middle East'. With the benefit of hindsight, some historians have judged this emphasis on the German threat to Persia and Iraq to be misplaced or exaggerated; at the time it seemed to be a very present danger – which is one of the reasons El Alamein was totemic for both sides. As Brooke noted with justifiable asperity, 'That the threat did not materialise is no evidence that I had exaggerated its importance. It was due solely to the fact that Hitler missed one of the great opportunities of the war.' It remains baffling that, even today, some historians dismiss the Middle East and the Mediterranean as 'peripheral' theatres in the Second World War merely because Hitler was unable to see that they were pivotal.

For Churchill, however, there was more at stake than even the Persian oil fields. 'During this month of July, when I was politically at my weakest and without a gleam of military success, I had to procure from the United States the decision which, for good or ill, dominated the next two years of the war.' On the 18th, Roosevelt's Chief of Staff, Marshall, accompanied by the stridently Anglophobic Chief of Naval Operations, Admiral King, and the President's confidant, Harry Hopkins, arrived in London for what promised to be an exceptionally uncomfortable round of negotiations.

Ten days earlier, after an exhaustive rehearsal of the arguments with the Chiefs of Staff and the War Cabinet, Churchill had written to Roosevelt without the constructive – or perfidious – ambiguity which had coloured the earlier dialogue between the two sides. Armed with advice that, with forty-seven Wehrmacht divisions in central Europe and twenty-seven in France, the Germans could comfortably see off a cross-Channel landing by thirty Allied divisions without drawing a single unit from the Russian Front, he informed the President baldly, 'No responsible British general, admiral, or air marshal is prepared to recommend *Sledgehammer* as a practicable operation in 1942.' Explaining why his Chiefs thought that the operation would not be a 'sound, sensible enterprise', he stated, with even greater clarity, 'It may therefore be said that premature action in 1942, while probably ending in disaster, would decisively injure the prospect of well-organised large-scale action in 1943.' Though he carefully refrained from saying so, a premature landing in France, even if it were militarily practicable, would have jeopardised the British position in the Middle East and placed the very survival of the British Empire in question, thus ruining his entire war strategy. Instead he argued – somewhat shakily – that *Gymnast* (the proposed Allied landings in North Africa) offered 'by far the best chance of effecting relief to the Russian front in 1942'. Then, exaggerating shamelessly but flatteringly, he went on to tell the President, 'This has all along been in harmony with your ideas. In fact it is your commanding idea.' Finally, after this classic example of high diplomacy, he delivered the coup de grâce: 'Here is the true Second Front of 1942.'

This clarion call sprang from Churchill's determination 'to bury' *Sledgehammer* which, in his own mind at least, 'had been dead for some time' in any case. But, in putting so much faith in Roosevelt's malleability, he reckoned without Marshall and the President's other advisors, who were by now more than ever dubious about the strategic value of an Allied invasion of North Africa to prop up the British Empire, let alone that it could seriously be conceived as a 'true Second Front'. On 15 July, two days before the American trio were due to arrive, Dill, who had established a warm personal relationship with Marshall, wrote to Churchill warning him that unless he made a convincing case for *Gymnast*, 'everything points to a complete reversal of our agreed strategy and the withdrawal of America to a war of her own in the Pacific, leaving us with limited American assistance to make out as best we can against Germany'.

Dill was not scaremongering. At a meeting with the US Secretary of War, Henry Stimson, Marshall had proposed 'a showdown' with the British. Goaded by what they evidently regarded as Churchill's 'obstinacy' over *Sledgehammer*, the American negotiators agreed that, as 'the British won't go through with what they've agreed to, we will turn our backs on them and take up the war with Japan'. In this spirit, on 10 July, Marshall cabled the President, who was at Hyde Park, to argue that unless the British were willing to demonstrate 'forceful, unswerving adherence' to a second front in Europe, 'we should turn to the Pacific and strike decisively against Japan.'

On Roosevelt's return to the White House on the 15th, the two men had what Stimson described as a 'thumping argument' as Marshall pressed the point again. Evidently forgetting his own largesse after the fall of Tobruk only a month earlier, Marshall not only declared himself to be opposed to *Gymnast*, but, in even more vehement terms, to any further American involvement in the Middle East whatsoever. Instead, he reiterated the case for concentrating all US efforts on the Far East. Had he been aware of Marshall's volte-face, Churchill would have been astonished and horrified. But he would also have been greatly relieved to discover that, rather than giving way, the President ended their discussion in unequivocal terms, telling Marshall that 'there would be no shift to the Pacific and no threat or ultimatum to the British'.

To settle the matter once and for all, Roosevelt despatched Marshall, Hopkins and King to London with written instructions requiring them 'to reach immediate agreement' on 'definite' plans for 1942 and tentative ones for 1943 or 1944. The President's overriding priority was to have US ground forces in action against the Germans during 1942, and – now that Churchill had ruled out *Sledgehammer* for that year – he ruled this should be either by the despatch of troops to support the British in Persia, Syria and Egypt or via landings in North Africa to 'drive in against the backdoor of Rommel's armies'. In either case, the task he set them was to save the Middle East. His injunction effectively put *Gymnast* firmly back at the top of the agenda.

Notwithstanding these instructions, the London talks started badly. Churchill was furious to learn that, rather than attending upon him first, his American visitors planned to precede their negotiations with an off-the-record briefing from their British military counterparts. Knowing that Brooke's commitment to *Gymnast* was less wholehearted than his own and suspecting that Roosevelt was driven principally by domestic political imperatives, he was so suspicious that when he met his most sympathetic transatlantic interlocutor, Harry Hopkins, he could not refrain from berating his unsuspecting visitor for what he clearly felt to be a break of courtesy and protocol. According to Hopkins, he even tore pages from a book of Army Regulations to prove the point that the [British] Chiefs of Staff were under his command. 'The Prime Minister threw the British Constitution at me with some vehemence,' the puzzled emissary reported back to the President, adding dryly, 'it is an unwritten document, so no damage was done'.

Not yet knowing Roosevelt's mind, Churchill's momentary attack of paranoia was a measure of his anxiety about what might be settled behind his back by edgy subordinates at a point when all he had striven for in the last two years appeared to depend on winning over Marshall and his colleagues in the days ahead. As his physician, Lord Moran, noted, 'My diary for 1942 has the same backcloth for every scene: Winston's conviction that his life as Prime Minister could be saved only by a victory in the field.' That victory could only come in the Middle East and only with American support.

The talks began in earnest on 20 July. Clearly ignoring their orders from the President to 'save the Middle East', Marshall and King not only reiterated the case for *Sledgehammer* but also argued that military action against the Japanese in the Pacific should precede the invasion of North Africa. Brooke and his team countered the Americans point by point. Much the same happened on the following day, leading the CIGS to note wearily in his diary, 'Disappointing start! Found ourselves much where we started yesterday morning.' The next day, they failed to break the impasse yet again. Marshall said that he would have to consult the President – as though he was quite unaware of Roosevelt's written instructions (which were very probably held securely in his briefcase). In the absence of any other explanation, it seems clear that Marshall was either defying his commander-in-chief or that Roosevelt had privately indicated that he was content to allow his advisors to test the British resolve to the limit regardless of his presidential instructions to them. Whatever the case, after three days of inconsequential negotiation, the two sides had expended a great deal of energy and time. The diplomatic quadrille could not go on indefinitely; a denouement was required.

That evening, at a meeting of the War Cabinet, Churchill went round the table asking each minister for his views. To a man, they took his part. Marshall was immediately informed that the British government had formally rejected *Sledgehammer*. When the news reached Washington, Stimson expostulated that Britain was led by 'a fatigued and defeatist government which had lost its initiative, blocking the help of a young and vigorous nation whose strength had not yet been tapped'. On the following day, however, a reassuring cable arrived from Roosevelt, allowing Churchill to inform the Chiefs of Staff that the President had accepted that a 'western front in 1942 was off' and also 'that he was in favour of attack in North Africa'. This was a seminal moment and a triumph for Churchill's obdurate diplomacy. It may be presumed – in the absence of clear evidence – that the President was convinced that the British government was not bluffing; that he was deeply reluctant to provoke a damaging breach with Churchill; that he was, in any case, persuaded by the thrust of the Prime Minister's strategic vision; and that, in the absence of any other alternative, North Africa offered the only available battlefield to which he could commit US troops to fight alongside the British in the run-up to the 1942 mid-term elections, a political imperative that weighed far more heavily with him than with his military advisors. To this extent, he had in effect swallowed Churchill's bait: North Africa was to be 'the true Second Front in 1942'. There were to be many more transatlantic wrangles and rows about the implications of the President's decision, but the formal burial of *Sledgehammer* breathed new life into *Gymnast* – which, at Churchill's behest, was now to be renamed *Torch* and to proceed at the earliest opportunity.

That evening Brooke was able to note that the Americans had delivered 'almost everything we had asked them to agree to from the start'. It had been, he wrote, a 'very trying week' but he and his team had 'got just what we wanted out of the USA Chiefs'.

With his emissaries back in Washington, the President cabled Churchill welcoming the agreement they had reached in London, adding, 'I cannot help feeling that the past week represented a turning-point in the whole war and that we are now on our way

shoulder to shoulder.' In fact, rather as seas remain rough even
when the storm has passed, the two sides were still mutually suspicious and sometimes at loggerheads while Stimson and Marshall
continued to agitate against what they still regarded as the folly
of Torch. But the crucial decision had been made. On 3 August,
in correspondence with the South African Prime Minister, Field
Marshal Jan Smuts, Roosevelt wrote, 'I believe that the holding
of the Middle East is of prime importance ... and the so-called
Second Front must be launched in 1942.' The fact that he used the
term 'so-called' suggests that he was referring to Churchill's 'true'
second front in North Africa and not (as some historians have suggested) still hankering after an early landing in Europe. Either way,
the die was cast. In what was a crucial victory for the partnership
between Churchill and Roosevelt, the military focus now shifted
unambiguously from Europe to North Africa and the Middle East.
In so doing, it not only charted the future course of the war in the
west but, in the words of Max Hastings, it also saved the Allies
from the 'colossal folly' of a premature second front in Europe.

The Prime Minister's satisfaction at this outcome was tempered
by the fact that Britain's Russian ally was proving no less intrac-
table – but far more disagreeable – than the Americans had been.
As the Red Army retreated before the renewed Nazi offensive
towards Stalingrad and the Caucasus, the clamour in Britain for
a 'Second Front Now' had not abated; in particular, the agonies
endured by the population of Leningrad served only to ignite
further public sympathy for the sufferings of the Soviet people
to which the Prime Minister, despite his warm words, seemed cal-
lously and unaccountably immune. Though Churchill was in a
better position to deflect this domestic pressure now that he and
Roosevelt had agreed to postpone any second front in Europe
until 1943 at the earliest, his uneasy relationship with Stalin had
sharply deteriorated.

Earlier in July, following the disaster which befell Convoy
PQ 17 – when twenty-four of thirty-five merchant vessels loaded
with 3,850 trucks, 430 tanks, and 250 warplanes were sunk in the
Arctic Ocean en route from Iceland to Archangel – the Prime

Minister had been prevailed upon by the Admiralty to suspend this flow of Anglo-American supplies to Russia. When he wrote to Stalin to explain this, the Soviet leader wrote back in fury to denounce the decision to 'stop' the supply of vital equipment to the Soviet Union when it was needed 'more than ever'. Although the accusation was not explicit, his tone was offensive enough to imply that the Prime Minister cared somewhat less about the mortal struggle of the Russian people than he did for the inevitable and much smaller loss of British maritime lives in the Arctic. Nor was that all. Clearly goaded by a brief reference which Churchill had made to devoting his efforts to the need to beat Rommel before all else, he wrote, 'I must state in the most emphatic manner that the Soviet Government cannot acquiesce in the postponement of a Second Front in Europe until 1943.' Now he was to be told that this was precisely what had happened.

Roosevelt was far more sensitive than Churchill to the way in which this disagreeable news should be conveyed to the Soviet leader. 'We have got always to bear in mind the personality of our Ally,' he counselled Churchill. 'No one can be expected to approach the war from a world point of view whose country has been invaded.' With Roosevelt's support, Churchill decided that the best way to explain their decision would be to do it face to face. Accordingly, on 30 July he wrote to Stalin to suggest a meeting at which 'we could then survey the war together and take decisions hand-in-hand ... [and] I could then tell you plans we have made with President Roosevelt for offensive action in 1942'. Vouchsafing that he would be flying to Cairo shortly, where he had 'serious business' to conduct, he suggested that he might fly on from there to Moscow. Stalin eagerly agreed.

Churchill's 'serious business' in Cairo was pressing. Without a decisive victory over Rommel, his own status at home and his lessening influence in the emerging Anglo-American-Soviet triumvirate would be further jeopardised. His impatience was aggravated by a message from Auchinleck on 31 July. 'Owing to a lack of resources and enemy's effective consolidation of his positions,' he wrote, 'it is not now feasible to renew our efforts to break enemy front or turn his southern flank. It is unlikely that an opportunity will arise for resumption of offensive operations before mid-September.' A delay of at least seven weeks was seven weeks too many for Churchill. He had had enough of what he – and some of those around him – regarded as yet another inexplicable and inexcusable procrastination.

The Prime Minister left RAF Lyneham bound for Cairo in the early hours of 2 August. It was a long and arduous flight via Gibraltar in a four-engined bomber that was neither pressurised nor insulated against the cold and so noisy that the only way to communicate was by writing notes. So far from being exhausted by this, the sixty-nine-year-old Prime Minister found the experience exhilarating. As they flew over Upper Egypt, he was enchanted by the 'endless winding silver ribbon of the Nile stretched joyously before us' and energised at the prospect of being 'the man on the spot' at the front. Brooke, who had flown in separately from Malta, was more circumspect. Big decisions were about to be made and he foresaw 'troublesome times ahead'.

The precise course of events in the next few days is riven by conflicting and bitterly contested versions from the principal protagonists and their competing apologists. What is not in dispute is that Churchill was on the warpath, that he wanted radical change, and that he had long ago lost faith in Auchinleck. Churchill himself intimated in his memoirs that he did not rush to judgement before reaching Cairo. But when Brooke stopped off in Malta on his way to Egypt, he had told Lord Gort (who had replaced the ailing and eccentric Dobbie as governor two months earlier) about 'the plans for a new Command in the Middle East'; and on their very first evening in Cairo, Churchill kept his CIGS up until the early hours to argue back and forth about Auchinleck's future. In a reversal of his previous contention, he now proposed that Auchinleck should surrender his command of the Eighth Army to concentrate on his overriding responsibilities as C-in-C, Middle East. As Brooke had already advocated this, their discussion moved to Auchinleck's successor as Eighth Army commander. Churchill favoured General 'Strafer' Gott, a veteran officer with a reputation for buccaneering optimism. Gott had commanded the 7th Armoured Division

– the 'Desert Rats' – during *Compass* and *Brevity* before being promoted to command XIII Corps, which had been prominent at Gazala and most recently during the First Battle of El Alamein. He was not universally admired: the South African official historian of the Second World War was to write, 'It has not been unknown for a commander to pass from disaster to disaster, but it is quite without precedent for any commander to pass from promotion to promotion as a reward for a succession of disasters.' But others revered him: Michael Carver was not alone when he wrote, 'I worshipped him as the ideal of all that I believed that a senior officer should be.' But Brooke believed Gott was worn out after nearly two years in the desert as a front-line commander and that he needed a break.

Thus baulked, Churchill suddenly and casually suggested that Brooke should himself take command of the Eighth Army. Professing that the Prime Minister's suggestion 'gave rise to the most desperate longings in my heart', the CIGS nonetheless failed to rise to the bait. Doubting his own qualifications for such a testing role, he consulted the South African Prime Minister Field Marshal Smuts – 'a most delightful old man with a wonderfully clear brain' – who, as the most trusted of all his fellow leaders, had been asked by Churchill to join them in Cairo. Smuts advised Brooke to stay at his post, where his presence was much needed; somewhat relieved, the CIGS duly rejected Churchill's proposal. Someone else would have to be found to lead the Eighth Army into battle.

Since their arrival, Auchinleck had been in several long meetings with both Churchill and Brooke, though he still had no idea what was brewing. But on the afternoon of 4 August, after another meeting with the CIGS, he agreed both to relinquish his front-line command and that he should be succeeded in that post by a relatively obscure colleague, Lieutenant General Bernard Montgomery, who was in England at South East Command, responsible for the defence of Kent, Sussex and Surrey. Brooke claimed later to have been surprised by Auchinleck's ready acquiescence as the two men were known to have had a decidedly abrasive relationship when Auchinleck had been Montgomery's commanding officer at Southern Command. In a waspish aside, Montgomery was to write of that period, 'I cannot recall that we ever agreed on anything'; much later Auchinleck confirmed (in a BBC interview with David Dimbleby) that 'I didn't approve of [his methods] and he didn't approve of me. Of my methods.' Despite this bad blood, Auchinleck insisted that he had himself proposed Montgomery as his successor. Nor is there reason to doubt him. Unlike his successor, 'The Auk' never showed any tendency to advance his own cause by spite or mendacity.

To Brooke's frustration, Churchill continued to press the case for Gott rather than Montgomery, on the implausible grounds that the latter could not possibly arrive from England in time to hasten the offensive against Rommel. That evening, at a meeting with Smuts and others, including General Wavell who had been summoned from India, Churchill cross-questioned Auchinleck about his forthcoming offensive. Not for the first time, Brooke was exasperated by the Prime Minister's attitude. 'He is again pressing for an attack before Auchinleck can possibly get ready!' he noted. 'I find him almost impossible to argue with on this point.' Churchill's obstinate refusal to accept the military case against premature action had become inextricably linked to his need to find almost any grounds for ridding himself of his obdurate commander-in-chief.

The Prime Minister's satisfaction at being 'on the spot' was enhanced by the 'princely' hospitality of the British ambassador, Sir Miles Lampson and his wife, who even moved out of their private quarters to make way for Churchill to accommodate his sybaritic tastes. 'The weather is delightful,' he purred in a letter home to Clemmie. 'My host and hostess are charming; the food pre-war. My rooms are air-cooled. The wonderful air of the desert with its fierce sunshine and cool breeze invigorates me so much that I do not seem to need as much sleep as usual.'

He was less appreciative of the spartan environment at Auchinleck's headquarters at Ruweisat Ridge, which he visited early in the morning on 5 August. There he and Brooke were offered a frugal breakfast in what he described disparagingly as 'a wire-netted cube, full of flies and important military personages' – one of whom was Auchinleck's clever but widely distrusted military guru, Eric Dorman-Smith, whom Brooke loathed. The heat, the sand, the flies, and the presence of Dorman-Smith did nothing to improve an atmosphere already strained by the incompatible temperaments of Auchinleck and Churchill. When Brooke departed for a guided tour of the front line, Churchill returned to the fray, 'his pudgy fingers stabbing at the map' as he urged various lines of attack against Rommel. 'No, sir, we cannot attack yet,' Auchinleck reiterated. When Churchill turned to him, Dorman-Smith agreed forcibly. It was, he said later, 'a bit like being caged with a gorilla' until the Prime Minister 'rose, grunted, stumped down from the caravan and stood alone in the sand, back turned to us'. If Auchinleck's fate had not already been sealed, it was certainly symbolised in that moment of silent censure.

Brooke meanwhile was driven to Gott's headquarters, where, over a cup of tea, the general confided that 'some new blood ... someone with new ideas and plenty of confidence in them' was needed in the desert and that he had by now 'tried' most of his ideas to no avail. This conversation confirmed Auchinleck in his opinion that Gott not only needed a break but that he was 'not the man to lead the 8th Army in an offensive to turn the tide of the war'.

For Brooke, the next day turned out to be 'one of the most difficult' in his life, 'with momentous decisions to take'. Early in the morning Churchill burst into his bedroom while the CIGS was still getting dressed. He was clearly elated as he informed Brooke that he had some ideas he needed to share with him. 'I rather shuddered and wondered what he was up to,' Brooke noted in his patronising fashion. After breakfast the Prime Minister elaborated his plans for dividing the Middle East Command in two, separating Iraq and Persia from Egypt. Auchinleck, in whom Churchill said he had 'lost confidence' would be despatched to take command of Iraq and Persia and – he hoped – Brooke himself would take his place as commander-in-chief in Egypt.

'This offer made my heart race very fast!!' Brooke wrote that evening, but he responded at once by saying it would be the wrong move, that he knew nothing about desert warfare, and that he 'could never have time to grip hold of the show to my satisfaction before the necessity to attack became imperative'. Churchill was not best pleased. In an attempt to win Brooke over, he set Smuts to work his magic. Though the South African Prime Minister had advised him against taking command of the Eighth Army, he now pressed him to accept Churchill's new offer. Reminding the CIGS of the leading part he had played in saving the British Expeditionary Force at Dunkirk, he laid out before him the 'wonderful future' that would be his after victory over Rommel. But even Smuts did not prevail.

Some of Brooke's detractors have intimated that his failure to seize the moment reflected a lack of valour or resolve. Brooke himself argued that he could better serve the nation by staying at Churchill's side though – for obvious reasons – he could hardly say this to the Prime Minister's face. 'I felt I could exercise some control over him,' he wrote later. 'I had discovered the perils of his impetuous nature. I was now familiar with his method of suddenly arriving at some decision without any kind of logical examination of the problem. I had, after many failures, discovered the best methods of approaching him. I knew that it would take at least six months for any successor taking over from me to become as familiar as I was with him and his ways. During those six months anything might happen.' According to his own account, Brooke turned down the offer with 'many heart-gnawing regrets'. It was a blessing that he did.

The haphazard and discursive attempts to find a general qualified to lead the Eighth Army into battle came to an abrupt end that afternoon when news arrived that Gott, who had been appointed to command the Eighth Army, had died in a plane crash. He had hitched a lift from the RAF's headquarters at Borg el Arab for a few days' leave in Cairo in a transport plane carrying fourteen wounded soldiers. Fifteen minutes after take-off, on what was a routine flight along a 'safe' corridor, the Bristol Bombay, lumbering along at less than 200 mph, was attacked by a small posse of Messerschmitt fighters. Within moments the Bombay was in flames. The pilot managed to make a safe landing (and survived), but most of the wounded were trapped inside, and Gott, who sitting in a jump seat at the rear of the plane, was trapped in the fuselage and died. The news of his death shocked and grieved Churchill who, only the day before, in the course of a long drive with the XIII Corps commander, convinced himself, as he wrote to Clemmie, that he was blessed with 'high ability, charming simple personality, and that he was in no way tired as was alleged'.

There was now only one possible candidate left. A telegram ordering Montgomery to proceed to the Middle East was despatched forthwith to the War Cabinet in London. Churchill knew that the new commander of the Eighth Army was a dyspeptic personality whose self-esteem knew few bounds; but he was also, in the Prime Minister's judgement, 'a highly competent, daring and energetic soldier'. Furthermore, he wrote to Clemmie, 'If he is disagreeable to those about him he is also disagreeable to the enemy.'

On 8 August, Colonel Ian Jacob, the Prime Minister's Military Assistant Secretary (later to be appointed Director-General of the BBC), carried a letter from Churchill to Eighth Army headquarters to inform Auchinleck that he was to be removed from his command. For Jacob, who liked and admired Auchinleck, 'it was like going to murder an unsuspecting friend'. That evening the commander-in-chief asked Brigadier de Guingand, his Director of Military Intelligence, to go for a walk with him. 'He put his arm in mine and said: "Freddy, I'm to go." … I felt intensely sorry for my Chief, for I had become very fond of him. It must have hurt.'

Shorn of surplus emotion or gratitude, Churchill's letter stated baldly, 'The War Cabinet have now decided … that the moment has come for a change.' Expressing the hope that Auchinleck would accept the lesser command of the Tenth Army in Iraq and Persia 'with the same disinterested public spirit that you have shown on all occasions', Churchill informed him that his successor as C-in-C, Middle East, would be General Alexander (who had just been designated to lead the British First Army in the *Torch* landings under the overall command of General Eisenhower). When Jacob reported back to the Prime Minister that his disagreeable task had been accomplished, he found Churchill pacing about his quarters with his mind on one thing and one thing only: 'Rommel, Rommel, Rommel, Rommel!' he kept repeating, 'What else matters but beating him?'

Auchinleck displayed little outward emotion as he contemplated his downfall although he later conceded that his notice of dismissal had come as 'a shock' to him. Many years later, in an interview with the broadcaster David Dimbleby, he confessed to being 'slightly humiliated but not hurt' by Churchill's decision which – by the latter's account – he accepted 'with soldierly dignity'. Brooke's version is rather different. Auchinleck, he noted at the time, was 'in a highly stormy and rather unpleasant mood' when he arrived in Cairo on 10 August wanting to know why he had been sacked. Unsurprisingly, Brooke's explanation that it was 'mainly lack of confidence in him' was not well received.

Later that afternoon, following a long conversation with Churchill, at which they discussed the Tenth Army Command, Auchinleck was still apparently 'in an unpleasant mood'. When he finally turned down the offer, Brooke noted coldly that he made an error of judgement because the Persia/Iraq front was 'the one place where he might restore his reputation'. Their conversation took place on the embassy lawn in Cairo and the two men were observed by Churchill's physician, Charles Moran, who was reading a book in the shade of a tree in another part of the garden. That evening he wrote in his diary,

> I could not hear what the CIGS was saying, nor could I see the expression on Auchinleck's face, but I did not need any help to follow what was happening. Auchinleck sat with his forearms resting on his thighs, his hands hanging down between his knees, his head drooping forward like a flower on a broken stalk … the whole attitude expressed grief: the man was completely undone. After a time they got up and went into the house. I tried to get on with my book, but I was somehow made miserable by what I had seen.

Brooke was unmoved. Accusing Auchinleck of 'behaving like an offended film star', he wrote later that it would have been 'a more "soldierly" act to accept what he was offered in war'. Auchinleck's refusal to accept demotion to the Tenth Army destroyed any latent sympathy that Churchill may have harboured on account of the 'blow' he had inflicted on his commander-in-chief: 'It is for him to settle whether he wishes to render further service to the Crown,' he commented dismissively when he received the news. Auchinleck himself insisted that his decision to turn down the new command was not taken in pique or anger – though he would never forget the 'slight' humiliation – but because 'I had a certain amount of pride and I did not think that I should have the same professional control over others after having stepped down in command.' Instead he decided that he would retreat to India, his spiritual homeland (where, a year later, he was to take up his previous role as commander-in-chief of the Indian Army). But his humbling in Egypt had not yet been fully accomplished.

Harold Alexander arrived in Cairo on 9 August followed two days later by Bernard Montgomery. Both generals were due to take up their posts (respectively as C-in-C, Middle East and Eighth Army commander) on 15 August. But while Alexander remained in Cairo, virtually incognito as his new appointment had yet to be announced, Montgomery – at Auchinleck's invitation – went up to the Eighth Army's forward headquarters at Ruweisat Ridge. Montgomery was unimpressed: 'no mess tent, work done mostly in trucks or in the open air in the hot sun, flies everywhere'. When he was told that Auchinleck was accustomed to sleeping outside on the ground, he was disparaging: 'everyone was to be as uncomfortable as possible, so that they wouldn't be more comfortable than the men ... the whole atmosphere was ... dismal and dreary'.

In his determination to present himself as the saviour of the Eighth Army, Montgomery had no qualms about undermining his soon-to-be predecessor. Two days before he was due to take over, in an act of calculated insolence for which he must have known there could be no effective reprimand, he despatched a telegram to GHQ, declaring, 'Lieut-Gen MONTGOMERY assumed command of the Eighth Army at 1400 hrs today.' Claiming that the situation he had inherited from Auchinleck was 'quite impossible, and in fact, dangerous', he noted with glee that 'I learnt later that the arrival of the telegram made Auchinleck very angry as he had told me not to take over until 15 August.'

Not content with subjecting his titular commander-in-chief to this petty indignity, Montgomery did not hesitate to stoop lower in his effort to diminish and discredit Auchinleck. Later that afternoon he summoned all staff officers to appear before him at his caravan at Eighth Army headquarters. In a clear, if not calculated, distortion of the truth, he barked, 'Here we will stand and fight; there will be no further withdrawal. I have ordered that all plans and instructions dealing with further withdrawal are to be burnt, and at once. We will stand and fight here. If we can't stay here alive, then let us stay here dead.' His intention was most certainly to rally support and imprint his abrasive personality on his own staff. But to achieve this he was not embarrassed to insinuate falsely that Auchinleck was a defeatist, planning to retreat once again, and unwilling to 'stand and fight'.

Montgomery had already been briefed by Auchinleck. No one knows precisely what passed between them but Montgomery claimed later he was told that 'If Rommel attacked in strength, as was expected soon, the Eighth Army would fall back on the Delta; if Cairo and the Delta could not be held, the army would retreat southwards up the Nile, and another possibility was a withdrawal to Palestine. I listened in amazement ... I got out of the room as soon as I decently could.' This account stretches credulity to the limit. Auchinleck may indeed have alerted Montgomery to the fact that he had retained, modified and updated the plans for a 'worst case' contingency, that had originally been drawn up by Wavell and approved by the Chiefs of Staff in London. This did indeed envisage a withdrawal to the Delta if, but only if, 'the worst came to the worst and we had to get out of Alamein'. As Montgomery must have appreciated, it would have been quite irresponsible for the commander-in-chief to have overlooked this possibility. But, by August 1942, with Rommel's advance halted by the Eighth Army at the First Battle of El Alamein, no one in the Middle East Command, least of all Auchinleck, was planning to retreat any further. It is virtually inconceivable that the outgoing commander-in-chief could have led Montgomery to believe that a headlong retreat to the Delta or beyond formed part of his battle plan. However, his aversion to Auchinleck knew few bounds: in a contemptuous diary note, he wrote scathingly of the 'Gross mismanagement, faulty command,

and bad staff work' which had led to the precipitous retreat from Gazala to El Alamein, for which calamity, he added 'the final blame must rest on General Auchinleck'.

Churchill was swift to endorse Montgomery's hyper-critical assessment. 'I am sure we were heading for disaster under the former regime,' the Prime Minister informed the War Cabinet from Cairo, a week after Auchinleck had relinquished his post. 'The Army was reduced to bits and pieces and oppressed by a sense of bafflement and uncertainty. Apparently it was intended in the face of heavy attack to retire eastwards to the Delta. Many were looking over their shoulders to make sure of their seat in the lorry.' When these words were reproduced in the fourth volume of Churchill's *Second World War*, Dorman-Smith – one of the principal architects of Auchinleck's plan to hold the Alamein line and to launch an all-out counter-attack against Rommel in September – sued Churchill for libel. The case was eventually settled out of court, but only after the most eminent military historian of the day, Basil Liddell Hart, acting as an 'honest broker', concluded that there was no shred of evidence to sustain this 'imputation of funk'. For good measure, he added that 'Montgomery's tendency to paint everything black prior to his arrival on the scene has long been a joke among his fellow soldiers. Also his tendency to sweeping and unfounded assertions.'

Eventually, Montgomery was also forced to withdraw his libellous allegations which he had made the mistake of repeating in his memoirs. A publisher's note in later editions made clear that he had misrepresented his predecessor's stated intention to 'launch an offensive from the Alamein position when his army was rested and had been regrouped'. For a long time, however, Montgomery's mud stuck, not least because his victim, with great self-restraint, kept his counsel for decades. It was only as an old man, when he told his BBC interviewer that Montgomery's aspersions were 'absolute rubbish', that the Auk allowed himself the last word.

The irony of this episode is that, as soon as he took over from Auchinleck, Montgomery's new commander-in-chief, General Alexander, moved hurriedly to implement a 'series of extreme measures' for the defence of Cairo and Alexandria which had originated with Wavell and Auchinleck. Montgomery may have torn up Auchinleck's redundant 'worst case' plans but this by no means entailed the abandonment of the defensive work which his predecessors had initiated in the Nile Delta. Under the direction of General 'Jumbo' Wilson, three army divisions began to 'construct rifle-pits and machine posts, to mine bridges, and flood access routes' with the purpose of protecting 'vital installations against raids which penetrate the Alamein position'. Not only was Wilson instructed to oversee the construction of these defences but, at Churchill's personal direction, he was charged 'to take responsibility from the moment when General Alexander told him that Cairo was in danger'.

On 21 August the Prime Minister reassured the War Cabinet that, to 'give the fullest manoeuvring power to the Eighth Army in the event of its being attacked next week, a strong line of defence is being developed along the Delta from Alexandria to Cairo'. The intensity of their focus on this threat may be gauged from the fact that the next day Churchill convened an hour-long meeting with Alexander and Brooke to review their 'worst case' options were Rommel to achieve 'a temporary breakthrough with a thrust on Cairo'. No detail was omitted from their discussion. When Brooke urged that 'petrol reserves at pumps [ordinary filling stations] should be reduced' in the hope of paralysing the Panzerarmee's takeover of the capital, Miles Lampson (the British ambassador) was summoned 'to attend to this danger'. If there was any significant difference between these preparations and the 'worst case' plans laid by Wavell and inherited by Auchinleck, it was a matter of scale and design. It had nothing to do with the military strategy or tactics of any of them. The evidence is compelling – as both Churchill and Montgomery were later obliged to concede – that Auchinleck was every bit as ready to do battle against Rommel as they were and had no intention of further withdrawal. By implying otherwise, Montgomery did a disservice not only to the truth but – eventually – to his own reputation as well.

Notwithstanding his unsavoury attempt to smear Auchinleck's reputation, Montgomery's first speech to his staff officers on the day he usurped command of the Eighth Army was an indisputable triumph. Favouring cricketing analogies over hunting metaphors, his simple, forthright promise – 'we ourselves will start to plan a great offensive; it will be the beginning of a campaign which will hit Rommel for six right out of Africa ... we will hit him with a crack and finish with him' – barked out in the short, sharp cadences that were to become so familiar, made a powerful impact on his audience. His officers forgot his vulpine looks, his wispy body and his strutting demeanour and instead wondered at the intensity and certainty of his will. De Guingand, who felt that Churchill had been right 'on balance' to dismiss Auchinleck and whom Montgomery had astutely promoted to be his Chief of Staff, was ecstatic. 'The effect of his address was electric – it was terrific. And we all went to bed that night with a new hope in our hearts, and a great confidence in the future of our Army.'

By this time, the Prime Minister and his party had left Cairo for Moscow, flying via Teheran to reach the 'sullen, sinister Bolshevik State' two days later. His task was to convince Stalin that it was more immediately important to defeat the Nazis in North Africa than to open a second front in Europe. It was his first meeting with the Soviet leader and he had taken a large entourage with him, including Brooke, Wavell, and, following a request to the President, Roosevelt's trusted emissary, Averell Harriman as well.

With the Red Army hard pressed on every front and enduring unspeakable casualties at the hands of the Wehrmacht in battles of a scale and savagery which – to Stalin – must have made the struggle in the desert seem like a weekend skirmish, the Anglo-American allies still feared that Hitler's brutal resolve would ultimately overpower the equally implacable and no less murderous will of the Soviet leader. Though Stalin showed no sign of sharing this analysis, he seethed with barely suppressed fury at the failure of the West to risk British and American lives on anything like the scale endured by their Soviet counterparts in the struggle against Germany. The first encounter between Churchill and Stalin in the late evening of 12 August at the Kremlin, promised to be exceedingly uncomfortable.

Churchill began by trying to explain why it would not be possible to launch a second front in Europe during 1942. The atmosphere, according to Churchill became 'bleak and sombre' as Stalin demurred, his mood veering from glum to agitated as he accused the Prime Minister of failing to take the risks required for victory. 'Why were we so afraid of the Germans?' Churchill recorded him as demanding, before going on to declare that it was important to 'blood your troops' in battle to discover their true worth. After two hours of such uncouth observations, there was 'an oppressive silence' which Churchill took as his cue to unfold a map of 'Southern Europe, the Mediterranean, and North Africa' and to outline the case for an alternative second front in that theatre instead of France.

At this point, according to Churchill, Stalin became 'intensely interested' as the Prime Minister outlined his Mediterranean strategy. In September, the British would win in Egypt and in October, North Africa would fall to *Torch*. Throughout this period and beyond, the panzer divisions in France would be pinned down against the risk of an Allied attack across the Channel. Once the Anglo-American operation in North Africa had achieved its purpose, Churchill explained, the Allies would be in a position 'to threaten the belly of Hitler's Europe' in conjunction with a second-front landing in France in 1943. To illustrate his point, Churchill drew a picture of a crocodile to show how the Western Allies would simultaneously attack 'the soft belly of the crocodile as we attacked his hard snout'. With the benefit of hindsight, it was an unfortunate metaphor; Italy was to prove anything but a 'soft belly'. However, it conjured a vivid image which demonstrated beyond peradventure that the Mediterranean – including the Middle East and North Africa – was pivotal to the overall Allied strategy.

At this point, according to Churchill, Stalin's interest reached such 'a high pitch' that he said – oddly for a dictatorial atheist prone to incarcerate and murder the Faithful – 'May God prosper this undertaking'. As he grasped Churchill's strategic purpose – rather more fulsomely than Britain's American allies – he declared that *Torch* would 'hit Rommel in the back'; it would overawe Spain; it would provoke fighting between Germans and French in France; and it would expose Italy to the full brunt of the war.

The Prime Minister was greatly impressed by Stalin's 'swift and complete mastery of a problem hitherto novel to him'. The conversation ended with Churchill informing his host that, with the replacement of Auchinleck by Montgomery, a 'decisive' battle was to be fought in the desert in late August or September. After a meeting which had lasted four hours, and in the belief that 'at least the ice had been broken and a human contact established', Churchill 'slept soundly and long'.

However, in the course of the next two days, the mood darkened as the two leaders covered the same ground again but, with the help of their military advisors, in rather more detail. On several occasions, Stalin went out of his way to be exceptionally offensive by implying that the Western Allies lacked the conviction and courage to fight with the same resolution as Soviet soldiers. Churchill responded with matching vehemence. 'The democracies would show very soon by their deeds that they were neither sluggish nor cowardly,' he avowed. 'They were just as ready as the Russians to shed blood.' Churchill's fierce defence of Western valour evidently earned him the bully's respect. Determined that Stalin should not miss the full import of his words, the Prime Minister prodded his hapless interpreter as he spoke. Seeing this, Stalin intervened and said with a smile, 'Your words are of no importance, what is important is your spirit.'

The parallel talks between their military advisors produced little of consequence which probably contributed to Brooke's jaundiced account of a banquet which Churchill described as a sober occasion which he had clearly enjoyed. According to his fastidious CIGS, it was a grotesque 'orgy' of oil and fish, suckling pig and vodka, at which almost everyone got drunk. Brooke was bored and disgusted by a nineteen-course meal which lasted for three hours and did not end until after midnight. And whereas Churchill described Stalin as a 'profound Russian statesman and warrior with whom I was to be in intimate, rigorous, but always exciting, and at times even genial association', Brooke observed he had 'an unpleasantly cold, crafty, dead face … whenever I look at him I can imagine him sending off people to their doom without ever turning a hair'.

Nonetheless, Churchill's immediate purpose had been achieved. On 17 August, after leaving Moscow, he was able to inform Roosevelt that, despite their 'grievous disappointment' about the postponement of the second front, the Russians 'have swallowed this bitter pill. Everything for us now turns on hastening TORCH and defeating Rommel'. This was to prove far harder and to take much longer than he had led Stalin to believe. Nor was the Soviet dictator as amenable as Churchill seemed to think. Though he had little choice but to swallow Churchill's 'bitter pill', the foul taste of it lingered. It did nothing to alter his belief that – in a commonly deployed Russian quip – the British were ready to fight for their Empire in the Middle East 'to the last drop of Russian blood'.

TWENTY-ONE

MONTGOMERY MAKES HIS MARK

'He told us everything ... what his plan was for battle, what he wanted the regiments to do, and what he wanted me to do ... What a man.'

Regimental sergeant major on Montgomery

In his first two weeks as commander of the Eighth Army, Montgomery had been exceptionally industrious. Initially his troops were sceptical, if not cynical, about the new arrival. Dubious about all senior ranks, their loyalties were first and foremost to their immediate colleagues in the platoons and units on which they depended for survival in the chaos of battle and for the camaraderie which sustained them in between. The higher the chain of command rose, the more remote it seemed to those at the bottom. Those senior officers who despatched them to the front with little explanation of why they were there or what they were supposed to achieve belonged to another world to which they had virtually no access.

However, according to Michael Carver, who was in the midst of it, this did not mean that the Eighth Army had become 'hopelessly dispirited ... Few parts of the Army had lost faith in themselves or even in their commanders.' The real problem was more subtle. The 'most general and dangerous tendency' was for different formations to blame each other when things went wrong. To those who expected to be led into yet another bloody and inconclusive battle against the apparently invincible Desert Fox, Montgomery was but another of these English generals about whom they knew little and, to begin with, cared less.

Montgomery, however, did not hesitate to exaggerate the degree of despondency which had affected the army and which he was resolved to extirpate. On the day after his arrival – when he had met only a handful of senior colleagues – he told his staff officers, 'I believe that one of the first duties of a commander is to create what I call "atmosphere" and in that atmosphere his staff, subordinate commanders and troops will live and work and fight. I do not like the atmosphere I find here.'

After the retreat from Dunkirk, Montgomery's military career had been confined to the south coast of Britain, but it had made him strongly aware of public opinion on the home front and of the difference between a force of career veterans and the civilian conscripts who formed the growing bulk of the Eighth Army. With his inimitable combination of chutzpah and conviction, Montgomery embarked on a 'hearts and minds' campaign to win the personal allegiance of the men under his command. Appreciating more clearly than his predecessors that the soldiers needed sound reasons to put their lives on the line, he was confident that they were biddable. But they had to know 'what was going on, and what you want to do – and why, and when ... and that [their] best interests will be absolutely secure in your hands ... If all these things are understood by the military leader, and he acts accordingly, he will find it is not difficult to gain the trust and confidence of such men.'

Driving from unit to unit, he soon made himself known to the officers and men of all ranks. His eccentric but highly visible attire – the Australian slouch-hat or the tank-beret, and the regimental badges with which they were bedecked – made him easy to distinguish in a khaki crowd. This did not always make the impact he may have wished. 'He was wearing this Australian hat, with all the badges that were around the brim, and a pair of "Bombay bloomers"' – K[haki] D[rill] shorts, which were a lot wider than normal,' Sergeant James Frazer, serving in the Royal Tank Regiment, noted. 'Now, dressed in that hat and shorts, and with his thin legs, he looked like matchsticks in a pair of boots. Very high-pitched voice – and he didn't look like a general at all.'

However, he not only drove through the ranks but he stopped

to talk to the men, both en masse and one to one, as though he were a politician campaigning for votes. 'Montgomery came to the southern sector ... and one of the first things he asked was, when did we leave England and had we had any post?' Sergeant John Longstaff noted. 'Not a single soldier had had a letter. Had we any NAAFI? We hadn't even seen the NAAFI. We were scrounging what we could from other units – cigarettes – and understandably, other units weren't prepared to give them away or even sell them.'

The NAAFI – or rather its absence – really mattered. When Longstaff and his platoon stumbled on an unexpected cache of supplies in a captured Italian truck, he immediately thought of the absent NAAFI. 'I went over and found a bottle of brandy and a couple of big carafes, holding probably about eight or nine litres of vino, and a load of french letters (which we used, funnily enough to carry water later on, and I used to keep my guns clean). We also found hundreds of packets of Italian cigarettes ... we'd not had a single issue of cigarettes – or of anything you would call the niceties of the NAAFI. We went into battle without a fag between us. I can tell you fags for a soldier were very important.'

When Montgomery showed a concern for the welfare of his men, he made a lasting impression. 'He wanted to know why our shirts were stained – because we had only one shirt and there was sweat – and they were hard, like bloody cardboard,' Longstaff recalled. 'He wanted to know if we'd had any leave. Nobody had had any leave at that stage. He made sure his adjutants took note of everything. He wasn't talking to the officers – he was talking to the riflemen – he was sitting inside little dugouts with the lads.'

Not everyone succumbed to this public relations blitz. 'Montgomery was a bit of a bull-shitter,' one British infantryman concluded, adding, 'but I think that was part of his act, and very effective, I think. He had to publicise himself and build up a reputation against Rommel ... We all thought the world of Rommel. If you were opposite Rommel, you expected something to happen. He did have a very demoralising effect on British troops. He was a bloody good general.' But, by comparison with what any senior officer before him had essayed, Montgomery put on a masterly performance that captivated his audience. 'He told us everything … what his plan was for battle, what he wanted the regiments to do, and what he wanted *me* to do … What a man,' an admiring regimental sergeant major said after one such personal encounter with the Eighth Army commander.

Of course Montgomery did not tell his men 'everything'. Most of his time was spent preparing a detailed plan of campaign for Rommel's next offensive, which, thanks to Ultra intercepts, he knew to be imminent. The origins of this plan were to become a matter of lasting dispute between acolytes of Montgomery, who would claim that it was entirely his own creation, and devotees of Auchinleck, who believed that the upstart newcomer had merely appropriated his predecessor's strategy and then taken the credit for it when it worked.

In the history of the Desert War, there is no greater confusion and contention than over the nomenclature used to identify the three main battles fought at or around El Alamein between July and November. It is now generally acknowledged, however, that The First Battle of El Alamein (under Auchinleck in July) stopped Rommel in his tracks; the Second Battle (under Montgomery in August, and more often known as the Battle of Alam el Halfa) forced Rommel on to the defensive; and the Third Battle (which ended with Montgomery's famous victory in November) finished him off. The cumulative effect of the three battles suggests that the First and Second were as important as the Third. So the question of how much credit is due to whom for the success of the Second Battle is of more than academic interest: the reputation of two generals, one of whom was widely traduced by his successor, was at stake.

The truth about Alam el Halfa appears to lie somewhere between the two extreme positions. According to Alexander, who had overriding responsibility for the decisions made by the new commander of the Eighth Army, Montgomery accepted 'in principle' his predecessor's plan 'to hold as strongly as possible the area between the sea and Ruweisat ridge and to threaten from the flank any enemy advance south of the ridge from a strongly defended prepared position on the Alam el Halfa ridge.' In truth,

Montgomery had no alternative as the proximity of the sea made it impossible to mount an outflanking attack to the north. The rest was a matter of tactical emphasis and detail which, inevitably, shifted day by day if not hour by hour.

Following the retreat to the El Alamein line, Auchinleck – working to guidelines devised by Dorman-Smith and Gott – had drawn up a blueprint both for the defence of that position and for the counter-offensive against the Panzerarmee which he had planned for September. But he had failed to convey this clearly to his own officers, let alone the rest of the Eighth Army. One official historian of the desert campaign judged Auchinleck to be 'hopeless' as a commander because he 'never seemed to be able to get anyone to obey him'. This was a silly exaggeration but it contained a kernel of truth. Unaware of his imminent demise, Auchinleck had not only conceived a new battle strategy to resist the forthcoming offensive but, to deliver it effectively, was determined to embark upon a wholesale reorganisation of the Eighth Army, integrating the armour, artillery and infantry to form flexible and mobile units, very similar to those favoured by Rommel. However, before he had time to convince his most senior commanders that this radical renewal was either necessary or desirable, he had been fired.

With the departure of Auchinleck, and several other senior officers, including Dorman-Smith, who were unceremoniously removed at the same time to be replaced by less-experienced officers, the Eighth Army was not so much leaderless as in limbo. More by force of personality than originality of thought, Montgomery seized the moment to stamp his mark. One of his new appointees, recruited to take command of XIII Corps, General Brian Horrocks – later to acquire renown as a 'television general' on account of his popular BBC documentaries – described his first briefing by Montgomery. 'One of the most remarkable military appreciations I ever heard,' he recalled. 'Remember he had arrived in Egypt only five days before; yet in this short space of time he had acquired a complete grip of the situation.' Brooke was similarly impressed by the speed with which Montgomery absorbed the military complexities of the battlefield and the clarity of his purpose. 'I was dumbfounded by the rapidity with which he grasped the situation facing him, the ability with which he had grasped the essentials, the clarity of his plans, and above all his unbounded self-confidence.'

However, in the words of Niall Barr, one of the most fair-minded historians of the Desert War, 'Montgomery's "complete grip of the situation" relied heavily upon the work of Auchinleck, Gott, and Ramsden [General William Ramsden, appointed commander of XXX Corps in July 1942].' Six weeks before Montgomery arrived to take command, Ruweisat Ridge and Alam el Halfa had already been clearly identified by this trio as vital to the defence of El Alamein and Montgomery must have known this. But if he was economical with the truth or lacked generosity of spirit, Montgomery's great talent was leadership: the ability to grasp the essence of the task ahead, to organise his resources accordingly, and to inspire his senior commanders with his own unquenchable will to win.

It was this quality that most affected Churchill on his return to Cairo from his meeting with Stalin. On 19 August, accompanied by Alexander, he drove through the desert to Eighth Army headquarters, which Montgomery had moved back from Ruweisat Ridge to Borg el Arab, which would co-locate him with the RAF's headquarters close to sea. Displaying a solicitous concern for the Prime Minister's well-being, Montgomery put his own caravan, complete with office, bedroom and bathroom, at Churchill's disposal. After a 'delicious' bathe in the Mediterranean – within sight of a thousand or so Eighth Army soldiers similarly disporting themselves naked in the waves – they repaired to Montgomery's map room where, according to Churchill, they were given 'a masterly exposition of the situation, showing that in a few days he had firmly grasped the whole problem'. The following day, after a whistle-stop tour of the front, Churchill claimed to have detected 'the reviving ardour of the Army. Everybody said what a change there had been since Montgomery had taken command. I could feel the truth of this with joy and comfort.'

Before he left for London, the Prime Minister went out of his way to emphasise the surpassing importance to him of the coming struggle, telling a press conference, 'We are determined to fight for Egypt and the Nile Valley as if it were the soil of England itself.'

The mood on the other side of the Alamein line was very different. Rommel was anxious and despondent. He knew that he was in a precarious position: that with the Eighth Army being rapidly replenished on an unprecedented scale but his own supplies beginning to run dangerously low, it would be impossible for the Panzerarmee to stay put for very much longer. Rommel's nightmare was a 'mechanised static warfare with a stabilised front, because this was just what the British officers and men had been trained for'. His only option, apart from a withdrawal – which Hitler would assuredly forbid – was to make a last-gasp lunge in the hope of breaking through at El Alamein and perhaps seizing the Delta.

Hitler's failure to grasp the potential of Operation *Herkules* – the capture of Malta – to eliminate the Eighth Army now haunted Rommel. For a while in the early summer, despite Hitler's half-hearted commitment, it had looked as though a combination of U-boats and German bombers, flying from Sardinia and Sicily and supported by the Italian navy, might just vanquish the British in the Mediterranean. By the end of July, as a result of these combined operations, Malta was once again on the verge of collapse.

On 11 August, to avert this disaster, a convoy of fourteen British merchant ships, loaded with vital supplies and escorted by two Royal Navy battleships, three aircraft carriers, seven cruisers and thirty-two destroyers, headed from the Atlantic through the Straits of Gibraltar bound for the Grand Harbour at Valletta. As they entered the Mediterranean, they came under furious bombardment from the air and the sea. By the 13th, five of the British warships had been sunk or put out of action and nine of the merchant vessels had gone to the bottom with a total loss of 350 British lives. But the gamble had not been in vain. Five of the supply ships made it to Malta, though the most important of them, the tanker *Ohio*, was so badly damaged that it limped into harbour lashed to two other vessels to prevent it from sinking. Although he did not yet realise it, the safe arrival of this convoy not only saved the British garrison but torpedoed the lingering visions of victory to which Rommel clung, albeit with a conviction that diminished by the day. The last chance to destroy the Eighth

Army by transforming Malta from a British to an Axis garrison had been irredeemably lost.

Rommel complained bitterly to Berlin and to Rome about his predicament and in particular about the refusal of Comando Supremo to deliver urgently needed supplies, without which he was virtually imprisoned on his side of the El Alamein line. In early August the Italian convoys responsible for supplying the Panzerarmee barely managed to deliver enough supplies to Tripoli, Benghazi and Tobruk to meet its daily requirements. Its front-line units were chronically short of men, weapons and ammunition; their tanks and trucks – 85 per cent of which were captured American or British vehicles – were running out of spare parts; and an acute lack of fuel was crippling the prospect of a sustained offensive. Undetected by the Axis powers, *Ultra* decrypts from Bletchley Park provided Alexander with precise details of all shipping movements between Italy and North Africa (to a level that Wavell and Auchinleck had never enjoyed). As a result, the RAF managed to sink more Axis tankers than reached their destination.

Rommel was rapidly running out of options. With retreat out of the question, he resolved to press forward, urged on by Comando Supremo, in the quixotic personage of Cavallero, who had hitherto almost invariably been averse to offensive action and whom he had previously dismissed as 'a weak-willed, office-chair soldier'. At this point, on 20 July, after waiting in vain to be granted an audience with the commander of the Panzerarmee, Mussolini flew back to Rome. However, evidently trusting that in due course he would still be called upon to enter Cairo in glory, he left his belongings behind in Derna – and presumably his white charger as well. Four weeks later, on 17 August, calling for 'the destruction of all British forces to the west of the Delta, as well as the seizure of Alexandria, Cairo, and the Suez Canal', he gave orders for Rommel's offensive to be renewed. This was hubris on stilts.

In the last week of August General Nehring, commanding the Afrikakorps, judged that his tanks could advance no more than seventy-five miles – assuming that the terrain was even and they did not have to engage in battle – before they would run out of fuel.

Rommel's most senior staff officers were aghast at the prospect of an offensive without the resources required to sustain it. Knowing that the commitments made by Berlin and Rome to deliver the means to achieve even a limited victory were most unlikely to arrive on schedule, they urged him to call off the action. So fierce were their objections that Kesselring flew to meet Rommel at his headquarters on 27 August to insist that, by sea or by air, the fuel to power his offensive would be delivered. Thus pressed by Kesselring on behalf of Hitler, and by Cavallero on behalf of Mussolini, Rommel decided to open his offensive on 30 August.

The simplest and most compelling explanation for what was to prove a disastrous démarche is that 'the dictators had lost all sense of reality'. However, this assessment is based on the somewhat dubious assumption that the two dictators had once been endowed with this useful quality of mind. The reality is that Mussolini had long inhabited a zone of his own where, psychologically, white chargers were to the fore, while Hitler's obsession with the conquest of Russia was as pathological as his global vision of a thousand-year Reich. 'For a long time, I have had everything prepared,' he told Albert Speer during an exultant tour d'horizon in August. 'As the next step, we are going to advance south of the Caucasus and then help the rebels in Iran and Iraq against the English. Another thrust will be directed along the Caspian Sea toward Afghanistan and India. Then the English will run out of oil. In two years we'll be on the borders of India. Twenty to thirty elite German divisions will do. Then the British Empire will collapse.'

From the Führer's perspective, it was not beyond the bounds of reason still to imagine that von Kleist's 1 Panzerarmee might storm through the Caucasus to strangle the British Empire. Somewhat more prosaically, Rommel knew that his last chance of contributing usefully to his leader's global delusions was to break the British at El Alamein before the arrival of the 300 Sherman tanks which had been promised by Roosevelt after the fall of Tobruk. He also knew that the enterprise was hazardous in the extreme. If Hitler and Mussolini had made dreams their master, Rommel had no choice but to risk it all 'on one turn of pitch-and-toss'.

To stack the odds against him even further, the Panzerarmee, which was already under strength, was stricken by sickness and diarrhoea. Rommel himself had been very unwell. In a letter to his wife Lu at the beginning of the month, he had confessed to feeling 'very tired and limp', a lassitude that he could not shake off and which frequently confined him to his bed. By 26 August his aide-de-camp, Lieutenant Berndt, felt bound to write personally to Lu, alerting her to 'the state of the Marshall's health'. Pointing out that her husband had been in the desert for nineteen months, which was longer than any other officer over the age of forty, Berndt warned that in addition to a heavy cold and 'the digestive disturbance typical of Africa', he had recently shown 'signs of exhaustion which have caused great anxiety to all of us who were aware of it'. According to Bayerlein, Rommel was having 'frequent attacks of faintness ... but was trying with all his strength to remain on his feet'. His medical advisor, Professor Horster, had signalled Berlin to inform OKW that he was 'not in a fit condition to command the forthcoming offensive'. But as no one else of comparable stature was available, he had little choice but to rouse himself for the fray.

On 30 August Rommel duly issued his fateful Order for the Day. 'Today, the army, supported by new divisions, will attack once again in order finally to destroy the enemy. I expect every soldier in my army to give his all in these decisive days. Long live fascist Italy! Long live the Greater German Reich! Long live our great Führer!' The tone of his letter to his wife on the same day was far more subdued. 'It's been such a long wait worrying all the time whether I should get everything I needed together to enable me to take the brakes off again,' he wrote. 'Many of my worries have by no means been satisfactorily settled and we have some very grave shortages. But I've taken the risk.'

It was a risk born of desperation. By eavesdropping on British radio frequencies, Rommel and his senior commanders knew that the forces at Montgomery's disposal were not only superior to his own in almost every respect, but ready and waiting for the Panzerarmee's last-gasp offensive.

The Eighth Army had spent the previous fortnight reinforcing and extending the positions established under Auchinleck on the Alam el Halfa ridge, which ran from north-east to south-west across the desert to the east behind the El Alamein line. Thanks to Ultra, Montgomery knew for certain that Rommel planned to make his main thrust at this point, in the hope of outflanking the Eighth Army and advancing on Alexandria with one panzer division and on Cairo with a further two divisions. But at Alam el Halfa, as a result of Montgomery's fastidious preparations, they would be confronted by a formidable array of military firepower: 400 tanks, 300 anti-tank guns and 240 field guns, dug in at key points on the south-western edge of the salient, directly in the path of Rommel's advancing army.

Garrisoning Alam el Halfa had been exhausting work. W. R. Garrett, a private in the 44th Division, newly arrived from Britain, described the reality of war with a piquant precision to match the misery:

> Our rations were bad, corned beef and biscuits and little else served with a sprinkling of sand and garnished with flies. Half a gallon of brackish water for all purposes per man per day. This inevitably led to stomach disorders, a raging thirst and filthy clothes. Above all in terms of torment were the flies. Flies swarmed round us all day. seeking moisture in our eyes, mouths and ears. The work was demoralising. Picks and shovels were our only tools and were soon blunted on the unyielding rock. We welcomed the night and a respite from the torment and toil and sweat. We welcomed the sunrise for its relief from the night's chill. Cuts and abrasions, and there were many, were constantly covered in flies and sand and developed into 'desert sores' that festered and refused to heal. If bandaged the flies would penetrate between the folds and search for blood.

Even as they worked, Garrett and his comrades lived in fear that 'our pathetic efforts' would not prevent Rommel's panzers from overrunning their positions: 'It all seemed quite hopeless and we despairingly slogged on in our own primitive way.' A terrifying reminder of what they would face once battle was joined in earnest came when Garrett's best friend was killed by a German bomber which seemed to come from nowhere out of a cloudless sky, leaving him 'writhing and squirming in agony with two stumps smothered in blood and sand where his legs had been severed'.

Just after midnight on 31 August 1942, with a full moon overhead, de Guingand was woken to be told that Rommel's advance had begun. 'I felt very "hit up" because I realised the importance of the issue,' he wrote, 'and in addition it was the first big battle that [the] Eighth Army had fought since I had become its Chief of Staff.' De Guingand decided to wake Montgomery. '"Excellent, excellent," he said and went back to sleep.'

Rommel's progress was soon hampered by a belt of minefields which were deeply buried and protected by booby traps. As the panzers nosed their way through this treacherous terrain, the sky was soon as bright as day as pathfinders released flares to guide wave upon wave of RAF bombers who dropped their loads with pinpoint accuracy on Rommel's men. The advance was further disrupted by a simple but effective ruse. At de Guingand's direction, a young intelligence officer with 7th Armoured Division, Captain Peter Vaux, compiled a false 'going map'. The 'going maps' were much like charts of the ocean, colour-coded to show where the 'going' was good, indifferent, or impassable; they were invaluable aids to navigation. Many of these maps had already been captured by the Germans. De Guingand decided that they should be allowed to 'capture' another but it would be falsely coded to trick them into 'wallowing in deep sand' at a point where the map suggested it was possible to go at 'a good gallop'. Vaux was given the task of ensuring that this precious document duly fell into the hands of the enemy. By one account, Vaux arranged for a scout-car containing the 'tea-stained, folded and refolded' map to be driven towards a German outpost where the crew abandoned it and fled as soon as it came under fire. In de Guingand's version, the scout car was deliberately blown up on a mine. In either case, the trick worked. From a vantage point on Alam el Halfa, Vaux apparently watched a German patrol approach the vehicle, ransack it, and walk away with its contents. In his official report of the battle, Alexander referred obliquely to the fact that the steps taken by de Guingand 'had borne fruit' as two panzer divisions became bogged in 'the very soft going of Deir el Agram'. Von Mellenthin later confirmed that the 'false going' map 'was accepted as authentic and served its purpose in leading the Afrikakorps astray'. These obstacles to Rommel's progress were of no small moment; they forced the panzers to burn up precious fuel and left them dangerously exposed to the mercy of the RAF. Any residual hope of success that Rommel may have harboured depended on making one of his lightning thrusts around or through the Eighth Army, the possibility of which became less likely by the hour.

In the early hours of 31 August the British units drawn up on Alam el Halfa were taut with anxiety. The very word 'panzer' still provoked a frisson of trepidation at every level in all ranks of the Eighth Army: on too many occasions Rommel's armour had metaphorically run rings round them. Montgomery's order that the tanks on Alam el Halfa had to resist the temptation to move but instead remain in their positions, dug-in and hull-down, was unequivocal, but their crews – officers and men – instinctively felt themselves to be sitting targets. It took great nerve to watch and wait without flinching while Rommel's tanks advanced slowly towards them.

Montgomery's instructions were well judged and effective. The British armour defended with such careful ferocity that by daylight the panzers had failed even to reach the front line, let alone breach it. Realising that his prospects of driving the defenders off the ridge were becoming ever more remote, Rommel almost abandoned the attack there and then. But, with reports that the Afrikakorps was belatedly closing in on the British positions, he saw a glimmer of hope. Despite the fact that the balance of forces was heavily weighted against him – Montgomery had almost twice as many tanks at his disposal (700 to 450, of which 240 on the Axis side were inferior Italian models) – there was still a chance, which was all that the Desert Rat had ever needed, that the panzers might break through.

The battle was won and lost in the fierce fighting at close

quarters which now ensued. 'I don't want you to think we're peeing in our bags here,' the commander of the 10th Armoured Division radioed to one of his junior commanders, as a squadron of panzers manoeuvred past a line of British tanks to threaten his headquarters, 'but you may have to come out of your position and attack him from the rear.' At this point, the panzers changed course and rumbled towards ground held by the City of London Yeomanry. This was their undoing. 'I saw tank after tank going up in flames or being put out of action, and this included my own ... through the fog of battle it was difficult to know which of their tanks had been knocked out ... [but] ... the great thing was that they were not coming on in front,' a Yeomanry commander, Major A. A. Cameron, recalled with satisfaction.

Although a sandstorm that raged throughout much of the day gave the Panzerarmee some respite from the RAF, the Afrikakorps' vehicles were rapidly running out of fuel. When the storm died down later that evening, the RAF – which had command of the skies – was given a free hand to complete the Eighth Army's work. Rommel watched and noted: 'With one aircraft flying circles and dropping a continuous succession of flares, bombs from the other machines, some of which dived low for the attack, crashed down among the flare-lit vehicles of the reconnaissance units [on which the RAF had concentrated its bombardment] ... Soon many of our vehicles were alight and burning furiously.'

By the morning of 1 September, any lingering hope of victory that Rommel may have harboured had evaporated. With the Afrikakorps pinned down under an aerial bombardment which inflicted severe casualties on men and machines, Rommel himself was fortunate to escape unscathed. 'On one occasion' he wrote, 'I only just had time to throw myself into a slit-trench before the bomb fell. A spade lying on the spoil beside the trench was pierced through by an 8-inch splinter and the red-hot metal fragment fell beside me in the trench. Swarms of low-flying fighter-bombers were coming back to the attack again and again and my troops suffered tremendous casualties. Vast numbers of vehicles stood burning in the desert.'

The onslaught continued long into the night. The Panzerarmee had never before been subjected to such an onslaught; the

RAF's domination of the air combined with the resolution of the British armour on the ground was decisive. The Battle of Alam el Halfa – the Second Battle of El Alamein, or, as Montgomery sometimes called it, the First Battle of El Alamein – was effectively over.

The following morning, 2 September, Rommel concluded that he could no longer hold even the ground the panzers had taken in their initial advance. 'Our offensive no longer had any hope of success, partly because we had no petrol and insufficient fighter cover and partly because the battle had now reached a stage where material strength alone would decide the issue.' But the lack of fuel – the price paid for the failure to seize Malta – made a rapid withdrawal impossible during daylight. As a result the Afrikakorps was subjected to an intense bombardment not only from the air but from the Eighth Army's gunners on the ground, who, on average, landed ten shells on the Panzerarmee for every one fired in reply. The bombardment continued throughout that night.

By 3 September Rommel's troops had retreated to the 'start' line from which they had advanced on Alam el Halfa three days earlier. They left behind some fifty tanks, fifty pieces of artillery and four hundred ruined vehicles. Up to this point, Montgomery had resisted the temptation to go on the offensive. Now, though, he initiated a cautious counter-attack – codenamed Operation *Beresford* – against the retreating German and Italian divisions. To the south, the New Zealand Division assailed the German 90th Light Division on one flank and the Italian Trieste Division on the other. It was a hard-fought engagement in which both sides sustained heavy casualties.

In his official report Montgomery's commander-in-chief, General Alexander, paid special tribute to the '28 (Maori) Battalion [for] fighting a particularly gallant action'. The New Zealanders were widely regarded by both sides to have formed the toughest and fiercest units in the Eighth Army but, after this engagement, Rommel took a dimmer view of their prowess on what he otherwise judged to be a remarkably chivalrous battlefield. When the commander of the 6th New Zealand Brigade, Brigadier George Clifton, was captured, he was taken to Rommel, who believed that the New Zealanders had been responsible for frequent and flagrant breaches of the Geneva Conventions. 'Repeated cases had occurred of prisoners and wounded being massacred by this particular division,' he charged. According to Rommel, Clifton replied – rather airily – that this was probably due to the 'large numbers of Maoris' in their ranks. Adding circumstantial weight to Rommel's complaint, a brigadier in the New Zealand Division wrote later of the exceptional number of Germans and Italians killed in this encounter. If Rommel's allegation was true, it was one of the few incidents of its kind in the Desert War. Although it is faintly ridiculous to romanticise a bloody conflict with tanks and artillery as though it were a medieval encounter between knights in armour, any abuses perpetrated by either side in the desert paled into insignificance by comparison with the atrocities committed by all sides in Europe and the Far East.

Rommel and Clifton evidently established a personal rapport and the German was amused when Clifton told him that he and his men had been ashamed to be captured by an Italian unit. The Italians were about to surrender and in the act of removing the bolts from their rifles when a German officer arrived on the scene. He stiffened their resolve and as a result Clifton's unit found itself surrendering instead. Rommel was even more entertained by the fact that his prisoner – a 'courageous and likeable' man – managed soon afterwards to escape from captivity via a lavatory window. (Clifton was recaptured and taken to Italy where he escaped from internment at his fifth attempt, dressed as a merchant sailor. Subsequently he was captured again and taken to Germany, where he finally made it to allied lines on his ninth attempt at escape, despite being wounded on the eighth.)

Notwithstanding its early promise of success, Operation *Beresford* – like so many earlier battles in the desert – petered out amid a shambles of poor planning, broken communications, inept co-ordination, lost battalions, burning vehicles and near panic. Officers and men were caught in the open, dive-bombed by Stukas and raked by artillery fire. The Royal West Kent regiment – fresh from Britain and without experience of desert warfare – suffered grievously in this mayhem. Most of its senior officers were killed or wounded and two of its battalions were routed, the survivors fleeing to the relative security of the positions held by the New Zealanders. As the stragglers made it back to safety, Major T. H. Bevan, noted bleakly that the exhausted arrivals 'all had the same story – that it was bloody murder out there'. But Rommel's panzer divisions, which had fought themselves to a standstill, were in no condition to take advantage of the Eighth Army's brief but devastating setback. By the time Operation *Beresford* had been called off, the Panzerarmee still had no alternative but to retreat.

'By the evening of the 5th September,' the Middle East Commander-in-Chief reported, 'Rommel's slow and stubborn withdrawal had brought him back to the area of our minefields. Here he turned to stand and it was clear that he intended to make a strong effort to retain this much at least of his gains.' Losses on both sides had been heavy (2,900 casualties in the Panzerarmee; 1,750 in the Eighth Army) but there was no doubt that Rommel had suffered by far the greater military setback. If the First Battle of El Alamein had arrested Rommel's advance on Cairo, the Second at Alam el Halfa had decisively turned the tide. 'With the failure of this offensive,' Rommel wrote, virtually repeating what he had already noted after the first encounter, 'our last chance of gaining the Suez Canal had gone.'

All that remained to settle the matter beyond any possible dispute was the outright defeat of the Panzerarmee by forcing Rommel out of the defensive laager which his troops had constructed along the El Alamein line and driving him out of Egypt altogether. It was for this – the Third Battle of El Alamein – that Churchill at once started to agitate with his usual impatience: Rommel had to be routed without delay.

TWENTY-TWO

CHURCHILL FEELS THE PRESSURE

'Victory finds a hundred fathers but defeat is an orphan.'

Count Galeazzo Ciano

The Prime Minister had returned to London on 24 August following his gruelling trip to the Middle East and Moscow in the confident belief that the planning for Operation *Torch* was well underway. Instead, he found himself on the receiving end of what he described as 'a bombshell' from Washington – a change of heart by the American Chiefs of Staff which promised to unravel the whole operation, and thereby torpedo Churchill's entire war strategy, which he had developed with such energetic diligence over the last six months.

While Churchill had been away, the old divisions between London and Washington over *Torch* had resurfaced with a vengeance. So far from moving towards agreement on the military details of an immensely complex operation, the American Joint Chiefs were at loggerheads with their British counterparts over virtually every significant part of the plan. On 6 August it had been agreed that General Eisenhower should be put in command of *Torch* but – as though to demonstrate that any agreement between allies is as hard to achieve as a treaty between adversaries – every other issue of any substance was in bitter dispute: from the number of troops required and where they should be landed, to the timetable of the operation and what role should be played by each part of the Allied coalition.

Torch had originally been designed as part of a co-ordinated pincer movement intended to eliminate the Axis presence from North Africa, the 'true Second Front' which Churchill had promised Roosevelt. The original plan envisaged an American-led assault on the North African coast at various points between Casablanca and Tunis while, simultaneously, Montgomery would drive Rommel back deep into Libya before Hitler had a chance to reinforce the Panzerarmee from the other side of the Mediterranean. The Allies would thus acquire complete control of the entire North African littoral, the island fortress of Malta would be saved, and, in turn, the 'soft underbelly' of Italy would be fatally exposed to an Anglo-American assault. As he had persuaded Roosevelt and advised Stalin, the 'true' second front would have been established in North Africa rather than in Europe. All this was suddenly in jeopardy.

In Churchill's absence, the initial character and scope of *Torch* had been scaled down by the Americans to such a degree as to convince the British that Washington had lost its stomach for a venture about which the American Chiefs had always been dubious. The competing demands from the commander-in-chief of the US Navy, Admiral King, for ships, men and weapons to sustain the American commitment in the Pacific had accelerated Washington's drift away from Churchill's 'Europe First' strategy, to which he had assumed the White House was now fully committed.

To complicate matters further, the British were fearful that, under pressure from Hitler, General Franco – who was ostensibly a non-belligerent bystander – might soon allow the Wehrmacht to cross Spain to seize Gibraltar, and thereby control the Western Mediterranean; even worse, were he to detect that the advantage in North Africa was slipping away from the Allies, the Spanish dictator might even decide to throw in his lot with Hitler and enter the war on the Axis side. The most effective way both to convince Franco otherwise and to persuade the Vichy French in North Africa to switch their allegiance from the Axis to the Allies was to deploy enough force to demonstrate that the most powerful nation in the world as well as the British really meant business. Unless *Torch* were to involve the use of overwhelming force it

would swiftly become a damp squib – with incalculable consequences for both the Middle East and the Empire.

London's deepening frustration was summed up by Kennedy
in a note for Brooke which he wrote the day before the CIGS and
Churchill arrived back in London on 25 August. 'The whole operation is at best extremely hazardous,' he wrote. 'The only hope of
success is if we and the Americans put our whole effort into it. It
is almost incredible that their share of the operations should be so
weak and half-hearted.' *Torch*, he warned, was at risk of becoming
'a tremendous disaster'.

The following day, Kennedy was summoned to Number 10
for an 11 a.m. meeting with Churchill, who was in bed, 'wearing
The Dressing Gown; a half-smoked cigar was in his mouth, and a
glass of water and some papers on the table beside him'. When he
asked for a progress report on *Torch*, Kennedy did not spare him:
three times as many troops were required as had been allocated,
the American contribution was quite inadequate, and their reluctance to do more was, he judged, 'a sign that our strategic policies
were diverging'.

Much disconcerted, Churchill immediately cabled Roosevelt,
urging that the two of them should instruct Eisenhower (who
sympathised with the British perspective) to launch *Torch* on
14 October. Only by forcing the issue in this way, he intimated,
would it be possible to ensure that the first Allied operation of
the war – which he cunningly and shamelessly described as 'your
great strategic conception' – would be a 'decisive success'. At the
end of a long and detailed elaboration of the means to this end,
he concluded, 'I feel that a note must be struck now of irrevocable
decision and superhuman energy to execute it.'

No sooner had Churchill despatched this rallying cry than the
'bombshell' from Washington arrived on his desk. It took the form
of a memorandum from the American Joint Chiefs, which – he was
soon to inform Roosevelt – 'profoundly disconcerted' the British
government. Their message – though implicit – was straightforward: they were unwilling to put their troops at great risk in the
Mediterranean by launching a major assault on Algiers – which
Churchill and his advisors regarded as an essential precondition for

defeating the Germans in North Africa. By limiting the operation to a landing at the port of Oran in western Algeria and the city of Casablanca on the Atlantic coast of Morocco, as the Americans had proposed, would, Churchill informed the President, be 'making the enemy a present not only of Tunis but of Algiers ... We are all convinced that Algiers is the key to the whole operation.'

Roosevelt's response, which arrived three days later, was far less emollient than the Prime Minister might have hoped. The President not only made it clear that he differed with the Prime Minister on matters of strategic substance but he also raised a new issue which was bound to aggravate Churchill's distress. Though the Americans shared the British concern that Franco might soon allow the panzers to transit Spain en route to North Africa, Roosevelt was more worried about the impact of the landings upon the Vichy French in North Africa, who were firmly entrenched in Morocco, Algeria and Tunisia with 125,000 troops that were still under the tutelage of the Nazis.

Judging the British to be loathed by the Vichy French to such a degree that, in Andrew Roberts's phrase, 'the Stars and Stripes might be welcomed in North Africa whereas the Union Jack would be fired on', the President was blunt:

> I feel very strongly that the initial attacks must be made by an exclusively American ground force. The operation should be undertaken on the assumption that the French will offer less resistance to us than they will to the British. I would even go so far as to say I am reasonably sure a simultaneous landing by British and Americans [who had maintained diplomatic relations with Vichy France] would result in full resistance by all French in Africa, whereas an initial American landing without British ground forces offers a real chance that there would be no French resistance, or only a token resistance.

The only crumb of comfort for Churchill in Roosevelt's disagreeable message was that he similarly hoped that the target date for the landings could still be met, though, somewhat reprovingly, he commented that the precise timing was not for either of them to determine but for the commander-in-chief, General Eisenhower.

So far from resolving the disagreements between the British and Americans, this initial exchange led to a to-and-fro of toughly worded cables in which neither held back from expressing their discomfort with the other's position; their correspondence was peppered with such phrases as 'This sudden abandonment of the plan on which we have hitherto been working will certainly cause grievous delay' (Churchill, 1 September), or 'I feel that the operation as herein outlined is as far as I can go towards meeting your views' (Roosevelt, 3 September). The tension between the two leaders was a reflection not only of the competing pressures on them but also from their differing perspectives, the fact that *Torch* was of surpassing importance for them both.

The stakes could hardly have been higher. *Torch*'s commander-in-chief, General Eisenhower, was caught between his loyalty to his superiors in Washington and his sympathy for the British. 'We are undertaking something of a quite desperate nature and which depends only in minor degree upon the professional preparations we can make or upon the wisdom of our military decisions,' Eisenhower noted in his diary. 'In a way it is like the return of Napoleon from Elba – if the guess as to psychological reaction is correct, we may gain a great advantage; if the guess is wrong, it would be almost as certain that we would gain nothing and lose a lot.'

Torch could easily have collapsed under the weight of the differing priorities and the self-regard by which both nations were animated; the tone of the correspondence, on both sides, contained more than a hint of resentful national pride. Churchill, for whom this episode marked the first unambiguous demonstration of the fact that he was now the junior partner in a grand alliance, was both bruised and dismayed by the unexpected turn of events. On 4 September he could not resist drafting a long letter to Harry Hopkins, his own good friend and the President's closest confidant, complaining that he was 'deeply perturbed' by the way *Torch* was being 'knocked about, and above all at the needless delays which add so much to our joint troubles'.

In the end, the letter was never sent. On the same day, a cable arrived from Roosevelt in which he avowed 'we are getting very close together'. Notwithstanding his senior status in the Alliance, he negotiated a way through the strategic thickets which threatened to jeopardise the project by demonstrating that readiness to compromise which marked him out as a great statesman: the Americans would, after all, land at Algiers alongside the British as well as at Oran and Casablanca. Churchill was relieved and gratified. 'We agree,' he replied on 5 September, even suggesting that the British Army's 'highly trained' troops under Eisenhower's command could disguise themselves from the Vichy French by wearing US Army uniforms. 'They will be proud to do so,' he avowed. When he heard this, Roosevelt cabled simply 'Hurrah' and Churchill responded 'O.K., full blast.'

But, as though to confirm Britain's diminished authority, the Prime Minister wrote once again to Roosevelt a few days later, in cunningly submissive terms. 'In the whole of *Torch*, military and political, I consider myself your lieutenant, asking only to put my view-point plainly before you … We British will come in only as and when you judge expedient. This is an American enterprise, in which we are your helpmates.' In this, he demonstrated a high degree of diplomatic acumen. Though he never forgot that *Torch* was his idea, or that it was inextricably connected to his imperial vision for the Middle East, and ultimately to victory in Europe, he astutely avoided claiming credit publicly for the first Anglo-American military operation of the Second World War. With *Torch* now reignited and Rommel repulsed at Alam el Halfa, the Prime Minister had grounds for cautious satisfaction: his grand plan for victory in North Africa, the Middle East and the Mediterranean showed every sign of moving towards fruition. Instead he was consumed by anxiety and gloom. At home he was beset on all sides by criticism of his leadership. Some agitated for him to surrender his role as Minister of Defence. Others complained that the public was infected by war weariness and low morale. Commentators in the press recalled the succession of military disasters over which he had presided – in the desert, in Greece and Crete, Hong Kong, Singapore, Burma, Tobruk and latterly (on 19 August) the fiasco of the Dieppe raid, during which, in the space of a few hours, more than three-fifths of the Canadian Second Infantry Division had been killed, wounded, or captured. The blame for this was generally laid firmly on the Prime Minister's shoulders. Even some of his previously loyal lieutenants began to murmur against him. To make matters worse, Sir Stafford Cripps, a lynchpin of the War Cabinet, chose this moment to proffer his resignation. Knowing that Cripps's apparent loyalty concealed the ambitions of an arch rival for the highest office, Churchill feared that his departure would precipitate a political crisis. Using all the guile at his command, the Prime Minister managed to persuade him – in the national interest, of course – to stay his hand.

Under these pressures, even Churchill's magnificent self-belief was dented and self-pity sometimes seeped to the surface. After a meeting with him on 24 September, Brooke described his 'very pathetic' mood. When the gloom descended on him, according to his CIGS, he lamented that 'he was the only one trying to win the war, that he was the only one who produced any ideas, that he was quite alone in all his attempts, no-one supported him … all we did was provide and plan difficulties … Frequently in this oration he worked himself up into such a state from the woeful picture he had painted, that tears streamed down his face!' Later, Churchill himself wrote, theatrically, of this 'bleak lull' when he might have been dismissed from office and thus have vanished from the scene, 'with a load of calamity on my shoulders' while 'the harvest, at last to be reaped, would have been ascribed to my belated disappearance'. As it turned out, his critics were to be denied that satisfaction and his own fortunes were about to take a turn for the better.

In the Western Desert Montgomery was preparing for battle in his own measured way. He was not a man to be hurried. Dogged and determined, he had a clear sense of what would be required before taking the offensive against Rommel. 'I would concentrate on three essentials: leadership, equipment, and training … We had just won a decisive victory, but it had been a static battle: I was not prepared to launch the troops in an all-out offensive without intensive prior training.' Although he wrote in self-congratulatory terms about the action at Alam el Halfa – or the 'Battle of Alamein' as he occasionally referred to it – claiming that 'there was no difficulty in seeing [Rommel] off', the victory had not been as easily achieved as he liked to boast. In particular, the shambles of Operation *Beresford* – in which one British brigade alone suffered more than 700 casualties within the space of twenty-four hours – contributed more than 1,000 of the 1,750 who were killed, wounded or captured in the course of the five-day action. This rate of attrition not only provided salutary testimony to the human cost of offensive warfare but served warning about the soaring rate of casualties which might be expected in the large-scale offensive for which the Eighth Army was now training in earnest.

Montgomery's resolve was not in doubt. Fanatically driven, obsessively focussed, clinically organised and pathologically egotistical, he was not a clubbable colleague. But he knew what he wanted from the Eighth Army and he would not rest until he got it. Every soldier under his command, from generals to corporals, would rehearse rigorously and repeatedly until the general was satisfied they were ready for the offensive. There was little respite. Under the previous regime, an Australian infantryman recalled wryly, 'When troops usually went out of the line to a "rest area" ... you either dug holes all day and guarded dumps all night or you trained all day and guarded dumps all night.' By contrast, under Montgomery, 'You trained all day and then you trained all night. Not every day and every night – but almost.' The Eighth Army was susceptible to neither blandishments nor oaths, but Montgomery offered something else: the icy precision of an outsider who had arrived to create order, discipline and certainty. In this respect, an otherwise stern critic, Correlli Barnett, likened him admiringly to 'Florence Nightingale putting a hospital in order'.

He was brutal with those he regarded as incompetent or who failed to meet his exacting standards. His reprimands were severe: he dismissed platoons of brigadiers and unit commanders with cavalier disdain for their feelings and even the most senior officers were despatched with a rare disregard for their self-esteem. After Alam el Halfa, General Ramsden, who had been appointed to command XXX Corps by Auchinleck, asked to take four days' leave in Cairo. Montgomery genially gave his consent. Thirty-six hours later, he was summoned back urgently to Eighth Army headquarters at Borg el Arab. Supposing that the offensive must be imminent, he went to see Montgomery, who abruptly informed him that he was to be replaced by General Sir Oliver Leese. When Ramsden remonstrated, Montgomery said coldly, 'This is war – this is war', adding for good measure, 'You're not exactly on the crest of a wave, Ramsden.'

Montgomery's charmless manner won him few friends but his allies in the Eighth Army – those who admired his clarity of purpose and who trusted his conviction – were numerous. That he not only knew his own mind but made sure that others knew it as well inspired confidence. His sympathetic biographer, Nigel Hamilton, has conceded that Montgomery was 'braggartly, vain, rude, dogmatic, and impossibly self-righteous' but likened him to the leader of an 'adopted tribe' providing not only leadership, but reassurance, confidence, and protection. Somewhat less persuasively, Hamilton attributed his acquisition of this status to the fact that the Eighth Army was 'jaded, bewildered' and 'baffled' by defeat. Jaded they may have been, tired they certainly were, but Auchinleck had not left his successor with the ramshackle, broken, lost tribe that Montgomery's apologists describe.

Far more corrosive were the rivalries and envies which had long beset the upper echelons and had seeped through to the rank and file of an army drawn from so many diverse sources. These were too deeply embedded to be expunged overnight but Montgomery at least gave the impression that, under his leadership, victory would be theirs so long as they were willing to follow his lead and obey his orders. He was helped in this by the fact that, unlike so many other British officers, he plainly did not derive his authority from his membership of the British upper classes. Fox-hunting metaphors were alien to him (though he would repeatedly promise to 'hit the enemy for six'), likewise the snobberies of the cavalry officers' mess or the Guard's Club, in which gentlemen had inherited a place at the top of a table to which only the vulgar would even refer. So far from belonging to this culture,

Montgomery was an outsider who had imposed himself upon his peers – many of whom disdained him – by the force of his disagreeable but magnetic personality. During the Battle of Alam el Halfa he had demonstrated a steely confidence which impressed even those who regarded him as an insufferable arriviste. But the real test of his leadership was yet to come.

Before his dismissal, Auchinleck had started to prepare for what was to become the final Battle of El Alamein. Whether or not Montgomery adopted his predecessor's battle plan has been contested by warring historians as bitterly as if their own academic reputations mattered as much as those of the generals over whose bodies they have fought with such ferocity. It is a sterile pursuit: if Montgomery derived his conceptual framework for the offensive from Auchinleck, he would never have seen fit to acknowledge his debt; if he did not, it is beyond doubt that their focus would, in any case, have been remarkably similar essentially because they faced the same logistical and territorial constraints.

Of more strategic significance was a very real difference of perspective between them. As C-in-C, Middle East, as well as commander of the Eighth Army, Auchinleck's responsibilities had been far greater than those with which Montgomery was tasked. While Montgomery's exclusive focus as a battlefield commander was on Rommel and the destruction of the Panzerarmee in Africa, Auchinleck had to give his attention equally to the defence of the northern as well as the eastern front. From that perspective, the defeat of Rommel was one part of a far more complex scenario than Montgomery ever had to contemplate. As commander of the Eighth Army, Montgomery had no strategic responsibilities of any kind; these now lay with Auchinleck's replacement, Alexander, whose task had also been made far simpler than his predecessor's by Churchill's decision to split the Middle East Command in two, charging 'Jumbo' Wilson's new Persia and Iraq Command with the prime responsibility for the defence of the northern flank. Alexander's overriding task, as Montgomery's commander-in-chief, was laid out for him by Churchill with unambiguous precision. 'Your prime and main duty will be to take or destroy at the earliest opportunity the German–Italian army commanded by Field Marshal Rommel, together with all its supplies and establishments in Egypt and Libya.' Nothing was to distract either him or Montgomery from that purpose.

For Montgomery, nothing else mattered. This obsession made a swift and powerful impression on Wendell Willkie, Roosevelt's former opponent in the 1940 US election campaign, who had since broken with the isolationist wing of his party to become a Special Envoy for the President. Warned by Roosevelt that by the time he reached the Middle East, Cairo might have fallen into German hands, Willkie arrived in the Egyptian capital on 4 September. He was soon subjected to all manner of rumour and counter-rumour about the British predicament in the region. He was thus mesmerised by the 'wiry, scholarly, intense, almost fanatical personality of General Montgomery' who kept insisting in a quiet voice that, so far from facing any kind of crisis, 'Egypt has been saved'. On a tour of the front, interrupted only by a lunch of 'sandwiches – and flies', he was dazzled by the Eighth Army commander's 'amazing' mastery of military detail as again and again he demonstrated more knowledge of the deployment of troops and tanks than the relevant unit commanders he met. When Montgomery assured him that the Eighth Army's superiority in tanks and planes meant that 'it is now mathematically certain that I will eventually destroy Rommel', Willkie did not doubt this for a moment; and he was right. For the first time in the Desert War, the Eighth Army had the preponderance of firepower required for victory.

He relayed this glowing assessment to a White House which still harboured grave doubts about the Eighth Army's prowess and remained anxious lest a Nazi pincer movement from the Caucasus and the desert might yet strangle the Middle East. This did much to reassure the President that his decision to press ahead with *Torch* – which he cabled to Churchill on the same day as Willkie's awestruck meeting with Montgomery – had not been so ill judged as his principal advisors had feared. But the key word in Montgomery's secret briefing was 'eventually'. Like Wavell and Auchinleck before him, he had no intention of being rushed into a premature offensive until his men were so well trained, armed and supplied as to ensure victory. But, unlike his predecessors, who eventually succumbed to Churchill's sustained war of attrition against them, he had time on his side. Auchinleck's ultimate and capital offence had been his point-blank refusal to launch an offensive before the middle of September. No such sword of Damocles hung over Montgomery, who not only was a newcomer who had just won a defensive battle (at Alam el Halfa), but who also represented the beleaguered Prime Minister's last throw of the military dice in the desert. Nonetheless, he was still to feel the goad from Downing Street.

In a prescient note, while the good news about Alam el Halfa was still being digested in London, Brooke wrote on 8 September, 'My next trouble will now be to stop Winston from fussing Alex and Monty and egging them on to attack before they are ready. It is a regular disease that he suffers from, this frightful impatience to get an attack launched.' As Brooke knew only too well, the Prime Minister was driven by both political and strategic demons. On 9 August, in a note to the First Sea Lord, pressing him to accelerate the delivery of the Sherman tanks which had been promised by America after the fall of Tobruk and were now on their way to Alexandria, Churchill wrote of 'the immense importance of beating Rommel as a prelude to *Torch*'. In part, the 'immense importance' he ascribed to this pre-emptive victory sprang from the plausible belief that if the Panzerarmee were to be destroyed at El Alamein, victory in Operation *Torch* would be far easier to accomplish. But there was another factor. Shorn of any diplomatic niceties, Churchill was desperate to secure the public triumph of a British victory over Germany which would otherwise be submerged by the even greater drama of the first Allied venture of the war, when the spotlight would inevitably be on the Americans.

But this political purpose was reinforced by a pressing strategic anxiety. Warned by the Turkish ambassador that Ankara was losing 'the will-power to resist' the diplomatic pressure coming from Berlin following Hitler's seizure of Sebastopol from the Red Army in July, Churchill sought urgently to stiffen Turkey's resolve. On 28 August he therefore instructed the Chiefs of Staff to make provision for more 'war material' to be despatched from

Egypt to Turkey by the end of October. However, he reminded them, the delivery of these tanks and guns by this date hung 'on the assumption of definite success in the Western Desert by the middle of October'.

For all these reasons, Churchill's impatience knew few bounds. Having instructed Alexander on his appointment to 'destroy' the Panzerarmee 'at the earliest opportunity', he now cabled his commander-in-chief to find out when the offensive was expected to begin. 'It would be a help to me to know about when you think it will come off,' he wrote, admonishing, 'I had hoped to have heard from you before.' Ignoring that rebuke, Alexander replied patiently but firmly, to explain that, though Rommel's army had been 'seriously weakened' at Alam el Halfa, Montgomery's attack was to be somewhat delayed because of it.

By this time, the Eighth Army commander had come to the view that Operation *Lightfoot*, as he had codenamed the opening phase of the final Battle of El Alamein, could not proceed until the second half of October – more than a month later than Auchinleck had planned. This was for several sound reasons: the 300 Sherman tanks, which had only just reached Egypt, were not yet readied for the particular hazards of desert warfare; the 1st and 10th Armoured Divisions required more training; and the final preparations for an offensive by almost 200,000 troops, many of whom had only just arrived in the country, could not possibly be completed before the middle of October at the earliest.

The commander of an Eighth Army which had already suffered 80,000 casualties since its formation did not intend to risk unnecessary bloodshed on account of incompetent leadership and inadequate training. He could issue all manner of morale-raising instructions – 'Morale is the big thing in war. We must raise the morale of our soldiers to the highest pitch. They must enter this battle with their tails high in the air and the will to win made' he liked to say – but without more preparation for the battle ahead, all the morale in the world would be in vain. Montgomery would not allow himself to be harried into a premature offensive.

For his part, Churchill's impatience to pre-empt *Torch* with a British victory in the desert, was intensified by Malta's predicament;

a lynchpin of Britain's military operations in the Mediterranean and North Africa, the garrison was once again running low on vital provisions. On 17 September, chafing for action, the Prime Minister cabled Alexander once again. 'I am anxiously awaiting some account of your intentions. My understanding with you was the fourth week in September. Since then you have stated that the recent battle, which greatly weakened the enemy, has caused delay in regrouping etc... . I must know which week it falls in, otherwise I cannot form the necessary judgements affecting the general war.'

Alexander, who was a diplomat as much as a soldier, did not reply at once but instead flew up to Eighth Army headquarters to consult Montgomery. According to Montgomery's Chief of Staff, 'Freddy' de Guingand, who took notes at their meeting, Montgomery was swiftly to the point. 'I won't do it in September,' he told his commander-in-chief, 'But if I do it in October it'll be a victory.' Alexander asked, 'Well, what shall I say to him?' At this, Montgomery took de Guingand's notepad and wrote the message he wished his commander-in-chief to despatch to London. Out of de Guingand's earshot, he told Alexander that if Churchill were to insist on a September attack, 'they would have to get someone else to do it'. Alexander duly informed London that it was 'essential' for the attack to be launched at night 'in the full moon period'; for this reason it would be wrong to start the offensive until 'minus 13 of *Torch*', which was by now scheduled for 4 November.

Churchill bowed to the inevitable. 'We are in your hands, and of course a victorious battle makes amends for much delay,' he wrote grudgingly on 23 September, before adding with rather more grace, 'Whatever happens we shall back you up and see you through.' By now Montgomery had settled on a date for the attack. It was timed to begin in the late evening of 23 October, when, as so often at crucial moments in this conflict, the desert would be helpfully illuminated by a full moon.

In marked contrast to the atmosphere at Eighth Army headquarters, Rommel's mood was bleak in the extreme. In the days following their retreat from Alam el Halfa, the Panzerarmee began strenuously to fortify a line, which ran along a forty-mile front between the sea and the Qattara Depression, a mere eight miles to the west of the Eighth Army's forward positions. On the face of it, the Axis forces had the advantage. As Rommel was to explain, 'we constructed our defensive system' to ensure that the Panzerarmee could hold out against 'even the heaviest British attack'. Once the British crossed the no-man's land between the two armies, they would find themselves entering a minefield, laid with some half a million explosive devices. Beyond the minefield, they would face the artillery, tanks and motorised divisions of the entire Panzerarmee, a formidable if not impenetrable barrier.

But fortifications alone would not be enough to stop what Rommel described, for the benefit of both Hitler and Mussolini, as 'the finest troops of the British Empire'. His confidence sapped by what he called 'the battle of supplies' which he now had to wage 'with new violence' against both Comando Supremo and OKW, Rommel nonetheless did what he could to alert the Axis leaders to his worsening predicament. The immediate cause of this crisis was the intensity and impunity with which the Royal Navy and the Royal Air Force bombarded both the Italian convoys and the North African ports held by the Axis powers. For some months the Panzerarmee had received only 40 per cent of what its commander regarded as their 'absolute minimum needs'.

Observing this shortfall, logistics officers in the German General Staff concluded that it had become impossible to sustain the African theatre. However their superior officers – with very few exceptions – drew the obvious lesson that at the root of the problem was the strategic failure of OKW and Comando Supremo to recognise, let alone to eliminate, the threat from the British garrison on Malta. In early September Rommel despatched a stark warning both to the Führer's headquarters and Comando Supremo in Rome, that without 'the uninterrupted flow of the supplies essential for life and battle ... the continued successful maintenance of the African theatre of war will be impossible'. The shortages were so acute, he complained, that the bread ration for the troops had been halved, they were undernourished, and many who had served in the desert for over a year were utterly exhausted. According to Rommel, this aggravated another predicament: the weakening performance of the Italians under his command. They were unable to make quick decisions, their tanks and artillery had limited range, their officers were inexperienced, their men were poorly led, and unless they were supported in the line of defence by German 'corset stays' they were incapable of withstanding a bayonet charge by the British.

Rommel's angry but woebegone litany may well have been affected by a recurrence of his debilitating sickness. He was once again suffering from low blood pressure and near-fainting fits caused by the gastrointestinal problems brought on by excessive physical and psychological stress. By September his ailments were serious enough for his physician to order him home on extended leave. Writing to his wife on 9 September, he affected to be in good spirits, but alerted her to the fact that 'the doctor is pressing me hard to have a break in Germany and doesn't want me to postpone it any longer ... On the one hand, I'm overjoyed at the prospect of getting away for a while and seeing you, but on the other I fear I shall never be free of anxiety about this place, even though I won't be able to get to the front myself.'

On the 23rd, with no sign of any improvement in either the flow of supplies or his health, he flew from Derna to Rome 'with a heavy heart' for an audience with Mussolini. Despite his stark warning that, unless the fuel, ammunition, weapons, and provisions he required were forthcoming, the Axis would be forced to abandon North Africa altogether, Il Duce still seemed incapable of recognising the gravity of the predicament, a failure Rommel attributed in part to the Panzerarmee's previous successes on the battlefield.

Mussolini's public utterances continued to be as bombastically fascistic and self-delusional as ever: the Americans posed no threat to the Axis because they were more interested in making money than war; he would in due course preside over a peace settlement as a result of which Italy would soon be able to 'direct the whole life of Europe'. In private he was far less assured. Comando Supremo had delivered him a pessimistic diagnosis of Axis prospects in North Africa which, for once, even he was unable to ignore.

During the summer, when their staffs warned of an imminent

Anglo-American invasion of North Africa – which, coincidentally, they also referred to as 'a second front' – both Mussolini and Hitler ridiculed the suggestion. In a letter to Il Duce in early August, the Führer went so far as to write, 'I consider this second front idea to be totally insane.' Quite what was in Mussolini's mind is impossible to discern. By his own account, Il Duce continued to believe – like many in OKW – that 'a great pincer movement with the Germans storming the Caucasus and Rommel's German–Italian armies conquering Egypt' would bring ultimate victory. However, Comando Supremo's prescient anxiety about a second front in North Africa – which they also advised would almost certainly lead to an invasion of southern Italy – clearly affected him; so much so that, by the autumn, he had already been persuaded of the need to reinforce and, if necessary, impose a formal occupation on Tunisia to repel any possible Anglo-American landings on the African shore of his Mediterranean Lake.

When Rommel's failure at Alam el Halfa was reported to him, he lapsed into what his Foreign Minister, Ciano, described as a 'black mood', during which he said nothing at all about Egypt for three days. When he finally gave vent to his dismay, he not only indulged in 'one of his periodic attacks on the Army' with which 'everything' was going wrong on all fronts, but also vented his anger specifically at Rommel. 'As always,' Ciano noted drily, 'victory finds a hundred fathers but defeat is an orphan.'

Mussolini's capricious behaviour was doubtless exacerbated by his persistent ill health. The gastro-enteritis by which he had long been afflicted in times of crisis now flared up so sharply that he was sometimes unable to conceal the pain. He lost a great deal of weight, which made him seem aged and haggard. On his return from his ill-fated visit to North Africa, where he had suffered acutely, he was diagnosed with amoebic dysentery, the prescribed cure for which failed to achieve its purpose. It was noted that he was increasingly stricken by indecision and that his once elephantine memory was deserting him. One of his physicians even feared that his ill health had been so aggravated by the stress of war that his days on earth were numbered. None of this was allowed to be mentioned in public; any suggestion that his health was failing him was forbidden and foreign journalists knew that to refer to it was to court instant expulsion.

On 27 September, after an absence of three weeks, Ciano had a meeting with Mussolini, at which he noted his father-in-law's loss of weight. Otherwise, he found him calm and clear-minded, though depressingly aware that 'military events' – the stouter than expected resistance by the Red Army at Stalingrad (where Italian troops were tied down alongside the Wehrmacht) as well as the humiliation in Albania and the setbacks in North Africa – had 'cut deeply into the morale of the population'. Ciano himself had just had a meeting with Rommel, who told him that he was about to take a six-week break from the front, prompting Mussolini to observe that the Panzerarmee commander would never return to the desert and that he was 'physically and morally shaken'. As Ciano observed morbidly, 'We are starting the winter with a state of mind in which, at the worst, we should be at the end of the winter.'

Rommel left Rome for Berlin bearing vague assurances of future supplies and a farewell injunction from Mussolini to the effect that it was imperative to seize the Nile Delta before the arrival of the Americans. In Berlin he discerned that a spirit of optimism still prevailed. In an attempt to prick this bubble of complacency, Rommel did not waste time on the niceties but instead laid out his troubles, reiterating that without greater support and more supplies of every kind it would not be possible even to hold on in North Africa, let alone defeat the Eighth Army. His list of demands included 11,000 reinforcements (to be drawn from the Wehrmacht and the Italian army) in addition to an unspecified number of thousands required to bring every unit of the Panzerarmee up to strength and 17,000 replacements for those members of his Afrikakorps who were exhausted by long service in the desert; more bombers and fighters to restore parity with the RAF and to deny Malta to the British; more submarines and motor torpedo boats; and more shipping to carry the many thousands of tons of fuel, ammunition and provisions needed to sustain the line at El Alamein. If these demands made sense in their own terms, Rommel must have known that they would be regarded as quite unrealistic, even 'preposterous', when every available Axis soldier, tank and aeroplane was being thrown at the Red Army, which was showing a degree of resistance on all fronts which Hitler had not anticipated.

Berlin appeared to be in denial about the situation at El Alamein. At one point, when Rommel stated that the RAF had 'shot up my tanks with 40-mm. shells', Goering retorted ludicrously, 'That's completely impossible. The Americans only know how to make razor blades.' Rommel replied, 'We could do with some of those razor blades, Herr Reichsmarschall.' To avoid any further dispute, he produced one of the offending shells which had been fired at a tank from a low-flying RAF bomber, killing almost the entire crew.

Hitler, focussing on gesture rather than strategy, seized the opportunity to present Rommel with the field marshal's baton which he had bestowed on him after his triumph at Tobruk the previous June. The ceremony took place in the Reich Chancellery, where obsequious courtiers noted that Rommel committed a faux pas by failing to remove his gloves before shaking hands with the Führer. Afterwards, Goebbels, as Propaganda Minister, made sure that Rommel was suitably fêted by the German populace. He was paraded alongside Hitler at the Berlin Sports Palace, where the Nazi Party staged a 'Winter Help' rally and where, by his account, he was 'somewhat alarmed to be greeted by an ecstatic crowd'. There was also a press conference at which – with a bravado that he certainly did not feel – he found himself declaring, 'We are now one hundred kilometres from Alexandria and Cairo and have the gateway to Egypt in our hands. We intend to go into action! We did not go all the way there in order sooner or later to be pushed back. You can be certain of one thing: we shall hang on to what we have.'

The ambiguity in this declaration of intent – which promised in one breath to advance, but in the next, not to retreat – was not apparently noted by his fans at the stadium. His speech not only served its rousing purpose but led Goebbels to note in his diary both that Rommel was 'just the sort of National Socialist general that we need', and that Hitler had declared his youngest field marshal to be gifted with 'personal courage and exceptional imagination' that would make him 'the future commander-in-chief of the army'.

None of this adulation impressed Rommel or solved his predicament. Despite abundant evidence to the contrary, the Führer's planning staff continued to believe that the Panzerarmee's position on the Alamein Line was secure and – unaccountably – that, in any case, Montgomery would not attack until early in 1943. By this time, they told themselves, Rommel would be strong enough to turn the tables once again and advance on the Delta. This complacency, betrayed in an official memorandum which stated, inter alia, that 'OKW does not consider the offensive has failed, on the contrary it reckons with its resumption', was shared by Hitler, who continued to believe that the Eighth Army would be unable to break through Rommel's defences. Thus, garlanded with his new baton and a chestful of false promises, Rommel retreated to the mountain resort of Semmering near Vienna, where, accompanied by his wife, he was supposed to rest and recuperate but where he succeeded only in worrying about 'the plight' of his army in Africa, as a result of which, he noted, 'I was of course incapable of attaining real peace of mind.'

If a small platoon of eminent historians, heavily armed with the wisdom of hindsight, had been in Churchill's shoes or commanding the Eighth Army on that night, the famous Battle of El Alamein that was about to commence would never have taken place. It was, in their minds, an 'unnecessary' as well as an excessively bloody affair which had been made redundant by the fact that, within a fortnight, an Anglo-American army of more than 100,000 men was to land on the North African coast some 1,500 miles away at the other end of the Mediterranean. *Torch*, they argued, would have forced Rommel to rush back from El Alamein to confront this far greater threat to the Axis position in North Africa. In these circumstances, all that Montgomery would have had to do was to wait for this moment and then give chase, harrying the Panzerarmee all the way back to Tunis and beyond until it found itself squeezed into surrender from the west and the east by the combined power of the two Allied armies. But such speculative analysis not only involves second-guessing the past or indulging the benefit of hindsight, it ignores the military uncertainties and the political imperatives which – at the time – made the Third Battle of El Alamein a strategic inevitability.

In London, it was still feared that the Wehrmacht might yet drive through the Caucasus to threaten the Middle East from the north. The German army still had Stalingrad in a stranglehold and, in his capricious fashion, it remained possible that Hitler would release enough aircraft from the Soviet front and enough U-boats from the Atlantic to blockade the British garrison on Malta. Nor, in the absence of any evidence to the contrary, was it unreasonable to suppose that the Führer might belatedly heed Rommel's demand for the men, weapons and provisions which, with Malta neutralised, would allow him once again to threaten the Nile Delta.

Alternatively, if Montgomery had merely stood his ground at El Alamein (as these historians have proposed) and had Rommel indeed withdrawn as soon as the threat from Operation *Torch* became apparent, it is not at all clear that the Eighth Army would have been able to inflict much damage on the Panzerarmee, with its armour virtually intact: even after its pulverising ordeal at El Alamein, the remains of Rommel's army retained enough discipline and agility to retire in orderly fashion all the way back to Tunisia to confront the Anglo-American invasion. It is not hard to imagine what Eisenhower would have thought – let alone his military and political superiors in Washington – as they contemplated their own casualties in North Africa, knowing that the British under Montgomery had allowed Rommel to steal away from El Alamein before a shot had been fired.

Moreover, given the conviction and guile with which the Axis forces fought to retain their strongholds in North Africa, it is reasonable to conjecture that, had the entire Panzerarmee been allowed to withdraw from Egypt and Libya without a fight at El Alamein, the combined might of the Axis forces which were rapidly assembled to confront the Anglo-American invaders would assuredly have given Eisenhower an even harder fight for very much longer than the six months it eventually took the Allied commander-in-chief to prevail. It is even possible that Rommel would have fought Eisenhower to a standstill. A military stalemate in North Africa would have revealed *Torch* as the fiasco which many in Washington had feared it would become, the fragile trust between the Joint Chiefs of Staff would have been severely strained, if not shattered, by Britain's failure to savage Rommel at El Alamein, and, as a result, the Prime Minister's standing and influence in the White House, no less than in Britain, would have been gravely eroded.

If it was militarily inconceivable for Montgomery to stay his hand at El Alamein, there were compelling political reasons for him not to do so. For two years – from Dunkirk to Tobruk – Britain had been buffeted by defeat after defeat in Europe and the Far East as well as North Africa, to the point where it had started to seem that victory was beyond the British Army. It had been demoralising both for the soldiers at the front and for the public at home. In the United States, it had created a widespread impression that Perfidious Albion had become a toothless lion as well. Despite the agreement which, after long and bruising negotiations, the Allies had reached over Operation *Torch*, the pressures on Roosevelt from those of his advisors who had only acquiesced in the venture with great reluctance, had not evaporated. Other theatres of war (the struggles against the Japanese in the Pacific and against the Germans in Russia) were hungry for American armaments which, Roosevelt's team continued to argue, should not be 'diverted' to North Africa.

The President had taken a significant strategic risk in overriding these objections. In deciding in favour of *Torch*, he had defined the Middle East and the Mediterranean as a theatre of major strategic interest for the United States. He had pledged his faith in the Eighth Army by sending 300 Sherman tanks and squadrons of USAF bombers to sustain the British struggle against Rommel. It cannot be imagined that he would have approved a stand-off at El Alamein by a British Army which enjoyed massive superiority thanks in large measure to this largesse. From the American standpoint, a stand-off would have been regarded as a 'no-show', confirming Anglophobes and isolationists across the United States that the President had been duped by a Prime Minister who was willing to see 'Our Boys' die on the battlefield to save British skins. It had never been stated quite so crudely, but, from Washington's perspective, Britain's will to win at El Alamein was a litmus test for the Anglo-American Alliance, a proving ground for the new partnership.

For the last two years, Churchill's overriding priority had been to prevent the defeat of both the United Kingdom and the British Empire. To achieve this, he had used every diplomatic and psychological wile at his command to secure Roosevelt's commitment to the same vision. In the testing and often acrimonious months of diplomacy leading up to El Alamein, they had together managed to forge the framework for a vital military alliance. But this partnership had yet to be put seriously to the test: in the months ahead, there were bound to be grave misunderstandings, severe arguments and sharp disagreements, clashes of temperament and personality – tensions which would surely be exacerbated as the more powerful partner, not always tactfully, began to assert its pre-eminent role in the relationship. In these circumstances Churchill needed to demonstrate that Britain was not only a political but a military force to be reckoned with, one gifted with a resolve on the battlefield in which the Americans could place their trust and trust with their lives. El Alamein offered the last opportunity before *Torch* to demonstrate this beyond reasonable doubt.

Of course, there were domestic and personal considerations as well. Churchill's authority at Westminster and in the country had been eroded by failure on the battlefield. Even his magisterial rhetoric, which rarely faltered, had begun to sound stale and repetitive, grandiloquent but hollow. A swelling chorus of sceptical voices began to ask – as it were – 'Where's the beef?' The criticism had been summed up earlier in the year by an influential newspaper columnist, William Connor – 'Cassandra' – of the *Daily Mirror*. Wielding his stiletto with neat cruelty, he commented, 'Upon the broad and powerful shoulders of Mr Churchill rests the entire burden of the criticism of the war effort. Who put it there?

None other than Mr Churchill himself.' It was a shallow jibe but it reflected the frustration of failure by which Britain seemed to be entombed.

Churchill's political enemies plotted for Sir Stafford Cripps, the only other politician of comparable stature, to replace him; were Cripps to resign from the Cabinet, it would have precipitated a major political crisis. Even the Prime Minister's friends, worrying about his health and his frame of mind, wondered if he could stay the course. Some of these asserted that he would be finished as Prime Minister if the Eighth Army were to endure another defeat at the hands of the apparently insuperable Desert Fox. Brendan Bracken, Churchill's Minister of Information, an acolyte who devoured gossip from the corridors of power like a vulture at a carcass, had convinced himself, 'If we are beaten in this battle it's the end of Winston.' Whether or not Bracken would have been proved right about that, El Alamein was certainly crucial to Churchill's authority as Prime Minister, and he knew it.

On the evening of 23 October, 'Winston was like a cat on hot bricks,' according to Sir Alan Lascelles, the King's Private Secretary. He was at a dinner given by George VI at Buckingham Palace for Eleanor Roosevelt, the President's wife. At one point, during the meal, Lascelles discreetly left the room. 'I had to go out in the middle', he noted 'to get the news by telephone from No. 10. After a brief interval, nothing would content Churchill but to go to the telephone himself. His conversation evidently pleased him, for he walked back along the passage singing "Roll Out the Barrel" with gusto, but with little evidence of musical talent. This astonished the posse of footmen through which he had to pass.' The Third Battle of El Alamein was about to commence.

TWENTY-THREE

INTO THE BREACH

'There are great possibilities and great dangers. It may be the turning point of the war leading to further success combined with the North African attacks, or it may mean nothing. If it fails I don't quite know how I shall bear it.'

General Alan Brooke

In the desert that same evening, the 23rd, the sky was clear. Hardly a soul moved. The battleground was illuminated by the full moon like the stage of a great theatre, but to the casual eye it would have seemed to be an empty quarter. There was no visible sign of guns or tanks or soldiers; all were hidden even from aerial reconnaissance. Though they were poised for battle, it was as though the 200,000 troops of the Eighth Army and the 100,000 men of the Panzerarmee had decided to hold their collective breath. On one side, the Germans knew that an attack was imminent but not precisely when to expect it. On the other, the British knew exactly what they were waiting for: the roar of an artillery barrage signalling that the offensive was underway.

As they waited in the dark poised for the signal to move out of their slit trenches towards the enemy line, every man in the Eighth Army knew what was expected of him. Earlier in the day, Montgomery had issued a 'Personal Message' to all of them (which, always mindful of his image, he was at pains to hand out during a press conference at Eighth Army headquarters):

The battle which is about to begin will be one of the decisive battles of history. It will be the turning point of the war. The eyes of the world will be upon us, watching anxiously which way the battle will swing. We can give them their answer at once, 'It will swing our way.' ... All that is necessary is that each one of us, every officer and man, should enter this battle with the determination to see it through – to fight and to kill – and finally, to win. If we do this there can be only one result – together we will hit the enemy for 'six', right out of North Africa.

He concluded his address with a phrase which owed much to the fact that he believed – with some justice – that in the past too many units in the Eighth Army had lain down their arms without good cause: in capital letters he therefore admonished, 'LET NO MAN SURRENDER SO LONG AS HE IS UNWOUNDED AND CAN FIGHT.' Earlier, in briefing his senior officers, he warned that the coming battle would be 'a killing match' which might last ten days and in which, he said privately, more than 13,000 British and Commonwealth troops would be killed or wounded. De Guingand was once again impressed by Montgomery's confidence and by the impact of his words, especially when he declared, 'everyone – *everyone* – must be imbued with the burning desire to "kill Germans". "Even the padres – one per weekday and two on Sundays."'

The two armies were very far from evenly matched either in quality or number. The Panzerarmee numbered 108,000 men, split evenly between its German and Italian components. The Eighth Army, with contingents from Britain, Australia, New Zealand, South Africa and India, as well as the 'free' Greek and French units – 220,000 men in total – was more than twice as large. But the more decisive imbalance was in armaments, both on the ground and in the air, where British superiority was technically as well as numerically overwhelming: more than 900 tanks (including the newly arrived Shermans) versus some 500 tanks (of which only 200 were panzers of various vintages and the rest outdated Italian models); more than 2,000 pieces of artillery and anti-tank guns versus 1,200; and at least 530 serviceable RAF fighters and bombers (with 650 others in reserve) versus a force of 350

Luftwaffe planes, a superiority which, following a series of devastating raids by the RAF, had left the Luftwaffe 'virtually unable to play any role in the battle of El Alamein'. Despite these numerical advantages, the quality of the fighting men on each side, the manner of their deployment, and their resolve remained critical to the equation. In these respects, a large question mark still hung over the Eighth Army.

To a far greater degree than Rommel, Montgomery was hampered by the outmoded traditions and multinational structure of his forces, some of which not only lacked any experience of desert warfare but, despite the intensive training to which they had been subjected, were not yet ready to meet the demands he was about to make on them. He also lacked flexibility in their deployment; it was impossible for him to restructure or reorganise the various elements of the Eighth Army (drawn from the Empire and the Dominions as well as from Britain) without the approval or the consent of the principal commanders who were answerable ultimately to their own governments. And, like Auchinleck before him, he could not count on every one of his divisional commanders to obey his orders without question. Even some British officers – for all his inspirational leadership – felt free on occasion to question and even to ignore his instructions.

A striking example of this had arisen earlier in the month when the commander of X Corps, General Herbert Lumsden, the most experienced tank commander in the Eighth Army and the only one who had survived Montgomery's cull, openly challenged the battle plan for the first phase of El Alamein. Lumsden was the quintessence of the dashing cavalry officer: a fine horseman with famous steeplechasing victories to his name and a recipient of the Military Cross in the First World War, who had already been wounded in the desert campaign. His combination of elegance and arrogance could not have been better tailored to irritate Montgomery and it was soon obvious that the two men could not abide one another.

Montgomery's offensive was planned as though it were an updated version of a First World War battle in which the 'poor bloody infantry' left their trenches to cross no-man's land under cover of darkness before hurling themselves upon the enemy. In the case of El Alamein, the foot soldiers – thus the unfortunate codename, Operation *Lightfoot* – were to clear a way through the German minefields for Lumsden's armoured divisions to pierce the enemy front line and then 'crumble' (Montgomery's term) Rommel's forward defences so that the tanks could 'break-out' in the early hours of the morning to drive through a multi-fractured front line.

However, at a meeting of X Corps, from which Montgomery was fortuitously absent, Lumsden and his divisional commanders decided that the plan was unworkable, that the logjams and road-blocks which would inevitably impede the advance were bound to leave their tanks trapped in the open and dangerously exposed to enemy fire. Lumsden wanted his tank units to be free-wheeling and independent, not hog-tied to the slow progress of the Eighth Army's foot soldiers. According to de Guingand, who was present at the X Corps meeting as Montgomery's Chief of Staff, Lumsden insisted, 'Tanks must be used as cavalry: they must exploit the situation and not be kept as supporters of infantry. So I don't propose to do that.'

After the meeting had broken up, de Guingand took Lumsden aside and said, 'Look here, my dear boy, you can't do this. You know Monty. You must know him well enough – he won't permit disobedience to his orders'. Lumsden airily dismissed the advice. The following morning, at an acrimonious meeting with his errant corps commander, Montgomery duly insisted that his battle plan was to be obeyed. For the moment – but only for the moment – that was the end of the matter.

Nonetheless, within the limits of time and talent, Montgomery had presided over an impressive reformation of the Eighth Army, to the point where 'as it was about to embark on the largest offensive of the desert war it was not a new force standing upon the grave of its successor but a renewed and reinvigorated military machine resting upon the shoulders of the "old" desert army'. Though he invariably claimed the credit for this transformation, he owed a great debt to the commanding officers over whom he presided – the 'multiple authors and contributors' – and who between them ironed out the flaws in Montgomery's conception of Operation *Lightfoot* and translated his intentions into a practical and detailed plan of attack.

At 9.40 p.m. on 23 October, the silence of the desert was broken in the most spectacular fashion. 'No fury of sound had ever assailed our ears like that before,' wrote a British bombardier from the Royal Horse Artillery, as he stood among the guns while they launched a deafening fusillade at the enemy's artillery positions on the no-man's land which separated the two armies.

> It cuffed, shattered and distorted the senses, and loosened the bowels alarmingly ... When I could focus, the faces I first saw looked blanched and then flushed brightly in a kaleidoscope of passionately flickering hues as every line and every detail was etched into relief by the flashes from the muzzles of the guns ... hundreds of guns almost hub to hub, all bucking and recoiling, spitting fire and snapping like a pack of vicious terriers, all at once, it was sheer horror.

An infantryman from the 5th Seaforth Highlanders wrote, 'The noise is unbelievable ... the whole sky is screaming ... The infantryman is a fly inside a drum ... The uproar swells and fades and swells again, deafeningly, numbing the brain.' For some it was too much. Even Sergeant-Major Harper, who had been through Tobruk and Gazala, was 'dumbfounded by the din' of the heavy artillery. 'Blimey, this is beginning to get hard work,' he thought to himself after ten or twelve rounds. Then he noticed that 'one bloke was missing, hiding in a slit trench behind the gun. So I dragged him out by the scruff of the neck ... I threatened to shoot him if he didn't get back on the job. I had to do something drastic because if you do that sort of thing in action it becomes contagious. I would have shot him if I had to ... He went back to the gun but was never quite the same again.'

Montgomery had ordered 750 guns – 300 in the south and, fifteen minutes later, 450 in the north – to open fire in a cacophony of sound and fury, an onslaught which reminded Alexander of the

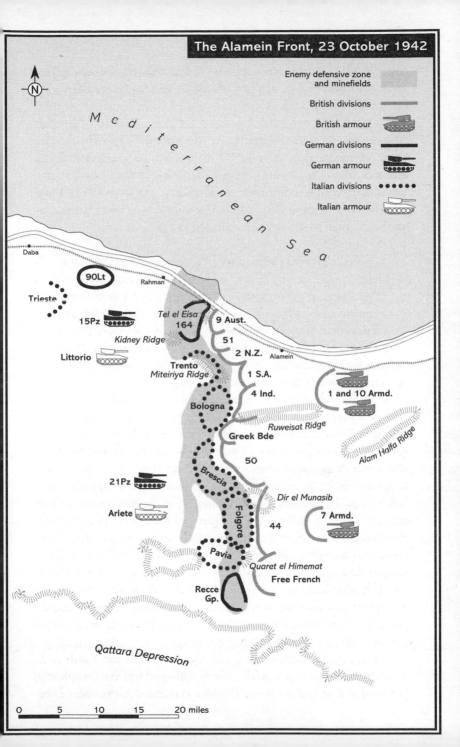

The Alamein Front, 23 October 1942

Enemy defensive zone and minefields
British divisions
British armour
German divisions
German armour
Italian divisions
Italian armour

Mediterranean Sea

Daba
90Lt
Rahman
Trieste
15Pz
Tel el Eisa
164
9 Aust.
Kidney Ridge
51
Littorio
2 N.Z.
Alamein
Trento
Miteiriya Ridge
1 S.A.
Bologna
4 Ind.
1 and 10 Armd.
Ruweisat Ridge
Greek Bde
Alam Halfa Ridge
50
21Pz
Brescia
Dir el Munasib
Ariete
Folgore
44
7 Armd.
Pavia
Quaret el Himemat
Free French
Recce Gp.

Qattara Depression

0   5   10   15   20 miles

First World War. Montgomery was to claim that he fell asleep just before the artillery opened fire, although he noted in his diary that the artillery barrage 'was a wonderful sight, similar to a Great War 1914/18 attack ... the effect was terrific'. De Guingand's account also suggests that the Eighth Army commander was more wakeful than Montgomery's post-war recollection suggests: his Chief of Staff, who was almost certainly with him at the time, was to describe having a quiet dinner and then, at 9.30 p.m., finding a vantage point overlooking the battlefield where 'we watched as the whole sky lit up, and a roar rent the air ... It was a great and heartening sight. I tried to picture what the enemy must be thinking, did he know what was coming? He must do now. How ready was he?'

This opening volley lasted for thirty minutes and it took the Panzerarmee totally by surprise. A few days earlier, General Georg Stumme, deputising for Rommel, who was still recuperating in Semmering, sought to raise the spirits of his senior colleagues. 'The enemy is by no means certain of victory,' he told them. 'We must increase that uncertainty every day ... The feeling of complete moral superiority over the enemy must be awakened and fostered in every soldier, from the highest commander to the youngest man. From this moral superiority comes coolness, confidence, and self-reliance and an unshakeable will to fight. This is the secret of every victory.'

Earlier that day, foiled by poor aerial reconnaissance and inadequate intelligence combined with the blanket secrecy which camouflaged the Eighth Army's preparations, the Panzerarmee's daily report had stated, 'Enemy situation unchanged. Quiet all day along the front.' A few hours later, as the shells crashed into their forward positions, the German and Italian troops were momentarily stunned by the onslaught. The 'inferno [was] an inhuman relentless series of explosions', wrote Ralph Ringler, serving in the 104th Panzergrenadier. 'The whole desert seemed to hum and shudder. As I surfaced from a deep sleep, the shock raced through my limbs ... The shells howled overhead and exploded, the ground rocked and the detonations shook me into confusion.' An Italian sergeant, Riccardo Poletto, was similarly shaken by the scale of the unexpected bombardment as 'shells suddenly fell all round. There was choking smoke. It seemed an avalanche of fire.'

In fact the impact of the British artillery barrage was as much psychologically as physically destructive. 'I could hear the shells howling over me. We thought this was the end,' recalled Martin Ranft, a gunner serving with the German 164th Light Division. When he finally dared to peek out of his foxhole, the surrounding area 'looked like a ploughed field. There wasn't much left, and we said, "How can anyone survive?" But we did. We had some casualties … One of my friends had his foot blown off by a shell. He died the next day. One had a direct hit in a bunker, one shell went right through and blew his head off.' Although its casualties were not as heavy as might have been expected, no soldier in the Panzerarmee could have been left with any doubt that they were about to face the severest test of the 'moral superiority' with which General Stumme had hoped to imbue them. Montgomery's 'shock and awe' bombardment – to destroy the Axis artillery and communications and thus leave each Axis unit fighting in isolation – was a morale-sapping foretaste of what was to come in what the Eighth Army commander had promised would be a 'dog-fight' to the finish.

In London that night, after the War Office informed him that the battle had started, Brooke was in turmoil. 'We are bound to have some desperately anxious moments,' he noted. 'There are great possibilities and great dangers. It may be the turning point of the war leading to further success combined with the North African attacks, or it may mean nothing. If it fails I don't quite know how I shall bear it.' Adding a further note later to explain 'the acute agony of expectation' of this moment, he placed El Alamein at the very heart of a military strategy (from which, in truth, he had wavered from time to time) 'to clear North Africa, open the Mediterranean, threaten Southern Europe, and at some later date liberate France'.

Forty minutes after the first deafening fusillade from the British artillery, tens of thousands of British infantrymen rose from their slit trenches where they had endured a long, cold and comfortless evening. In a scene reminiscent of Ypres or the Somme, they began to march in steady columns towards the Axis front line. Each man carried rations for twenty-four hours, ammunition and hand grenades. As they picked their way through the enemy minefields their path was illuminated not only by the moon but by the interplay of searchlights and tracer fire. There was little exuberance, just a resolute sense of purpose. Only the Highland Division, each man carrying a saltire (less from patriotism than for identification), stood out from the marching host, the 'eerie, exhilarating and frightening music' of their pipers piercing 'the din of shell and mine exploding and the racket of gunfire'. Piper Charles Miller, serving with the Argyll and Sutherland Highlanders, led his battalion without flinching. 'We had orders to keep on and ignore the wounded. They were left for people behind: the stretcher-bearers. It was a matter of not showing to your pals that you were frightened ... Pipers are very important to a Scottish regiment. We had to play the boys in; there were quite a lot of casualties among the pipers.'

The stretcher-bearers, who had the gruesome task of picking up the dead and wounded, navigated their way through the night by following the bodies lying in their path. The cries of the wounded were piteous against the background venom of shell-fire and explosions. 'One of the casualties has both legs and an arm blown off,' one stretcher-bearer wrote. 'While I stand there he regains consciousness and starts pleading, "Kill me, God, please kill me." I find I am incapable, and with tears in my eyes cover the body with a greatcoat, thinking how small he looks.'

Accompanying the infantry, the engineers and sappers, under intense pressure to maintain the momentum of the advance, swept the sand for mines. It was not always done by the rule book. 'I walk along like this, and I give a kick here and a kick there,' an Australian engineer explained, 'They were as thick as thieves these mines, and booby-traps in between them.' A sapper described the peculiarly lethal impact of the S mines, 'When a foot trod on the detonator there were two distinct explosions. The first flung the mine up in the air and the second explosion was at waist height and it spewed out hundreds of ball bearings horizontally. I felt sorry for the infantry boys. They had to walk across the minefield and take up defensive positions to keep the Jerries off while our lads got to work.'

The 'killing match' as Montgomery chose to describe the battle became just that. 'The rotten part about an attack is that it must go on, and if your mate goes down beside you, you can't stop,' an infantryman with the New Zealand Division wrote home. 'It seems hard and callous, but its unavoidable.' There were twenty-five men in his platoon at the start of the attack; by the time they were ordered to halt, there were twelve of them left.

The 'break-in' on the northern front, which was to bear the main thrust of the attack, was spearheaded by the infantry divisions of XXX Corps, under the command of General Leese (who had replaced Ramsden). Its task was to open two main corridors across a deep minefield for Lumsden's tanks to file across towards Rommel's front line, advancing like twin battering rams to trap the defenders and cut them off from the rest of the Panzerarmee.

At 2 a.m. on the 24th, the first tank brigades removed their gun covers, loaded their weapons, started their engines and lumbered forward, their drivers peering through swirling mists of fine sand, kicked up by their tracks, as they tried to locate the white tapes which had been laid by the sappers and engineers to mark a safe route through the minefields. There was a bitter chill in the air. 'Most of us', one crew member recalled, 'were frozen to the marrow and not feeling particularly brave. The first flush of excitement had given place to the knowledge that in a very few hours we would once more be at grips with the enemy armour and that the slaughter would begin all over again.'

For *Lightfoot* to succeed, it was essential for Lumsden's two armoured divisions to cross the minefields to take up positions at the very front of the battle line before dawn to avoid being exposed to a blizzard of enemy fire with no room to manoeuvre or turn round and with no means of escape. It was a precise and inflexible plan which allowed for virtually no errors or unforeseen hazards. And that rigidity of purpose and design was almost its undoing. Although the infantry advancing along the southern corridor towards Miteiriya Ridge initially made good progress, overrunning the Panzerarmee's forward defences in their path and crossing more than five miles of desert, they were brought to an abrupt halt as they reached the ridge by the discovery of a scatter of mines about which they had no advance knowledge.

As the starlit night gave way to the dull grey of dawn, the advance was further slowed by the stiffening resistance of the Axis artillery. The disciplined reports from brigade and divisional commanders give little indication of the gruesome confusion that now bloodied the battlefront as the enemy guns drilled into Montgomery's infantry. 'There was a terrific explosion, and something flew past my head,' one man reported. 'It was a leg with a boot on it. A round of HE [High Explosive] had taken Chalky White's leg off. He was looking at me with astonishment and pointing to the raw, bleeding stump with the white bone sticking through. I went towards him with the idea of helping him, I think. Just then the machine gun opened up again and poor Chalky got it full in the face.' Another described his own moment of horror. 'A bullet smashed into my hand causing me to drop my rifle. I felt something boring into my shoulder and a taste of blood in my mouth. Nearly everyone seemed dead or dying, and I ran away from the senseless slaughter, unable and unwilling to stay and let myself be shot full of holes like a colander.'

As dawn broke, the first tank squadron to reach Miteiriya Ridge found itself in the direst possible predicament, unable to 'break-out' and caught in the cross-hairs of the Axis artillery. With his characteristic penchant for understatement, de Guingand wrote later, 'Miteiriya Ridge was a very unpleasant place to be, and very fierce fighting took place.' With less restraint, a crew member in one of the tanks described the moment when 'suddenly all hell broke loose. Every kind of tracer fire came flying towards us from all directions. The tank crews waiting behind in the packed gaps through the minefield saw armour-piercing tracer shells screaming from all over the place towards A Squadron's tanks – then the explosions of tanks blowing up, sheets of flame as they caught fire, and the dull cherry-red of red-hot tank turrets.'

Soon there was a gridlock of vehicles along the ridge with

some 200 tanks trapped into immobility along a two-mile front, unable to advance and unable to retreat. A traffic jam of tanks, trucks, and armoured cars – the full panoply of a great army on the march – was soon queued back for five miles or more across the congested desert. Without the air supremacy of the RAF, these columns of stranded vehicles would have been sitting targets for the Stuka dive-bombers which in the past had posed such a threat to the Eighth Army's progress back and forth across the North African littoral.

This impasse brought to a head the long-simmering animosities which had bedevilled relations between the Eighth Army's armour and infantry and which, despite his much-vaunted powers of command, even Montgomery had been unable to resolve. In this case, General Freyberg, commanding the New Zealand (Infantry) Division, and General Gatehouse, commanding the 10th Armoured Division, held diametrically opposed views about how to escape their predicament. As they were unable to communicate with each other directly – for inexplicable reasons, given their crucial roles in Operation *Lightfoot* – they had to argue with each other indirectly via their respective headquarters. Although Gatehouse had managed to find a measure of security from the enemy fire on the least exposed flank of the ridge, he was determined not to send his tanks forward to face what were certain to be heavy casualties, informing Freyberg bluntly, 'Don't want to go out and get A/ Tked [anti-tanked] and shelled to hell.' Freyberg, who knew much about infantry but little about armour, clearly believed that Gatehouse lacked the will, and even the courage, to take the battle to the enemy. But had Gatehouse yielded to Freyberg's pressure, he would have been responsible for a military disaster of inexcusable proportions. Those tanks fortunate enough to survive the enemy bombardment would have swiftly run out of fuel and ammunition, at which point, without any prospect of replenishment, they would have sat plumply in the sand waiting to be picked off one by one. In vain, therefore, Freyberg kept calling his headquarters to demand that 10th Armoured Division be infused with 'some energy'.

The advance along the other northern corridor fared no better. As Alexander put it in his formal report, 'the deployment of 1st

380 DESTINY IN THE DESERT

Armoured Division [commanded by General Raymond Briggs] was even more seriously held up because the northern lane was still blocked by minefields under fire from the enemy strongpoints which the Australian and Highland Divisions had been unable to overcome'. By dawn on the 24th, the 2nd Armoured Brigade, following the infantry, was still floundering in the minefield that blocked the northern corridor.

'The inferno that was the great battle of Alamein continued unabated,' a padre serving with the Royal East Kent Regiment ('the Buffs') noted. 'The appalling din of guns firing and shells bursting, the grim sights of mangled men and twisted corpses, the nauseating smell that was a mixture of sulphur and rotting human flesh, the mental strain from sleeplessness and responsibility, the fear of breaking down in front of the men.' A corporal in the Argyll and Sutherland Highlanders, Vernon Scannell, had anguished memories of 'the voices of those who'd been badly wounded, their voices raised in terror and pain. I can remember one particular sergeant who'd always seemed to me almost a kind of father figure … he was badly wounded and hearing his voice sort of sobbing and calling for his mother seemed to be so demeaning and humiliating and dreadful'.

There was no better news from XIII Corps, which had been deployed some twenty miles further south on the approaches to Himeimat Ridge. During the weeks of preparation before the battle, elaborate efforts had been made to dupe the enemy into believing that the Eighth Army's main thrust was to come from this end of the line. Operation *Bertram* involved the construction of dummy railway tracks, water reservoirs, storage tanks, pump houses, bivouacs, and tanks. One morning at dawn, during these preparations, Major John Harris of the 2nd Derbyshire Yeomanry was standing with his commanding officer watching a squadron of tanks manoeuvring nearby. 'What's strange about those tanks?' the CO asked. 'I don't know. Are they these new Shermans?' Harris replied. His CO said, 'They make no noise, they've got no tracks, they are lorries with canvas over them made to look like tanks' – a deception first practised by Rommel on his arrival in

Tripoli eighteen months earlier. Whether or not these ruses were successful, Rommel's intelligence most certainly believed that the Eighth Army's main attack was to come from the south.

More weightily, the presence of XIII Corps, under the command of General Horrocks, served false notice on the Germans that the southern flank was indeed as crucial as their intelligence had led them to believe. Horrocks was charged by Montgomery to mount a series of diversionary attacks against the three panzer divisions protecting the Himeimat salient to tie them down well away from the northern front where the real breakthrough was planned. To this end, as XXX Corps and the X Armoured Corps tried to make progress in the north, the 7th Armoured Division, under the recently promoted General John Harding, advanced on the Axis forces dug in defensively around the Himeimat salient. As Harding's tanks lumbered slowly over what he described as 'a long, open stretch of heavy sand' towards Himeimat, they had to navigate through the minefields by which the approaches to the ridge were protected. 'If you are stuck in a minefield' he noted, 'tanks are a dead duck to anti-tank fire'. They managed to cross safely to the other side but soon came under heavy fire. To avoid losing too many tanks, Harding decided to call a halt.

The Free French Brigade, which was also under Harding's command, had advanced along an escarpment to the south of the ridge until it came under fierce bombardment from the German tanks above; as their own anti-tank guns had been bogged in soft sand, the Free French were unable to return fire and had little choice but to retreat. With his infantry battalions subjected to a similar battering, Horrocks was forced to abandon the assault altogether. This was not what Montgomery had intended. As Harding put it, 'we were stuck. This was the position for the next couple of days.'

Nonetheless, these diversionary attacks served some purpose. For a time at least, the 21st Panzer Division and the most formidable of the Italian units, the Ariete Division – which might otherwise have hurried north to reinforce the hard-pressed defences around Miteiriya Ridge, where the genuine 'break-in' and 'crumbling' was to be attempted – were instead detained by Montgomery's feint to the south.

Though he was never to admit it, Montgomery had under-estimated the time it would take for his armoured divisions to navigate a path through the minefields in the heart of the battlefield. The resilience and ferocity with which the Axis artillery had arrested the British onslaught inflicted a heavy toll in life and limb. With 3,000 soldiers killed or wounded after only twenty-four hours of battle, the casualty rate was alarmingly high. Moreover, by dawn on the second day of the battle, Operation *Lightfoot* was already worryingly behind the schedule Montgomery had devised. Despite the fact that the initial British bombardment had virtually destroyed the Panzerarmee's communications network – which meant the Axis forces had been obliged to rely on runners to keep contact between the army, corps, and divisional headquarters – the Panzerarmee's defences had held up disturbingly well along the entire front from north to south.

The Eighth Army commander's reaction to this setback was characteristically unforgiving. Before the battle he had ordered that if the corridors were still blocked by dawn, the armoured units were to fight their way out through the minefields towards the Axis defences regardless of the cost in tanks or lives; an instruction, he commented later with evident glee that 'was not popular with the armoured units' but one which 'I was determined to see … carried out to the letter'. Now, with *Lightfoot* bogged down, he turned on his bête noire, General Lumsden. 'So far he has not impressed me by his showing in battle,' he noted; 'perhaps he has been out here too long; he has been wounded twice. I can see that he will have to be bolstered up and firmly handled … There was not that eagerness on the part of senior commanders to push and there was a fear of casualties.' Summoning the X Corps commander to his presence, he instructed him to 'drive his divisional commanders', warning that 'if there was any more hanging back I would remove them from their commands and put in more energetic personalities'.

This was unfair on both Lumsden and his commanders, many of whose tanks were still trapped in the minefields, unable to manoeuvre with the freedom required to break free without incurring significant – and needless – tank losses. So far from

'hanging back', Lumsden was already in consultation with the
XXX Corps commander, General Leese, who was hatching a plan
– which Montgomery would later claim shamelessly as his alone
– by which the two tank divisions in the northern corridors would
break free of the minefields later that evening. In the course of
these discussions, Lumsden made it clear that the key question
was 'whether you are going to sit down and accept static phase
or whether we go for it bald-headed. We may get through where
his guns are now. It is a tremendous decision. If we don't do it
the battle just fizzes out.' Lumsden's measured appreciation of the
alternatives by which he was faced suggests that Montgomery's
defamatory insinuations about the courage of the most experienced tank commander in the Eighth Army were not only harsh
but baseless.

TWENTY-FOUR

'AN UNFORGETTABLE NIGHTMARE'

*'Some of the tanks continued to advance even after they had
been hit and set on fire, with only dead and dying men inside
them, like huge self-propelled funeral pyres, a dead man's
foot still pressing down the accelerator.'*

Dino Contini, Littorio Division captain

The Eighth Army's setbacks might have been even more serious if the Panzerarmee had been under Rommel's command at the time. But the Desert Fox was still in Germany on sick leave. In the early hours of the 24th, with all other means of communication severed, his stand-in, General Stumme was driven to the front in his staff car, accompanied only by his chief signals officer, to find out what was happening and to what extent the Eighth Army had penetrated the Panzerarmee's forward positions. At some point during the night, they blundered into a unit of the Australian Division. According to the corporal driving them, 'They told me to get out of the firing area as quickly as possible.' What happened next is unclear but it appears that the signals officer was gunned down by a sudden burst of machine-gun fire and that the driver took off at high speed with Stumme clinging to the side of the car until he fell off, the victim of a fatal heart attack. For several hours the Panzerarmee was thus leaderless – though, given the ability of the Wehrmacht to respond flexibly to any crisis, not entirely headless: by midday on the 24th, General Wilhelm von Thoma, the commander of the Afrikakorps, had been appointed on a temporary basis to take Stumme's place.

Von Thurma faced a virtually insuperable challenge. Although the British offensive had stalled, it was not about to fizzle out. In a forlorn attempt to avert the inevitable, the panzers moved back and forth along the front, hoping to find a weak spot at which to launch a counter-attack. But, where the British armour had come to a standstill, the Shermans now came into their own. For the first time in the desert conflict, the Eighth Army had a tank capable of firing high-explosive rounds to pick off the 88mm guns which had hitherto inflicted so much damage; the Sherman could also destroy the panzers in a long-range duel, with armour-piercing shells that were devastating even at a range of 1,000 yards. Armed with such superior weaponry, Montgomery had the freedom to fight a battle of attrition which was slowly but inevitably to transform the balance of power on the battlefield.

When the RAF joined the fray – flying no less than 1,000 bombing and fighter raids on the 24th alone – the German gunners reacted by using the 88mms in their original anti-aircraft role. But as their barrels reared up towards the sky, they simultaneously exposed their precise location to the British tanks and artillery which subjected them to immediate and merciless bombardment: the once mighty 88mm no longer enjoyed the tactical advantage that had made it so devastating a weapon in every previous battle.

Moreover, as Rommel had repeatedly forewarned, the panzers were also hampered by the acute shortage of fuel. No longer able to range widely and freely to make the lightning thrusts that used to cause such havoc, their need to conserve petrol combined with their relative inferiority in both numbers and technical potency now dramatically limited their ability to secure any tactical advantage against the Eighth Army.

With Rommel still on sick leave in the Austrian Alps, OKW followed the course of the battle at El Alamein with mounting concern. According to Rommel, Field Marshal Keitel rang him on the afternoon of the 24th with the news that 'the British had been attacking at Alamein with powerful artillery and bomber support since the previous evening. Stumme was missing. He asked me whether I would be well enough to return to Africa and take over command again. I said I would.' Rommel spent the next few hours in what he described as a state of 'acute anxiety' until he received a personal call from Hitler himself. 'Rommel, there is bad news from Africa. The situation looks very black. No one seems to know what has happened to Stumme. Do you feel well enough to go back and would you be willing to go?' Rommel was still in treatment for his recurring stomach ailments and, according to his biographer, was 'still a very sick man and in no condition to return to the Desert', but he at once assented. As though to reassure himself that Rommel meant what he said, the Führer rang again just before midnight to reaffirm that the enemy offensive was reaching 'dangerous proportions'. Rommel made plans to fly back the following morning. His spirits were low; defeat seemed inevitable. There were 'no more laurels to be earned in Africa', he was to write, 'for I had been told in the reports I had received from my officers that supplies had fallen far short of my minimum demands. But just how bad the supply situation really was I had yet to learn.'

At about 11 a.m. on 25 October his plane landed in Rome, where General von Rintelen (OKW's liaison officer at Comando Supremo) briefed him to the effect that, partly because the Italian navy had failed to provide the necessary shipping and partly because the Royal Navy had destroyed several supply vessels, the Axis vehicles in the desert had only enough fuel apiece for a journey of 300 kilometres. As the distance between El Alamein and the Panzerarmee's headquarters at Tripoli was five times that, Rommel was bitterly resentful. 'This was sheer disaster,' he wrote later. With so little petrol available, the Panzerarmee was 'crippled'.

By the time he landed in North Africa that evening, the news had gone from bad to worse. A devastating display of firepower from the British artillery and a relentless bombardment by the Desert Air Force had reduced the 15th Panzer Division, which had made several thwarted attempts to counter-attack, from 119 to 31 serviceable tanks. The petrol crisis was deepening and, with the sinking of yet another fuel tanker outside the harbour at Tobruk, there was no prospect of any relief. A little before midnight, Rommel sent a brief signal to every Panzerarmee unit: 'I have taken command of the army again.' This may have boosted morale but Rommel was deeply pessimistic. Nevertheless, his sole hope of staving off defeat – 'to throw the enemy out of our main defence line at all costs and to reoccupy our old positions' – was not quite so forlorn as he had allowed himself to believe.

In the early hours of the same day, the 25th, Montgomery was chafing more than ever at the failure of his armour to achieve the objective he had set them. Although the 1st Armoured Division had 'broken out' of the minefields earlier in the day, the price had been high with 'dozens of shattered burning vehicles, and dead and wounded soldiers, littering the desert'. A little to the south on the same northern flank, the 10th Armoured Division was still ensnared on Miteiriya Ridge, amid a mass of burning fuel tankers incinerated by a squadron of Stuka dive-bombers which had managed to evade the RAF's marauding Spitfires. The tanks were unable to advance beyond the ridge without taking what its commander, General Gatehouse, regarded as a 'suicidal and stupid' risk.

At 3.30 that morning, both corps commanders, Lumsden and Leese, were summoned to a crisis meeting with Montgomery, which had been hastily arranged by his Chief of Staff. De Guingand had been dismayed by the failure of the 10th Armoured Division to make any significant progress. 'I think I could count the number of times I have awakened [Montgomery] at night on my two hands. I went along to his caravan and woke him up. He appeared to be sleeping peacefully – in spite of a lot of attention from the enemy airforce outside. He told me to bring the two Corps commanders along to his map lorry.' Inside, Montgomery was sitting on a stool looking closely at a map of the battlefield which was fixed to the wall.

In his memoirs, Montgomery contrasted the performance of the two armoured divisions under Lumsden's command on the northern front. Praising the 1st Division, under General Briggs, which was 'out in the open and was being furiously attacked by the enemy armour, which was exactly what the doctor ordered', he accused the 10th Division, under Gatehouse, of finding excuses to remain hull down on the slopes of Miteiriya Ridge (as a result of which – though Montgomery failed to concede this – his

Grants and Shermans were able to repel an all-out attack by the 15th Panzer Division). In the presence of Leese and Lumsden, he refrained from making this crude comparison but – although, in de Guingand's phrase, 3 a.m. was 'not a good time to hold a conference' – he merely asked them to explain their situation. This prompted Lumsden to make clear once again that he objected to the role that Montgomery had allotted to his armour.

Montgomery's battle plan required the tanks to 'leap-frog' the infantry and advance on open ground in the hope of luring the enemy into a counter-attack which would end with the panzers being impaled on the guns of his artillery; inevitably British tank losses would be severe, but it was, he judged, the only way to achieve victory. Lumsden thought that to use tanks as bait in this way was to invite catastrophe. However, he apparently bowed to Montgomery's demands and, implicitly, also to his fellow corps commander, Leese.

Whatever Leese may have said face-to-face during this conference, the gulf between him and Lumsden (respectively personifying infantry and armour) surfaced brutally in a letter he wrote to his wife later that day. 'I'm afraid they've no stomach for a fight and are not given a lead to have the will to succeed. Sometimes I feel quite ashamed to have been in Armour [he had previously served in the Guards]. All my infantry think nothing of them.'

Montgomery then demanded to speak directly to Gatehouse by phone. Though each was to dispute what passed between them, de Guingand reported that Montgomery 'clearly and quickly made it very plain that there would be no alteration to his orders. The armour could and must get through'. In his account of their terse and tense exchange, Montgomery claims to have discovered 'to my horror' that Gatehouse was at the 10th Division's headquarters some ten miles behind his leading armoured brigades. 'I spoke to him in no uncertain voice, and ordered him to go forward at once and take charge of his battle; he was to fight his way out, and lead his division from in front and not from behind.'

Even by Montgomery's standards this libellous insinuation was cruelly unwarranted. Gatehouse may have lacked strategic perspective but he was justly renowned as one of the most fearless commanders in the Eighth Army, known to have led his units into battle careless of his own safety. His decision to pitch his divisional headquarters well behind the Miteiriya front was to avoid aggravating the congestion of vehicles by which the ridge had been saturated; a dangerous chaos of vehicles which Montgomery had failed to foresee and for which he bore significant responsibility.

At the end of their pre-dawn conference, when Leese had departed, Montgomery took Lumsden to one side and, by his own account, 'spoke very plainly to him'. Reaffirming that the armoured divisions had to break out of the minefields onto open ground, and reiterating that 'any wavering or lack of firmness now would be fatal', he concluded their exchange by warning that if either he or Gatehouse was not 'for it' then 'I would appoint others who were'. In short he required their tanks to extricate him from a critical impasse, the blame for which should properly lie with his overly optimistic battle plan rather than the lack of 'stomach for a fight' with which he charged them.

Nonetheless, despite their profound misgivings, neither Lumsden nor Gatehouse had any intention of disobeying their superior officer. The 10th Armoured Division was duly ordered to renew the offensive. The carnage was almost immediate. Within the hour, 8th Armoured Brigade came under heavy fire from no more than 400 yards away. Tanks burst into flames, providing a flaring beacon for a swarm of German bombers which inflicted further casualties. According to the official history of the Staffordshire Yeomanry, the scene was 'an unforgettable nightmare never to be erased from the memory of all those present'. At 6 a.m., despite Montgomery's instructions, Gatehouse ordered the 8th Armoured Brigade to withdraw to the relative security of Miteiriya Ridge, to avoid further losses. Either he and Montgomery had misunderstood one another or Gatehouse had refused to persist with the 'suicidal and stupid' attack which had already severely depleted his armour for no discernible military advantage.

By midday, it was clear that – from the British perspective – the 'general situation' was, in Leese's term, 'critical'. The British advance had stalled. The New Zealanders, who had fought heroically, were 'exhausted'; the South African Division had 'fought to a standstill' and its two brigades were 'now too weak for further offensive operations'; one brigade only of the Indian Division was 'as yet capable' of 'a sustained attack'; two brigades of the Highland Division 'had had a good hammering'; and the armour 'had lost a lot of tanks and had to be re-equipped for any further offensive action'.

At this point, even Montgomery realised that he could not persist with a plan that was starting to unravel at an alarming rate. Unless he could find some other way of 'breaking-out' and 'crumbling' the enemy's defences, the battle would be stalled indefinitely. Following an urgent conference with his senior commanders at the headquarters of the New Zealand Division at noon, he acted accordingly and with impressive speed. Showing an unexpected ability to think flexibly as well as clearly, he abandoned the attempt to drive forward from Miteiriya to the southwest. Instead, he ordered XXX Corps to attack to the north-west. Without conceding that he shared any responsibility for the shambles at Miteiriya Ridge, he blithely noted that his revised plan entailed a 'new thrust or axis of operations ... a switch of 180 degrees [psychologically perhaps; the physical switch was 90 degrees] ... a completely new direction of attack' which, he hoped, 'might catch the enemy unawares'.

His quick thinking justified his optimism: the Panzerarmee was taken wholly by surprise in an operation which marked the real turning point of the Battle of El Alamein. To that extent, Montgomery's decision could fairly be described as a master stroke for which – on this occasion – he deserved the credit he invariably gave himself.

Over the course of the next two days, as the British edged forward, the battle raged with ferocity and bitterness on both the northern and southern fronts. The casualties mounted on both sides and so did the stress and exhaustion of twenty-four-hour warfare, throughout which the tanks and artillery pounded away with relentless, accurate monotony. On the northern front, the infantry, with the Australians and Scottish Highlanders to the fore, slogged their way forward with extraordinary resolution from minefield to minefield, across open ground, forcing their way into the Axis defences, often fighting at close quarters, even hand to hand.

On one occasion Captain Hugh Samwell, serving with the 7th Argyll and Sutherland Highlanders, overran an Italian position. They took several prisoners. He was standing in the middle of the melee when he heard a shout, 'Watch Out!' There was a blinding explosion at his feet. Miraculously unhurt, he looked round for the sergeant who was with him. He was on his back, groaning, his leg 'a tangled mess'. One of the Italians, who had come out of the slit trench in which he had been cowering, apparently in the act of surrender, had thrown a grenade at Samwell and his men.

By his own account Samwell was overcome with a sudden fury as

> an absolute uncontrollable temper surged up inside me. I swore and cursed at the enemy now crouching in the corner of the trench; then I fired at them at point-blank range – one, two, three, and then click! I had forgotten to reload. I flung my pistol away in disgust and grabbed a rifle – the sergeant's I think – and rushed in. I believe two of the enemy were sprawled on the ground at the bottom of the square trench. I bayoneted two more and then came out again.

Even at El Alamein, the decency and chivalry which distinguished the desert campaign, did not always prevail against the rage of the moment.

Some of the fiercest fighting was around Kidney Ridge, a shallow depression to the north-west of Miteiriya Ridge which was captured by the 1st Armoured Division just before midnight on the 25th. In response, Rommel ordered units of the 15th Panzer Division and the Italian Littorio Division to retake the ridge. As the British poured fire onto the advancing tanks, the desert became an inferno, the memory of which was seared in the mind of one of the Littorio's junior officers, Captain Dino Contini:

> Some of the tanks continued to advance even after they had been hit and set on fire, with only dead and dying men inside

them, like huge self-propelled funeral pyres, a dead man's foot still pressing down the accelerator … A procession of blazing monsters, shaken by explosions and emitting coloured flashes as the shells inside went off … The souls of the dead men must have been trapped in their vehicle; how else could a smashed and blazing tank continue to advance towards the enemy?

The intensity of the British barrage forced the Axis armour to fall back. By the end of the day, the 15th Panzer Division had been shredded while one Italian regiment lost all but two of its forty-one M13s. Rommel, who had arrived at the front in time to observe the engagement, wrote afterwards with an uncharacteristic blend of horror and bemusement, 'Rivers of blood were poured out over miserable strips of land which, in normal times, not even the poorest Arab would have bothered his head about.'

The battle was no less intense in the air. Late in the afternoon of the 25th, a formation of German and Italian aircraft dived towards a column of British trucks. But some sixty RAF fighters 'pounced on these slow machines', forcing the Italians to jettison their bombs over their own lines and leading the German planes into a 'self-immolating' attempt to press home the attack, incurring heavy losses in the process. 'Never before in Africa had we seen such a density of anti-aircraft fire,' wrote Rommel. 'Hundreds of British tracer shells criss-crossed the sky and the air became an absolute inferno of fire.' At the end of the day, in a cryptic letter to his wife Lu, he wrote 'Situation critical. A lot of work! After my wonderful weeks at home it's not easy to acclimatise myself to the new surroundings and the job in hand.' Moreover he was rapidly running out of options.

The following day, the 26th, Rommel saw no alternative but to order the panzers to renew their attacks on the ridge. Finally realising that the offensive by XIII Corps (under Horrocks) in the south was probably a diversionary tactic, he summoned the 21st Panzer Division from Himeimat to reinforce his counter-offensive at Miteiriya. It was a calculated gamble as he was horribly aware that the 21st Panzers would not have enough fuel to return to the south if Horrocks were to prove him wrong.

But with the British tanks 'hull-down' and the anti-tank guns well dug in on Miteiriya Ridge, the panzers made no headway in a tank-to-tank combat of high military drama. During what he described as 'an exciting day', de Guingand stood by Montgomery's command vehicle listening to a loudspeaker which was tuned into the wireless 'net' that served the forward tanks. The chatter was instructive. 'Look out, Bob, a couple sneaking up your right flank – you should see them any moment now.' And then, after a tank commander had given the order to fire: 'Well done – good shooting – another brew up [a tank in flames].' By the end of the day both 15th Panzer and the Littorio Division had been severely damaged and the newly arrived 21st Panzer Division had been reduced from 106 to 45 serviceable tanks.

That evening Rommel wrote to his wife again: 'A very hard struggle. No one can conceive the burden that lies on me. Everything is at stake again and we're fighting under the greatest possible handicaps. However, I hope we'll pull through. You know I'll put all I've got into it.' Reflecting on the tactics adopted by the armour on each side, the leading military historian of that period, Basil Liddell Hart, commented that both armies 'successively provided an object lesson in the cost and futility of the "direct approach" – the offensive spirit unguided by subtlety of mind'.

To those trapped in the swirl of sand, the crump of shells and the cries of the wounded, the battlefield was confused and incomprehensible. Entire units got lost in a dense web of minefields (christened 'the Devil's Garden' by the Germans) which did more even than the Axis tanks and artillery to impede the Eighth Army's progress. Sometimes units fired on one another in mistake for the enemy; 'friendly' fire was a perpetual hazard in a featureless environment where one landmark was almost indistinguishable from another and where planes and tanks found it virtually impossible to tell friend from foe.

Sergeant John Longstaff had bitter memories of a horror which was replicated up and down the line:

I thought we'd had our chips that night. I think it was the only time I really felt I was going to be killed ... I think there was a real balls-up. They had decided that the Royal Artillery and supporting guns would give an artillery barrage to our left flank and to our right flank ... but we would go in silently. So we went in again and another bastard accident took place. An order was given for one of our platoons to attack a machine gun. They attacked it – but it was our own machine-gunners. Half of my bloody platoon was killed in that one bloody battle by my own mates.

Though the chain of command from Montgomery via corps, divisional, and brigade commanders prepared and elaborated instructions in great detail, these orders had to be modified, cancelled or ignored by battalion and company commanders in the heat of a battle where contact between one platoon and another was easily lost and where individual units found themselves unexpectedly pinned down or surrounded by enemy artillery. To the soldier at the front, in a slit trench or a tank or a minefield, the battlefield was a great and ghastly muddle. The chaos was eloquently summed up by Michael Carver, serving in the 7th Armoured Division, who wrote later, 'There was always somebody firing at something and usually somebody being fired at, but who and what it was and why was generally a mystery.'

While the fighting on the northern front continued near the coast and around Kidney Ridge, Montgomery decided to call a halt to the offensive everywhere else to refresh and regroup his forces. The New Zealand Division, led by General Freyberg, and Lumsden's armoured X Corps were both withdrawn from the front at Miteiriya Ridge. XXX Corps had endured three days of attrition on the battlefield and many of its units were close to exhaustion. 'Hard fighting had been going for the previous three days,' Montgomery was to write, 'and I began to realise from the casualty figures [4,600 in XXX Corps alone] that I must be careful.'

Once again, he also had to rethink his battle plan. From Ultra intercepts, he knew that Rommel had now brought the

reinforcements from the south up to defend the northern corridor to the west of Kidney Ridge. This meant it would be excessively hard, if not impossible, to achieve a breakthrough where he
had hoped. If his offensive was not to peter out, he would need to
change tack once again. His 'pause', as Alexander described it, was
thus to rest, replenish, and reinvigorate the Eighth Army and, at
the same time, to devise a new line of attack.

This was not what Montgomery had intended or expected.
Although he chose to lay the blame for the failure of Operation
Lightfoot squarely on the shoulders of Lumsden and his tank
commanders, this was unfair. The truth was that it had proved
impossible to use tanks in the way that he had envisaged; to
deploy them as 'an armoured shield with which to protect the
infantry's "crumbling" attacks and draw upon itself the German
armoured counter-attacks' was to court disaster. For this reason
he was forced to go back to the tactical drawing board. That he
managed to achieve this about-face without conceding that he had
made any mistakes was not only testament to his vanity but to
his remarkable powers of recovery. If he had felt any doubt, he
did not show it; he invariably gave the impression of both being
certain of victory and knowing exactly how to achieve it. In the
words of one of his senior officers, General Charles Richardson,
who saw him most mornings at breakfast, 'I don't think relaxed is
the right word because his style was in fact very taut. Of course
there was never any hurry, no flap ... His philosophy really went
like this: that a commander must radiate confidence at all times ...
and if he couldn't control his emotions and conceal his fears, then
he shouldn't be a commander at all!' Thus, as he used the 'pause'
which had been imposed upon him to recast the next stage of the
Battle of El Alamein, he betrayed no concern at all. In 10 Downing
Street, however, the atmosphere was distinctly less sanguine.

When the Prime Minister heard about Montgomery's decision
to suspend the offensive, he reacted with peevish anxiety. On 28
October the Foreign Secretary, Anthony Eden, went for a late-
night drink to Number 10, where he apparently took it upon
himself to tell Churchill that neither Alexander nor Montgomery

was 'gripping' the situation or showing the requisite offensive spirit. The Alamein battle, in which so much had been invested, was, Eden advised, petering out. Later that night Churchill drafted a telegram – 'not a pleasant one' – which he sent to Brooke for despatch to Alexander. In an accompanying message summoning his CIGS to a meeting the following morning, the Prime Minister wrote, 'The Foreign Secretary and I are agreed that this or something like it should be sent in view of the evident slowing down of the battle ... It is most necessary that the attack should be resumed before "Torch". A standstill now will be proclaimed as a defeat. We consider the matter most grave.'

As soon as Brooke arrived at 10 Downing Street, Churchill met him with what the CIGS described as a 'flow of abuse' about Montgomery: 'What was *my* Monty doing now, allowing the battle to peter out (Monty was always *my* [i.e. Brooke's] Monty when he was out of favour!). He had done nothing now for the last three days, and he was now withdrawing troops from the front. Why had he told us he would be through in seven days if all he intended to do was to fight a half hearted battle? Had we not got a single general who could even win one single battle? etc. etc.'

When he discovered that Eden was responsible for Churchill's rant, Brooke could barely contain his anger. 'The strain of the battle had had its effect on me, the anxiety was growing more and more intense each day and my temper was on edge.' Why, Brooke demanded, had the Prime Minister consulted his Foreign Secretary when he wanted advice on strategic and tactical matters? At this rebuke from the CIGS, Churchill flared up, reminding him that as Prime Minister he was entitled to consult anyone he liked. Moreover, he would chair a meeting of the Chiefs of Staff at 12.30 p.m. to discuss the issue formally.

The Chiefs duly met and Churchill at once asked Eden to repeat his criticisms and concerns. The Foreign Secretary obliged. Then it was Brooke's turn. The CIGS did not even attempt to disguise his disdain for Eden, retorting that 'the Foreign Secretary's view of the battle must have been very superficial' if he had really come to conclude that it was petering out. Outlining Montgomery's reasons for the 'pause', he laced his comments with sarcasm, wondering icily if the Foreign Secretary had 'forgotten that the fundamental principle of all strategy and tactics lay in immediately forming new reserves for the best blow?' When the South African Prime Minister Jan Smuts added his voice in support, Brooke quelled all doubters. Later that day, clearly chastened if not mollified, Churchill cabled Alexander to congratulate him on 'the resolute and successful manner in which the decisive battle which is now proceeding has been launched by you and Montgomery'.

Perhaps because he looked back on his earlier outburst with some embarrassment, Churchill excluded any reference to this incident in an otherwise comprehensive passage in his memoirs. But it was a measure of the intense strain he was under with the date of the Torch landings only a little over a week away. It remained of supreme importance to him that Rommel should be beaten at El Alamein before the Americans landed in North Africa. In his congratulatory cable to Alexander, the only hint of his underlying anxiety was when he wrote that Torch 'moves forward with complete secrecy and good fortune', adding, 'Your battle continuing at full blast will play a memorable part.'

In his diary, Churchill's physician confirmed Brendan Bracken's diagnosis that 'Winston is finding the suspense almost unbearable'. When Moran went to give the Prime Minister a sleeping pill, he was warned by the PM's staff that he would find his patient 'in an explosive mood'. They were right. 'I was with him only a few moments,' Moran wrote, 'but as I left he grunted, half under his breath: "If this goes on, anything may happen." Moran found Brooke waiting for him outside. "Is the PM all right, Charles? I thought he was going to hit me when he demanded: 'Haven't we got a single general who can even win one battle?'"'

Brooke was not nearly so confident about Montgomery's progress as he had declared himself to be at the Chiefs of Staff meeting. 'I was far from being at peace,' he wrote later. 'On returning to my office I paced up and down, suffering from a desperate feeling of loneliness ... there was just the possibility that I was wrong and that Monty was beat. The loneliness of those moments of anxiety, when there is no-one one can turn to, have to be lived through to realise their intense bitterness.' It was these doubts, which were evidently shared in other parts of Whitehall, that had led to Eden's ill-judged interference in matters beyond his competence. But the Foreign Secretary's meddling was not entirely without consequence.

While Churchill raged against Montgomery, Alexander and the resident Minister of State, Richard Casey, flew up from Cairo to the Eighth Army's tactical headquarters where Montgomery was finalising his plans for the next and final stage of the battle, which he had codenamed Operation *Supercharge*. The Eighth Army commander swiftly concluded that his decision to 'draw divisions into reserve' had caused 'consternation' in London and that Whitehall 'thought I was giving up', but left it to de Guingand to tell Casey that Whitehall should not 'bellyache'.

When the meeting broke up, Casey made the error of taking de Guingand to one side to ask whether he was really happy about 'the way things were going'. Montgomery's Chief of Staff did not appreciate this sidelong approach behind his boss's back and said abruptly 'We are certain of success.' When Casey suggested that it might be necessary to send Churchill a signal 'preparing him against the possibility of a reverse', de Guingand exploded, 'If you send that signal I will see that you are hounded out of political life!' Casey was wise enough firstly to refrain from pointing out that he was not a British politician but an Australian civil servant on secondment, and secondly to bury any thought of cabling the Prime Minister in the proposed terms. Instead he reported that both Alexander and Montgomery 'fully realise importance of achieving breakthrough at earliest possible moment and are directing themselves strenuously to that end'. Later, Montgomery commented dismissively that 'Whitehall thought I was giving up, when in point of fact I was just about to win'. And, for good measure, he added, 'I never heard what signal was sent to London after the visit and was too busy with *Supercharge* to bother about it.'

Had London been fully aware of Rommel's predicament, Casey's visit to the front would have been even less opportune. As he surveyed the remains of 'his' demesne and the noose that was tightening around him, the Desert Fox was close to despair – as nearly certain that he was about to lose as Montgomery was that he was about to win. By 27 October it was already quite 'obvious' to him that 'the British would destroy us bit by bit as we were virtually unable to move on the battlefield'. In the space of forty-eight hours two tankers and two ammunition ships had been sunk before reaching the North African coast, leaving the Panzerarmee bereft of fuel and ammunition. Not the least ironic aspect of the Desert War is that on the very day that Brooke was driven to pace about his office in an agony of apprehension lest '*his* Monty' should fail, Rommel was almost simultaneously pacing back and forth in the sands of North Africa, no less agitated by the near-certainty that Montgomery would succeed. Although the Panzerarmee's commander had sought to rally his troops, telling them, 'The present battle is a life and death struggle … I therefore require that every officer and man will give of his utmost and therefore contribute to its success,' he knew it was almost certainly in vain. On the evening of the 29th he wrote once again to his wife: 'The situation continues very grave … At night I lie with my eyes wide open, unable to sleep, for the load that is on my shoulders. In the day I'm dead tired. What will happen if things go wrong here? That is the thought that torments me day and night. I can see no way out if that happens.' At that moment, the commander of the Eighth Army was in the process of working out how best to ensure that the Desert Fox would find no way of escape.

On 30 October Montgomery sat in his caravan and wrote out his 'MOST SECRET' instructions for Operation *Supercharge*. As usual, these were a product of collaboration (notably with de Guingand), cool thinking and bold leadership. But, yet again, Montgomery was to refrain from sharing the credit with anyone else. 'I always wrote such orders myself and never let the staff do it,' he was to boast in his memoirs. Not content with such vainglory, he added with comical self-regard, 'This was the master plan and only the master could write it.' In outline, the 'master plan' was neither complex nor inventive nor – in so far as warfare can ever be – elegant. It relied on brute force, ruthless determination, and the will of the Eighth Army to sustain a blood-soaked slugfest. In the time available, it was also the only conceivable way to be certain of forcing Rommel to yield before the *Torch* landings began.

As drafted by Montgomery, *Supercharge* was designed to '(a) Destroy the enemy armoured forces. (b) Force the enemy to fight in the open, and thus make him use petrol by constant and continuous movement. (c) Get astride the enemy supply route, and prevent movement of supply services. (d) Force the enemy from his forward landing grounds and aerodromes. (e) Bring about the disintegration of the whole enemy army by a combination of (a), (b), (c), and (d).' Through Ultra intercepts and precise field intelligence, Montgomery knew that the Panzerarmee was in a critical condition. He had no doubts: *Supercharge* would deliver a 'staggering' blow against Rommel, from which, he asserted, 'I do not consider he will be able to recover.'

Montgomery was elated by the approaching climax. 'So far it has been a complete slogging match, carried out on an enormous battlefield,' he wrote in a private letter on the eve of *Supercharge*. In a letter to Brooke, he boasted,

> I have managed to keep the initiative throughout and so far Rommel has had to dance entirely to my tune ... I think he is now ripe for a real hard blow which may topple him off his perch. It is going in tonight and I am putting everything I can into it; I think we have bluffed him into where it is coming ... There will be hard and bitter fighting as the enemy is resisting desperately and has no intention of retiring. I am enjoying this battle ... if we succeed it will be the end of Rommel's army.

Rommel had persuaded himself that the Eighth Army's final assault would be at the northern end of the front, close to the Mediterranean, as, indeed, Montgomery had initially planned and where, in de Guingand's phrase, the 'most savage fighting of the campaign' was already in progress. Understandably but fatally, the Desert Fox was about to fall into the trap – the bluff – to which Montgomery had referred in his letter to Brooke: the full and final thrust of *Supercharge* was – in a stroke of tactical brilliance – to be launched in almost the opposite direction from that which Rommel now expected.

Montgomery had intended to unleash *Supercharge* on the night of 31 October to give Rommel no time to regroup his battered units. But General Freyberg, whom he had chosen to lead the assault, resisted. The commander of the New Zealand Division was regarded by Montgomery as 'superb ... the best fighting Divisional Commander I have ever known. He has no great brain power and could never command a Corps. But he leads his Division into battle, going himself in front ... the only way to find him in a battle is to look for a group of 3 Honey tanks in the NZ area; it will be Freyberg.' The grizzled New Zealander may have been of modest intellect but he knew how to organise a fighting unit, especially when the battlefield that was about to embrace them promised to be a Valley of Death.

He also knew that his men had been battered by the struggles around Miteiriya Ridge. He was not a man to be bounced against his better judgement. He told Montgomery, 'I will lead any infantry you like but I will not take my New Zealanders into another assault.' So far from angering Montgomery with this refusal to comply, he forced the Eighth Army commander to yield. If he was unwilling to lead his own men in *Supercharge*, Freyberg could have two British infantry brigades and a British armoured brigade instead. 'I had to bribe him brigade by brigade!!' Montgomery wrote later, with an uncharacteristic display of humour and self-deprecation, adding, 'it took me some hours to complete the bribery'. Eventually Freyberg relented. 'I could see that the old warhorse was itching to fight again,' Montgomery noted with satisfaction, 'This sort of show was very much his cup of tea and I knew he was the right man for it.'

But it was quite impossible for Freyberg to take the offensive until he had created order out of the organisational chaos which confronted him. It took time to locate the new units; the infantry was 'greatly fatigued' and the artillery was in a state of disarray. He concluded that his new division would not be ready to move off at the appointed hour on 31 October. Montgomery acquiesced without protest and delayed *Supercharge* by twenty-four hours, until just after midnight on 2 November.

Meanwhile, on the northern front, the Australian Division, under General Morshead, had been fighting tenaciously for almost a week, seeking both to 'crumble' a strongly defended German garrison near the railway track which ran close to the coast road and to retain their own positions on a crucial salient against wave after wave of counter-attacks. It was a raw and bloody struggle during which, according to de Guingand, 'no quarter was given' and individual acts of gallantry were legion.

When 2/13 Battalion came under fire from no more than 800 metres away, a platoon was despatched to eliminate the mortars and machine guns responsible. 'The Commanding Officer handed me a compass, gave me a bearing, and wished me luck,' the platoon leader, Lance-Sergeant Reginald McKellar recalled. 'Luck! – my platoon consisted of ten men plus Lady Luck.' His platoon crossed a minefield until they were close to the enemy post, at which point they came under fire. McKellar ordered his men to hurl their grenades towards the guns. 'They fell thick and heavy. The Germans were rattled and put up feeble resistance.' The patrol then rushed the mortars and captured four German soldiers, but only after 'one Aussie had a fist-fight with a German twice his size'.

The following morning the battalion found itself isolated and exhausted, without artillery or armoured support. 'Why can't our chaps be relieved?' Corporal Jack Craig complained. 'Human endurance can only stand so much. This cannot go on much longer. I wonder what the top brass really want from a human being.' But like hundreds of other stoics, Craig just endured as slowly, day by day, hour by hour, the Australians strengthened their hold on the northern salient.

By the early hours of 1 November the resulting tally of human life was scattered gruesomely across the battlefield. 'The first light of dawn revealed a sight that was none too good for chaps with weak stomachs. Dead and mutilated bodies were to be seen with burnt out guns, tanks and weapons of all descriptions,' an infantryman serving in the Australian Division reported. At a makeshift funeral service for a colleague, Captain Peter Lewis noted that when the moment came for the padre to inter his body, 'it was difficult to find a little bit of desert to bury him in, the area was so packed'.

But Morshead's men had served their purpose. By fighting indomitably, they had not only forced Rommel to withdraw the bulk of his dwindling number of panzers from the south and the centre of the El Alamein line to arrest what he wrongly supposed to be the main thrust of Montgomery's final assault, but in a battle of the cruellest attrition, the Australians had weakened his army beyond repair.

TWENTY-FIVE

THE END OF THE BEGINNING

'It's got to be done. If necessary I am prepared to accept one hundred per cent casualties in both personnel and tanks.'
General Bernard Montgomery

With the odds against them worsening by the hour, Rommel's troops fought with rare resolve and, in some cases, a remarkable degree of self-delusion. Even on 1 November, a junior officer in the Ariete Armoured Division, Second Lieutenant Vincenzo Formica, was still convinced that victory was possible:

At 1300 we had two pieces of good news, the English had tried to break through but had lost entire detachments without any result. To the north during heavy fighting with the 21st Panzers around eighty tanks had been surrounded and destroyed. It seemed that the British had given up any further attempt to break through. Our morale, always high, turned positively euphoric. Officers and soldiers who had lived through the fighting and had suffered for months in the middle of the Egyptian desert during the hottest part of the year saw finally that all their suffering and sacrifices were rewarded with the fighting man's most wanted prize: Victory. We assumed we would be launching a counter-offensive to the final victory. The word was 'Christmas at Alessandria.'

Rommel knew better. That afternoon, during a lull in the

fighting, he went to inspect the northern battlefront for himself. There was a Red Cross Flag flying on a hut by the railway line, which the Australians had named 'Thomson's Post'. He counted some thirty or forty ruined armoured vehicles scattered in the desert, but the German artillery had called a halt to their bombardment because, he noted, 'the British were obviously getting their wounded out'. That reprieve for the enemy was also a respite for his own forces. When the battle resumed, the Panzerarmee was now so short of ammunition that, to preserve its supplies, the artillery was ordered to engage the enemy with 'harassing fire only and not by concentrated fire'.

Rommel had already cabled General Rintelen, OKW's official linkman with Comando Supremo. 'Over and over again the army has pointed out the absolute necessity for sufficient provisions, fuel and ammunition. Responsibility for the present acute crisis rests squarely on those who are in charge of supplies,' he wrote in uncontained fury. It was to no avail. That evening, when he returned from the front to his headquarters, he wrote to his wife, 'Some supplies are supposed to be on their way. But it's a tragedy that this sort of support only arrives when things are almost hopeless.' The third Battle of El Alamein was about to reach its climacteric.

In Berlin and Rome, the Axis generals appeared to be inhabiting another realm of reality. In so far as they were aware of Rommel's predicament, they were incapable of appreciating its severity or doing anything on the scale required to rescue him. Mussolini was not only out of touch but ailing. On 28 October he had presided at the twentieth anniversary of his 'March on Rome' looking 'thin and tired'. It was a lacklustre occasion from which the passion which had once inspired the Fascist Party – now run by 'incapable, discredited, and questionable men', as Ciano described them – was noticeable by its absence. Not only had the fire which had once animated the Fascist Party burnt itself out but Mussolini himself had lost the animal vitality which had once excited the faithful.

Although he was momentarily roused to good humour by an 'extremely laudatory and sugar-coated' letter from Hitler to mark the twentieth anniversary of that intoxicating year when he had founded the Fascist Party to save the Italians from themselves, he was a much diminished and deflated figure. Often too frail to appear in public or so unwell that he had to cancel meetings at short notice, he was sometimes in severe discomfort. 'My father is very ill,' wrote his daughter, Edda Ciano. 'Stomach pains, irritability, depression etc.' According to his personal attendant, Quinto Navarra, 'He would on occasions abandon himself to his pain and throw himself on the floor to roll about, groaning in agony.' A woman who visited him at his residence noted that his appearance was so haggard that 'he didn't look real any more. It was like looking at a caricature.'

The condition of the Italian people, of whom he continued to despair, had also sharply deteriorated. Almost all foodstuffs were rationed and in the south the peasantry was close to starvation. When angry crowds gathered to demonstrate against the privations which fascism and the war had inflicted on them, the police reacted with violence, firing volleys over their heads to disperse them. In increasing numbers, intellectuals were emboldened to face arbitrary arrest and imprisonment for voicing anti-fascist sentiments. Communists produced samizdat newspapers and painted slogans on public buildings demanding liberty and peace. This surge of unrest merely confirmed Mussolini's conviction that the Italians were a degenerate race, capable only 'of singing and eating-ice cream'; his army was 'useless', his generals were 'paralytic' and his admirals were even worse. His subjects returned the compliment by concluding, in the words of his biographer, Christopher Hibbert, that Il Duce 'must be a part of every rankling injustice, every defeat, every hardship, every fresh disaster that showed the Fascist system which he had created was not capable of dealing with the emergency into which he had plunged it'.

In so far as Mussolini focussed at all on El Alamein, it was with a glassy, self-delusional stare. By 30 October Cavallero – hitherto the wildest of optimists – had reached the conclusion that defeat was inevitable and that 'the end of the army' was imminent. But Il Duce's Chief of Staff evidently failed either to share this insight with his commander-in-chief or to reconnect him with reality. On 1 November, a few hours before the launch of Operation *Supercharge*, Rommel received a signal from Cavallero: 'Il Duce authorises me to convey to you his deep appreciation of the counter-attack led personally by you. Il Duce also conveys to you his complete confidence that the battle now in progress will be brought to a successful conclusion under your command.'

Hitler was equally out of touch, but for different reasons. As Mussolini celebrated the twentieth anniversary of the Fascist Party, the Führer was preparing a similar ritual to mark the anniversary of his 1923 putsch. In thrall to his grotesque sense of indomitability, he had taken to contrasting himself with Kaiser Wilhelm, whom he dismissed as 'a man lacking the strength to resist his enemies'; in contrast, he bragged that 'in me they have found an adversary who does not even think of the word capitulation'. The Führer was more than ever obsessed by the titanic struggle that was still underway in Russia, but where the Wehrmacht was beginning to falter. In the north, the people of Leningrad, some of whom had been driven by starvation into acts of cannibalism, had nonetheless failed to succumb; the siege of the city, though it would not end for another fourteen months, was starting to hurt the attackers as much as the defenders. In the south, the twin thrusts into the Caucasus and towards Astrakhan via Stalingrad had both been arrested hundreds of miles short of their final destinations.

After seizing Sebastopol and Novorossiysk, Panzergruppe von Kleist's slow advance was starting to splutter out in the foothills of the Caucasian mountains. So far from seizing the Black Sea littoral and the western shore of the Caspian Sea, as Hitler had ordered, his fifteen divisions had stumbled to a halt at Nalchik, some 450 miles short of the oil wells at Baku, and very far indeed from his vision of seizing Britain's Empire in the Middle East.

At Stalingrad, where the ferocity of the fighting knew no limits and had already reached unspeakable levels of depravity, General Paulus's Sixth Army was unable to finish the other great task set by Hitler, to 'smash' the Red Army and occupy the city. On both sides of this terrible encounter on the Russian steppe, young men were forced to the limits of endurance by the manic ruthlessness of both Hitler and Stalin. Grappling with each other in close combat, struggling across every pile of rubble and through every ruined cellar, they fought for every inch of every street. Stalingrad was filled with the stench of dead bodies and blood. It was an urban killing ground of unspeakable horror but, with winter approaching, the Russians were slowly gaining the advantage.

Despite the overwhelming evidence that his grand vision was crumbling about him, Hitler forbade any discussion which suggested that, in Stalin's Red Army, the German panzers may have met their match. When his Army Chief of Staff, General Halder, tried to point out that the Russians were thought to be preparing a massive counter-attack at Stalingrad, Hitler accused him and his colleagues of cowardice. When a formal statement was read to him which showed that the Russians were likely to muster at least another million men on the Stalingrad front and a further 500,000 in the Caucasus, the Führer 'flew at the man who was reading, with clenched fists and foam in the corners of his mouth and forbade him to read such idiotic twaddle'. So tenuous was his hold on reason, that according to Halder, his decisions no longer bore any relation to strategic reality but 'were the product of a violent nature which acknowledged no bounds to possibility and which made its wish father to the deed'. For failing to comply with the implications of this military madness, Halder was summarily dismissed on 24 September.

His successor, General Zeitzler was more amenable. For this reason, if the Führer's senior staff officers so much as glanced at what was happening at El Alamein, it was through the prism of Hitler's hallucinatory conviction that victory was as inevitable in the Middle East as it was in Russia: Rommel was a military magician who, by one means or another, would always conjure victory out of prospective defeat. As a result, urgent warnings from the German Naval Command that the situation in the Mediterranean had become critical were dismissed by OKW as 'overly pessimistic'. Thus, like Hitler, they were wholly unprepared for the shock which was about to shatter this collective delusion.

At precisely 1.05 a.m. on 2 November, under cover of an artillery barrage from 360 guns, Freyberg ordered his men to advance from their 'start line' near Kidney Ridge towards the Rahman track which ran north to south from the Sid Abd el Rahman mosque near the coast towards the Qattara Depression. This lateral 'highway' through the rocks and boulders strewn across this part of the desert still lay behind Rommel's retreating front line, allowing him rapidly to redeploy his dwindling forces to fill the breach at any point where the Eighth Army might try to pierce a way through. To seize the Rahman track would eliminate that tactical expedient.

The initial attack was led by two infantry brigades. 'As far as could be seen, to both left and right of us, men were advancing with their rifles in port position, their bayonets glinting in the pale moonlight,' Roy Cooke, serving with 5th Seaforth Highlanders, noted. 'As we advanced the feeling of pride and exhilaration was unmistakable. We didn't realise or think of the danger we were in; we were doing a job, and the thought of being killed or wounded was far from our minds ... There were reddish coloured explosions ahead of us and bullets, both tracer and otherwise, coming our way. I remember seeing forms sink to the ground, but our orders were to keep going and not to stop for the wounded or dying.' In the early hours of the 2nd, *Supercharge* was going according to the 'master plan'.

To begin with, thanks in part to the heroic diversion created by the Australians in the north, all went well. Freyberg's men advanced at good speed along a front 4,000 yards wide and some 6,000 yards deep, protected by a creeping barrage of artillery fire. 'Twenty-five pound shells don't make a bang and a thud when they go over your head, they sound like a whiplash,' Colonel William Watson, leading the 6th Battalion, Durham Light Infantry, recalled. 'It was nerve-wracking to start with, but then the whole thing started to be like a song. The shells came over and exploded ahead of us.'

As they tramped through the acrid smoke, lurid forms emerged from the fog, walking towards them with their hands in the air, surrendering. 'I aired my schoolboy German telling them which way to go. The Italians were terrified and kept yelling out

"Madre!". It was a very cold night and we only wearing our KD shirts and shorts, yet we were all in a sweat.'

By no means all the German and Italian units in their path surrendered or fled. Watson described how 'in our keenness to get on we must have walked over lone enemy soldiers who lay doggo as we passed, and some of them killed my RSM Page and the MO who was tending him, as well as Sergeant Fairlie, who played cricket for the battalion, and young Second Lieutenant Vickers who had just joined the battalion. It was a great blow.' But, though the casualties mounted on both sides, the Eighth Army's disproportionate strength in men and weaponry was inexorable.

As dawn approached, the British infantry reached the German front line. Captain Peter Lewis recalled 'the mass of shell holes, lots of German and Italian dead. We started taking prisoners of war, some of them in a daze and hysterical. They wandered about, and unfortunately some got shot, as it was sometimes difficult to tell if they were trying to surrender or making off for a slit trench.' But Lewis was nonetheless impressed by 'the bloody good soldiers' against whom his battalion was pitted. 'One German came out of a dugout as if he had been shot out by a launcher, and came straight at me with a pistol ... One bloke waited until we had got beyond him, and chucked a stick grenade at us. One of my chaps went back and found him already dead; he had thrown it while actually about to die.'

Advancing with implacable tread, Freyberg's men fought their way slowly forward, until by 6.30 a.m., they had reached their immediate destination near Tel el Aqqaqir, a mound of slightly higher ground just to the west of the Rahman track. Here they were to form a bridgehead from where the 9th Armoured Brigade was to pierce an opening through Rommel's anti-tank defences and so lead on to victory.

But the stones and boulders which covered the sand made this task far harder than they had anticipated. As they tried frantically to dig their slit trenches, the Axis artillery opened up with furious accuracy. 'For the next five hours my group just lay as the shells came over,' one junior officer reported. 'They were dead on range. All the time we were trying to dig. It was the worst ever. Stuff was landing continually within twelve yards of us, and some shells were as close as four feet.' Despite this barrage of fire, the infantry held its ground and gradually consolidated its position. Nonetheless, *Supercharge* was faltering.

Montgomery's plan of attack required the tanks to be used as though they were battering rams, 'breaking out' from the bridgehead created by the infantry and heading directly towards the Rahman track and the formidable anti-tank shield which Rommel had positioned there. But the Eighth Army's commander had once again failed to take full account of either what this entailed or the fact that the best-laid plans on paper could not always be delivered on schedule in the desert. On this occasion, however, he had been given due warning.

At the pre-battle briefing, Freyberg had conceded, 'We all know that for armour to attack a wall of guns sounds like another Balaclava; it is properly an infantry job. But there are no more infantry available, our armour must do it.' In response, the commander of the 9th Brigade, John Currie, warned that he would probably lose 50 per cent of his tanks if they were to be used in this role. When Colonel Sir Peter Farquhar discovered what was expected of his 3rd Hussars, he sought out the Eighth Army commander and told him bluntly that his plan would be 'suicide'. Montgomery did not demur but merely replied, 'It's got to be done. If necessary I am prepared to accept one hundred per cent casualties in both personnel and tanks.'

Montgomery's sangfroid was about to be put fully to the test. Following behind the infantry, the 9th Brigade, with 133 tanks, trundled through the dark towards the front in the early hours of 2 November. 'It was like driving through the rush hour,' wrote one crew member. 'It was pitch dark and we were in a very thick cloud of dust. It was a real pea-souper.' Inevitably, units became separated from one another, some got lost, some broke down, and some were disabled or destroyed by enemy fire. By the time the brigade reached the bridgehead prepared by the infantry at Tel el Aqqaqir, it was almost dawn. They had arrived too late for most of them to 'break out' before sunrise, which was essential if *Supercharge* was to have the overwhelming impact which Montgomery had intended. By continuing, as they had been ordered by Montgomery and Freyberg, the 9th Armoured Brigade would soon be lethally exposed.

'We knew what to expect and that at any moment the sun would come up,' Captain C. B. Stoddart recalled. 'I gave all my crew a sip of whisky and we were off. Very slowly at first in the half light. Nothing happened for a few minutes and then hell was let loose ... I was the first of the whole regiment to be hit ... We were very nearly run over by our own friends and Jerry was shooting hard and it was not yet properly light.'

Very soon the desert turned into precisely that Balaclava to which Freyberg had so blithely referred. Currie led the charge of the 9th Brigade standing on the outside of his tank. Though it was not yet light, the German anti-tank screen soon pinpointed the advancing British squadrons. A crewman in a Crusader squadron of the Royal Wilts regiment described the moment as 'great balls of fire seem to leap out of the sand and hurtle towards the oncoming tanks. Some miss their mark and bounce on the sand. Others land with a sickening metallic clang on the Crusaders and explosions add dull thuds to the pandemonium of sounds that fills the shattered air.'

As the sun broke the horizon, the Shermans and Grants, the heavy armour, lumbered after the Crusaders into the enemy line of fire, the outline of each vehicle clearly silhouetted in the light of dawn. As they veered towards the Axis artillery, which was dug in below the skyline and virtually invisible, the anti-tank gunners targetted them one by one. Soon they became entwined with panzer units as well as the artillery. The mayhem was indeed of Crimean proportions. Private William Knowles observed the disaster as it slowly unfolded. 'The Shermans were slowly being picked off, it was a terrible thing to watch. If a tank was hit it burst into flames. I didn't see anyone get out. Some shells hit the tanks and ricocheted off, you could actually see the shell twisting over and up into the air making a peculiar noise. Then it would come down making a whirring noise ... I couldn't do anything: just sit there.' Captain Ian English a company commander with the Durham Light Infantry was similarly appalled. 'This was a ghastly sight … The Germans had marvellous targets. Within two or three hundred yards of my company about twenty tanks were hit, and not many men seemed to get out of the tanks.'

Currie surveyed the detritus caused by the folly which had been imposed on him by Montgomery. 'As far as the eye could see,' one of his senior officers wrote, 'lay the terrible record – tank after tank burning or wrecked, the smoke of their burning mingled with the cold mist, the crimson shafts from the eastern sky tincturing all objects with the hue of blood. Only here and there could Currie see a tank still defiantly shooting it out with the more distant guns and the tanks of the Afrikakorps. He was very angry, very bitter.'

Within little over an hour, the 9th Armoured Brigade had lost seventy-five of the ninety-five tanks with which Currie had begun the charge, while 230 officers and men were dead from an original total of 400. Statistically this was even more than the 50 per cent losses that Currie had predicted, though short of the 'one hundred per cent casualties' his commander had been willing to accept. Oddly, however, his anger was not directed at either Montgomery or Freyberg. Instead, in the heat of the moment, he turned his ire on Brigadier Arthur Fisher, whose 2nd Armoured Brigade was supposed to have followed the 9th into the doomed assault but which was nowhere to be seen. When the leading regiment of Fisher's brigade eventually reached Currie's position, the 9th's commander called up its commanding officer, Lieutenant Colonel Gerald Grosvenor. 'Well, we've made a gap in the enemy tank screen, and your brigade has to pass through, and pass through bloody quick,' Currie fumed. Surveying the litter of burning tanks around them, Grosvenor retorted drily, 'I have never seen anything, sir, that looks less like a gap.'

Later, writing as though the 9th Division's valiant self-immolation had been an act of atonement for earlier failures by the British armour, Montgomery commented portentously, 'If the British armour owed any debt to the infantry of the Eighth Army, the debt was paid on 2 November by 9th Armoured Brigade in heroism and blood.' But many of Montgomery's peers not only thought that no such debt was owing but that Currie's suicidal charge had inflicted on his men a price which was far too high for what little they had been able to achieve. In another age, Montgomery's conduct would assuredly have merited a formal inquiry if not a court martial. Currie himself seemed almost to acknowledge this when he wrote simply, but with restraint and pride, 'This action, condemned by many as an incorrect and costly way of using armour, was fought to a finish with great gallantry and devotion to duty.'

Freyberg remained stolidly immune to the calamity which had befallen the 9th Brigade. Instead he urged the 1st Armoured Division's commander, General Briggs, to take over where Currie had left off. But Briggs had no intention of emulating such reckless gallantry. 'The plain truth is that armour cannot charge concealed or semi-concealed guns just behind a crest and get away with it,' he declared later. 'These have to be dealt with methodically by stalking, High Explosive fire and artillery concentrations and this takes time.' Briggs was adamant that if he had followed Currie's lead – as Montgomery had planned – his tanks would have suffered a similar fate for very little, if any, tactical advantage. Despite the protestations of Freyberg to the contrary, the evidence is compellingly in favour of Briggs. Either way, despite the Eighth Army's massive preponderance of men and weapons, *Supercharge* had stalled.

None of this gave comfort to Rommel, who knew with certainty that the battle of attrition to which his exhausted forces were now committed could have only one outcome. By his own account it was only by the desperate firing of all available artillery and anti-tank guns, regardless of the ammunition shortage, that a further British penetration was prevented. His headquarters had very little idea of what was happening along the front as a combination of the RAF and British artillery had severed the Panzerarmee's lines of communication while the engineers had jammed its radio frequencies. As a result, 'complete chaos' reigned at many points along his line of defence.

Nevertheless the Desert Fox still tried to seize the initiative. Taking advantage of the British armour's loss of momentum at Tel el Aqqaqir, he summoned virtually all that was left of his Panzer-armee to a last-ditch attempt to halt the Eighth Army's offensive. In mid-morning the 21st Panzer Division launched a desperate counter-attack at Tel el Aqqaqir against the 2nd Armoured Brigade and the remnants of the 9th.

As a test of endurance, the tank battle which ensued rivalled any other such encounter of the Second World War. 'For hours on end the whack of armour-piercing shot on armour plate was unceasing,' the 9th Lancers official history was to relate. 'Then the enemy tank attacks started. Out of the haze in serried lines they came, the low black tanks ... It went on like this through-out the day, tanks regularly running out of ammunition and the lorries rushing forward to replenish them.' But, with the British tanks outnumbering the panzers by at least four to one, there was no doubt about the outcome. As the official report of Rommel's 90th Light Division stated, 'Smoke and dust covered [the] battlefield and visibility became so bad that the general picture was of one immense cloud of smoke and dust. Tanks engaged in single combat; in these few hours the battle of Alamein was decided.'

The Eighth Army's superiority in infantry and tanks was matched in the skies above the battlefield, where the RAF's Desert Air Force flew back and forth at will over the Panzer-armee's positions, wreaking havoc on the vehicles and command posts below and inflicting significant psychological damage in the process. One bombing raid alone, in the mid-afternoon of 2 November, prompted 200 German infantrymen to throw down their arms and surrender. 'Where are our fighters, our Stukas and AA?' a German artillery officer wrote in his diary, 'Can't see a thing of them. Tommy comes every quarter of an hour with eighteen heavy bombers.' On that day, the Desert Air Force flew a total of 881 bomber and fighter sorties (against the Luftwaffe's 175) and dropped a total of 352 tons of bombs (against 20 tons). Even Rommel was affected by the constant roar of the bombers flying overhead, complaining that within the space of less than an hour 'seven formations each of 18 bombers, unloaded their bombs on my troops'. When General Horrocks visited Eighth

Army headquarters he found Montgomery relaxing in a deck-chair watching the bombers flying overhead. 'They are winning this battle for me,' he said.

As the day wore on, two of the better Italian divisions – the Littorio and the Trieste – began to disintegrate under the relentless bombardment. One unit after another fell back and then turned to flee from the front line, their resistance broken. At 2 p.m. on the 2nd, Rommel was forced to summon the Italian Ariete Armoured Division, to join the panzers at Tel el Aqqaqir. As he set off towards the front, Lieutenant Formica, who only a day earlier had been confident that 'Alessandria' would be in Axis hands by Christmas, was in a very different frame of mind. 'Long columns of vehicles belonging to different detachments and even different divisions were moving in such a chaotic way as to make it apparent that they were not detachments moving in an ordered fashion towards set objectives. Conditions (bad visibility, vehicles clogging up with sand, accidents) were appalling. From my vehicle I could see soldiers on my right who were exhausted and silent.'

By the end of the day, Rommel had lost a total of 117 tanks, including 77 panzers; his elite Afrikakorps was reduced to 35 serviceable tanks. Exhausted and crippled by a shortage of men and material, he judged that the Panzerarmee would no longer be 'capable of offering any effective opposition' to the Eighth Army's next attempt to break through. That evening he wrote despairingly to his wife, 'Very heavy fighting again, not going well for us. The enemy, with his superior strength is slowly levering us out of our position. That will mean the end. You can imagine how I feel.'

For once even the Desert Fox could not imagine any way out of his predicament except to withdraw in as discreet and orderly a fashion as possible. This would not be easy. Already thousands of Italian infantrymen had surrendered, walking with their hands held above their heads towards the British lines; others were fleeing haphazardly across the desert towards the certainty of extreme hunger and thirst and very often death. Without enough vehicles or fuel to transport those who were still at their posts, Rommel had little choice but to order the Panzerarmee's infantry – Germans and Italians – to begin the retreat towards a new defensive position which he hoped to establish at Fuka, some fifty-five miles along the coast to the west.

That evening he signalled Comando Supremo in Rome to advise that he had no choice but 'to extricate the remnants' of the Panzerarmee but warning that it would be impossible to save many of his Italian units from destruction at the hands of the enemy. He also cabled OKW in similarly stark terms. With fuel for less than two days and an acute shortage of ammunition, he explained that he intended to lead his entire force back to Fuka to avoid annihilation by the combined might of the Eighth Army and the RAF. 'In this situation,' he concluded, 'I have to reckon with the gradual destruction of the army, in spite of its heroic resistance and the troops' exceptional spirit.' This dreadful – almost unbelievable – news had a devastating impact in Berlin.

In the early hours of 3 November, OKW received a further message from Rommel reporting that the withdrawal had started at 10 p.m. the previous evening. But the message did not reach General Warlimont, the Führer's Deputy Chief of Operations Staff, until 9 a.m. because the desk officer on duty failed to recognise its significance. As soon as he read the terrible news, Warlimont sent Rommel's cable to his immediate superior, General Jodl, who passed it on to Hitler's Chief of Staff Field Marshal Keitel, who in turn took it to Hitler.

At 12 p.m., Hitler's adjutant stormed into the office where Warlimont had just begun his daily briefing to demand an explanation for the delay. He was followed soon afterwards by Hitler himself, who was almost beside himself with fury. Blaming Keitel for the late delivery of the message, he instructed the Supreme Commander to stay behind after the midday conference, at which point the Führer yelled at him 'in such a hysterical tone that his words could be clearly heard through double doors'. Soon afterwards, Warlimont was summoned to appear before the Führer along with the hapless major who had been responsible for the inadvertent delay in forwarding Rommel's message to Hitler's office. Detecting a conspiracy by OKW to conceal the truth until Rommel's decision had become a fait accompli, Hitler demanded an explanation for what had happened, threatening that if he

failed to tell the truth, the major would very soon be a dead man.
The truth soon emerged, but it did nothing to mollify the Führer.
The major was posted to a detention battalion, and Warlimont was
summarily dismissed from his post without being given a chance
to explain his innocent part in what had occurred. Later, Hitler was
persuaded to countermand these orders but, in a rare moment of
defiance, Warlimont initially refused to accept his reinstatement.
However, he was soon obediently back at his desk.

Hitler found it impossible to digest the fact that Rommel – his
favourite soldier on whom he had lavished great honours and high
praise – could really have been outfought to the point of defeat on
the battlefield; it was out of the question. He therefore despatched
a message to Rommel which betrayed both great ignorance and
pathetic hubris:

> It is with trusting confidence in your leadership and the
> courage of the German–Italian troops under your command
> that the German people and I are following the heroic struggle
> in Egypt. In the situation in which you find yourself there
> can be no other thought but to stand fast, to yield not a yard
> of ground and to throw every gun and every man into the
> battle … Your enemy, despite his superiority, must also be at
> the end of his strength. It would not be the first time in history
> that a strong will has triumphed over the bigger battalions. As
> to your troops, you can show them no other road than that to
> victory or death.

Rommel declared himself to be 'stunned' by Hitler's ludicrous
demands. He was also outraged. 'This order demanded the impossible,' he wrote. 'In spite of our unvarnished situation reports, it
was apparently still not realised at the Führer's H.Q. how matters
really stood in Africa … for the first time during the African campaign I did not know what to do.' For several hours he was tormented by the enormity of the dilemma Hitler had forced on him.
Eventually, however, he persuaded himself that, since he demanded
unconditional obedience from others he should apply the same
principle to himself. Calling a halt to the retreat, he ordered all

units to turn and face the enemy once again – even though he was well aware that every soldier under his command would know that further resistance was pointless. 'A kind of apathy took hold of us,' he wrote, 'as we issued orders for all existing positions to be held on orders from the highest authority.'

That night, in his last letter to his wife from El Alamein, he wrote, 'Dearest Lu, The battle is going very heavily against us. We are simply being crushed by the enemy weight ... At night I lie open-eyed, racking my brains for a way out of this plight for my poor troops. We are facing very difficult days, perhaps the most difficult that a man can undergo. The dead are lucky, it's all over for them. I think of you constantly with heartfelt love and grati-tude. Perhaps all will be well and we shall see each other again.'

Rommel was still in a state of perplexed fury when Kesselring arrived at his headquarters on the following morning, the 4th. When the Mediterranean C-in-C opined that Hitler's experience on the Eastern Front had taught him that, even in the direst situ-ation, his armies should hold the line at all costs, he could not contain himself. 'So far I've taken it for granted that the Führer left the command of the army to me. This crazy order has come like a bombshell. He can't just blindly apply experience he's gained in Russia to the war in Africa. He really should have left the deci-sion to me.' Kesselring sought to mollify Rommel by saying, 'I would be inclined to regard Hitler's order as an appeal, rather than a binding order.' When Rommel demurred, Kesselring insisted, 'The Führer cannot have intended for your army to perish here.'

Later, Rommel came to the conclusion that the real explana-tion for Hitler's 'crazy' diktat sprang from OKW's habit of subor-dinating military imperatives to propaganda priorities. 'They were simply unable to bring themselves to say to the German people and the world at large that Alamein had been lost, and believed that they could avert its fate by a "Victory or Death" order.'

In Whitehall, there was euphoria as it became clear that the Desert Fox was finally on the run. Two days before Rommel gave his order for a full retreat, Brooke had received a personal letter from Montgomery:

A real hard and very bloody fight has gone on now for eight days. It has been a terrific party ... I have managed to keep the initiative throughout, and so far Rommel has had to dance entirely to my tune; his counter-attack and thrusts have been handled without difficulty up to date. I think he is now ripe for a real hard blow which may topple him off his perch. It is going in to-night and I am putting everything I can into it ... If we succeed it will be the end of Rommel's army.

At lunchtime on the 3rd, while he was doing the rounds of various military units in the south of England, Brooke was called to the telephone to be told that Ultra decrypts of messages Rommel had sent OKW and Hitler showed him to be in desperate straits. 'It can be imagined what the receipt of this ... meant to me. I dared not allow myself to attach too much importance to it, but even so felt as if I were treading on air for the rest of that day,' he noted. The following morning he was summoned to see Churchill, who showed him an intercept of Hitler's notorious 'Victory or Death' order. 'PM delighted,' Brooke noted. Later Alexander cabled Churchill with the news for which he had waited so long. 'After twelve days of heavy and violent fighting the Eighth Army has inflicted a severe defeat on the German and Italian forces under Rommel's command. The enemy's front has broken.'

The Prime Minister was so elated that he summoned Brooke once again to propose that the church bells of Britain should at once be rung out in celebration. Brooke implored him to wait until they were quite certain of victory. That evening in Downing Street, the CIGS found the Prime Minister in 'a great state of excitement' as he dictated messages to Roosevelt, Stalin, and a host of other luminaries. He also cabled Alexander to congratulate him and his 'brilliant lieutenant', Montgomery on masterminding 'an event of the first magnitude ... which will play its part in the whole future course of the World War. If the reasonable hopes of your telegram are maintained, and wholesale captures of the enemy are maintained and a general retreat apparent,' he continued, 'I propose to ring the bells all over Britain for the first time this war. Try to give me the moment to do this in the next few days. At least 20,000 prisoners would be necessary.' Then, in a reference to the wider importance of this, he went on, 'You will realise that such a demonstration would be timely in the immediate advent of "Torch", both in encouraging our friends in the "Torch" area and in taking the enemy's eyes off what is coming to him quite soon.'

Brooke was almost as elated. 'The Middle East news has the makings of the vast victory I have been praying for. A great deal depends on it.' The CIGS hoped and expected that the victory at El Alamein would make a salutary impression on the Vichy French in North Africa and on Franco (whose ambiguous 'non-belligerency' was a persistent cause of anxiety); if so, the prospects for *Torch* would be greatly enhanced. 'And if "Torch" succeeds' he noted, 'we are beginning to stop losing this war and working towards winning it.'

When General von Thoma, the commander of the Afrikakorps, received Rommel's' 'No Retreat' order – 'You are to fight to the utmost … You have got to instil this order into your troops … they are to fight to the very limit' – he was incredulous. 'The Führer's order is unparalleled madness. I can't go along with this any longer,' he fumed at his Chief of Staff, Bayerlein. The entire Panzerarmee was left with at most 80 tanks to face some 600 on the British side. Rommel's shock was the greater because Wehrmacht commanders were accustomed to using their own initiative in seeking to realise the Führer's directives; Hitler's message was not only 'madness' but, at the worst possible moment, violated this well-established procedure.

However, by the early hours of 4 November, von Thoma had deployed his severely depleted armour to form a thin defensive line alongside what was left of the 90th Light Division and the Italian XX Corps (consisting of the Ariete and the surviving remnants of the Littorio and Trieste Divisions). After a battle lasting more than three hours, the Panzerarmee still held the line against a British infantry attack which was supported by 200 tanks. By midday the once-mighty Afrikakorps had been reduced to a mere two dozen battle-worthy panzers.

Bayerlein was at Rommel's headquarters when he received

news that von Thoma's force had been virtually wiped out. He leaped into a reconnaissance vehicle and hastened to the front, where he saw the Afrikakorps commander standing alongside one of his burning tanks. As he approached, a British machine gun turned its fire on his vehicle. Bayerlein ordered his driver to beat a swift retreat. A few moments later, Grant Washington Singer, a captain in the Tenth Royal Hussars, arrived at the scene in his scout car. The Afrikakorps commander was still standing where Bayerlein had left him, upright and immobile. Not recognising von Thoma, Singer described how he was accosted by a 'distinguished looking chap, rather forlorn [who] came out of the dustcloud, wearing field uniform and equipment, not like a British brass hat.' The general handed over his pistol to Singer and the two officers shook hands.

That evening, as Churchill celebrated in London, the German commander was invited to take dinner with Montgomery. Ever quick to seize a photo opportunity, his host arranged for the cameras to snap him shaking hands with his prisoner. When the pictures appeared in the British press, Brendan Bracken, Churchill's Minister of Information, wrote disapprovingly to the Prime Minister. 'The incident, trifling in itself, roused an altogether disproportionate amount of disapproval,' he commented, 'Montgomery remains the hero of the hour, but that he should entertain a German general to dinner and allow himself to be photographed receiving him appears to have struck the home public as symptomatic of an attitude they fear and resent.' However Churchill, who admired von Thoma, was unruffled and would assuredly have been even less inclined to heed Bracken's stricture, had he known that two days earlier, on hearing that Singer had been killed in action, von Thoma wrote a letter of sympathy to the captain's mother: 'I shall always keep an honourable memory of this knightly foe on the battlefield, who also took me to General Montgomery, and beg to express my sincere sympathy with you, most honourable gracious lady.' This was chivalry of a Churchillian order.

Not every German prisoner was treated so considerately. Among the 20,000 prisoners captured in the Third Battle of El Alamein, Corporal Fritz Neumaier, reported that, though he and his fellow prisoners were treated well enough to start with, 'as we went back towards Alexandria our treatment became progressively worse. At one point we had rotten tomatoes thrown at us and were hit by rifle butts when we had to get into trucks.' According to Fritz Zimmermann, a gunner in the 15th Panzers, 'We were driven like cattle in a pen. It was very cold and we had no blankets … a British soldier wanted to shoot us all. But one of our men spoke English and told him we were under the protection of the Geneva Convention [the Third, signed in 1929] … but he still took watches and rings and other valuable things from us. Somebody protested and he was hit. So we went into captivity with a heavy heart. But many of us were glad that the fighting was over'.

However magnanimity in victory was not entirely absent. A lieutenant in the Italian Folgore Parachute Regiment, which had earned a fearsome reputation for itself, described what happened when his unit surrendered. 'The British separated us according to rank. One British soldier took my dagger then felt my tunic, looking for more hidden weapons. He found the parachute badge that we had been told to remove from our sleeves. "Folgore" he said, and, obviously impressed, he picked up my dagger and handed it back to me – an honour of the kind that we'd never had from our own lousy government. I shall never forget that moment. The British soldier's gesture was worth more than a medal to me.'

As German and Italian prisoners streamed eastwards into captivity or westwards towards the Libyan border in varying degrees of disorder, the Eighth Army finally burst through what remained of the German defences in both the north and the south. The final assault was spearheaded by the 5th Indian Brigade and the Argylls, who finally seized Tel el Aqqaqir. Squadrons of armoured cars accelerated across the desert laying waste to those enemy units which had not already melted away in front of them or offered themselves up for surrender. 'It was full daylight and getting among the soft transport vehicles, our work of destruction began,' a Highlander reported with relish. 'In the first quarter of an hour the two squadrons destroyed forty lorries, simply by putting a bullet through the petrol tank and setting a match to the leak.' When their own lorries got bogged down in soft sand, their crews commandeered German and Italian vehicles and forced their 'pan-icked' occupants to lie in nearby slit trenches. There were no nice-ties. 'We had no time to take prisoners. We just took their weapons and told them to start walking east. Only those who refused were shot. Few refused.'

With the British armour carving a swathe through the ruins of the Axis defences from south, centre and north, the Panzer-armee was almost encircled and facing the risk that its only line of retreat into Libya would very soon be blocked. At 3.30 p.m. on 4 November, at about the same moment as Alexander sent his victory message to London, Rommel bowed to the inevitable. Defying Hitler's 'crazy' instructions, he ordered a general retreat to avoid the mass surrender or annihilation of his entire army.

Initially, the Panzerarmee's retreat from El Alamein was disorderly to the point of chaos as infantry and armoured units scrambled for the same narrow avenues of escape. In their urgency, soldiers who had fought with cold tenacity at the front now muscled one another aside as they tried to scramble aboard those few trucks which were not already overflowing with the sick and wounded.

To cover their retreat, the remains of the Afrikakorps and the Ariete Division were ordered to hold the line for as long as pos-sible. Second Lieutenant Formica found himself at the front just before dawn. Unaware of the disaster by which the Panzerarmee was now engulfed, he watched in disbelief as 'vehicles of every sort crossed my path, with men on board who were pale and bat-tered … I had the impression that the whole of our line had given up. It seemed impossible! And my division, the glorious Ariete? There they were stationary in front of the enemy while all around them pulled back … Our orders were to resist to the bitter end – the classic order of a desperate situation.'

When they were little more than 2,000 yards from the British front line, Formica's commanding officer pointed out the enemy tanks, hull down in the sand. 'I saw the enemy for the first time, silent and still like a treacherous wild beast, half hidden in the early morning mist.' He also saw German soldiers retreating on foot, 'very tired but in perfect order while enemy shells were landing between their lines'.

Rommel, who was rarely disposed to speak well of the Italian components of the Panzerarmee, made an exception of the Ariete Division, which now found itself facing a hundred heavy tanks, supported by a constant barrage of artillery, for which the light and inefficient Italian armour could offer no riposte. Nonetheless it was not until the middle of the afternoon that the Italian division signalled Rommel: 'Enemy tanks penetrated south of Ariete. Ariete now encircled.' There was then radio silence. One by one the Italian tanks were blown up or split asunder. By the evening, XX Corps had been completely destroyed after what Rommel described as 'a very gallant action'. Of the Ariete, he wrote with rare generosity, 'we lost our oldest Italian comrades, from whom we had probably always demanded more than they, with their poor armaments, had been capable of performing'.

Formica stayed at the front until the end, recalling proudly those who had fought and perished in the Ariete Division, 'It will never be said of them that they retreated.' As he joined the dejected throng, he was moved by the distress of those whose only means of escape was by foot. At one point he came across a unit of the Bologna Infantry Division. 'It was a truly pitiful scene when all those men desperate from thirst and exhaustion went down on their knees around me so that I could give them a drink,' he wrote. Their elderly commanding officer, wizened and wearing a black patch over his left eye, the other sharp with resolve, commented bleakly, 'We officers have other spiritual resources but for my soldiers, poor things, they only can think of their thirst.' The zealous second lieutenant forbore to recount whether or not the one-eyed officer took on water himself. In any event, the battlefield was everywhere spattered by such harrowing scenes as the defeated foot soldiers of a once awesome army stumbled out of Egypt to begin the arduous trek back towards Tunis, 1,800 miles to the west. None of them would see Egypt again.

The next morning, 5 November, with the Panzerarmee in full retreat and the Eighth Army in cautious pursuit, Corporal Wagnell, serving in the Royal Army Service Corps (which had the crucial role of providing transport and supplies), passed 'the wrecks of vehicles and tanks … In many places the dead were as yet unburied, lying starkly on the ground, and once we had to swerve to avoid a couple on the road.' Later they came on a great store of German supplies or, 'a great deal of loot', as Wagnell put it.

> Personnel of *all* [his emphasis] ranks were out to see what they could find. In a German camp on the beach were many tents which clearly showed how hastily the enemy had evacuated the place. Tables laid for a meal, clothing and equipment strewn about in great disorder. There were bottles of wine and spirits … binoculars and toilet requisites. There was an abandoned Italian camp with a large quantity of clothing and whole barrels of wine … Some of our men fitted themselves out with new boots on the spot and many brought away brand new shirts, underwear etc.

As they advanced, they passed trucks filled with prisoners on their way back to Alexandria; the 'Prisoner of War cages were filled to overflowing'.

With the battlefield silent, a group of Gordon Highlanders was waiting for the arrival of its platoon commander, Lieutenant Ewen Frazer, who recalled:

> The last thing I remember … was Sgt. Dunlop calling my platoon and bringing them smartly to attention for my inspection. Of the two lines drawn up in the desert only the front line of six had made it through the ten day battle with me. They looked slight figures, tired and grey, but amazingly smart and proud. A chirpiness returned to the ranks and Pte Edwards I think called out 'We did it then Sir.' He was not being boastful and I choked back a hasty reply. 'Nae bad men' I managed. He had said it all.

On the same day, when it was too late to make any difference, a message reached Rommel from Hitler (and, in so far as it mattered, Mussolini as well) countermanding their 'Victory or Death' orders and authorising a retreat. The Third Battle of El Alamein was finally and formally over. For the first time in the Second World War, the Germans (as well as the Italians) had been comprehensively beaten in battle and, between them, the men who fought in the British, Australian, New Zealand, South African and Indian divisions which comprised the might of Montgomery's Eighth Army, could claim an unequivocal victory over the Axis enemy.

For the Panzerarmee the human cost was some 20,000 men killed or wounded and 30,000 taken prisoner, of whom 10,000 were Germans; a total of 50,000 of the 100,000 who had gone into battle twelve days earlier. Before the battle, Montgomery had calculated that the 200,000-strong Eighth Army would incur 13,000 casualties. He was not far out: the total number of those killed, wounded or listed as missing in action was 13,500 (a sacrifice endured disproportionately by the 2,827 Australians, 2,388 New Zealanders and the 2,495 men serving with the 51st Highland Division who had borne the brunt of the infantry assault).

Certain by now that the Eighth Army had taken the required number of prisoners to justify a celebration, Alexander cabled Churchill: 'Ring out the bells!' But, with the vanguard of the *Torch* armada – 400 ships in fourteen convoys – heading towards the Straits of Gibraltar, Churchill reflected how easily the near certainty of success could turn to the absolute disaster of failure (as it had at Cambrai in the First World War). That night he decided to postpone the bell ringing until he could be sure that the landings in North Africa had been accomplished without undue mishap.

Characteristically, Montgomery was to attribute the victory at El Alamein to his own military genius. Nor did he bestow many bouquets on others who had played their part in his triumph; his immediate colleagues who had helped steer the course of the battle and his predecessors who had helped shape its design were excised almost entirely from his account of the triumph over which he presided. Perhaps inevitably, the combination of a famous victory and his assiduous self-promotion ensured that 'Monty' was almost instantly elevated to the status of a national hero, hailed as one of the greatest commanders in the annals of British warfare. It is not to detract from a memorable achievement to observe that the truth is somewhat more prosaic than he would have had it be.

The future Chief of Defence Staff, Michael Carver, was to offer one of the more judicious appraisals of the 'slogging-match' at El Alamein. 'It was a battle of attrition ... It may have been expensive and unromantic but it made certain of victory, and the certainty of victory at that time was all important. Eighth Army had the resources to stand such a battle while the Panzerarmee had not and Montgomery had the determination, will power and ruthlessness to see such a battle through.'

In Germany, Hitler swiftly put the defeat at El Alamein to the back of his mind. As Rommel led his defeated army back into Libya, the Führer was in Munich to celebrate the nineteenth anniversary of the Nazi revolution by heralding an imminent triumph at Stalingrad before an audience of 'Old Combatants' gathered loyally in the city's Burgerbraukeller. Unaware that Stalin was within days of unleashing *Uranus*, the brilliantly conceived military operation that was finally to entrap Paulus's Sixth Army, he was also oblivious to the signs and portents which should have provided ample evidence that the Wehrmacht was soon to face the 'beginning of the end' in Russia. Addicted to destruction, he could think only of conquest. No realities were allowed to impede this purpose. The fact that his young combatants at the Russian Front were already strained to the point of exhaustion, demoralised, hungry, homesick and prey to disease and dysentery, was of no consequence to him. That – with a cruel winter already upon them – they were rapidly losing what little strength or stomach they might once have had for the victory that he required of them, was quite beyond his reckoning. So, when he harangued the faithful in the Burgerbraukeller on 8 November – as reports reached OKW that a huge enemy convoy was heading through the Mediterranean to an unknown destination – he assuredly believed his own rhetoric. 'I wanted to reach the Volga,' he told them, 'to be precise at a particular spot, at a particular city. By chance it bore the name of Stalin himself ... I wanted to capture it and, you should know, we are quite content, we have as good as got it!' As Stalingrad's historian, Antony Beevor, has noted, 'His speech ranked among the greatest examples of hubris in history ... The fatuous boasts about

Stalingrad ... were not merely hostages to fortune: they were to trap him into a course for disaster.'

Meanwhile, in the absence of any messages or instructions from his Führer, Rommel unburdened himself in letters to his beloved wife, Lu: 'Heading West again. I'm well in myself, but you won't need to be told what's going on in my mind ... What will become of the war if we lose North Africa? How will it finish? I wish I could get rid of these terrible thoughts.' With the Führer's own terrible thoughts elsewhere, Rommel's fateful questions were left to hang in the air.

In Italy, Rommel's failure to hold the line at El Alamein caused consternation. On 3 November Ciano noted, 'A new and more violent English attack renders our Libyan situation very dangerous. Our forces are wearing out and supplies are arriving as if delivered through an eyedropper ... That crook of a Cavallero continues to give the watchword of optimism at headquarters, but on the sidelines they see the future very black.' By the 5th, Mussolini finally accepted that Rommel's forces were on the retreat. In his diary for that day Ciano noted, 'He is pale. His face is drawn; he is tired. But he still keeps his balance.' Ciano added that, 'for some time past an irrepressible pessimism has taken possession of the Italians'. On the 6th he noted, 'The Libyan retreat is assuming more and more the character of a rout ... Even Il Duce thinks that as matters stand Libya will probably be lost.' But, so far from conceding failure, Mussolini swiftly went on to assert that the loss of Libya would allow him to 'better concentrate on the defence of Italy itself'. There were no limits to his hubris.

In Moscow, the British victory at El Alamein caused no rejoicing at all. Indeed it was hardly noticed. If Stalin was impressed at all, he failed to communicate his congratulations to Churchill. His long-standing antipathy towards the British government, exacerbated by the decision to suspend the Arctic convoys in July following the disaster that struck PQ 17, had sharpened yet again in the intervening months.

On 9 October, when Churchill alerted Stalin to the imminence of both Montgomery's forthcoming offensive and the *Torch* landings, his message contained a bitter pill which even a lavish coating of prime ministerial sugar could not conceal. Pointing out that the relative success of PQ 18 (twenty-seven of the forty merchant vessels survived the U-boats and the Luftwaffe to land their cargoes in Murmansk) had been achieved only because seventy-seven warships had been employed on the operation, he advised the Soviet leader that the Arctic convoys were to be suspended forthwith, because the escort ships were now needed for *Torch*. Stalin's reply was eloquent: 'I received your message of October 9th. Thank you.' When Churchill and Roosevelt compared notes about this response, the President, who had cabled Stalin separately in similar vein, wrote, 'I am not unduly disturbed ... I have decided they [the Russians] do not use speech for the same purposes as we do.' Nonetheless, as Churchill noted later, 'The atmosphere was heavily charged with suspicion.'

This was hardly surprising, given the enormous strains placed on the Soviet Union as the Red Army prepared finally to prise the Wehrmacht from its grip on Russia. With the Caucasus still occupied by German armies, Leningrad still under siege and – though its hold was weakening – the Sixth Army still threatening Stalingrad, the Soviet leader was not only preoccupied with the Herculean struggle against Hitler's invading armies but angry about the continuing failure of the Anglo-American Alliance to commit itself to a timetable for a second front in Europe. By comparison with this urgent and overarching need, El Alamein was a small blip on a bleak and distant horizon.

In America, Roosevelt wasted little time complimenting Churchill on the victory at El Alamein. His attention was almost entirely focussed on *Torch* and, more especially, the first deployment of American troops on the Second World War battlefield. He knew that the operation was fraught with danger: what if the U-boats were to detect the Allied convoys on their way to their North African destinations? Or if a sudden storm turned gentle seas into mountainous waves crashing on the Atlantic or Mediterranean shores to imperil the landings? Or if the Germans decided to occupy Spain and seize Spanish Morocco and thereby close the Straits of Gibraltar, trapping tens of thousands of American soldiers inside the Mediterranean? Although he had refrained from campaigning during the American mid-term elections, choosing instead to remain above the fray, he was more than sensitive about public opinion: a military disaster in the Mediterranean would be a political disaster in Middle America and for him.

American attitudes towards Roosevelt's commitment to the war had evolved, but many voters were still less than wholeheartedly convinced that 'their boys' should be fighting a 'European' war. In early October, Roosevelt had written to Dr George Gallup (the founder of the American Institute of Public Opinion, later the Gallup Organization) to thank him for one of the regular confidential reports which the pollster had just sent him. 'I am a bit appalled by the percentage of people who have no idea of what the war is about,' Roosevelt complained drily. 'I am inclined to think that this group includes a large proportion of those who were referred to by a radio commentator some months ago when he said "There are three groups in this country who say they want to win the war (a) if, at the same time Russia is defeated, (b) if, at the same time, Roosevelt is defeated, (c) if, at the same time, England is defeated."' His sparkle of humour notwithstanding, the President needed *Torch* to be a success. After a low turnout, the Republicans made big gains in the November elections, winning seventy-seven seats in the House of Representatives, only seven short of an overall majority. This was assuredly a significant enough outcome to divert Roosevelt's attention from the British victory at El Alamein, which happened to coincide precisely with the announcement of the results – though, once Rommel was on the retreat, he did cable Churchill to say 'I am very happy with the latest news of your splendid campaign in Egypt.' Indeed, Roosevelt's most fulsome reaction to El Alamein was not to materialise for another four months, after he had watched a British propaganda film about the Battle. 'That new film *Desert Victory* is about the best thing that has been done about the war on either side,' he confided in a letter to Churchill on 17 March, 'Everyone here is enthusiastic. I gave a special showing for the White House

Staff ... everyone in town is talking about it; and I understand that within ten days it will be in the picture houses. Great good will be done.'

In Britain, on 10 November, Churchill seized the opportunity of a prime ministerial speech at the Lord Mayor's Luncheon in the Mansion House, to rouse the nation. 'I have never promised anything but blood, toil, tears and sweat,' he reminded his audience, 'Now, however, we have a new experience. We have victory – a remarkable and definite victory. The bright gleam has caught the helmets of our soldiers, and warmed and cheered all our hearts.' But there were few, if any, street parties or other signs of national rejoicing. Instead, in homes where the wireless had for so long brought news of setbacks and disasters, the discourse around the fireplace or over the supper table was more of relief than exhilaration. In public houses, they raised their glasses to the men who had fought and died in a faraway desert, but the hardships everyone knew were still to be endured at home, as well as on the battlefield, could not be wished away even by their Prime Minister's mellifluous oratory.

Nor did the press of events allow the government to dwell for long on the Eighth Army's triumph. Within days Churchill and Roosevelt were in detailed correspondence – and somewhat at loggerheads – over the future direction of Allied strategy following the final defeat of the Axis armies in North Africa, which they already presumed to be a foregone conclusion. Should Sicily or Italy be the focus of further operations? And, if so, how should the invasion of Europe – Operation *Roundup*, later and more famously to be renamed *Overlord* – be scheduled: for 1943 or 1944? Misunderstandings, doubts, and anxieties piled upon one another as they negotiated their way towards the next phase of the war.

But the renewed focus on these vast and complex challenges could not detract from the intense satisfaction that Churchill derived from El Alamein. The Eighth Army's victory against Rommel had proved to the world that the British could triumph on the battlefield and that Hitler was not invincible. The Americans could no longer be in any doubt that the partner with whom they were about to mount the first Allied offensive of the Second World War was a brother-in-arms to be reckoned with. And though the conduct of the war would henceforth be determined by Washington, he could savour the fact that its contours and its direction had already been defined in London. It is hard to imagine that this would have been achieved without the Prime Minister's own passion for the British Empire, an undimmed – though anachronistic – vision of Britain's role in the world which had inspired his obsessive demands for victory in the desert and of which the triumph at El Alamein formed the decisive climax.

When he advised his audience at the Mansion House, 'This is not the end, it is not even the beginning of the end, but it is, perhaps, the end of the beginning,' Churchill not only etched a potent aphorism on the collective memory of the British people, he also stated the truth – and an important one at that.

TWENTY-SIX

THE BEGINNING
OF THE END

*'All enemy resistance has ceased. We are masters of the
North African shores.'*
General Harold Alexander to Winston Churchill

Two days before the Prime Minister delivered himself of that famous phrase, Brooke made a laconic note in his diary. Concealing his relief, he wrote, on 8 November, 'This morning, the landings at Casablanca, Oran and Algiers, or rather in the vicinity of these places, were carried out almost like clockwork.' It was a momentous day, the product of immaculate planning, good timing and luck. It had been a long and troubled gestation but Operation *Torch* – the first Allied operation of the Second World War – was finally underway. Churchill had achieved his great objective: to corral the Americans into his strategic vision for victory by ensuring that the second front, which would signal the beginning of the end, should begin on the shores of North Africa rather than the French coast. *Torch* was his inspiration and without his relentless insistence it would not have been accomplished. It was a singular triumph, and as important as any he achieved in the course of the war.

Though Churchill was to describe the 'assault phase' of *Torch* as a 'brilliant success' he was soon mired in the military and political complexities of the events which followed. The struggle for victory in North Africa became a major campaign in its own right that was to take far longer and to exact a much greater toll than he or anyone else had foreseen. Nonetheless its salient features are clear enough. The initial phase of *Torch* involved a total of 110 troop ships carrying altogether 107,000 Allied soldiers, escorted by more than 200 British and American warships, which headed for three different destinations on the North African coast, running the gauntlet of U-boats in the Atlantic and the Mediterranean. Although OKW and Comando Supremo were aware of the naval build-up, they were unable to discern its purpose or timing. The planning for *Torch* had been shrouded in a veil of secrecy so tightly drawn that no word of it found its way to either Axis power. As a result, even when Berlin and Rome became aware of a military armada sailing into the Mediterranean, they had no idea of its destination until the first Allied battalions began to wade ashore on the beaches of Morocco and Algeria.

The Allied commander-in-chief, General Eisenhower, had very little idea of whether the 60,000 Vichy troops in North Africa would lay down their arms or resist. It was therefore of great immediate relief that the three Anglo-American task forces, supported by Canadians, Dutch and Free French troops, met virtually no resistance. Within hours of landing, Algiers was in Allied hands, by the following day Oran had fallen, and on the 11th – after a brief but spirited effort to repel the invaders – Casablanca surrendered to General George S. Patton, who was to become famous later as the most gung-ho of all US commanders.

But the landings were the easy part. Far more challenging, and of critical importance to the success of *Torch*, was the second stage of the operation: the advance on Tunis, 400 miles to the east. The Tunisian capital was little more than a hundred miles across the Mediterranean from the Axis air bases in Sicily. For this reason the Allied foothold in North Africa would remain tentative and fragile until this Vichy stronghold had been conquered as well. However, precisely because of the proximity of Sicily, the Americans had ruled out an initial landing at or near Tunis, judging that the threat of an aerial onslaught by the Luftwaffe posed an unacceptable risk. This caution was to prove an expensive postponement of the inevitable.

The Allies had foreseen that Hitler and Mussolini were likely to respond to the landings in Morocco and Algeria by sending reinforcements to Tunisia but they reckoned without the speed or ferocity of Hitler's reaction. By the time Eisenhower's two armies – led respectively by Patton and a far less colourful British commander, Lieutenant General Kenneth Anderson – were ready to embark on the arduous route march towards the mountainous terrain by which Tunisia was girdled, the first panzer regiments had already landed in the capital.

The news of the Allied landings had kindled near panic at OKW, where, for the first time, the dreadful implications of an Anglo-American conquest of North Africa began to sink in. Belatedly realising that if Tunis were to fall, his southern flank in Europe – in France, Italy, or the Balkans – would be exposed to an Allied invasion from North Africa, Hitler was finally roused to treat this theatre as vital to the survival of the Third Reich. By the end of December he had despatched 50,000 German troops to Tunisia, soon to be followed by a further 100,000; from Italy Mussolini contributed another 28,000 men.

Still harbouring the delusion that Rommel's defeat at El Alamein was a temporary setback and that in due course the Germans would destroy the Eighth Army and reach the Suez Canal, Hitler, so far from regarding North Africa as a sideshow, now insisted that Tunisia was 'the cornerstone of the southern flank of the European war' and was to be held at all costs.

Eisenhower needed to reach Tunis before Hitler's reinforcements had a chance to seal a vital bridgehead to the west of the capital. But his forces were waterlogged by the torrential winter rains which swept through the mountain passes through which they had to advance into Tunisia. It was not until late November that elements of the First Army, under the lacklustre command of Anderson, managed to seize an airfield some twenty-five miles to the west of Tunis – only to be routed a few days later. Anderson was over-promoted and the Americans under his command were inexperienced. Mercifully from the Allied standpoint, however, this unhappy combination was matched by a rudderless Axis command. The panzers in Tunisia lacked the inventive and incisive leadership of Field Marshal Rommel, who was still in Libya beating a rapid but nonetheless masterly retreat from El Alamein to Tunis.

Rommel had just reached Tobruk, 360 miles from El Alamein, with the remnants of his Panzerarmee when he heard about *Torch*. He was filled with dread. With his own forces 'being simply crushed by the enemy superiority' and with Eisenhower's forward troops taking the Algerian port of Bone, barely fifty miles from the Tunisian border, he concluded – prematurely – that the battle for North Africa was all but over. The following day, 14 November, he wrote again to his wife, 'What will become of the war if we lose North Africa? How will it finish? I wish I could get rid of these terrible thoughts.' He had not yet entirely succumbed to despair but he had a far clearer grasp of reality than his Führer, whose hold on reason had become more tenuous by the day.

A few days later, the retreating Panzerarmee reached Agedabia, almost 300 miles from Tobruk, remarkably unscathed despite running out of fuel. On 28 November, lacking the means to conduct an effective counter-attack against the Eighth Army, and in the absence of any directive from OKW about the future of the campaign in North Africa, Rommel flew to the Wolfsschanze, where, like a crazed behemoth, Hitler was presiding over the gruesome denouement at Stalingrad. Nine days earlier the Red Army had launched Operation Uranus, a brilliantly conceived and executed pincer movement, trapping the Sixth Army in the city itself. Hitler refused to countenance a break-out. Instead General Paulus was ordered to hold Stalingrad whatever the cost; his troops would be supplied, via an 'air-bridge' masterminded by Reichsmarschall Goering, with all the resources required to resist and in due course defeat the encircling Russian armies. Logistically Goering's plan was idiotic; its consequence was to consign scores of thousands of both German and other Axis soldiers to a slow death from starvation, disease, and hypothermia in the sub-zero conditions of the Russian winter. November was the beginning of the end for Hitler's Russian delusions. Though the full scale of the hideous catastrophe was yet to be unveiled – the Sixth Army did not officially surrender until 1 February, the day after Paulus was captured – the Russian Front in the north, the south and the east was at the point of disintegration. This was only too apparent to Hitler's craven military advisors in OKW who still did not dare to confront the truth which their commander-in-chief still denied.

This was hardly the most propitious moment for Rommel to descend on the Führer's headquarters uninvited and demanding an audience. He had not only abandoned his post in North Africa but had done so without permission – an act of insubordination which evidently infuriated Hitler – but, to make matters worse, so far from committing himself to a last-ditch stand against the Eighth Army at Marsa el Brega (50 miles to the east of Agedabia), he was planning to abandon any effort to hold the line in any part of Libya. Instead he advocated a retreat all the way to Tunis, a suggestion that was greeted with a stony lack of goodwill by his superiors in OKW. When he was summoned to the Führer's office, Rommel went even further, advising him that in due course all North Africa would have to be abandoned to the enemy. According to Rommel, the mere mention of this strategic option evidently 'worked like a spark in a powder barrel. The Führer flew into a fury and directed a stream of unfounded attacks upon us.' Rommel left the Wolf's Lair empty-handed, bemused and embittered by his treatment and with only vague promises of further assistance.

From Poland, he travelled by train with Goering to see if Mussolini would be more responsive. Still furious at OKW's refusal to grasp the realities of North Africa and at the readiness of Hitler's military acolytes to blame the troops at the front 'for their own mistakes', Rommel was revolted by Goering's behaviour on the journey as the Reichsmarschall 'plumed himself, beaming broadly at the primitive flattery heaped on him by imbeciles from his own court, and talked of nothing but jewellery and pictures.' Stalingrad had clearly slipped his mind.

At their meeting with Il Duce, Rommel was further infuriated when Goering sought to ingratiate himself with Mussolini by volunteering that Rommel had 'left the Italians in the lurch at El Alamein', to which Mussolini apparently retorted, 'That's news to me; your retreat was a masterpiece, Marshal Rommel.' However, these reassuring words were no more than that. With all available shipping and aircraft requisitioned to support the Fifth

Panzerarmee now being formed to defend Tunisia from Eisenhower's forces, Rommel was no more successful in Rome than he had been at the Wolfsschanze.

With Hitler once again obsessed to the exclusion of all else by the disintegration of his Soviet fantasies at Stalingrad, the confusion within and between OKW and Comando Supremo over North Africa reached stratospheric levels of incoherence as senior officers contradicted and countermanded themselves and each other with a fanciful abandon which suggested that none of them had any grasp of the facts on the ground. But these facts were ineluctable.

Although he was repeatedly rescued from imminent disaster by the extreme caution of Montgomery's dogged pursuit, Rommel was compelled to yield. On 12 December he abandoned the Marsa el Brega Line; by 22 January he had given up the defence of Tripoli, allowing Montgomery's Eighth Army to occupy the city without resistance; and by the middle of February his dwindling army had crossed the border into southern Tunisia, where his exhausted men took up positions along the Mareth Line, a natural defensive barrier which ran for some twenty-two miles between the sea to the north and the Atlas mountains to the south.

Against all the odds, Rommel had contrived a near-miracle. In what has been widely judged 'one of the most brilliant retreats in the history of warfare' he had led a broken army, stricken by lack of fuel, weaponry and ammunition across more than 1,800 miles of desert from El Alamein to Tunis, and it had been accomplished with minimal loss of life or equipment. In the process the Desert Fox had yet again flouted the orders of his superior officers in Berlin and Rome, he had refused to succumb to a cascade of incompetent demands from above instructing him to 'stand and fight' in the wrong places at the wrong time, and for this insubordination, he had been rebuked, defamed, undermined and excoriated. But he had saved himself and his men from annihilation.

Mercifully from Rommel's perspective, Montgomery was reluctant to make the bold moves required to finish off the Panzerarmee. Refusing to accept the risks entailed by an outflanking movement or an unexpected head-on assault, he failed to cut off the

Panzerarmee's retreat. Even the Eighth Army commander's most loyal acolytes were bemused at his failure to seize the initiative. De Guingand, his Chief of Staff, complained that 'he ought to have rounded up the enemy', and even his admiring biographer, Nigel Hamilton, has noted that a combination of 'lethargy, confusion, lack of communications and administrative chaos' – for which he absolves Montgomery from any personal blame – was responsible for the failure to prevent Rommel from reaching Tunisia. The magisterial Basil Liddell Hart spoke of the 'magnificent opportunity' which had been missed thanks to Montgomery's 'caution, slow motion, and narrow manoeuvre.' Rommel himself, while allowing that from time to time he had been put under great pressure during the retreat, attributed his escape from the Eighth Army's clutches to Montgomery's 'absolute mania for always bringing up adequate reserves behind his back and risking as little as possible.'

As it was, Rommel's reprieve meant that the Allied victory in North Africa was severely delayed. How much longer it might have taken, or whether it would have been accomplished at all, had Rommel been allowed to reach Tunisia without doing battle at El Alamein, is mere conjecture. In the event, it took until May 1943, six months after El Alamein, before Hitler's armies in North Africa were finally forced to surrender. If confirmation were needed that the Alamein slugfest was a military as well as a political necessity, it is the realisation that the final struggle for victory in North Africa would have been far more protracted and expensive had Rommel been allowed to escape from Egypt with his Panzerarmee virtually intact.

In any case, Eisenhower's armies, under the command of General Alexander (who had been transferred from the Middle East to serve as the Supreme Commander's deputy) had to fight a long series of gruelling engagements against combined German and Italian forces which had been massively reinforced from Sicily with men and materiel between November 1942 and January 1943. For a while the struggle seemed evenly balanced, worryingly so for the British CIGS, who was dismayed by the 'bad news from Tunisia'. Complaining on 21 February that 'the American troops will take a great deal more training before they will be any use', he noted that he was 'very doubtful if Alexander is man enough to pull it straight'.

Rommel was not for a moment deluded by transitory moments of tactical advantage. His sense of encroaching doom was aggravated by his rapidly deteriorating health. 'Heart, nerves, and rheumatism are giving me a lot of trouble,' he confided to his wife on 26 February. 'But I intend to stick it out as long as humanly possible.'

His men faced an impossible task: to defend a front of 370 miles – which was roughly as long as the Western Front in the First World War – against an Allied army which had almost twice as many fighting troops (210,000 versus 120,000) and eight times as many tanks (1,200 versus 150). Nonetheless he made one last attempt to dislodge the Allied forces in Tunisia. In late February, with an echo of the daring which had earned the Desert Fox his reputation, he masterminded a series of battles at and around the Kasserine Pass during which Eisenhower's inexperienced troops were forced to fall back. For a moment, it seemed that the Americans might even be routed. But it proved impossible to sustain this effort for more than a few days. When – despite his earlier fall from the Führer's favour – he was rewarded for his prowess at Kasserine with an offer to command the newly formed Heeresgruppe Afrika (the African Army Group, comprising the 1st and 5th Panzer armies), he declined.

By this time Rommel had reached the conclusion that it would be 'plain suicide' for the Axis armies to remain any longer in North Africa. On 9 March, he duly flew once more to see Mussolini (who concluded that he was a 'defeatist') and Hitler (who told him he was a 'pessimist'). Clearly 'very upset' by the Red Army's triumph at Stalingrad, the Führer not only gave Rommel short shrift but, refusing his plea to be allowed to remain at his post for a few more weeks, instructed him to take sick leave at once. Rommel was never to return to Africa.

On 20 March 1943 Montgomery launched a two-pronged attack against the Mareth Line. Uncharacteristically, he underestimated the enemy's resolve. Amid scenes of chaos reminiscent of the worst days of El Alamein, a brilliant German counter-attack forced Montgomery to call off the offensive four days later. It took a further two days before the RAF managed to inflict enough damage on the Italian and German defenders to allow the 1st Armoured Division to break through. But by 28 March the Mareth Line was in Allied hands.

With the way now open for Patton's force to close in from the west and Montgomery's from the south and east, the Allied noose started to tighten around Tunis. Although the 88,000 American troops under Patton took heavy casualties as they began to plough slowly forward, the Eighth Army moved relentlessly on the capital. On 29 March, General Juergen von Arnim (who, in Rommel's stead had been appointed to command Heeresgruppe Afrika) signalled OKW in desperation. 'Supplies disastrous. Ammunition for 1–2 days, nothing left in the depot for heavy artillery. Petrol similar, major movements are no longer permitted. No ships for several days. Supplies and provisions only for one week.'

The final assault on the capital began on 6 May. Meeting very little resistance, the Allies entered Tunis the next day. By now the Fifth Panzerarmee had virtually ceased to exist as a fighting force obliging Hitler and Mussolini finally to accept that the battle for North Africa was over. On 10 May, Hitler sent a message to Arnim, lauding the 'heroic and awe-inspiring struggle of our soldiers in Tunisia … [which] will be seen as a gallant page in the military history of Germany'. Not to be outdone Mussolini wrote of Heeresgruppe Afrika's 'stalwart heroism and unbending heroism against the enemy's superiority in numbers. History will pay tribute to these heroic acts.'

Such lavishly insincere sentiments were of little if any comfort to the 238,243 German and Italian soldiers who formally surrendered on 12 May, a loss of manpower comparable to the numbers taken prisoner by the Red Army at Stalingrad. Nor was there any other source of comfort. In his final commentary on the debacle in North Africa, Rommel wrote, 'Terrible as it was to know that all my men had found their way into Anglo-American prison camps, even more shattering was the realisation that our star was in decline and the knowledge of how little our command measured up to the trials which lay ahead.'

As long lines of German troops drove westwards either in their own vehicles or in commandeered horse-carts in search of the prisoner-of-war cages which had been hastily constructed to receive them, Alexander signalled Churchill on 13 May, 'Sir, It is my duty to report that the Tunisian campaign is over. All enemy resistance has ceased. We are masters of the North African shores.' Churchill commented, 'No one could doubt the magnitude of the victory of Tunis. It held its own with Stalingrad.' This was hyperbole of an extravagance which should have brought a blush to the cheek even of the statesman who was allegedly to say, 'History will be kind to me for I intend to write it', but Churchill's triumphalism was understandable. The British Empire had fought back and won, the Mediterranean was in Allied hands, and the 'soft underbelly' of Europe beckoned; and – to a very great degree – the vision had been his.

At the Casablanca Conference in January 1943, the Western Allies had mapped out a strategy for the liberation of Europe which was to begin with landings in Sicily and Italy. They also agreed that the invasion of northern Europe could not be undertaken until 1944. As Churchill had long intended, and as the Americans had long resisted, North Africa rather than Normandy was confirmed unequivocally as the second front from which to launch the liberation of continental Europe from the Nazi domination.

It was to take far longer and to prove far more arduous than any of the Allied commanders had imagined. Although the assault on Sicily, which liberated the Mediterranean sea lanes, took no more than a month to complete, it cost 25,000 American, British and Canadian casualties while the greater part of the Axis forces managed to escape to the mainland relatively unscathed. Even though the loss of Sicily precipitated the overthrow of Mussolini, and soon afterwards the collapse of Italian resistance, the Allies still had to fight for almost every inch of Hitler's southern flank on the mainland in what were to prove some of the bloodiest battles of the European war.

The invasion of Italy was launched on 3 September. Five days later, Marshal Badoglio, the Army Chief of Staff appointed by King

Victor Emmanuel to replace Mussolini as the country's political leader, concluded an armistice with the Allies. But the Wehrmacht, which had already occupied France following the *Torch* landings, moved rapidly to reinforce its front-line defences across Italy. It took more than a month for the Allies to secure southern Italy and another eight months of bitter fighting – notably at Anzio and Monte Cassino – before they had the upper hand in the north as well. Even by June 1944, as the Allies prepared to launch the D-Day landings in northern France, the Germans still occupied the mountainous borderlands between Italy and France. It was not until 29 April 1945 that Kesselring formally surrendered Italy to the Allies.

So far from being the Third Reich's 'soft underbelly' – assuredly the unhappiest phrase ever to escape Churchill's lips – Italy had proved to be virtually invincible. The cost in human life during the nineteen-month battle for Italy which began in September 1943 far exceeded even the worst fears of the Allied commanders. In total, these amounted to 320,000, of whom at least 60,000 were killed in action (as against 336,000 German casualties, of whom 50,000 were fatalities). Yet, though victory was hard won, the struggle for Italy helped to exhaust the Wehrmacht and, alongside the D-Day landings and the Red Army's march on Berlin, played a key part in the strangulation of Nazism.

If 'the end of the beginning' was symbolised by the Battle of El Alamein, the invasion of Italy – to which it was inextricably linked by *Torch* – may fairly be judged, along with Stalingrad, to signal 'the beginning of the end'. The end itself was announced by Churchill on 8 May 1945, the day which came to mark the liberation of Europe from the monstrous tyranny personified in Adolf Hitler.

The ultimate fates of the leading *dramatis personae* whose destinies were shaped, in a variety of ways, by the conflict in the desert reflected their diverse and conflicting roles. Some died or were killed before the end of the war, some survived to live out their final days humiliated or forgotten, others reached positions of great authority and prestige. The lives of all of them were intertwined by a Desert War which had ended with either victory or defeat at El Alamein.

Among the Germans

On 30 April 1945, ADOLF HITLER died by his own hand in his *Führerbunker*. Afterwards his corpse was carried up to the Reich Chancellery garden, where it was incinerated.

After the Allied victory, FIELD MARSHAL KESSELRING, who had been in overall command of the Mediterranean and North African fronts, was charged with responsibility for the massacre of civilians by German troops during the Italian campaign. He was sentenced to death by firing squad but the sentence was commuted to life imprisonment after both Alexander and Churchill intervened on his behalf. He was released in 1952 on grounds of ill health. He died in 1960 at the age of seventy-four.

In 1943, ADMIRAL RAEDER, the principal advocate in OKW of a Mediterranean strategy, was forced to resign as commander of the German Navy following a series of disastrous errors and was subsequently demoted. He was sentenced to life imprisonment at the Nuremberg trials but was released in 1955. He died five years later at the age of eighty-six.

FIELD MARSHAL ROMMEL recovered from his fall from grace to play a leading role in preparing the defence of Normandy against the expected D-Day landings. He went on to lead the military resistance to the Allies until, on 17 July 1944, he was severely wounded in the head and taken to hospital. He was diagnosed with a quadruple fracture of the skull. He played no further part in the fighting, which, in any case, he had come to regard as futile.

His disillusionment with Hitler led him to offer tacit support to the 20 July plot against the Führer's life. Though he was not one of the plotters, he soon knew himself to be a marked man. On 14 October a dark green car with a Berlin number plate drove up to his house. Two generals went inside to talk to him. According to his son Manfred, who was there at the time, he emerged a few moments later to tell his wife and his son, who were waiting upstairs, that he had been given two options: he could either take poison or expect to die in a shoot-out with Gestapo agents who had ringed the area. Ten minutes later, he left the house and drove to a nearby wood. There he swallowed the poison and, as he had been advised by the generals, he died within three minutes.

The official cause of death was ascribed to the injuries he had endured in Normandy. With ghastly cynicism, Hitler wrote a note of condolence to Frau Rommel: 'Accept my sincerest sympathy for the heavy loss you have suffered with the death of your husband. The name of Field Marshal Rommel will be for ever linked with the heroic battles in North Africa.' At the age of fifty-two, Germany's youngest field marshal, once the Führer's favourite general, was duly accorded a state funeral with full military honours.

Among the Italians

MARSHAL BADOGLIO lost control of Italy's armed forces after signing the secret armistice with the Allies and was forced to flee Rome to seek refuge. On 13 October his government officially declared war on Germany. However, his past loyalty to the fascist cause was to be his undoing. Following the liberation of Rome by the Allies, he was sacked as Prime Minister. He died, at the age of eighty-five, in 1956.

GENERAL 'ELECTRIC WHISKERS' BERGONZOLI, who had been captured at Beda Fomm in February 1941, was released at the end of the war and died in 1973 at the age of eighty-nine.

MARSHAL CAVALLERO, Rommel's bête noire as the mercurial Chief of Comando Supremo, was arrested by Mussolini's successor, Badoglio, in 1943. When Badoglio surrendered to the Allies, Cavallero was 'rescued' by the Germans, who assumed he was still loyal to the fascist cause. But they came across a letter which he had written to Badoglio seeking exculpation, and concluded that he was a traitor. Trapped between the Nazis and Badoglio, he appears to have committed suicide on 13 September 1943. His death was caused by a gunshot wound to his head. He was sixty-three.

Until the very end, COUNT CIANO's fate was intimately entwined with that of his father-in law. Sacked by Mussolini in February 1943, he was one of those members of the Fascist Grand Council whose overwhelming votes helped seal his father-in-law's downfall in July 1943. Ciano tried to flee to Spain but he was captured by Mussolini's acolytes and jailed in Verona.

On 23 December 1943, in his final diary entry, written from his prison cell, he wrote of the 'sham tribunal' which he knew would sentence him to death. 'It is hard to think that I shall not be able to gaze into the eyes of my three children or to press my mother to my heart, or my wife ... But I must bow to the will of God, and a great calm is descending upon my soul.' He concluded, 'I am preparing myself for the Supreme Judgement.' On 11 January 1944 he was tied to a chair and executed by firing squad.

MARSHAL GRAZIANI, the 'butcher' of Ethiopia, who led the Italian invasion of Egypt in September 1940, remained loyal to Mussolini until the end. At the end of the war he was held in custody by the Allies until 1948, when he was sentenced to nineteen years' imprisonment for collaborating with the Nazis. However he was released a few months later. An unrepentant fascist, he died in 1955 at the age of seventy-two.

In July 1943 MUSSOLINI was arrested and imprisoned at a mountain resort in Abruzzo but was rescued in a daring raid by a German commando unit two months later. He was taken to Hitler, who was evidently shocked by his haggard and woebegone appearance but nonetheless set him up as the titular head of the 'Italian Socialist Republic' in the far north of Italy. For a while Il Duce continued to harbour dreams of recovering his lost empire but, sick and downhearted, the founder of Italian fascism gradually became a pathetic relic of the braggart who had once mesmerised the nation. 'I am finished. My star has set ... I await the end of the tragedy, strangely detached from it all,' he confided to an interviewer in January 1945. The end came three months later when he was captured by communist partisans as he tried to flee Italy disguised as a German soldier. On 28 April 1945 he, like Ciano, was executed by firing squad along with fifteen members of his retinue and his mistress Clara Petacci. Their corpses were taken by truck to Milan to be hung upside down from the wall of a garage in the Piazzale Loreto, where they were mocked and stoned by the very same people who had once revered Il Duce as their saviour.

Among the Americans

HARRY HOPKINS, who had done so much to broker the Anglo-American Alliance, and who had lived through those years suffering from stomach cancer, finally succumbed at the age of fifty-five in January 1946.

GENERAL MARSHALL continued to serve as the US Chief of Staff until the end of the war. In 1947 he was appointed by Roosevelt's successor, Harry Truman, as Secretary of State. In this role he initiated the European Recovery Programme – the Marshall Plan – for which he was later to be awarded the Nobel Peace Prize. He resigned on the grounds of ill health in January 1949 but returned as Secretary of Defense the following year, retiring from public office in 1951. In 1953 he represented the US government at the Coronation of Queen Elizabeth II. He died in 1959, a little before his seventy-ninth birthday.

PRESIDENT ROOSEVELT was re-elected for a fourth term in 1944, but his health was in sharp decline. After his return from the Yalta Conference in February 1945, he went to rest at the Little White House at Palm Springs to prepare himself for the inaugural conference of the United Nations. He died there of a massive stroke on the afternoon of 12 April 1945. A little under four weeks later, on 8 May, President Truman dedicated Victory in Europe Day to his memory, advising the American people that his only wish was that 'Franklin D. Roosevelt had lived to witness this day'.

ADMIRAL ERNEST KING, the Chief of Naval Operations, whose Anglophobia played its part in the strained negotiations between London and Washington, was promoted to the newly created post of Fleet Admiral in December 1944. After retirement in 1945, he remained in Washington to serve as advisor to the Secretary of the Navy. A severe stroke in 1947 forced him to spend his latter years in hospital. He died in 1956 at the age of 75.

GENERAL 'VINEGAR JOE' STILWELL went on to serve in China and India during the Burma Campaign. His abrasive relations with the Chinese and, in India, with General Wavell, led to his recall by Roosevelt. He later served as Commander of Army Ground Forces, US Tenth Army. He died of stomach cancer in October 1946 while still on active service.

In his capacity as Secretary of State for War, HENRY STIMSON took overall responsibility for the US Occupation zone in Germany following Hitler's downfall. He was instrumental in establishing the legal framework for the Nuremberg Trials. He resigned in 1945 and died at the age of 83 in October 1950.

Among the British

Following his success in Tunisia, GENERAL ALEXANDER was appointed to command two Allied armies during the invasion of Sicily. Remaining as commander of the 15th Army Group throughout the Italian campaign, he took the German surrender on 29 April 1945 as the overall commander of the Mediterranean theatre. After the war, at the invitation of the Canadian Prime Minister, he was appointed Governor General of Canada. In 1952 he returned to serve Churchill as Minister of Defence, retiring two years later. As Earl Alexander of Tunis, he died in June 1969 aged seventy-seven and was buried near his family home in Hertfordshire.

When GENERAL AUCHINLECK was sacked by Churchill as C-in-C, Middle East, in August 1942, he took a sabbatical year in India until he replaced Wavell there as commander-in-chief on the latter's elevation to Viceroy. He remained in that post until 1947, when he retired as a field marshal. He returned to England but later moved to Marrakesh, where, always an outsider, he lived alone until his death in 1981, at the age of ninety-six.

GENERAL BROOKE continued to serve as Chief of the Imperial Staff until his retirement in 1946 as Field Marshal Lord Alan-brooke. The asperity and candour of his *War Diaries*, first edited in an abridged version by the historian Sir Arthur Bryant in 1957, caused a sustained frisson of controversy. Though he was vain, Brooke was not a self-publicist and – somewhat to his chagrin – he was thereby denied the public recognition which was assuredly his due. Nonetheless – unlike Montgomery, whose reputation had initially eclipsed his – the judgement of posterity was to grow in his favour as his name faded. He died at his home in Hampshire in 1963 at the age of seventy-nine.

O'Connor's successor GENERAL CUNNINGHAM was summoned back to Britain after Auchinleck's reluctant decision to remove him from the command of the Eighth Army. Although he became commander of the Army Staff College at Camberley, he never again saw active service. In 1945 he was appointed High Commissioner of Palestine when British rule was being subverted by terrorists belonging to various Zionist underground movements. In 1948 he presided over Britain's departure from Palestine and the creation of the state of Israel. He died in Tunbridge Wells in 1983, aged ninety-six.

Montgomery's Chief of Staff, 'FREDDY' DE GUINGAND, continued to serve loyally in that role until the end of the war, a testing and exhausting responsibility which required him constantly to mend the diplomatic fences with colleagues through which Montgomery wilfully blundered. In 1946 he was rewarded for his long-suffering service with a knighthood, and, as a major general, retired to Southern Rhodesia to write his memoirs, which did not refrain from identifying Montgomery's many weaknesses as well as his considerable strengths. He died on 29 June 1979 at the age of seventy-nine.

FIELD MARSHAL SIR JOHN DILL continued to serve the British government in Washington until his premature death from aplastic anaemia in November 1944. He was accorded a memorial service in the capital's National Cathedral and the route of his funeral cortège to the Arlington National Cemetery was lined by thousands of US soldiers. Reflecting the strong feelings of his close friend Marshall, the American Chiefs sent a message of condolence to their British counterparts, extolling his virtues and mourning 'the passing of a great and wise soldier, and a great gentleman'. He was sixty-two.

'CHINK' DORMAN-SMITH, Auchinleck's strategic *alter ego*, returned to England after Montgomery (who judged him to be 'a menace'), sacked him in August 1942 with the enthusiastic endorsement of Brooke (who thought him 'a sinister influence'). Although Liddell Hart judged him to be one of the 'outstanding' soldiers of his generation, his military career took a sharp downwards trajectory. Although he was given command of a brigade at Anzio, his abrasive and intolerant nature led lesser but more senior talents to regard him as unfit for this role and he was soon removed. After the war he returned to his Irish roots and became embroiled in Irish politics. In 1951 he ran for the Dáil for a party closely allied to the IRA, an enthusiastic dalliance with Irish republicanism which continued for several years. He died on 11 May 1969 in County Cavan at the age of seventy-three.

'PUG' ISMAY continued to work at Churchill's side until the end of the war, attending every major Allied conference up to and including Potsdam in February 1945. Promoted by this time to become a full general, he took his seat in the Lords as Baron Ismay in 1947. In the same year he offered to serve Mountbatten as Chief of Staff in the months leading up to the partition of India. Later he briefly served Churchill as Secretary of State for Commonwealth Relations. In 1952 he became the first Secretary-General of NATO, allegedly defining the role of the new Alliance as 'to keep the Russians out, the Americans in, and the Germans down'. He retired in 1957 and died eight years later, on 17 December 1965, at his home in Gloucestershire. He was seventy-eight.

MAJOR GENERAL JOHN KENNEDY was promoted from his role as Director of Military Operations in 1943 to work even more closely with Brooke as Assistant Chief of the Imperial General Staff, where he served until the end of hostilities. From 1947 to 1953 he served as Governor of Southern Rhodesia. He died in 1970 at the age of seventy-seven.

As though to confirm the impression that 'to the victor belong the spoils', GENERAL MONTGOMERY followed his triumphs in North Africa by playing a leading role in the Italian campaign, the D-Day landings, and the subsequent victory in Europe, where his arrogance and self-regard, which led the usually emollient Eisenhower to describe him later as 'a psychopath', earned him the lasting enmity of his fellow commanders. After the war, as Field Marshal Viscount Montgomery of Alamein, he succeeded Brooke as Chief of the Imperial General Staff, a post in which the limits of his strategic abilities were rudely exposed. At the age of sixty-nine he retired from the army but not from public gaze. His iconic status gave him a platform from which to give the nation the benefit of his views on almost any matter of controversy (inter alia, he admired Chairman Mao's leadership of China, he supported apartheid in

South Africa and he opposed the 1967 Sexual Offences Act which he described as 'a charter for buggery'). He died in 1976 at his home in Hampshire aged eighty-eight, the most famous British general of the Second World War and – in the judgement of many, if not most, military historians – the most overrated as well.

GENERAL O'CONNOR, the Desert Fox of the British commanders, who had run into an enemy patrol in April 1941, escaped from an Italian POW camp two years later. On his return he was presented with the knighthood which had been awarded to him after his capture. In 1944 he commanded VIII Corps in Normandy. He retired in 1948, and died aged ninety-one in 1981.

GENERAL NEAME, who was captured with O'Connor, escaped captivity at the same time. He died three years before O'Connor at the age of eighty-nine.

GENERAL RITCHIE, Cunningham's successor as the Eighth Army commander, also recovered from being sacked by Auchinleck and commanded XII Corps in Normandy following the D-Day landings. After his retirement at the end of the war, he emigrated to Canada where he died at the age of eighty-six in 1983.

Following his dismissal as C-in-C, Middle East, GENERAL WAVELL served as C-in-C, India. Promoted to field marshal in January 1943, he became Viceroy and Governor-General a few months later. He was replaced by Lord Mountbatten in 1947 and returned to England, where he died three years later. He was accorded a full military funeral at Westminster Abbey which Churchill did not attend.

On the evening of VE Day WINSTON CHURCHILL stood on a Whitehall balcony to address a vast crowd gathered below, 'My dear friends, this is your hour,' he told them. 'It is not victory of a party or of any class. It's a victory of the great British nation as a whole. We were the first, in this ancient island, to draw the sword against tyranny.' The crowd responded with renditions of 'Land of Hope and Glory' and 'For He's A Jolly Good Fellow'.

Two months later the Labour Party, under Clement Attlee, won a landslide victory over the Conservatives. After six frustrating years of opposition, during which he made his famous

'Iron Curtain' speech in Fulton, Missouri, Churchill returned to government in October 1951, serving as Prime Minister until his resignation in 1955, when he was succeeded by his Foreign Secretary, Anthony Eden. In October 1964, at the age of ninety, he finally stood down from Parliament. Four months later, succumbing to the latest of a series of severe strokes, he died at his home in London on 24 January 1965.

In his 'Finest Hour' speech, following the evacuation from Dunkirk, Churchill had spoken as though he believed that the 'British Empire' might 'last for a thousand years'. By the time of his death – partly as a result of the haemorrhage of energy and strength caused by the glorious victory to which he had led the nation – Britain was in full retreat from that anachronistic vision and casting around for a role in a world where its power and status was in inexorable decline. But at his lying-in-state at Westminster Hall in the last week of January, tens of thousands of British citizens filed past his coffin in mourning. The BBC's commentator at the scene, Richard Dimbleby, spoke barely above a whisper, as he found the words to express their feelings as, one by one, they paused momentarily before the catafalque. 'We shall never see Winston Churchill again, but we may do well to print this scene deep in our memories, for many will talk of him that are yet unborn.' It was a simple sentence and it was so.

ACKNOWLEDGEMENTS

I am indebted to Antony Beevor, Sir Max Hastings and Andrew Roberts, whose initial counsel and enthusiasm spurred me to enter this fray.

My researcher, Guy Gibbs, helped me to chart a course through the fog of the Desert War and guided me to many of the key military documents of the period. Ross Mahoney unearthed some powerful 'voices' from the warfront which had not hitherto been published. Serena Sissons generously gave me the fruits of her labours in the Italian vineyard of wartime memories.

The staff at the Imperial War Museum in London and the Leeds University Library's Liddle Collection confirmed their reputation for expertise and co-operation. I have drawn extensively from the IWM's archive, and especially from the remarkable testimony from the front line of the Desert War collected in *Forgotten Voices, Desert Victory*, edited by Major-General Julian Thompson.

I owe a great debt to three specialists in the history of the Desert War: Dr Niall Barr, Stephen Bungay and Professor Martin Kitchen read the manuscript with scholarly diligence and offered me astute advice. Needless to say any errors of fact or inadequacies of judgement are mine, not theirs or anyone else's.

I am grateful to my editor, Daniel Crewe, whose commitment

and judgement have been invaluable, and to his colleagues at Profile Books, Penny Daniel, Cecily Gayford, Ruth Killick and Drew Jerrison, whose combined expertise and enthusiasm has been a constant source of encouragement. My copyeditor, Trevor Horwood, has spared me much embarrassment with his meticulous attention to important detail, and Diana Lecore has brought an enviable precision and clarity to her task as indexer. My thanks to Sasha Joelle Achilli and her colleagues at FreshOne Productions for unearthing most of the photographs; and to Martin Lubikowski for the clarity of his maps.

Veronique Baxter, my agent at David Higham Associates, has been shrewd and persistent on my behalf. I am also grateful to her colleagues, Nann du Santoy and Laura West. My PA, Stella Keeley, who deciphered and organised copious notes, has been astonishingly patient throughout her ordeal.

My thanks also to my good friend, Robin Barnwell, the producer of *The Road to El Alamein – Churchill's Desert Campaign*, the BBC 2 documentary which was based on *Destiny in the Desert*; as he constructed a 90-minute television film from my manuscript, we had many stimulating discussions about the desert campaign for which I am much in his debt. Similarly, Peter Grimsdale, the film's executive producer, was a source of great encouragement throughout.

Most of all, I am grateful to my wife, Jessica, who has coped brilliantly with the fact that, for much of the last two years, I have been living in the past when our young children have wanted me to inhabit the present. Her gentle and enduring support has been the rock without which I would surely have foundered.

Jonathan Dimbleby
August 2012

LIST OF ILLUSTRATIONS

1. Lieutenant-General Bernard Montgomery © CORBIS
2. General Erwin Rommel – the Desert Fox © dpa/Corbis
3. General Cavallero, head of the Italian Comando Supremo
4. Marshall Graziana © 2012 White Images/Scala
5. General John Dill © Getty Images
6. General Andrew Cunningham © Bettmann/CORBIS
7. General Claude Auchinleck © Getty Images
8. General Wavell © CORBIS
9. Hitler and Mussolini on the Brenner Pass © 2012 Cinecitta Luce/Scala
10. Stuart tanks © The Tank Museum
11. German Stuka planes (aerial view) © Getty Images
12. Soldiers prior to departure to Greece. Photo courtesy of the Australian War Memorial
13. The 'Imperial Army of the Nile' © Hulton-Deutsch Collection/CORBIS
14. Australian soldiers in the field. Photo courtesy of the Australian War Memorial
15. The Eighth Army in action © Imperial War Museum
16. Churchill, Auchinleck, Wavell, Brooke, Harwood and Casey in the garden of the British Embassy in Cairo © Getty Images
17. Churchill in Cairo © Imperial War Museum
18. Hitler promoting Rommel to Field Marshall © Getty Images
19. Churchill with Roosevelt at the White House © Press Association
20. Churchill's first meeting with Stalin © CORBIS
21. Lietenant-General Richard O'Connor in Derna, Libya © Imperial War Museum

22. General Alan Brooke © Getty Images
23. General George Marshall © Getty Images
24. Ships burning in Tobruk harbour (P05342.023). Photo courtesy of the Australian War Memorial
25. Surrender at Tobruk © Press Association
26. 'Wolf's Lair', 1941© 2012 Photo Scala, Florence/BPK, Bildagentur fuer Kunst, Kultur und Geschichte, Berlin
27. The Fall of Tobruk © Press Association
28. Regimental aid post of 2nd NZEF 20th Battalion at Sidi Rezegh, Libya. Photo courtesy of Alexander Turnbull Library, Wellington, New Zealand
29. Early morning Communion service, Baggush. Photo courtesy of Alexander Turnbull Library, Wellington, New Zealand.
30. Axis prisoners on the roadside during pursuit from Alamein, Egypt. Photograph by H. Paton. Alexander Turnbull Library, Wellington, New Zealand
31. Rommel © Bettmann/CORBIS
32. American troops landing in North Africa. Photo courtesy of the US National Archives

While every effort has been made to contact copyright-holders of illustrations, the author and publishers would be grateful for information about any illustrations where they have been unable to trace them, and would be glad to make amendments in further editions.

List of Maps

NOTES

Preface: A Pivotal Struggle

p. xv 'This is not the end ...', Winston S. Churchill, *The End of the Beginning* (Cassell, 1943), pp. 264–5.

p. xvi 'it is evident ...', 'Before Alamein ...', Winston S. Churchill, *The Second World War*, Vol. IV, *The Hinge of Fate* (Cassell, 1951), pp. 537, 541.

p. xviii 'the carotid artery of empire', Douglas Porch, *Hitler's Mediterranean Gamble: The North American and the Mediterranean Campaigns in World War II* (Cassell, 2004), p. 7.

p. xviii 'I have not become ...', Churchill, *The End of the Beginning*, pp. 264ff.

p. xix 'We are determined ...', Statement to Press Corps, 22 August 1942, Prime Minister's Office Papers, 1940–45.

p. xxii 'The civilian population ...', quoted in Richard Holmes, *The World at War* (Ebury Press, 2007), p. 270.

p. xxii 'the turning of the hinge of fate', Churchill, *Second World War*, Vol. IV, p. 541.

1 Starting Points

p. 1 'I have nothing to offer ...', Parliamentary Debates, House of Commons (Hansard), Vol. 360, Cols 1501–25.

p. 1 'Now we must stand ...', William L. Shirer, *The Rise and Fall of the Third Reich* (Pan, 1959), p. 883.

p. 2 'We shall fight on the beaches ...' Hansard, Vol. 361, Cols 787–98.

p. 2 'We're finished ...', David Howarth, *Pursued by a Bear*, cited in Max Hastings, *Finest Years: Churchill as Warlord, 1940–45* (Harper Press, 2009), p. 28.

p. 2 'where we owned nothing …', Winston S. Churchill, *The Second World War*, Vol. II, *Their Finest Hour* (Cassell, 1949), p. 372.

p. 3 'fount of British military power …', ibid., p. 117.

p. 4 'suspicious of politicians …' et seq., John Connell, *Wavell: Scholar and Soldier* (Collins, 1964), pp. 254, 255.

p. 4 'comprised an extraordinary amalgam …' Churchill, *Second World War*, Vol. II, p. 376.

p. 4 'Winston's tactical ideas …' Connell, *Wavell*, p. 256.

p. 5 'a prolonged hard fight …', 'I put my case …', Churchill, *Second World War*, Vol. II, pp. 373, 376.

p. 5 'succeeded in convincing', 'I convinced him …', 'I am pretty sure …', Connell, *Wavell*, p. 256.

p. 5 'to assemble and deploy …', Churchill, *Second World War*, Vol. II, p. 379.

p. 6 'Blackshirts of the Revolution …', 'an atmosphere of gloom …', Christopher Hibbert, *Mussolini* (Palgrave Macmillan, 2008), pp. 124–5.

p. 6 'Is it too late …', 'May I remind you …', Churchill, *Second World War*, Vol. II, pp. 107, 108.

p. 7 'War alone brings …' Benito Mussolini, 'Doctrine of Fascism', *Enciclopedia Italiana* (1932).

p. 7 'a few thousand dead …', Hibbert, *Mussolini*, p. 124.

p. 7 Ciano's observations, Hugh Gibson, ed., *The Ciano Diaries, 1939–1943: The Complete, Unabridged Diaries of Count Galeazzo Ciano, Italian Minister of Foreign Affairs, 1936–1943* (Simon Publications, 2001), pp. 280, 282, 285, 287.

p. 9 'Spent morning in the office …', Field Marshal Lord Alanbrooke, *War Diaries 1939–45*, ed. Alex Danchev and Daniel Todman (Weidenfeld and Nicolson, 2001), p. 107.

p. 9 'meant business', Charles Stuart, ed., *The Reith Diaries* (Collins, 1975), p. 263.

p. 9 Hitler on Russia, Halder's Diary, 31 July, 1940, cited in Alan Bullock, *Hitler: A Study in Tyranny* (Pelican, 1962), p. 598.

p. 10 Churchill's Secret Session briefing, 'A Statement to the House of Commons, September 17, 1940', in Charles Eade, comp., *Secret Session Speeches by Winston Churchill* (Cassell, 1946).

p. 11 'thinking in global …', Martin Kitchen, *Rommel's Desert War* (Cambridge University Press, 2009), p. 4.

p. 11 'doubtful whether an advance …', Bullock, *Hitler*, p. 600.

p. 11 'weeks of cajoling …', Kitchen, *Rommel's Desert War*, p. 4.

p. 12 'were subjugated or starving', 'with all its power and might …', Churchill, *Second World War*, Vol. II, p. 104.

p. 13 Telegram, Churchill to Roosevelt, 15 May 1940, ibid., p. 23.

p. 14 'I don't know what …', Leonard Mosley, *Marshall, Hero for Our Times* (Hearst Books, 1982), p. 138.

p. 14 'to parley amid ...', Churchill, *Second World War*, Vol. II, p. 51.

p. 15 'If we go down ...', ibid., p. 167.

p. 16 'on their last legs', 'extremely low', *The Roosevelt Letter*, ed. Eleanor Roosevelt, Vol. III, *1928–1945* (Harrap, 1952), pp. 329, 330.

p. 16 'from being neutral ...', Churchill, *Second World War*, Vol. II, p. 358.

p. 16 'spontaneously', Hansard, Vol. 364, Col. 1170.

p. 17 'I have said this before ...', Robert Dallek, *Franklin D. Roosevelt and American Foreign Policy, 1932–1945* (Oxford University Press, 1995), p. 252.

p. 17 'Couldn't they put up ...', Edward Crankshaw, *Khrushchev Remembers*, cited in Laurence Rees, *World War II: Behind Closed Doors – Stalin, The Nazis and The West* (BBC Books, 2008), p. 72.

p. 18 'The Soviet "mass" ...' et seq., Alan Bullock, *Hitler and Stalin, Parallel Lives* (HarperCollins, 1991), p. 731.

2 Opening Salvos

p. 20 'The English are withdrawing ...', Gibson, *Ciano Diaries*, p. 293.

p. 21 'In September I was taken ...', 'were tired and wanted ...', Julian Thompson, *Forgotten Voices: Desert Victory* (Ebury Press, 2011), pp. 5, 7.

p. 21 'Never has a military operation ...', Gibson, *Ciano Diaries*, p. 291.

p. 22 'a pantomime offensive', 'a birthday party ...', Porch, *Hitler's Mediterranean Gamble*, p. 46.

p. 22 'was effected with admirable skill ...', 'made little attempt ...', *London Gazette* (*LG*) 37609, 11 June 1946, pp. 2999, 3001.

p. 22 'Small in stature ...', Leeds University Library, Liddle Collection (1939–45), Army 090, Earl Haig, unpublished manuscript, p. 110.

p. 23 'A general came up ...' et seq., Thompson, *Forgotten Voices*, p. 13.

p. 23 'When he brought back ...' et seq., Liddle Collection, Earl Haig, unpublished manuscript, p. 117.

p. 24 'continually engaged and harassed the enemy', *LG* 37609, p. 3001.

p. 24 'The desert roused ...', Jonathan Dimbleby, *Richard Dimbleby: A Biography* (Hodder and Stoughton, 1975), p. 108.

p. 24 'The sandstorm came ...' et seq., Jon Latimer, *Alamein* (John Murray, 2002), p. 23.

p. 24 'Our worst enemy ...', Thompson, *Forgotten Voices*, p. 10.

p. 25 'it flapped in the wind ...', ibid., p. 14.

p. 25 'There were no flies ...', ibid., p. 15.

p. 25 'Here in the desert ...', Dimbleby, *Richard Dimbleby*, p. 105.

p. 25 'playing chess ...', *Time*, 30 September 1940.

p. 26 'I began to see ...', Alan Moorehead, *The Desert War: The Classic Trilogy on the North American Campaign 1940–43* (Aurum Press, 2009), p. 11.

p. 26 Richard Dimbleby, *The Frontiers Are Green* (Hodder and Stoughton, 1943), p. 21.

p. 26 'pervaded by the familiar smell …', Artemis Cooper, *Cairo in the War 1939–45* (Penguin 1995), p. 4.

p. 27 'sprang to his feet …', ibid., p. 5.

p. 27 'Wavell had an …', IWM file no. 2778; www.iwm.org.uk/collections/item/object/80002764.

p. 28 'A side of him …', Holmes, *World at War*, p. 151.

p. 28 'Such a country …', Cooper, *Cairo in the War*, pp. 79–80.

p. 29 'I realised Winston's …', Connell, *Wavell*, p. 277.

p. 29 'fretted at the delays …', Sir John Kennedy, *The Business of War* (Hutchinson, 1957), p. 62.

p. 29 'splendid enterprise' et seq., Churchill, *Second World War*, Vol. II, pp. 479, 480.

p. 30 'magnified the possible …', 'the hard realities …', Kennedy, *Business of War*, p. 62.

p. 30 'From time to time …' to 'grieved and vexed', Churchill, *Second World War*, Vol. II, pp. 392, 396, 397, 399.

p. 31 'hungry for a turn to the offensive', 'I fear that the proportion …', ibid., p. 448.

p. 32 'News from every quarter …', ibid., p. 483.

p. 32 'Gentlemen …', 'This is not an offensive …', Moorehead, *Desert War*, p. 60.

p. 32 'Feel undue …', 'If with the situation …', 'I always meant …', Connell, *Wavell*, pp. 288, 289.

p. 33 'gutted tanks …', Dimbleby, *Frontiers Are Green*, p. 102.

p. 33 'The Italians were …', 'It was a complete …', 'The first time …', Thompson, *Forgotten Voices*, pp. 18, 19.

p. 34 Moorehead's Italian booty descriptions, Moorehead, *Desert War*, pp. 62, 64.

p. 35 'piles of Italian kit …', 'take that bloody stuff off …', 'God watch and keep …', Thompson, *Forgotten Voices*, p. 19.

p. 35 'But for the cowardice …', Moorehead, *Desert War*, p. 65.

p. 36 'that seemed at first …', 'plodded four abreast …', ibid., p. 71.

p. 36 'a screaming sound', 'There was this …', Thompson, *Forgotten Voices*, p. 12.

p. 36–7 'all we heard …', 'We have about …', Moorehead, *Desert War*, pp. 47, 46.

p. 37 'The Army of the Nile …', Churchill, *Second World War*, Vol. II, pp. 542–3.

p. 37 'I am sure …', ibid., p. 541.

3 Mussolini's Mistake

p. 38 'a thunderbolt' et seq., Gibson, *Ciano Diaries*, pp. 321–2.

p. 39 'We must speak …', ibid., p. 322.

p. 39 'This snow and cold …', ibid., p. 327.

p. 39 'It is the material …', 'soft and unworthy people', Hibbert, *Mussolini*, p. 131.

p. 40 'a hopeless situation …' et seq., Kitchen, *Rommel's Desert War*, pp. 26–7.

p. 41 'Hitler keeps confronting …' et seq., Gibson, *Ciano Diaries*, p. 300.

p. 41 'This time he really …', Hibbert, *Mussolini*, p. 133.

p. 41 'He is pessimistic …' et seq., Gibson, *Ciano Diaries*, pp. 312–13.

p. 42 'a gramophone with seven records', Kitchen, *Rommel's Desert War*, p. 15.

p. 42 'through political intervention', Hibbert, *Mussolini*, p. 132.

p. 42 'This is grotesque …' et seq., Gibson, *Ciano Diaries*, p. 318.

p. 42 'plunged in the depths …', Hibbert, *Mussolini*, p. 133.

p. 43 'complete and very unpleasant …', O'Connor, in Adrian Gilbert, ed., *The Imperial War Museum Book of The Desert War 1940–1942* (Sidgwick and Jackson, 1995), p. 4.

p. 44 'I have given …', Correlli Barnett, *The Desert Generals* (Phoenix, 1999), p. 42.

p. 45 'All hell was let loose' et seq., Leeds University Library, Liddle Collection (1939–45), Army 025, J. Tramp.

p. 45 'We came across a battery …', Gilbert, *Desert War*, p. 5.

p. 45 'Eyetie [prisoners] trying …', ibid., pp. 6–7.

p. 45 'We admired the Australians …', Thompson, *Forgotten Voices*, pp. 22–3.

p. 46 'They looked pathetic …', ibid., p. 26.

p. 46 'On either side …' et seq., Dimbleby, *Frontiers Are Green*, p. 107.

p. 47 'cannon-fodder' et seq., Thompson, *Forgotten Voices*, p. 27.

p. 47 'the litter of a rout' et seq., Dr Stephanides in Gilbert, *Desert War*, pp. 10–11.

p. 48 'Hunt is still going …', 'The enemy's position …', John Sadler, *El Alamein: The Story of the Battle in the Words of the Soldiers* (Amberley, 2010), p. 33.

p. 48 'The enemy's position was desperate …', LG 37628, p. 3267.

p. 49 'It was a really …', Gilbert, *Desert War*, p. 12.

p. 49 'Fox killed in the open', ibid.

p. 49 'I thought you'd like …', Thompson, *Forgotten Voices*, p. 29.

p. 49 'You have done …', Connell, *Wavell*, p. 329.

4 A Change of Plan

p. 50 'I ought to have …', Thompson, *Forgotten Voices*, p. 34.

p. 51 'We read it together …', Francis de Guingand, *Operation Victory* (Hodder and Stoughton, 1947), pp. 47–9.

p. 51 'This grave step …', Winston S. Churchill, *The Second World War*, Vol. III, *The Grand Alliance* (Cassell, 1950), p. 83.

p. 51–2 Churchill–Eden cables, Churchill, *Second World War*, Vol. II, pp. 474–6.

p. 52 'It is quite clear …', Churchill, *Second World War*, Vol. III, p. 9.

p. 52 'a move in the war …', TNA CAB 105/1, No. 42, 10 January 1941.

p. 53 'at least twenty …' et seq., Kennedy, *Business of War*, p. 72.

p. 53 'Our information contradicts …' et seq., Churchill, *Second World War*, Vol. III, p. 16.

p. 54 'lost his temper …', Kennedy, *Business of War*, p. 75.

p. 54 'was now trying …' et seq., ibid., pp. 75–6.

p. 55 Churchill–Eden cables, Churchill, *Second World War*, Vol. III, pp. 63, 69.

p. 55–6 'The hazards of the enterprise …', 'to have fought …', ibid., pp. 89, 93.

p. 56 'to push on from …' et seq., F. L. Loewenheim et al., *Roosevelt and Churchill: Their Secret Wartime Correspondence* (Barrie and Jenkins, 1975), p. 132.

5 Rommel to the Rescue

p. 57 'on normal reasoning', 'such reckoning …', Basil Liddell Hart, ed., *The Rommel Papers* (Da Capo, 1982), p. 105.

p. 57 'great error … that the enemy …', Connell, *Wavell*, p. 384.

p. 58 'I didn't know …', Thompson, *Forgotten Voices*, p. 34.

p. 58 Hitler's New Year message to Mussolini, Churchill, *Second World War*, Vol. III, p. 12.

p. 58 'a detour through …', Porch, *Hitler's Mediterranean Gamble*, p. 28.

p. 59 'deliver a devastating blow …', Kitchen, *Rommel's Desert War*, p. 42.

p. 59 'There are no hidden condolences …' et seq., Gibson, *Ciano Diaries*, p. 338.

p. 60 'shattered', Kitchen, *Rommel's Desert War*, p. 46.

p. 60 'Britain could hold …', Desmond Young, *Rommel* (Collins, 1950), p. 62.

p. 62 'the pilot, ignoring …', Liddell Hart, *Rommel Papers*, p. 105.

p. 62 'We wanted an adventure …', Leeds University Library, Liddle Collection (1939–45), Private Papers of Fritz Herman Zimmermann, File No. 13406.

p. 63 'The engineer looked …', Thompson, *Forgotten Voices*, p. 36.

p. 63 'no intention of striking …', Liddell Hart, *Rommel Papers*, p. 105.

p. 63 'We saw tanks …', Gilbert, *Desert War*, p. 17.

p. 64 'Our intention was …', *LG* 37638, 2 July 1946, p. 3428.

p. 64 'It is painful …', Gilbert, *Desert War*, p. 86.

p. 64 'I found Neame …', Connell, *Wavell*, p. 386.

p. 64 'Suddenly the road …', Thompson, *Forgotten Voices*, p. 38.

p. 64 'spirals of black smoke …', Gilbert, *Desert War*, pp. 87–8.

p. 65 'signs of panic …', Thompson, *Forgotten Voices*, p. 44.

p. 65 'I was surprised …', ibid., p. 40.

p. 65 'things here are going …' et seq., Pietro Ostellino, *Ariete Tanks Fight! The Ups and Downs of the Ariete Armoured Division in the letters of Lt. Pietro Ostellino, North Africa Jan. 1941 to March 1943* (in Italian) (Prospettiva Editrice, 2009).

p. 65–6 Rommel and Gariboldi; Rommel's letter of 3 April 1941, Liddell Hart, *Rommel Papers*, p. 111.

6 Dangerous Diversions

p. 67–8 'incandescent with rage', 'The brutality can …', Andrew Roberts, *Masters and Commanders* (Allen Lane, 2008), p. 124.

p. 68 'On the beaches …', Moorehead, *Desert War*, p. 151.

p. 69 Cairo Communiqué, 1 May 1941, ibid., p. 147.

p. 69 'the expedition to Greece …', LG 37638, p. 3432.

p. 69 'You have done …', Loewenheim et al., *Roosevelt and Churchill Correspondence*, p. 138.

p. 70 'the admiration …', 'supplies in so far …', *Roosevelt Letters*, Vol. III, p. 364.

p. 70 'moving into the war …', 'I could make out …', 'Do you play poker?' Kennedy, *Business of War*, p. 79.

p. 71 'Slowly and in spite of …', *Roosevelt Letters*, Vol. III, p. 265.

p. 71 'When will you Irishmen …', ibid., p. 370.

p. 71 'unless the advance …', ibid., p. 267.

p. 71 'Britain's War', Dallek, *Roosevelt and American Foreign Policy*, p. 264.

p. 72 'We've been attacking …', 'long black columns …', 'Several men laid …', 'It was a miracle …', Liddell Hart, *Rommel Papers*, p. 116.

p. 72 'He got into my car …', Thompson, *Forgotten Voices*, p. 41.

p. 73 'I soon realised …', Connell, *Wavell*, p. 392.

p. 73 Harding account, Bolton account, Thompson, *Forgotten Voices*, pp. 40, 41.

p. 73 'We reached Derna …', ibid., p. 41.

p. 74 'It was a great shock …', Gilbert, *Desert War*, p. 16.

p. 74 'This tragic accident …', Barnett, *The Desert Generals*, p. 65.

p. 75 'essential', LG 37638, pp. 3429–30.

p. 75 'I got a pick …' Thompson, *Forgotten Voices*, p. 46.

p. 75 'it seems to be …', Churchill, *Second World War*, Vol. III, p. 183.

p. 75 'I think we can …', Thompson, *Forgotten Voices*, p. 43.

p. 76 'unthinkable that …', Churchill, *Second World War*, Vol. III, p. 183.

p. 76 'We feel it vital …', 'an invaluable bridgehead', ibid., pp. 187, 185.

p. 76 Churchill's conversation with Harriman, Roberts, *Masters and Commanders*, p. 4.

p. 77 'If you don't ...', 'there should be no ...', Kitchen, *Rommel's Desert War*, pp. 74, 65.

p. 77 'race against time', 'There'll be no Dunkirk ...', Connell, *Wavell*, p. 407.

p. 78 'The tanks came ...', Thompson, *Forgotten Voices*, p. 46.

p. 78 'which demoralised the enemy ...', ibid., p. 48.

p. 78 'Some of our tanks ...', Robert Lyman, *The Longest Siege: Tobruk – The Battle that Saved North Africa* (Macmillan, 2009)

p. 79 'Their morale is definitely low', Connell, *Wavell*, p. 410.

p. 79 'Perhaps it was ...', Churchill, *Second World War*, Vol. III, p. 186.

p. 79 'We have too few ...', Liddell Hart, *Rommel Papers*, p. 130.

p. 79 'For days Rommel ...', Kitchen, *Rommel's Desert War*, p. 100.

p. 80 'Perhaps he is ...', ibid., p. 95.

7 Trouble at Home and Away

p. 82 'worn and anxious' et seq., Kennedy, *Business of War*, pp. 91, 93.

p. 82 'battle-worthy ...' et seq., ibid., pp. 102, 103.

p. 83 Kennedy at Chequers, ibid., p. 106.

p. 83 'The loss of Egypt ...', Directive by the Prime Minister and Minister of Defence, 28 April, 1941, cited ibid., p. 102.

p. 84–5 Dill and Churchill on the defence of Egypt, Churchill, *Second World War*, Vol. III, pp. 375, 376.

p. 85 'I am sure that ...', Kennedy, *Business of War*, p. 116.

p. 85 'no difficulty in convincing ...', Churchill, *Second World War*, Vol. III, p. 377.

p. 85 'the effects of his ...', Kennedy, *Business of War*, p. 116.

p. 86 'It might be said ...', Churchill, *Second World War*, Vol. III, p. 308.

p. 86 'I was threatened ...', *LG* 37638, pp. 3432–3.

p. 87 'I feel that ...', 'Your glorious defence ...', Churchill, *Second World War*, Vol. III, pp. 260, 262.

p. 88 'to advance in North Africa ...', Kitchen, *Rommel's Desert War*, p. 93.

p. 89 'to give all aid ...', Porch, *Hitler's Mediterranean Gamble*, p. 572.

p. 90 'The security of Egypt ...', Churchill, *Second World War*, Vol. III, p. 237.

p. 90 'Your message ...', 'Wavell gives me ...', Connell, *Wavell*, pp. 438, 439.

p. 91 'The Arab Freedom Movement ...' et seq., Churchill, *Second World War*, Vol. III, p. 234.

p. 92 'What a baby ...', 'Yes, what a baby ...', Kennedy, *Business of War*, p. 117.

p. 92 'Hitler certainly cast ...', Churchill, *Second World War*, Vol. III, p. 236.

p. 92 'Rashid Ali ...', *LG* 37638, p. 3439.

p. 92 'I told Winston ...', Connell, *Wavell*, p. 446.

p. 93 'The Prime Minister ...', Kennedy, *Business of War*, p. 116.

p. 93 'gave us the feeling ...', Churchill, *Second World War*, Vol. III, p. 236.

p. 93 'favourable', 'you must trust ...', Kennedy, *Business of War*, p. 120.

p. 93 'Our view is that ...', Churchill, *Second World War*, Vol. III, p. 290.

p. 94 'What a time you are having ...', Connell, *Wavell*, p. 463.

p. 94–5 Despatch from Cairo, LG 37638, p. 3440.

p. 95 'gladly lay down ...', John Colville, *The Fringes of Power: Downing Street Diaries Volume One, 1939 to October 1941* (Hodder and Stoughton, 1985), Sunday, 25 May 1941, p. 464.

p. 95 Free French encounter with Foreign Legion, Dimbleby, *Frontiers Are Green*, p. 128.

p. 96 'We must again ...', LG 37638, p. 3431.

8 A Fightback Fails

p. 97 'the enemy strength ...', 'a good jumping off place ...', LG 37638, p. 3431.

p. 98 Churchill's demands of Wavell in Cyrenaica, Churchill, *Second World War*, Vol. III, Appendix III, p. 684.

p. 98 'One thing seemed ...', Kennedy, *Business of War*, p. 133.

p. 98 'Everything must now ...', 'My dear Prime Minister ...', Connell, *Wavell*, p. 481.

p. 99 'I think it right ...' et seq., Kennedy, *Business of War*, p. 128.

p. 100 'question of Wavell ...', ibid.

p. 100 'You have at the present ...', Churchill, *Second World War*, Vol. III, p. 707.

p. 101 'The fate of the war ...' et seq., Churchill, *Second World War*, Vol. III, p. 218.

p. 101 'the brilliant success of Tiger', 'the risks I had ...', ibid., pp. 223, 308.

p. 101 Wavell's final despatch, LG 37638.

p. 102 Durham Light Infantry recollections of Capuzzo, Thompson, *Forgotten Voices*, pp. 64, 65, 66–7, 68.

p. 103 'I am sorry ...', Kennedy, *Business of War*, p. 119.

p. 103 'the only time ...', Thomson, *Forgotten Voices*, p. 68.

p. 103 'The three-day battle ...', Liddell Hart, *Rommel Papers*, p. 146.

p. 104 'wandered about the valley ...', Churchill, *Second World War*, Vol. III, p. 308.

p. 104 'The operation which went ...' et seq., de Guingand, *Operation Victory*, p. 88.

p. 104 'after the long strain ...', Churchill, *Second World War*, Vol. III, p. 310.

p. 104 'The Prime Minister's ...', Connell, *Wavell*, p. 505.

p. 104 'sorry he had not done better', Churchill–Dill exchange, Kennedy, *Business of War*, pp. 143, 145.

p. 105 'His fine head ...', Moorehead, *Desert War*, p. 283.
p. 105 'his dark face ...', Victoria Schofield, *Wavell, Soldier and Statesman* (John Murray, 2006), p. 211.
p. 105 'saw suddenly ...', Moorehead, *Desert War*, p. 184.
p. 106 'a military genius,' Young, *Rommel*, p. 95.
p. 106 'He looked tired ...', Schofield, *Wavell*, p. 184.
p. 106 'never less than three ...' et seq., Barnett, *Desert Generals*, p. 77.
p. 107 'Whether we can ...', Kennedy, *Business of War*, p. 139.
p. 107 'I suppose you realise ...', 'Well that depends ...', ibid., p. 133.
p. 108 Churchill's broadcast, Churchill, *Second World War*, Vol. III, pp. 331–2.
p. 109 'We don't think ...', Kennedy, *Business of War*, p. 148.
p. 110 'Not even I ...' et seq., Gibson, *Ciano Diaries*, pp. 369–72, passim.
p. 110 'Few lovers expended ...', Hastings, *Finest Years*, p. 190.
p. 111 'quite understood ...', Colville, *Fringes of Power*, p. 334.
p. 111 'I feel you will ...', Churchill, *Second World War*, Vol. II, p. 489.
p. 112 'like a disorderly day's rabbit-shooting', Hastings, *Finest Years*, p. 191.
p. 112 'They are a quaint lot ...', ibid., p. 188.
p. 112 'had some reason ...', ibid., p. 185.
p. 113 'It was plain ...', Churchill, *Second World War*, Vol. II, p. 493.
p. 113 'whether Churchill's government ...', Hastings, *Finest Years*, p. 172.
p. 113 'England still has ...', 'they aren't bust', Dallek, *Roosevelt and American Foreign Policy*, pp. 252, 253.
p. 113 'The more rapid ...', Churchill, *Second World War*, Vol. II, pp. 500–501.
p. 114 'everything possible ...', 'Suppose my neighbour's ...', Basil Rauch, ed., *Franklin D. Roosevelt: Selected Speeches, Messages, Press Conferences, and Letters* (Easton Press, 1957), p. 269.
p. 114 'There is danger ahead ...', Dallek, *Roosevelt and American Foreign Policy*, pp. 256–7.
p. 115 'This will disturb ...', Churchill, *Second World War*, Vol. II, p. 507.
p. 115 'The thing to do ...', Dallek, *Roosevelt and American Foreign Policy*, p. 255.
p. 116 'A wonderful story ...', Churchill, radio speech broadcast from London to America on receiving the Honorary Degree of Doctor of Laws of the University of Rochester, 16 June 1941.

9 A New Broom in the Desert

p. 118 '[H]e was a soldier ...', Philip Warner, *Auchinleck: The Lonely Soldier* (Cassell, 1981), p. 138.
p. 118 'The fact is ...', Kennedy, *Business of War*, pp. 134–5.
p. 119 'President Roosevelt is now ...', Churchill, *Second World War*, Vol. III, p. 707.
p. 119 'the greatly increased ...', ibid., p. 313.

p. 120 'by converging attacks …', Kitchen, *Rommel's Desert War*, p. 120.

p. 121 'would secure the land bridge …', ibid., p. 121.

p. 122 'artificers, engineers …', Arthur Bryant, *The Turn of the Tide* (Alanbrooke Diaries 1939–1943) (Collins, 1957), p. 325.

p. 122 'invite failure on both fronts', 'there were serious …', Churchill, *Second World War*, Vol. III, pp. 354, 356.

p. 122 'Appreciation', *LG* 37695, 20 August 1946, pp. 4215–16.

p. 122 'naturally prefer certainty …', 'hard and decisive …', Churchill, *Second World War*, Vol. III, pp. 357, 359.

p. 122 'most people near him …', Warner, *Auchinleck*, p. 83.

p. 123 'to launch an offensive …', Churchill, *Second World War*, Vol. III, p. 360.

p. 123 'What I would like …', Warner, *Auchinleck*, p. 91.

p. 123 'unquestioned abilities …', 'a mistake and a misfortune', Churchill, *Second World War*, Vol. III, pp. 363, 364.

p. 124 'Churchill *is* the War Cabinet …', 'I suppose Churchill …', 'too tired even …', Simon Berthon, *Allies at War: The Bitter Rivalry among Churchill, Roosevelt, and de Gaulle* (Caroll and Graf, 2001), pp. 96, 97.

p. 124 'to tell you that …', 'here was an envoy …', Churchill, *Second World War*, Vol. III, p. 21.

p. 125 'Now Mr Prime Minister …' et seq., Kennedy, *Business of War*, pp. 156, 153.

p. 125 'the new situation …', 'large numbers of tanks …', Kennedy, *Business of War*, p. 157.

p. 125–6 Churchill–Hopkins meeting, 24 July 1941, Churchill, *Second World War*, Vol. III, pp. 378–9.

p. 126 'cruise away from …', *Roosevelt Letters*, Vol. III, p. 383.

p. 126 'Even at my ripe old age …', Roberts, *Masters and Commanders*, p. 52.

p. 126 'brooded on the future …', Churchill, *Second World War*, Vol. III, p. 382.

p. 128 'The Battle of the Atlantic …', Dallek, *Roosevelt and American Foreign Policy*, p. 266.

p. 128 'It is time …', ibid., p. 288.

10 Auchinleck Stands Firm

p. 129 'One lies in bed …', Liddell Hart, *Rommel Papers*, p. 148.

p. 130 'Water was unobtainable …', Thompson, *Forgotten Voices*, pp. 75–6.

p. 130 'There is an enervating quality …', Moorehead, *Desert War*, p. 198.

p. 130 'There was through this quiet time …', ibid., pp. 194–5.

p. 131 'It was like …', ibid., p. 225.

p. 131 'We were working …', *LG* 38177, 13 January 1948, p. 311.

p. 131 'thought that troops …', Warner, *Auchinleck*, p. 92.

p. 131 'long personal chatty letter ...', ibid., p. 107.

p. 132 'It is impossible ...', Churchill, *Second World War*, Vol. III, p. 481.

p. 132 'could not only ...' et seq., ibid., p. 344.

p. 132 'felt very deeply ...', ibid., p. 421.

p. 133 'I have hitherto ...', ibid., p. 481.

p. 133 'Weekly and often ...', ibid., p. 478.

p. 133–4 'a victory in Cyrenaica ...', 'Turkey may be ...', ibid., p. 484.

p. 134 'Nothing gives us greater ...', ibid., p. 488.

p. 135 'Whenever an idea ...', Kennedy, *Business of War*, p. 173.

p. 135 'I have in command ...', Churchill, *Second World War*, Vol. III, p. 493.

p. 135 'We were working ...', *LG* 38177, p. 311.

p. 136 'real danger ...', Young, *Rommel*, p. 23.

p. 136 'I am not nervous ...', General Lord Ismay, *The Memoirs of Lord Ismay* (Heinemann, 1960), p. 271.

p. 137 'not just to master ...', Stephen Bungay, 'The Road to Mission Command: The Genesis of a Command Philosophy', *British Army Review* 137 (Summer 2005), pp. 22–32.

p. 137 'which specified ...', ibid.

p. 139 'An engagement occurred ...', Gibson, *Ciano Diaries*, p. 404.

p. 139 'a decisive area ...', 'already tottering ...', Kitchen, *Rommel's Desert War*, p. 139.

p. 140 'I cannot accept ...', ibid. 136.

p. 140 'further relief', Churchill, *Second World War*, Vol. III, p. 462.

p. 140 'This was the beginning ...', ibid., p. 492.

p. 140 'It rained in squalls ...', Moorehead, *Desert War*, p. 232.

p. 142 'I hear you wish ...', Young, *Rommel*, p. 102.

p. 142 'Mercifully for us ...', Friedrich von Mellenthin, *Panzer Battles* (Spellmount, 2008), pp. 63–4.

p. 143 'It was a wild ...', 'orchestrating tanks ...', John Bierman and Colin Smith, *Alamein: War Without Hate* (Penguin, 2003), pp. 107–8.

p. 143 'sat on his tank ...', Moorehead, *Desert War*, pp. 234–5.

p. 144 'like a man berserk ...', ibid., p. 238.

p. 144 'I cannot describe ...', Gilbert, *Desert War*, p. 55.

p. 145 'went through the back ...', 'An anti-tank rifle ...', Gilbert, *Desert War*, pp. 55–6.

p. 145 'This was a momentous ...', Michael Carver, *Tobruk* (Pan, 1964), p. 44.

p. 145 'With luck earth ...', Churchill, *Second World War*, Vol. III, p. 504.

p. 145 'the destruction of ...', Liddell Hart, *Rommel Papers*, p. 154.

p. 145 'our difficulties began', *LG* 38177, pp. 312ff.

p. 146 'We headed straight ...', Carver, *Tobruk*, p. 72.

p. 146–7 2nd Rifle Brigade at Sidi Rezegh, ibid., p. 54.

p. 147 'When I came to ...', Thompson, *Forgotten Voices*, p. 98.

p. 147 Auchinleck's despatch, *LG* 38177.

p. 147 'the tanks shone …', von Mellenthin, *Panzer Battles*, p. 67.

p. 148 Bayerlein's account of Sidi Rezegh, Liddell Hart, *Rommel Papers*, pp. 161–2, 169.

p. 148 'The sights were horrible …', Thompson, *Forgotten Voices*, p. 106.

p. 149 'excited exultation', 'The battle seems …', Liddell Hart, *Rommel Papers*, pp. XXX, 162.

p. 149 'annihilation', 'shifting in the balance …', LG 38177.

p. 149 'under great strain', Barnett, *Desert Generals*, p. 112.

p. 149 'lost his nerve …', *The Auk at Ninety*, BBC TV (1974).

p. 149 'with the intuition …', 'I thought Rommel …', Barnett, *Desert Generals*, p. 112.

p. 149–50 'I am convinced …', 'Am immensely heartened …', Churchill, *Second World War*, Vol. III, p. 505.

11 The Tables Are Turned

p. 151 'the contagion of bewilderment …', 'I came to understand …', Moorehead, *Desert War*, pp. 239–40.

p. 152 'grossly over-estimated', 'prevented the enemy …', 'A British truck …', LG 38177, p. 312.

p. 153 'a strong sun-burned …' et seq., Barnett, *Desert Generals*, p. 114.

p. 154 'His position is desperate …', Barnett, *Desert Generals*, p. 116.

p. 154 'I have formed the …', 'It is no use …', Warner, *Auchinleck*, p. 110.

p. 155 'straightforward and absolutely honest …', 'handsome and authoritative …', 'Ritchie was perforce …' et seq., Barnett, *Desert Generals*, pp. 123, 124.

p. 156 'We just assumed …', Robert Crisp, *Brazen Chariots*, cited in Porch, *Hitler's Mediterranean Gamble*, p. 249.

p. 156 'the Afrikakorps …', von Mellenthin, *Panzer Battles*, p. 70.

p. 156 'Night was the …', Thompson, *Forgotten Voices*, p. 51.

p. 157 'Dust, flies …', ibid., p. 54.

p. 157 'We had no pleasures …', Gilbert, *Desert War*, p. 25.

p. 157 'What are you doing here?' ibid., p. 88.

p. 157 'I took the rifle …', ibid., p. 58.

p. 158 'They were quite …' et seq., IWM file no. 19956, www.iwm.org.uk/collections/item/object/80019410.

p. 159 'It was a journey …', Leeds University Library, Liddle Collection (1939–45), Army 087, V. Gray.

p. 160 'Tobruk is relieved …', Thompson, *Forgotten Voices*, p. 106.

p. 160 'Several aircraft …' et seq., Moorehead, *Desert War*, pp. 245–6.

p. 161 'I've had to break off …', 'We're pulling out …', Liddell Hart, *Rommel Papers*, pp. 172, 175.

p. 161 'gone through the township …', Moorehead, *Desert War*, p. 254.

p. 162 'It was an exhilarating journey ...' et seq., Liddle Collection, V. Gray, p. 177.

p. 163 'a bitter taste remained' et seq., Young, *Rommel*, p. 116.

p. 164 'Here then ...', Churchill, *Second World War*, Vol. III, pp. 574ff.

p. 164 'I banged the old piano ...', Dimbleby, *Frontiers Are Green*, p. 141.

12 Roosevelt Joins the Fray

p. 165 'Mr President ...', Churchill, *Second World War*, Vol. III, p. 537.

p. 165 'Being saturated ...', ibid., pp. 539–40.

p. 166 'In the past ...', Hastings, *Finest Years*, p. 215.

p. 166 'Oh! that is the way ...', Bryant, *Turn of the Tide*, p. 282.

p. 166 'The forces endeavouring ...', Dallek, *Roosevelt and American Foreign Policy*, p. 317.

p. 167 'I have sworn ...', 'I foresee ...', Gibson, *Ciano Diaries*, pp. 373, 374.

p. 167 'review the whole war plan ...', Churchill, *Second World War*, Vol. III, p. 541.

p. 167 'the overpowering personality ...', Hastings, *Finest Years*, p. 216.

p. 167 'it would be disastrous ...', Churchill, *Second World War*, Vol. III, p. 542.

p. 168 'from Africa eastwards ...', Bryant, *Turn of the Tide*, p. 226.

p. 169 'that the defeat ...', Churchill, *Second World War*, Vol. III, p. 571.

p. 169 'an immense feat ...', Roberts, *Masters and Commanders*, p. 69.

p. 169 'the total destruction ...' et seq., Churchill, *Second World War*, Vol. III, pp. 574ff.

p. 170 'We were conscious ...', ibid., p. 568.

p. 170 'as a mark of respect', Loewenheim et al., *Roosevelt and Churchill Correspondence*, p. 172.

p. 171 'Here, in the midst ...', 'found peace ...', Churchill, *Second World War*, Vol. III, p. 594.

p. 171–2 Roosevelt–Churchill strategy correspondence, Loewenheim et al., *Roosevelt and Churchill Correspondence*, pp. 138, 140, 141.

p. 172 'considered it very ...', Dallek, *Roosevelt and American Foreign Policy*, p. 321.

p. 000 'the Limeys', 'jolly old England', Roberts, *Masters and Commanders*, p. 83.

p. 173 'The Limeys want us in ...', Dallek, *Roosevelt and American Foreign Policy*, p. 322.

p. 174 'You know, my friend ...', ibid., p. 324.

p. 174 Boxing Day speech, Churchill, *Second World War*, Vol. III, p. 596.

p. 175 'against savage and brutal forces ...', ibid., p. 606.

p. 175 'breathed freezing cold ...', Roberts, *Masters and Commanders*, p. 85.

p. 175 'a very dangerous operation', 'take no chances ...', Dallek, *Roosevelt and American Foreign Policy*, p. 322.

p. 176 'our thoughts flowed ...', 'the first step towards ...', 'stubborn resistance ...', Churchill, *Second World War*, Vol. III, pp. 606, 621.

p. 178 'everything that he needed', Kitchen, *Rommel's Desert War*, p. 185.

p. 178 'mostly excuses', 'cheered', Gibson, *Ciano Diaries*, p. 431.

p. 178 'has used big figures ...', 'reminds one only ...', 'never in the course of history', ibid., pp. 435, 423, 358.

13 The Desert Fox Goes Hunting

p. 180 'The situation is developing ...', Liddell Hart, *Rommel Papers*, p. 179.

p. 180 'the enemy seemed ...', LG 38177, p. 137.

p. 181 'infuriated the forward troops ...', Bierman and Smith, *Alamein*, p. 133.

p. 181 'greatly increasing ...', von Mellenthin, *Panzer Battles*, p. 74.

p. 181 'the island's defiant guns ...', Bryant, *Turn of the Tide*, p. 286.

p. 181 'hard-pressed more than ...', Churchill, *Second World War*, Vol. III, p. 21.

p. 182 'I was at relative peace ...', Liddle Collection, V. Gray, p. 179.

p. 182 'leapfrogged from one ...', Bierman and Smith, *Alamein*, p. 135.

p. 183 'I wonder what ...', Liddell Hart, *Rommel Papers*, p. 181.

p. 183 'We obtained further things ...', Bierman and Smith, *Alamein*, p. 135.

p. 184 'I am much disturbed ...', Churchill, *Second World War*, Vol. IV, p. 25.

p. 184 'defeat of our armour ...', ibid., p. 28.

p. 185 'skilful and bold' ...', ibid., p. 29.

p. 185 'it soon became apparent ...', von Mellenthin, *Panzer Battles*, p. 76.

p. 186 'any reasonable hope ...', Churchill, *Second World War*, Vol. IV, p. 29.

p. 186 'Make it no more ...', Liddell Hart, *Rommel Papers*, p. 182.

p. 186 'shortage of fuel ...', 'nobody but the Führer ...', Kitchen, *Rommel's Desert War*, p. 191.

p. 187 'Second Benghazi Handicap', Warner, *Auchinleck*, p. 118.

p. 187 'went like greased lightning', Liddell Hart, *Rommel Papers*, p. 183.

p. 187 'He came out continually ...', Alanbrooke, *War Diaries 1939–45*, p. 226.

p. 187–8 'his brain was ...' et seq., Kennedy, *Business of War*, p. 161, 178, 179.

p. 188 'repulsive', Alanbrooke, *War Diaries 1939–45*, p. 192.

p. 188 'the de facto British Ambassador ...', 'a key figure ...', Roberts, *Masters and Commanders*, p. 76.

p. 189 'like a peevish child ...' et seq., Alanbrooke, *War Diaries 1939–45*, p. 207.

p. 190 'it had been ...' et seq., Churchill, *Second World War*, Vol. IV, pp. 58, 59.

p. 191 'many ebbs and flows' et seq., House of Commons Official Report, 27 January 1942.

p. 191 'Although I feel …', Churchill, *Second World War*, Vol. IV, p. 62.

p. 191 'I have during …', Alanbrooke, *War Diaries 1939–45*, pp. 228–9.

p. 192 'almost certain', Kennedy, *Business of War*, p. 196.

p. 192 'impregnable fortress', Loewenheim et al., *Roosevelt and Churchill Correspondence*, p. 184.

p. 192 'in these trying weeks' et seq., ibid., pp. 179, 181, 238.

p. 192 'I am anxious …', Eade, *Secret Session Speeches*, p. 54.

p. 193 'utterly inadequate', 'We refuse to accept …', 'Night and day …', Churchill, *Second World War*, Vol. IV, pp. 6, 7, 9.

p. 194 'an inexcusable betrayal' et seq., ibid., pp. 139, 144.

14 Trouble at the Top

p. 196–7 'he was showing …', 'I just sit silent …', Kennedy, *Business of War*, pp. 208, 203.

p. 197 Churchill's response to Auchinleck's 'Appreciation', Churchill, *Second World War*, Vol. IV, p. 261.

p. 197–8 'he poured abuse …', 'I am positive …', 'another example …', Alanbrooke, *War Diaries 1939–45*, pp. 235, 206.

p. 198 'armies were not …', Kennedy, *Business of War*, p. 205.

p. 198 'Viewing the war …', 'so signally …', Warner, *Auchinleck*, p. 131.

p. 198 'defensive', ibid., p. 205.

p. 198 'the longer he waited …', Kennedy, *Business of War*, p. 205.

p. 199 'almost one of …', 'This tiny island …', *Memoirs of Lord Ismay*, p. 273.

p. 199 'his feelings would …', Kennedy, *Business of War*, p. 206.

p. 199 'Found the PM …', Lord Charles Moran, *Churchill at War, 1940–45* (Robinson, 2002), p. 54.

p. 199 'at your earliest convenience', Churchill, *Second World War*, Vol. IV, p. 262.

p. 200 'infuriated …', Bryant, *Turn of the Tide*, p. 338.

p. 200 'extreme regret', 'I have done everything …', 'It seemed to me …', 'at least fifteen …', Churchill, *Second World War*, Vol. IV, pp. 262–3.

p. 201 'We have got to face the fact …', Warner, *Auchinleck*, pp. 122–3.

p. 202 'the growth of …', ibid., p. 123.

p. 203 'our hardness and fighting spirit …', Kennedy, *Business of War*, p. 198.

p. 203 'were undoubtedly softer …', ibid.

p. 203–4 'The more I see …' et seq., Alanbrooke, *War Diaries 1939–45*, p. 170.

p. 204 'drastic measures' et seq., Kennedy, *Business of War*, p. 199.

p. 205 'The British soldier …', Liddell Hart, *Rommel Papers*, p. 185.

p. 205 'Contrary to the principle …', ibid., p. 184.

p. 205 'The last day ...', Alanbrooke, *War Diaries 1939–45*, pp. 243–4.

p. 206 'the cumulative and accelerating ...', Barnett, *Desert Generals*, p. 110.

p. 206 'The third-rate mind ...', Lavinia Greacen, *Chink: A Biography* (Macmillan, 1989), p. 151.

p. 207 'I have given Dorman-Smith ...' et seq., ibid., pp. 191, 183.

p. 208 'I am very satisfied ...' et seq., Churchill, *Second World War*, Vol. IV, pp. 263–4.

p. 209 'If we had judged ...', Kennedy, *Business of War*, p. 197.

p. 209 'purely a temporary ...', 'He is a mass ...', 'YOU MUST COME HOME ...', Warner, *Auchinleck*, p. 136.

15 Deadlock

p. 210 'These holes ...', John Ellis, *The Sharp End* (Aurum, 1990), pp. 38–9.

p. 210–11 Snell and Lewis recollections, Thompson, *Forgotten Voices*, pp. 116, 117.

p. 212 'a complete clown ...', Gibson, *Ciano Diaries*, p. 442.

p. 212 'under no circumstances whatsoever', Kitchen, *Rommel's Desert War*, p. 197.

p. 213 'As I have completed ...', 'What Harry and ...', Churchill, *Second World War*, Vol. IV, pp. 280, 281.

p. 213 'I think we realize ...', *Roosevelt Letters*, Vol. III, p. 424.

p. 214 'Communism under Stalin ...', Hastings, *Finest Years*, p. 287.

p. 214 'My darling ...', Mary Soames, ed., *Speaking for Themselves: The Personal Letters of Winston and Clementine Churchill* (Black Swan, 1998), p. 464.

p. 215 'I had to make ...', *Roosevelt Letters*, Vol. III, p. 423.

p. 215 'I doubt if any ...', Roberts, *Masters and Commanders*, p. 125.

p. 215 'in which a powerful offensive ...', Bryant, *Turn of the Tide*, p. 345.

p. 215 'the extreme hazards', Roberts, *Masters and Commanders*, p. 120.

p. 216 'Western Europe is favoured ...', Churchill, *Second World War*, Vol. IV, p. 281.

p. 216–7 'the stupidity', 'so ridiculous ...', Kennedy, *Business of War*, p. 224.

p. 217 'What he did not realise ...', Mosley, *Marshall*, p. 203.

p. 217 'a pleasant and easy man ...', Alanbrooke, *War Diaries 1939–45*, p. 246.

p. 217 'Brooke made ...', 'In our opinion ...', Roberts, *Masters and Commanders*, pp. 141, 142.

p. 217 'selfless men ...', Moran, *Churchill at War*, p. 41.

p. 218 'impossible to imagine ...', *Memoirs of Lord Ismay*, p. 251.

p. 218 'extremely closely together', Alanbrooke, *War Diaries 1939–45*, p. 246.

p. 218 'initial joust', 'adept in the use ...', Roberts, *Masters and Commanders*, pp. 147–8.

p. 218 'virtually accepted *in toto* ...', ibid., p. 151.

p. 218 'in full agreement …', Churchill, *Second World War*, Vol. IV, p. 283.

p. 218 'in 1942 perhaps …', Alanbrooke, *War Diaries 1939–45*, p. 248.

p. 219 'They had not begun …' et seq., ibid., pp. 248, 249

p. 219 'stopping up rat holes', Roberts, *Masters and Commanders*, p. 128.

p. 219–20 'Unless the Middle East …', 'disastrous consequences', 'in every practical way', ibid., p. 127.

p. 220 'it was essential …', 'we could not entirely …', Churchill, *Second World War*, Vol. IV, p. 283.

p. 220 'resolved to march forward …' et seq., ibid., p. 287.

p. 221 'The plans are fraught …', Alanbrooke, *War Diaries 1939–45*, p. 250.

p. 221 'reservations about this or that' et seq., Bryant, *Turn of the Tide*, p. 356.

p. 221 'influence and diplomacy …', 'more difficult …', Churchill, *Second World War*, Vol. IV, pp. 290, 289.

p. 222 'No doubts were expressed …', *Memoirs of Lord Ismay*, p. 240.

16 Stretched to Breaking Point

p. 223 'He has already …', 'Just imagine …', Bullock, *Hitler and Stalin*, pp. 859, 832.

p. 224 'can be considered …', 'the strategic consequences …', Kitchen, *Rommel's Desert War*, p. 199.

p. 224 'make it impossible …', Michael Howard, *The Mediterranean Strategy in the Second World War* (Greenhill, 1968), p. 12.

p. 225 'capture or total neutralisation', Kitchen, *Rommel's Desert War*, p. 199.

p. 225–6 'suppression of Malta', 'neutralise', 'People fled …', 'Civilians queued …', Porch, *Hitler's Mediterranean Gamble*, pp. 262, 261, 263.

p. 226 'it is obvious …', Churchill, *Second World War*, Vol. IV, p. 272.

p. 226 'when only five …', Bierman and Smith, *Alamein*, p. 122.

p. 227 'too much should not …' et seq., Warner, *Auchinleck*, pp. 136–7.

p. 227–8 'If the immediate …', 'every resource …', 'to check the Japanese …', 'The matter most …', 'very nice for us …', 'I feel very strongly …', ibid., p. 137.

p. 228 'Kitchener's machine guns …', 'To give peace …', Jeremy Paxman, *Empire: What the World Did to the British* (Viking, 2011), p. 120.

p. 229 'on the subject of India …', ibid., p. 259.

p. 229 '*volunteered*', 'mercenaries …', Churchill, *Second World War*, Vol. IV, p. 187.

p. 230 'I have given much thought …' et seq., Loewenheim et al., *Roosevelt and Churchill Correspondence*, pp. 191–2.

p. 230 'full independence …', Churchill, *Second World War*, Vol. IV, p. 191.

p. 231 'I feel that …', 'I was thankful …', ibid., p. 194.

p. 231 'would not have hesitated …', et seq., ibid., pp. 194–5.

p. 232 'deeply disturbed', ibid., p. 231.

p. 232 'With very great respect …', 'disastrous consequences', 'I beg you …', ibid., p. 232.

p. 233 'While we are grateful …', ibid., p. 275.

p. 234 'would be a disaster …', ibid., p. 275.

p. 234 'This was an incredible …', 'The manner in which …', Kennedy, *Business of War*, p. 226.

p. 234–5 'a most unusual procedure', 'obey or be relieved', Churchill, *Second World War*, Vol. IV, p. 275.

p. 235 'We are determined …', 'very latest date…', ibid., pp. 275–6.

p. 235 'It is necessary …', 'My intention is …' et seq., ibid., p. 276.

p. 236 'We have full confidence …', 'I am now absolutely …', ibid., p. 277.

p. 236 'bloated', Porch, *Hitler's Mediterranean Gamble*, p. 264.

p. 237 'treated Hitler …', Kitchen, *Rommel's Desert War*, p. 208.

p. 238 'The usual scene …', Gibson, *Ciano Diaries*, p. 477.

p. 238 'British Conservatives …' et seq., ibid., p. 478.

p. 238 'Nothing much to report …', Liddell Hart, *Rommel Papers*, p. 188.

p. 239 'strengths, positions …', 'under the gimlet eyes', C. J. Jenner, 'Turning the Hinge of Fate: Good Source and the UK-US Intelligence Alliance, 1940–1942', *Diplomatic History*, 32, 2 (April 2008), pp. 165–205.

p. 239 'General Wavell told me …', Bierman and Smith, *Alamein*, p. 44.

p. 240 'The trouble is …', 'stupefying in its openness', 'contributed decisively …', Jenner, 'Turning the Hinge of Fate', p. 166.

p. 240 'all we needed …', ibid., p. 171.

17 The Worst of Times

p. 241 'There is a cloud of dust …', Gilbert, *Desert War*, p. 100.

p. 242 'It will be hard …', 'I was tense …', Liddell Hart, *Rommel Papers*, pp. 204, 206.

p. 242–3 'Do not think …' et seq., LG 38177, Appendix 16, pp. 390–91.

p. 243 'this great force', 'in a swirling cloud …', Liddell Hart, *Rommel Papers*, p. 207.

p. 243 'an awful muck of a battle', Kitchen, *Rommel's Desert War*, p. 221.

p. 244 'I didn't realise …', 'those two lads …', 'gabbling out the message' et seq., Thompson, *Forgotten Voices*, p. 122.

p. 245 'in some cases …', von Mellenthin, *Panzer Battles*, p. 81.

p. 245 'fled away …', 'The advent of …', Liddell Hart, *Rommel Papers*, p. 207.

p. 245 'Eighth Army were …', de Guingand, *Operation Victory*, p. 115.

p. 246 'Shells flew all round …', 'took us for hostile …', Liddell Hart, *Rommel Papers*, p. 209.

p. 247 'a crushing victory', von Mellenthin, *Panzer Battles*, p. 81.

p. 247 'Although his lightning attack …', 'Our armour strove …', 'had succeeded …', LG 38177, p. 356.

p. 248 'in a really desperate position ...' et seq., Young, *Rommel*, p. 103.

p. 248–9 'Yoicks. Tally ho ...' et seq., 'Bob, you are to stand ...' et seq., 'He was terrified ...' et seq., Thompson, *Forgotten Voices*, pp. 129, 131, 137.

p. 249–50 'it was just ...', 'it really became ...', Major A. H. G. Dobson in Gilbert, *Desert War*, p. 102.

p. 250 'If we had not ...', Young, *Rommel*, p. 101.

p. 250 'Our mines ...', de Guingand, *Operation Victory*, p. 116.

p. 250–1 'leaving the toes ...' et seq., Dimbleby, *Frontiers Are Green*, p. 262.

p. 251 'Most of them ...' et seq., ibid., p. 270.

p. 251 'Coming at us ...', Robert Lee, Events in North Africa, Experiences on the Gazala Line, Second World War Experience Centre: www.war-experience.org/history/keyaspects/nafrica0642/pagetwo.asp.

p. 252 'I am distressed ...', 'I *think* Ritchie ...', Barnett, *Desert Generals*, p. 155.

p. 252 'It seemed to me ...', 'We appeared to be ...', *LG* 38177, p. 357.

p. 253 'The 32nd Army Tank Brigade ...', ibid., p. 358.

p. 253 'gravely embarrassing', 'the heavy British tanks ...', von Mellenthin, *Panzer Battles*, p. 86.

p. 253 'In the first second ...', Bierman and Smith, *Alamein*, p. 171.

p. 254 'had, indeed recovered ...', Young, *Rommel*, p. 105.

p. 254 'form a new ...', *LG* 38177, p. 359.

p. 254 'in the whole course ...', von Mellenthin, *Panzer Battles*, p. 86.

p. 254–5 'General Koenig ...', 'We are surrounded ...', Bierman and Smith, *Alamein*, p. 173.

p. 255 'some of these ...', 'When a ray ...', Bierman and Smith, *Alamein*, p. 174.

p. 255 'tremendous courage and tenacity', Liddell Hart, *Rommel Papers*, p. 222.

p. 255 'The English Guards ...', Moorehead, *Desert War*, p. 347.

p. 256 'Well done, 8th Army ...', Michael Carver, *Dilemmas of the Desert War: The Libyan Campaign 1940–1942* (Spellmount, 2002), p. 88.

p. 256 'I don't understand ...', Moorehead, *Desert War*, p. 349.

p. 256 'Germans and Italians alike ...', Dimbleby, *Frontiers Are Green*, p. 272.

p. 257 'we were bombed ...', 'slaughter of British tanks ...', Liddell Hart, *Rommel Papers*, p. 221.

p. 258 'evidently', 'losses on both sides ...', Carver, *Dilemmas of the Desert War*, p. 104.

p. 258 'I was lucky ...', 'we were shot up ...', Thompson, *Forgotten Voices*, pp. 144, 147.

p. 258 'like horses in a race ...', Liddle Collection, Earl Haig, unpublished manuscript, pp. 130–31.

p. 259 'was a very messy business ...', Liddle Collection, Earl Haig, tape-recorded interview with Earl Haig by Peter Liddle.

p. 259 'courage of the German ...'et seq., 'The battle has been ...', Liddell Hart, *Rommel Papers*, pp. 222–3, 224.

p. 259 'Your decision to fight ...' et seq., Churchill, *Second World War*, Vol. IV, p. 331.

p. 260 'the firm and unanimous decision ...', Andrew B. Cunningham, *A Sailor's Odyssey: The Autobiography of Admiral of the Fleet, Admiral Cunningham*, pp. 464–5, cited in Niall Barr, *Pendulum of War* (Pimlico, 2005), p. 16.

p. 260 'It is not my intention ...', LG 38177, Appendix 6, pp. 377–8.

p. 260 'If, for any reason ...', Kennedy, *Business of War*, p. 243.

p. 260 'At home we had ...', Churchill, *Second World War*, Vol. IV, p. 372.

p. 260 'War Cabinet interpret ...', ibid., p. 332.

p. 261 'War Cabinet interpretation ...', 'was glad to know ...', 'business of the highest ...', ibid., pp. 332, 334.

p. 261 'To every man of us ... .', Liddell Hart, *Rommel Papers*, p. 225.

p. 261–2 'like the crenellated battlements ...' et seq., 'Indeed ...', Moorehead, *Desert War*, p. 370.

p. 262 'tinned tomatoes ...' et seq., ibid., p. 372.

p. 262 'Things are going ...', Carver, *Dilemmas of the Desert War*, p. 119.

p. 263 'Kesselring had been good ...', von Mellenthin, *Panzer Battles*, p. 90.

p. 263 'terrifying', 'we didn't know ...', Bierman and Smith, *Alamein*, p. 181.

p. 264 'weak resistance', von Mellenthin, *Panzer Battles*, p. 91.

p. 264 'hundreds', 'at the sight of ...', Vittorio Vallicella, *Diario di Guerra da El Alamein all tragica ritirata, 1942–1943* (Edizioni Arterigere, 2009), p. 18.

p. 264 'By nightfall ...', von Mellenthin, *Panzer Battles*, p. 92.

p. 264 'got as drunk as lords ...', 'Deutschland uber Alles', Bierman and Smith, *Alamein*, p. 183.

p. 265 'Situation shambles', 'An order was circulated ...', LG 38177, p. 362.

p. 265 'Bodies lay everywhere ...', Bierman and Smith, *Alamein*, p. 183.

p. 265 'Practically every building ...', Liddell Hart, *Rommel Papers*, p. 231.

p. 265 'We have only ...', Vallicella, *Diario di Guerra*, p. 20.

p. 265 'Tobruk! It was a wonderful battle', 'Soldiers of the Panzer Army ...' et seq., Liddell Hart, *Rommel Papers*, pp. 231, 232.

p. 265 'destiny's gift ...', Kitchen, *Rommel's Desert War*, p. 244.

18 The Americans Come Good

p. 267 'the risks of ...', Roberts, *Masters and Commanders*, p. 199.

p. 267 'No responsible British ...', Churchill, *Second World War*, Vol. IV, p. 342.

p. 268 'imperative' et seq., Roberts, *Masters and Commanders*, p. 190.

p. 268 'blunt and stand-offish ...', *Memoirs of Lord Ismay*, p. 253.

p. 268 'abandoned, or ...', Roberts, *Masters and Commanders*, p. 187.

p. 269 'the plans that ...', 'brewing up', 'a bit peevish ...', Alanbrooke, *War Diaries 1939–45*, pp. 267, 268.

p. 270 'It was a bitter moment ...' et seq., Churchill, *Second World War*, Vol. IV, pp. 343–4.

p. 270 'This was a hideous ...', 'used to stroll ...', *Memoirs of Lord Ismay*, pp. 254, 256.

p. 270 'vividly', 'tact and real heartfelt sympathy', Alanbrooke, *War Diaries 1939–45*, p. 269.

p. 270 'no reproaches ...', Churchill, *Second World War*, Vol. IV, p. 344.

p. 270 'It was at moments ...', *Memoirs of Lord Ismay*, p. 255.

p. 271 'Give us as many ...', 'a terrible thing ...', Churchill, *Second World War*, Vol. IV, p. 344.

p. 271: 'threatened a complete collapse ...', Sherwood, Eyre and Spottiswoode, *An Intimate History*, 1949.

p. 271 'may lead to USA ...', Alanbrooke, *War Diaries 1939–45*, p. 270.

p. 272 'completed in all details ...', Roberts, *Masters and Commanders*, p. 201.

p. 272 'great difficulty to get ...', Alanbrooke, *War Diaries 1939–45*, p. 272.

p. 273 'With numerically superior ...', Jenner, 'Turning the Hinge of Fate', p. 176.

p. 274 'a large American force', 'not trusting himself ...', Roberts, *Masters and Commanders*, p. 205.

p. 275 'Fellers is a ...', ibid.

p. 275 'deny the probability ...', 'You are familiar with ...', ibid.

p. 275 'Whitehall handled Washington's disgrace ...', Jenner, 'Turning the Hinge of Fate', p. 175.

p. 276 'The Briton-in-the-street ...', *Time*, 29 June 1942.

p. 276 'We all felt immensely ...', 'another unfrequented little club ...', Kennedy, *Business of War*, p. 248.

p. 276 'I squirmed beneath ...' et seq., Hastings, *Finest Years*, p. 303.

p. 277 'There is no doubt ...' et seq., Churchill, *Second World War*, Vol. IV, p. 354.

p. 277 'Dimbleby's facts ...', Dimbleby, *Richard Dimbleby*, p. 154.

p. 277 'There is no doubt ...', ibid.

p. 277 'emphasise our general ...', 'Fundamentally our task ...', ibid., p. 151.

p. 278 'It is really disgraceful ...', ibid., p. 155.

p. 278 'suppressed', 'in the hope that ...', 'The Cairo mind ...', Dimbleby, *Frontiers Are Green*, p. 274.

p. 278 'glowing news ...', 'was justified ...', Dimbleby, *Richard Dimbleby*, p. 156.

p. 278 'The BBC should ...', 'come to loathe ...', ibid., p. 158.

p. 279 'The Prime Minister wins ...', 'whenever we have disasters ...', 'We may lose Egypt ...', Hansard, Vol. 381, Cols. 527, 313, 582.

p. 279 'on the ground ...', 'the Prime Minister ...', 'the debate was ...', Churchill, *Second World War*, Vol. IV, p. 357.

p. 280 'military misfortunes', 'We are at this moment ...', 'If there are any ...', 'bitter pang', 'Some people assume ...', 'Lobby gossip ...', Hansard, Vol. 381, Cols 584, 585, 588, 610.

p. 281 'He had not yet ...', *Time*, 13 July 1942.

19 The Auk's Last Stand

p. 282–3 'I deeply regret ...', 'Whatever views I may have ...', 'ration strength', 'for three or four weeks', 'every fit male ...', Churchill, *Second World War*, Vol. IV, pp. 348, 349.

p. 283–4 'Kesselring maintained ...', 'the reasoned and powerful ...', 'it is only once ...', von Mellenthin, *Panzer Battles*, p. 93.

p. 284 'We got off very lightly ...', ibid., p. 96.

p. 284 'I pointed out to him ...', Bierman and Smith, *Alamein*, p. 201.

p. 285 'Morale in good units ...', Thompson, *Forgotten Voices*, p. 162.

p. 285 'Well, Briel ...', Latimer, *Alamein*, p. 54.

p. 285 'Get out your frocks ...', Cooper, *Cairo in the War*, p. 192.

p. 286 'All day ...', Moorehead, *Desert War*, p. 383.

p. 286 'were burnt in the open ...', Latimer, *Alamein*, p. 56.

p. 286 'in the most dreadful state ...', Lampson anecdote, Cooper, *Cairo in the War*, pp. 195, 196.

p. 287 'They thought Rommel ...', BBC WW2 People's War, Article A2927054, www.bbc.co.uk/history/ww2peopleswar/stories/54/a2927054.shtml

p. 287 'assuring him that ...', Cooper, *Cairo in the War*, p. 193.

p. 287–8 'all people are God's people ...' et seq., Kitchen, *Rommel's Desert War*, p. 113.

p. 288 'altogether too provocative ...', ibid., p. 114.

p. 288 'once the enemy ...', Cooper, *Cairo in the War*, p. 197.

p. 289 'much pain' et seq., Gibson, *Ciano Diaries*, pp. 502, 505.

p. 290 '[W]e are stuck ...', Vallicella, *Diario di Guerra*, p. 39.

p. 291 'furious artillery fire ...', 'an enterprise and audacity', Liddell Hart, *Rommel Papers*, pp. 246, 254.

p. 291 'The struggle for the last ...', 'Unfortunately, things are not ...', ibid., p. 249.

p. 292 'We come out of our holes ...', TNA AIR 41/50, The Middle East Campaign, Vol. IV.

p. 292 'For 16 months ...', Vallicella, *Diario di Guerra*, p. 46.

p. 292 'longed to have had ...', 'did not seem able ...', IWM AL 879/1: '90 Light Div (Afrika), War Diary'; EDS Collection, Doc. 11929, www.iwm.org.uk/collections/item/object/1030011787.

p. 292–3 'with an almost unbelievable ...', 'the men's amazing spirit ...', 'a series of violent ...', Liddell Hart, *Rommel Papers*, pp. 243, 245.

p. 294 Morshead–Auchinleck exchange, Barr, *Pendulum of War*, p. 101.

p. 294–5 'These fellows were bloody heroes ...', 'The Germans concentrated ...', 'I turned my company ...', Thompson, *Forgotten Voices*, pp. 164, 166, 167.

p. 296 'We don't have to bother ...' et seq., pp. 112, 113, 114.

p. 296 'saw great clouds ...', Latimer, *Alamein*, p. 70.

p. 297 'trapped in a saucer', 'Shells were now landing ...', Liddle Collection, Earl Haig, unpublished manuscript, p. 154.

p. 297 'fundamental cause ...', 'I was firm ...', LG 38177, pp. 367, 366.

p. 297 'great opportunity ...', 'still possible ...', von Mellenthin, *Panzer Battles*, p. 99.

p. 297–8 'very serious situation' et seq., Liddell Hart, *Rommel Papers*, pp. 254–9.

p. 298 'You have done well ...', Warner, *Auchinleck*, p. 157.

p. 298 'the price to Auchinleck ...', Liddell Hart, *Rommel Papers*, p. 260.

20 Enter Montgomery

p. 300–1 'the retention of Iraq ...', 'If the Russians ...', Kennedy, *Business of War*, pp. 219, 220.

p. 301 'much closer to achieving ...', Kitchen, *Rommel's Desert War*, p. 277.

p. 302 'the only way in which ...', 'they were of fundamental ...', 'I quite understand ...', Barr, *Pendulum of War*, p. 97.

p. 302–3 'with his back ...', 'If Rommel's army ...', 'much hangs on this battle', 'even if Auchinleck ...', 'how narrow we considered ...', Kennedy, *Business of War*, pp. 254, 256, 257.

p. 303 'That the threat did not materialise ...', Bryant, *Turn of the Tide*, p. 477.

p. 303 'During this month of July ...', Churchill, *Second World War*, Vol. IV, p. 390.

p. 303 'No responsible British general ...' et seq., ibid., p. 392.

p. 304 'to bury', 'had been dead ...', ibid., p. 390.

p. 304 'everything points ...', ibid., p. 397.

p. 304 'a showdown', 'obstinacy', 'the British ...', 'forceful, unswerving adherence ...', Roberts, *Masters and Commanders*, p. 231.

p. 305 'thumping argument', ibid., p. 239.

p. 305 'there would be no shift ...', Dallek, *Roosevelt and American Foreign Policy*, p. 349.

p. 305 'to reach immediate agreement', Roberts, *Masters and Commanders*, p. 242.

p. 305 'drive in against ...', Dallek, *Roosevelt and American Foreign Policy*, p. 349.

p. 306 'The Prime Minister threw ...', Roberts, *Masters and Commanders*, p. 243.

p. 306 'My diary for 1942 ...', Moran, *Churchill at War*, p. 54.

p. 306 'Disappointing start! ...', Alanbrooke, *War Diaries 1939–45*, p. 283.

p. 307 'a fatigued and defeatist ...', 'western front in 1942 ...', Roberts, *Masters and Commanders*, pp. 251, 252.

p. 307 'almost everything ...' et seq., Alanbrooke, *War Diaries 1939–45*, p. 285.

p. 307 'I cannot help ...', Churchill, *Second World War*, Vol. IV, p. 405.

p. 308 'I believe that ...', *Roosevelt Letters*, Vol. III, p. 435.

p. 308 'colossal folly', Hastings, *Finest Years*, p. 314.

p. 309 'stop', 'more than ever', 'I must state ...', 'We have got ...', Churchill, *Second World War*, Vol. IV, pp. 241, 242.

p. 309 'we could then survey ...', ibid., p. 409.

p. 309 'Owing to a lack ...', Michael Carver, *El Alamein* (Fontana, 1962), p. 22.

p. 310 'endless winding silver ribbon ...', Churchill, *Second World War*, Vol. IV, p. 412.

p. 310 'troublesome times ahead', 'the plans for a new Command ...', Alanbrooke, *War Diaries 1939–45*, pp. 289, 288.

p. 311 'It has not been ...', Barr, *Pendulum of War*, p. 118.

p. 311 'I worshipped him ...', ibid.

p. 311 'gave rise to ...', 'a most delightful ...', Alanbrooke, *War Diaries 1939–45*, p. 290.

p. 311 'I cannot recall ...', Bernard Montgomery, *The Memoirs of Field-Marshal the Viscount Montgomery of Alamein, KG* (Collins, 1958), p. 71.

p. 312 'I didn't approve ...', Warner, *Auchinleck*, p. 240.

p. 312 'He is again pressing ...', Alanbrooke, *War Diaries 1939–45*, p. 291.

p. 312 'The weather is delightful ...', Soames, *Speaking for Themselves*, p. 467.

p. 312 'a wire-netted cube ...', Churchill, *Second World War*, Vol. IV, p. 415.

p. 313 'his pudgy fingers ...' et seq., Greacen, *Chink*, p. 236.

p. 313–4 'some new blood ...' et seq., Alanbrooke, *War Diaries 1939–45*, pp. 292, 294.

p. 315 'high ability ...', 'a highly competent ...', Soames, *Speaking for Themselves*, p. 467.

p. 315 'it was like going ...', Barr, *Pendulum of War*, p. 204.

p. 315 'He put his arm in mine ...', de Guingand, *Operation Victory*, p. 135.

p. 315 'The War Cabinet ...', Warner, *Auchinleck*, p. 165.

p. 315 'Rommel, Rommel, Rommel ...', Bierman and Smith, *Alamein*, p. 221.

p. 316 'a shock', Barnett, *Desert Generals*, p. 237.

p. 316 'slightly humiliated …', *The Auk at Ninety*, BBC TV.

p. 316 'with soldierly dignity', Churchill, *Second World War*, Vol. IV, p. 422.

p. 316 'in a highly stormy …', Alanbrooke, *War Diaries 1939–45*, p. 297.

p. 316 'I could not hear …', Moran, *Churchill at War*, p. 63.

p. 316 'behaving like an …', Alanbrooke, *War Diaries 1939–45*, p. 296.

p. 317 'It is for him to settle …', Warner, *Auchinleck*, p. 168.

p. 317 'I had a certain amount …', Barnett, *Desert Generals*, p. 237.

p. 317 'no mess tent …', Montgomery, *Memoirs*, p. 100.

p. 317 'Lieut-Gen MONTGOMERY …', 'quite impossible …', 'I learnt later …', Nigel Hamilton, *The Full Monty: Montgomery of Alamein, 1887–1942* (Penguin, 2001), pp. 519, 521.

p. 318 'Here we will stand …', ibid., p. 531.

p. 318 'If Rommel attacked …', Montgomery, *Memoirs*, p. 94.

p. 318 'the worst came …', Warner, *Auchinleck*, p. 240.

p. 318 'Gross mismanagement …', Hamilton, *The Full Monty*, p. 548.

p. 319 'I am sure we were heading …', Churchill, *Second World War*, Vol. IV, p. 465.

p. 319 'imputation of funk', 'Montgomery's tendency …', Greacen, *Chink*, p. 308.

p. 319 'launch an offensive …', Barnett, *Desert Generals*, p. 338.

p. 319 'absolute rubbish', *The Auk at Ninety*, BBC TV.

p. 319 'series of extreme measures', Churchill, *Second World War*, Vol. IV, p. 469.

p. 320 'construct rifle-pits …', *LG* 38196, p. 842.

p. 320 'to take responsibility …', Churchill, *Second World War*, Vol. IV, p. 469.

p. 320 'give the fullest …', ibid., p. 467.

p. 320 'petrol reserves at pumps …' et seq., Alanbrooke, *War Diaries 1939–45*, p. 311.

p. 321 'we ourselves will start …', Bierman and Smith, *Alamein*, p. 232.

p. 321 'on balance', de Guingand, *Operation Victory*, p. 135.

p. 321 'The effect of …', ibid., pp. 136–7.

p. 321 'sullen, sinister Bolshevik State', Churchill, *Second World War*, Vol. IV, p. 428.

p. 322–3 Churchill–Stalin meeting, ibid., pp. 429–35, passim.

p. 323 'The democracies would show …', 'Your words are of no …', 'profound Russian statesman …', ibid.

p. 324 'an unpleasantly cold …', Alanbrooke, *War Diaries 1939–45*, p. 301.

p. 324 'grievous disappointment', 'have swallowed …', Churchill, *Second World War*, Vol. IV, p. 444.

21 Montgomery Makes His Mark

p. 325 'hopelessly dispirited ...', Carver, *El Alamein*, p. 24.

p. 326 'I believe that one ...', Latimer, *Alamein*, pp. 98–9.

p. 326 'what was going on ...', Montgomery, *Memoirs*, pp. 89–90.

p. 326–7 'He was wearing ...', 'Montgomery came to ...', 'I went over ...', 'He wanted to know ...', Max Arthur, *Forgotten Voices of the Second World War* (Ebury Press, 2004), pp. 199–202, passim.

p. 327 'Montgomery was a bit ...', Sadler, *El Alamein*, p. 106.

p. 328 'He told us everything ...', Latimer, *Alamein*, p. 100.

p. 328 'in principle', 'to hold as strongly ...', *LG* 38196, 3 February 1948, p. 841.

p. 329 'hopeless', 'never seemed ...', Barr, *Pendulum of War*, p. 216.

p. 329 'One of the most remarkable ...', ibid., p. 212.

p. 329 'I was dumbfounded ...', Alanbrooke, *War Diaries 1939–45*, p. 478.

p. 330 'Montgomery's "complete grip ..."', Barr, *Pendulum of War*, p. 212.

p. 330 'delicious', 'a masterly exposition ...', 'the reviving ardour ...', Churchill, *Second World War*, Vol. IV, pp. 462–3, 464.

p. 331 'We are determined ...', Churchill, Statement to Press Corps, 22 August 1942, TNA Prime Ministerial Office Papers, 1940–1945 (PREM) 4/71/4, Churchill Archive, cited in Jenner, 'Turning the Hinge of Fate'.

p. 331 'mechanised static warfare ...', Liddell Hart, *Rommel Papers*, p. 262.

p. 332 'a weak-willed ...', ibid., p. 352.

p. 333 'the destruction of all ...', Kitchen, *Rommel's Desert War*, p. 296.

p. 333 'the dictators had lost ...', Kitchen, *Rommel's Desert War*, p. 298.

p. 333 'For a long time ...', Gordon A. Craig, *Germany 1866–1945* (Oxford University Press, 1978), p. 753.

p. 334 'very tired and limp', 'the state of the Marshall's health' et seq., Liddell Hart, *Rommel Papers*, p. 263.

p. 334 'frequent attacks ...', Barr, *Pendulum of War*, p. 271.

p. 334 'not in a fit condition ...', Liddell Hart, *Rommel Papers*, p. 271.

p. 334 'Today, the army ...', Kitchen, *Rommel's Desert War*, p. 300.

p. 334 'It's been such ...', ibid., p. 275.

p. 335–6 'Our rations were bad ...' et seq., IWM Doc. 2405, www.iwm.org.uk/collections/item/object/1030001986.

p. 336–7 'I felt very ...', 'a good gallop', de Guingand, *Operation Victory*, pp. 146, 148.

p. 337 'tea-stained, folded', Tim Clayton and Phil Craig, *End of the Beginning* (Hodder and Stoughton, 2002), p. 319.

p. 337 'had borne fruit', 'the very soft going ...', *LG* 38196, p. 845.

p. 337 'was accepted as authentic ...', von Mellenthin, *Panzer Battles*, p. 104.

p. 338 'I don't want you to think ...', Bierman and Smith, *Alamein*, p. 236.

p. 338 'I saw tank after tank ...', Latimer, *Alamein*, p. 112.

p. 338–9 'With one aircraft ...', On one occasion ...', 'Our offensive no longer had ...', Liddell Hart, *Rommel Papers*, pp. 279, 280.

p. 340 '28 (Maori) Battalion ...', *LG* 38196, p. 846.

p. 340 'Repeated cases had occurred ...', 'large numbers of Maoris', Liddell Hart, *Rommel Papers*, p. 281.

p. 340 'courageous and likeable', Liddell Hart, *Rommel Papers*, p. 281.

p. 341 'all had the same story ...', Barr, *Pendulum of War*, p. 245.

p. 341 'By the evening ...', *LG* 38196, p. 846.

p. 341 'With the failure ...', Liddell Hart, *Rommel Papers*, p. 283.

22 Churchill Feels the Pressure

p. 342 'a bombshell', Churchill, *Second World War*, Vol. IV, p. 475.

p. 344 'The whole operation ...' et seq., Kennedy, *Business of War*, pp. 263, 264.

p. 344 'your great strategic conception' et seq., Churchill, *Second World War*, Vol. IV, p. 474.

p. 344–5 'profoundly disconcerted' et seq., ibid., p. 475.

p. 345 'the Stars and Stripes ...', Roberts, *Masters and Commanders*, p. 279.

p. 345 'I feel very strongly ...', Churchill, *Second World War*, Vol. IV, p. 477.

p. 346 'This sudden abandonment ...' et seq., Loewenheim et al., *Roosevelt and Churchill Correspondence*, pp. 246, 248.

p. 346 'We are undertaking ...', Roberts, *Masters and Commanders*, p. 279.

p. 346–7 'deeply perturbed' et seq., Churchill, *Second World War*, Vol. IV, p. 486.

p. 347 'we are getting ...', 'We agree' et seq., Loewenheim et al., *Roosevelt and Churchill Correspondence*, pp. 249, 250.

p. 347 'Hurrah', 'O.K., full blast', 'In the whole of *Torch* ...', Churchill, *Second World War*, Vol. IV, pp. 487, 488.

p. 348 'very pathetic' et seq., Alanbrooke, *War Diaries 1939–45*, p. 324.

p. 348 'bleak lull' et seq., Churchill, *Second World War*, Vol. IV, p. 494.

p. 348 'I would concentrate ...', Montgomery, *Memoirs*, p. 112.

p. 349 'Battle of Alamein', 'there was no difficulty ...', Barr, *Pendulum of War*, p. 249.

p. 349 'When troops usually ...', Latimer, *Alamein*, p. 120.

p. 349 'Florence Nightingale ...', Barnett, *Desert Generals*, p. 268.

p. 350 'This is war ...', ibid.

p. 350 'braggartly, vain, rude ...' et seq., Hamilton, *The Full Monty*, pp. 562–3.

p. 352 'Your prime and main duty ...', Churchill, *Second World War*, Vol. IV, p. 424.

p. 352 'wiry, scholarly, intense ...' et seq., Wendell L. Willkie, *One World* (Simon and Schuster, 1943), pp. 4–10.

p. 353 'My next trouble ...', Alanbrooke, *War Diaries 1939–45*, p. 319.

p. 353 'the immense importance ...', Churchill, *Second World War*, Vol. IV, p. 787.

p. 354 'war material', 'on the assumption ...', ibid., p. 788.

p. 354 'destroy ... at the earliest opportunity', Churchill, *Second World War*, Vol. IV, p. 424.

p. 354 'It would be a help ...', Barr, *Pendulum of War*, p. 255.

p. 354 'Morale is the big thing ...', Bierman and Smith, *Alamein*, p. 249.

p. 355 I am anxiously awaiting ...', Churchill, *Second World War*, Vol. IV, p. 527.

p. 355 'I won't do it ...' et seq., Bierman and Smith, *Alamein*, p. 241.

p. 355 'they would have to get ...', Montgomery, *Memoirs*, p. 117.

p. 355 'essential' et seq., Churchill, *Second World War*, Vol. IV, p. 527.

p. 355 'We are in your hands ...', ibid., p. 528.

p. 356 'we constructed our defensive system', 'even the heaviest ...', Liddell Hart, *Rommel Papers*, pp. 297–8.

p. 356 'the finest troops of the British Empire' et seq., ibid., p. 289.

p. 357 'corset stays', Kitchen, *Rommel's Desert War*, p. 307.

p. 357 'the doctor is pressing me ...', Liddell Hart, *Rommel Papers*, p. 290.

p. 358 'direct the whole life ...', Denis Mack Smith, *Mussolini* (Paladin, 1981), p. 319.

p. 358 'I consider this ...', Kitchen, *Rommel's Desert War*, p. 319.

p. 358 'a great pincer movement ...', Benito Mussolini, *My Rise and Fall* (Da Capo, 1948), p. xxvii.

p. 358 'black mood' et seq., Gibson, *Ciano Diaries*, p. 521.

p. 359 'cut deeply into ...' et seq., ibid., p. 525.

p. 360 'preposterous', Kitchen, *Rommel's Desert War*, p. 315.

p. 360 'shot up my tanks ...' et seq., Liddell Hart, *Rommel Papers*, p. 295.

p. 360–1 'We are now one hundred ...', 'just the sort of ...', Kitchen, *Rommel's Desert War*, p. 317.

p. 361 'OKW does not ...', ibid., p. 325.

p. 361 'the plight', 'I was of course ...', Liddell Hart, *Rommel Papers*, p. 294.

p. 365 'Upon the broad ...', Angus Calder, *The People's War: Britain 1939–1945* (Granada, 1971), p. 313.

p. 365 'If we are beaten ...', Moran, *Churchill at War*, p. 91.

p. 365 'Winston was like ...', 'I had to go out ...', Hastings, *Finest Years*, p. 338.

23 Into the Breach

p. 366 'The battle which is ...', Montgomery, *Memoirs*, pp. 127–8.

p. 367 'everyone – *everyone* ...', de Guingand, *Operation Victory*, pp. 160–61.

p. 368 'virtually unable ...', Kitchen, *Rommel's Desert War*, p. 325.

p. 369 'Tanks must be used ...', 'Look here, my dear boy ...', Hamilton, *The Full Monty*, p. 671.

p. 369 'as it was about to embark ...', 'multiple authors and contributors', Barr, *Pendulum of War*, p. 301.

p. 370 'No fury of sound ...' et seq., Latimer, *Alamein*, p. 177.

p. 370 'The noise is unbelievable ...' Ellis, *The Sharp End*, p. 68.

p. 370 'dumbfounded by the din' et seq., Bierman and Smith, *Alamein*, p. 277.

p. 370 'was a wonderful sight ...', Barr, *Pendulum of War*, p. 309.

p. 371 'we watched as ...', de Guingand, *Operation Victory*, p. 164.

p. 371 'The enemy is by no means ...', 'Enemy situation unchanged ...', Barr, *Pendulum of War*, p. 306.

p. 371 'inferno [was] an inhuman ...', G. Forty, *Afrika Korps at War*, Vol. II, *The Long Road Back* (Ian Allen, 1978), pp. 71–3.

p. 371 'shells suddenly fell ...', Latimer, *Alamein*, pp. 178–9.

p. 372 'I could hear the shells ...', Thompson, *Forgotten Voices*, p. 197.

p. 372 'We are bound ...' et seq., Alanbrooke, *War Diaries 1939–45*, p. 333.

p. 373 'eerie, exhilarating and frightening ...', B. Pitt, *The Crucible of War: Year of Alamein 1942* (Cape, 1982), p. 302.

p. 373 'We had orders ...', Thompson, *Forgotten Voices*, p. 198.

p. 373 'I walk along like this ...', Latimer, *Alamein*, p. 181.

p. 373 'When a foot trod ...', Hamilton, *The Full Monty*, p. 699.

p. 374 'The rotten part ...', ibid., p. 700.

p. 374 'Most of us ...', Barr, *Pendulum of War*, p. 322.

p. 375 'There was a terrific explosion ...', 'A bullet smashed into ...', Sadler, *El Alamein*, pp. 154, 155.

p. 375 'Miteiriya Ridge was a very ...', de Guingand, *Operation Victory*, p. 197.

p. 375 'suddenly all hell broke loose ...', Barr, *Pendulum of War*, p. 323.

p. 376 'Don't want to go out ...', 'some energy', ibid., pp. 324, 325.

p. 376 'the deployment of 1st Armoured Division ...', LG 38196, p. 853.

p. 377 'The inferno that was ...', Sadler, *El Alamein*, p. 159.

p. 377 'the voices of those ...', Arthur, *Forgotten Voices*, p. 196.

p. 377 'What's strange about those tanks?' et seq., Thompson, *Forgotten Voices*, p. 195.

p. 378 'a long, open stretch ...', 'we were stuck ...', ibid., p. 201.

p. 379 'was not popular ...', Montgomery, *Memoirs*, p. 120.

p. 379 'So far he has not ...', Bierman and Smith, *Alamein*, p. 283.

p. 379 'drive his divisional commanders', Montgomery, *Memoirs*, p. 29.

p. 380 'whether you are going ...', Barr, *Pendulum of War*, p. 330.

24 'An unforgettable nightmare'

p. 381 'They told me to get ...', Latimer, *Alamein*, p. 199.

p. 382 'the British had been attacking ...', Liddell Hart, *Rommel Papers*, p. 302.

p. 383 'Rommel, there is bad news ...', 'still a very sick man ...', Young, *Rommel*, p. 172.

p. 383 'no more laurels ...', 'This was sheer disaster ...', Liddell Hart, *Rommel Papers*, p. 304.

p. 383 'I have taken command ...', Bungay, 'The Road to Mission Command', p. 174.

p. 384 'to throw the enemy ...', Liddell Hart, *Rommel Papers*, p. 306.

p. 384 'dozens of shattered ...', 'suicidal and stupid', Barr, *Pendulum of War*, pp. 334, 337.

p. 384 'I think I could count ...', de Guingand, *Operation Victory*, p. 199.

p. 384 'out in the open ...', Montgomery, *Memoirs*, pp. 129–30.

p. 385 'not a good time ...', de Guingand, *Operation Victory*, p. 199.

p. 385 'I'm afraid they've no stomach ...', Hamilton, *The Full Monty*, p. 723.

p. 385 'clearly and quickly ...', de Guingand, *Operation Victory*, p. 199.

p. 385 'to my horror', 'I spoke to him ...', Montgomery, *Memoirs*, p. 130.

p. 386 'spoke very plainly ...' et seq., ibid.

p. 387 'critical' et seq., Hamilton, *The Full Monty*, p. 723.

p. 387 'new thrust or axis ...' et seq., ibid., p. 724

p. 388 Samwell account, John Strawson, *The Battle for North Africa* (Pen and Sword Military Classics, 2004), p. 139.

p. 389 'Some of the tanks ...', Bungay, 'The Road to Mission Command', p. 175.

p. 389 'Rivers of blood ...', Liddell Hart, *Rommel Papers*, p. 306.

p. 389 'pounced on these ...' et seq., 'Situation critical ...', ibid., pp. 307, 308.

p. 390 'an exciting day', 'Look out, Bob ...', 'Well done ...', de Guingand, *Operation Victory*, p. 344.

p. 390 'A very hard struggle ...', 'successively provided ...', Liddell Hart, *Rommel Papers*, pp. 309, 307.

p. 391 'I thought we'd had ...', Arthur, *Forgotten Voices*, p. 207.

p. 391 'There was always somebody ...', Carver, *El Alamein*, pp. 208–9.

p. 391 'Hard fighting had been ...', Montgomery, *Memoirs*, p. 131.

p. 392 'pause', LG 38196, p. 855.

p. 392 'an armoured shield ...', Hamilton, *The Full Monty*, p. 743.

p. 392 'I don't think relaxed ...', ibid., p. 742.

p. 392–3 'gripping', 'not a pleasant one', Alanbrooke, *War Diaries 1939–45*, p. 335.

p. 393 'The Foreign Secretary and I ...', Barr, *Pendulum of War*, p. 366.

p. 393–4 'flow of abuse' et seq., 'The strain of the battle ...' et seq., Alanbrooke, *War Diaries 1939–45*, pp. 335, 336.

p. 394 'the resolute and successful ...', 'moves forward ...', 'Your battle continuing ...', Churchill, *Second World War*, Vol. IV, pp. 534–5.

p. 394 'Winston is finding ...' et seq., Moran, *Churchill at War*, p. 92.

p. 394 'I was far from ...', 'On returning to ...', Alanbrooke, *War Diaries 1939–45*, p. 336.

p. 395 'draw divisions into reserve' et seq., Montgomery, *Memoirs*, pp.132–3.

p. 395 'the way things were going' et seq., Barr, *Pendulum of War*, p. 369.

p. 395 'Whitehall thought I was ...', 'I never heard ...', Montgomery, *Memoirs*, pp. 132–3.

p. 396 'obvious', 'the British would ...', Liddell Hart, *Rommel Papers*, p. 310.

p. 396 'The present battle is ...', Barr, *Pendulum of War*, p. 361.

p. 396 'The situation continues ...', Liddell Hart, *Rommel Papers*, p. 312.

p. 396 'I always wrote ...', 'This was the master plan ...', Montgomery, *Memoirs*, p. 117.

p. 397 '(a) Destroy the enemy ...', 'I do not consider ...', Montgomery, *Memoirs*, pp. 133–6.

p. 397 'So far it has been ...', 'I have managed ...', Hamilton, *The Full Monty*, pp. 754, 755.

p. 397 'most savage fighting ...', de Guingand, *Operation Victory*, p. 202.

p. 398 'superb ... the best ...', Hamilton, *The Full Monty*, p. 755.

p. 398 'I will lead ...', 'I had to bribe him ...' et seq., ibid., pp. 740, 741.

p. 398 'greatly fatigued', LG 38196, p. 856.

p. 399 'no quarter was given,' de Guingand, *Operation Victory*, p. 202.

p. 399 'The Commanding Officer ...' et seq., 'Why can't our chaps ...' et seq., Latimer, *Alamein*, p. 263.

p. 399 'The first light of dawn ...', Barr, *Pendulum of War*, p. 379.

p. 400 'it was difficult ...', Thompson, *Forgotten Voices*, p. 212.

25 The End of the Beginning

p. 401 'At 1300 we had ...', F. Formica, ed., *Diary of Second Lieutenant Vincenzo Formica*, www.fereamole.it.

p. 402 'the British were obviously ...', 'harassing fire only ...', Liddell Hart, *Rommel Papers*, p. 315.

p. 402 'Over and over again ...', Kitchen, *Rommel's Desert War*, p. 337.

p. 402 'Some supplies are supposed ...', Liddell Hart, *Rommel Papers*, p. 316.

p. 402 'thin and tired', 'incapable, discredited ...', Gibson, *Ciano Diaries*, p. 534.

p. 402 'extremely laudatory and sugar-coated', ibid., p. 536

p. 403 'My father is very ill' et seq., Hibbert, *Mussolini*, p. 150.

p. 403 'He would on occasions ...', 'he didn't look real ...', ibid., p. 143.

p. 403 'of singing and eating-ice cream' et seq., 'must be a part of ...', ibid., pp. 147, 159.

p. 403 'the end of the army', Kitchen, *Rommel's Desert War*, p. 341.

p. 404 'Il Duce authorises ...', Liddell Hart, *Rommel Papers*, p. 316.

p. 404 'a man lacking ...', 'in me they have found ...', Bullock, *Hitler and Stalin*, p. 688.

p. 405 'flew at the man ...', 'were the product ...', ibid., p. 686.

p. 405 'overly pessimistic', Kitchen, *Rommel's Desert War*, p. 341.

p. 406 'As far as could be seen ...', James Lucas, *War in the Desert: The Eighth Army at El Alamein* (Arms and Armour Press, 1982), p. 237.

p. 406 'Twenty-five pound shells ...', Thompson, *Forgotten Voices*, pp. 217–18.

p. 406 'I aired my schoolboy German ...', Sadler, *El Alamein*, p. 185.

p. 407 'in our keenness ...', 'the mass of shell holes ...', Thompson, *Forgotten Voices*, pp. 220, 222.

p. 407–8 'For the next five hours ...', 'We all know ...', Barr, *Pendulum of War*, pp. 385, 386.

p. 408 'It's got to be done ...', Bierman and Smith, *Alamein*, p. 318.

p. 408 'It was like driving ...', Barr, *Pendulum of War*, p. 386.

p. 409 'We knew what to expect ...', Hamilton, *The Full Monty*, p. 758.

p. 409 'great balls of fire ...', Barr, *Pendulum of War*, p. 387.

p. 409–10 'The Shermans were slowly ...', 'This was a ghastly ...', Thompson, *Forgotten Voices*, pp. 226, 227.

p. 410 'As far as the eye could see ...', Hamilton, *The Full Monty*, p. 760.

p. 410 'Well, we've made a gap ...', 'I have never seen ...', Barr, *Pendulum of War*, p. 389.

p. 410 'If the British armour ...', ibid.

p. 411 'This action ...', Latimer, *Alamein*, p. 291.

p. 411 'The plain truth ...', Hamilton, *The Full Monty*, p. 761.

p. 411 'complete chaos', Liddell Hart, *Rommel Papers*, p. 318.

p. 412 'For hours on end ...', Latimer, *Alamein*, p. 289.

p. 412 'Smoke and dust covered ...', Barr, *Pendulum of War*, p. 390.

p. 412 'Where are our fighters ...', Sir Brian Horrocks, *A Full Life* (Collins, 1960), p. 139.

p. 412 'seven formations each ...', Liddell Hart, *Rommel Papers*, p. 318.

p. 413 'They are winning ...', Latimer, *Alamein*, p. 292.

p. 413 'Long columns of vehicles ...', *Diary of Vincenzo Formica*.

p. 413 'capable of offering ...', 'Very heavy fighting again ...', Liddell Hart, *Rommel Papers*, pp. 319, 317.

p. 414 'to extricate the remnants', Bierman and Smith, *Alamein*, p. 328.

p. 414 'In this situation ...', Kitchen, *Rommel's Desert War*, p. 341.

p. 414 'in such a hysterical tone ...', ibid., p. 342.

p. 415–6 'It is with trusting confidence ...', 'This order demanded ...', 'A kind of apathy ...', Liddell Hart, *Rommel Papers*, p. 321.

p. 416 'Dearest Lu, The Battle ...', ibid., p. 320.

p. 416 'So far I've taken it ...', ibid., pp. 323–4.

p. 416 'I would be inclined ...', 'The Führer cannot have intended ...', Latimer, *Alamein*, p. 302.

p. 416 They were simply unable …', Liddell Hart, *Rommel Papers*, p. 324.

p. 416–7 'A real hard …', 'It can be imagined …', Bryant, *Turn of the Tide*, p. 515.

p. 417 'PM delighted', Alanbrooke, *War Diaries 1939–45*, p. 338.

p. 417 'After twelve days …', Churchill, *Second World War*, Vol. IV, p. 537.

p. 417 'a great state of excitement', Bryant, *Turn of the Tide*, p. 516.

p. 417–8 'brilliant lieutenant' et seq., Churchill, *Second World War*, Vol. IV, pp. 537–8.

p. 418 'And if "Torch" succeeds …', Alanbrooke, *War Diaries 1939–45*, p. 338.

p. 418 'You are to fight …', 'The Führer's order …', Latimer, *Alamein*, pp. 295, 294.

p. 419 'distinguished looking chap …', ibid., p. 303.

p. 419 'The incident …', ibid., p. 329.

p. 419 'I shall always …', Bierman and Smith, *Alamein*, p. 320.

p. 419 'as we went back …', ibid., p. 331.

p. 420 'We were driven …', Liddle Collection, Private Papers of Fritz Herman Zimmermann, File. No. 13406.

p. 420 'The British separated us …', Bierman and Smith, *Alamein*, p. 332.

p. 420–1 'It was full daylight …' et seq., Sadler, *El Alamein*, p. 192.

p. 421 'vehicles of every sort …' et seq., *Diary of Vincenzo Formica*.

p. 422 'a very gallant action' et seq., Liddell Hart, *Rommel Papers*, p. 325.

p. 422 'It will never be said …' et seq., *Diary of Vincenzo Formica*.

p. 422–3 'the wrecks of vehicles …' et seq., Leeds University Library, Liddle Collection (1939–45), E. G. Wagnell.

p. 423 'The last thing I remember …', Leeds University Library, Liddle Collection (1939–45), Army 075, E. Frazer.

p. 424 'Ring out the bells!' Churchill, *Second World War*, Vol. IV, p. 539.

p. 425 'slogging-match' et seq., Carver, *El Alamein*, pp. 205–6.

p. 425 'I wanted to reach …' et seq., Antony Beevor, *Stalingrad* (Penguin 1999), p. 214.

p. 426 'Heading West again …', Liddell Hart, *Rommel Papers*, p. 351.

p. 426 'A new and more violent …' et seq., Gibson, *Ciano Diaries*, pp. 538, 539.

p. 427 'I received your message …', 'I am not unduly disturbed …', 'The atmosphere was …', Churchill, *Second World War*, Vol. IV, pp. 520, 521.

p. 428 'I am a bit appalled …', *Roosevelt Letters*, Vol. III, p. 439.

p. 428 'I am very happy …', Churchill, *Second World War*, Vol. IV, p. 566.

p. 428 'That new film …', *Roosevelt Letters*, Vol. III, p. 461.

p. 429 'I have never promised …', Churchill, *The End of the Beginning*, p. 264.

p. 430 'This is not the end …', ibid., pp. 264–5.

492   DESTINY IN THE DESERT

26 The Beginning of the End

p. 431 'This morning, the landings ...', Alanbrooke, *War Diaries 1939–45*, p. 339.

p. 431 'brilliant success', Churchill, *The End of the Beginning*, p. 564.

p. 433 'the cornerstone of ...', Kitchen, *Rommel's Desert War*, p. 356.

p. 434 'being simply crushed ...', Liddell Hart, *Rommel Papers*, p. 351.

p. 435 'worked like a spark ...', 'for their own mistakes', 'plumed himself ...', 'left the Italians ...', 'That's news ...' ibid., pp. 365, 366, 367.

p. 436 'one of the most brilliant ...', Kitchen, *Rommel's Desert War*, p. 420.

p. 437 'he ought to have ...', 'lethargy, confusion ...', cited ibid.

p. 437 'magnificent opportunity' et seq., cited ibid., p. 419.

p. 437 'absolute mania ...', Liddell Hart, Rommel Papers, p. 395.

p. 437 'bad news from Tunisia' et seq., Alanbrooke, *War Diaries 1939–45*, p. 384.

p. 438 'Heart, nerves, and rheumatism ...', 'plain suicide' et seq., Liddell Hart, *Rommel Papers*, pp. 410, 416, 418, 419.

p. 439 'Supplies disastrous ...', Kitchen, *Rommel's Desert War*, p. 450.

p. 439 'heroic and awe-inspiring ...', 'stalwart heroism ...', ibid., p. 455.

p. 439 'Terrible as it was ...', Liddell Hart, *Rommel Papers*, p. 422.

p. 440 'Sir, It is my duty ...', 'No one could doubt ...', Churchill, *The End of the Beginning*, p. 698.

p. 443 'Accept my sincerest ...', Liddell Hart, *Rommel Papers*, p. 505.

p. 444 'sham tribunal' et seq., Gibson, *Ciano Diaries*, p. 584.

p. 444 'I am finished ...', Hibbert, *Mussolini*, p. 280.

p. 445 'Franklin D. Roosevelt ...', Speech broadcast from White House, 8 May 1945, Harry S. Truman Library.

p. 447 'outstanding', Greacen, *Chink*, p. 134.

p. 448 'a psychopath', Antony Beevor, *D-Day* (Viking, 2009), p. 523.

p. 449 'My dear friends ...', Hastings, *Finest Years*, p. 570.

p. 450 'We shall never see ...', Dimbleby, *Richard Dimbleby*, p. 385.

SOURCES

It would be possible to fill a substantial library with the wide range of military and political histories, biographies, memoirs, diaries, letters, speeches, debates, reports, bulletins, interviews, documentary films and dramas, which have been inspired by the Battle of El Alamein and the events leading up to it. I have gained from many of these but not all of them. So far as possible, I have drawn from original sources, almost all of which have been in the public domain for some time, and many of which have been reproduced in other writings. Where I have relied on secondary sources for these references, I have generally credited the secondary rather than the primary source.

The sources listed below are those, from many, which I have found particularly helpful and illuminating.

Archive material
BBC, WW2 People's War: www.bbc.co.uk/history/ww2peopleswar/
Imperial War Museum, London (IWM): www.iwm.org.uk/
Leeds University Library, Liddle Collection: http://library.leeds.ac.uk/
    liddle-collection
The National Archives, London (TNA): www.nationalarchives.gov.uk/
Parliamentary Debates, House of Commons (Hansard): http://hansard.
    millbanksystems.com/
Second World War Experience Centre: www.war-experience.org/

TV and periodicals
The Auk at Ninety (BBC TV, 1974)
London Gazette: www.london-gazette.co.uk/
Time magazine

Published sources

Alanbrooke, Field Marshal Lord, *War Diaries 1939–45*, ed. Alex Danchev and Daniel Todman (Phoenix Press, 2001)

Andrew, Christopher, *Secret Service: The Making of the British Intelligence Community* (Sceptre, 1986)

Arnold-Forster, Mark, *The World at War* (Collins, 1973)

Arthur, Max, *Forgotten Voices of the Second World War* (Ebury Press, 1988)

Atkinson, Rick, *An Army at Dawn: The War in North Africa 1942–1943* (Abacus, 2004)

Barnett, Correlli, *The Desert Generals* (Phoenix, 1999)

Barr, Niall, *Pendulum of War: The Three Battles of El Alamein* (Pimlico, 2005)

Bates, Peter, *Dance of War: The Story of the Battle of Egypt* (Leo Cooper, 1992)

Beevor, Antony, *D-Day* (Viking, 2009)

——, *Stalingrad* (Penguin, 1999)

Berthon, Simon, *Allies at War: The Bitter Rivalry among Churchill, Roosevelt, and de Gaulle* (Caroll and Graf, 2001)

Bierman, John and Colin Smith, *Alamein: War Without Hate* (Penguin, 2003)

——, *The Battle of El Alamein: Turning Point of World War II* (Viking, 2002)

Blake, Robert, *The Decline of Power 1915–1964* (Granada, 1985)

Bright, Joan, *Ninth Queen's Royal Lancers 1936–1945: The Story of an Armoured Regiment in Battle* (Gale & Polden, 1951)

Bryant, Arthur, *The Turn of the Tide* (Alanbrooke Diaries 1939–1943) (Collins, 1957)

Buckingham, William F., *Tobruk: The Great Siege* (History Press, 2009)

Bullock, Alan, *Hitler: A Study in Tyranny* (Pelican, 1962)

——, *Hitler and Stalin, Parallel Lives* (HarperCollins, 1991)

Bungay, Stephen, *Alamein* (Aurum, 2002)

——, 'The Road to Mission Command: The Genesis of a Command Philosophy', *British Army Review* 137 (Summer 2005)

Burleigh, Michael, *Moral Combat: A History of World War II* (HarperPress, 2010)

Calder, Angus, *The People's War: Britain 1939–1945* (Granada, 1971)

Carver, Michael, *Dilemmas of the Desert War: The Libyan Campaign 1940–1942* (Spellmount, 2002)

——, *El Alamein* (Fontana, 1962)

——, *Tobruk* (Pan, 1964)

Churchill, Winston S., *The End of the Beginning* (Cassell, 1943)

——, *The Second World War*, Vol. II, *Their Finest Hour* (Cassell, 1949); Vol. III, *The Grand Alliance* (Cassell, 1950); Vol. IV, *The Hinge of Fate* (Cassell, 1951)

Clayton, Tim and Phil Craig, *End of the Beginning* (Hodder and Stoughton, 2002)

Colville, John, *The Fringes of Power: Downing Street Diaries 1939–1955* (Weidenfeld and Nicolson, 2004)

——, *The Fringes of Power: Downing Street Diaries Volume One, 1939 to October 1941* (Hodder and Stoughton, 1986)

Connell, John, *A Biography of Field Marshal Sir Claude Auchinleck* (Cassell, 1959)

——, *Wavell: Soldier and Scholar* (Collins, 1964)

Cooper, Artemis, *Cairo in the War 1939–45* (Penguin, 1989)

Craig, Gordon A., *Germany 1866–1945* (Oxford University Press, 1980)

Dallek, Robert, *Franklin D. Roosevelt and American Foreign Policy, 1932–1945* (Oxford University Press, 1995)

de Guingand, Francis, *Generals at War* (Hodder and Stoughton, 1964)

——, *Operation Victory* (Hodder and Stoughton, 1947)

Dimbleby, David and David Reynolds, *An Ocean Apart* (Hodder and Stoughton, 1988)

Dimbleby, Jonathan, *Richard Dimbleby: A Biography* (Hodder and Stoughton, 1975)

Dimbleby, Richard, *The Frontiers Are Green* (Hodder and Stoughton, 1943)

Eade, Charles, comp., *Secret Session Speeches by Winston Churchill* (Cassell, 1946)

Elliot, Peter, *The Cross and the Ensign: A Naval History of Malta 1798–1979* (HarperCollins, 1994)

Ellis, John, *The Sharp End* (Aurum, 1990)

Farren, Roy, *Winged Dagger: Adventures on Special Service* (Grafton, 1988)

Formica, F., ed., *Diary of Second Lieutenant Vincenzo Formica*, www.fereamole.it

Forty, G., *Afrika Korps at War*, Vol. II, *The Long Road Back* (Ian Allen, 1978)

Gibson, Hugh, ed., *The Ciano Diaries, 1939–1943: The Complete, Unabridged Diaries of Count Galeazzo Ciano, Italian Minister of Foreign Affairs, 1936–1943* (Simon Publications, 2001)

Gilbert, Adrian, ed., *The Imperial War Museum Book of The Desert War 1940–1942* (Sidgwick and Jackson, 1995)

Greacen, Lavinia, *Chink: A Biography* (Macmillan, 1989)

Hamilton, Nigel, *The Full Monty: Montgomery of Alamein, 1887–1942* (Penguin, 2001)

Hastings, Max, *All Hell Let Loose: The World at War 1939–1945* (HarperPress, 2011)

——, *Finest Years: Churchill as Warlord, 1940–45* (HarperPress, 2009)

Hibbert, John Christopher, *Mussolini: The Rise and Fall of Il Duce* (Palgrave Macmillan, 2008)

Hinsley, F. H. et al., *British Intelligence in the Second World War* (HMSO, 1979)

Holland, James, *Together We Stand: North Africa 1942–1943: Turning the Tide in the West* (HarperCollins, 2006)

Holmes, Richard, *Churchill's Bunker* (Profile Books, 2009)

——, *The World at War: The Landmark Oral History from the Previously Unpublished Archives* (Ebury Press, 2007)

Holt, Thaddeus, *The Deceivers: Allied Military Deception in the Second World War* (Phoenix, 2005)

Horrocks, Sir Brian, *A Full Life* (Collins, 1960)

Howard, Michael, *The Mediterranean Strategy in the Second World War* (Greenhill, 1968)

Ismay, General The Lord, *The Memoirs of Lord Ismay* (Heinemann, 1960)

Jackson, Ashley, *The British Empire and the Second World War* (Hambledon Continuum, 2006)

James, Lawrence, *Raj: The Making and Unmaking of British India* (Abacus, 1997)

Jenner, C. J., 'Turning the Hinge of Fate', *Diplomatic History*, 32, 2 (April 2008), pp. 165–205

Johnson, J. E. *Full Circle: The Story of Air Fighting* (Cassell, 2001)

Kennedy, Sir John, *The Business of War*, ed. Bernard Fergusson (Hutchinson, 1957)

Kitchen, Martin, *Rommel's Desert War* (Cambridge University Press, 2009)

Latimer, Jon, *Alamein* (John Murray, 2002)

Liddell Hart, Basil, *History of the Second World War* (Pan, 1977)

Liddell Hart, Basil, ed., *The Rommel Papers* (Da Capo, 1982)

Loewenheim, Francis L., Harold D. Langley and Manfred Jonas (eds), *Roosevelt and Churchill: Their Secret Wartime Correspondence* (Barrie and Jenkins, 1975)

Lucas, James, *Panzer Army Africa* (MacDonald and James, 1977)

——, *War in the Desert: The Eighth Army at El Alamein* (Arms and Armour Press, 1982)

Lyman, Robert, *The Longest Siege: Tobruk – The Battle that Saved North Africa* (Macmillan, 2009)

Mack Smith, Denis, *Mussolini* (Paladin, 1981)

Montgomery, Bernard, *The Memoirs of Field-Marshal the Viscount Montgomery of Alamein, KG* (Collins, 1958)

Moorehead, Alan, *The Desert War: The Classic Trilogy on the North American Campaign 1940–43* (Aurum Press, 2009)

Moran, Lord Charles, *Churchill at War, 1940–45* (Robinson, 2002)

Mosley, Leonard, *Marshall, Hero for Our Times* (Hearst Books, 1982)

Mussolini, Benito, *My Rise and Fall* (Da Capo, 1948)

Nicolson, Nigel, *Alex: The Life of Field Marshal Earl Alexander of Tunis* (Weidenfeld and Nicolson, 1973)

Norman, Bruce, *Secret Warfare: The Battle of Codes and Ciphers* (David and Charles, 1973)

Ostellino, Pietro, *Ariete Tanks Fight! The Ups and Downs of the Ariete Armoured Division in the letters of Lt. Pietro Ostellino, North Africa Jan. 1941 to March 1943* (in Italian) (Prospettiva Editrice, 2009)

Paxman, Jeremy, *Empire: What the World Did to the British* (Viking, 2011)

Pitt, B., *The Crucible of War: Year of Alamein 1942* (Cape, 1982)

Plesch, Dan, *America, Hitler and the UN* (I. B. Tauris, 2011)

Porch, Douglas, *Hitler's Mediterranean Gamble: The North American and the Mediterranean Campaigns in World War II* (Cassell, 2004)

Ranfurly, The Countess of, *To War with Whitaker: The Wartime Diaries of the Countess of Ranfurly 1939–1945* (Mandarin, 1997)

Rauch, Basil, ed., *Franklin D. Roosevelt: Selected Speeches, Messages, Press Conferences, and Letters* (Easton Press, 1957)

Rees, Laurence, *World War II: Behind Closed Doors – Stalin, The Nazis and The West* (BBC Books, 2008)

Roberts, Andrew, *Masters and Commanders* (Allen Lane, 2008)

———, *The Storm of War: A New History of the Second World War* (Penguin, 2009)

Robson, Mark, *Italy: The Rise of Fascism 1915–1945* (Hodder Education, 2006)

Roosevelt, Eleanor, ed., *The Roosevelt Letters*, Vol. III, *1928–1945* (Harrap, 1952)

Sadler, John, *El Alamein: The Story of the Battle in the Words of the Soldiers* (Amberley, 2010)

Schofield, Victoria, *Wavell, Soldier and Statesman* (John Murray, 2006)

Shirer, William L., *The Rise and Fall of the Third Reich* (Pan, 1959)

Smith, Michael, *The Spying Game: The Secret History of British Espionage* (Politico, 2003)

Soames, Mary, ed., *Speaking for Themselves: The Personal Letters of Winston and Clementine Churchill* (Black Swan, 1998)

Strawson, John, *The Battle for North Africa* (Pen and Sword Military Classics, 2004)

Stuart, Charles, ed., *The Reith Diaries* (Collins, 1975)

Thompson, Julian, *Forgotten Voices: Desert Victory* (Ebury Press, 2011)

Tucker, F. *Approach to Battle* (Cassell, 1963)

Vallicella, Vittorio, *Diario di Guerra da El Alamein all tragica ritirata, 1942–1943* (Edizioni Arterigere, 2009)

von Mellenthin, Friedrich W., *Panzer Battles* (Spellmount, 2008)

Warner, Philip, *Auchinleck: The Lonely Soldier* (Cassell, 1981)

———, *World War Two; The Untold Story* (Cassell, 2002)

Whiting, Charles, *The Poor Bloody Infantry 1939–1945* (Spellmount, 2007)
Willkie, Wendell L., *One World* (Simon and Schuster, 1943)
Young, Desmond, *Rommel* (Collins, 1950)
Ziegler, Philip, *Mountbatten* (Fontana, 1986)

INDEX